On Our Own
Americans in the Sixties

On Our Own
Americans in the Sixties

Douglas T. Miller
Michigan State University

D. C. Heath and Company
Lexington, Massachusetts   Toronto

Address editorial correspondence to:

D. C. Heath and Company
125 Spring Street
Lexington, MA 02173

Acquisitions Editor: James Miller
Developmental Editor: Lauren Johnson
Production Editor: Anne Rebecca Starr
Designer: Jan Shapiro
Photo Researchers: Judy Mason, Martha Friedman
Production Coordinator: Charles Dutton
Permissions Editor: Margaret Roll

To Arden and Gilman,
Children of the Sixties

They had their rules and regulations,
their corrupt corporations, their racist presumptions,
and their woeful war. We had our visions,
our love, and each other. We were on our own.

Henry Douglass
(poet and former antiwar activist)

There's one line in "Hey Jude" that sort of
sums up what the period was about:
"Take a sad song and make it better."

Paul Krassner
(editor, writer, and former Yippie)

Those of us who were there will not forget.
And the effects of that explosion in the sixties
have by now permeated every nook and cranny of our culture.

Rennie Davis
(former SDS leader)

The nineteenth century came to an end in America
only in the nineteen-sixties; the desperate pretense that the
two World Wars had left the world as unchanged as the Boer War
had left it was finally stripped away by the sexual revolution,
the women's movement, the civil-rights movement,
the environmental movement, the Vietnam War protests.

Janet Malcolm
(writer and former University of Michigan student)

P r e f a c e

The sixties, broadly conceived as encompassing the years from the midfifties through the early seventies, was an extraordinary period in American history, a time when an unprecedented number of people sought to transform their society. Through massive civil-rights and antiwar movements; struggles for the rights of women, gays, Native Americans, Hispanics; and concern for the environment, a generation emerged into maturity and took responsibility for reshaping the world that it had inherited. Of course, innumerable Americans either opposed these social movements or remained indifferent to them, and ultimately these idealistic dreams of changing America into a "beloved community" went unrealized. Nevertheless, a series of boisterous upheavals profoundly shook society. *On Our Own: Americans in the Sixties* attempts to comprehend and explain this highly complex and still-controversial era. Trying to make sense of the sixties has been an enterprise of personal and intellectual discovery for me; one that has made *On Our Own* an enlivening book to write, as I hope it will be to read.

My goal in appraising America in the 1960s is to synthesize: to integrate my own primary research over the past twenty years with the best of the new social history as well as with the more customary political, economic, diplomatic, and intellectual histories. This approach, both interdisciplinary and analytical, aims to create a holistic account that makes comprehensible the issues, conflicts, and human struggles of this absorbing period.

Several key premises guide *On Our Own.* First, I assume that the 1960s stand as one of the most important decades in the annals of America and that what occurred then has given direction to much of subsequent U.S. history. Second, I argue that the various social movements—from civil rights to feminism, pacifism to environmentalism, gay rights to red power, counterculture to commune—stand as the most momentous developments of the decade and the chief catalysts of political and cultural change. Third, I stress that the legacies of the sixties have transformed America irrevocably. In manifold ways, the various social movements interconnected to form the larger "Movement" that raised fundamental questions about the nation's democratic system. Fourth, I contend that the theme of coming apart or unraveling, which predominates published political histories and studies of the New Left, has been overemphasized. Finally, I believe that the periodization of much sixties scholarship is flawed and that, to comprehend the decade, one must show its roots in the fifties and its ramifications in the seventies and beyond.

Americans never made it "back to the garden," of which Joni Mitchell sang the ideal in her 1969 lyrics to "Woodstock," but the quest left no aspect of U.S. society, culture, and politics unchanged. The sixties bequeathed numerous legacies, although its full promise remains for future generations to fulfill.

• • •

Everyone, it seems, has an opinion about the sixties, and over the years many people have shared their views with me. Although agreement even on what happened—let alone why, or what it meant—is not always easily reached, these discussions nevertheless have stimulated many insights. My students, too, have helped to shape my views through their critical exchanges and research projects. I particularly wish to thank the following friends, students, and colleagues who read earlier drafts of the book: Pat Cruza, Lisa Fine, Dave Guard, Victor Howard, Joe Janeti, Jeff Janowick, Bellis Miller, Jeff Miller, Troy Paino, Irene Shim, and Dave Stramecky. I owe special appreciation to Eloise and Paul MacIsaac, who in my summer of need, following the demise of my old laptop, generously lent me their personal computer. The courteous and knowledgeable staffs of the libraries of Michigan State University, the University of California at Berkeley, and the New York Public Library helped me to locate hard-to-find sources, and in other ways assisted me with my study. Grants and a research leave from Michigan State University and a grant from D. C. Heath gave me the time and sustenance necessary to complete *On Our Own*.

This book derives in part from my own primary research that has focused particularly on the New Left and counterculture of the sixties and seventies, and more generally on postwar American social and cultural history. Of necessity, however, *On Our Own* depends on the scholarship of hundreds of others whose articles and monographs make it possible to offer an interpretive synthesis. The most important of these scholars are cited in the bibliographic essays at the end of each chapter.

D. C. Heath commissioned the following historians to review various drafts of manuscript chapters: Linda Alkana, California State University—Long Beach; Ray Arsenault, University of South Florida; Hyman Berman, University of Minnesota; Scott Bills, Steven F. Austin State University; John Braeman, University of Nebraska; Russell Buhite, University of Tennessee—Knoxville; David Castle, Muskingum College; James Clayton, University of Utah; Robert Collins, University of Missouri—Columbia; David Conrad, Southern Illinois University; John D'Emilio, University of North Carolina—Greensboro; Karen Duddy, University of Massachusetts—Boston; James Farrell, St. Olaf College; John Guilmartin, Ohio State University; Mitchell Hall, Central Michigan University; Jack Hammersmith, West Virginia University; Samuel Hand, University of Vermont; Robert Harris, State University of New York—Binghamton; David Horowitz, Portland State University; Christopher Kimball, Augsburg College; Steven Lawson, University of North Carolina—Greensboro; Norman Markowitz, Rutgers University; Lorraine McConaghy, University of Washington; Ann McLaurin, Louisiana State University—Shreveport; Jesse Moore, Jr., University of Rochester; Carol Petillo, Boston College; Peter Ripley, Florida State University; Warren Roberts, State University of New York—Albany; David Schmitz, Whitman College; Jordan Schwarz, Northern Illinois University; Edward Shapsmeier, Illinois State University; Chris Smith, Arizona State University; Thomas Sugrue, University of Pennsylvania; Marcia Synnott,

University of South Carolina; Allan Wald, University of Michigan; Brian Ward, University of Newcastle-Upon-Tyne; and Stephen Waring, University of Alabama—Huntsville. Their written commentary, replete with constructive suggestions and enthusiastic encouragement, proved indispensable in the development of this book. I also owe an enormous debt to the highly competent staff at Heath and especially wish to acknowledge senior history editor James Miller, developmental editor Lauren Johnson, senior production editor Anne Rebecca Starr, and permissions editor Margaret Roll.

Throughout the years it took to research and write *On Our Own,* my wife Sus not only read and discussed the book with me, she also bolstered my spirits and kept me cognizant of what truly matters.

Finally, this book is dedicated to my children Arden and Gilman Miller. Born in the sixties, their lives exemplify the best of that decade's humane idealism.

D. T. M.

Contents

P R O L O G U E

I came upon a child of God,
He was walking along the road,
And I asked him, "Tell me,
Where are you going?"

"I am going down to Yasgur's farm,
I'm going to join a Rock an' Roll band,
I'm going to get back to the land,
And try to get my soul free."

We are stardust,
We are golden,
We are caught in the Devil's barter
And we've got to get ourselves
Back to the Garden.

Then can I walk beside you? . . .
By the time we got to Woodstock
We were half a million strong
And everywhere there was a song
And celebration.

       Joni Mitchell, "Woodstock" (1969)

Tin soldiers and Nixon's coming
We're finally on our own
This summer I hear the drumming
Four dead in Ohio.

       Neil Young, "Ohio" (1970)

In the mideighties, the motion picture *The Big Chill* scored a major success. The movie portrayed idealists of the sixties, now living in the Reagan years, as either virtuous failures or compromised successes—both equally powerless to change the world. Only the Vietnam veteran in the film has preserved his integrity, yet he is impotent, literally and figuratively. For the others, dreams of a new Eden have long since given way to various versions of the personal quest for riches. In the end, the sixties for them mean little more than memories, friendships, and old record albums.

This nostalgic yet cynical view of the sixties, common in U.S. popular culture, is only one way to judge the decade. Most conservatives see the era as the terrible time when America lost its way in a morass of drugs, sex, wasteful welfare programs, and radical politics. Right-wing columnist George Will categorizes the sixties as ''noisy with the voices of fundamentally frivolous people feigning seriousness,'' an ''age of intellectual rubbish,'' of ''sandbox radicalism,'' and of ''almost unrelieved excess.'' Similarly, journalist Jonathan Yardley claims that the '' '60s were adolescent rebellion masquerading as a political movement,'' an ''unfettered self-indulgence on the part of the privileged children of the middle class. . . . For all their noisy rhetoric and noisy music, the '60s contributed nothing to America's national heritage, at least nothing that anyone in his right mind would care to treasure.'' New Right intellectual journals such as Hilton Kramer's *The New Criterion* routinely blame the sixties for America's current ills. In 1993 the *Wall Street Journal* editorialized that the murder of a Florida physician by an antiabortionist was the consequence of the antiwar protests at the 1968 Democratic National Convention.

Unrepentant radicals, on the other hand, solemnize the era as a golden age of revolt, a time of utopian dreams that shattered in the reactionary Reagan-Bush years. As the editors of the recent radical anthology *The 60s Without Apology* see it, the ''trashing'' of the sixties by conservatives ''has become a strategic feature of the current struggle for hegemony.'' Certainly there is much truth in this argument.

If, as many believe, the sixties serve as a fulcrum of postwar American history, then controlling the historic image of that decade helps to shape current policies and perceptions. These conflicting historic interpretations form part of a larger clash of cultures and values that the decade unleashed and that Americans have yet to resolve. If, as the Right believes, the sixties witnessed excessive permissiveness, anarchistic antiauthoritarianism, and fiscal irresponsibility, then conservative policies make sense. But for those who perceive the decade as a time of caring, sharing, equality, and freedom that produced what former Students for a Democratic Society (SDS) leader Todd Gitlin called ''an incomplete Reformation'' of American life, then the need to sustain that change appears pressing. Recent presidential-campaign debates over welfare, women's rights, health care, gay rights, abortion, art censorship, the environment, and America's role in the world have reflected this ongoing controversy.

The ideological struggle between Right and Left, and the nostalgia of the mass media have generated lively interest in the 1960s but have not brought us closer to an accurate historical assessment of those tempestuous years. And though it would be foolhardy to claim that any scholar will ever achieve complete objectivity in analyzing such a controversial subject as American society in that pivotal decade, this book nevertheless represents a serious effort to produce a fresh analysis.

Many of the books that have attempted to synthesize the period strike a polemical note, especially evaluations written in the heat of the late sixties such as Theodore

Roszak's *The Making of a Counter Culture* (1969) and Lewis Feuer's *The Conflict of Generations* (1969). More recent works, too, continue either to glorify or to damn the sixties. George Katsiaficas's *The Imagination of the New Left* (1988) and Edward P. Morgan's *The Sixties Experience* (1991) exemplify the former approach; Joseph Conlin's *The Troubles* (1982) and Stanley Rothman's and S. Robert Lichter's *Roots of Radicalism* (1982) typify the latter. One recent study, Peter Collier's and David Horowitz's *Destructive Generation* (1989), even recalls post–World War II confessions by former leftists turned conservative. During the sixties, Collier and Horowitz edited the radical *Ramparts* magazine; now born-again conservatives, they denounce the drug taking, promiscuity, anti-Americanism, and violence of that decade as if those are the period's only legacies. Other studies, such as Herbert Hendin's *Age of Sensation* (1975) and Morris Dickstein's *Gates of Eden* (1977), try to tell the story of the sixties through metaphor: one aspect of American life—sexual attitudes in Hendin's case, literature in Dickstein's—serves as metaphor for the entire period.

Controversy over the meaning of the sixties has simmered from the outset. Writing at the end of the decade, Yale Law School professor Charles Reich and journalist David Halberstam published very different appraisals. In his best-selling *The Greening of America* (1970), Reich saw America enduring an extraordinary transformation as a new, liberated consciousness arose "out of the wasteland of the Corporate State, like flowers pushing up through the concrete pavement." In *McCall's* that year, Halberstam bade "good-by to all that, to the Sixties, to all that hope and expectation. It started so well, a belief that . . . all the pieces would come together for a golden era of American social and cultural progress, victory over the darker side of our nature, victory over injustice. It ended in pain, disillusionment, bitterness, our eyes expert in watching televised funerals."

Arguments over the nature of the 1960s persist in historical assessments of the period, though most scholars have agreed more with Halberstam's negative evaluation than Reich's positive one. In 1971 historian William O'Neill expressed in the title of his book *Coming Apart* what would become the dominant interpretation of the sixties: the increasing polarization and then fragmentation of American politics and culture.

In *America in Our Time* (1976), a book with a more precise thesis than O'Neill's, Godfrey Hodgson, a British correspondent long based in America, attempted to pinpoint what had come apart in the sixties. Referring to the years between John F. Kennedy's election in 1960 and Richard Nixon's resignation in 1974 as "the time of lost hopes," Hodgson traced the rise and fall of America's governing consensus, beginning with the emergence of the United States from World War II as the most powerful and prosperous country in the world. During this exceptional period, Hodgson argued, American policymakers came to accept what he termed the "liberal consensus." "Confident to the point of complacency about the perfectibility of American society, anxious to the point of paranoia about the threat of communism," this consensus culminated in the Kennedy-Johnson years.

From the start, however, the consensus had fissures, and encouraged two particularly risky illusions: first, that "the inequalities and injustices of American society were residual, and could be abolished by the expenditure of resources on a scale that need not involve any hard choice between priorities"; second, that "the United States could use its military power to change the world in conformity with its wishes and not itself be changed in the process." The struggle of blacks at home and the Vietnam War abroad exposed the fatal flaws in the liberal consensus. By the end of the sixties, in Hodgson's view, the "illusion of omnipotence" had shattered, revealing "the bankruptcy of the American model for most of the developing world." Ultimately, Hodgson concluded, "the crisis of the sixties posed questions . . . about the legitimacy of [the] system itself." From the perspective of the midseventies, Hodgson predicted that America's only hope was to build a new consensus "on the ruins of illusion."

Allen Matusow's influential *The Unraveling of America* (1984), although less sweeping in its chronological coverage than Hodgson's study, also found the United States coming apart by the late sixties. Concerned largely with domestic liberalism in the Kennedy-Johnson years, Matusow noted that "liberals came to identify the main problems confronting the country as unemployment, racism, and poverty. The solutions they sponsored were Keynesian management of the economy, civil rights laws, and special measures to bring the poor into the economic mainstream." Like Hodgson, Matusow maintained that the measures by which liberals tried to cure the nation's ills proved inadequate and provoked an uprising against liberalism from both the Left and the Right. By 1968, he concluded, "optimism vanished, fundamental differences in values emerged to divide the country, social cohesion rapidly declined, and the unraveling of America began."

Both Hodgson and Matusow examined the New Left and related counterculture, but they addressed that phenomenon (what activists referred to as "the Movement") as a short-lived curiosity of significance chiefly for its role in the collapse of liberalism. Historians who focus exclusively on the New Left are more likely to attribute long-range legacies to the Movement, yet they also emphasize the theme of coming apart. Scholars such as Kirkpatrick Sale, Edward J. Bacciocco, Jr., Irwin Unger, George Vickers, Nigel Young, Milton Cantor, and Alan Brinkley have concerned themselves primarily with the organizational and political failures of the New Left. They have particularly emphasized the late-sixties implosion of the most important New Left organization, Students for a Democratic Society. SDS, in Brinkley's words, "collapsed on itself in a paroxysm of frustration, nihilism, and violence."

The two best books on the Movement were written by former SDS activists: Todd Gitlin, *The Sixties: Years of Hope, Days of Rage* (1987), and James Miller, *"Democracy Is in the Streets": From Port Huron to the Siege of Chicago* (1987). Both treat the Movement sympathetically, though with serious reservations. As Miller concluded in his compassionate study of SDS: "The New Left was obviously in some respects a dead end." Both these past participants established a dichotomy between a good, early New Left and a bad, later New Left, a division that allowed them to praise the initial years of the student and civil-rights movements while disparaging the increasing militancy and violence of the later sixties. Nevertheless, the resultant story still told of an unraveling. In Gitlin's account, for instance, the "years of hope" were relatively few, easily equaled by years of confusion and finally self-destruction.

Thus, the predominant theme of most examinations of the sixties, whether from the perspective of mainstream politics or from the New Left, is that of coming apart. Certainly it would be presumptuous to deny that in many ways the ties that had traditionally held America together came unknotted in the late sixties. Still, the standard interpretation of the decade overemphasizes the extent of America's unraveling, leads to a false sense that the era came to an abrupt end, and thereby downplays the enormous impact and legacies of the decade.

Writing from the perspectives of the Nixon and Reagan years, respectively, it is not surprising that Hodgson and Matusow saw liberalism as having expired in the sixties. Conservatism, of course, remains a powerful force in American politics. Yet the victory of Democrat Bill Clinton in the 1992 presidential election indicated that liberalism had not died; rather, it saw a period of reassessment. Hodgson and Matusow correctly analyzed the flaws of the earlier liberal vision: America was neither omnipotent abroad nor rich enough to solve all its problems at home without a radical redistribution of the nation's wealth. But these misperceptions in no way proved the bankruptcy of liberal aspirations to use the government as a positive force in resolving foreign and domestic dilemmas.

Similarly, by concentrating on the demise of SDS, histories of the New Left create the notion that the whole Movement self-destructed between 1968 and 1969 in an orgy of mindless Marxism and quixotic violence. This premise gives the erroneous impression that the Movement failed and thus minimizes the immense impact that the social movements of the sixties did exert. Focusing on the fate of SDS also overemphasizes the extent of violence within the Movement. Despite the publicity generated by riotous New Leftists such as the Weatherman faction of the SDS, the overwhelming majority of Movement activists in fact remained nonviolent. Unfortunately, the self-destructive terrorism of a few tended to discredit the entire Movement in the media at the time and continues to do so in recent historical scholarship.

Finally, by focusing on the fate of SDS as a national organization, scholars overlook the mass movement that flourished in the late sixties and early seventies after SDS expired. Although SDS had served as a major focus of community organizing and antiwar activism, the national organization diminished in significance as the Movement mushroomed in the mid- to late sixties. In addition, most SDS chapters were campus based and had little connection to the larger society. Tellingly, many chapters continued calling themselves SDS even after the demise of the national organization in 1969.

Yet during these years, thousands of other Movement organizations, ad hoc committees, and coalitions blossomed, mostly at the grass-roots level. In 1969 Movement mailing lists contained the names of some seventeen hundred organizations. The years 1968–1972 witnessed the largest and most influential antiwar demonstrations, a flowering of communes, and the spread of counterculture values and lifestyles to a broad base of the population. That period also saw the rise of major new movements for women, the environment, gays, Hispanics, and Native Americans. By 1970 the Movement and the related counterculture had expanded numerically, had gained importance in the lives of participants, and had penetrated or influenced virtually every aspect of American society, from the armed forces to religion, from business to sports. Whereas some viewed this development as a tragic unraveling, others saw it as a healthy opening up of political and cultural dialogue that would lead to a more democratic and pluralistic America than before. For millions of activists and those influenced by the Movement, the late sixties and early seventies were a time of ecstatic liberation, not disastrous decline.

The ongoing nature of the Movement also throws into question the way in which scholars have periodized the sixties. Many writers regard the decade as a unit beginning with the lunch-counter sit-ins and the Kennedy election in 1960 and closing with the Nixon presidency; the Manson murders and the Altamont violence of 1969; and the May 4, 1970, killings at Kent State. Such history oversimplifies. The sixties cannot be understood as a self-enclosed ten-year span. The decade did not represent some sort of remarkable about-face, some mysterious transformation of the genial fifties. As *On Our Own: Americans in the Sixties* tries to show, the seeds of social activism that flowered in the sixties were sown in that earlier, more quiescent period. Nor did the social movements of the sixties and the various issues raised come to a crashing end in the violence of 1968 and 1969. Many movements have endured, and political debate continues to center on issues raised in that decade.

Students of the New Left are particularly prone to treat the much publicized late-sixties breakup of SDS and the Black Power movement as the end of an era. Yet feminism, gay liberation, ecological radicalism, conservation, and communal living are just a few of the movements that have since flourished. What is needed, therefore, is an approach that elucidates the period's political, social, and cultural roots in earlier American history and their manifestations that have persisted. *On Our Own* offers such a perspective.

COLD WAR REALITIES, AMERICAN DREAMS

"My son and his family, who live in California not too far from the atomic-bomb testing grounds in Nevada, are becoming used to seeing a flash and some minutes later feeling the house rock," a woman told the *Reader's Digest*. "One night recently he woke from a sound sleep and asked, 'What's that?' 'Oh, go back to sleep,' said his wife. 'It's only an atomic bomb.' My son settled back. 'All right. I was afraid one of the kids had fallen out of bed.'"

The couple in this 1952 *Digest* story were part of the newly affluent postwar middle class: they owned their home and, like many young couples of the time, had at least two children, on whom they doted. Yet they, like many other postwar Americans, faced a profound ambivalence. On the surface, the lives of such families bubbled along with prosperity and success. Yet however much they tried to pretend otherwise, fears of nuclear destruction simmered just beneath the surface.

Most Americans, of course, lived far enough away from nuclear test sites to avoid seeing the flash and feeling the house rock, and weighty questions concerning the world's fate seldom cropped up during family dinner discussions. Still, no one could ignore the atomic age. Throughout the midcentury years, the Cold War and the related nuclear-arms race provoked widespread fears of nuclear annihilation. By the midfifties, public apprehension also grew concerning the dangers of radioactive fallout from the United States' and the Soviet Union's atmospheric tests of nuclear weapons. Newspapers regularly discussed the possibility—even the probability—of World War III. Schools routinely held air-raid drills: Teachers taught schoolchildren to lie flat on their stomachs or to curl up in a fetal position with their heads tucked between their knees under desks or in windowless hallways and wait for the A-bomb or the all-clear. Families built and stocked underground survival shelters and even armed them to keep out less-prepared neighbors when the Bomb fell.

Hollywood, capitalizing on the nation's nuclear jitters, produced a spate of films depicting alien monsters that threatened American civilization. Many such monsters—either mutants created by radiation or prehistoric brutes resuscitated by nuclear blasts—arose from atomic explosions. *The Beast,* the giant octopus in *It Came from Beneath the Sea, The Deadly Mantis, The Spider,* and *The Crab Monster* are just a few of the deadly atomic offspring stalking or slithering through post-Hiroshima cinema. In the 1954 horror hit *Them!* ants mutate to enormous proportions as a result of radioactive fallout from bomb tests in New Mexico. After terrorizing a small town, the ants eventually are destroyed, but the scientist-hero ominously concludes that in the atomic age the rise of such monstrous mutants is inevitable.

Domestic communist infiltration also haunted Cold War America, especially in the early fifties. During these years, the trials of accused Soviet agents Alger Hiss and Julius and Ethel Rosenberg, combined with Wisconsin senator Joseph McCarthy's loud accusations of spies in government, convinced millions that communist agents lurked everywhere.

Such apprehensions and problems contradict the recent outpouring of nostalgia for the "nifty fifties." Since the early seventies, the popular image of America's midcentury years has been one of peace and prosperity: "Happy Days," bunny hops and bobby sox, Mickey Mantle and Willie Mays, Marilyn Monroe and James Dean, Elvis Presley and Chuck Berry, cruising and panty raids, Howdy Doody and Kukla, Fran, and Ollie. This positive picture has more to do with relieving recent anxieties than with what really happened, although, of course, the recent vision contains grains of truth. For the white middle class, the fifties offered affordable suburban houses equipped with the latest appliances, powerful automobiles and cheap gas, secure jobs and good wages, all presided over by a trusted and lovable president, Dwight D. Eisenhower. While fifties front-page headlines screamed of spies, the Cold War, Korea, and H-bombs, opinion polls revealed that the great majority of Americans concerned themselves mostly with their own lives and those of their families and immediate friends. Such people embraced the fifties, although the more menacing actualities never lay far from the surface of this complex decade. Ultimately, the contrast between dreams and realities produced tensions that would climax in the 1960s.

Conflict and Containment

The United States emerged from the Second World War as the most powerful and wealthy nation on earth. Americans enjoyed formidable advantages; they had triumphed in battle and had proved their ability to wage successful conventional war, they had sole possession of the atomic bomb, and they savored an economy that had more than doubled while the economies of other nations had declined or collapsed. Not surprisingly, America's leaders thus saw the United States as an omnipotent giant capable of shaping the world's future. What magazine magnate Henry Luce had prophesied at the outset of the war appeared to be coming true: the "American Century" was dawning, a century in which, Luce predicted, the United States, "the most powerful and vital nation in the world," would act "for such purposes as we see fit and by such means as we see fit." Columnist Walter Lippmann intoned, "What Rome was to the ancient world, what Britain has been to the modern world, America is to be to the world of tomorrow." Triumphant in a just war, Americans anticipated a postwar period that would be, in the words of a popular 1946 film, "The Best Years of Our Lives."

But something went wrong. Soon after the war, a sinister new enemy, the communist Soviet Union, appeared, threatening America's vision of a peaceful world order. Although the two countries had cooperated as allies in World War II, their more typical antagonisms had long roots in the past. Anti-Soviet and anticommunist sentiments had pervaded the American political temper since the 1917 Bolshevik revolution. At the end of World War I, the United States and the other Allies had sent troops into Russia in an unsuccessful effort to crush the nascent communist regime. Soviet distrust of the United States was equally entrenched, dating not only from the 1918 intervention but also from the U.S. failure to recognize the Soviet state until 1933, Americans' unwillingness to join the Soviets during the 1930s in an antifascist coalition, and their own belief that communism must inevitably triumph over capitalism. The Soviets, particularly their leader, Joseph Stalin, viewed the United States as head of the worldwide capitalist bloc, irrevocably hostile to socialism. In this respect, the two nations' wartime alliance proved ephemeral, and with the end of that global clash a new pattern of international conflict surfaced—the Cold War. With Germany and Japan defeated and Great Britain and France enfeebled, the United States and the Soviet Union emerged as the two great powers. Although America dominated in military might, it nevertheless cast a fearful eye on the Soviet Union.

Soon after the war, President Harry S Truman and other top policymakers took offense that the Soviets refused to allow free elections in Poland and other areas of Eastern Europe that Soviet troops had liberated from Nazi Germany. In March 1946, Britain's wartime prime minister, Winston Churchill, speaking in Fulton, Missouri, warned Americans of a communist "peril to Christian civilization." From the Baltic to the Adriatic, Churchill claimed, "an iron curtain has descended across the [European] continent."

A year later, on March 12, 1947, in a controversial speech before a joint session of Congress, the president announced the Truman Doctrine: "It must be the policy of the United States to support free peoples who are resisting attempted subjugation by armed minorities or by outside pressures." Here was a new version of the American mission: the United States would serve as the guardian of free peoples everywhere in a world irreconcilably divided between the forces of good and evil. If America should fail in this mission, Truman warned, "we may endanger the peace of the world—and we shall surely endanger the welfare of our own nation." Although initially voiced in support of a bill to send military aid to Greece and Turkey, the message meant that the United States must contain communism everywhere. Containment thus became the keystone of American Cold War policy and in the coming years would lead the United States into armed conflicts in Asia, the Middle East, and Latin America.

In retrospect, it is clear that after World War II, both the Soviets and the Americans attempted to pursue their own interests, yet each viewed the other's actions through distorted ideological lenses. Thus the Russians, having twice in the twentieth century suffered invasions through Eastern Europe, saw the creation of pro-Soviet regimes in that region as essential to their national security. American leaders, for their part, judged this behavior an illegitimate violation of the Eastern European countries' right to self-determination and part of a Soviet plot to spread communism.

In the late 1940s and early 1950s, the Cold War intensified. In 1948 a communist coup in Czechoslovakia toppled the last democratic government in Eastern Europe. That same year, the Soviets cut off western access into Berlin, and the United States and Great Britain responded by airlifting supplies into West Berlin for nearly a year before the Russians agreed to reopen the borders. In 1949 the Soviets exploded their first atomic bomb, and Mao Zedong's communist forces triumphed in China, sobering events that caused many Americans to blame communist agents and sympathizers at home for every setback.

In 1950, after less than five years of peace, communist North Korea invaded South Korea. Assuming that the Soviets had directed the invasion, Harry Truman concluded that "if the Russian totalitarian state was intending to follow in the path of the dictatorship of Hitler and Mussolini, they [had to] be met head on in Korea." Without consulting Congress, Truman ordered in U.S. forces under General Douglas MacArthur. The UN Security Council, minus the Soviet Union, which was boycotting the organization on an unrelated matter, branded North Korea an aggressor and called on member states to assist South Korea. Although from start to finish about 90 percent of the UN forces were American, Truman's war had international sanction. For the next three years, U.S. troops fought a stalemated war against both North Korean and Chinese soldiers in far-off Asia.

Containment marked a drastic change in American policy. From a traditionally isolationist nation concerned largely with the Western Hemisphere, the United States now saw itself as the world's policeman. In earlier periods of peace, the United States had possessed meager defense budgets, a small standing army with no troops on foreign soil, and no military alliances. Now America became a garrison state with a massive military establishment, huge defense budgets, a global ring of military bases, and military treaties with some forty nations. The United States also launched a nuclear-arms race with the Soviets. Soon after learning of the Soviet Union's first atomic test, President Truman gave the go-ahead for building the hydrogen bomb, a weapon over a thousand times more powerful than the bombs that had destroyed the Japanese cities of Hiroshima and Nagasaki at the close of World War II. On November 1, 1952, the Americans exploded the first H-bomb; the Soviets soon followed suit. The balance of power had become a balance of terror.

To muster congressional and public support for the administration's Cold War policies, Truman and other policymakers routinely portrayed the complex postwar international scene in dramatic but simplistic terms of good versus evil. As Senator J. William Fulbright recalled, "After World War II, we were sold on the idea that Stalin was out to dominate the world." Communism, the government insisted, was a monolithic, conspiratorial force, controlled and directed by Moscow and aimed at world rule. This official version of the Cold War portrayed the United States as the shield of free peoples against the hosts of totalitarianism. In effect, the war was an irrevocable global

Testing the Bomb. More than two thousand U.S. marines witnessed this atomic blast at Yucca Flat, Nevada, in April 1952, and many later suffered from radiation-related illnesses. Throughout the 1950s, the United States conducted above-ground atomic and hydrogen bomb tests with little regard for health risks.

struggle that pitted the individualistic, capitalistic, and God-fearing democrats against the collectivist, socialistic, and atheistic communists. With the battle seen in these terms, America could ill afford to lose.

By the early fifties, politicians and public alike unquestioningly accepted this over-simplified, bipolar picture. But although such a worldview catalyzed near-unanimous support of Cold War policies, it fostered paranoia. Americans began to see isolated events in various parts of the world as part of a global communist conspiracy, one that millions believed operated even within the United States itself.

Loyalty Under Fire

Soon after the Second World War, as relations between the two superpowers soured, vehement fears of an internal communist threat emerged. As anti-Soviet feeling grew, conservatives exploited this sentiment as a way to attack liberals. In the 1946 congressional elections, Republican propaganda tried to equate New Deal liberalism with the red menace. Such smear tactics helped Republicans to gain control of Congress and to elect anticommunist stalwarts, including Richard Nixon of California and Joseph McCarthy of Wisconsin.

But although conservative Republicans took full advantage of national fears for political purposes, by 1947 Harry Truman and the Democrats would boost the status of conservative anticommunists by exaggerating the Soviet threat and depicting the Cold War as an ideological struggle between the forces of decency and malevolence. On March 22, 1947, just ten days after announcing the Truman Doctrine, the president launched a domestic crusade against communism. By executive order, he initiated a loyalty review program for government employees with the stated purpose of effecting "maximum protection" to "the United States against infiltration of disloyal persons into the ranks of its employees." Truman later complained of the "great wave of hysteria" sweeping the nation, yet his commitment to victory over communism and to safeguarding the United States from external and internal threats contributed to that very hysteria.

The loyalty program lent credence to the correlation of dissent with disloyalty and legitimated guilt by association. Between the security program's launch in March 1947 and December 1952, the government investigated some 6.6 million people. Not a single case of espionage was thereby uncovered, although more than five hundred individuals were dismissed for "questionable loyalty." With utter disregard for individual civil liberties, Truman's review board conducted loyalty checks using undisclosed evidence, secret and often paid informers, and neither judge nor jury.

To establish a criterion of loyalty, the president's attorney general, Tom Clark, drew up a list of supposedly subversive organizations. Clark, a conservative Texas lawyer, took his role of safeguarding American security seriously. "Those who do not believe in the ideology of the United States," he proclaimed, "shall not be allowed to stay in the United States." He compiled his list on the basis of secret Federal Bureau of Investigation (FBI) files, with no public hearings. Although originally classified, the list soon became publicly known as "the Attorney General's List," thereby giving official sanction to blacklisting. In determining disloyalty, the government considered not only membership in organizations on the list but also "sympathetic association" with any listed group. By the early fifties, the government deemed hundreds of groups subversive. Besides the Communist party and its affiliates, the list included many civil-rights, peace, and other left-of-center organizations.

Truman bolstered the budget and power of the FBI, allowing it to play the role of America's ideological watchdog. FBI director J. Edgar Hoover warned that "behind this force of traitorous Communists constantly gnawing at the very foundations of American society, stand a half million fellow travelers and sympathizers ready to do the Communists' bidding." During Hoover's tenure as head of the FBI, until his death in 1972, his uncompromising attitude toward suspected subversives never wavered. In the 1960s, he and his agency became the implacable foes of civil-rights, antiwar, and other protest movements.

In addition to the FBI, other government organizations were involved in the search for subversives: the Central Intelligence Agency, which although founded in 1947 with a mandate to gather foreign intelligence, soon turned its attention to domestic surveillance as well; the Post Office Intelligence Division; the Customs Bureau of the Treasury; the Civil Service Commission; the Passport Division of the State Department; the Immigration and Naturalization Service of the Justice Department; and the various branches of military intelligence.

Despite the failure to uncover large-scale subversion, the broad scope of the official red hunt gave popular credence to the notion that the government crawled with spies. Most Americans became convinced of the need for absolute security and the preservation of the status quo, even if they had to violate individuals' civil liberties. Soon states, cities, and counties followed the federal government's lead and established their own loyalty programs, utilizing the now well-publicized list. So too did many corporations, educational institutions, and labor unions. Hollywood and the television networks purged themselves of and blacklisted suspected subversives. The city of Dearborn, Michigan, even crowned a "Miss Loyalty" at a beauty pageant complete with loyalty oaths. Publicly pledging fidelity to God, country, and Constitution while abjuring communist affiliations became a basic feature of American life. Under the guise of loyalty checks, conservatives often ferreted out not communists but nonconformists of all sorts: liberals, New Dealers, radical labor leaders, civil-rights activists, pacifists, and atheists.

As the Cold War heated up in the late forties and early fifties, fears of internal communist subversion escalated. No major spy rings were uncovered, but several well-publicized trials convinced most Americans that a serious threat existed. On July 20, 1948, a federal grand jury indicted eleven leaders of the Communist party of the United States. Although not charging them with espionage, the prosecution proved that these communists believed in the ideas of Marx and Lenin and therefore advocated the violent overthrow of the government. In the atmosphere of the time, this link was enough to convict them of conspiracy.

On January 21, 1950, a jury found Alger Hiss guilty of perjury. The Hiss case came to national attention in August 1948 when, at a House Un-American Activities Committee (HUAC) hearing, Whittaker Chambers, a confessed ex-communist, accused Hiss of having been a party member while employed in the State Department during the 1930s. Initially Chambers's charges were vague, but with prodding from HUAC member Richard Nixon, he soon told a dramatic story of stolen documents passed from Hiss to himself to the Soviets. A first trial ended in a hung jury, but a second trial, much publicized and still controversial, resulted in Hiss's conviction for perjury.

The Hiss case convinced millions that Republican charges of spies' infesting the Democratic administrations of Franklin Roosevelt and Harry Truman had merit. To many Republicans and right-wing superpatriots, Alger Hiss—a bright, urbane, handsome, Harvard-educated, eastern aristocrat with an odd-sounding name—came to symbolize New Deal treachery. Republican Nixon called the Hiss case only "a small part of the whole shocking story of Communist espionage in the United States."

On February 3, 1950, only two weeks after Hiss's conviction, the British government announced the arrest of Dr. Klaus Fuchs, a high-level atomic scientist who had worked on the Manhattan Project. Fuchs confessed to having spied for the Soviet Union. Investigators linked him to Americans Harry Gold, Morton Sobell, and Julius and Ethel Rosenberg. Arrested and tried for espionage, Gold and Sobell received long jail terms. The Rosenbergs, professing their innocence to the end, received the death sentence and were executed on June 19, 1953.

Truman's loyalty program had spurred national outrage against subversives, and now events had raged out of control. Instead of maintaining leadership over the crusade against communist and internal subversion, the president saw hysteria mushrooming everywhere, to the benefit of the Republicans. Americans wanted answers: How could Russia have the bomb? How could China have fallen to the communists? How many more Alger Hisses still lurked in government?

Joseph McCarthy, a junior senator from Wisconsin, claimed to have the answers to these frightening questions. On February 9, 1950, less than a week after the Fuchs story broke and while Americans agitated over Hiss, China, and the Soviet bomb, McCarthy held up a piece of paper while addressing the Women's Republican Club in Wheeling, West Virginia. "I have here in my hand a list of 205 that were known to the Secretary of State as being members of the Communist party and who, nevertheless, are still working and shaping policy in the State Department," he thundered. With these words, McCarthy's anticommunist career took center stage, where he remained for four and a half years, pushing the nation's mania to new heights of irrationality. McCarthy did not create the national paranoia over communism; he merely capitalized on it. His rhetoric and tactics, although extreme, were well within the established framework of Cold War politics. McCarthy never turned up a single subversive, but his rash, false outbursts mirrored the political climate of the day.

In these years, American society reflected a strange amalgam of fear and consensus. Supposed communist infiltration, spy trials, loyalty investigations, Korean fighting, and the Bomb spawned widespread anxieties. In the name of national security, McCarthy and his ilk trampled on basic civil liberties. Dissent was suppressed, conformity demanded. Yet such fear and repression, coupled with phenomenal and unprecedented prosperity, also prompted Americans to unite under a national faith. Seeing the world in dualistic terms, people celebrated the United States as the bastion of freedom, democracy, and "people's capitalism." Indeed, the combined anxiety and optimism of the time is revealed in the title of a 1950 song: "Jesus Is God's Atomic Bomb."

"Easy Street"

The United States had gone to war in 1941 as merely one among several global powers. It emerged in 1945 as the world's superpower. Western Europe, the traditional center of world authority, resembled, in Churchill's words, "a rubble heap, a charnel house, a breeding ground of pestilence and hate." Europe's industrial production had plummeted, food was scarce, capital was lacking. In complete contrast, the United States sprang from the war with a booming, expansive economy. The Gross National Product (GNP), less than $100 billion in 1940, skyrocketed to nearly $212 billion by 1945. Unemployment, the major prewar problem, virtually disappeared. So preponderant was American economic supremacy that in 1947, even with economic recovery well under way in Europe, the United States produced about half the world's manufactures, including 80 percent of new automobiles made that year. Although many Americans at war's end braced themselves for a new depression, in fact the United States stood on the brink of the most spectacular economic expansion in history. From World War II through the early 1970s, except for brief periods of recession, the boom pushed Americans to levels of prosperity undreamed of in prewar times.

New highs in consumer spending drove the postwar boom. During the depressed thirties, millions of Americans had made do with what they had. Although the war had brought full employment and bigger paychecks, the government had regulated production, urging industries to concentrate on manufacturing war materials, not consumer items. During most of the war years, no automobiles were built, and, except for government projects around war plants, new housing was rare. With little to buy, Americans saved, and by 1945 they had accumulated more than $140 billion. After a decade and a half of scrimping, the national mood was anything but frugal.

For nearly three years after the war, consumer demand outstripped production. People put their names on long waiting lists to buy new automobiles and snapped up household appliances as fast as producers could ship them. These years saw the advent of one new item of profound future importance: television. The Radio Corporation of America (RCA) had first marketed television sets in 1939, even opening that year's World's Fair, in New York, with a television broadcast. Yet as late as 1946, only seven thousand sets stood in American homes. Two years later, annual output reached close to one million, and the three major radio networks—ABC, CBS, and NBC—offered regular national televised broadcasts. A new industry and a revolutionary medium of communication had arisen.

Massive postwar consumer spending also eased the reconversion from wartime to peacetime production. So too did the GI Bill. Passed in June 1944 to aid returning veterans, this legislation stimulated long-term prosperity by providing home, farm, and business loans, readjustment allowances, preferential employment status, hospital care, and generous education grants. Soon after the war, about a million former soldiers entered college under the GI Bill, receiving both tuition and subsistence allowances. The bill had manifold benefits. It reduced the number of returning veterans' seeking jobs by diverting them to college, allowed the training of a generation of professionals and skilled technicians, and facilitated the rapid growth and democratization of the American university system. An additional million veterans established their own businesses with guaranteed loans of up to $2,000. Finally, the bill helped a generation of GIs to buy homes at low interest rates with no down payment. These benefits accelerated the postwar marriage and baby boom and the suburban explosion in the late forties and fifties that fueled postwar prosperity.

Personal income grew annually in the fifties despite three mild recessions. Between 1945 and 1960, the average wage earner's real purchasing power rose by more than 22 percent; from 1960 to 1970, it leaped ahead by an additional 38 percent. Although the nation had enjoyed other periods of sustained economic growth, the boom from World War II to the early 1970s differed in one important way: rather than spending these increases in real wages solely on necessities—better food, shelter, and clothing— as they had in the past, millions earned incomes sufficient for nonessential items as well. This development prompted economist Walt Rostow to dub America's postwar economic development the "high mass consumption" stage.

American culture in these years transformed from one dominated by the ethic of self-denial to one of self-indulgence, a shift strongly encouraged by corporate advertising, particularly on television. Advertisers dazzled Americans with visual images of the good life. In the comfort of their living rooms, Americans were tantalized by flashy automobiles, labor-saving appliances, and prepared foods and urged to enhance their status and pleasure by purchasing these products.

To sell the plethora of consumer goods that corporate America produced and advertisers touted, entrepreneurs built vast, luxurious shopping centers, especially in the

The Ultimate Automobile. Advertisements for the Cadillac Le Mans implied that buying this 250-horse-power, tail-finned model bestowed instant status on its owner.

burgeoning suburban communities. Shopping, once a chore, now became a joy, and almost a way of life for some people. A writer for *Life* in the midfifties boasted that Americans could browse in a ''$5 million grocery store, picking from the thousands of items on the high-piled shelves until their carts became cornucopias filled with an abundance that no other country in the world has ever known.''

The spurt in consumer credit also fueled high levels of personal spending. Between 1946 and 1970, as Americans came to rely on home mortgages and auto loans to finance these major purchases, short- and intermediate-term loans increased from $8.4 billion to $127 billion. Then in 1950 came that magic, small plastic rectangle—the credit card—beginning with Diners Club. Soon shoppers could charge everything from electric toothbrushes to two-week vacations and pay for everything in installments. All-purpose charge cards such as American Express and Visa as well as cards issued by companies such as Sears and Standard Oil multiplied in the fifties and sixties. Cards and installment buying stimulated consumption. One study concluded that ''on the average, people who charge purchases spend about 35 percent more than those who pay cash.''

The postwar spending boom had a marked effect on American industry. Big business, already powerful in the prewar period, grew even larger. Between 1940 and 1960, the percentage of the total labor force classified as self-employed dropped from 26 to 11 percent. Most people now worked for giant corporations, and in major industries a few huge firms dominated. In the manufacture of automobiles, agricultural machinery, tires, cigarettes, aluminum, liquor, meat products, copper, tin cans, and office machinery, three companies prevailed; in steel, chemicals, and dairy products, about six reigned.

Beginning around midcentury, a wave of mergers swept American business. In addition to the traditional combining of companies in the same field, the postwar years saw the conglomerate merging of companies in totally unrelated fields. So great was the concentration of industry that by 1968 the two hundred largest manufacturing corporations held the same proportion of total manufacturing assets as had the thousand largest companies in 1941. These giant firms not only employed millions of Americans, they also served in some ways as social and welfare institutions. Between 1940 and 1965, corporate investment in pension funds grew from $4 billion to $100 billion and profoundly affected the stock market. Generally unrestrained by competition, the large corporations made many of the nation's fundamental decisions concerning prices, production, wages, and technological change.

As they consolidated, major industries invested an average of $10 billion a year in new plants and machinery, prompting a jump in productivity per labor-hour. From 1945 through the midfifties alone, per-capita production shot up 200 percent. A new word came into use in the immediate postwar years: *automation,* the use of self-regulating machinery to perform manufacturing operations. Automation, begun before the war, made rapid advances in the postwar years, often at the expense of labor. Employment in the textile industry, for example, declined 35 percent between 1947 and 1961, largely owing to automated machinery.

The most dramatic advances in automation came after 1960 with the introduction of computers in business operations. Although the first operable computer was developed at Harvard University during World War II, not until 1948, with the invention of the transistor at Bell Telephone Laboratories, did computer technology become practical. As late as 1954, only twenty computers were in business use. By 1960, however, computer sales exceeded $1 billion—and this was just the beginning. Computers accelerated automation and augmented productivity but brought technological unemployment as well.

Postwar changes in corporate structure and productivity transformed industrial employment. Traditional unskilled and semiskilled blue-collar workers proved increasingly expendable. Even the employment of skilled machinists declined by 27 percent from 1950 to 1970. On the other hand, during the postwar years of bureaucratization, specialization, and technological change, the percentage of salaried white-collar workers exploded. Clerical employees, salespeople, engineers, scientists, computer programmers, public relations experts, teachers, and various managerial personnel multiplied in number and importance. From 1947 to 1957, salaried middle-class employees grew by 61 percent, while the number of factory operatives declined by 4 percent. By 1956 white-collar workers outnumbered the blue-collar labor force for the first time. The United States had entered what some experts have called a ''postindustrial'' state.

These changes in the work force weakened organized labor. Few of these new types of employees belonged to unions or even identified their interests with those of organized labor. Between 1945 and 1960, the number of nonagricultural workers belonging to unions fell by 14 percent. The Congress of Industrial Organizations (CIO), the nation's largest labor organization, which had enjoyed spectacular success unionizing mass-production industries in the late 1930s, grew cautious in the postwar years. In the late 1940s, under pressure from the government, the CIO had expelled eleven communist-dominated unions and purged known communists from other unions such as the United Auto Workers (UAW). By these actions, the CIO became more acceptable to the American public, but communist labor leaders had been effective union organizers, and their expulsion enfeebled the CIO. In 1950, nationally televised Senate hearings linking some unions with organized crime further tainted the labor movement. In an effort to marshal stability and power, the American Federation of Labor (AFL) and the CIO agreed to merge in 1955, but labor problems continued. In 1957 the AFL-CIO ousted its largest union member, the Teamsters, because of the organization's continued connections with organized crime. During these years, the labor movement also suffered from the migration of many industries to the strongly antiunion South and the rise in nonunion white-collar employees.

For unionized blue-collar workers who did not lose their jobs to automation, however, the postwar economic boom offered higher wages that enabled many to enjoy new affluence. As early as 1948, General Motors and the UAW agreed to automatic cost-of-living wage hikes. This practice, as well as such benefits as paid vacations and pension plans, soon spread to other unionized industries and allowed millions of workers the time and money to join the buying frenzy.

Although celebrants of the postwar economic abundance tend to bestow most credit on private industry and the free-enterprise system, government played a crucial role: its expenditures during the war had ignited the boom. Immediately after the war, the GI Bill aided the prosperous transition from war to peace. During the fifties, federal funds for highways, welfare benefits, farm subsidies, and housing loans spurred the nation's prosperity, as did military spending, which became the government's most important economic function. The onset of the Cold War in the late forties and the fighting in Korea from 1950 to 1953 accelerated defense expenditures. Between 1947 and 1957, defense budgets, exclusive of veterans' benefits, totaled over $325 billion. Hydrogen bombs, B-52 bombers, a nuclear navy, guided missiles, and the space program provided the bulwarks of the nation's affluence. Indeed, business and government grew increasingly interdependent. Well before President Eisenhower warned the nation against the "military-industrial complex" in his 1961 farewell address, corporate America had become entwined with government through an intricate web of defense contracts. Because most large corporations both depended on and influenced government defense spending, the nation became locked on a martial course.

Federal funding of research and development tightened the connection between government and private industry. During the war, government-supported scientists had made major discoveries in nuclear physics, aerospace, chemicals, and electronics. In the Cold War years, Washington, D.C., continued to finance more than half the nation's research and development, much of which earned these industries high profits. The government also served as the country's largest single employer. By 1970 the federal payroll boasted nearly 13 million people, a figure that had more than doubled from 1950.

Reveling in the abundance of the midcentury years and seeking to forget the crises of the Cold War, Americans luxuriated in self-congratulation. The Great Celebration was under way. In a popular 1952 book, *The Big Change,* author Frederick Lewis Allen chose as his theme "the changes which have taken place in the character and quality of American life by reason of what might be called the democratization of our economic system, or the adjustment of capitalism to democratic ends." From the days of the Carnegies, Rockefellers, and Morgans, when "America seemed in danger of becoming a land in which the millionaires had more and more and the rest less and less," Allen unfolded a tale of unrevolutionary but steady progress toward what he saw as the nearly classless utopia of midcentury. The editors of *Fortune* concurred: "It is not the capitalists who are using the people," they claimed, "but the people who are using the capitalists. Capital has become, not the master of this society, but its servant.'' ''Easy Street,'' chimed in *Time* editor Thomas Griffith, ''now stretches from coast to coast.''

Intellectuals joined the celebratory chorus. Historians, searching the nation's past for those enduring values that held America together, proclaimed the United States a consensual and exceptional society, free of the conflicts that plagued class-ridden Europe. Thus they saw America's midcentury affluence as the natural outgrowth of the country's unique, providential past. ''Why should *we* make a five-year plan for ourselves,'' asked historian Daniel Boorstin, ''when God seems to have had a thousand-year plan ready-made for us?''

Although scholarly celebrants of American abundance influenced their colleagues and the educated public, it was television that most powerfully convinced Americans that they had never had it so good. TV both exemplified the new consumer culture and stimulated it. Along with TV advertising, numerous shows cultivated the notion of America as a land of plenty. Popular programs such as ''Father Knows Best'' and ''The Adventures of Ozzie and Harriet'' featured attractive people dressed in the latest fashions, living in well-appointed suburban homes. Quiz shows offering participants cash or luxury prizes became audience favorites; on ''The Price Is Right,'' contestants competed for various goods by trying to guess each item's exact cost.

In reality, though, the postwar boom, impressive as it was, did not eliminate economic problems. For example, growth had failed to redistribute income. The rich amassed wealth much faster than the rest of society. The share of the nation's riches held by the top half of 1 percent of the population increased from 19.3 percent in 1949 to 25 percent in 1956. In 1960, 1 percent of the country's population held 33 percent of its wealth; the population's bottom 20 percent possessed less than 0.005 percent of the bounty. If middle-class status in the 1950s is defined as an annual income of at least $3,000, then fewer than 60 percent of Americans had achieved that level by middecade.

Poverty, too, persisted. The postwar movement of basic industries from the older industrialized Northeast and Midwest to the South created regional pockets of deprivation, and many small towns and farming regions languished. The decline of trade unions also contributed to impoverishment of nonunion workers. In 1960 government statisticians classified nearly 40 million Americans as poor—fully 22 percent of the population. While most people celebrated what economist John Kenneth Galbraith labeled *The Affluent Society* in his 1958 best-selling study, African-American blues singer J. B. Lenoir sang the ''Eisenhower Blues'':

Ain't got a dime, ain't even got a cent.

I don' even have no money to pay my rent.

My baby needs some clothes, she needs some shoes.

Peoples I don't know what is I'm gonna do.

I got them Eisenhower blues.

Many poor were nonwhites. Rural poverty had long scourged African-Americans in the South, but the mass migrations of southern blacks to northern cities to escape destitution often ended in disappointment. With limited education and few skills, urban blacks competed for menial positions at a time when most cities offered fewer blue-

The Other Fifties. Poverty, usually ignored by the prosperous middle class, still plagued millions of midcentury Americans. This migratory worker camp outside of Phoenix, Arizona, was just one type of slum where the poor were forgotten.

collar jobs than ever. Most central cities thus teemed with unemployed and underemployed minorities.

But Americans who did enjoy rising incomes and easy credit found it easy to forget that not everyone could afford the new house, the new car, and the other trappings of the good life. With scholars and media alike singing variants of "America the Bountiful," who could blame the average citizen for complacency and materialism? Had not such abundance always been the promise of American life? And was not such well-being a just reward after the hardships of depression and war? Middle-class Americans believed that they deserved such wealth and looked ahead to an even brighter future.

Levittown and Miltown

Optimism among the middle class fueled the baby boom. To celebrate its seventy-fifth anniversary, General Electric announced in January 1952 that the company would award five shares of common stock to any of its 226,000 employees or their wives who had a baby on October 15. Company officials predicted 13 such births, but on the appointed day, GE families produced an astounding 189 babies.

General Electric couples, like Americans everywhere, avidly joined the postwar baby boom. From 1946 through 1964, births hit record highs. During these years, Americans delivered some 75.9 million babies, compared with only 44.4 million during the depression and war years of 1929–1945. By the midfifties, America's birthrate rivaled that of India. The number of mothers who bore three or more children doubled compared to prewar years. Between 1940 and 1960, the population of the United States grew by 50 million, the largest twenty-year jump in American history. As a result, the nation's median age dropped. In 1945 the percentage of children under age fourteen constituted less than a quarter of the total population; by 1960 this figure had increased to nearly a third. Men and women married younger and had larger families. The sheer size of this generation alone ensured its long-lasting significance. When millions of baby boomers reached adolescence in the mid- to late sixties, they would shape a unique youth culture.

The exploding birthrate made child rearing a national concern and reinforced the prevalent notion that women's proper place was in the home. Dr. Benjamin Spock— whose *Baby and Child Care,* first published in 1946, outsold every other book except the Bible for the next twenty years—touted motherhood as an all-important, all-consuming vocation. Spock even urged a government subsidy for at-home mothers. Drawing on the ideas of pioneer Viennese psychoanalyst Sigmund Freud and American philosopher John Dewey, Spock instructed a generation of women to create an atmosphere of warmth and intimacy for their children. He advised on-demand breast feeding, a relaxed schedule of toilet training, and reasoned discussion rather than physical punishment as a means of discipline, and he encouraged adults not to fear spoiling their children.

Where could parents find the "comforting and loving" home environment that Spock advocated? Postwar middle-class Americans believed that they had the answer in suburbia. The suburbs both filled a need and fulfilled a dream. One of the most pressing domestic problems confronting the nation at the end of the war had been a severe housing shortage. With the drop in housing construction from the thirties through the war years, returning veterans, many of them newly married, could not find places to live. But by the late forties, federal financing, low interest rates, small down payments, and guaranteed mortgages for veterans stimulated builders. William Levitt, Augus Wynne, and Henry Kaiser, among others, turned out mass-produced tracts of Cape Cod and ranch-style houses on sites within commuting distance of central cities but in open country, where land was cheap and restrictions few. Builders in the 1950s alone constructed a phenomenal 13 million new homes. By 1960 some 60 million Americans lived in suburbia, about equal to the number dwelling in cities.

Although suburban development devastated forest and farmland, it tapped into the human urge to get back to pastoral paradise, away from urban grime, crime, and crowding. Tracts sprang up with such names as "Wildwoods," "White Hills Estates," and "Crystal Stream," although no woods, hills, streams, or estates lay in sight. But with patio doors opening onto outdoor barbecues and picture windows framing vistas of green lawns and shrubs, millions of families felt that the American dream had come true. In the early fifties, $7,000 could buy a house with separate bedrooms for the children, a kitchen filled with the latest appliances, wall-to-wall carpeting in the living room (which often also featured a built-in TV), and a garage for the new car. Low down payments (as little as $1 for veterans) and a monthly mortgage of about $65 made such housing affordable.

Because neither suburban builders nor the federal government envisioned a need for improved mass public transportation to serve the needs of suburban dwellers, subur-

The American Dream. Large, homogenous suburbs spread rapidly in the postwar years, altering the American landscape and lifestyle.

banites came to depend on the automobile. Americans purchased some 58 million new cars during the fifties alone, and the number of registered automobiles jumped by 21 million. In response, local, state, and federal governments financed an improved and expanded road system. In 1956 Congress passed the Highway Act, which authorized construction of some forty-one thousand miles of interstate highways. Sold to Congress and the public in part as a defense measure to allow evacuation of cities in case of nuclear attack, the act intensified America's already strong commitment to the private automobile and encouraged suburbs to sprawl still farther from central cities. More expensive than all the New Deal welfare measures combined, the Highway Act was President Eisenhower's major piece of domestic legislation. New highways stimulated an ever-widening ring of suburban developments around the nation's cities, as well as a proliferation of shopping centers, motels, gas stations, and food chains such as Howard Johnson's and McDonald's. Banks, offices, and factories also moved to the suburbs.

Americans' addiction to private autos came with huge costs. Some of them stemmed directly from the auto itself: dependence on petroleum, pollution, congestion, and carnage, as annual highway deaths topped forty thousand by the late fifties and seat belts remained unadvertised, extra-cost options. But others were more subtle, though just as devastating. Ground public transportation declined and in many cases was dismantled altogether. Central cities, increasingly the residence of the poor and nonwhites, deteriorated. But in the 1950s, when gas cost only about twenty-five cents a gallon and new, open highways beckoned, few Americans noticed these warning signs. Automakers kept building bigger and flashier cars and changed models yearly to encourage status buying. The Ford Edsel, for example, was advertised as ''the smart car for the young executive or professional family on the way up.'' The smooth, curved lines and solid colors of the late forties gave way to the soaring tail-finned, two-toned, and even three-toned models of the late fifties. Advertisers described motors in terms of raw power—"Rocket 88" and then "98"; "Strato-Streak V-8."

Autos and freeways quickened the pace of migration not only from city to suburb but also from north to south and from east to west. During each year of the fifties, nearly one-fifth of the population changed residences. Lured by the sun and new job opportunities, northern and midwestern citizens began an exodus to what would later be called the Sun Belt. Florida, Texas, and Arizona attracted many of these new residents, but most migrants, such as the Brooklyn Dodgers and the New York Giants, headed for California, where the population swelled by more than 5 million over the decade.

Americans traveled not only for new jobs but also for the sheer pleasure of it. Trips to Europe, once limited to the very rich, became commonplace. Visiting various parts of the United States grew even more popular. The new freeways, motels, and fast-food chains made such recreation easy, and new tourist attractions such as Disneyland, which opened outside Los Angeles in 1956, dazzled and delighted.

Yet for all the plenitude that suburbanites enjoyed in the 1950s, evidence suggested that not all of them were content in this New World Eden. In 1959 the *New York Times* reported the findings of a medical and psychiatric study of one suburban community: "Life in growing suburbia . . . is giving people ulcers, heart attacks and other 'tension-related psychosomatic disorders.' " Doctors found that "everything from crab grass to high taxes played a role in emotional difficulties." Drinking increased in the fifties, especially in the suburbs. Perhaps the clearest index of suburban tensions came with the jump in consumption of the new tranquilizer drugs Miltown and Thorazine—a joining of the twin themes of outward abundance and inward anxiety. Tranquilizer sales soared from $2.2 million in 1955, the year that Miltown was introduced, to $150 million by 1957. Apart from their use in mental hospitals, these drugs were taken almost exclusively by middle-class men and women. The use of sleeping pills and—for those who could afford it—psychiatric help also skyrocketed.

That anxieties should accompany affluence is not surprising. Millions of middle-class Americans enjoyed an abundance that few would have dreamed possible only a decade earlier. But no standards existed by which to measure success. What was enough? People worried about keeping up with their neighbors or about obtaining the newest goods. Americans' very mobility also made them anxious, as frequent moves engendered a sense of rootlessness. Suburbs fostered transient communities of newcomers with unknown antecedents. To offset these feelings, people joined civic groups, held neighborhood backyard barbecues, and regularly got together for bridge, canasta, and even TV watching. But insecurities persisted. In addition to concerns about belonging and success, fears of communism, the Cold War, and, of course, the Bomb festered. All was not well in paradise.

Least enamored of America's suburban utopias were the intellectuals. Cultural historian Lewis Mumford asserted that the new suburbs were "a multitude of uniform, unidentifiable houses, lined up inflexibly at uniform distances, on uniform roads, in a treeless communal waste, inhabited by people in the same class, the same income, the same age group, witnessing the same television performances, eating the same tasteless pre-fabricated foods from the same freezers, conforming in every outward and inward respect to a common mold." Mumford charged suburban developers with destroying the nation's once vital and viable cities. John Keats, in his 1957 book *The Crack in the Picture Window,* similarly lamented builders' desecration of the countryside with rows of "identical boxes spreading like gangrene," breeding "swarms of drones . . . [who] cannot be said to have lives of their own."

Other critics saw suburban life spawning a new, undesirable, national character type as Americans lost their independent individualism and turned to group conformity. They feared that Americans would become a mediocre people incapable of sustaining creative, independent thought. Their picture of the mass sameness of U.S. society mirrored the popular, critical stereotype that most Americans held of totalitarian societies like the Soviet Union.

The two most popular and influential studies belittling the supposed emergence of a docile, conformist character type were David Riesman's *The Lonely Crowd* (1950) and William Whyte, Jr.'s, *The Organization Man* (1956). According to Riesman, nineteenth-century Americans were typically "inner-directed," relying on their own conscience to make moral decisions. This character type had given way, he said, to the "other-directed" American of modern mass society, whose morality derived from a compulsion to fit in with the crowd. Riesman's evaluation implied a shift from true self-reliance to a value system driven by adjustment and a need for conformity.

Fortune editor Whyte, in his study of the residents of suburban Park Forest, a postwar development outside Chicago, argued that the Protestant ethic of hard work, frugality, and individualism was being supplanted by a new "social ethic" based on cooperation, security, and "a belief in the group as the source of creativity." Whyte worried that the need to adjust to one's peers, with "belongingness" as the highest goal, stifled individualism.

Even religion in the 1950s, argued theologian Will Herberg in his influential *Protestant-Catholic-Jew* (1955), became "a way of sociability or 'belonging,' rather than a way of reorienting life to God." During the 1950s, organized religion reached a historic high point in modern America. Some 96 percent of the populace claimed belief in God, and the percentage of the population regularly attending religious services reached an all-time high. President Eisenhower assured the nation that the United States was "the mightiest power which God has seen fit to put upon His footstool." But Herberg believed that this massive revival constituted a "religiousness without religion." Like Riesman and Whyte, he perceived postwar America as increasingly homogenized and suburbanized. Claimed Herberg, "The people in the suburbs want to feel psychologically secure, adjusted, at home in their environment. Being religious and joining a church is, under contemporary American conditions, a fundamental way of 'adjusting' and 'belonging.'" Whereas Americans once identified themselves in terms of their ancestors' country of origin, in postwar America, Herberg believed, people no longer valued their ethnicity. Now, being a Protestant, Catholic, or Jew—rather than a Dane, Italian, or Pole—became a way "of being an American and locating oneself in American society."

Herberg, Riesman, Whyte, and other critics made valid statements about postwar American life. People did face tremendous pressures to conform. New suburbanites, living apart from relatives and ethnic urban neighborhoods, did yearn to ease their isolation and rootlessness. The growth of the huge, bureaucratic corporations with their stress on teamwork did pressure Americans to fit in. IBM even laid out standards of workers' dress and decorum. And given the furor over the supposed domestic infiltration of communists, nonconformists risked being branded as subversive. In a larger sense, the general conformity paralleled the period's drive for consensus.

Yet intellectuals were only partly accurate that the conformist trends that they decried marked a new, permanent shift in the national character. For one thing, the conformity and peer orientation that they depicted strongly resembled what the great French thinker Alexis de Tocqueville had already characterized as "the tyranny of the majority" in the America of the 1830s. Tocqueville suggested that Americans, lacking a fixed class structure, have always searched for groups to join. A second criticism of the intellectuals' theses has become more obvious in the decades after the publication of their books. Clearly the social upheavals since 1960 have revealed Americans to be a heterogeneous people with a variety of lifestyles. Indeed, social observers today question whether an American national character even exists.

Most important, these writers erred in utterly disregarding the working class, the poor, and nonwhites. Their studies imply that only the affluent white middle class constituted the real America and that suburban life represented American life in general. Researchers seldom studied unionized factory employees and ignored the growing number of blue-collar suburbs. They overlooked consciously ethnic urban neighborhoods and dismissed poverty as a vanishing trifle that a few more years of economic growth would eliminate. As historian Richard Hofstadter wrote in the midfifties, "The jobless, distracted, and bewildered men of 1933 have become homeowners, suburbanites, and solid citizens."

Intellectuals were not the only ones who viewed America as a homogeneous and classless society. The mass media joined in the chorus as well. Popular television situation comedies from the midfifties, for example, fostered an image of America as middle class and family centered. In the early years of TV, just after the war, producers adapted shows directly from radio, many of them originating in the depression years and featuring somewhat realistic urban, working-class families of different ethnic backgrounds. In the late forties, such borrowed-from-radio TV shows as "The Goldbergs," "Life with Luigi," "The Life of Riley," and "I Remember Mama" portrayed, respectively, the problems and comic mishaps of working-class Jewish-, Italian-, Irish-, and Swedish-Americans who lived in urban neighborhoods. TV also adapted the long-running radio hit "Amos 'n' Andy," which, although it ignored racial prejudice, at least used an all-black cast and characterized African-American families with a degree of dignity and wit. Such early TV fare reflected America as it actually was—heterogeneous and pluralistic. In the early fifties, however, as America became affluent and suburbanized, such shows were canceled. The three major networks, seeking high ratings and profits, grew cautious and turned the medium into a celebration of conformity and consumerism. By middecade, only Jackie Gleason's hilarious "Honeymooners" regularly presented working-class families. In nearly all other family situation comedies, suburban, white, middle-class people defined the norm.

From 1953 to 1962, "Father Knows Best" exemplified the "ideal" American family. Robert Anderson, the father (played by Robert Young), seemed the model suburban organization man: wise and kindly, patriarchal but benign, bland and other-directed. Jane Wyatt acted the role of his wife, Margaret, the "perfect" homemaker. Although an able cook, family budget balancer, and chauffeur for the children, she was portrayed as scatterbrained and in need of frequent husbandly advice. The three teenage children, though sometimes boisterous, were well mannered and cautious, and doted on their parents. The show focused solely on this affluent, suburban family, but it seldom depicted the real complexities and pressures inherent in family life.

The TV Andersons epitomized America's public self-image in the midfifties, an image that some critics lamented but that television, other mass media, and most people cheered. In 1954 *McCall's* magazine coined the term *togetherness* to celebrate this new domestic ideal. Americans, the editors claimed, "are creating this new warmer way of life not as women *alone* or men *alone,* isolated from one another, but as a *family* sharing a common experience." Although the magazine stressed shared domestic responsibilities, the editors stopped short of advocating complete equality: "For the sake of every member of the family, the family needs a head. This means Father, not Mother." *McCall's* even ran a contest to define togetherness; though tens of thousands of entries failed to produce an acceptable answer, the concept nevertheless struck a chord. Soon editorial writers, advice columnists, marriage counselors, and the clergy began touting family togetherness almost as if it were America's national purpose.

And so, despite widespread individual anxieties and certain caustic intellectual criticisms, the Great Celebration dominated midfifties American life. The suburbs spread; huge, tail-finned cars sold in record numbers; and uplifting books like Reverend Norman Vincent Peale's simplistic *The Power of Positive Thinking* (1952) topped the best-seller list—all while the reassuring Eisenhower, when not on the golf course, sat in the Oval Office. Racism, sexism, poverty, pollution, the Cold War, and the nuclear-arms race still threatened America, but most people had eyes only for the ideal of domestic bliss.

Eisenhower Equilibrium

In 1952 Americans elected General Dwight D. Eisenhower to the presidency. Except for cynical intellectuals and diehard Democrats, people liked Ike. Seldom in American history has a president been so in tune with the national mood. By the time Eisenhower took office in 1953, Americans had endured nearly a quarter-century of disruptions: the economic devastation of the depression, the upheavals of world war, the Cold War threat, the hysteria over supposed domestic communist subversion, and the fear of nuclear annihilation. Weary of national and international disasters and fed up with partisan politics, they craved tranquility, security, and unanimity. Ike promised to deliver. As columnist Walter Lippmann put it, Eisenhower seemed the "dream boy embodying all the unsatisfied wishes of all the people who are discontented with things as they are."

Born in 1890, Eisenhower had grown up in Abilene, Kansas. His hard-working, God-fearing parents instilled in him a strong belief in traditional moral values and small-town mores. His West Point education reinforced his sense of duty, service, and patriotism. Although not an innovative thinker, he nevertheless proved an able administrator and organizer. Working his way up the military ranks, in 1944 he accepted the post of supreme commander of the Allied forces on the Western Front. In that position, he demonstrated his talents for genial, conciliatory leadership, uniting the often divided Allied military leaders in the greatest single operation of the war—the D-Day invasion of Europe—and the final drive to victory over Hitler's Germany. Ike emerged from the war a hero.

Ike. War hero turned president, Dwight D. Eisenhower, with his winning smile, convinced millions that the nation was in good hands.

Winning the Republican nomination over the more conservative, isolationist Ohio senator Robert Taft, Eisenhower, a moderate Republican with an internationalist outlook, tried to heal the party breach. He selected as his running mate California senator Richard Nixon, a man known for his strong anticommunist views and popular with the Republican Right. Ike pledged to ''end the mess in Washington'' and to ''go to Korea,'' while Nixon, Joseph McCarthy, and other right-wing Republicans lashed out at what they called ''twenty years of Democratic treason.'' The aggressive campaign worked; Eisenhower easily defeated his Democratic opponent, Adlai Stevenson, the urbane, witty, intellectual governor of Illinois.

Untainted by experience in electoral politics, Ike seemed a truly national leader above the political fray. His public image as a plain, honest man of the people inspired confidence. His grandfatherly demeanor, sparkling blue eyes, and infectious boyish grin; his sincere platitudes about God, country, motherhood, and family; his circumlocutions at thorny press conferences—all endeared him to millions and made him a symbol not of party but of national consensus. Tired of the recent barrage of crises, Americans ascribed hope and confidence to Ike. As a Pennsylvania homemaker remarked: ''It's like America has come home.''

Concerned about the spiraling costs of the Korean conflict and attuned to the growing American disapproval of that war, President-elect Eisenhower kept his campaign pledge and visited the front in December 1952. Armistice negotiations with the North Koreans and the Chinese, begun during Truman's presidency, had broken down. Through diplomatic channels, Eisenhower hinted that he might use nuclear weapons if peace were not forthcoming. This intimidation persuaded the communists to return to the negotiating table, and on July 23, 1953, an armistice restored the boundary between North and South Korea to essentially its prewar position. The agreement preserved South Korean sovereignty, and American troops remained stationed there to deter further aggression. Despite the lack of a clear-cut victory, most Americans welcomed the end of the three-year war, and American policymakers deemed Korea a partial success, for containment had halted communist aggression. Henceforth Asia would remain a major Cold War battleground, with the United States committed to combat any Chinese or Soviet expansion in the region.

During the remainder of the fifties, except for the activities of military advisers in South Vietnam (see Chapter 6) and a brief marine landing in Lebanon in 1958, Eisenhower kept the United States out of overt military involvement. Korea had taught him that limited wars fought with conventional weapons cost too much and upset the public. Instead, he and Secretary of State John Foster Dulles called for a "New Look" in American defense policy. Dulles, a deeply religious Presbyterian, saw the Cold War as a moral struggle between the forces of good and evil. He called not for containment but for "liberation." In place of conventional weapons, Dulles's and Eisenhower's New Look relied on expanding the nation's nuclear arsenal and threatening massive retaliation to deter communist aggression. Such a policy, in the words of Eisenhower's secretary of defense, Charles Wilson, would "get more bang for the buck." Indeed, in the years after Korea, the Eisenhower administration allowed conventional forces to decline and stockpiled large numbers of nuclear weapons.

This strategy, based on U.S. nuclear superiority, carried a high price. By precluding all options other than nuclear war, the Eisenhower-Dulles policy sacrificed flexibility. Judging nuclear war in Europe too risky, the United States chose to do nothing while the Soviets crushed popular uprisings in East Germany in 1953 and three years later in Hungary. This failure to act forced the Eisenhower government to abandon its commitment to liberate Eastern Europe and return to the Truman Doctrine of containment.

The policy of massive retaliation proved particularly ineffective with underdeveloped countries, where peoples struggled to throw off colonialism, military dictatorships, and poverty. Looking through their Cold War lenses, American policymakers worried lest rebels in such areas favor the communists. But because nuclear weapons did not present a viable option in squelching upheavals in small, emerging nations, the Eisenhower administration turned to clandestine operations carried out by the Central Intelligence Agency (CIA). Headed by Allen Dulles, brother of the secretary of state, the CIA secretly helped to overthrow the government of Mohammed Mossadegh of Iran in 1953 and the democratically elected head of Guatemala, Colonel Jacobo Arbenz Guzman, in 1954. These successes encouraged the White House to try further clandestine operations, and throughout the remainder of the fifties the CIA carried on covert maneuvers in such countries as Vietnam and Cuba. Such activities not only violated traditional norms of international conduct but stirred widespread anti-American sentiment throughout the non-Western world that would spark future crises.

Most Americans remained ignorant of these CIA activities, seeing only that Ike had gotten them out of Korea, had reduced the military budget, and had kept the peace. Eisenhower also benefited when the hated Soviet dictator Stalin died in 1953. Subsequent Soviet leaders took a more conciliatory attitude toward the West, and in 1955 Ike attended the first postwar U.S.-Soviet summit conference in Geneva, Switzerland. Neither side agreed to any concessions, but the talks were cordial and the media puffed the "Spirit of Geneva." Many Americans began to hope for a thaw in the

Cold War and an alternative to all-out hostilities. This reassurance served to boost Ike's popularity.

In domestic matters, too, Eisenhower possessed a talent for pleasing the majority. Taking office during turbulent times, he exuded much-needed calm and conciliation. To the new president, politics meant compromise; he offered no bold, innovative schemes of social reform and shunned abstract theories in favor of pragmatism. He cultivated a relaxed demeanor and spent much well-publicized time golfing, fishing, or playing bridge. While his unruffled mien led Democrats to criticize him as a do-nothing president, Eisenhower in fact kept a firm, though discreet, hand on affairs. He made skillful use of subordinates and thus avoided confrontations that might demean his office.

Eisenhower's approach to domestic issues was conservative but not reactionary. He believed in a balanced federal budget, minimum government intervention in the economy, and returning power to the states and to private interests where possible. Although his policies favored big business, he did not seek to repeal the New Deal reforms. He accepted the need for government welfare and supported a modest expansion of Social Security, minimum wage, unemployment insurance, and public housing, as well as instigating the massive interstate highway construction program. The terms *modern Republicanism* and *dynamic conservatism* caught on as labels for his policies. His brother and close adviser, Milton Eisenhower, characterized the president's approach as follows: "We should keep what we have, catch our breath for a while, and improve administration; it does not mean moving backward." This cautious, middle-of-the-road course disappointed both Democratic liberals and right-wing Republicans, but to millions of Americans, tired of conflict, Ike's moderation and morality delivered exactly what they wanted.

An adept administrator, Eisenhower also enjoyed extraordinary good luck. His handling of Joseph McCarthy provides one example. Personally Eisenhower loathed McCarthy, describing him privately as a "pimple on the path to progress." In the 1952 campaign, however, Ike declined to criticize the reckless, anticommunist senator, even standing on the same platform with him in Wisconsin. When McCarthy falsely accused General George Marshall of supporting communism, Eisenhower refused to defend his old friend and mentor.

Once in office, Ike still avoided confronting the senator, vowing to a close associate that he would not "get into a pissing contest with a skunk." In part to counteract McCarthy, the president broadened Truman's loyalty review program in 1953 and dismissed a number of presumed security risks from government jobs. These actions in no way quieted the Wisconsin senator, who continued to lash out at supposed subversives in government, much to the embarrassment of the administration. In 1953 McCarthy accused the Voice of America and the United States Information Agency (USIA), both propaganda agencies of the State Department, of furthering left-wing causes. He forced USIA libraries to remove the books of such "communists, fellow travelers, et cetera" as Henry David Thoreau, Ralph Waldo Emerson, Mark Twain, and Theodore Dreiser.

In 1954 McCarthy began to investigate alleged communists in the army. At last he had overreached himself. On the evening of March 9, distinguished newscaster Edward R. Murrow devoted his popular CBS program, "See It Now," to an attack on McCarthy. Using a compilation of films of the senator in action, the program depicted McCarthy at his worst: berating witnesses, contradicting himself, belching, laughing at his own crude jokes. At the end of the documentary, Murrow told his audience, "The line between investigation and persecution is a very fine one, and the junior senator has stepped over it repeatedly." McCarthy's actions, he claimed, "have caused alarm and dismay amongst our allies abroad and given considerable comfort to our enemies, and whose fault is that? Not really his; he didn't create the situation of fear, he merely exploited it, and rather successfully. Cassius was right: 'The fault, dear Brutus, is not in our stars, but in ourselves.'" For years anticommunists like McCarthy had terrorized network TV. Actors had been blacklisted, and producers had shunned controversial subjects. Not until Murrow had anyone in the industry dared to speak the truth. McCarthy lashed back, calling Murrow "the leader and cleverest of the jackal pack which is always found at the throat of anyone who dares to expose individual communists and traitors." But Murrow's courage spelled the end of the Wisconsin senator's ability to intimidate.

The following month, the networks aired a series of Army-McCarthy hearings before a congressional committee. Even more Americans than had watched Murrow's "See It Now" witnessed the senator's verbal bludgeoning of witnesses and constant interruptions with cries of "point of order!" McCarthy ranted at one general of impeccable loyalty, "You are a disgrace to the uniform. You're shielding Communist conspirators. . . . You're not fit to be an officer. You're ignorant." Finally, after McCarthy crudely slurred the reputation of a young lawyer not even involved in the hearings, Joseph Welch, counsel for the army, turned on the senator and asked: "Have you no sense of decency?" The gallery erupted in applause, and McCarthy's popular support plummeted. As *Washington Post* reporter Alfred Friendly explained, "The American people could not believe just how ugly that ugly man was until they saw him, finally, on television during the Army-McCarthy hearings." Even before the hearings concluded, the Senate began an investigation of McCarthy's conduct. In December, his colleagues voted to censure him. Although he retained all his senatorial privileges, McCarthy's power evaporated, and in 1957 he died of complications from alcoholism.

The senator's fall from grace in no way curbed the nation's anticommunism, but it enhanced the tranquility of midfifties America and Eisenhower's vast popularity. With Stalin dead, the Korean War ended, and McCarthy silenced, Americans breathed easier and turned to reaping the rewards of peace and prosperity.

• • •

The sting seemed gone from the times, and in 1956, a cheerful nation overwhelmingly reelected Eisenhower, again over Democrat Adlai Stevenson. Just before the election, sociologist David Riesman visited a new suburb south of Chicago to interview voters. "Most of the people we spoke to were young housewives, often interrupted in their midday television program"; they were educated but complacent. He found respondents vague about politics but liking Ike. "As one looked over that flat Illinois prairie at all the signs of prosperity," generalized Riesman, "it was not hard to see why these people were so bland politically and responded to the same qualities in Ike. . . . These people were not self-made men who remembered their struggles against hardship but, rather, a society-made generation who could not believe society would let them down."

Liberal intellectuals such as Riesman dismissed Eisenhower as bumbling and ineffectual and criticized his inaction and lack of vision. Scholarly evaluation written soon after his presidency, animated by the liberal and radical movements of the sixties, continued to fault his lack of leadership and initiative. When a post-Vietnam generation of historians reappraised Eisenhower, however, they found him a much more effective, shrewd, and forceful leader than previous scholars had supposed. Recent scholars credit Ike for ending the Korean War, avoiding further military involvement, and keeping the United States out of a nuclear showdown with the Soviets. He brought both dignity and popularity to the presidential office and genially led Americans to the peace and prosperity that they so craved.

There is much truth in this revisionist reevaluation. Nevertheless, if Eisenhower deserves praise for granting the nation a respite from postwar perils, his administration also left less commendable bequests. It suppressed or ignored civil-rights issues, urban decay, poverty, unemployment, environmental pollution, and health care and thereby sowed the seeds of future crises. Although he kept the peace abroad, Ike's failure to end the Cold War, his covert use of the CIA, his stockpiling of nuclear weapons and swaggering threats to use them, and his commitment of military advisers to South Vietnam proved troubling legacies.

Eisenhower's personal popularity remained high through his second term in office, but those years revealed how precarious the midfifties repose actually was. Increasingly, the disjuncture between realities and dreams widened. Even at middecade, careful observers had noted a rising dissent, particularly among certain youth, intellectuals, women, and African-Americans. These discontents would challenge and ultimately shatter the image of America as an affluent, homogeneous, happy suburb. Despite the prevailing complacency, the fifties harbored revolts that would shape the tumultuous sixties.

Selected Bibliography

Four comprehensive accounts of the social and cultural developments in the 1950s are Douglas T. Miller's and Marion Nowak's *The Fifties: The Way We Really Were* (1977); Geoffrey Perrett's *A Dream of Greatness* (1979); Mary Jezer's *The Dark Ages: Life in the United States, 1945–1960* (1982); and J. Ronald Oakley's *God's Country: America in the Fifties* (1986). Less critical evaluations of the midcentury years include David Halberstam, *The Fifties* (1993); John Diggins, *The Proud Decades, 1941–1960* (1989); William O'Neill, *American High* (1986); Paul A. Carter, *Another Part of the Fifties* (1983); and Jeffrey Hart, *When the Going Was Good: American Life in the Fifties* (1982). On the impact of the Bomb on American culture, see Paul Boyer, *By the Bomb's Early Light* (1985), and Alan Winkler, *The Atom and American Life* (1993).

Three excellent recent reassessments of the Cold War are John L. Gaddis, *The United States and the Cold War* (1992); Melvyn Leffler, *A Preponderance of Power: National Security, the Truman Administration, and the Cold War* (1992); and Fred Inglis, *The Cruel Peace* (1991). Other important Cold War studies include Walter LaFeber, *America, Russia, and the Cold War* (1976 ed.); Daniel Yergin, *The Shattered Peace: The Origins of the Cold War and the National Security State* (1977); Stephen E. Ambrose, *Rise to Globalism* (1988 ed.); Lloyd C. Gardner, *Architects of Illusion: Men and Ideas in American Foreign Policy, 1941–1949* (1970); Gregg Herken, *The Winning Weapon: The Atomic Bomb in the Cold War, 1945–1950* (1980); Gar Alperovitz, *Atomic Diplomacy* (1985 ed.); Thomas G. Paterson, *On Every Front: The Making of the Cold War* (1979); and Joyce Kolko and Gabriel Kolko, *The Limits of Power: The World and United States Foreign Policy, 1945–54* (1972).

A persuasive account of the post–World War II red scare is Richard M. Fried, *Nightmare in Red: The McCarthy Era in Perspective* (1990). Also helpful are David Caute, *The Great Fear: The Anti-Communist Purge Under Truman and Eisenhower* (1978), and Stanley I. Kutler, *The American Inquisition* (1982). Athan Theoharis, *Seeds of Repression: Harry S Truman and the Origins of McCarthyism* (1971), and Richard Freeland, *The Truman Doctrine and the Origins of McCarthyism* (1985 ed.), are critical studies of the Truman administration's loyalty program. Two thorough biographies of Joseph McCarthy are Thomas C. Reeves, *The Life and Times of Joe McCarthy* (1982), and David M. Oshinski, *A Conspiracy So Immense: The World of Joe McCarthy* (1983). Athan Theoharis and John Stuart Cox, *The Boss: J. Edgar Hoover and the Great American Inquisition* (1988), emphasizes the FBI's role in the red scare. The Hiss and Rosenberg cases are treated, respectively, in John Chabot Smith, *Alger Hiss* (1976), and Ronald Radosh and Joyce Milton, *The Rosenberg File* (1983). Stephen J. Whitfield, *The Culture of the Cold War* (1991), examines the impact of anticommunism on popular culture.

David P. Calleo, *The Imperious Economy* (1982), is a worthwhile study of postwar economic developments. The standard economic history of the fifties is Harold G. Vatter, *The U.S. Economy in the 1950s* (1963). Other economic aspects of that period are considered in John Kenneth Galbraith's influential *The Affluent Society* (1958). Three books reflecting both the midcentury economic optimism and Cold War urgency are Frederick Lewis Allen, *The Big Change* (1952); Editors of *Fortune, U.S.A. The Permanent Revolution* (1951); and Peter Drucker, *The New Society* (1950). Postwar poverty first came to national attention through Michael Harrington's *The Other America* (1962).

The baby boom is the subject of Landon Y. Jones, *Great Expectations* (1980). Kenneth Jackson, *Crabgrass Frontier* (1985), is the best history of suburban development. For a sampling of the vast literature on suburbia, see Philip C. Dolce, ed., *Suburbia: The American Dream and Dilemma* (1976). Other important studies include Robert Fishman, *Bourgeois Utopias* (1987); Herbert J. Gans, *The Levittowners* (1967); Dolores Hayden, *Redesigning the American Dream* (1984); Zane L. Miller, *Suburb* (1982); and Gwendolyn Wright, *Building the Dream: A Social History of Housing in America* (1981). The two most influential midcentury accounts of the supposed impact of suburbs and corporations on national character are David Riesman et al., *The Lonely Crowd* (1950), and William H. Whyte, Jr., *The Organization Man* (1956).

For the impact of television in the postwar years, see Michael Arlen, *The Camera Age* (1982); Erik Barnouw, *Tube of Plenty* (1982 ed.); Todd Gitlin, *Inside Prime-Time* (1983); and William Boddy, *Fifties Television: The Industry and Its Critics* (1990). Peter Biskind, *Seeing Is Believing: How Hollywood Taught Us to Stop Worrying and Love the Fifties* (1983); Nora Sayre, *Running Time: Films of the Cold War* (1982); Tino Balio, ed., *Hollywood in the Age of Television* (1990); and Gordon Gow, *Hollywood in the Fifties* (1971) probe the influence of movies.

A good starting point for exploring the Eisenhower presidency is Robert F. Burk, *Dwight D. Eisenhower* (1986). Other important studies of Ike and his administration include Stephen E. Ambrose, *Eisenhower* (2 vols., 1983–1984); Fred I. Greenstein, *The Hidden-Hand Presidency* (1994 ed.); Piers Brendon, *Ike* (1986); Peter Lyons, *Eisenhower* (1974); Herbert Parmet, *Eisenhower and the American Crusades* (1972); and Joann P. Krieg, ed., *Dwight D. Eisenhower* (1987).

CHAPTER

2

DISILLUSIONMENT AND PROTEST:

THE MIDFIFTIES

On April 12, 1954, crooner Perry Como's romantic ballad "Wanted" sat atop *Billboard*'s singles chart, while the big band soundtrack from *The Glenn Miller Story* headed the album category. But that same day, in New York's Pythian Temple, Bill Haley and the Comets recorded "Rock Around the Clock," a song that would soon head the top-ten list for eight weeks. Strongly influenced by black artists, Haley's rendition, with its insistent beat, would forever change the world's conception of popular music. July 5, 1954, saw an even more important recording session: Elvis Presley cut his first Sun Record in Memphis. That September, powerful WINS radio in New York hired Cleveland disc jockey Alan Freed to bring his popular "Moondog's Rock 'n' Roll Party" to the Big Apple. Freed's show soon became New York's most listened-to music program. Rock and roll, now entrenched in the music industry, swiftly helped to define a new youth culture that markedly differentiated the young from their parents.

Other forces too disrupted the conservative, family-oriented values of midfifties America. The tremendous popularity among young people of movie stars Marlon Brando and James Dean revealed youthful alienation from adult assumptions. Brando in *The Wild One* (1954) and Dean in *Rebel Without a Cause* (1955) portrayed defiant, anguished young rebels too sensitive to adjust to society's expectations. From 1954 on, Hollywood produced a spate of such films targeting adolescent audiences and so stimulated the youth culture.

A group of nonconformist writers, the Beats, voiced an even more sweeping rejection of middle-class mores. Allen Ginsberg's poem *Howl* (1956) and Jack Kerouac's rambling prose epic *On the Road* (1957) mocked the "square" world of corporate jobs and mindless consumption. Kerouac dismissed suburban America as "rows of well-to-do houses with lawns and television sets in each living room with everybody looking at the same thing and thinking the same thing at the same time." These writers instead extolled personal and sexual freedom. By the late fifties, the Beats' literature and lifestyle had influenced numerous educated young people and ushered in a counterculture that would flourish in the 1960s.

As the fifties wore on, a growing number of women began to chafe at their circumscribed roles as wives and mothers. Although it would take some time for their discontent to coalesce into a major feminist movement, clearly the postwar domestic ideal had flaws. Radical intellectuals, too, came to question the complacent, celebratory consensus. In 1954 literary critic Irving Howe launched *Dissent,* a journal that excoriated the conformism and complacency of the age. Other radical journals followed, and by the late fifties such intellectuals as C. Wright Mills and Paul Goodman challenged mainstream America's most basic beliefs.

Finally and most significant, African-Americans began taking an active role in opposing centuries of racial injustice. The civil-rights movement shifted gears in 1954 with the Supreme Court's *Brown* v. *Board of Education of Topeka* decision, which declared segregation in public schools unconstitutional. In 1955 and 1956, blacks in Montgomery, Alabama, boycotted the discriminatory bus system for more than a year and eventually won when the Supreme Court struck down the city's bigoted bus laws. This spreading black revolt intensified, inspiring activism among white pacifists and college students, especially in the nation's more prestigious universities.

Most Americans, of course, continued to follow the moral strictures of Eisenhower's America and accept the predominant values of complacency and conformity, home and family, getting and spending, the Cold War and anticommunism. But in retrospect, it becomes clear that the mid- to late fifties were a time of transition, with a number of developments portending a changing America: alienated youth, Beats, dissatisfied homemakers, radical intellectuals, civil-rights activists, and nonconformist pacifists.

The "Silent Generation" Speaks

"The teenagers of today," declared a California youth authority in 1954, "are stronger, smarter, more self-sufficient and more constructive than any generation of teenagers in history." Many midfifties commentators advanced similar claims. Young Americans embraced their parents' values, these observers insisted, and like their elders, made security a top priority. For young women, security meant marrying a successful man and raising a family. For young men, it also meant marriage and family, plus a safe, rewarding corporate job. In a 1956 study, social scientist Philip Jacob concluded that college students "fully accept the conventions of the contemporary business society. They expect to conform to the economic status quo and to receive ample rewards."

Indeed, some professors found their students too prudent and apolitical and dubbed them the "Silent Generation." But most adults applauded youthful emulation of their beliefs.

Even as adults extolled youth's integral role in the Great Celebration, however, the young themselves showed signs of restlessness. Indeed, several factors set this generation apart from their parents. For one thing, they had grown up in a society wealthy enough to keep them in school for a longer period. Compulsory education now included high school, and for the first time, college became the norm for children of the middle class. These trends extended youth into what previous generations considered early adulthood. The term *adolescence* came into general use to describe the years from puberty to the early twenties. Now instead of entering the adult world of work early, young people spent years together in the relatively pampered environment of schools and universities. Not surprisingly, a unique youth culture emerged.

The widely different historical periods in which parents and their children matured also planted the seeds of the "generation gap" of the sixties. Adults, however successful, remained haunted by memories of the depression. Although they relished the new abundance, adults found it difficult to throw off the traditional values of thrift and self-denial. Middle-class baby boomers, on the other hand, took affluence for granted, never having known anything else. Television reinforced this tendency of the young to scorn their parents' scarcity mentality. For most adolescents, TV became the major medium through which they learned adult values, and television shows and advertising propagandized an ethic of instant gratification.

Youthful hedonism also was an outgrowth of the nuclear terror that touched this generation, the first to grow up under the shadow of the Bomb. (Their parents seem not to have been affected so deeply. Adults, after all, had seen atomic bombs used in what they deemed a righteous cause: winning the war against Japan.) Their children, on the other hand, squeezed under school desks in regular civil-defense drills, knew that nuclear weapons could destroy all life in a flash. Their awareness of the potential for imminent destruction fostered their existential, live-for-the-present philosophy.

If nuclear war erupts, stated a character in J. D. Salinger's *The Catcher in the Rye,* "I'm going to sit right to hell on top of it. I'll volunteer for it, I swear I will." This 1951 novel's immense popularity among high school and college students revealed the uneasiness that numerous young people harbored. Holden Caulfield, the novel's privileged, alienated adolescent hero, rebels against the crass, "phony" adult world. Ultimately Holden's rebellion proves quixotic and futile. Unable to adjust to society's rigid norms, he suffers a nervous collapse and retreats into his imagination. Throughout the fifties, *The Catcher in the Rye* ranked as the most popular book among middle-class adolescents, and its leading character became a symbol for a generation of estranged youth. Not surprisingly, many parents' groups fought to ban *Catcher* from school and public libraries and even from bookstores.

Like Holden, most postwar American children spent much more time with their peers than with their parents. Living increasingly in suburbia, often with commuter fathers absent until well into the evening, children in schools, summer camps, clubs, cliques, and eventually colleges developed a peer-oriented culture. And affluence, combined with indulgence, provided the young with money to spend. Capitalizing on this new source of consumers, corporate America manufactured and advertised products targeting the burgeoning youth market. Young people chose their own fashions, television shows, movies, and other goods ranging from soft drinks to acne creams. By the midfifties, they also had their own music.

"Hooby-Dooby Oop-Shoop": Rock Rolls

Rock and roll became the bedrock of the youth culture. Before the midfifties, the music industry had marketed the same pop tunes for both teens and their parents—songs performed by singers such as Perry Como, Patti Page, Nat "King" Cole, Eddie Fisher, and Rosemary Clooney that affirmed society's strict and cautious values. Although love songs predominated, most were sentimental ballads in which sex was expressed only through euphemism, as in Rosemary Clooney's 1951 hit, "Come On-a My House" ("I'm gonna give you candy").

Yet even as early as 1951, change was in the air, for in that year, Cleveland disc jockey Alan Freed began playing black rhythm-and-blues music for youthful white audiences. Originally an announcer on a classical music program, Freed had become interested in rhythm-and-blues programming after he had noticed white adolescents gyrating to this African-American music at a downtown record store. He persuaded his station manager to begin a new show, "Moondog's Rock 'n' Roll Party." (*Rock 'n' roll* was an urban black slang expression meaning both sex and dancing, as an old blues song proclaimed, "My baby rocks me with a steady roll.") Freed's program scored an instant hit among white teens.

With its long roots in the southern blues tradition, rhythm and blues had evolved into urban black music during the thirties and forties with the mass migration of African-Americans to the North. Unlike pop, it was raw and uninhibited, featuring passionate, often sexually explicit lyrics, screaming tenor saxophones, blues guitars, and a heavy beat. In the early fifties, while white pop entertainers crooned about "Mama Kissing Santa Claus" or the price of a "Doggie in the Window," black rhythm-and-blues singers belted out such songs as "Work with Me Annie," which pleaded, "Annie, please don't cheat. Give me all my meat. . . . Work with me, Annie. Let's git it while the gitting is good"; and "Sixty Minute Man," about a lover's staying powers. White adults, who quailed when they heard the words *virgin* and *seduction* in Otto Preminger's 1953 film *The Moon Is Blue,* found the new music appalling.

The popularity of the new sound was spread by radio stations, which had turned to a low-cost format of recorded music, often aimed at particular listeners, after TV had eclipsed it as the medium of mass entertainment. Most large cities had stations that programmed rhythm and blues for African-Americans, but the music's raucous energy and blatant sexuality attracted more and more white adolescents. As station managers recognized the new youth market, they followed Freed's example and by the midfifties increasingly presented rhythm and blues, now more often called rock 'n' roll. Disc jockeys with names such as Fat Daddy, Jumpin' George, Rockin' Robins, and Wolfman Jack proliferated across the country. Playing rock music and speaking a jivetalk in imitation of black deejays, these radio personalities brought the once denigrated African-American culture to young listeners, a perspective that challenged the most basic premises of the mainstream Cold War ideal.

White artists, sensing the rising popularity of rock, began imitating it as they had copied black jazz earlier in the century. Bill Haley's 1953 hit, ''Crazy, Man, Crazy,'' was the first rock record to sell more than a million copies. In 1954 ''Shake, Rattle and Roll'' and ''Sh-Boom'' hit the charts. Both songs had originally been performed by the black artists Joe Turner and the Chords, respectively, but it was cover versions by white groups—Bill Haley and the Comets, and the Crew Cuts—that sold. Typically, whites' recording material originally aimed for black audiences amended what they deemed offensive lyrics. Turner's recording of ''Shake, Rattle and Roll,'' for example, contained the lines

> Well you wear low dresses,
> The sun comes shinin' through.
> I can't believe my eyes,
> That all of this belongs to you.

In Haley's more guarded cover version, the lines became

> You wear those dresses,
> Your hair done up so nice.
> You look so warm,
> But your heart is cold as ice.

Yet as rock songs by black performers grew popular and profitable, racism began to lessen, although it still ran rampant in the record industry. Here, too, Freed played an important role. On his popular radio show, he championed black artists and refused to play white cover versions of their material. His success in reaching predominantly white audiences with this format led other disc jockeys to follow suit. Freed also staged large-scale rock concerts featuring African-American performers.

By 1955 black artists such as Little Richard, Fats Domino, Chuck Berry, Bo Diddley, and Ray Charles had achieved stardom, and their records generally outsold white cover versions. Little Richard's original ''Tutti-Frutti'' and ''Long Tall Sally,'' for instance, far outsold the insipid copies by white crooner Pat Boone. But the midfifties also witnessed the emergence of a number of southern white singers such as Carl Perkins, Jerry Lee Lewis, and Buddy Holly who developed their own rock styles. Above all, the middecade produced rock and roll's first superstar, Elvis Presley.

Born in 1935 of working-class parents in Tupelo, Mississippi, Elvis grew up in the blues town of Memphis, Tennessee. In Memphis's Beale Street clubs he heard blues greats Muddy Waters, Howlin' Wolf, and B. B. King. Fusing this black southern musical tradition with white gospel singing and country and western, Presley crafted his own brand of music. Although he was discovered by Sam Phillips of Memphis's Sun Records in 1954, not until RCA signed Presley late in 1955 did his career blossom. With his first RCA releases, including ''Hound Dog'' and ''Heartbreak Hotel,'' Presley became a national sensation and in two years sold more than 28 million records.

Elvis exuded sexuality and strength. To most middle-class adults, long familiar with the melodic crooning of singers like Bing Crosby, Presley's textured voice sounded crude and even threatening as it shifted from wailing blues to throaty ballads. And Elvis's stage presence outright offended them. With his purple and black striped

Rock and Roll's First Superstar. Elvis Presley, seen here in June of 1956, epitomized the rebellion of the midfifties that launched a unique youth culture.

pants, white buck shoes, and a pink sports coat, shirt collar rolled up, long black hair slicked back, and outrageously long sideburns, Presley sneered, rolled his hips, and flailed his legs in what struck critics as a burlesque house "bump and grind." During 1956–1957, the national TV programs "Stage Show," "The Milton Berle Show," "The Steve Allen Show," and the "Ed Sullivan Show" exposed millions of Americans to "Elvis the Pelvis," although on one of his three Sullivan show appearances, censors kept the cameras above Elvis's famed hips. Looking back from the perspective of the late sixties, celebrated composer and conductor Leonard Bernstein would credit Elvis with being "the greatest cultural force in the twentieth century. . . . He introduced the beat to everything and he changed everything—music, language, clothes, it's a whole new social revolution—the Sixties comes from it."

At the time, however, adults recoiled, from Elvis in particular and from rock and roll in general. The music seemed too sexual, too primitive, too rooted in the alien traditions of southern blues singers, poor-white country and gospel musicians, and northern rhythm-and-blues artists of the urban black ghettos. "Beware of Elvis Presley," warned the Catholic magazine *America*. Elvis, claimed a Los Angeles reporter, was a "sexhibitionalist" whose music was a "lascivious steaming brew." Testifying before the Senate Subcommittee on Delinquency, a witness claimed that Elvis's "strip-tease antics threaten to 'rock-n-roll' the juvenile world into open revolt against society. The gangster of tomorrow is the Elvis Presley type of today." In Nashville, disc jockey Great Scott publicly burned six hundred Elvis records. In San Francisco, two high school girls who won a "Why I Love Elvis" contest were expelled from school. "We don't need that kind of publicity," pronounced the principal.

Adults everywhere blamed the music for corrupting morals and instigating violent behavior. To upholders of "the American way of life," the vastly popular midfifties rock explosion represented outlawed forces bursting forth to challenge the old verities. Southern segregationists, for their part, saw rock as a plot by the National Association for the Advancement of Colored People (NAACP) to further interracial sex. The Reverend David Noebel opined that the communists had instigated the rock revolution to subvert America. While Noebel's view was extreme, most adults probably agreed with a reporter's comments on the merits of rock published in the *Denver Post:* "This hooby-dooby, oop-shoop, ootie-ootie, boom-boom, de-addy boom, scoobledy goobledy clump—is trash." To suburbanized, middle-class, white adults, rock threatened the very foundations of their lives.

Although adults exaggerated the new music's menace—typical lyrics explored teen love, jealousy, desire, loneliness, and adult misunderstanding—their charges were not without merit. The popularity of rock and roll among the young revealed the failure of mainstream society to enforce its ideal of conformity. Americans in the shifting postwar years wanted their traditional vision of normality to be immutable. Instead, millions of white youth reveled in a music associated with a despised black subculture. Had adults not recoiled so, rock and roll might have remained simply another form of entertainment. In part, adult disapproval ensured its place in young people's growing sense of uniqueness.

Youthful celebration of this music thus became a way to defy adult authority, but this was not the primary reason that rock and roll appealed to young people. Rather, it allowed the young to break free from the world of decorum, affluence, and expectations imposed on them by adults. The amplified beat energized the young, giving expression to the restlessness and anguish that so many youths felt growing up in the circumspect world of the midfifties. The music put them in touch with their emotions and with one another. It made them want to dance, to let go, and offered adolescents release, vitality, sexuality, and autonomy.

Rock also extricated white middle-class youth from the rigid barriers of race and class. For most suburbanized adolescents, rock and roll was their introduction to African-American culture and to the equally alien traditions of poor southern whites. As the music drew the black and white South into the American mainstream, white youth sensed the pulse of black America. And although cavorting at integrated rock concerts seldom led to the interracial sexual liaisons so feared by middle-class adults, not surprisingly young white Americans proved much more sympathetic than their parents to the emerging civil-rights movement.

Rock and roll, then, became more than just a new form of popular entertainment.

It linked teens around the country and soon around the world and expressed the ideas, values, and emotions that stirred their generation. Rock and roll gave adolescents a sense of belonging to a unique social group; as such it provided a form of entitlement. It was theirs. There were groups with teen names—the Teen Queens, Frankie Lymon and the Teenagers, the Six Teens—and teen songs—"Teen-Age Prayer" (1955), "Teen Angel" (1957), "Sixteen Candles" (1958), and "Teenager in Love" (1959). Meanwhile, the generation gap widened. By the late fifties, rock and roll artists mocked the parental generation: "Hail rock 'n' roll. Deliver me from the days of old," belted out Chuck Berry; "Yakkety Yak," a teen mockingly answered his parents in a Coasters' song.

The Trouble with Teenagers

As the popularity of rock and roll rose, juvenile delinquency too took a jump—and some adults saw connections between the new music and youthful deviance. *Blackboard Jungle,* a sensationalistic 1955 movie portraying delinquency in an urban high school and featuring Bill Haley's "Rock Around the Clock," seemed to confirm adults' worst fears.

As adolescent alienation from adult values intensified, juvenile delinquency spread from slums to suburbs and cut across geographic, racial, ethnic, and class barriers. By the midfifties, some 400,000 juveniles were convicted annually. Although this figure represented only 2 percent of those in the ten-to-seventeen age bracket and some juvenile "crimes" consisted of absences from school, breaking curfews, or entering pool halls, the media and much of the adult public nevertheless fretted.

Magazine articles with titles such as "Why Teenagers Go Wrong" proliferated. In a 1955 Senate hearing on delinquency, one witness exclaimed, "Not even the Communist conspiracy could devise a more effective way to demoralize, disrupt, confuse, and destroy our future citizens than apathy on the part of adult Americans to the scourge known as Juvenile Delinquency." Experts cited a range of supposed causes of youthful rebellion—rock and roll, comic books, working mothers, poverty, schools, television—but were unable to agree on the most important cause. Nevertheless, nearly all specialists and most of the public concurred that juvenile delinquency somehow represented a breakdown in the nation's most basic institution, the family. This failure of the postwar domestic ideal of affluent family togetherness plagued adults.

In reality, the seeming upsurge in youthful deviance stemmed more from media hype than reality. Even delinquent adolescents often misbehaved only to scoff at adult authority and assert their autonomy. To set themselves apart from the adult generation, for example, some teens joined gangs and cultivated their own dress, hair styles, and language.

Contrasts between adult and juvenile reactions to delinquency come to the light in responses to two important midfifties films about youthful defiance. *The Wild One* (1954) starred Marlon Brando as the leader of a motorcycle gang that rampaged through a small California town. Brando's crude, inarticulate character mumbled his lines and refused to get along with anyone. Adult audiences saw the film as a condemnation of senseless juvenile crime, but young viewers perceived Brando as a rebel hero. When

Rebel Without a Cause. Teenagers by the millions identified with the brooding, sensitive, and alienated James Dean, who died tragically in a 1955 car crash.

an adoring waitress asked, ''What are you rebelling against?'' Brando sneered, ''Whadda ya got?'' Adolescent audiences assumed that beneath Brando's coarse exterior lay a sensitive core.

A year later, Hollywood released the even more influential *Rebel Without a Cause,* starring James Dean, Natalie Wood, and Sal Mineo as disturbed teens from an affluent California suburb. Grown-ups saw *Rebel Without a Cause* as an indictment of youthful deviance. Although the film's title suggested that delinquency had no roots, the movie actually faulted the parents. Dean's father and mother failed to play the conventional gender roles: the father cooked and wore an apron, the mother dominated; Wood suffered an overbearing father; Mineo's family had deserted him. Thus, the film confirmed what the experts and politicians told parents: a proper family environment prevented delinquency.

Teens almost invariably identified with the young rebels, especially James Dean. To TV playwright Rod Serling, who had given Dean his first starring role in a 1953 television drama, the young actor embodied the emerging youth culture. ''There was a post-war mystification of the young,'' claimed Serling, ''a gradual erosion of confidence in their elders, in the so-called truths, in the whole litany of moral codes. They just didn't believe in them anymore.'' The moody, enigmatic, defiant Dean captured the imagination of adolescent audiences as no other film star has before or since. His tragic auto death at twenty-four, just three days before the release of *Rebel,* elevated him permanently to a symbol of the moral outsider too sensitive to survive the rigidities of adult society. For years after his death, Dean received more fan mail than any other Hollywood star, most of it from teens.

Dean and Brando, and Elvis, too, who was making his first hit records just as *Rebel* became a box-office smash, exuded an undisciplined, primitive energy and sexuality. They seemed to urge young audiences to demand personal liberation. Unlike adult society's ideal male—the responsible husband-father and successful businessman—Dean and Brando portrayed individuals incapable of living in a society dominated by conformity and moral compromise.

Adolescent Americans also learned contempt for middle-class mores through *Mad* magazine. Begun as a comic book in 1952, *Mad* changed to magazine format in the midfifties when comics came under fire as a cause of juvenile delinquency. *Mad* parodied and ridiculed virtually everything—movies, TV shows, the suburbs, Eisenhower, the Cold War, the smugness of the age. Walt Disney's beloved Mickey Mouse became "Rickey Rodent," G.I. Joe appeared as "G.I. Shmoe." In a spoof of the popular children's television show "Howdy Doody" (called "Howdy Dooit"), "Buffalo Bill" asked a kid in the "peewee gallery," "What would you like to be when you grow up? . . . A police chief? . . . A fireman? . . . An Indian? . . . Or (hot-dog) maybe a JET FIGHTER PILOT? Huh?" The kid answered: "What I want to do when I grow up is to be a hustler like Howdy Dooit! I want to be where the cash is . . . the green stuff . . . moolah . . . pound notes . . . get it? MONEY!" For young readers, *Mad*'s irreverent humor subverted the bourgeois complacency of the age.

Adolescents' worship of comic-book superheroes such as Plasticman, Captain Marvel, and the Human Torch also laid bare youthful alienation from adult values. In an age of conformity, these mythic heroes had unique histories. At first they lived as ordinary people; then, through a fluke of fate or an industrial accident, they gained superhuman powers. Spurning the moral caution of midcentury America, the superheroes boldly used their powers to fight the world's evils.

A Howl in the Darkness: The Beats

The incipient Beat movement contributed to the transformation of midfifties America and definition of the youth culture.[1] In October 1955, the same month in which *Rebel Without a Cause* opened, an unheralded event unfolded in San Francisco's Six Gallery. About 150 people packed the small art gallery to attend a poetry reading. Novelist Jack Kerouac livened things up by passing gallon jugs of wine through the crowd. Soon people were cheering the poets on with shouts of "Go! Go! Go!" as jazz aficionados did at jam sessions of that time.

The highlight of the evening was Allen Ginsberg's reading of *Howl,* a poem he had written two weeks earlier while under the influence of peyote and other drugs. Arms outstretched, weaving, bobbing, and dancing, Ginsberg electrified the audience with his passion:

---

[1] In the 1940s, jazz musicians used the term *beat* to mean "frustrated," "played out," or "beaten," as in "I'm beat right down to my socks." Novelist and jazz aficionado Jack Kerouac, who christened himself and his friends the Beat generation, defined *beat* as "a sort of furtiveness . . . a weariness with all the forms, all the conventions of the world." On other occasions, however, Kerouac claimed that *beat* stood for "beatitude," or spiritual blessedness.

I saw the best minds of my generation destroyed

by madness, starving hysterical naked,

dragging themselves through the negro streets at dawn

looking for an angry fix, . . .

Thus began Ginsberg's lament against what he saw as the destructive forces of midfifties America, forces that he symbolized in the figure of Moloch, a deity whose worship called for the parental sacrifice of children:

Moloch whose mind is pure machinery! Moloch whose

blood is running money! Moloch whose fingers are

ten armies! Moloch whose breast is a cannibal

dynamo!

At the conclusion of Ginsberg's reading, the audience jumped to its feet and cheered wildly. As poet Michael McClure later recalled, everyone knew ''at the deepest level that a barrier had been broken, that a human voice and body had been hurled against the harsh wall of America.'' Ginsberg called *Howl* his ''original blow for freedom,'' and Kerouac proclaimed the reading as ''the birth of the San Francisco Poetry Renaissance.''

Although the reading symbolized the public genesis of the Beat movement, doubtless little would have come of it without subsequent events. In 1956 Ginsberg's *Howl and Other Poems* was published by poet Lawrence Ferlinghetti, who ran City Lights Books, a gathering place for the burgeoning bohemian community of artists, writers, and musicians who clustered in San Francisco's North Beach area. Police confiscated *Howl* as an ''obscene and indecent'' publication. A much-publicized civil liberties trial ensued, and in a landmark legal decision, the court judged *Howl* literature, not pornography. Suddenly Americans discovered that they harbored a genuine literary avant-garde, and *Howl and Other Poems* became one of the best-selling poetry books in publishing history.

Ginsberg dedicated *Howl* ''to Jack Kerouac, new Buddha of American prose,'' and *Howl*'s publicity prompted the 1957 publication of Kerouac's novel *On the Road*. Unprecedented aesthetically and thematically, *Road* depicted an underground subculture that departed almost entirely from middle-class mores. Instead of the cautious conformity of Eisenhower's America, the book reveled in release and joy. Kerouac recounted adventures going back to the late forties that he had shared with Ginsberg, novelist William Burroughs, and other friends, particularly the crazed, petty thief, drifter, and womanizer Neal Cassady. As the character Dean Moriarty, Cassady was portrayed as an archetypal American hero, a symbol of freedom and rebelliousness, ''mad to live, mad to talk, mad to be saved, desirous of everything at the same time.''

Kerouac, Ginsberg, and other Beats scoffed at the corporate world and found no fulfillment in suburban life. Outcasts by choice, they romanticized those whom they regarded as estranged from middle-class life—homosexuals, hobos, junkies, Mexicans, Indians, and particularly African-Americans, whose culture they saw as an antidote for anesthetized white America. Sal Paradise, the narrator and Kerouac's persona in *On*

A Different Beat. Beat poets Allen Ginsberg and Peter Orlovsky, shown here in Paris in 1956, helped to shape a literary movement that challenged some of America's most sacrosanct values. Ginsberg would later become a guru to the sixties counterculture.

the Road, related how "at lilac evening I walked with every muscle aching among the lights of 27th and Welton in the Denver colored section, wishing I were a Negro, feeling that the best the white world had offered was not enough for men, not enough life, joy, kicks, darkness, music, not enough night." Throughout the novel, as Sal and Dean restlessly sped back and forth across the country, they encountered and celebrated the vitality and energy of America's underclasses.

Critics attacked *On the Road* for its "degeneracy" and disregard for social custom. But for many middle-class adolescents, *Road* became the book that most articulated their discontent with parental expectations, conformity, materialism, and puritanical notions of sex. The novel's uninhibited adventures spelled liberation. *On the Road* quickly became a best-seller, and more than ever the Beat generation came to national attention.

America's mass media feasted on the Beats. Reporters swarmed over such bohemian enclaves as New York's Greenwich Village and San Francisco's North Beach and churned out titillating accounts of Beat life. Reporter Mike Wallace interviewed Kerouac on television's most widely watched talk show. The Beat movement became a fad. Walt Kelly's comic strip "Pogo" added a Beat character, and *Playboy* magazine, launched in 1953, featured a female Beat as Playmate of the Month. TV began a series, "Route 66," that echoed the themes of *On the Road.* In cities across the country, coffeehouses sprang up featuring poetry reading, jazz, and folk music. These places attracted young people disaffected with middle-class life and drawn, however superficially, to the Beat alternative.

Yet most of the attention bestowed on the Beats had a hostile tone, typified by

Paul O'Neil's 1959 *Life* article, "The Only Rebellion Around." "The wide public belief that Beats are simply dirty people in sandals is only a small but repellant part of the truth," wrote O'Neil. In his view, the Beats intended "to offend the whole population." They "have raised their voices against virtually every aspect of current American society: Mom, Dad, Politics, Marriage, the Savings Bank, Organized Religion, Literary Elegance, Law, the Ivy League Suit and Higher Education, to say nothing of the Automatic Dishwasher, the Cellophane-wrapped Soda Cracker, the Split-level House, and the clean, or peace-provoking H-bomb."

But O'Neil and the other critics failed to recognize that the Beat movement was not all negation. From protesting the stultification of middle-class life, Beat writers like Kerouac and Ginsberg went on to exalt spontaneity, emotion, participation, sexuality, spirituality, community, love, and freedom. Strongly attracted to Zen Buddhism, they found in Zen and other Eastern religions an alternative to the hard-driving, individualistic Protestant ethic. Zen counseled them to be at peace with the universe and to live in harmony with nature rather than seek dominion over it, an alternative vision that would strongly influence the sixties counterculture and the later environmental movement.

Just as adults' rejection of rock only stimulated young people's fascination with the music, so too did the belittling of the Beats enhance their popularity among adolescents and open what would become a chasm between mainstream and avant-garde counterculture in the sixties. If there had been no hostile and sensational publicity, the Beat movement might well have remained a minor literary phenomenon. But once the media drew attention to the Beats, their literature, values, and lifestyle won them terrific popularity among the younger generation. By scorning the cultural priorities of hard work and material success, the Beats created an insurgent culture that gave millions of middle-class youth a sense of possibility, and that eased their apathy and impotence. Kerouac, Ginsberg, and other Beats had scraped an American nerve.

The Feminine Dilemma

Despite the manifold threats to the social order, family ideology held firm. In countless ways, psychiatrists, clergy, teachers, politicians, and other authority figures told women that fulfillment came through their roles as wives and mothers. An advice booklet written for teenage girls described homemaking and birthing as "very rich and rewarding experiences. You yourself feel more completely a woman, as, indeed, you are." Speaking before the all-women graduates of Smith College in 1955, Democratic presidential hopeful Adlai Stevenson asserted that "this assignment for you, as wives and mothers, has great advantages. . . . Women in the home [can] have an important political influence on man and boy. I think there is much you can do about our crisis in the humble role of housewife. I wish you no better vocation than that." By 1957 an amazing 92 percent of adult Americans had taken marriage vows at least once. In a national poll that year, 80 percent of respondents pronounced people who chose not to marry sick and immoral. If anything, the rise of delinquency and youth culture in the midfifties made the family, with the woman at its center, seem more than ever the bulwark of America. Not surprisingly, the custodians of American culture viewed working mothers as a dire threat.

During World War II, with men off fighting and industry booming, women had entered the work force in record numbers. All told, nearly 6.5 million had taken wartime jobs, and the proportion of women in the work force jumped from 25 to 36 percent. But in the immediate postwar years, women faced tremendous governmental and public pressures to abandon their jobs. The number of women workers declined right after the war. By 1949, however, this trend had reversed: throughout the fifties, a growing number of women took jobs, and by 1960 women constituted 40 percent of the nation's employees. More than half of these women workers were married. Indeed, between 1940 and 1960, the number of mothers at work jumped an incredible 400 percent. Some women worked to supplement their families' income so that they could afford the new house, car, and other trappings of affluence. But many more women worked for the same reasons that men did: for money, of course, but also for the challenge, companionship, autonomy, prestige, and power that a job offered.

Despite the reality of more and more women working outside the home, society still urged them to remain homebodies. This dilemma naturally instilled feelings of guilt and inadequacy, particularly among working mothers with young children. One distressed woman wrote to famed baby doctor Benjamin Spock: "I try to give [my son] a great deal of affection, although I am a working woman. . . . Sometimes it is so difficult to maintain my control that my hands shake. . . . Does he need help or do I?" Traditionalists struggled to reconcile the domestic ideal with the growing trend of female employment outside the home and to distinguish between employment and a career. It became culturally acceptable for women to work for a brief period, but to pursue a career was deemed too "masculine." As a reporter for *Look* instructed, "She gracefully concedes the top job rungs to men." Employment statistics reflected this biased thinking. Over one-third of working women held clerical jobs, while less than 6 percent had any sort of administrative positions. Moreover, women's pay on average was a full 40 percent below that of men. Even when men and women held the same job, the women received much lower salaries than the men.

Another paradox facing midcentury women centered on sex. The neo-Victorian fifties offered an image of women strictly polarized between the supposedly "good" and "bad" girl. As the midfifties advice book *On Becoming a Woman* told teenage girls, "Boys will only respect you if you say no." *Scholastic* magazine warned young ladies that "if you . . . kiss the boys goodnight, you're running the risk of having yourself footnoted as 'an easy number.'" Society expected women to remain virgins until their wedding night, but, paradoxically, they were also supposed to be sexually attractive. A male writer advised in a 1953 *Coronet* article, "The smart woman will keep herself desirable. It is her duty to herself to be feminine and desirable at all times in the eyes of the opposite sex." "The outer you," counseled *Seventeen,* the magazine for teenage girls, "is a reflection by which all other persons measure the inner you. You will want to remove underarm hair and perhaps the hair on your legs." The purpose of such constant attention to allure was, of course, to attract a man and, once wedded, to please him. Society expected the woman to adopt a passive role in marriage and to devote herself to satisfying her husband and her children more than herself.

Ambiguity clouded the cultural messages about sex that women received. Numerous magazine advertisements portrayed the cheery, stolid housewife smiling as she scrubbed the floor with a mop and the latest detergent. But other advertisements featured sexy, glamorous, bejeweled models clad in tight-fitting silk cocktail dresses. Both

Conflicting Images of Postwar Women. In the ad on the left, a wife extols the virtues of her Magic Chef gas range, contrasting markedly with Hollywood sex goddess Elizabeth Taylor. Domestic housewife or glamorous seductress—women were left with ambiguous images of what the ideal woman should be.

types of ads stimulated women's consumption, but the female roles that they depicted were mutually exclusive. How could women be both? Movies sent something of the same mixed message. Many films reflected the ideal of the meek, nurturing, domestic female. Actresses Doris Day, Debbie Reynolds, and June Allyson regularly played such roles. Yet films starring blatantly sexual stars like Marilyn Monroe, Elizabeth Taylor, and French actress Brigitte Bardot scored far more successes at the box office.

In 1953 Dr. Alfred Kinsey created a national scandal with the publication of his study, *Sexual Behavior in the Human Female.* Kinsey's findings revealed that despite all the public preaching about chastity before marriage and passivity in the marriage bed, half of the six thousand women interviewed admitted to having sex before marriage, and a quarter to intercourse outside marriage. Kinsey reached the shocking conclusion that women valued sexual fulfillment as much as men did. The media and politicians scorned Kinsey's findings and continued to preach a puritanical ethic. One New York congressman tried to bar *Sexual Behavior in the Human Female* from the mails and charged Kinsey with "hurling the insult of the century against our mothers, wives, daughters and sisters."

Growing up female in such a repressive and ambivalent culture and finding fulfillment in the limited roles allowed women remained difficult. By the midfifties, dissatisfaction among women bubbled to the surface. Poet Sylvia Plath satirized expected sexual conventions in "The Applicant":

A living doll everywhere you look.

It can sew, it can cook.

It can talk, talk, talk.

It works, there is nothing wrong with it.

Will you marry it, marry it, marry it.

Diane Di Prima, a Beat poet, also lamented the feminine self-suppression and male self-absorption found even in the bohemian domestic scene. In "The Quarrel," the poet resents washing dishes while her lover works on his paintings, but she knows that it would be "uncool" to gripe. She thereby angrily complies in her own powerlessness. "Hey, hon," her lover notes in the poem's last line: "It says here Picasso produces fourteen hours a day."

A Barnard graduate who admitted to having "played dumb" to catch her man found marriage upsetting: "The plunge from the strictly intellectual college life to the 24-hour a day domestic one is a terrible shock. We stagger through our first years of childrearing wondering what our values are in struggling to find some compromise between our intellectual ambition and the reality of everyday living." Another young mother confessed, "I've tried everything women are supposed to do—hobbies, gardening, pickling, canning, and being very social with my neighbors. . . . I love the kids and Bob and my home. . . . But I'm desperate. I begin to feel that I have no personality. . . . Who am I?"

A growing number of magazine articles acknowledged the problems afflicting women. In 1956 *McCall's*, the magazine of family "togetherness," printed a story entitled "The Woman Who Ran Away" and was astounded when it attracted more readers than any previous piece. Another study, written by a male doctor for *Coronet*, noted all sorts of "vague and disturbing" signs of female psychosomatic illnesses. Some women, the doctor found, suffered behind "a mask of placidity" that "hides an inwardly tense and emotionally unstable individual seething with hidden aggressiveness and resentment." "The unhappy wife," observed columnist Max Lerner in 1957, "has become a characteristic American culture type." By the late fifties, the divorce rate was rising and the birthrate declining as more and more women broke free from the constraints of marriage. These trends would continue and magnify through the sixties and seventies.

In 1957, Betty Friedan, wife, mother, and author, began research for some articles on what had become of the women in her 1942 Smith College class. She found nearly all of her respondents to be affluent suburban wives and mothers; she also perceived a pattern of frustration among these women, including herself. She later described this dilemma as "the problem that has no name" and attributed it to the "strange discrepancy between the reality of our lives as women and the image to which we were trying to conform." Society's "mystique of feminine fulfillment," according to Friedan, left many women feeling "empty" and "incomplete." Yet in a culture dominated by "the feminine mystique," women not "gaily content in the world of bedroom, kitchen, sex, babies and home" worried that they were neurotic. Friedan expanded her research over the years and in 1963 published her findings in *The Feminine Mystique,* a book that shocked and then galvanized millions of female readers.

A Radical Awakening

In the early fifties, America's intellectual Left languished in political limbo. The Cold War and anticommunist crusade created a political climate so stifling that even the mildest criticisms of the existing order seemed positively un-American. But although such pressures hastened the virtual demise of the Communist party, independent radical thinkers continued their work. Moreover, with the lessening of Cold War and anticommunist tensions in the midfifties, dissent gained some respectability and independent radical thinkers attracted a new audience. The end of the Korean War, the death of Stalin, and the censuring of McCarthy, combined with the growing challenges of alienated youth and blacks, further legitimized dissent.

Sociologist C. Wright Mills won repute as one of the new radical thinkers. Mills had long estranged himself from mainstream values. A burly Texan who wore boots and army fatigues throughout the fastidious fifties, Mills further shocked his contemporaries by driving a motorcycle to his classes at Columbia University and toting his papers in a duffel bag. But it was his scholarship that most disturbed his tweedy, buttoned-down colleagues. At a time when academic sociology increasingly tangled itself in jargon, statistics, and pedantry, Mills wrote with the imaginative skills of a novelist and the power of a radical pamphleteer. While most social scientists stressed their intellectual objectivity, Mills saw the intellectual's role as that of moral and political advocate. He condemned supposedly "value-free" sociology, claiming that it masked a profoundly conservative bias. To Mills the intellectual had a duty to resist conformity and "to unmask and to smash the stereotypes of vision and intellect with which modern communications swamp us."

In *White Collar* (1951) and *The Power Elite* (1956), Mills attacked what he saw as postwar America's drift toward a militarized, centralized, undemocratic bureaucracy. To him the ideal political system was the direct democracy of the New England town meeting or the city-states of ancient Greece. Democracy in contemporary America was a fiction, "more a formal outline than an actuality." Under the guise of Cold War necessity, Mills argued, the United States had become dominated by an interlocking directorate of military leaders, corporate commanders, and government bureaucrats. This was a world of "manipulated consent," in which "the young complacents of America, the tired old fighters, the smug liberals, the shrill ladies of jingoist [militaristic] culture . . . are all quite free," wrote Mills. "Nobody locks them up. Nobody has to. They are locking themselves up."

Against the Grain. In *The Power Elite, The Causes of World War III,* and other publications, sociologist C. Wright Mills sharply challenged the prevailing Cold War consensus. His writings helped to shape the New Left of the 1960s.

From the late fifties until a heart attack killed him at age forty-five in 1962, Mills grew increasingly polemical. In his widely circulated paperbacks *The Causes of World War Three* (1958) and *Listen Yankee* (1960), he lashed out at American foreign policy and defended Fidel Castro's Cuban revolution. "The immediate cause of World War III," he contended, "is the preparation of it." America's Cold War strategy was based on what he termed "crackpot realism," although the approach made perfect sense if one accepted its basic premise: the need to contain communism throughout the world. He particularly lamented the lack of serious discussion of possible alternative policies. "It is no exaggeration to say," he wrote in 1960, "that since the end of World War II in . . . the United States smug conservatives, tired liberals and disillusioned radicals have carried on a weary discourse in which issues are blurred and potential debate muted; the sickness of complacency has prevailed, the bi-partisan banality flourished."

In a similar vein, historian William Appleman Williams deplored America's myopic anticommunism and continued frontier-expansionist mentality. Like Mills, he perceived the United States as democratic in name only. As he saw it, this apparently liberal society was actually dominated by the large corporations in what he termed "corporate liberalism." Williams decried persistent postwar calls for more military spending to ensure U.S. superiority over the Soviets. This stubborn endurance of "the frontier outlook made it extremely difficult for American leaders to accept the reality of nuclear stalemate, let alone to negotiate the kind of fundamental compromises that would make disarmament feasible and realistic."

In 1959 Williams published *The Tragedy of American Diplomacy,* a revisionist critique of the origins of the Cold War markedly at odds with the consensus histories of the time that wholly blamed the Soviets. "At the apex of its power," wrote Williams, the United States found itself progressively thwarted in its efforts to inspire, lead, and reform the world. This supreme paradox of American history becomes comprehensible when viewed as a direct result of the nation's conception of itself and the world in terms of open-door expansion. For America's weakness in strength was the product of its ideological definition of the world. The United States not only misunderstood the revolutions in economics, politics, color and anticolonial nationalism, it asserted that they were wrong or wrong-headed and that they should be ignored or opposed in favor of the emulation of American expansion.

A professor of history at the University of Wisconsin, a school with a long tradition of radicalism, Williams attracted a group of graduate students who accepted his views of American history and in their own work extended the revisionist perspective. In 1959 Williams and some of his students, including Lloyd Gardner, Lee Baxandall, and Saul Landau, founded the journal *Studies on the Left,* which became a key forum for the emerging young intellectual Left.

Another trenchant, although less systematic, critic of corporate America and the Cold War was novelist Norman Mailer. First achieving fame as the young author of the World War II novel *The Naked and the Dead* (1948), Mailer refused to follow the official line. In 1952 he complained that "everywhere the American writer is being dunned to become healthy, to grow up, to accept the American reality, to integrate himself, to eschew disease, to re-evaluate institutions." By the midfifties, he claimed, "We live in a climate so reactionary that the normal guides to understanding contemporary American politics are reversed. . . . Radical political life has become difficult, and to hold the position of a libertarian socialist is equivalent to accepting almost total intellectual alienation from America."

Still, Mailer persisted with what he described as "the courage to be individual, to speak with one's own voice." In 1957 he published a widely discussed essay, "The White Negro," which celebrated the white urban "hipster" as the embodiment of rebellion from society's "slow death by conformity."[2] An existential, apocalyptic hero, the hipster lived with violence and death, releasing primitive energies before a repressive society. Like the rugged pioneer, the tough cowboy, and the sensual black, the hipster transcended the sham of respectability and domesticity that crushed "every creative and rebellious instinct." Mailer's essay predicted that the hip consciousness would spread as white America came to recognize the African-American. He prophesied a time of rebellion when the complacency of the fifties would shatter.

The idea of the hipster linked white and black cultures. To Mailer the hipster was "the first wind of a second revolution in this century, moving not forward toward action and more rational equitable distribution, but backwards toward being and the secrets of human energy." The Beat writers, too, celebrated what Allen Ginsberg called the "angelheaded hipster." Kerouac's *On the Road* extolled the hipster consciousness, the search for a life free from constraint, lived with the "ragged and ecstatic joy of pure being."

Like Mailer, Paul Goodman—poet, novelist, essayist, educational theorist, city planner, Gestalt psychologist, and general intellectual gadfly—interpreted hipsters,

---

[2] *Hipster* was a term popularized by black jazz musicians. It meant someone "in the know."

Beats, delinquents, and drop-outs not as problems but as natural responses to the absurdities and constraints of mainstream society. Goodman contended that corporate-dominated America provided little meaningful work for young people. Horatio, the hero of his 1959 novel *The Empire City,* steals his official school identity cards at age six and opts out of the system. The rest of the novel recounts Horatio's unconventional education and creation of a fulfilling communal life beyond the reach of the "Organized System."

In contrast to most fifties intellectuals, who prided themselves on being pragmatic realists, Goodman was an unashamed anarchistic, utopian romantic. In 1960 he published *Growing Up Absurd,* a book that became something of a manifesto for the sixties New Left and counterculture. In place of corporate capitalism and the warfare state, Goodman called for small, sharing, decentralized communities. Rather than a hierarchical society run by elites, he advocated an egalitarian society in which everyone took part in decisionmaking. Modern capitalism with its technological requirements, he believed, forced people to repress their true feelings, the capacity of their bodies to experience pleasure, and their instinct for play. His ideal society would offer spontaneity, sexuality, love, joy, and work with tangible value.

The emergence of radical periodicals stoked an alternative culture. In 1953, amid McCarthy's intimidation of the Left, independent journalist I. F. Stone began publishing *I. F. Stone's Weekly,* a radical newsletter that attacked the Cold War, McCarthyism, the arms race, and the Eisenhower administration. Although it never reached a mass audience, *Stone's Weekly* over the years influenced liberal and radical intellectuals on issues ranging from government corruption to U.S. policies in Vietnam.

As another early indication of intellectual discontent, in 1954 literary critic Irving Howe founded *Dissent,* a journal intended "to dissent from the bleak atmosphere of conformism that pervades the political and intellectual life of the United States; to dissent from support of the *status quo* now so noticeable on the part of many former radicals and socialists; to dissent from the terrible assumption that a new war is necessary or inevitable." Besides Howe, early contributors included Mills, Goodman, and other radical New York intellectuals. Beginning cautiously with articles criticizing McCarthyism and the extremes of the Cold War, *Dissent* editors took heart at the emerging civil-rights movement. Howe praised the Montgomery bus boycott as "a political and social innovation of a magnitude approaching the first sit-down strikes in the 1930s." By the late fifties, *Dissent* became a significant voice for the growing intellectual Left.

A year later, Norman Mailer helped to establish the *Village Voice,* published in New York's Greenwich Village. The *Voice,* the first of the underground newspapers that would gain importance in the sixties, was staffed by young writers such as Nat Hentoff, Jill Johnston, Jack Newfield, and John Wilcox and featured the artful photographs of Fred MacDarrah and the engaging comic strips of Jules Feiffer. It espoused radical politics and praised the Beats and the avant-garde art scene. By the late fifties, the *Voice* enjoyed a growing readership on college campuses across the country.

In 1956 pacifists Dave Dellinger, A. J. Muste, and Bayard Rustin launched *Liberation* magazine. In the first issue, the editors disparaged "the gradual falling into silence of prophetic and rebellious voices." *Liberation* radicals were anti-Marxist pacifists and believed in civil disobedience as advocated and practiced by Thoreau and Gandhi.

Hoping to avoid the mistakes of liberalism and Marxism, they set out to find a pacifistic approach, a "third way," that relied on "the individual ethical insights of the great religious leaders and the collective social concern of the great revolutionists." Like Paul Goodman, a frequent contributor to *Liberation,* the editors favored utopian thinking, humanized technology, decentralized power, and participatory democracy in which decisionmaking was based on consensus. *Liberation* prefigured much of the direct-action, nonviolent protest of the sixties New Left.

Less political and more outrageous was Paul Krassner's the *Realist.* Begun in 1958, it satirically attacked virtually every icon of Eisenhower's America: politics, the Cold War, the Bomb, advertising, TV, suburbia, and especially religion. Fusing fact and fantasy, his scandalous satire tried to deflate America's sacrosanct self-image. In a typical Krassner stunt, he printed a large red-white-and-blue poster reading FUCK COMMUNISM. Although Krassner's message expressed the essence of America's postwar political ideology, the outraged postal department refused to deliver the poster through the mail.

Besides a widening range of radical publications, a few independent radio stations sprouted up. Pacifica Foundation, established by pacifists just after World War II, began listener-supported radio station KPFA in San Francisco. Later it opened WBAI in New York and an affiliate of KPFA in Los Angeles. These stations' programming, in addition to folk, jazz, and classical music, included innovative public-affairs shows that discussed such controversial issues as nuclear disarmament, Beat literature, anticommunism, homosexuality, and communal living. Throughout the fifties and sixties, these noncommercial stations advanced the cause of radicalism and cultural dissent.

Even commercial radio accelerated the rise of a new sensibility. Disc jockeys such as Alan Freed and Wolfman Jack Smith promoted black rhythm and blues, just as Jocko, Hal Jackson, "Symphony" Sid Torin, and Daddy-O Daylie popularized black jazz. A primary radio personality abetting the subversion of mainstream culture was Jean Shepherd. Broadcast nightly from midnight to 3 A.M. on New York's powerful WOR, Shepherd's monologues regaled the Northeast. A Village regular and an original contributor to the *Voice,* Shepherd proved a superb storyteller with a razor-sharp sense of detail. His monologues described a world peopled by "day people," who "lived in an endless welter of train schedules, memo pads and red tape," and the "night people," who shared his late-night sphere. The day people took society's mandates seriously and acquiesced to the demands of consumer culture, thus furthering what Shepherd referred to as "creeping meatballism." Shepherd's regular listeners felt like true night people who understood the system's absurdity.

In a vein similar to Shepherd's, the late fifties also witnessed the emergence of new stand-up comedians—Mort Sahl, Shelly Berman, Dick Gregory, Elaine May and Mike Nichols, Jonathan Winters, and Lenny Bruce—who affronted bourgeois sensibilities with nightclub routines satirizing everything from politics to sex. In 1959 *Time* dubbed these comedians "sickniks," claiming that their humor represented a "personal and highly disturbing hostility toward all the world." Sahl raised national ire by cracking jokes about FBI director J. Edgar Hoover; Bruce, whose favorite routine was called "Religion, Inc.," was arrested several times for using obscene language. These comics, who cut through the pretenses and fatuities of postwar life, appealed especially to restless, alienated, college-educated audiences.

Black Uprising

Although various specters hovered over the social complacency of the midfifties, neither intellectuals, women, nor youths organized a full-scale protest movement during those years. Despite their alienation, these groups depended too much on the affluent Eisenhower consensus to see their way clear to an alternative vision.

African-Americans, on the other hand, were excluded from that consensus. They were relegated to the lowest rungs of the economic ladder and denied basic constitutional and human rights. In the midfifties, inspired by a volatile mix of frustrations and hopes, African-Americans launched a civil-rights struggle that would flower into a political and moral awakening. In the long run, this movement would not only effect a revolution in race relations but would inspire Hispanic-Americans, women, homosexuals, Native Americans, and other groups to demand recognition of their rights.

Black novelist Ralph Ellison's 1952 masterpiece *Invisible Man* opens with his unnamed narrator explaining: "I am an invisible man. . . . I am invisible, understand, simply because people refuse to see me." The novel explored the limited options open to African-Americans: life in rural poverty or in a northern city ghetto, promises offered by a black southern college whose president cringed before white "benefactors," or "brotherhood" held out by the white-dominated Communist party. Each option ended in betrayal. Whites saw nonwhites only as stereotypes, not as people. Constantly deceived by his supposed white supporters, Ellison's hero ends up living in a secret room beneath the streets of New York. His hermit life symbolized the position of African-Americans at midcentury: disillusioned, wanting change, hiding to rest. But Ellison did not depict this postponement as a defeat: "It is incorrect to assume that, because I'm invisible and live in a hole, I am dead. I am neither dead nor in a state of suspended animation. Call me Jack-the-Bear, for I am in a state of hibernation [and] a hibernation is a covert preparation for a more overt action."

The overt action that Ellison predicted seemed remote when his novel was published—the era of Senator Joseph McCarthy and the extremes of anticommunist witch hunting, a time when most people deemed all protest un-American. In 1952 neither Democrats nor Republicans supported civil-rights legislation. Indeed, Adlai Stevenson, the Democratic presidential nominee, chose white supremacist John Sparkman of Alabama as his running mate, and Republican Eisenhower had recently testified against the desegregation of the armed forces.

Blatant racism pervaded every aspect of life in the early fifties. In the South, African-Americans faced a solidly entrenched system of segregation upheld by law, custom, and white violence. Most southern whites firmly believed in the natural superiority of their race. Fearing the sexual "amalgamation of the races" and job competition, whites in the years after the Civil War had passed a jumble of local and state Jim Crow laws that imposed strict segregation in schools, parks, public buildings, restaurants, buses, trains—even cemeteries. Throughout the South, "White" and "Colored" signs separated everything from drinking fountains to hospitals. Separate schools and other facilities provided for blacks were inevitably inferior, but blacks lacked the political power to confront the problem. Only in certain areas, largely in the upper South, could blacks even exercise their constitutional right to vote. At midcentury, three out of four adult African-Americans in the South were disfranchised. The Democratic party dominated the region, and politicians did not get elected without endorsing segregation and black disfranchisement.

To escape discrimination, and to replace jobs lost through mechanization of cotton production, African-Americans had fled the rural South since the early years of the twentieth century. This exodus climaxed between 1940 and 1970 when more than 4.5 million blacks deserted the South—nearly 2 million in the fifties alone. They moved north and west, settling mostly in cities in the hopes of finding work and a rewarding life. In 1960 more than half of the nation's blacks, compared with only one-third of whites, lived in central cities. In the suburbs, on the other hand, whites outnumbered nonwhites by more than thirty-five to one. By the early fifties, a clear pattern had emerged: as whites exited the cities for the suburbs, African-Americans and other non-whites took their places. This pattern of *de facto* segregation only intensified racial and class distinctions.

Adjustment to city life proved difficult for blacks. Lacking money, skills, and education, many migrants became trapped in a desperate cycle of poverty that gave them little or no chance of entering the American mainstream. Ellison described these urban newcomers as "shot up from the South into the busy city like wild jacks-in-the-box broken loose from our springs—so sudden that our gait becomes like that of deep sea divers suffering from the bends." The exodus of affluent whites, along with industries and businesses, slashed urban tax bases and exacerbated the problem. This loss of tax revenues, combined with exploitive landlords and indifferent politicians, spelled doom for city services and housing.

In an effort to reverse urban decay, Congress in 1949 had passed the National Housing Act aimed at ensuring "a decent home and a suitable living environment for every American family." This urban renewal plan failed dismally. During the fifties, developers took advantage of loopholes in the government's program and destroyed far more lower-class housing than was rebuilt. In Los Angeles, the Hispanic barrio of Chavez Ravine was leveled to make room for Dodger Stadium; elsewhere developers demolished tenements and replaced them with shopping centers, colleges, parks, or highways. Often the slums that they bulldozed had been lively neighborhoods. The high-rise apartments that replaced many slums seldom proved as habitable as the older, sturdier housing. By the end of the fifties, most major cities were more segregated and dilapidated than ever.

Many African-Americans living in the urban North were too impoverished to escape the ghetto, but even those who could afford better housing found few choices. Real-estate agents often refused to show homes in white neighborhoods to nonwhites, and banks denied them mortgages. Many suburban communities made formal covenants to ensure racial exclusivity, which zoning laws also furthered. Even the federal government encouraged residential segregation. "If a neighborhood is to retain stability," advised a Federal Housing Administration underwriters' manual, "it is necessary that properties shall continue to be occupied by the same social and racial class."

Most politicians saw no pressing need to change the racist status quo. Indeed, few whites realized how discriminatory America was. With the media focusing almost exclusively on the affluent, white middle class and with that class increasingly segregating itself in all-white suburbs, it was easy for whites to assume, as liberal intellectual Max Lerner wrote, that "the Negro is entering into the full stream of our effort."

Northern whites who recognized racism generally saw it as a southern problem. The legal attack on segregation appeared to confirm this view. On May 17, 1954, the Supreme Court handed down its landmark decision, *Brown* v. *Board of Education*. Chief Justice Earl Warren, announcing the Court's hard-won unanimous decision, asked, "Does segregation of children in public schools solely on the basis of race, even though the physical facilities and other 'tangible' factors may be equal, deprive the children of the minority group of equal educational opportunities?" Warren answered, "We believe that it does." Citing studies of the psychological effects of segregation, the chief justice charged that keeping black children "from others of similar age and qualifications solely because of their race generates a feeling of inferiority as to their status in the community that may affect their hearts and minds in a way unlikely ever to be undone." Warren resolutely concluded that "in the field of public education, the doctrine of 'separate but equal' has no place. Separate educational facilities are inherently unequal."

The *Brown* case derived from years of legal effort by the National Association for the Advancement of Colored People (NAACP). Spearheaded by the courageous black lawyer, Thurgood Marshall, director of the NAACP's Legal Defense Fund, the NAACP had won a series of postwar cases concerning higher education, voting rights, transportation, and real estate. But *Brown* proved by far the group's most impressive victory. In striking down the separate-but-equal doctrine that federal courts had accepted as constitutional since 1896, the case shook the very foundation of legalized segregation. Here, declared the *Chicago Defender*, was "a second emancipation proclamation . . . more important to our democracy than the atom bomb." When asked by a Supreme Court justice whether he feared that southern hostility might undermine the ruling, Marshall answered, "Every single time that this Court has ruled, they have obeyed it, and I for one believe that the rank and file of the people in the South will support whatever decision in this case is handed down."

Initially, Marshall's optimism seemed well founded. Within a few months of the decision, most border states and those states with local options allowing segregation made provisions to integrate their classrooms. The schools of the nation's capital also abolished segregation. Even the white-supremacist governor of Arkansas declared that his state would obey the law. Hopes of rapid compliance, however, quickly evaporated. The original *Brown* decision did not contain any implementation decree and left responsibility for carrying out desegregation to local school officials. In May 1955, little more than a year after the verdict, the Supreme Court issued a second *Brown* decision calling for district courts to handle desegregation cases. Although this second decision demanded that desegregation proceed "with all deliberate speed," in effect it sanctioned a go-slow approach. For the first time in history, the Court had vindicated a constitutional right and then had deferred its exercise.

Still, Southerners might have complied with the decision had President Eisenhower taken a strong stand in supporting and enforcing it, as was his responsibility. But Eisenhower had little sympathy for the cause of racial equality, and this decision, which complicated his political life, annoyed him. "I don't believe you can change the hearts of men with laws or decisions," he pronounced. Rather than publicly endorse the

Brown ruling, the president stated that he would express neither "approbation nor dis-approval." He later reportedly confided to an aide that his appointment of Earl Warren to head the Court was "the biggest damnfool mistake I ever made."

Eisenhower's refusal to uphold the Court's decision encouraged southern segrega-tionists to defy the ruling. States that initially showed signs of compliance now reneged, and the South launched a bitter, determined campaign to preserve segregated schools. Long-dormant doctrines of states' rights and state nullification of federal law revived, along with the violent white-supremacist Ku Klux Klan and new terrorist organizations such as the White Citizens' Council.

Southern whites used every possible means to prevent integration: laws turning public classrooms into so-called private schools, special pupil-placement decrees that preserved segregation, and laws giving authority over schools to local boards to avoid statewide suits by the NAACP. Several states legally barred the very existence of the NAACP, and private businesses fired black or white employees known to support de-segregation. Where legal and economic measures failed, southern whites resorted to mob violence. By the end of 1956, in the eight states of the Deep South, not one black student attended school with white children, and only a few did so in the upper South. Not only did southern black children continue attending squalid, segregated schools after *Brown,* but in all areas of life, separation of the races remained the rule. Yet although the *Brown* decision failed to eliminate segregation, it did legitimate African-American aspirations for first-class citizenship. The Court's verdict had elated blacks, but many realized that they would have to act on their own behalf. The Emmett Till case in the summer of 1955 particularly awakened African-Americans to the nature of white racism.

Fourteen-year-old Emmett "Bobo" Till from Chicago was spending the summer at his uncle's home in the small town of Money, Mississippi. One Wednesday evening late in August, Carolyn Bryant, a young white mother, sold Till, an African-American, two cents worth of gum over her husband's grocery counter. Mrs. Bryant later told her husband that Till had whistled at her and asked her for a date. That Sunday, Carolyn's husband, Ray Bryant, and his half brother, J. W. Millam, kidnapped Till at gunpoint. Till's body was later recovered from the Tallahatchie River. The back of his head had been shot off. In Chicago, more than ten thousand mourners attended Till's funeral. But in Tallahatchie County, Mississippi, where nineteen thousand blacks and eleven thousand whites lived and no blacks were registered to vote, the all-white, all-male grand jury deliberated for less than an hour before dismissing all charges against those accused of Till's murder. Reflecting on the case, I. F. Stone wrote in his *Weekly* on October 3, "To the outside world it must look as if the conscience of white America has been silenced." With keen foresight, Stone went on to write: "The American Negro needs a Gandhi to lead *him,* and we need the American Negro to lead *us.*" That Decem-ber witnessed the beginning of the fulfillment of Stone's wish.

On December 1, 1955, in Montgomery, Alabama, Rosa Parks, a seamstress and an active member of the local NAACP chapter, boarded a city bus after a long day's work. The law required blacks, who constituted more than three-quarters of all passen-gers riding the public buses, to pay at the front of the bus, then reenter through the back door, sit only in the rear, and relinquish their seats to standing whites. As more and more whites boarded the bus that day, Mrs. Parks, seated in the front row of the "colored" seats, refused to stand to accommodate a white man. When the bus driver demanded she move, she stayed put. "I felt it was just something I had to do," she later said. Her courageous refusal would change the course of history.[3]

When officials arrested Rosa Parks and locked her in the city jail, black leaders, already infuriated by the flagrant violations of the *Brown* decision and the recent Till case, took action. E. D. Nixon, president of the Alabama NAACP and head of the local chapter of the Brotherhood of Sleeping Car Porters, posted bond to secure Parks's release and drove her home. Then Nixon talked with Jo Ann Robinson, a black English professor at Alabama State College and president of the Women's Political Caucus. The two had searched for a cause around which to rally Montgomery's black community. The arrest of Mrs. Parks, widely known among local blacks as a respectable person with a firm belief in racial equality, convinced Nixon and Robinson that the time had come to act. Professor Robinson and other members of the Women's Political Caucus spent the night mimeographing a flier that urged blacks to protest Parks's arrest by refusing to ride the buses.

The next day, Nixon called leaders from the black community and persuaded the somewhat reluctant Reverend Martin Luther King, Jr., the newly appointed twenty-six-year-old pastor of the Dexter Avenue Baptist Church, to host the meeting. There the group unanimously supported the call for a bus boycott. King, an Atlanta native with a recent doctorate from Boston University, became inspired. "There comes a time when people get tired," he declared, "tired of being segregated and humiliated; tired of being kicked about by the brutal feet of oppression."

When Montgomery's buses began rolling the next day, virtually no blacks were on board. This was just the beginning. For more than a year, Montgomery's fifty thousand black residents united. They walked; they drove in car and taxi pools; they rode mules. Daily, they faced legal harassment and mob violence. One handbill circulated by whites read: "When in the course of human events it becomes necessary to abolish the Negro race, proper methods should be used. Among these are guns, bows and arrows, sling shots and knives. We hold these truths to be self evident, that all whites are created equal with certain rights: among these are life, liberty, and the pursuit of dead niggers." Authorities arrested King and other black leaders on trumped-up speeding charges, and whites bombed a number of black houses, including King's. White employers fired many blacks because of their participation in the boycott; other blacks suffered attacks and beatings. But they remained peaceful, and they continued the boycott. "My feets is tired," one elderly black woman explained, "but my soul is rested." "A miracle has taken place," Reverend King claimed. "The once dormant and quiescent Negro community is now fully awake."

In November 1956, the boycotters won a major victory when the Supreme Court ruled the Alabama law requiring segregated buses unconstitutional. On December 21, the boycott finally ended. Montgomery's buses were at last integrated. This small triumph held significant consequences. Out of the boycott emerged an eminent leader, a forceful new tactic for social change, and a determination among African-Americans

---

[3]Evidence suggests that Rosa Parks chose arrest rather than humiliation as a conscious political act. In addition to her long involvement in the NAACP, in 1953 she had attended a two-week training session at Highlander Folk School in Monteagle, Tennessee, an institution dedicated to racial integration.

Montgomery Bus Boycott. Parking lots such as this one became transfer points for an intricate system of car and taxi pools used to replace the buses, as most of Montgomery's fifty thousand African-Americans united in the triumphant bus boycott.

to eradicate centuries of injustice. Montgomery marked the first time since Reconstruction that southern blacks protested en masse, and—largely owing to the influence of King—they acted nonviolently. The boycott stimulated King to develop and put into practice his philosophy of massive nonviolent resistance.

Although inspired by the nineteenth-century transcendentalist Henry David Thoreau and the leader of the Indian independence movement Mohandas Gandhi, as well as contemporary pacifists A. J. Muste and Bayard Rustin, the real source and effectiveness of King's philosophy of passive resistance derived from the African-American Christian faith so central to southern black culture. "If you will protest courageously, and yet with dignity and Christian love," King told his followers, "when the history books are written in future generations, the historians will have to pause and say, 'There lived a great people—a black people—who injected new meaning and dignity into the veins of civilization.'"

King was only one of many important boycott leaders, yet because of his articulate defense of nonviolence and the media attention that he generated, he arose from Montgomery a world-renowned figure and a symbol of black determination. To direct future civil-rights campaigns, King and a network of southern black ministers founded the Southern Christian Leadership Conference (SCLC) early in 1957, laying the groundwork for the civil-rights movement. Montgomery had catalyzed new self-confidence and resolve among African-Americans everywhere. The time of waiting patiently for the courts and the politicians to grant basic rights was over. In 1959 Dr. King prophesied that the near future would witness massive black "direct action against injustice." The new decade would barely begin before King's prediction proved true.

During the late fifties, the civil-rights movement gained momentum. Although no other single event such as Montgomery captured national attention, resistance to racism percolated. Following Montgomery, for instance, protesters organized similar bus boycotts in Tallahassee, Florida; Rocky Mount, North Carolina; and Birmingham and Tuskegee, Alabama. In May 1957, on the third anniversary of *Brown,* more than thirty thousand participants gathered in the nation's capital for a Prayer Pilgrimage. The crowd cheered as Martin Luther King, Jr., A. Philip Randolph, and others called on the country's leaders to accelerate civil-rights progress. In 1958 and 1959, Bayard Rustin and King organized Youth Marches for Integrated Schools, attracting some twenty-five thousand black and white participants. In 1958 a youth group affiliated with the Oklahoma City NAACP held a lunch-counter sit-in in which a group of blacks and whites asked to be served at a segregated eatery. Inspired, other young blacks held similar sit-ins in Oklahoma and Kansas, and in 1959, Congress of Racial Equality (CORE) members sat in at a W. T. Grant's lunch counter in Miami. During these same years, black organizations grew in membership and honed their strategic skills. Although none of these developments received widespread media coverage, they hinted at a new mood of urgency and hope.

The Faces of Protest

In addition to civil-rights activism, the late fifties saw the emergence of several other protest movements. Although the effects of the Cold War and the anticommunist witch hunts had virtually annihilated the Marxist Left, nonviolent, non-Marxist radicalism surfaced in the more relaxed environment of the midfifties.

In 1955, the same year in which the civil-rights struggle began in Montgomery, radical pacifists in New York City organized a civil defense protest. Every spring from 1951 through 1961, New York City, like other cities throughout the country, required residents to take shelter during mock nuclear attacks. On June 15, 1955, a group of pacifists defied the macabre exercise. As they saw it, civil defense drills were part of the government's effort to hoodwink the American public into believing that they could survive a nuclear war. When the civil defense sirens wailed, Dorothy Day, A. J. Muste, Dave Dellinger, Bayard Rustin, Jim Peck, and twenty-three other peace advocates gathered on the lawn outside city hall and refused to take shelter. They were arrested, and the presiding judge denounced them as "murderers." Each June through the remainder of the fifties, the group reenacted the ritual protest against civil defense and the nuclear-arms race. Despite regular prison sentences, the number of participants multiplied annually. By the end of the decade, such protests spread to other cities and to several college campuses.

In 1957 these protests prompted a group of activists to found the Committee for Nonviolent Action (CNVA), which aimed to organize nonviolent civil disobedience against deadly atmospheric nuclear-bomb tests. On August 6, 1957, the twelfth anniversary of the bombing of Hiroshima, the CNVA marched to the Nevada site of a planned nuclear detonation in an attempt to block the scheduled test. Federal officials arrested eleven of the pacifists. In May the following year, the committee endeavored to sail the *Golden Rule* into the South Pacific, where the United States planned a series of H-bomb tests. Albert Bigelow, a prominent Bostonian highly decorated in World War II naval operations, served as the ship's skipper. When the *Golden Rule* neared the test site, the Coast Guard seized the ship and arrested Bigelow and his crew. Their adventure and arrest caught the world's attention and inspired support demonstrations in various American cities, as well as in London and Montreal. Speculating on the significance of Bigelow's courage, Martin Oppenheimer wrote in *Dissent* that summer:

> If, as they admit, their effort may bring no real change, why do it at all? . . . They did it because they could do no other, because no one else did it for them, because politics failed to do it, because the hour was late and because they had to. Effectiveness had little to do with it. This was the individual act undertaken against a state and a condition which seemed omnipotent; above all, this was propaganda of the deed, one's physical body thrown into a void where no other bridge seemed to exist.

Opposition to nuclear weapons, particularly their atmospheric testing, proliferated. *Village Voice* cartoonist Jules Feiffer lampooned testing in his comic-strip story of the "Big Black Specks." His characters inhabited a world in which big black specks from nuclear fallout filled the skies. Feiffer's self-righteous government officials assured the people that nuclear tests had "added no appreciable amount of radioactive fallout to the atmosphere." Unsuccessful with this lie, the officials then launched an ad campaign. Huge billboards proclaimed that "Big Black Floating Specks Are Very Pretty!" and "Big Black Floating Specks are Good for You!"

In November 1957, Norman Cousins, the editor of the *Saturday Review,* helped to organize the National Committee for a Sane Nuclear Policy (SANE), calling for immediate suspension of all nuclear testing. More moderate than CNVA, SANE grew rapidly and by the summer of 1958 boasted some 130 chapters with an estimated membership of twenty-five thousand. By then opposition to the Bomb and nuclear testing had swelled owing to such publications as Nobel Prize–winning scientist Linus Pauling's exposé of the dangers of nuclear fallout, *No More War!* (1958); Jim Peck's eloquent, personal defense of pacifism, *We Who Would Not Kill* (1958); C. Wright Mills's polemical *The Causes of World War Three* (1958); and Nevil Shute's doomsday novel and later popular film, *On the Beach* (1957). Late in 1958, the Eisenhower administration, which had regularly dismissed proposals to cease testing as "catastrophic nonsense," agreed with the Soviets to halt above-ground tests. Ike's capitulation proved a major victory for SANE and other antinuclear activists worldwide.

In addition to adult protest, the younger generation of the late fifties began to shake the "silent" and "apathetic" labels. Racial inequality, nuclear testing, militarism, compulsory Reserve Officer Training Corps (ROTC) membership for all male students, and civil defense all stirred students to active protest. In 1958 concerned students at Cornell University founded the student auxiliary of SANE (Student SANE). The Student Peace Union arose at the University of Chicago in 1959. The Cuban revolution that year also galvanized many young Americans, especially as the United States government, in support of U.S. corporations such as the United Fruit company, grew increasingly hostile toward Castro's regime. By late 1959, several campuses had organized Fair Play for Cuba groups.

Older radical intellectuals took heart when they saw what the *Nation* described in 1959 as the "Tension Beneath Apathy" on university campuses. "The kids are fed up," wrote Beat poet Kenneth Rexroth in July 1960. "During the past couple of years, without caring about the consequences, making up their techniques as they went along, organizing spontaneously in the midst of action, young people all over the world have intervened in history." In his prescient essay "The New Left" in September 1960, C. Wright Mills praised the growing youthful radicalism: "Let the old men ask sourly, 'Out of apathy—into what?' The age of Complacency is ending. Let the old women complain wisely about the 'end of ideology.' We are beginning to move again." Similarly, Paul Goodman concluded *Growing Up Absurd* with the statement that "we of the previous generation who have been sickened and enraged to see earnest and honest effort and humane culture swamped by . . . muck, are heartened by the crazy young allies." He ventured to predict that "perhaps the future may make more sense than we dared hope."

• • •

Writing at the end of the fifties, Goodman described the decade as "extraordinarily senseless and unnatural." American society, in his words, was "a Closed Room with a Rat Race as the center of fascination, powerfully energized by fear of being outcasts." Norman Mailer went so far as to characterize the fifties as "one of the worst decades in the history of man." Poet Robert Lowell, in a less caustic account, referred to the fifties as "tranquilized." Reminiscing about growing up in the midcentury years, sixties radical Tom Hayden claimed that for "young people like myself the world of the fifties was largely a one-dimensional one . . . lacking in any real social conflict. There seemed to be only one reality, one set of values: those of the comfortable middle class. There being only that one reality, life was already programmed: You went to high school, then college, then got married and found a job."

Although exaggerated, these critiques contained much truth: many people found mainstream American society confining. But this was not the only fifties. From mid-decade on, dissent smoldered under the smooth surface of the Eisenhower era as malcontents began to articulate their long-suppressed grievances. Whether voiced by Chuck Berry's "Roll Over Beethoven," Allen Ginsberg's "Moloch," the sardonic *Mad* figurehead Alfred E. Neuman's "What, me worry?", C. Wright Mills's faulting of America's "crackpot realism," or Martin Luther King, Jr.'s teaching of human dignity through peaceful resistance, new energies and possibilities burst forth. The Silent Generation of youth haltingly found its voice. Women increasingly chafed against the demands of domesticity. Radical intellectuals challenged the prevailing consensus. Above all, African-Americans developed powerful tactics with which to attack the nation's blatant racism.

The mid- to late fifties stands as a time of transition. Seeds sown in these years would flower in the intensely activist era that followed.

Selected Bibliography

Useful treatments of the growing dissent in the later fifties are found in Douglas T. Miller and Marion Nowak, *The Fifties* (1977); W. T. Lhamon, Jr., *Deliberate Speed: The Origins of a Cultural Style in the American 1950s* (1990); Morris Dickstein, *Gates of Eden* (1977); Marty Jezer, *The Dark Ages: Life in the United States, 1945–1960* (1982); Todd Gitlin, *The Sixties* (1987); and David Halberstam, *The Fifties* (1993).

The best book on fifties youth and the specter of juvenile delinquency is James B. Gilbert, *A Cycle of Outrage: Juvenile Delinquency and the Mass Media in the 1950s* (1986). Paul Goodman's prophetic *Growing Up Absurd* (1960) is also a wise assessment of youth and delinquency in the 1950s. See also Edgar Z. Friedenberg, *The Vanishing Adolescent* (1959); Benjamin Fine, *1,000,000 Delinquents* (1955); and Harrison E. Salisbury, *The Shook-Up Generation* (1958). Reading J. D. Salinger's *Catcher in the Rye* (1951) provides a sense of midcentury youthful alienation.

The origins and early development of rock and roll are covered in Charlie Gillett, *The Sound of the City* (1984 ed.). Also valuable are Philip H. Ennis, *The Seventh Stream: The Emergence of Rocknroll* (1992); Arnold Shaw, *The Rockin' '50s* (1974); Nik Cohn, *Rock: From the Beginning* (1969); Jim Miller, ed., *The Rolling Stone Illustrated History of Rock and Roll* (1976); Carl Belz, *The Story of Rock* (1969); Jeff Greenfield, *No Peace, No Place: Excavations Along the Generational Fault* (1973); Herbert London, *Closing the Circle: A Cultural History of the Rock Revolution* (1985); and John Orman, *The Politics of Rock Music* (1985). Herb Hendler's *Year by Year in the Rock Era* (1983) offers a fact-filled chronology of rock history. On Elvis, see Jane Stern and Michael Stern, *Elvis World* (1987); Albert Goldman, *Elvis* (1981); Steve Dunleavy, *Elvis* (1982); and Peter Guralnick, *Last Train to Memphis: The Rise of Elvis Presley* (1994).

The best historical study of the Beats is Michael Davidson, *The San Francisco Renaissance* (1989). Other helpful studies include John Tytell, *Naked Angels* (1976); Bruce Cook, *The Beat Generation* (1971); Lawrence Lipton, *The Holy Barbarians* (1959); Michael McClure, *Scratching the Beat Surface* (1982); and Joyce Johnson, *Minor Characters* (1983). Two excellent biographies of Kerouac are Ann Charters, *Kerouac* (1973), and Gerald Nicosia, *Memory Babe* (1983). See also Barry Gifford and Lawrence

Lee, *Jack's Book* (1978). Barry Miles, *Ginsberg* (1989), and Jane Kramer, *Allen Ginsberg in America* (1969), are fine biographies. See also Gordon Ball, ed., *Allen Verbatim* (1974). The best way to appreciate the Beats is through their writings, especially Allen Ginsberg, *Howl and Other Poems* (1956), and Jack Kerouac, *On the Road* (1957) and *The Dharma Bums* (1958).

Elaine Tyler May's *Homeward Bound* (1988) links the stress on domesticity in the postwar years to the larger imperatives of the Cold War. The problems of feminists in the conservative fifties are analyzed in Leila Rupp and Verta Taylor, *Survival in the Doldrums: The American Women's Rights Movement, 1945 to the 1960s* (1987), and Cynthia Harrison, *On Account of Sex: The Politics of Women's Issues, 1945–1968* (1988). Other studies worth consulting include Eugenia Kaledin, *Mothers and More: American Women in the 1950s* (1984); Betty Friedan, *The Feminine Mystique* (1963); Wini Breines, *Young, White, and Miserable: Growing Up Female in the Fifties* (1992); and the relevant chapters of William Chafe, *The Paradox of Change: American Women in the 20th Century* (1991 ed.).

Maurice Isserman's *If I Had a Hammer* (1987) examines the fate of the Left in the fifties and the Old Left's relationship to the emerging New Left. Also helpful are Lawrence Lader, *Power on the Left: American Radical Movements Since 1946* (1979); Milton Cantor, *The Divided Left: American Radicalism, 1900–1975* (1978); James Weinstein, *Ambiguous Legacy: The Left in American Politics, 1900–1975* (1975); and John P. Diggins, *The American Left in the Twentieth Century* (1973). Works by radical intellectuals discussed in this chapter are C. Wright Mills, *White Collar* (1951), *The Power Elite* (1956), *The Causes of World War Three* (1958), and *Listen Yankee* (1960); William Appleman Williams, *The Tragedy of American Diplomacy* (1959); Norman Mailer, "The White Negro" (1957), reprinted in his *Advertisements for Myself* (1959); and Paul Goodman, *The Empire City* (1959) and *Growing Up Absurd* (1960). Paul Goodman edited a collection of articles from *Liberation* published as *Seeds of Liberation* (1964).

Ralph Ellison's classic novel *Invisible Man* (1952) is a fascinating portrayal of the position of blacks in midtwentieth-century America. Overviews of the black struggle since World War II are Harvard Sitkoff, *The Struggle for Black Equality, 1954–1992* (1993); Manning Marable,

Race, Reform and Rebellion: The Second Reconstruction in Black America from 1945 to 1982 (1984); Doug McAdam, *Political Process and the Development of Black Insurgency, 1930–1970* (1982); Juan Williams et al., *Eyes on the Prize: America's Civil Rights Years, 1954–1965* (1987), based on the PBS television documentary; Thomas R. Brooks, *Walls Come Tumbling Down: A History of the Civil Rights Movement, 1940–1970* (1974); and Robert H. Brisbane, *Black Activism: Racial Revolution in the United States, 1954–1970* (1974). The *Brown* case is astutely treated in Richard Kluger's *Simple Justice* (1976). The aftermath of that desegregation decision is the theme of Benjamin Muse, *Ten Years of Prelude* (1964), and Anthony Lewis, *Portrait of a Decade* (1964).

Taylor Branch's superb *Parting the Waters: America in the King Years, 1954–1963* (1988) places Martin Luther King, Jr., in the larger political and social context of the era. Equally impressive is David Garrow's *Bearing the Cross: Martin Luther King, Jr., and the Southern Christian Leadership Conference, 1955–1968* (1986). Other excellent studies of King and SCLC include David L. Lewis, *King: A Biography* (1978 ed.); Stephen B. Oates, *Let the Trumpet Sound: The Life of Martin Luther King, Jr.* (1982); and Adam Fairclough, *To Redeem the Soul of America: The Southern Christian Leadership Conference and Martin Luther King, Jr.* (1978). King's own account of the Montgomery bus boycott and the development of his nonviolent philosophy is found in his *Stride Toward Freedom* (1958).

Lawrence Wittner, *Rebels Against War, 1941–1960* (1969), covers rising pacifism and antinuclear protest in the late fifties. Also important are Nat Hentoff's biography of A. J. Muste, *Peace Agitator* (1963); Jim Peck's personal testament, *We Who Would Not Kill* (1958); and Linus Pauling's plea for an end to atmospheric nuclear testing, *No More War!* (1958).

CHAPTER

3

T H E   K E N N E D Y
P R O M I S E

On the eve of the 1960 presidential election, novelist Norman Mailer wrote discontentedly, "Not all the roots of American life are uprooted but almost all." The "essence of the new postwar SuperAmerica," he charged, was "the supermarket, that homogeneous extension of stainless surfaces and psychoanalyzed people, packaged commodities and ranch homes, interchangeable, geographically unrecognizable."

What the nation needed, claimed Mailer, was "a hero central to his time, a man whose personality might suggest contradictions and mysteries which could reach into the alienated circuits of the underground." Many Americans, of course, had thought of President Eisenhower as just such a man. But to Mailer, Ike "could stand as a hero only for that large number of Americans who were most proud of their lack of imagination. . . . The incredible dullness wreaked upon the American landscape in Eisenhower's eight years has been the triumph of the corporation. A tasteless, sexless, odorless sanctity in architecture, manners, modes, styles has been the result. Eisenhower embodied half the needs of the nation, the needs of the timid, the petrified, the sanctimonious, and the sluggish." Ike was "the anti-Hero" representative of the "dull anxiety" of the 1950s. With the twin crises of the late fifties—a racial showdown at home and Soviet space successes abroad—"the fatherly calm of the General," Mailer lamented, "began to seem like the uxorious mellifluences of the undertaker."

65

Yet with the dawning of the new decade and the Democrats' nomination of John F. Kennedy as their presidential candidate, the radical novelist took heart. To Mailer, Kennedy "was unlike any politician who had ever run for President in the history of the land, and if elected he would come to power in a year when America was in danger of drifting into a profound decline." Categorizing Kennedy's political record to date as merely "conventional," Mailer nevertheless found promising qualities in the handsome young candidate. He possessed "a cool grace," showed "the poise of a fine boxer," and, like the Beats, had the "patina of that other life, the second American life, the long electric night with the fires of neon leading down the highway to the murmur of jazz." Here stood a champion who could tear the nation "loose from the feverish ghosts of its old generals" and "face into that terrible logic of history which demanded that the country and its people must become more extraordinary and more adventurous, or else perish."

Mailer titled his extraordinary preelection article on Kennedy "Superman Comes to the Supermarket." According to Mailer, as existential Superman, Kennedy would help Americans to throw off the slough of materialism and conformity and would push the country to reach uncharted depths. "We as a nation would finally be loose again in the historic seas of a national psyche which was willy-nilly and at last again, adventurous."

Millions of Americans shared Mailer's sense of expectation. On TV and in public appearances, John F. Kennedy projected commitment and vigor. His campaign called on Americans to pursue a New Frontier "of unknown opportunities and perils." Although he was narrowly elected, his vitality and style nevertheless captured the imagination of millions worldwide. He came to seem, in the words of *New York Times* columnist James Reston, "a story-book President," attractive, vibrant "with poetry on his tongue and a radiant young woman at his side." Promising to confront the global communist challenge and "to get America moving again," he inspired hopes for peace, prosperity, and social justice and encouraged thousands of idealistic young activists to work to end war, poverty, and segregation. As one Peace Corps volunteer put it, "We had such faith in what Kennedy was doing, and we all wanted to be part of it."

With his self-confidence and ambitious notions about the powers of his office, Kennedy vowed to galvanize not only America but the rest of the world. His achievements, however, fell far short of his ambitions, and on November 22, 1963, an assassin's bullets killed him. JFK's brief presidency, coinciding with and ultimately spurred by the growing clamor for civil rights, left a legacy of rising expectations and stimulated a flowering of social criticism and activism.

Little Rock and *Sputnik:* Crises in the Late Fifties

Despite a rising clamor of dissent, the Great Celebration was still in full swing in late summer 1957. The economy seemed more prosperous than ever. Auto manufacturers sold record numbers of cars, especially that year's two-toned Chevrolet. The New York Yankees were about to clinch the American League pennant, as usual, while in the National League the upstart Milwaukee Braves excited fans in the nation's beer capital. Even the specters that troubled Americans at middecade—juvenile delinquency and rock and roll—appeared on the wane. Some young people still committed crimes, but

Showdown at Little Rock. African-American students Richard Richardson and Harold Smith brave a hostile crowd in their effort to integrate Central High School in Little Rock, Arkansas.

the congressional hearings on delinquency had ended, and the media paid less attention to the issue. Instead, adults read about a new college prank, the panty raid, in which young men stormed women's dormitories to capture female undergarments.

The year 1957 also saw Dick Clark launch the nationally televised "American Bandstand." Shown every weekday from 3 to 5 P.M. for adolescent audiences, "Bandstand" sanitized and commercialized rock. The show played records by such white teen rockers as Paul Anka, Frankie Avalon, Fabian, and Bobby Vinton, while neatly dressed, mostly white teens demurely danced the latest steps. It all looked and sounded tame, even to adults. That March an editorial in the trade paper *Cash Box* asserted, "The type of rock 'n' roll that originally excited the kids and made it a subject for national and international debate, has quietly receded into the background and has been replaced with a softer version with emphasis on melody and lyric."

Racial tensions, earlier inflamed by *Brown* and Montgomery, also seemed to ebb by 1957. That September, Congress passed the first civil-rights bill since Reconstruction. Although of limited value in enforcing racial equality, this act established the U.S. Commission on Civil Rights to investigate such matters as voting discrimination. Early that same month, Althea Gibson became the first black to win the women's championship of the traditionally lily-white United States Lawn Tennis Association.

Then, on September 25, America's domestic tranquility shattered. National attention focused on Little Rock, Arkansas, where President Eisenhower had dispatched federal troops to enforce the court-ordered integration of nine black students into hitherto all-white Central High School. For the first time, television cameras and newspaper photographers revealed to the nation the ugly face of white racism as mobs jeered at the young black students with chants of "two, four, six, eight, we ain't gonna integrate!'' and ''Niggers, keep away from our school. Go back to the jungle!'' Little Rock was the first in a long series of televised racial confrontations in the South in which the contrast between screaming white racists and clean-cut nonviolent blacks roused widespread support for the civil-rights cause. Yet despite this instance of federally backed integration, school desegregation moved at a snail's pace. To avoid showdowns similar to Little Rock, the South increasingly set up all-white private academies, leaving blacks in underfunded segregated public schools.

On October 4, 1957, while troops, mobs, and cameras still swarmed over Little Rock, an even more shocking message came through the teletype: the Soviet Union had launched the world's first earth-orbiting satellite. Incredibly, the 184-pound *Sputnik* circled the earth every ninety-six minutes. All across the country, Americans could pick up the regular ''beep, beep, beep'' of *Sputnik*'s transmitter on their radios. People shuddered as they realized that the Russians had scored a scientific and technological victory in an area that the Americans had long expected to dominate. *Sputnik*, screamed nuclear scientist Edward Teller, amounted to a ''technological Pearl Harbor.''

At first the Eisenhower administration tried to play down the Soviet achievement. Sherman Adams, the president's White House staff chief, declared that the United States had no interest in ''an outer-space basketball game.'' But on November 3, 1957, the Soviet Union performed an even more astounding feat when it rocketed into orbit a second satellite, *Sputnik II*, weighing more than 1,120 pounds and carrying a live dog. Suddenly Adams's comic concept of space basketball gave way to doomsday visions of Soviet space-launched missiles raining destruction on New York, Los Angeles, and Kansas City. More than any time since the Cold War began, the Russians truly seemed a menace. Senate majority leader Lyndon Johnson fumed, ''The Roman Empire controlled the world because it could build roads. Later—when men moved to the sea the British Empire was dominant because it had ships. Now the Communists have established a foothold in outer space. It is not very reassuring to be told that next year we will put a 'better' satellite into the air. Perhaps it will even have chrome trim—and automatic windshield wipers.''

Sputnik rekindled Cold War fears and touched off an unprecedented national debate over America's goals and values. Although Eisenhower remained personally popular, his administration came under sharp attack. Critics warned that Soviet success in propelling a satellite into space gave the Russians a long lead in missile technology. Surely, they argued, the Soviets would take advantage of this superiority in their presumed drive for world domination. ''We find ourselves as a nation on the defensive, and as a people seemingly paralyzed in self-indulgence,'' protested the president of Princeton University. The very things that most midfifties Americans had cherished—material comfort and a complacent, middle-of-the-road president—now seemed a mistake.

But the government's hurried efforts to join the space race ended in fiasco. On December 6, 1957, amid much fanfare, the United States attempted to launch its first satellite, the *Vanguard*. At 1:44 P.M. the countdown began. The huge rocket fired, lifted slowly, and then exploded in flames. When the smoke cleared, the rocket's nose cone could be seen leaning precariously against a support pole; the cantaloupe-sized satellite had been thrown clear and rested on the ground a short way off, emitting a steady radio signal.

''Sputternik,'' ''flopnik,'' ''kaputnik'' were a few of the epithets the world's wits dubbed the failed *Vanguard*. It mattered little that two months later the United States managed to orbit a small satellite; the damage had already been done. The Soviet *Sputniks,* claimed American ambassador to Italy Clare Booth Luce, were an "outer-space raspberry to a decade of American pretensions that the American way of life is a gilt-edge guarantee of our national superiority."

The cover of the January 20, 1958, issue of *Newsweek* depicted the globe as a chessboard with the banner headline: "Mortal Challenge: Are We Up to It? A World at Stake—In Science, Education, Diplomacy, Economics, Defense." Inside, *Newsweek* editors warned that

> to every civilization, at some moment in its existence, the mortal challenge comes. Now Red Russia's dictatorship has thrust such a challenge upon the West. The challenge is not simply military; it is total—intellectual, spiritual, and material. To survive, the free world, led by the United States, must respond in kind. Amid a clamor of alarm and self-criticism, America is preparing to shoulder this burden of great historical responsibilities.

Waves of apprehension roiled the placid surface of American life. Looking for a scapegoat to blame for America's humiliation, politicians and the media hit upon the public school system. The Soviets, they argued, boasted a rigorous educational curriculum that emphasized science and mathematics, whereas the U.S. school system stressed mediocrity at the expense of excellence.

Educational reform became a national crusade. Special educational commissions solemnly assembled. Congressional hearings droned. TV and radio programmers preempted regular shows to air educational grievances. From cover to cover, four successive, self-proclaimed "Urgent" issues of *Life* warned of a "crisis in education." "The schools are in terrible shape," accused the *Life* editors. "What has long been an ignored national problem, Sputnik has made a recognized crisis."

From an official government report, *Education in the U.S.S.R.* (1957), to a bestseller entitled *What Ivan Knows and Johnny Doesn't* (1958), to the *Life* "crisis" issues, the same cry reverberated: the Soviets turn out more scientists and engineers yearly; America must catch up. "Education," argued Admiral H. G. Rickover, the creator of the nation's nuclear navy, "is our first line of defense—make it strong."

Congress responded in 1958 with the National Defense Education Act, aimed at cultivating a technological elite of scientists and engineers to serve the needs of the military-industrial complex. Throughout the nation, administrators revamped school curricula to place special emphasis on the sciences, encourage gifted students, and strengthen discipline. More than ever, Americans saw higher education as the keystone of national security. College enrollments jumped from 2.5 million students in 1955 to 3.6 million in 1960. By then the federal government channeled over $1.5 billion to universities, mostly to support defense-related research.

The *Sputnik* crisis also spurred obsessive concern over national security. General Maxwell Taylor, a top military official, warned that a "missile gap" endangered the very existence of the American republic. Pressure to raise defense spending clamored from all sides. Critics called for more conventional military forces, claiming that Eisenhower's reliance on nuclear weapons as the main deterrent would not stop Soviet-instigated wars of national liberation. Politicians and military leaders also urged the

New American Heroes. The Soviet launch of *Sputnik* escalated Cold War fears and spurred obsessive concern over national security. Belatedly, the flights of America's astronauts, culminating in the 1969 moon landing, would reassure the nation that the United States had finally surpassed the Soviets in space.

government to launch a massive effort to overtake the Soviets in what was now referred to as a space race.

Less than a year after the first *Sputnik,* Eisenhower created the National Aeronautics and Space Administration (NASA) to coordinate efforts to surpass the Soviets. In April 1959, Americans were introduced to their first astronauts, seven military test pilots. All were fathers in their thirties; all were white, Protestant, and natives of small-town America; all but one had a crewcut. With reassuring Anglo-Saxon names such as Shepard, Carpenter, and Cooper, they conjured up images of honest work and old-fashioned virtue. To *Time* magazine, they were "seven men cut out of the same stone as Columbus, Magellan, Daniel Boone, Orville and Wilbur Wright."

The astronauts and the space program supplied Americans with heroes and national triumphs. Yet initially the Soviets kept scoring all the successes. More than a month before upstaging the United States with the *Sputnik* launches, the Soviet Union had triumphantly tested an intercontinental ballistic missile (ICBM). The event, not highly publicized to the American people, alarmed U.S. policymakers. The government gave missile development top priority, but the United States would fail to perfect a similar ICBM until late November 1958. The Soviets also achieved satellite orbits about the moon and sun well in advance of the United States, and in 1959, they landed a rocket on the moon carrying their hammer-and-sickle flag.

Space shots and ICBMs were not the only problems confronting Americans in the last years of the fifties. The U.S. economy also began to falter. By the spring of 1958, the country found itself in the midst of the worst recession of the postwar era; unemployment climbed from about 4 percent to over 8 percent, the highest rate since the depression. Professional economists, influenced by British economist John Maynard Keynes (1883–1946), advocated stopping the recession through monetary expansion and increased government spending, even if the strategy entailed deficit financing. But Eisenhower, worried about inflation and the budget deficit, rejected recommendations for a tax cut and new public-works projects. As the recession deepened, discontent mounted.

To make matters worse, in 1958 congressional committees disclosed conflict-of-interest violations by presidential appointees and charges of influence peddling by Vice President Richard Nixon's former campaign manager. Even Ike's trusted and influential adviser Sherman Adams resigned after a congressional subcommittee revealed that he had accepted expensive gifts from a millionaire businessman seeking government favors. "Things are in an uproar," charged the hitherto pro-Eisenhower *Chicago Daily News.* "But what is Eisenhower doing? All you read about is that he's playing golf. Who's running the country?"

Exploiting the discontent generated by *Sputnik,* recession, and corruption, the resurgent Democrats swept the 1958 off-year elections and after November enjoyed a 283–153 margin in the House and 64–34 in the Senate. The party looked eagerly ahead to the 1960 presidential race. One Democrat in particular—John F. Kennedy, the handsome, youthful senator from Massachusetts—emerged as a highly articulate critic of the Republican administration and a prime prospect for the Democratic presidential nomination. Eisenhower's foreign policy, Kennedy charged, was a hodgepodge of "piecemeal programs, obsolete policies, and meaningless slogans." The president had sacrificed military strength to the dogma of balanced budgets. In his speeches, Kennedy often drew parallels between Winston Churchill's efforts in the 1930s to warn a complacent Britain of the Nazi menace and his own attempts to awaken an equally indifferent American citizenry to the immensity of the Soviet threat: "No Pearl Harbor, no Dunkirk, no Calais is sufficient to end us permanently if we but find the will and the way. In the words of Sir Winston Churchill in a dark time of England's history: 'Come then—let us to the task, to the battle and the toil—each to our part, each to our station. Let us go forward together in all parts of the [land]. There is not a week, nor a day, nor an hour to be lost.'"

Eisenhower, hoping to calm growing Cold War tensions and recoup Republican prestige, revived attempts to negotiate with the Soviets and invited Russian leader Nikita Khrushchev to visit America. In the fall of 1959, the Soviet premier met with Eisenhower at the presidential retreat Camp David in Maryland, where the two leaders made plans to hold a formal summit meeting in Paris the following spring.

The attempt at rapprochement fizzled. On May 1, 1960, two weeks before the scheduled summit, Moscow announced that it had shot down an American U-2 spy plane twelve hundred miles inside the Soviet Union. Eisenhower first denied U.S. involvement in espionage, but Soviet officials exposed his lie by displaying Francis Gary Powers, the captured CIA pilot, and the pictures that he had taken of Russian military installations. Although he finally accepted responsibility for the U-2 flight, the proud Eisenhower refused to apologize. When the Paris summit convened, the Soviets walked out, and an opportunity to advance world peace was lost.

By this time, the American penchant for critical self-scrutiny had grown obsessive. The president's Commission on National Goals established after *Sputnik* produced a massive report, *Goals for Americans*. Mass-circulation magazines and learned journals alike devoted whole issues to discussing national purpose and America's future. Books with titles such as *The Ugly American* and *America the Vincible* shot to the tops of best-seller lists.

Much of the national debate focused on dissatisfaction with the quality of American life. Critics suddenly saw material prosperity, once the nation's pride, as enfeebling the populace. "Have We Gone Soft?" asked novelist John Steinbeck. "If I wanted to destroy a nation, I would give it too much and I would have it on its knees, miserable, greedy, and sick." "Our goal has become a life of amiable sloth," complained *Time* editor Thomas Griffith. To economist Robert Heilbroner, American society had developed into "an immense stamping press for the careless production of underdeveloped and malformed human beings, and that, whatever it may claim to be, it is not a society fundamentally concerned with moral issues, with serious purposes, or with human dignity." The Great Celebration had given way to the Great Lamentation.

Economist John Kenneth Galbraith, in his best-selling 1958 book *The Affluent Society,* brought new depth to the post-*Sputnik* arguments against materialism. Excessive concentration on the private production of consumer goods, he maintained, led to an orgy of wasteful spending that left the public sector of the economy impoverished. Americans wallowed in "an atmosphere of private opulence and public squalor." Schools suffered from crowding, inadequate facilities, and poorly paid teachers. Hospitals, mental institutions, clinics, and prisons were insufficient in number, understaffed, and overfilled. With profit the dominant value, essential public services naturally lagged. Galbraith proposed to reverse these priorities: private spending on consumer items should shrink while government spending on public needs should expand.

Not all post-*Sputnik* economists supported Galbraith's call for a boost in government expenditures, but virtually all emphasized the importance of economic growth as an axiom of the Cold War consensus. Just as opinion makers perceived the United States and the Soviet Union as locked in an arms and space race, economists believed that the superpowers had entered a growth race too. Only systematic economic growth would show the world that capitalism, not communism, had the most to offer developing nations. Heightened production would allow democratic nations to solve social problems peaceably. Regular, nonrevolutionary capitalist growth, in the words of future Kennedy adviser Walt Rostow, would serve as "an anti-Communist manifesto."

But was the United States growing fast enough? Many post-*Sputnik* observers thought not. Even discounting the recession of 1957–1958, America's growth rate during the fifties trailed that of the Soviets by more than 4 percent annually. Demands for accelerated productivity became a basic feature of the late-fifties Great Lamentation and another tool that the Democrats used to attack the Eisenhower administration.

Outside politics, several well-publicized scandals fueled the late-fifties American malaise. In 1959 Charles Van Doren, an attractive young English professor from Columbia University who had become a national hero through his apparent brilliance in answering difficult questions on a popular TV quiz program, confessed to congressional investigators that the show had been rigged. Soon after, famed disc jockey Alan Freed was convicted of having received payoffs from record companies for pushing particular songs. Other shocking revelations exposed widespread cheating in colleges, even West Point, and in New York City a group of police officers were caught working for a burglary ring.

Passing the Torch: The Election of 1960

Americans take for granted that any young schoolboy can grow up to be president, but few have fathers who literally groom their sons for the nation's highest office. Such was the case with the thirty-fifth president of the United States, John Fitzgerald Kennedy. The patriarch of the Kennedy family, Joseph P. Kennedy, was a self-made multi-millionaire. A proud, competitive, and insecure Irish-American Catholic, the elder Kennedy raised his four sons to achieve political power and with it the social recognition that had eluded him. The oldest son, Joe, Jr., seemed the embodiment of the father's ideal—athletic, handsome, bright, and outgoing. But with Joe's death in World War II, the father shifted his ambitions to his second son, Jack.

Like all the other Kennedy children, Jack was driven to excel as a student and an athlete. Although he suffered from a chronic bad back, he played sports at Harvard and served in the navy during the Second World War. He emerged from the conflict a hero, having rescued members of his crew after Japanese destroyers sank the PT boat that he commanded. In 1946, prodded and financed by his father, the young Kennedy campaigned in Boston for a seat in the House of Representatives. He won handily and, despite an undistinguished record as a congressman, successfully ousted the aristocratic incumbent, Henry Cabot Lodge, Jr., from the United States Senate in 1952. His marriage to the beautiful and socially prominent Jacqueline Bouvier in 1953 proved a key political asset. In 1956 he published the Pulitzer Prize–winning book *Profiles in Courage,* a study of politicians who had acted on principle rather than expediency. Kennedy took full credit for this book, but in fact most of *Profiles in Courage* had been ghost-written by his staff member Ted Sorensen.

Although Kennedy had sponsored no important legislative measures, his eloquent post-*Sputnik* attacks on the Eisenhower administration for failing "to maintain the minimum conditions for our survival" ensured him widespread support. Backed by an effective political organization and his father's finances, Kennedy won a series of Democratic primaries and in July 1960 gained a first-ballot nomination at the Democratic convention in Los Angeles. He chose Senate majority leader Lyndon Baines Johnson (LBJ) from Texas as his running mate. The choice was a case of politics' making strange bedfellows. JFK and LBJ, two men who would dominate the politics of the sixties, harbored a mutual distrust of and dislike for one another. Kennedy embraced Johnson out of expediency, to balance the ticket and win southern support. The ambitious Johnson accepted, giving up his powerful position in the Senate in the hopes that the vice presidency would ultimately catapult him into the Oval Office.

Meanwhile, the Republican party nominated Vice President Richard Nixon. Although the lack of serious opposition to his candidacy cost Nixon some national publicity, he struck a pose as a statesman above party faction. As his running mate, Nixon picked Henry Cabot Lodge, Jr., whom Kennedy had defeated in the 1952 Senate race.

The two young presidential candidates (Kennedy was forty-three; Nixon, forty-seven) launched their campaigns within the context of the post-*Sputnik* debate over national purpose. The Cold War formed the centerpiece for each man's strategy. Today people remember Kennedy as a martyred liberal and Nixon as a corrupt conservative, but in 1960, judged by their stated policies, they were virtually indistinguishable. Both vehemently reinforced the nation's Cold War commitments. Each perceived communism as a monolithic world threat masterminded by the Soviet Union, and the United States as the leader of the free world with a moral and military right to intervene. Both men's worldviews had been shaped by the Great Depression and the rise of fascism in the thirties, the sacrifices and victory in World War II (both had served as naval officers in the Pacific), the emergence of the Cold War, and the domestic anticommunist crusade. Each candidate believed that the chief executive should play a more active role than did the incumbent, but neither urged drastic changes in the nation's social and economic system or foreign policy.

Nixon had the advantage of more national recognition and executive experience as Eisenhower's vice president. He particularly stressed his competence in foreign affairs. In 1959 he had gotten into an argument with Soviet leader Nikita Khrushchev in a model kitchen at an American exhibition in Moscow. The press had puffed this minor squabble into the "Kitchen Debate," and Nixon gained a reputation as an adroit negotiator, able to stand up to the Russians.

Nixon also presumably had the blessing of being the chosen successor of Eisenhower. Yet the ailing Ike personally disliked Nixon and remained aloof during the campaign. Asked at a press conference in August, "What major decision of your administration has the vice-president participated in?" he quipped, "If you give me a week, I might think of one." Despite this barb, Nixon was closely connected in the public mind with the beloved Ike, and he entered the campaign the clear favorite.

Kennedy faced an uphill battle but had his own advantages. For one thing, his hard-fought victory in the Democratic primaries and at the convention had given him national campaign experience and recognition. It had also granted him time to develop an effective political organization. He possessed an excellent mind for political detail, and from the outset he attracted many talented subordinates. Also, because virtually every critical evaluation of America faulted the Eisenhower-Nixon administration, Kennedy had the good fortune to capitalize on the post-*Sputnik* mood more than his opponent. "Mr. Nixon says 'We never had it so good,'" Kennedy campaigned. "I say we can do better." His speeches echoed the theme of reassessment. He emphasized the need to speed up the economic growth rate. "Public interest," Kennedy insisted, must take priority over "private comfort." He charged that "we have as a nation gone soft, physically, mentally, spiritually soft . . . losing our will to endure. . . . We stick to the orthodox, to the easy way and the organization man. . . . Profits are up, but so is our crime rate. So is the rate of divorce and juvenile delinquency and mental illness. So are the sales of tranquilizers and the number of children dropping out of school."

Like so many others, Kennedy assumed that the Soviets would take advantage of their presumed superiority in missile technology and economic growth rate to launch a worldwide offensive. His campaign struck a note of crisis; the United States must be prepared to face the supreme challenge. As he proclaimed, "Each day we draw nearer the hour of maximum danger." He declared his intention to base his campaign on the single assumption that

> the American people are tired of the drift in our national course, . . . they are weary of the continual decline in our national prestige. . . . I run for the presidency because I do not want it said that in the years when our generation held political power America began to slip. I don't want historians writing in 1970 to say that

the balance of power in the 1950s and 1960s began to turn against the United States and against the cause of freedom.

In the post-*Sputnik* mood of recrimination, Kennedy's appeals moved millions of Americans. Besides his outstanding political organization and ability to capitalize on the debate over national purpose, Kennedy possessed a third edge: personality. Born to great wealth, he was well educated, handsome, youthful, urbane, witty, and charming. His fashionable and attractive wife, Jacqueline, added to his appeal. In sum, Kennedy was blessed with true political charisma. By contrast, the self-made Nixon often came across as tense, self-conscious, insecure, and insincere. A shrewd man, he lacked warmth, wit, and grace. Having risen to power by exploiting the anticommunist issue, he struck many liberals as little better than a cleaned-up Joe McCarthy. Other Americans remembered the secret ''slush fund'' that he had received from California businessmen in his 1952 campaign for the vice presidency. Thus, despite his success in politics, public doubts about the man persisted. Even in his home town of Whittier, California, when supporters proposed naming a street in his honor, residents rejected the idea in a storm of angry protest. When the trustees of Duke University, where Nixon had studied law, tried to grant him an honorary degree, the faculty voted no. In the minds of millions of Americans, Nixon was ''Tricky Dick.'' The appeal of the two young candidates, according to Norman Mailer,

> no matter how close, dull, or indifferent their stated politics might be, were radical poles apart, for one was sober, the apotheosis of opportunistic lead, all radium spent, the other handsome as a prince in the unstated aristocracy of the American dream. So, finally, would come a choice which history had never presented to a nation before—one could vote for glamour or for ugliness, a staggering and most stunning choice.

The personality differences between the two candidates emerged most clearly in the one unique feature of the campaign: four nationally televised face-to-face debates. Few substantive disagreements arose in the discussions; Nixon even admitted that he and Kennedy shared the same policies and differed ''only about the means to reaching those goals.'' Despite highlighting the candidates' common commitment to the Cold War consensus, these TV encounters revealed the two men's widely disparate personas. The differences came to light especially in the first debate, which more than seventy million viewers watched. Nixon, suffering from a knee infection and general weariness, appeared pale, haggard, stiff, and ill at ease. Sweat oozed through the pancake makeup, ill concealing his five o'clock shadow. The well-tanned Kennedy, on the other hand, seemed natural and relaxed. The air of competence and confidence that he projected dispelled worries about his youth and inexperience.

Nixon, however, proved an effective debater, and radio listeners judged the first contest about even. But the TV audience clearly deemed the Democratic challenger the winner. Of the four million voters who admitted to pollsters that they had based their choice on the televised debates, three million voted for Kennedy. TV had made its political mark. Henceforth, being telegenic would give any political candidate a crucial edge.

The absence of clear-cut issues in the campaign, in addition to TV's importance,

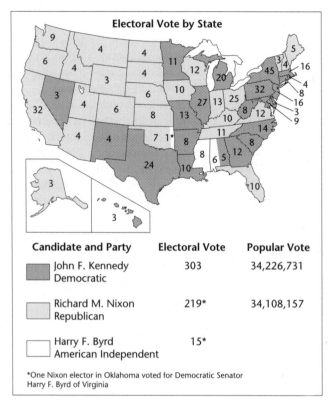

Presidential Election of 1960.

also accentuated Kennedy's Catholicism. No Catholic had ever been elected president. In 1928 the overwhelming defeat of Democratic nominee Al Smith, the first Catholic nominated by a major party, convinced many political analysts that only Protestants could win the presidency. Nixon's frequent dismissal of the religion issue only accentuated it. Throughout the campaign, conservative Protestant ministers charged that Kennedy would subordinate American interests to those of the pope. Jokes also circulated; one wit suggested that Kennedy would rename the Statue of Liberty "Our Lady of the Harbor." Kennedy did all he could to defuse this tension. Speaking before the hostile Houston Ministers Association, he pledged his belief in an America "where there is no Catholic vote, no anti-Catholic vote, . . . and where religious liberty is so indivisible that an act against one church is treated as an act against all." Post-election analyses suggest that while Kennedy's religion cost him votes in rural, Protestant regions, on balance his Catholicism helped him, especially in key blue-collar, northern urban areas, where 78 percent of Catholics voted for him.

Public interest in the long, grueling campaign ran high. A Gallup poll taken in late October found the race too close to call. On election eve, CBS computers predicted a Nixon victory. The popular vote proved the closest since 1888. Not until noon the day after the election did the press declare Kennedy the winner. With two-thirds of eligible voters going to the polls, Kennedy received a popular majority of only 118,574 votes. His victory in the electoral college was wider, 303–219; yet a shift of only 35,000 votes in a few key states could have reversed the final results. In one of those crucial states, Illinois, Republicans suspected that Chicago mayor Richard Daley's political machine had illegitimately secured JFK's slim triumph.

One key to Kennedy's victory was the African-American vote. After *Brown*, Montgomery, and Little Rock, politicians of both parties had grown sensitive to racial issues. During the election year, a massive sit-in movement had swept the South and captured national attention (see Chapter 4). By the time of the political conventions that summer, protesters were using nonviolent, direct-action tactics to challenge every form of public segregation. Although the two candidates kept their campaign focused on the Cold War, both parties adopted platforms that promised to support civil-rights legislation.

The Republicans seemed to have a good chance to garner a large share of the African-American vote. The Eisenhower administration had not strongly supported black rights, but Ike's actions in Little Rock and his signing the 1957 Civil Rights Act into law had won approval within the black community. Furthermore, the Republicans were Lincoln's party, whereas the Democrats remained tainted by the power of southern segregationists.

As a congressman and senator, Kennedy had compiled a lackluster record on civil rights. As a presidential candidate, however, he knew the importance of gaining black votes, so in addition to supporting his party's proposals for new civil-rights legislation, he criticized Eisenhower for failing to provide executive leadership in civil-rights matters. "If the president does not himself wage the struggle for equal rights," he argued, "if he stands above the battle—then the battle will inevitably be lost." He pledged that if elected he would with the "stroke of a pen" do what Eisenhower had not done: eliminate racial discrimination in federally aided housing by executive order.

Such campaigning raised Kennedy's standing among blacks, but it was an incident in late October that most improved his popularity among nonwhite voters. While leading a demonstration against a segregated Atlanta department store, Martin Luther King, Jr., was arrested for his participation in a sit-in. On October 25, less than two weeks before the election, a Georgia judge sentenced the civil-rights leader to four months of hard labor in a penitentiary. King's friends and family feared for the black leader's life. The Eisenhower administration did nothing; and Nixon, when reporters asked his opinion about the case, replied that he had none.

Sensing an opportunity, Kennedy took action. On October 26 he phoned the distraught Mrs. King and promised his help. The following day he had his brother Robert call the Georgia judge on King's behalf. That day King was released unharmed. Although King's freedom actually stemmed from a legal technicality, Kennedy got the credit. "For him to be that courageous," pronounced King, "shows that he is really acting upon principle and not expedience. . . . I am convinced he will seek to exercise the power of his office to fully implement the civil-rights plank of his party's platform." King's father, Reverend Martin Luther King, Sr., like many other Protestant black clergy, had supported Nixon for religious reasons. Now he announced his intention to vote for Kennedy. On the Sunday before the election, Democrats outside black churches distributed some two million copies of a pamphlet relating Kennedy's role in King's release and quoting King and other members of his family in praise of the Democratic candidate. Kennedy received black support in the election so overwhelming that it clinched his victory in such key states as Michigan and Illinois.

Kennedy's election stimulated high expectations. The new president exuded promise and purpose, and he fascinated the media with his vigor and glamour. African-Americans looked forward to a completion of the nation's racial reconstruction. Young people saw in Kennedy the personification of public virtue and moral commitment. The aged poet Robert Frost, whom Kennedy invited to participate in his inauguration, hailed the coming decade as "the next Augustan age. . . . A golden age of poetry and power." The enthusiasm of Kennedy's close supporters knew no bounds. To historian Arthur Schlesinger, Jr., who would soon be appointed an adviser, the election foretold "a new epoch" of "vitality" and "identity," with "new values . . . straining for expression and release."

Kennedy's campaign and charisma had convinced millions that he was not simply another politician seeking office but a true leader armed with vision, determination, and a sense of mission. For the young in particular, 1960 seemed to open a new era of hope, rich with the promise of freedom and opportunity. In retrospect, the country probably expected too much of one man and his administration. Even were Kennedy the Superman whom Mailer imagined, it is doubtful that he could have fulfilled all the bright hopes that his election had engendered. His tragically brief presidency would leave most promises unrealized.

Cautious Liberalism: The New Frontier at Home

The new president shared America's optimism. Radiating self-confidence, he hoped to turn the tide of international affairs in America's favor. The times, he believed, called for heroic presidential leadership. At his gala inauguration, the first to be nationally televised, the tanned president, braving cold January winds without hat or topcoat, summoned the nation to action: "Let the word go forth from this time and place, to friend and foe alike, that the torch has been passed to a new generation of Americans . . . tempered by war, disciplined by a hard and bitter peace, proud of our ancient heritage." In the most memorable line from the inaugural, the president challenged his listeners: "And so, my fellow Americans: ask not what your country can do for you— ask what you can do for your country."

During the campaign, Kennedy had claimed that the nation stood "on the edge of a New Frontier—the frontier of the 1960s—a frontier of unknown opportunities and peril . . . of unfulfilled hopes and threats." The New Frontier, he had explained, "sums up, not what I intend to offer the American people, but what I intend to ask of them. It appeals to their pride, not their pocketbook." Yet despite the civil-rights movement's dramatization of basic social injustice, Kennedy saw no need for profound change on that front. Wary of alienating white southern Democrats, he made no mention of race or poverty in his inaugural address. Rather, he maintained his focus on the Cold War. "Let every nation know," he pronounced, "whether it wishes us well or ill, that we shall pay any price, bear any burden, meet any hardship, support any friend, oppose any foe to assure the survival and success of liberty."

The first weeks of the new administration brimmed with an energy and excitement

America's Royalty. John F. Kennedy, Jacqueline Bouvier Kennedy, daughter Caroline, and son John with their good looks and vigorous style appeared to millions as the perfect American family.

not seen in Washington since the first hundred days of the New Deal. The highly cultured president and his wife surrounded themselves with intellectuals and artists. Rhodes scholars and other eminent academics, including such notables as historian Arthur Schlesinger, Jr., and economists John Kenneth Galbraith, Walter Heller, and Walt W. Rostow, enthusiastically agreed to serve their country. Distinguished musicians, poets, and painters gathered at elaborate White House celebrations. World-renowned cellist Pablo Casals performed in the East Room; the American Shakespeare Festival Theatre entertained at a state dinner. Art, beauty, and brilliance illuminated the White House.

From the outset, Kennedy embraced a dynamic style aimed at widening his popular support. In frequent television interviews and press conferences, he reiterated his promise "to get America moving again." His polished speeches, full of Shakespearean and Churchillian quotations, infused audiences with a sense of challenge, sacrifice, and heroism. Kennedy's style and grace awed the media and captured the imagination of millions of Americans. Between the election and the inauguration, a lavish musical based on the heroic legend of King Arthur and his court, *Camelot,* opened a long run on Broadway. Soon the media and much of the public reveled in the image of the Kennedy White House as a modern-day Camelot. Jack and Jackie became America's royalty.

Kennedy awarded major government appointments to people with reputations as shrewd, skilled administrators. As secretary of defense, Kennedy selected Robert McNamara, a statistical expert and president of Ford Motor Company. Dean Rusk, the head of the Rockefeller Foundation, became secretary of state. As special assistant for national-security affairs, Kennedy tapped McGeorge Bundy, a forty-one-year-old Harvard dean. He picked C. Douglas Dillon, millionaire Wall Street investment banker and undersecretary of state in the outgoing Eisenhower administration, as secretary of the treasury. Kennedy's most controversial appointee was his younger brother Robert as attorney general. When asked about his thirty-five-year-old brother's lack of background and maturity for the position, the president joked, "I see nothing wrong with giving Robert some legal experience before he goes out to practice law."

Kennedy advisers, whether from academic, business, or government backgrounds, had much in common. Like the president, most were relatively young and prided themselves on being staunch pragmatists. In Schlesinger's words, "The New Frontier put a premium on quick, tough, laconic, decided people; it was easily exasperated by more meditative types." These men, Schlesinger added, harbored "a mistrust of evangelism" but had huge self-confidence in their abilities as scientific managers and experts. Kennedy described himself as an "idealist without illusions"; his appointees viewed themselves likewise.

The new president aroused strong emotions in his followers and called for active citizen involvement in public affairs, yet he had no desire to lead a populist crusade. "Most of the problems . . . that we now face are technical problems and are administrative problems," he declared. "They are very sophisticated judgments which do not lend themselves to the great sort of 'passionate movements' which have stirred this country so often in the past." Thus, while the president and his associates strove to rekindle and reshape national dedication, they also sought to maintain control of popular opinion. Foreign-policy matters, Kennedy claimed, "are so sophisticated and so technical that people who are not intimately involved week after week, month after month, reach judgments which are based on emotion rather than knowledge of the real alternatives."

Kennedy's men enjoyed their power. Schlesinger recalled "a sense of New Frontier autointoxication. The pleasures of power . . . were now being happily devoured." Although they accepted the Cold War consensus, Kennedy and his appointees expected to take a bolder stand than their predecessors in implementing traditional Cold War policies. These ambitious people, in the words of *New York Times* reporter David Halberstam, were "the best and the brightest." Yet as time would show, their expectations would far outstrip their accomplishments.

Even before taking office, the president-elect appointed special task forces to draw up reports on various national issues. Once in power, Kennedy sent Congress proposals on a number of domestic matters—transportation, housing, urban affairs, education, medical care, poverty, and eventually civil rights. He achieved some success: in 1961

Congress passed bills that supplemented unemployment benefits, increased Social Security payments, provided aid to depressed areas, and mandated a higher minimum wage. That year, at the urging of Assistant Secretary of Labor Esther Peterson, Kennedy's only female appointment to a policymaking position, the president catalyzed interest in women's issues by establishing the President's Commission on the Status of Women. The following year, the government legislated a manpower retraining act, a small public-works act, and a trade-expansion bill.

These accomplishments proved relatively limited, however. Major administration reforms—Medicare for the aged, federal aid to education, comprehensive tax reform, a mass transportation program, creation of a cabinet-level department of urban affairs, and a civil-rights bill—Congress either defeated or bottled up in committee during Kennedy's abbreviated administration. Overall, Kennedy's domestic legislative record failed to contrast markedly with Eisenhower's. There never was a domestic New Frontier.

Why did this ambitious administration yield such minimal results? The narrowness of Kennedy's electoral victory offers one clue: the New Frontier lacked a strong national mandate. Although the Democrats enjoyed a two-thirds majority in the Senate and nearly a 100-member majority in the House, a powerful, conservative coalition of southern Democrats and Republicans consistently blocked domestic reform measures. But much of the blame lay with Kennedy himself. Despite the fervor and idealism of his campaign rhetoric, he came to the White House believing that major domestic problems had already been solved and that the nation could eliminate its remaining inequities without restructuring society. Maintaining his focus on foreign policy, he proffered no persuasive vision of reform at home. As I. F. Stone noted, "Kennedy, when the tinsel was stripped away, was a conventional leader, no more than an enlightened conservative, cautious as an old man for all his youth, with a basic distrust of the people and an astringent view of the evangelical as a tool of leadership."

Had Kennedy shown a deeper commitment to domestic reform and a stronger willingness to pressure Congress, he undoubtedly would have improved his legislative record. But unlike his vice president and successor, Lyndon Johnson, Kennedy had never been part of the congressional inner circle. He lacked the know-how and skill to challenge Capitol Hill and tended to defer to his elders in Congress. Rarely pressing Congress on domestic matters, neither did he appeal directly to the people. He tried to avoid alienating legislators and losing their backing on foreign-policy matters, which he considered most important. Moreover, he feared putting presidential prestige on the line by fighting for bills that might fail. "There is no sense in raising hell," he maintained, "and then not being successful."

Although social reform lagged, the administration still hoped to promote economic growth and ease unemployment. Kennedy took office at a time when the recession showed signs of waning, but the economy nevertheless still plodded along, and unemployment in 1961 stood at more than 7 percent. Expenditures for welfare, relief, and social programs increased only modestly during his years in office. Indeed, it was government spending for defense and space that exerted the strongest impact on the national economy. In an ironic farewell address, General Eisenhower had warned Americans of a growing "military-industrial complex." Yet Kennedy, having won the presidency as a critic of Eisenhower's military preparedness, chose to emphasize defense spending over social welfare.

Kennedy during his campaign had promised to end the missile gap. But early in his administration, intelligence sources revealed that no such gap existed; in fact, the United States enjoyed a substantial lead over the Soviet Union in strategic weapons. Nevertheless, in 1961 the president persuaded Congress to expand the defense budget by 20 percent, procuring five times more ICBMs than Eisenhower had thought necessary and multiplying the number of medium-range missiles and nuclear submarines armed with Polaris missiles. Kennedy also allocated large sums to conventional (nonnuclear) weapons. In addition, to counter guerrilla warfare in developing nations, he augmented the Special Forces, a highly trained counterinsurgency unit popularly known as the Green Berets. In his first year in office, his defense budget rose by $7 billion to a total of $47.5 billion, by far the largest peacetime military budget in history. Similar expansions went to the space program as Kennedy, desperate to recoup national prestige, launched what became a $25 billion program to put a man on the moon before the end of the decade.

The massive military and space spending strengthened the United States' international status and stimulated domestic economic growth, which Kennedy believed would both shore up the nation's Cold War standing and eliminate inequalities at home. During the Eisenhower years, the Gross National Product (GNP) had risen at an annual average of 2.5 percent, while the Soviets had enjoyed a rate of 7 percent. Kennedy's campaign pledge to "get America moving again" targeted this disparity. To thus stimulate the GNP growth rate, Kennedy encouraged business productivity and efficiency. He began by sponsoring successful bills granting business tax credits for new investments in machinery or plant modernization and liberalizing business-depreciation allowances. Late in 1962, he proposed a major tax cut on both corporate profits and private incomes in hopes of accelerating spending. This proposal, influenced by Walter Heller, head of the Council of Economic Advisers, marked Kennedy's conversion to the Keynesian "new economics," a willingness to use fiscal policy, including deficit spending, to intensify economic expansion. Submitted to Congress in January 1963, Kennedy's tax cut would not pass until 1964.

But despite Kennedy's cautious, probusiness policies and his numerous administration appointees with business backgrounds, the president's relations with big business often soured. Many business leaders mistrusted Kennedy's liberal rhetoric and feared government interference in corporate policies. When stock-market prices dipped sharply in May 1962, business slapped the blame on the White House. The finger pointing angered Kennedy. "I understand every day why Roosevelt, who started out such a mild fellow, ended up so ferociously antibusiness," he griped. "It's hard as hell to be friendly with people who keep trying to cut your legs off."

Business hostility toward the president came to a head in April 1962. To keep inflation down while spurring economic growth, the Kennedy administration had pressured labor and management to maintain noninflationary wage-and-price increases. The steel industry appeared the key to wage-price stability. As Heller had written Kennedy in 1961, "Steel bulks so large in the manufacturing sector of the economy that it can upset the price applecart all by itself." The steel union's acceptance of a modest wage increase of 2.5 percent early in April 1962 elated Kennedy officials. Shortly after publication of the new contract, however, U.S. Steel announced plans to raise steel prices six dollars per ton, in clear violation of the wage-price guidelines. A furious Kennedy publicly denounced the price hike as "a wholly unjustifiable and irresponsible defiance of the public interest.'' Privately he fumed, ''My father once told me that all business-men were sons-of-bitches, but I never believed it till now.''

Kennedy used all the resources of his administration to thwart the steel industry's challenge. The Federal Trade Commission announced that it would look into price agreements among steel producers. Congress threatened antitrust action. Kennedy let it be known that he would review his probusiness tax policies. Ultimately the president forced the steel industry to rescind the price increases, but despite his unstinting efforts later to curry favor with business, including allowing two steel price increases the following year, Kennedy never won over the corporate community.

Even without enthusiastic business backing, the president, at least in part, lived up to his pledge to quicken economic growth. Massive defense and space spending, combined with business incentives and a modest rise in social spending, pushed the annual GNP growth rate to 5.6 percent. Unemployment dropped to a little over 5 per-cent, while inflation held to just over 1 percent per year. Yet many liberals demanded that he do more. Critics complained about ''the third Eisenhower administration.'' Influential *New Republic* columnist Richard Strout groused, ''We get awfully sick of this 'moderation.' All during the Eisenhower administration there was moderation . . . and now instead of Kennedy urgency there is more moderation.''

Liberals particularly lamented Kennedy's failure to redistribute income or to plug the large tax loopholes that benefited business and the rich. Corporate profits, they pointed out, had risen five times faster than personal income. And they protested the promotion of military spending at the expense of social welfare. Even Kennedy adviser John Kenneth Galbraith grumbled about the lack of spending on the public sector:

> I am not sure what the advantage is in having a few more dollars to spend if the air is too dirty to breathe, the water too polluted to drink, the commuters are losing out on the struggle to get in and out of the cities, the streets are filthy, and the schools so bad that the young, perhaps wisely, stay away, and hoodlums roll citizens for some of the dollars that they save in taxes.

Norman Mailer was disappointed too. He observed in the president and his close associates ''a total and depressing lack of attention for that vast heart of political matter which is utterly resistant to categorization, calculation, or statistic.'' Obsessed with such quantifiable measurements as the GNP, Kennedy seemed oblivious to the impassioned struggle for racial equality that raged around him. Only in 1963, his last year, would events force him to confront the most pressing domestic problems of his presidency: racism and poverty.

Containing Communism: The New Frontier Abroad

Economic growth and an agenda of unfinished social reforms became two legacies of the Kennedy years, but the administration left an even more profound inheritance: its activities in foreign affairs. Cautious to a fault with domestic matters, Kennedy took the opposite approach to foreign policy. Like his postwar predecessors, Truman and Eisenhower, Kennedy intended to contain communist expansion by force if necessary. All three leaders had learned what they considered a historic lesson from the events leading up to World War II: appeasement in response to aggression could backfire. The failure of British and French negotiations with Hitler at Munich in 1938 had taught them that a superpower like the United States could maintain credibility only through its willingness to use force. Kennedy also believed that the Cold War had reached a crisis, with the very survival of the free world at stake. "Before my term has ended," he warned on taking office, "we shall have to test anew whether a nation organized and governed such as ours can endure. The outcome is by no means certain."

Seeking personal greatness but lacking a bold vision of domestic reform, Kennedy saw the Soviet challenge as his opportunity for distinction. In *Profiles in Courage,* he had written, "Great crises produce great men, and great deeds of courage." Indeed, Kennedy perceived foreign policy in personal terms. Standing up to the Soviets would provoke a welcome test of wills. "We must not tempt them with weakness," he had pronounced in his inaugural.

Unlike Eisenhower, who had relied on the threat of massive nuclear retaliation as a deterrent to aggression, Kennedy and his advisers stressed the need for a flexible military establishment capable of fighting on any level, from guerrilla warfare to all-out nuclear combat. Such versatility, they assumed, would especially control revolutions in developing countries, as well as lessen the likelihood of nuclear war. Yet in practice the scheme easily led to military intervention. America's deepening involvement in Vietnam would become the worst legacy of Kennedy's new military strategy.

But it was Cuba that provided the first public test of JFK's approach to revolutionary regimes in underdeveloped regions. In 1959 guerrilla leader Fidel Castro had toppled the notoriously ruthless and corrupt Cuban dictator Fulgencio Batista. Initially many Americans sympathized with the bearded, charismatic young Castro, who promised the long-oppressed Cuban people social justice and land redistribution. However, when the new Cuban leader began nationalizing land holdings of American-owned companies, an alarmed Eisenhower retaliated by curtailing the amount of Cuban sugar that the United States would import. Infuriated, Castro stepped up nationalization and turned to America's enemy, the Soviet Union, for aid. Although the Cuban leader's reforms won strong support from working-class Cubans, numerous upper- and middle-class citizens, who had profited under Batista, fled the island and took refuge in the United States, many of them settling in Florida.

Determined now to drive Castro from power, the Eisenhower administration ended all American imports of Cuban sugar and pressured the Organization of American States, an alliance that the United States had forged with the Latin American nations in 1947, to expel Cuba. Yet rather than toppling Castro, these heavy-handed measures stirred Cuban nationalism and propelled the Cuban leader closer to Moscow. In 1960 the Soviets bought up the Cuban sugar crop at a price above world market levels. A frustrated Eisenhower ordered the CIA to begin secretly training an invasion force of Cuban exiles in Guatemala.

By the time Kennedy took office in January 1961, American policymakers had grown obsessed with Cuba. JFK shared their concern, claiming that Castro represented "a clear and present danger to the authentic and autonomous revolution of the Americas." The picture the CIA painted—the disgruntled Cuban people would welcome an invasion force of exiles and would join them in an uprising against Castro—encouraged the new president. For Kennedy, this news both presented an opportunity to reassert

The Bay of Pigs. Cuban leader Fidel Castro examines an American plane shot down on the beach of Playa Giron, the site of the abortive U.S.-sponsored invasion.

American influence in Cuba and offered a chance to test the use of limited force to counter a revolutionary regime. He gave the CIA permission to invade.

On April 17, 1961, some fourteen hundred American-trained and -supplied Cuban exiles landed on the southern coast of Cuba at the Bay of Pigs. But disaster awaited them: the CIA had drastically overestimated Cuban discontent, and no popular uprising took place. Within three days, Castro's army killed or captured all the invaders.

At first the Kennedy administration denied involvement in the invasion. As evidence of U.S. complicity mounted, however, the president reluctantly admitted responsibility. The debacle, in violation of international law and American principles, undermined the new administration's integrity while tightening Castro's control and reinforcing his dependence on the Soviets. Meanwhile, anti-American feeling intensified throughout Latin America.

Despite this humiliation, Kennedy and his advisers remained cocky. The president expressed regret only for the mission's failure, not for the invasion itself. Rather than question the ethics of counterinsurgency, Kennedy and his chief advisers continued to assert the United States' right to intervene when and where it judged necessary. "Let the record show that our restraint is not inexhaustible," Kennedy declared soon after the Bay of Pigs. Rephrasing the Truman Doctrine, JFK vowed that "if the nations of this Hemisphere should fail to meet their commitments against outside Communist penetration—then I want it clearly understood that this Government will not hesitate in meeting its primary obligations which are to the security of our Nation!"

The president also steeled himself to get tough. Through his brother Robert, he instructed the CIA to let ''no time, money, effort—or manpower—be spared'' in efforts to destroy Castro. His directive led to a variety of covert actions in Cuba. On at least eight occasions, CIA operatives attempted to assassinate the Cuban president, even resorting to such James Bondian devices as a poisoned fountain pen and exploding seashells.

Elsewhere in Latin America, the Kennedy administration relied on the Alliance for Progress to prevent the spread of Cuban-type revolutions. A foreign-aid program launched in March 1961, the alliance promised ''a vast cooperative effort . . . to satisfy the basic needs of the American peoples for homes, work and land, health and schools.'' The United States promised $20 billion over ten years to aid economic development in the region. Yet the alliance fell short of its goals to end illiteracy, eliminate malaria, and introduce basic land and tax reforms. Most of the aid took the form of loans that had to be repaid with interest, and these funds had to be spent in the United States. As a result, Latin America grew more debt ridden and dependent on Yankee dollars than ever. Reluctant Latin American leaders, encouraged by American business interests, undermined plans for substantive economic and social reforms. Poverty and instability continued to plague the region, and in 1962–1963 alone, six military coups took place.

The Peace Corps, another Kennedy foreign-policy innovation, also aimed to win friends, cultivate dependence on American goods and technology, and assist developing nations. Established by executive order in March 1961, the program quickly attracted thousands of idealistic young volunteers. Indeed, more of the Harvard class of 1962 applied to join the Corps than sought jobs with Fortune 500 companies. One Peace Corps alumnus recalled that his generation had ''been stirred by the Kennedy inaugural speech—the idea of giving, not getting. And we had the desire to do something for people somewhere in the world.'' By the end of the sixties, more than ten thousand volunteers had journeyed abroad to teach; to build houses, hospitals, schools, and roads; and to aid in irrigation and sanitation projects. Although it never received priority funding, the Peace Corps made positive contributions, and the sacrifices and dedication of American volunteers became legendary.

In contrast to the objectives of the Alliance for Progress and the Peace Corps, most of Kennedy's foreign policy struck a belligerent note. Twice during his first twenty months in office, JFK confronted Soviet leader Khrushchev, and on both occasions he plunged the world into crises that threatened nuclear holocaust. The initial incident centered on the fate of Berlin, the city partitioned between East and West at the end of World War II and located within Soviet-controlled East Germany. In June 1961, Kennedy traveled to Vienna for his first summit conference with Khrushchev. There the Soviet leader bluntly told the American president that he intended to sign a separate peace treaty with East Germany by December unless the United States and the Soviet Union could agree on a general German treaty. The Soviets sought to halt the embarrassing flow of East German refugees seeking freedom in the West through the divided city.

Khrushchev's proposed treaty would have placed access routes from West Germany to Berlin in the hands of the East Germans and thereby threaten Western rights in that city. Kennedy interpreted the Soviet premier's announcement as a personal attack. ''If Khrushchev wants to rub my nose in the dirt,'' he told a reporter, ''it's all over.'' Returning abruptly from Vienna, the president told the nation, ''The immediate threat to free men is in West Berlin. But that isolated outpost is not an isolated problem.

The threat is worldwide.'' Kennedy called up reserve units of the army and rushed a $3.2 billion supplemental military appropriation through Congress (his third such move in his first six months in office). He also persuaded Congress to allocate $207 million for an expanded civil-defense program and on national television urged the public to build private bomb shelters. Late that summer, *Life* featured a cover photo of a man digging a shelter and an article claiming that ''97 out of 100 people can be saved.'' The administration and the media thus tried to brace the public against nuclear war while implying that they could survive it.

In August 1961, tensions heightened again. The Soviets and East Germans built a concrete-block wall dividing East and West Berlin to stop the exodus of East Germans. Later that month, the Soviets resumed atmospheric nuclear testing. The United States in turn initiated a series of underground blasts that September and atmospheric explosions the following March. But with the infamous barricade in place, the Soviets no longer felt the need for a separate treaty with East Germany, and the crisis eased. Berlin remained a pawn in Cold War politics, and the wall literally and symbolically cemented the division between East and West.

The second clash between Kennedy and Khrushchev once more centered on Cuba. Following the Bay of Pigs disaster, Castro's anti-American sentiment naturally intensified. He became more overtly Marxist and turned increasingly to the Soviets for arms and trade. During the summer and fall of 1962, Moscow began to supply Cuba with medium-range nuclear missiles, ostensibly for defense against future U.S. threats. In mid-October, American reconnaissance planes took aerial photos that revealed several missile sites. The strategic value of these Soviet missiles was limited, however. Presidential adviser Ted Sorensen later noted, ''Those Cuban missiles alone . . . did not substantially alter the strategic balance in fact.'' But, Sorensen added, the missiles altered that balance ''in appearance.''

To revive American prestige, Kennedy demanded that the missiles be removed, then secretly summoned an executive committee to ponder U.S. options. Smarting from the Bay of Pigs humiliation and the Berlin standoff, the New Frontier leaders wanted victory, not compromise, and they never considered negotiation. The committee overwhelmingly favored offensive action: an air strike to wipe out the missiles or an invasion to seize them. (In 1992, after the Cold War had ended, Russian officials would reveal that the Soviets had battlefield nuclear weapons in Cuba and that Soviet field commanders had authority to use them if the United States bombed or invaded. Had the United States launched an attack, nuclear war almost certainly would have erupted. The two superpowers came far closer to nuclear holocaust than anyone knew at the time.) Fortunately, Robert McNamara proposed a milder course of action: a naval quarantine to prevent future arms shipments to Cuba, combined with a demand that existing missiles be removed. Kennedy accepted this advice.

In a TV address on October 22, the president told a startled and dismayed world that Soviet actions constituted an ''unjustified change in the status quo which cannot be accepted by this country, if our courage and our commitments are ever to be trusted again either by friend or foe.'' Kennedy gave Khrushchev an ultimatum to remove the missiles and warned that the United States would not ''shrink'' from the risk of ''worldwide nuclear war.''

The world reeled at the terrifying prospect of all-out nuclear war. Khrushchev condemned American actions as ''outright banditry'' and charged Kennedy with forcing the globe "to the abyss." Some city-dwelling Americans drove to the countryside, hoping to avoid obliteration; most hovered around their radios and TVs and awaited news of their fate. Bob Dylan wrote "A Hard Rain's Gonna Fall," evoking the end of human life. "We're eyeball to eyeball," pronounced Secretary of State Rusk.

The next few days proved the most frightening since the Cold War began, as the world teetered on the brink of destruction. At the UN, a member of the Soviet delegation told an American associate, "This will be our last conversation. New York will be blown up tomorrow by Soviet nuclear weapons." But to overwhelming global relief, the Soviets backed down. In a long, emotional letter to Kennedy on October 26, Khrushchev wrote, "Only lunatics or suicides, who themselves want to perish and to destroy the whole world," would trigger a nuclear war. The Soviet leader agreed to remove the missiles if the United States lifted the blockade and pledged not to invade Cuba. Kennedy accepted these conditions, and the crisis passed.

JFK, his advisers, and most New Frontier partisans hailed the Cuban missile crisis as the administration's finest hour. Walt Rostow called it "the Gettysburg" of the Cold War, while Arthur Schlesinger, Jr., described the president's technique as "a combination of toughness and restraint, of will, nerve, and wisdom, so brilliantly controlled, so matchlessly calibrated, that it dazzled the world." Yet one has to ask what would have happened if Khrushchev had not capitulated. Was it worth risking nuclear war to remove missiles of admittedly limited threat? In the midst of the crisis, Adlai Stevenson, whom Kennedy had appointed ambassador to the United Nations, had suggested that the president swap U.S. missiles in Turkey for the Soviet missiles in Cuba, a settlement that would have been acceptable to the Soviets. But Kennedy, though he had earlier ordered the removal of the obsolete Turkish missiles, refused to bargain with the Kremlin. Instead he brought the world to the edge of nuclear war for the sake of American prestige, political "face," and personal grandeur. Were it not for Nikita Khrushchev's restraint and willingness to accept public humiliation, the Cuban missile crisis could well have ended in utter catastrophe. Kennedy himself later estimated that there had been between a third and a half probability of thermonuclear war. His estimate was probably low.

Unquestionably, the crisis chastened President Kennedy and Premier Khrushchev, who both soon set about working to improve Soviet-American relations. In June 1963, a hot line was installed in the White House and the Kremlin to allow instant communication between the two capitals. In a speech at American University in Washington, D.C., that same month, Kennedy called for a reexamination of Cold War attitudes: "We must deal with the world as it is, and not as it might have been had the history of the last eighteen years been different. . . . If we cannot now end our differences, at least we can help make the world safe for diversity." The first fruits of these tentative moves toward détente came later that summer when the United States and the Soviet Union signed a limited nuclear-test-ban treaty outlawing atmospheric and underwater testing.

Despite these steps toward peace, however, Kennedy never really modified his Cold War perceptions. The test-ban treaty in no way diminished the administration's commitment to a massive arms build-up. Nor did it end the president's Cold War rhetoric or his escalation of America's military presence in Vietnam. In a speech that he planned to deliver in Dallas on November 22, 1963, Kennedy once again made clear his uncompromising worldview: "We in this country, in this generation, are, by destiny rather than choice, the watchmen on the walls of freedom."

November 22, 1963

In November 1963, Kennedy and Vice President Lyndon Johnson made a campaign swing through Texas in an effort to ensure that state's vote in the presidential election a year hence. On November 22, the smiling president, his wife by his side, waved from an open limousine as their motorcade made its way past the cheering crowds lining the streets of Dallas. Suddenly shots rang out. Kennedy slumped forward. Blood spurted from his head and throat. Within an hour, doctors at Parkland Memorial Hospital pronounced the president dead. The thousand days of Camelot were over, John Fitzgerald Kennedy's promise snuffed out.

Beeps from the circling Soviet *Sputnik* in the fall of 1957 had plunged Americans into a search for national purpose. Six years later, in the fall of 1963, the tragic shooting in Dallas once again brought that question of purpose to public attention. Perhaps no other moment in American history has had such a profound impact as the assassination of President Kennedy. Even the murder of Abraham Lincoln, the attack on Pearl Harbor, and the bomb dropped on Hiroshima never evoked such an immediate and intense public reaction as did the killing of JFK. To this day, people recall precisely where they were and what they were doing when they first heard the news. Television transformed the assassination into an intense, shared national experience. For four days, normal life seemed suspended as millions followed events on their sets without commercial interruption. Grim images haunted them—the president's hunched body, Jacqueline's bloodstained clothes and grief-stricken face, their small son saluting his father's casket, the somber funeral procession. Rolling drums and tolling bells interspersed with film clips of the living president and his family, so youthful, glamorous, and vibrant.

Almost instantaneously, Kennedy passed from history to legend. The nation—and the world—had never before suffered such an outpouring of grief. On CBS-TV, veteran anchorman Walter Cronkite wept as he announced the news. In far-off Guinea, President Sekou Touré pronounced, "I have lost my only true friend in the outside world." In France the tricolor flew at half-staff above the Elysée Palace; a bicycle race in Brussels slowed to a walk; in London the bells of Westminster Cathedral tolled in sorrow. The traditional Harvard-Yale football game was postponed. Like millions of others, Martin Luther King, Jr., sat in stunned silence when he heard of Kennedy's killing. Turning to his wife, Coretta, he prophetically murmured: "This is what is going to happen to me. This is such a sick society."

Throughout the United States, public buildings, schools, airports, streets, even shopping malls were named or renamed after the slain president. Portraits, plates, and other Kennedy memorabilia sold out immediately and became instant treasured family possessions. Whereas in 1960 one out of every two voters had chosen Kennedy, after his murder, two out of three claimed that they had.

Within hours after Kennedy's death, Dallas police announced the arrest of accused assassin Lee Harvey Oswald, a former marine who had lived for a short time in the

A Time to Weep. A sailor cries at John F. Kennedy's funeral.

Soviet Union. Two days later, before a stunned national TV audience, Jack Ruby, a nightclub owner and small-time gangster, fatally shot Oswald as Dallas police transferred him to a new jail. Oswald's peculiar death raised numerous questions. Had he acted as the lone assassin, or was he innocent, as he had steadfastly proclaimed? Was Ruby a hit man hired to kill Oswald to keep him quiet?

Rumors that Kennedy's death was part of a larger conspiracy ran rampant. Hoping to squelch these, the new president Johnson authorized a top-level committee headed by Chief Justice Earl Warren to make an official inquiry. Following a sloppily conducted ten-month investigation, the Warren Commission pronounced Oswald the lone assassin. Despite the Johnson administration's and the mass media's claim that the Warren Commission report had closed the books on the case, doubts and rumors would persist. Critics of the commission found significant flaws in the hastily researched and carelessly documented report. Soon best-selling books such as Mark Lane's *Rush to Judgment* (1965) and Edward Jay Epstein's *Inquest* (1966) revealed substantial evidence that cast doubt on the single-killer hypothesis.

Over the years, conspiratorial theories have continued to crop up. Some attribute Kennedy's death to Castro, others to the Kremlin, or to southern segregationists, or to the Mafia. The most bizarre conspiratorial theories have linked the assassination to the CIA, the FBI, and even to JFK's successor, Lyndon Johnson. In 1979 a congressional investigation concluded, on the basis of new evidence, that Kennedy's killing had "probably" resulted from a plot. In 1991 the controversial Oliver Stone movie *JFK* embraced a conspiracy thesis and convinced millions of Americans that the full truth about the assassination was not yet known. Perhaps it never will be.

• • •

Kennedy's presidency lasted two years and ten months. His partisans argue that had he lived, he would have been a great leader. Enthusiastic followers extol even his short tenure in office. Richard Goodwin, a Kennedy aide and speechwriter, for example, claimed that Kennedy "took a country that was on its back, fat and purposeless, lifted it up, gave it momentum, direction, purpose and a sense of its own strength and possibility."

Critics, on the other hand, fault Kennedy's militancy abroad and excessive cautiousness at home. He stood up to the Soviets, but at the risk of nuclear annihilation. He proposed peaceful revolution in Latin America, yet failed to fund it adequately. He signed a test-ban treaty with the Soviets, but presided over the most massive arms build-up in history. He created the Peace Corps to alleviate world suffering, yet carried on a vicious vendetta against Cuba and Fidel Castro.

Above all, John F. Kennedy was a man of his times. In foreign affairs he inherited and acted on a set of Cold War assumptions. In domestic matters, his narrow electoral victory could scarcely be interpreted as a public demand for bold new reforms. Nor did Kennedy think such reforms necessary. For most of his tenure, his courageous talk of charting a New Frontier was more rhetoric than reality.

Yet like that other U.S. president felled by an assassin's bullet just short of a century earlier, John F. Kennedy exhibited a capacity to change under the pressures of external events and inner experience. He assumed office in 1961 a conventional politician inclined toward conservatism. By 1963 he had grown more liberal. Recoiling from the frightful view at the brink of the Cuban missile crisis, Kennedy took the first tentative steps toward détente with the Soviets. That year he also belatedly recognized the urgency of the civil-rights struggle, committed his administration to racial equality, and began planning a national war on poverty.

The same adoring nation and world that had revered Kennedy for his charisma and promise in life mourned him deeply in death. Wrote British journalist Godfrey Hodgson, "This was the death of a democratic prince." To *New York Times* columnist James Reston, "What was killed [in Dallas] was not only the president but the promise. . . . The death of youth and the hope of youth, of the beauty and grace and the touch of magic. . . . He never reached his meridian: we saw him only as a rising sun."

Despite the dearth of concrete accomplishments, Kennedy had stirred a nation. His altruistic rhetoric, his appeals to idealism, his enunciation of personal and national destiny and mission had fired the imaginations and energies of millions, especially the young. He stimulated some to join the Peace Corps, some to march on Washington, some to work in urban slums. By the time of his death, the forces of social criticism and activism alike were rising.

Selected Bibliography

Norman Mailer's audacious preelection article on Kennedy, "Superman Comes to the Supermarket" is republished in Harold Hayes, ed., *Smiling Through the Apocalypse: Esquire's History of the Sixties* (1987). Elizabeth Huckaby, *Crisis at Central High: Little Rock, 1957–1958* (1980), is a personal account by one of the first black students at that school. Also useful is

Daisy Bates, *The Long Shadow of Little Rock* (1962). Little Rock is put in the larger perspective of fifties politics in Robert F. Burk, *The Eisenhower Administration and Black Civil Rights* (1984).

James R. Killian, Jr., *Sputnik, Scientists, and Eisenhower* (1976), is a memoir treating the effects of *Sputnik* on the American scientific community. Willy Ley, *Rockets, Missiles, and Men in Space* (1968), chronicles the impact of *Sputnik* on the American space program. The post-*Sputnik* debate over education is well documented in Barbara B. Clowse, *Brainpower for the Cold War: The Sputnik Crisis and the National Defense Education Act of 1958* (1981). Admiral Hyman Rickover's *Education and Freedom* (1959) reveals the contemporary sense of Cold War urgency to bolster education. No book adequately analyzes the theme of national reassessment from the *Sputnik* crisis through the 1960 election, but a good starting point is Eric Larrabee's contemporaneous study, *The Self-Conscious Society* (1960). John Kenneth Galbraith's influential plea for more public spending is *The Affluent Society* (1958). The U-2 crisis and its repercussions is the subject of Michael Beschloss, *MAYDAY* (1986).

Theodore H. White, *The Making of the President, 1960* (1961), is a lively and painstaking account of the Kennedy-Nixon contest. See also Angus Campbell et al., *American National Election Study, 1960* (1974), and Lucy S. Davidowicz and Leon J. Goldstein, *Politics in a Pluralist Democracy: Studies of Voting in the 1960 Election* (1963). Richard Nixon's account of the election is contained in his *Six Crises* (rev. ed. 1978).

Herbert S. Parmet's biography *Jack* (1980) on the prepresidential years and *JFK* (1982) on the presidency are thorough, balanced, and well documented, if a bit pedestrian. Thomas Reeves, *A Question of Character: The Life of John F. Kennedy in Image and Reality* (1991), is an excellent reexamination of the man and the myth. Four other recent reassessments are Thomas Brown, *JFK: History of an Image* (1988); David Burner, *John F. Kennedy and a New Generation* (1988); James Giglio, *The Presidency of John F. Kennedy* (1991); and Richard Reeves, *President Kennedy: Profile of Power* (1993). Laudatory biographies by Kennedy insiders include Arthur

Schlesinger, Jr., *A Thousand Days* (1965); Theodore Sorenson, *Kennedy* (1965); Pierre Salinger, *With Kennedy* (1966); and Kenneth O'Connell and David Powers, *Johnny We Hardly Knew Ye* (1972). These books should be contrasted with the following more critical studies: Garry Wills, *The Kennedy Imprisonment* (1983); Henry Fairlie, *The Kennedy Promise* (1973); and Bruce Miroff, *Pragmatic Illusions: The Presidential Politics of JFK* (1976). A good general history of the Kennedy and Johnson administrations is Jim F. Heath, *Decade of Disillusionment* (1975); Heath is also the author of *John F. Kennedy and the Business Community* (1969).

Roger Hilsman's *To Move a Nation* (1967) is a laudatory reminiscence centered on Kennedy foreign policy, as is Walt W. Rostow's *View from the Seventh Floor* (1964). In contrast, Louise FitzSimons, *The Kennedy Doctrine* (1972), and Richard J. Walton, *Cold War and Counterrevolution Doctrine* (1972), depict Kennedy as an unreconstructed Cold Warrior. On the Bay of Pigs, see Peter Wyden, *Bay of Pigs* (1980). Jack M. Shick, *The Berlin Crisis, 1958–62* (1971), places the Kennedy-Khrushchev confrontation over Berlin into larger historical context. Robert F. Kennedy's *Thirteen Days* (1969) presents the president's version of the Cuban missile crisis. More critical of Kennedy's handling of this are David Detzer, *The Brink* (1979), and Graham T. Allison, *Essence of Decision: Explaining the Cuban Crisis* (1971).

JFK's assassination is the subject of William R. Manchester's detailed *The Death of a President* (1967). Bradley S. Greenburg and Edwin B. Parter, *The Kennedy Assassination and the American Public* (1965), and P. Scott et al., *Dallas and Beyond* (1976), place that tragedy in a larger social context. The basic findings of the Warren Commission are set out in *A Concise Compendium of the Warren Commission Report* (1964). For a look at various conspiracy theories, consult Henry Hurt, *Reasonable Doubt* (1985); Michael L. Kurtz, *Crime of the Century* (1982); Anthony Summers, *Conspiracy* (1980); Edward Jay Epstein, *Legend: The Secret World of Lee Harvey Oswald* (1978) and *Inquest* (1966); and Mark Lane, *Rush to Judgment* (1965).

CHAPTER

THE CIVIL-RIGHTS
REVOLUTION

It was February 1, 1960. Four freshmen from North Carolina Agriculture and Technical College in Greensboro— Ezell Blair, Jr., Franklin McCain, Joseph McNeil, and David Richmond—sat down at the lunch counter at the local Woolworth store and ordered coffee and doughnuts. The waitress rebuffed them with the flat statement, "We do not serve Negroes." Yet the four young men remained seated until the store closed. The next day they returned, this time with twenty-three classmates. By the end of the week, hundreds of African-American students, including the A&T football team, had joined the protest. The Greensboro demonstrations attracted national attention, and soon black students and sympathetic whites launched similar sit-ins throughout the segregated South. The pace of already changing race relations accelerated.

These four freshmen were part of a generation of young blacks who had come of age in the years after the *Brown* decision. Tired of waiting for their rights, they held dormitory bull sessions in which they discussed the indignities that blacks suffered. "We challenged each other, really," one of them recalled. "We used to question, 'Why is it that you have to sit in the balcony? Why do you have to ride in the back of the bus?'" As Blair remembered, Montgomery had been "like a catalyst. It started a whole lot of things rolling." Martin Luther King, Jr., had spoken in Greensboro in 1958, and young Blair recollected King's sermon as "so strong that I could feel my heart palpitating. It brought tears to my eyes." Gaining confidence from one another, the four took action. McCain, elated by the sit-in, later marveled, "I felt as though I had gained my manhood."

The Greensboro protesters helped to spark a revolution in civil rights that in a few years would destroy Jim Crow, the southern system of segregating and disfranchising African-Americans. As thousands of blacks joined the freedom struggle, they transformed themselves from objects of white liberals' patronizing concern into the driving force behind the liberation movement. Blacks knew that positive change depended on their taking action. "That's what we gonna work forward to," claimed African-American activist Maggie Mae Horton, "tryin to get peoples to quit waitin for God to come do somethin for me. . . . Nobody can come here and get my rights for me. I got to get it myself." At grave risk, blacks forced civil-rights reform onto the political agenda of the white liberal establishment.

Victory would not come easily. Launched with idealism and optimism, the nonviolent civil-rights movement spread. Organizations such as the Southern Christian Leadership Conference (SCLC), the Congress of Racial Equality (CORE), and the Student Nonviolent Coordinating Committee (SNCC) staged sit-ins, freedom rides, marches, and mass demonstrations. At every turn, the movement met with brutal, racist resistance. Southern white supremacists burned churches, bombed buildings, and beat, shot, and even murdered civil-rights workers. This well-publicized extremism only steeled the resolve of the civil-rights crusaders. Spurring resistance among blacks outside the organized movement, the brutality provoked a national groundswell in favor of civil-rights legislation.

The beleaguered Kennedy and Johnson administrations and Congress ultimately supported legal changes in race relations, and the alliance between blacks and white liberals carried the day. The nation finally acknowledged the evil of racism, and with the Civil Rights Act of 1964 and the Voting Rights Act of 1965, the federal government eliminated much of the legal basis of public discrimination.

Yet despite the new laws, prejudice, poverty, and ghetto slums endured; real economic and social equality for nonwhites remained elusive. Stubborn barriers to racial justice compelled African-Americans to question the commitment of white liberals and to challenge America's liberal creed. Many younger blacks in particular lost faith in American society and ultimately took a militant stand. Rejecting the white liberal establishment, they turned to black separatism, racial pride, and sometimes revolutionary violence. Thus, just as the black and white liberal coalition registered its greatest victories, their alliance began to disintegrate.

"More Than a Hamburger": The Sit-Ins

The courage of the Greensboro four struck a chord in the South. For years, anger and determination had simmered within the southern black community, especially among its college students. In black colleges throughout the South, the Greensboro sit-ins awakened a generation of young activists.

John Lewis epitomized the new mood. Born in 1940 in segregated rural Alabama, he was fourteen when the Supreme Court issued its decision on school desegregation. "I remember it very well," stated Lewis. "I thought that the next year I would go to a real high school, and not the kind of training school that blacks were sent to. I thought

I wouldn't have to be bused forty miles each day, past white schools, to maintain a system of segregation. I thought we would have new buses.'' Like most of his peers, John Lewis had his hopes dashed, and in 1957 he graduated from high school without ever having attended a desegregated school. That year, deeply moved by the Montgomery bus boycott and the emergence of independent black nations in Africa, Lewis joined the Nashville chapter of the NAACP as well as the Nashville Christian Leadership Council, the local SCLC branch.

In 1958 Lewis met James M. Lawson, a gentle, bright, Christian pacifist who had spent three years as a missionary in India, where he had familiarized himself with the ideas of Mohandas Gandhi. Like Gandhi, Lawson thought organized nonviolence the most important force for change in the twentieth century. He also surmised that neo-Gandhian tactics fit the needs of black protest in the South, where whites held an overwhelming preponderance of power. At the time, Lawson served as southern field secretary for the Fellowship of Reconciliation, a small but influential pacifist organization. Traveling throughout the South, he held nonviolence workshops for blacks.

In the fall of 1958, Lawson organized the first of these workshops in Nashville and recruited John Lewis, Diane Nash, and a number of other local black students. In weekly sessions, Lawson taught the philosophy and discipline of nonviolence, tracing the principle from the early Christians to the present. Participants watched documentary films of Gandhi's resistance movement and discussed its relevance as a tactic for change in the South. They learned that Gandhi had been deeply affected by Henry David Thoreau's essay ''On Civil Disobedience,'' and they too studied the transcendentalist's powerful tract. They learned the lessons of the Montgomery bus boycott and read the writings of Martin Luther King, Jr. They also role-played the tactic of nonviolence. Lawson's visionary Christian ideals inspired the younger students. ''In his own right,'' claimed Lewis, ''he was a great moral force. We regarded him as our real teacher in nonviolence.''

In 1959 Lewis and other workshop participants established the Nashville Student Movement and the smaller, coordinating Central Committee. Comprising about twenty-five young men and women, including Lewis and later civil-rights leaders Marion Barry, James Bevel, and Diane Nash, the Central Committee in November 1959 decided to launch a campaign aimed at desegregating downtown Nashville's stores and restaurants. Late that month, the students conducted ''test sit-ins'' to gauge whites' reactions when blacks challenged Jim Crow. Students sat in at department-store restaurants and lunch counters; when refused service, they tried to engage the management in dialogue. To avoid attracting national attention, the local media paid scant attention to these incidents.

In late January 1960, the Central Committee organized an all-out assault against Nashville's segregation. More than five hundred students attended the planning meeting, but before the campaign could begin, the Greensboro sit-ins had gotten under way. Nashville students soon followed suit, commencing sit-ins on February 13. Leaders passed out to students a list of ''Rules of the Sit-Ins,'' which included ''Sit up straight. Don't talk back. Don't laugh. Don't strike back. Remember the teachings of Jesus, Gandhi, Thoreau, and Martin Luther King, Jr.'' Of all the sit-ins in the South that year, the Nashville protest proved the largest, best disciplined, and most influential.

The city's white establishment, confronted by the well-dressed, courteous black students' persistent requests for service at segregated facilities, at first reacted with

Jail Not Bail. SNCC leader John Lewis is arrested for his participation in a civil-rights demonstration in Nashville. Numerous black activists, like Lewis, dramatized their cause by choosing to serve time in jail rather than pay bail.

bewilderment. Many businesses simply closed. But police soon allowed white hecklers to pour ketchup over the protesters' heads, spit on them, hit them, and even grind out lighted cigarettes on their backs. The police seized only the blacks. John Lewis recalled:

> It was the first time in my life I had ever been arrested. This cop came up and said, "You're under arrest," and hundreds, maybe thousands, of angry whites who were standing on the streets applauded when they took us away. I had a certain amount of fear, because growing up in rural Alabama I had instilled in me that you don't get in trouble with the law. . . . Yet, in a strange way, I found it was also a good feeling. I felt at the time it was like a crusade. All of us then believed that we were in a holy war.

Convicted of disorderly conduct, Lewis, Nash, and fourteen others followed the principles of Thoreau and Gandhi: they chose jail rather than pay the fifty-dollar fine. By filling the prisons, they hoped to tax the resources of the state and highlight the system's injustice. Jail thus became transformed from a place of shame to one of political honor.

Arrests and harassment only bolstered the demonstrators' resolve. The sit-ins persisted, and hundreds of new recruits joined the movement. In addition to large-scale sit-ins, protesters organized boycotts of department stores with segregated lunch counters, conducted prayer vigils at city hall, and tried to attend white churches on Sunday mornings. These pressures, and the publicity that they engendered, soon bore fruit. On April 20, 1960, Nashville's mayor endorsed an end to segregation.

The next day, Martin Luther King, Jr., joined the celebration there. Thousands of blacks and whites crowded into the gymnasium at all-black Fisk University to listen to the famed civil-rights leader. Praising the demonstrations in Nashville as "the best organized and the most disciplined in the Southland," King added, "I came to Nashville not to bring inspiration but to gain inspiration from the great movement that has taken place in this community." "Segregation," he promised the jubilant crowd, "is on its deathbed now, and the only uncertain thing about it is the day it will be buried."

By the time of the Nashville victory, the sit-in movement had swept the South. Close to seventy thousand people participated in more than two hundred cities. As in Nashville, impatient young blacks and sympathetic whites elsewhere expanded the strategies of direct action. They held "kneel-ins" in churches, "swim-ins" in pools, "sleep-ins" in hotel and motel lobbies, "read-ins" in libraries, and "watch-ins" at movie theaters. This combination of moral and economic pressure yielded results. In 1960 alone, demonstrators desegregated the lunch counters and other public facilities not only of Greensboro and Nashville but of more than two hundred other cities.

The sit-in movement had ignited what John Lewis called a crusade "to redeem the soul of America." Gaining the right to sit at a lunch counter was a significant victory. Demonstrators at Chapel Hill carried signs that told the larger story: "We do not picket just because we want to eat. We can eat at home or walking down the street. We do picket to protest the lack of dignity and respect shown us as human beings." The sit-ins also earned blacks self-respect and revealed the cracks in the South's system of white supremacy. Every small success convinced the demonstrators that real equality lay within their grasp.

But the protesters paid a high price. More than thirty-six hundred of them ended up in jail. As in Nashville, whites often resorted to violence. In Houston, Texas, masked whites seized a black demonstrator, beat him with chains, carved "KKK" on his chest, and hung him by his knees from a tree. In Biloxi, Mississippi, a white mob attacked blacks with guns and clubs, seriously wounding ten people. Law-enforcement officials, too, often assaulted protesters with billy clubs, tear gas, and dogs. In Orangeburg, South Carolina, police in subfreezing weather turned high-pressure fire hoses on demonstrators and then arrested more than 500 African-Americans, locking some 350 into a small, unheated chicken coop.

Yet the more savagely the white South confronted the demonstrators, the more deeply the nonviolent blacks moved the rest of the nation. As the sit-in movement gathered momentum and attracted more and more media attention, the protesters touched the national conscience. In northern cities, white and black students began picketing chain stores such as Woolworth and Kresge that practiced segregation in the South.

The mass-supported southern sit-ins and northern pickets signified as well a new era: the end of the complacent fifties. Many young people watched with fascination as their peers made history. Some youths abandoned school or career to join the burgeoning civil-rights movement. In Harlem, Bob Moses, a twenty-five-year-old black schoolteacher with a master's in philosophy from Harvard, felt so moved by the sit-ins that he quit his job to join the struggle. The protesting students, he recalled, ''had a certain look on their faces, sort of sullen, angry, determined. Before, the Negro in the South had always looked on the defensive, cringing. This time they were taking the initiative. They were kids my age, and I knew this had something to do with my life.'' Moses became one of the most influential civil-rights activists in the South.

Nor were the young the only ones to take heart at the new activism. Ella Baker was nearly sixty when the sit-ins began. Raised in North Carolina's black belt, she had fought racism throughout her life. In the 1940s, as field secretary for the NAACP, she had traveled throughout the South seeking black recruits. It was dangerous work, but she had dedication and talent. In 1943 she had roused the young blacks of Greensboro to form an NAACP youth chapter. Seventeen years later, that chapter inspired the young men who boldly sat down at the local Woolworth's lunch counter and asked for coffee.

Since 1958 Baker had served as the first executive secretary of SCLC. In 1960, hoping to galvanize the younger generation, she marshaled $800 of SCLC money and sent out a call for sit-in leaders to meet at her alma mater, Shaw University in Raleigh, over Easter weekend. Expecting about a hundred attendees, Baker was astounded and pleased when more than three hundred showed up. They came from fifty-six colleges in the South and nineteen in the North.

In her opening address, Baker explained to the assembled students that it was ''more than a hamburger'' they were after. ''What's the use of integrating lunch counters when Negroes can't afford to sit down to buy a hamburger?'' she asked. The whole social structure needed to change. The real goal, she maintained, should be complete social, political, and economic freedom. Martin Luther King, Jr., delivered the keynote address, urging students to establish a permanent organization to sustain the sit-ins' momentum and to ''take the freedom struggle into every community in the South.''

King and his aides Ralph Abernathy and Wyatt Walker assumed that the students would form a youth affiliate of SCLC. But although the young protesters deeply respected Dr. King, many hesitated to ally themselves too closely with him and his group. Some students deemed SCLC, the NAACP, and other adult civil-rights organizations overly cautious and conservative. Despite her position in SCLC, Ella Baker encouraged this independence. With her guidance, the convention delegates created the Temporary Student Nonviolent Coordinating Committee. At a second conference held that October, student leaders dropped the word *temporary* and made SNCC (pronounced ''Snick'') permanent.

SNCC's statement of purpose proclaimed that ''the philosophical and religious idea of non-violence [is] the foundation of our purpose, the presupposition of our faith and the manner of our action.'' Flush with the success of the sit-ins, the membership embraced the principle of nonviolence. For members of the Nashville group, nonviolence had become a way of life. However, for most student protesters, peaceful resistance to racism was merely one tactic that had worked in the sit-ins. In the enthusiasm of the time, no one considered this difference of opinion a problem; later in the decade, it would become a major obstacle.

Another issue that protesters only partially addressed in 1960 concerned students from the North. The sit-ins had excited both black and white college students on northern campuses. Delegates traveled to the Raleigh meeting from such elite universities as Harvard, Yale, Berkeley, Chicago, and Michigan. Many of these well-educated northerners displayed sharper debating skills than did their southern counterparts, although few from the northern contingent had put their lives on the line in the same way that the southern students had done. After much deliberation, delegates decided that a northern student movement should be established as an auxiliary and that full northern membership in the main organization would be decided on an individual basis. This decision ensured the dominance of southern blacks in SNCC, but the place of northern whites in the movement would remain controversial.

The role of women in the movement also would stir debate within SNCC. Unlike SCLC—largely an alliance of southern, black, male ministers—SNCC attracted numerous young women, both black and white, determined to fight for racial equality, even at risk of their lives. Legends telling of the heroism and courage of movement women grew. Ruby Doris Smith was a seventeen-year-old student at Spelman College when she joined the sit-in at Rock Hill, South Carolina, just a week after the Greensboro protests. She spent thirty days in prison after practicing the ''jail-no-bail'' tactic. From Rock Hill, Smith took part in freedom rides and numerous demonstrations throughout the Deep South, enduring the anger of white mobs and the horrors of southern jails. A powerful figure, Smith would become SNCC's executive secretary and what another member called the ''heartbeat'' of the organization.

Diane Nash became another civil-rights icon. Born in Chicago, Nash never felt the stifling Jim Crow system until she enrolled at Fisk University in Nashville, then joined James Lawson's nonviolent workshop and played a leadership role in the Nashville sit-ins. A Catholic, she viewed the sit-ins as an example of ''applied religion,'' advancing ''appreciation of the dignity of man.'' Nash became SNCC's first paid field staff member, noted for her militancy and bravery. Other African-American women renowned for their fearlessness and determination included Cynthia Washington, who, riding a mule, organized blacks in an Alabama county where no civil-rights workers had ventured alone. Lucretia Collins dropped out of school to continue the freedom rides, feeling ''certain that we were writing history,'' although knowing that ''some of us would be killed.'' Annie Pearl Avery, appalled by a white policeman's savagery, grabbed his club and demanded, ''Now what you going to do, motherfucker?'' Annell Ponder, lying in a Mississippi jail so brutally beaten that she could barely talk, looked up at a visiting SNCC worker and whispered one word: ''Freedom.''

Female volunteers kept various SNCC field offices functioning, and when SNCC workers went in to organize a community, they often garnered the fiercest support from local black women. Writing about his experiences in Georgia, SNCC staff member Charles Sherrod noted that ''there is always a 'mama.' She is usually a militant woman in the community, outspoken, understanding, and willing to catch hell, having already caught her share.''

White women, too, joined the cause. Some of the most important whites in the movement, including Casey Hayden, Mary King, and Jane Stembridge, had grown up in the South. To participate in the civil-rights crusade, they had to relinquish the revered ideal of the ''southern lady.'' Having broken with their traditional culture, young white activists often looked to the movement's black women as role models.

Clearly women played crucial roles in SNCC, yet many movement men, dominating debate and decisionmaking, discriminated against them, relegating them to typing and clerical work, taking notes at meetings, and preparing refreshments. SNCC's sexism mirrored attitudes of the larger society, but eventually male dominance would inspire a feminist rebellion within the organization (see Chapter 11).

At the time, however, this and other problems seemed minor. Inflamed with idealism and impatience, the activists eagerly anticipated a quick end to segregation. "What happened in Greensboro, the kick-off place, can happen and is happening all across the South," claimed Jane Stembridge. "People can come to an understanding, barriers can be removed, a new South can be born, and America can become an actual democracy." The student movement would not stop, promised SNCC leader Charles McDew, until "every vestige of racial segregation and discrimination are erased from the face of the earth."

Drawing strength from one another and from the early sit-in victories, these young activists endured beatings and jailings in the belief that they were building the "beloved community." "Through nonviolence," proclaimed James Lawson, "courage displaces fear; love transforms hate. Acceptance dissipates prejudice; hope ends despair. Peace dominates war; faith reconciles doubt." The spiritual power of nonviolence, SNCC members believed, would create the Christian ideal of a racially and sexually integrated community "permeated by love." "Finally it all boils down to human relationships," explained Stembridge, "whether *I* shall go on living in isolation or whether there shall be a we. . . . Love alone is radical."

In the early 1960s, SNCC workers fanned out through the South in an effort to create local African-American community organizations. They advocated consensual rule, a political philosophy that would strongly influence the early white New Left (see Chapter 7). According to Mary King, "a spirit of egalitarianism permeated the organization and, even if every individual did not always speak out, everyone's opinion counted. No one was unimportant. As much as possible, policy decisions were made by consensus."

The music of the movement well expressed its ardor. Spirituals from the days of slavery, labor and protest songs from the thirties, and newly written freedom songs all affirmed the solidarity of the crusade. The songs gave voice to a yearning for freedom and a message of collective resistance, as in "We Shall Not Be Moved." The music, claimed Mary King, "had an unparalleled ability to evoke the moral power of the movement's goals, to arouse the spirit, comfort the afflicted, instill courage and commitment, and to unite disparate strangers into a 'band of brothers and sisters' and a 'circle of trust.'" Demonstrators sang on marches; they sang when confronted by police; they sang in the darkness of cold jail cells; they sang in the black churches so central to their lives and to the freedom cause. The songs captured their conviction that revolutionary nonviolence and redemptive love would break down the barriers of racial prejudice. "We Shall Overcome," an old spiritual rewritten for the movement by folk-music great Pete Seeger, became the civil-rights anthem:

Deep in my heart, I do believe
We shall overcome some day. . . .
We are not afraid. . . .
We'll walk hand in hand. . . .
Black and white together. . . .
We shall overcome.

© Copyright 1960

It was a forceful music and a mighty faith. The impatient young blacks, confident in the rightness of their cause, looked forward to imminent victory. As an Atlanta sit-in leader proclaimed, "We do not intend to wait placidly for those rights which are already legally and morally ours to be meted out to us one at a time."

The election of John F. Kennedy in November 1960 amplified their conviction. The new president, radiating promise and purpose, had campaigned in favor of civil-rights legislation and executive action on behalf of African-Americans, and he had intervened to save Reverend Martin Luther King, Jr., from months of hard labor and possible death in a Georgia penitentiary. In return, African-Americans had voted overwhelmingly for JFK. Surely now, student activists reasoned, Kennedy would support the struggle against Jim Crow.

Promises Unfulfilled: Kennedy and Civil Rights

Kennedy's decision to aid the jailed Martin Luther King, Jr., just before the 1960 election had won him the extensive black backing vital to his victory. Like the SNCC activists, most civil-rights leaders assumed that the new president would back their desegregation drive. Yet in office Kennedy shied away from civil-rights issues, worried that a struggle for racial justice would split the Democratic party, jeopardize the rest of his legislative program, and hurt his chances for reelection four years hence. To win support for his foreign-policy initiatives and New Frontier domestic programs, Kennedy sought to curry favor with southern Democratic congressmen, many of whom had seniority and held crucial committee positions. In the president's mind, only the communist threat demanded immediate action; solving racial problems, he believed, called for moderation, not coercion.

In the first two years of his administration, Kennedy never empathized with the moral passion and urgency of the civil-rights cause. A cool pragmatist, he viewed civil rights with the same detachment as he did other domestic political issues such as tax reform and trade expansion. Absorbed with crises abroad, he assigned low priority to the drive against racism. Politics for him consisted of bargains and compromises among elite factions. He neither grasped nor appreciated the new democratic mass politics emerging among African-Americans in the early 1960s. By nature, he distrusted populist politics, and he disliked a movement that inflamed an issue beyond his control.

Instead of throwing his support behind racial equality, Kennedy chose the difficult and contradictory path of trying to conciliate the civil-rights movement while wooing the white South. Although he named numerous blacks to high office, including Thurgood Marshall as a federal circuit court judge, Carl Rowan as ambassador to Finland, and Andrew Hatcher as his associate press secretary, he also appointed white segregationists to federal judgeships. Kennedy's first judicial appointment went to William Harold Cox of Mississippi, who once referred to black litigants in his courtroom as "niggers" and compared them to "chimpanzees." Kennedy's dilemma was a long-time Democratic party problem. Black voters, particularly in northern urban areas, made up a large part of the Democrats' constituency, but pursuing their rights risked alienating the all-important white southern Democrats.

Initially the administration avoided advocating civil-rights legislation that the president feared would get bogged down in Congress and offend southern political leaders. JFK also delayed delivering on his campaign promise of an executive order barring discrimination in federally financed housing. When pressed, he said simply that the matter was under consideration. Only through Justice Department litigation aimed at implementing the 1957 legislation on voting rights did the early Kennedy administration show commitment to racial equality. However, the law required that the government proceed case by case, an expensive and cumbersome process.

But much as the administration sidestepped the racial issue, the movement forced the government's hand. The sit-ins blossomed through 1960 and spread into 1961. That spring, CORE, a small northern-based interracial group founded in 1942, reintroduced a nonviolent tactic that the organization had first applied in 1947, the freedom ride.

In December 1960, the Supreme Court in *Boynton* v. *Virginia* had forbidden discrimination in bus and train terminals serving interstate carriers. The following February, James Farmer, the newly appointed director of CORE, decided to test the court ruling by sending an interracial group on a bus trip through the Deep South, demanding service at all the terminal facilities along the way. The real intention of these freedom rides, according to Farmer, "was to provoke the southern authorities into arresting us and thereby prod the Justice Department into enforcing the law of the land."

On May 4, 1961, seven blacks and six whites split into two interracial groups and left Washington, D.C., one group on a Greyhound bus and the other on a Trailways bus. The carefully chosen passengers included Farmer and Jim Peck, a white pacifist, and two others from CORE; several SNCC activists, including John Lewis, by this time a veteran with five civil-rights arrests; and members of the pacifist Quaker organization, the American Friends Service Committee, including the prominent Bostonian and World War II veteran Albert Bigelow. In 1958 Bigelow had skippered the *Golden Rule* into the Pacific to protest U.S. H-bomb tests. The riders harbored no illusions as to what awaited them; according to Farmer, they were "prepared for anything, even death."

As the buses made their way south, tension mounted. On May 8, at the depot in Charlotte, North Carolina, police arrested freedom rider Charles Perkins when he asked for a shoeshine in a white-only barbershop. Arriving the next day at the Greyhound terminal in Rock Hill, South Carolina, John Lewis, upon entering the white waiting room, met several young white hoodlums in leather jackets blocking the door. "Nigger, you can't come in here!" they screamed. Lewis replied, "I have every right to enter this waiting room according to the Supreme Court of the United States in the *Boynton* case." "Shit on that," the hoods snarled, and they clubbed him to the floor. Only after Lewis and Albert Bigelow had suffered severe beatings did police intervene. No arrests were made.

Nevertheless, the freedom ride ground on. After an overnight stop in Atlanta, where the riders dined with Martin Luther King, Jr., they began the dreaded trip across the Deep South, where newspaper coverage of the ride had paved the way for violence. When the first bus arrived in Anniston, Alabama, a white mob brandishing chains, iron bars, knives, and sticks broke the bus windows, slashed the tires, and dragged the freedom riders out and beat them. Belatedly the police drove off the attackers, and the bus departed, but the mob pursued in cars. Six miles out of town, one of the bus's slashed tires burst. The hoodlums threw a fire bomb into the disabled Greyhound, and it erupted in flames. As the protesters fled the burning vehicle, the mob closed in on

Riding for Freedom. On May 14, 1961, outside of Anniston, Alabama, a white mob set fire to this freedom-ride bus. Such incidents created enormous sympathy for the nonviolent freedom riders and forced the reluctant Kennedy administration to take steps to protect them.

them again. Only the arrival of an armed caravan of blacks in cars from Birmingham, led by Reverend Fred Shuttlesworth, saved the battered riders.

When the second contingent of freedom riders on the Trailways bus met with similar trouble in Birmingham, Farmer and other CORE officials reluctantly decided to call off the ride. Yet John Lewis would not hear of it. He believed too much in freedom to stop the ride, and he feared that giving in would signal the triumph of violence and segregation. Lewis contacted Diane Nash, James Bevel, and other Nashville SNCC members, and they hastily gathered a new group of riders to continue what CORE had started. When the Nashville contingent arrived in Birmingham, police stopped their bus and dragged them to jail. At about midnight, Birmingham's police commissioner, Eugene ''Bull'' Conner, drove the unwilling protesters to the Tennessee state line. They managed to make their way back to Birmingham, joined by fresh SNCC recruits from Nashville and Atlanta, and reassembled at the Greyhound station, but no bus driver would take them to Montgomery.

The Kennedy administration, focused on the president's upcoming summit with Khrushchev and the fermenting Berlin crisis, had done nothing to protect the freedom riders. ''Tell them to call it off. Stop them,'' Kennedy ordered his civil-rights adviser, Harris Wofford. Attorney General Robert Kennedy mused to Wofford, ''I wonder whether [the freedom riders] have the best interest of their country at heart. Do you know that one of them is against the atom bomb—yes, he even picketed against it in jail! The President is going abroad and this is all embarrassing him.''

The massive publicity that the freedom rides had generated particularly annoyed the Kennedys. TV reports, front-page photos, and banner headlines revealed to the world the brutality of southern racism. Not only did most of the American news media voice abhorrence at the violence, but throughout the world the bloodshed in Alabama tarnished America's image. The communist press claimed that racist brutality ''exposed'' the ''savage nature of American freedom and democracy.'' Editorials in developing nations emphasized the disparity between America's professed belief in equality and racial discrimination. Even the West European press condemned American racism for provoking anti-Western passions. Under this harsh spotlight, the Kennedy administration finally determined to act. Robert Kennedy persuaded Greyhound to supply a driver to take the freedom riders on to Montgomery. Through his aide John Siegenthaler, the attorney general received Alabama governor John Patterson's assurances of state protection for the demonstrators.

Early on the morning of May 20, 1961, John Lewis and twenty SNCC activists boarded a Greyhound bus in Birmingham, bound for Montgomery. At first police cars escorted the vehicle, and helicopters hovered overhead. As the bus entered Montgomery's city limits, however, the escorts vanished, and when the vehicle pulled into the station, Lewis became uneasy. The place seemed deserted; there were no other buses, no cabs, no people in sight. As the freedom riders stepped off the bus, a mob of several hundred whites charged them from around a corner. A woman shrieked, ''Kill the nigger-lovin' son of a bitch,'' as a surge of men with ax handles attacked Jim Zwerg, a young white student. Several toughs cornered Lewis, knocked him to the ground, and smashed his head with a soda crate, leaving him bleeding with a concussion. As Lewis lay unconscious, Alabama's attorney general, the state's chief law enforcement officer, stood over him and read an injunction prohibiting white and black groups to travel together through the state of Alabama on public transportation. In the mayhem, Siegenthaler, who had followed the bus in his car, tried to rescue two female freedom riders. Several whites clubbed him from behind, knocking him unconscious as well. The rioting raged for more than an hour before the police halted it. As Montgomery's police commissioner explained, ''We have no intention of standing guard for a bunch of troublemakers coming into our city.''

Furious at Siegenthaler's beating and feeling betrayed by Alabama officials, JFK termed the violence ''a source of the deepest concern'' and pledged that the federal government would take ''all necessary steps'' to meet its responsibilities in Alabama. Later that day, Robert Kennedy ordered some four hundred federal marshals to Montgomery ''to assist state and local authorities in the protection of persons and property and vehicles.'' Yet the following night in Montgomery, an enraged mob assaulted a freedom-ride rally assembled in Ralph Abernathy's First Baptist Church. Only Governor Patterson's decision to send in the National Guard brought the melee under control. Robert Kennedy now urged the black militants to accept a ''cooling-off period.'' Fumed Farmer, ''We had been cooling off for a hundred years. If we got any cooler we'd be in a deep freeze.'' The freedom riders, reinforced by additional volunteers, resolved to go on, this time into Mississippi, a state with a reputation for even harsher racism and violence than Alabama.

''We were all scared about going into Mississippi,'' admitted Farmer. ''I had seen fear in the eyes of some of the kids as they climbed the steps of the bus. But there was also something there that transcended fear.'' The young SNCC volunteers asked

Martin Luther King, Jr., to accompany them. He refused, on the grounds that participating would violate his parole on a previous civil-rights conviction. Because most of the riders were on similar probations from past arrests, King's excuse struck them as cowardly. John Lewis, Diane Nash, and other young activists who had once revered King would never see him in the same light again.

On May 24, twenty-seven freedom riders, escorted by the Alabama National Guard, ate breakfast at the terminal's white-only lunch counter and departed by bus for Jackson, Mississippi. As they crossed the state line, Mississippi state police took over the task of safely conveying the riders to Jackson. With forced cheer, the demonstrators sang:

Hallelujah, I'm traveling
Down Freedom's main line.

To everyone's relief, the bus entered the Jackson terminal without incident. Unbeknown to the riders, Attorney General Robert Kennedy had made a deal with Mississippi senator James Eastland and Governor Barnett: Mississippi officials pledged that there would be no mob violence, and the federal government agreed not to interfere if the state arrested the demonstrators. As the freedom riders walked into the terminal to test the facilities, police seized them. They nabbed Farmer at the white lunch counter; Lewis, as he stepped up to the white-only urinal. Rather than post bail or pay fines, the riders chose jail. Soon new groups of freedom riders took up the cause, and by late summer 1961, over a thousand people had participated. More than three hundred had been arrested in Jackson alone. Mississippi officials sent some sentenced riders to serve hard time at the infamous Parchman Penitentiary.

Finally, the federal government took action. On September 22, the Interstate Commerce Commission (ICC), under pressure from Attorney General Kennedy, announced that interstate carriers and terminals must display signs stating that seating "is without regard to race, color, creed or national origin." The ICC also prohibited interstate carriers from using any terminal that practiced segregation. Some Deep South terminals tried to evade the order, but most complied, and by the end of 1962, CORE declared a victory in the battle of interstate travel.

The freedom riders had triumphed, although at the cost of severe physical and psychological abuse. The rides exposed to the world the savagery of southern racism and southern officials' connivance with the mobs. The rides also had forced the reluctant Kennedy administration into the fray. Yet while the violence shocked most Americans, the president avoided discussing it. Had he voiced his support of the simple right of freedom to travel, condemned racist violence, and praised the courage of the freedom riders, he could have done much to educate the American public on the urgent need for justice. Instead, he limited his involvement to preserving law and order.

In late September 1962, circumstances again obliged JFK to take action when Mississippi governor Ross Barnett defied a federal court order for the admission of black air-force veteran James Meredith to the all-white University of Mississippi. Barnett appointed himself a deputy registrar at Ole Miss and pledged personally to block Meredith's admission at the doors of the administration building. Retired major general Edwin Walker, a member of the ultra-right-wing John Birch Society, worsened the crisis. Speaking on radio station KWKH in Shreveport, Louisiana, Walker urged mob action: "It is time to move. We have talked, listened and been pushed around far too much by the anti-Christ Supreme Court. Rise to stand beside Governor Ross Barnett." White Citizens' Councils also broadcast radio appeals for Mississippians to resist federally forced integration. On September 30, 1962, thousands of men, many toting lead pipes, chains, knives, and guns, thronged the university.

On television, JFK implored the people of Mississippi to accept the rule of law and dispatched hundreds of federal marshals to Oxford, Mississippi. Nevertheless, that night the mob attacked the officers, and in the ensuing riot, two died and several hundred were injured. Only the arrival of a National Guard armored cavalry unit and regular army troops saved the marshals and restored order. The next day, flanked by troops, James Meredith enrolled and attended his first class. The color barrier at Ole Miss had fallen.

Yet as the government finally moved to uphold the rights of one black student, it provided virtually no federal protection, despite Robert Kennedy's promise, to thousands of young black activists working to register voters in the Deep South. In the fall of 1961, SNCC and CORE, with assistance from the NAACP, SCLC, and other civil-rights groups, established the Voter Education Project. Attorney General Kennedy had encouraged the project in the hopes that voter registration would generate less conflict than the freedom rides. At a June 1961 meeting, he had told civil-rights leaders, "If you'll cut out this freedom riding and sitting-in stuff, and concentrate on voter registration, I'll get you a tax exemption." Kennedy also arranged grant money from liberal foundations and assured the black leaders of government protection.

Between 1961 and 1964, hundreds of SNCC and CORE field secretaries worked to register voters and to organize blacks in states such as Mississippi, Alabama, and Georgia. For months they talked to poor blacks on porches, in tarpaper shacks, and in churches, trying to educate prospective voters on their rights. These dedicated young men and women spoke the language and lived the life of the oppressed people. Fannie Lou Hamer, a worker on a Mississippi cotton plantation, lauded the SNCC workers: "Nobody never come out into the country and talked to real farmers and things. . . . They treated us like we were special and we loved 'em. . . . We trusted 'em, and I can tell the world those kids done their share in Mississippi."

As the volunteers set up offices in dusty small towns and traveled backcountry roads, they faced violence at every turn. Racist whites resorted to arson, bombings, beatings, and assassinations. Bob Moses, who had left his teaching position in Harlem after the sit-ins started, had joined SNCC and established a voter-education project in McComb County in the Mississippi delta. As he led a group of blacks to a voter-registration office in Liberty, Mississippi, a prominent citizen attacked him with the butt end of a knife. A few weeks later, a black farmer, Herbert Lee, who supported Moses's work, was shot and killed in broad daylight by a state legislator named E. H. Hurst. An African-American witness to the murder was later shot and killed. No one was ever charged in the deaths. Indeed, southern police often jailed civil-rights workers on trumped-up charges and then beat and even shot them. Time and again, SNCC and CORE workers appealed to the Justice Department for the protection that Robert Kennedy had promised. In virtually every case, national authorities did nothing.

The most visible federal presence in the Deep South was the FBI. Yet director J. Edgar Hoover sabotaged efforts to protect civil-rights workers. Convinced that Martin

Registering Voters. Hundreds of SNCC and CORE volunteers worked to register voters in the south. Although constantly threatened with violence, they toiled for years in their efforts to educate and organize blacks of the Deep South.

Luther King, Jr., was a communist conspirator, he limited the FBI's role in civil-rights cases to investigation. While SNCC workers fell to racist mobs or officials, FBI agents often stood passively in the background taking notes. Most of the agents themselves hailed from the South and sought to maintain good relations with local officials. Like Hoover, they dismissed the activists as troublemakers and a threat to public order. Martin Luther King, Jr., who led a series of demonstrations in Albany, Georgia, in 1962, claimed, "Every time I saw FBI men in Albany, they were with the local police force." Not surprisingly, wariness of the FBI ran rampant in the movement, and blacks grew disillusioned with the Kennedy government. King noted sadly that "if tokenism were the goal, the administration [has moved] us adroitly toward it." An October 1962 editorial in a black newspaper charged liberals with not delivering on their promises. Blacks, the editorial suggested, should bid white liberals "a fond farewell with thanks for services rendered, until [they] are ready to re-enlist as foot soldiers and subordinates in a Negro-led, Negro-officered army, under the banner of Freedom Now."

But as black activists and their white supporters kept exerting pressure on segregation and discrimination, the Kennedy administration cautiously stepped up its involvement. In November 1962, the president finally signed the executive order outlawing segregation in federally financed housing. Although this order had only limited impact, it held symbolic meaning. In February 1963, Kennedy sent a modest civil-rights bill to Congress and for the first time spoke out about racial discrimination in moral terms: "Let it be clear, in our own hearts and minds, that it is not merely because of the Cold War, and not merely because of the economic waste of discrimination, that we are committed to achieving true equality of opportunity. The basic reason is because it is right.''

Events in the spring of 1963 would intensify the president's budding commitment. That April, Martin Luther King, Jr., and SCLC launched a campaign for racial justice in Birmingham, Alabama, one of the most segregated cities in the nation. Virtually all public facilities in Birmingham were racially separated. The public library even banned a children's book picturing black and white rabbits playing together. Birmingham's racism also proved violent; between 1957 and 1963, eighteen antiblack bombings and more than fifty cross burnings terrorized the city's African-Americans. Police commissioner Eugene "Bull" Connor fit the stereotype of a southern sheriff—paunchy, jowly, brutal, and determined to keep blacks down. When the first freedom riders had arrived in Birmingham in 1961, Connor had promised the Klan fifteen minutes to beat the riders until "it looked like a bulldog got hold of them." Clearly Birmingham would not acquiesce peacefully to the protesters' demands. King and his associates hoped that a confrontation in that city would awaken the national conscience and "break the back of segregation all over the nation."

Day after day, the protesters marched and demonstrated in Birmingham. Connor's police clubbed them, jabbed them with electric cattle prods, assaulted them with dogs, and attacked them with high-pressure fire hoses. More than twenty thousand blacks went to jail, including King. The home of King's brother, Reverend A. D. King, was bombed, as was the motel that served as SCLC's headquarters. Still, the protests continued, and as television stations and newspapers throughout the country showed the appalling pictures of marchers, many of them youths and children, set upon by dogs and beaten by police, outrage swept the nation.

Inspired by Birmingham, demonstrators took to the streets in Jackson, Raleigh, and Tallahassee. Blacks, as well as white supporters, staged protests outside the South, too, in cities such as Los Angeles, Philadelphia, Chicago, and St. Louis, where demonstrators focused less on segregation than on jobs and housing. In May alone, an estimated seventy-five thousand Americans participated in civil-rights demonstrations.

President Kennedy, sickened by the violence and impressed by the demonstrators' determination, eventually sent federal troops to restore order in Birmingham. On June 11, when Governor George Wallace threatened to block the court-ordered admission of two blacks to the University of Alabama, JFK federalized the Alabama National Guard and forced the governor to back down. Later that evening, the president spoke about civil rights with a fervor that he had never before exhibited. America, he told a national TV audience, faced "a moral issue. . . . Events in Birmingham and elsewhere have so increased the cries for equality that no city or state or legislative body can prudently choose to ignore them." He warned that "the fires of frustration and discord are burning in every city." This moral crisis, he concluded, "cannot be met by repressive police action" or "quieted by token moves or talk. It is time to act in the Congress, in your state and local legislative body, and, above all, in all our daily lives. . . . A great change is at hand, and our task, our obligation, is to make that revolution, that change, peaceful and constructive for all."

Later that night, a white sniper shot and killed Medgar Evers, the leader of the Mississippi NAACP. A World War II veteran, Evers had spent his life trying to register black voters and had earned the reputation as "the Negro most feared by the segrega-

We Shall Overcome, Birmingham, Alabama, 1963. Hands locked together to resist the force of high-powered firehoses, these three young blacks challenge segregation. Their courage, and that of thousands of other demonstrators, created a groundswell of sympathy and support for civil-rights legislation.

tionists of Mississippi.'' By order of the president, he was buried at Arlington National Cemetery with full military honors.

On June 19, 1963, Kennedy submitted a broad new civil-rights proposal to Congress. Although late in throwing his full support behind the cause, he now endorsed most of the activists' demands. His bill called for the desegregation of public facilities, requested power to enable the Justice Department to initiate school-desegregation suits, and urged authorization for the government to withhold funds from federally assisted programs in cases of discrimination.

Kennedy also turned his attention to poverty in America. Moved by the civil-rights crusade and by Michael Harrington's stirring exposé of poverty, *The Other America* (1962), he asked his chief economic adviser, Walter Heller, to draw up a plan that would wage war on poverty through such measures as job training, education, nutrition, and direct aid to the poor.

On August 28, 1963, a coalition of civil-rights and labor organizations staged a march on Washington in support of jobs and freedom. Kennedy had hoped to fend off the event, fearing potential violence and public disapproval of his civil-rights bill. Once the march became inevitable, the administration pressured civil-rights leaders to keep it moderate. Under this coercion, John Lewis, now SNCC's chairman, agreed to tone down the militant speech that he had planned denouncing Kennedy's civil-rights efforts.

To Move a Nation. Martin Luther King, Jr., delivers his historic "I Have a Dream" speech at the March on Washington on August 28, 1963. The march awakened the nation to the urgency of racial justice.

Despite these tensions, the March on Washington proved pivotal to the civil-rights movement. About a quarter of a million blacks and whites gathered at the Lincoln Memorial on a sunny day that transformed into a vast celebration. The massive crowd joined hands and sang along as Joan Baez performed "We Shall Overcome." They listened to Bob Dylan's ballad about the murder of Medgar Evers; they clapped as Odetta intoned, "If they ask you who you are, tell them you're a child of God." The crowd endured heat, humidity, and a long procession of speakers exhorting the nation to its moral duty. Then Martin Luther King, Jr., stepped up. As he sermonized in the rhythmic tradition of black preaching, his rich, deep voice evoked a utopian vision: "I have a dream that one day even the State of Mississippi, a state sweltering with the heat of injustice, sweltering with the heat of oppression, will be transformed into an oasis of freedom and justice." King's speech, more than anything else that day, turned the March on Washington into a historic event. His vision lifted blacks' spirits and moved the hearts of whites. Broadcast on national TV, the march transmuted public opinion. Before the event, polls showed that only one-quarter of the population considered civil rights a pressing national issue; afterward a majority validated its urgency.

Yet southern Democrats and conservative Republicans persisted in stalling the civil-rights bill in Congress. In November 1963, still hoping to win the South in his forthcoming presidential campaign, Kennedy made his fatal trip to Dallas. At the time of his assassination, Congress had taken no action on the civil-rights bill.

Cautious Victories: Johnson and Civil Rights

Momentum for the civil-rights bill accelerated tremendously after Kennedy's murder, as President Lyndon Baines Johnson called on Congress to pass the measure as a tribute to the slain leader. "We have talked long enough in this country about equal rights," the new president asserted. "It is now time . . . to write it in the books of law." As a congressman and later a senator from Texas in the 1940s and early 1950s, Johnson had consistently voted against civil-rights bills. By 1957, however, he had become senate majority leader with presidential aspirations. To win the White House, he knew that he would have to gain the support of liberals and northern Democrats; thus, that year he guided an emasculated civil-rights bill through the Senate. By 1964, as an accidental southern president seeking to don the Kennedy mantle and build national support for the November presidential election, Johnson threw his support behind the bill. Acutely aware that African-American protest had changed the nation's domestic political agenda, he now championed civil-rights reform. LBJ succeeded primarily by pressuring Congress and gaining key backing from powerful Republicans, including Senate minority leader Everett Dirksen of Illinois. In a June 1964 showdown vote, the necessary two-thirds of the Senate called for an end to the debate, halting a fifty-seven-day southern filibuster.

On July 2, 1964, Johnson proudly signed the Civil Rights Act into law. Strengthened by liberal amendments, the act outlawed discrimination in employment and places of public accommodation on the basis of race, religion, or sex; authorized the government to withhold federal funds from public programs practicing discrimination; established the Equal Employment Opportunity Commission; and provided aid to communities desegregating their schools. The law rendered Jim Crow legally dead. Euphoric white liberals and blacks celebrated this "second Reconstruction."

Nevertheless, many tasks remained. The new law had little effect on such problems as endemic black poverty and widespread *de facto* segregation. To SNCC and CORE activists, who for years had risked their lives in the South, the most pressing concern was still enfranchisement. Whites had developed a variety of techniques to keep blacks from the polls, including manipulating literacy tests to deny even well-educated blacks the right to vote, devising complex voter-registration forms, and refusing to register blacks who made the slightest error on the forms. In the rural Deep South, where African-Americans often composed a majority, whites profoundly feared black political empowerment. Nonwhites seeking to register might be fired, turned off the land that they farmed, denied credit by local merchants, beaten, or shot. For years, these efforts had discouraged all but a small number of blacks from attempting to register. In Mississippi only 6 percent of adult blacks had joined voter rolls. In Alabama about 19 percent registered, although in Lowndes and Wilcox counties, where African-Americans constituted over two-thirds of the population, not a single black could cast a ballot.

Bob Moses and other SNCC field secretaries had made heroic efforts to register black voters in Mississippi. Between 1961 and 1963, some seventy thousand Mississippi blacks courageously tried to gain the right to vote; fewer than five thousand succeeded. As the November 1963 state elections approached, Moses hit upon a scheme to dramatize the political plight of Mississippi blacks: the Freedom Election. On election day, some eighty thousand disfranchised blacks scored a symbolic victory by casting "freedom ballots" for Aaron Henry, the head of the state NAACP, for governor.

About a hundred white students from Stanford and Yale had taken time off from college to assist in the Freedom Election. Their presence brought national attention to the campaign and new federal protection. Reflecting on the role that the white students had played, Moses thought of yet another plan to subvert Mississippi's white establishment: the Freedom Summer for 1964. His strategy was to enlist hundreds of white students to aid SNCC and CORE in a well-publicized effort to register Mississippi blacks.

Several black activists complained that bringing in white students would perpetuate notions of black inferiority. Others worried that whites would come in for the summer, monopolize publicity, stir things up, and then leave blacks to face reprisals alone. But Moses stressed the need for the national attention and federal protection that he assumed a substantial white presence would bring. It was not a question of ''Negro fighting white,'' he argued. ''It's a question of rational people against irrational people.''

Moses's reasoning prevailed, and SNCC and CORE, with nominal support from the NAACP, SCLC, and other civil-rights groups, formed the Council of Federated Organizations (COFO) and launched Mississippi Freedom Summer. SNCC workers and supporters established recruitment offices on major campuses, and students responded enthusiastically. On June 15, 1964, the first three hundred of the more than eight hundred young project volunteers met for a training session at the Western College for Women in Oxford, Ohio. Addressing the group, Moses warned, ''The guerrilla war in Mississippi is not much different from that in Vietnam. . . . Our goals are limited. If we can go and come back alive, then that is something.'' Several days later, as Moses began to address a batch of fresh recruits, a SNCC worker called him aside and whispered a message. Moses relayed the news: ''Yesterday morning, three of our people left Meridian, Mississippi, to investigate a church-burning in Neshoba County. They haven't come back, and we haven't had any word from them.'' The training sessions continued, but fear for the fate of the missing freedom fighters mounted. News came soon that investigators had discovered the badly burned car that the three had been driving. ''The kids are dead,'' predicted Moses.

The missing three were Michael Schwerner, a twenty-four-year-old white social worker from New York and a CORE staff member; James Chaney, a twenty-one-year-old Mississippi black also affiliated with CORE; and Andrew Goodman, a twenty-one-year-old white summer volunteer from Queens College in New York. After an intensive six-week investigation ordered by President Johnson, FBI agents unearthed the three bodies from a recently bulldozed dam in rural Neshoba County. The two whites had been shot once; Chaney had been brutally beaten and shot three times. Subsequent FBI investigations linked the deaths to the Ku Klux Klan and the sheriff and deputy sheriff of Neshoba County, although it would take years before any of the murderers would be convicted.

The killings aroused widespread publicity, and the Johnson administration promised to strengthen federal authority in Mississippi. Nevertheless, violence against the Mississippi Freedom Summer workers ground on. White racists burned some thirty-seven churches, bombed thirty homes, and beat and shot at hundreds of civil-rights activists. To harass the project further, local police made more than a thousand arrests, mostly on trumped-up charges. SNCC and CORE leaders pleaded in vain for Johnson's promised federal protection. J. Edgar Hoover traveled to Jackson, Mississippi, in midsummer and announced that the FBI ''most certainly'' would not provide special security for the student volunteers. By this time, most of the battle-hardened SNCC and CORE workers dismissed the FBI and the national government as little better than Mississippi's white racists.

The brutal pressures of the voting project eroded the movement's faith in the tactic of nonviolence. The once-pacifist David Dennis of CORE spoke for many when he cried at Chaney's funeral, "I'm sick and tired of going to the funerals of black men who have been murdered by white men. I'm not going to stand here and ask anyone not to be angry, not to be bitter tonight. . . . I've got vengeance in my heart." Dennis and many other SNCC and CORE field secretaries began carrying guns, and within a year both organizations would cease advocating peaceful resistance.

Tensions between the movement's black veterans and white volunteers also surfaced that summer. Living communally under the pressures of daily terrorism, blacks and whites sometimes vented their frustrations on each other. SNCC and CORE regulars resented the fact that the white volunteers garnered most of the national publicity but would soon be safely back at their prestigious colleges. Many blacks regarded the northern whites as pushy and patronizing. A white female volunteer wrote that the black activists "were automatically suspicious of us . . . ; throughout the summer they put us to the test, and few, if any, could pass. . . . It humbled, if not humiliated, me to realize that *finally they will never accept me.*" Instances of interracial sex further strained relationships for both blacks and whites. Although these sexual liaisons challenged the South's most basic racial bias, they also provoked jealousies and hostilities within the movement.

Even with these internal conflicts, the Summer Project managed to establish about a hundred Freedom Schools where young blacks received academic instruction as well as classes on African-American history and race relations. The volunteers worked tirelessly to educate and organize local black communities and to set up community centers. They also generated widespread publicity and nourished a national consensus opposed to Mississippi's racist policies. Yet for all their efforts, they managed to register only about twelve hundred new voters.

Frustrated, Moses and the Freedom Summer leaders established the nondiscriminatory Mississippi Freedom Democratic party (MFDP), in which more than sixty thousand disfranchised African-Americans enrolled. At local and state conventions, the MFDP selected sixty-eight delegates to attend the Democratic National Convention in Atlantic City and demand the ouster of the lily-white Mississippi regulars. By the time of the convention, which began on August 24, 1964, a liberal groundswell had arisen in support of the Freedom Democrats. In nationally televised hearings of the credentials committee, witnesses attested to the brutality and coercion used to keep blacks from registering. Moved by graphic descriptions of what MFDP delegate Fannie Lou Hamer called the "woesome times" that she faced after attempting to register, liberal members of the credentials committee rallied to the insurgents' cause.

Lyndon Johnson feared the political consequences of fully supporting the Freedom Democrats. He confided to his friend, Texas governor John Connally, "If you seat those black buggers, the whole South will walk out." Applying tremendous pressure on liberal Democrats and established civil-rights leaders, the president forced through a compromise: the MFDP would be given two delegates-at-large, and the Mississippi regulars would remain. Martin Luther King, Jr., and other older black leaders supported this compromise, but the outraged Freedom Democrats and young SNCC workers felt betrayed. "We didn't come all this way for no two votes," proclaimed Hamer.

SNCC and CORE workers and Freedom party delegates stormed out of the Atlantic City convention convinced that Johnson and the white liberal establishment had double-crossed them. "Never again," claimed SNCC's Cleveland Sellers, "were we lulled into believing that our task was exposing injustices so that the 'good' people of America could eliminate them. We left Atlantic City with the knowledge that the movement had turned into something else. After Atlantic City, our struggle was not for civil rights, but for liberation.'' Although not yet apparent, internal divisions had begun splintering the movement as younger black activists grew increasingly militant and separatist.

Among battle-scarred SNCC veterans, black nationalism began to replace civil rights as a goal. In September 1964, soon after the Democratic convention, SNCC leaders John Lewis, Bob Moses, James Forman, and Julian Bond and MFDP stalwart Fannie Lou Hamer traveled to Guinea to what Forman called ''Mother Africa.'' They rejoiced that, in Forman's words, ''there were no sheriffs to dread, no Klan breathing down your neck, no climate of constant repression.'' They came to see the African-American struggle as international. In February 1965, Lewis remarked that whether in Angola or Harlem, Mozambique or Mississippi, ''the struggle is . . . the same. . . . It is a struggle against a vicious and evil system that is controlled and kept in order for and by a few white men throughout the world.'' That month, a disillusioned Bob Moses changed his last name to Parris (his middle name). No longer speaking to whites, he cut his ties with SNCC and went to teach school in a remote village in Tanzania.

By 1965, with SNCC and CORE increasingly alienated from white liberals and more moderate civil-rights groups, Martin Luther King, Jr., and SCLC once again captured the movement's center stage. With an eye toward enacting a strong voting-rights law, SCLC leaders instigated a series of protests in Selma, Alabama, in January 1965. The city had a black majority, yet even though SNCC workers had worked to register voters there since 1962, only 320 blacks succeeded in enrolling, compared with nearly 10,000 of the white minority. For nearly three months, demonstrators marched and staged peaceful protests. As in Birmingham, white violence attracted national attention. Time and again, police, directed by Sheriff Jim Clark, attacked protesters, flailing nightsticks, chains, and electric cattle prods. Each night the TV networks bombarded Americans with reports from Selma, and when whites murdered two white civil-rights participants in March, pro–civil-rights sympathies swept the country. As had been the case since the Montgomery bus boycott, the media, particularly television, buttressed the civil-rights cause. Early on, a bitter irony had dawned on movement members: their success depended on provoking violence. The contrast between the peaceful, well-dressed, resolute demonstrators and the caterwauling, incensed mobs released yet another torrent of national outrage and calls for a voting-rights bill. As SCLC leader Andrew Young explained it, ''The movement did not 'cause' problems in Selma. . . . [I]t just brought them to the surface where they could be dealt with. Sheriff Clark has been beating black heads in the back of the jail for years, and we're only saying to him that if he still wants to beat heads he'll have to do it on Main Street, at noon, in front of CBS, NBC, and ABC television cameras.''

On March 15, 1965, in the midst of the Selma crisis, Lyndon Johnson asked Congress to pass a voting-rights bill. Although sympathetic with the civil-rights movement and well aware that 94 percent of the 1964 black vote had gone to him, he had tried to avoid further alienating southern congressmen to ensure passage of other domestic reforms. The delay also stemmed from the president's dislike of Martin Luther King, Jr. Johnson, vain about his 1964 accomplishments, resented King's selection as *Time*'s Man of the Year and his winning the Nobel Peace Prize. Damning reports on King from FBI director Hoover also turned Johnson against the civil-rights leader. With

President Kennedy's approval, the FBI had begun collecting information on King in 1962 through secret wiretaps and bugging devices. This illegal surveillance continued under Johnson. Hoover believed that SCLC was "spearheaded by Communists and moral degenerates" and hoped to defame King, whom he denounced as "the most notorious liar in the country." Although the FBI found no evidence of subversion, King, like Kennedy and Johnson, had extramarital affairs. The FBI recorded them and tried to blackmail King into silence or even suicide.[1]

The FBI nevertheless failed to divert King from his mission, and mounting national outrage at the violence in Selma forced Johnson's hand. In his speech of March 15, 1965, he compared Selma to Lexington, Concord, and Appomattox as turning points in "man's unending search for freedom." Using the language of the civil-rights movement, Johnson vowed, "All of us . . . must overcome the crippling legacy of bigotry and injustice—and we shall overcome." With strong presidential support and a bipartisan effort in Congress, the Voting Rights Act became law. Johnson signed the measure on August 6, 1965, and testified to the courage of African-Americans: "They came in darkness and they came in chains. Today we strike away the last major shackle of those fierce ancient bonds."

The Voting Rights Act abolished literacy tests for registrants and empowered the attorney general to appoint federal examiners to supervise voter registration in states practicing political discrimination. Together with the Twenty-third Amendment outlawing the poll tax in federal elections (ratified in 1964) and the 1966 Supreme Court decision annulling the poll tax in all elections, the new law reshaped southern politics. Although white economic and political coercion of African-Americans persisted in many areas of the South, by 1968 more than 2 million southern blacks nevertheless would join voter registration lists. In Mississippi the proportion of black registrants jumped from 7 percent of African-Americans eligible to vote in 1964 to 60 percent in 1968. In Selma, Alabama, the law wielded an even more striking impact: within two months after Congress passed the bill, the number of black voters soared from 320 to 6,789. In the spring of 1966, these new voters helped to oust Jim Clark, Selma's white supremacist sheriff. By 1969 more than 400 blacks had won elective office in the Deep South. For the first time since Reconstruction, African-Americans had formed a political force with clout in the South. Shrewd white politicians would soon relinquish their traditional obsession with race and adopt moderate nonracist policies.

●　●　●

Between the midfifties and the midsixties, American society witnessed a revolution in race relations. Pushed by judicial decisions, legislative acts, and above all by the persistent, organized black struggle for justice, the United States had undergone a revolutionary transformation. At dire personal risk, African-Americans had taken charge of their own liberation and confronted brutal bigotry without resorting to violence. Their bravery and the publicity that violent resistance to them generated had inspired a broad national consensus in favor of civil rights that forced the liberal political establishment

---

[1] Johnson reportedly amused himself by playing the tapes of King's trysts.

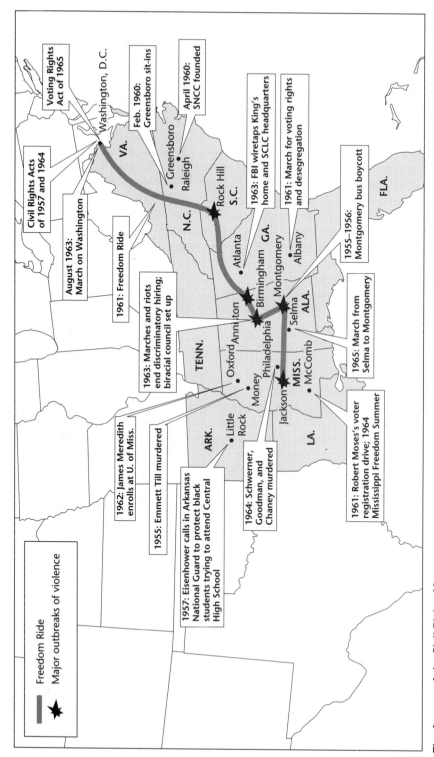

The Apogee of the Civil-Rights Movement.

to act. By 1965 blacks could buy a hamburger at a white restaurant in North Carolina, ride a bus through Alabama, and vote in Mississippi—all impossible in 1960. Public facilities were desegregated; universal suffrage thrived. Jim Crow lay prostrate.

Yet these triumphs, although pivotal, did not bring equality. White prejudice persisted, along with black poverty and its accompanying powerlessness. The civil-rights movement, so effective in fighting legal segregation, had no program for economic equity. Some African-Americans, of course, directly benefited from new educational and economic opportunities. From the midsixties on, the black middle class swelled. But for millions of nonwhites, the legal and judicial victories made little difference in their daily lives. Low levels of education, limited economic opportunities, and relentless prejudice doomed numerous rural and urban blacks to a life of destitution.

Furthermore, the momentum of the civil-rights revolution faltered by middecade. For some within the movement, the legislative and judicial victories that they had struggled to secure brought a sense of completion, and they relaxed. Other younger activists, especially members of SNCC and CORE, had broken with the mainstream civil-rights coalition and grown increasingly militant. After passage of the Voting Rights Act, the movement also shifted its focus to the North, where the majority of the nation's blacks now lived, and where the much-touted civil-rights revolution had made little difference. These blacks could already vote and patronize integrated restaurants. What they needed were solutions to poverty, poor housing, limited job opportunities, *de facto* school segregation—problems that the reforms of 1964–1965 had not even addressed. Increasing numbers of northern blacks languished in urban ghettoes, victimized by discrimination, police brutality, low-paying jobs, and political neglect. For them, the well-publicized civil-rights victories only stirred high expectations that reality would soon dash.

Thus, at the moment of apparent victory, the civil-rights movement began to collapse. In a few years, black militancy, urban rage, white backlash, and the war in Vietnam would destroy the most powerful movement for racial equality ever to arise in American history.

Selected Bibliography

The literature on the civil-rights revolution is immense. Overviews of the movement include Rhoda Lois Blumberg, *Civil Rights: The 1960s Freedom Struggle* (1991 ed.); Robert Weisbrot, *Freedom Bound: A History of America's Civil Rights Movement* (1990); Steven F. Lawson, *Running for Freedom* (1990); Hugh Davis Graham, *The Civil Rights Era: Origins and Development of National Policy, 1960–1972* (1990); Harvard Sitkoff, *The Struggle for Black Equality, 1954–1992* (1993 ed.); Manning Marable, *Race, Reform and Rebellion: The Second Reconstruction in Black America from 1945 to 1982* (1984); Doug McAdam, *Political Process and the Development of Black Insurgency, 1930–1970* (1982); Juan Williams et al., *Eyes on the Prize: America's Civil Rights Years, 1954–1965* (1987), based on the PBS television documentary; and Robert H. Brisbane, *Black Activism: Racial Revolution in the United States, 1954–1970* (1974).

Richard H. King's pathbreaking book, *Civil Rights and the Idea of Freedom* (1992), shows how the movement promoted individual and collective self-transformation in addition to its stated agenda. Aldon D. Morris, *The Origins of the Civil Rights Movement: Black Communities Organizing for Change* (1984), examines the roots of the freedom struggle in earlier leadership networks and stresses the crucial role of the black church.

Taylor Branch's monumental *Parting the Waters: America in the King Years, 1954–1963* (1988) places Martin Luther King, Jr., in the larger political and social context of the era. Equally impressive is David Garrow's *Bearing the Cross: Martin Luther King, Jr., and the Southern Christian Leadership Conference, 1955–1968* (1986). Other excellent studies of King and SCLC include David L. Lewis, *King: A Biography* (1978 ed.); Stephen B. Oates, *Let* the Trumpet Sound: The Life of Martin Luther King, Jr. (1982); and Adam Fairclough, To Redeem the Soul of America: The Southern Christian Leadership Conference and Martin Luther King, Jr. (1987). Essential for understanding King and his philosophy is King's Why We Can't Wait (1964), which contains his "Letter from Birmingham Jail" defending the tactics of direct-action, nonviolent protest.

The Greensboro sit-in that touched off sixties civil-rights protest is the subject of Miles Wolff, Lunch at the Five and Ten: The Greensboro Sit-ins: A Contemporary History (1970), and more impressively in William H. Chafe, Civilities and Civil Rights: Greensboro, North Carolina, and the Black Struggle for Freedom (1980). Studies of activist organizations engaged in civil disobedience include Clayborne Carson, In Struggle: SNCC and the Black Awakening of the 1960s (1981); Howard Zinn, SNCC: The New Abolitionists (1965); and August Meier and Elliott Rudwick, CORE: A Study in the Civil Rights Movement, 1942–1968 (1973).

Carl Brauer's partisan John F. Kennedy and the Second Reconstruction (1977) should be contrasted with Victor Navasky's critical Kennedy Justice (1970). JFK's civil-rights adviser Harris Wofford discusses the administration's efforts on behalf of blacks in his Of Kennedys and Kings: Making Sense of the Sixties (1980). An important study of both the Kennedy and Johnson administrations' role in civil rights is Mark Stern's Calculating Visions: Kennedy, Johnson, and Civil Rights (1992).

Doug McAdam, Freedom Summer (1988), and Mary Aickin Rothschild, A Case of Black and White: Northern Volunteers and the Southern Freedom Summers, 1964–1965 (1982), probe the experiences and interactions of black southern and white northern civil-rights workers in Mississippi. FBI director J. Edgar Hoover's efforts to crush King and the civil-rights movement is detailed in David Garrow's The FBI and Martin Luther King, Jr. (1983). Kenneth O'Reilly, Racial Matters: The FBI's Secret File on Black America, 1960–1972 (1989), examines FBI harassment of the civil-rights movement from a larger perspective.

Congressional debate and maneuvering over the 1964 Civil Rights Act is analyzed in Charles Whalen and Barbara Whalen, The Longest Debate: A Legislative History of the 1964 Civil Rights Act (1985). The impact of the most significant 1965 demonstration is the focus of Charles E. Fager's Selma, 1965: The March That Changed the South (1985 ed.), and David Garrow's Protest at Selma, Martin Luther King, Jr., and the Voting Rights Act of 1965 (1978).

One of the best ways to comprehend the courage, conflict, and complexity of the civil-rights activists and their movement is to read firsthand accounts by participants. Two excellent oral histories are Howell Raines, My Soul Is Rested: Movement Days in the Deep South Remembered (1983), and Henry Hampton and Steve Fayer, Voices of Freedom (1990). Other outstanding movement memoirs include Mary King, Freedom Song: A Personal Story of the 1960s Civil Rights Movement (1987); James Peck, Freedom Ride (1962); Anne Moody, Coming of Age in Mississippi (1970); Sally Belfrage, Freedom Summer (1965); Elizabeth Sutherland, ed., Letters from Mississippi (1965); James Meredith, Three Years in Mississippi (1966); James Forman, The Making of Black Revolutionaries (1972); and James Farmer, Lay Bare the Heart: An Autobiography of the Civil Rights Movement (1985).

5

IN QUEST OF
THE GREAT SOCIETY

For a unique historic moment, John F. Kennedy's death united Americans as none of his accomplishments in life had. The ultimate impact of this crisis-driven consensus would hinge on the role of the slain president's successor, Lyndon Baines Johnson.

Vice President Johnson accompanied Kennedy that tragic November day in Dallas, riding in an open car a short distance behind the president. When the fatal shots rang out, a secret-service agent pushed Johnson to the floor of the car and covered him with his own body. After doctors pronounced Kennedy dead, Dallas police drove Johnson to Love Field, where he boarded *Air Force One* and took the oath of office standing beside a stunned Jacqueline Kennedy. When the aircraft landed at Andrews Air Force Base outside Washington early that evening, it bore both the living and dead presidents. ''I will do my best,'' Johnson told the mourning crowd. ''That is all I can do. I ask for your help, and God's.''

Johnson faced a formidable task. Many people harbored misgivings about him because he hailed from Texas, the state where Kennedy was assassinated. Among liberals, he had a reputation as an untrustworthy backroom wheeler-dealer. African-Americans worried that as a southerner, Johnson might make even less of a commitment to civil rights than had the slain president. Reporters distrusted him. Postassassination memories of Kennedy recalled his polish and charisma as well as the aristocratic image that he had cultivated. Handsome, articulate, witty, and courageous, Kennedy had seemed a statesman above "dirty" politics. By contrast, LBJ came across as a poorly educated Texas provincial who could never hope to shake his "mere politician" image.[1]

Burly, loud, and coarse, Johnson struck many observers as arrogant, ambitious, suspicious, vain, and vulgar. His private, earthy invectives were legendary. Johnson called one person so dumb that "he couldn't pour piss from a boot with instructions written on the heel." He was known to conduct business while sitting on the toilet in full view of his associates. In small gatherings, his endless anecdotes and salty humor captivated listeners, but before large audiences and on television, his attempts at humility and solemnity sometimes sounded forced, and his Texas drawl grated on many northern ears.

Yet Johnson enjoyed important assets. He brought vast political experience to the presidency, having served in Washington since the New Deal, first as a congressman's aide, then as a congressman, later as senator, as senate majority leader, and finally as vice president. Possessing limitless energy, he was an immensely skilled politician who knew the workings of Capitol Hill intimately. He also had cultivated close relationships with powerful senators, both liberal and conservative.

Johnson had another advantage in the national mood. Shocked and confused by Kennedy's assassination, Americans yearned for strong leadership, and LBJ filled this need. As senate majority leader, he had earned an unequaled reputation for pressuring and plotting to win legislative victories. Now as president he applied his skills to coax Congress into passing reform bills, to win where Kennedy had lost, and to build a solid base for the 1964 presidential election.

Keenly aware of the vast outpouring of pro-Kennedy feeling, Johnson did everything in his power to assure the nation that his objectives matched his predecessor's, and he portrayed himself as the "dutiful executor" of Kennedy's program. Wrapping himself in the slain president's mantle, he pleaded with Kennedy's staff to stay on in the new administration. Some of JFK's high officials would become key figures in the Johnson administration. Others who soon left the government nevertheless provided an important symbol of continuity.

Addressing both houses of Congress five days after the assassination, Johnson intoned, "All I have, I would have given gladly not to be standing here today." He went on to exhort lawmakers to enact the "ideals" of the Kennedy administration: "Let us here highly resolve that John Fitzgerald Kennedy did not die in vain." He especially emphasized the need to pass the pending civil-rights bill as a tribute to the late president: "No memorial oration or eulogy could more eloquently honor President Kennedy's memory than the earliest possible passage of the civil-rights bill for which he fought."

From the outset, Johnson aspired to be a great president, and he embraced his new responsibilities with high energy and optimism. As a Texan and a southerner, however,

---

[1] Lyndon Baines Johnson liked to be referred to as LBJ and put the LBJ brand on those around him. Although his wife, Claudia, had been called Lady Bird since childhood, he christened his daughters Lynda Bird and Lucy Baines and called his dog Little Beagle. When he bought a ranch in 1951, he dubbed it the LBJ Ranch.

he realized that to succeed he must gain recognition as a national leader. By focusing on civil rights and identifying himself closely with Kennedy, he hoped to achieve this goal.

A man of paradox, Johnson clearly lusted for power, yet he exhibited sincere concern for victims of poverty or racial prejudice. Despite his desire to dominate and his support for sweeping, controversial reforms, he craved consensus and love. For a time, he scored successes in building both national unity and social progress. He brilliantly finessed the difficult transition of power; he cajoled Congress into passing virtually all of the blocked Kennedy agenda; he won a landslide victory in 1964; and in 1965–1966 he pushed through Congress one of the most massive outpourings of liberal legislation in American history.

Ultimately, however, his efforts to create what he termed the "Great Society" failed. His rhetorical emphasis on equality and social justice ran far ahead of legislative reality and provoked passionate but unfulfilled expectations among blacks and the economically disadvantaged. From the mid- to late sixties, frustration bred of dashed hopes erupted in violence, especially among African-Americans in the ghettoes of the nation's largest cities. Concurrently, the civil-rights movement splintered as SNCC and CORE came to advocate Black Power rather than integration. These developments spurred a conservative backlash that would challenge the very premises of liberal social reform. Above all, LBJ's conduct of the war in Vietnam undermined all that he had hoped to achieve.

LBJ

Born in 1908 near Johnson City in southwestern Texas, Lyndon Baines Johnson endured a painful childhood. A bright, sensitive boy, he suffered from his parents' conflicting demands. Sam Johnson, his father, was a hard-drinking, storytelling farmer and speculator who drove the family fortune from boom to bust. His back-slapping populist campaigning won him several terms in the state legislature. He tried to domineer his son and taught young Lyndon the crude, gregarious ways of southwest Texas Democratic party politics.

LBJ's mother, Rebekah Baines Johnson, was cut from a different cloth. The granddaughter of the founder of Baylor University and the descendant of a long line of Baptist ministers, she was a pious, genteel woman ill suited to the boorishness of small-town Texas. While Sam Johnson attempted to bestow his sense of manliness on young Lyndon, the boy's mother strove to raise her child as a well-bred patrician, curling his hair, reading him refined Victorian poetry, and coaxing him into taking violin lessons.

When Lyndon sought to win his mother's affection by adopting her values, he alienated his father and his peers. Yet when the boy failed to behave in what his mother deemed a proper manner, she dramatized her disapproval with long, stony silences. LBJ ultimately emulated his father in most ways, becoming a whiskey-drinking wheeler-dealer politician disdainful of intellectuals and proud of his masculinity. Nevertheless, a sense of failure would haunt him for not having lived up to his mother's standards. Throughout his life, he would battle feelings of insecurity and seemingly seek the approval that his mother had withheld. Tortured by his parents' opposing values, as an adult he aspired to unite persons of contending factions and to forge consensus.

Upon graduating from high school, Lyndon spurned his mother's advice to attend college. He escaped the family squabbles and traveled to California, where for more than a year he worked at picking fruit, washing dishes, and pumping gas before taking a position as a clerk with a Los Angeles lawyer, a cousin of his mother. Finally returning to Texas, he enrolled in 1927 at Southwest Texas State Teachers' College at San Marcos, where he became the trusted student assistant of the college president and a dominant force on campus.

After a brief stint at teaching Mexican-American children in the south Texas town of Cotulla and high school in Houston, Johnson, with his father's help, secured a job as an administrative assistant to Texas congressman Richard Kleberg. Washington politics now became the center of LBJ's universe. Befriending powerful people, particularly influential Texas congressman Sam Rayburn, LBJ quickly earned recognition as an up-and-coming young politician. In 1934 he married Claudia "Lady Bird" Taylor, also of Texas. Lyndon's bride was gracious, bright, politically astute, and devoted to her husband's career.

With Rayburn's backing, LBJ returned to Texas in 1935 to direct the state's branch of the National Youth Administration, a New Deal work-relief agency aimed at helping unemployed youths. Throwing himself into his new position, within six months Johnson had found employment for more than eighteen thousand young people and had won notice in Washington. On a visit to Texas in 1936, Eleanor Roosevelt publicly praised his efforts.

Running for Congress in 1937 to fill a vacant seat in his home district, Johnson distinguished himself in a ten-man field by being the only candidate to support the New Deal unequivocally. With the endorsement of the Roosevelt administration, LBJ triumphed in the election. Soon President Franklin Roosevelt, vacationing on the Texas Gulf Coast, took the opportunity to meet the new congressman. Captivated by the younger man's energy and flattery, FDR took a fatherly interest in LBJ's career and helped him to gain appointment to the prestigious House Naval Affairs Committee. For his part, Johnson became Roosevelt's strongest southern supporter, although on occasion he found it expedient to vote against the president in order to court his increasingly conservative Texas constituents.

In 1941 Johnson narrowly lost his bid for a Senate seat to Governor W. Lee "Pappy" O'Daniel, a former country-and-western radio personality and archconservative. Returning to the House, Johnson, without resigning his seat, served for seven months as a lieutenant commander in the navy after Pearl Harbor. He won a Silver Star for gallantry, before FDR ordered all congressmen to return to their duties on Capitol Hill.

After FDR's death in 1945, Johnson, like many other former New Dealers, moved to the political right. Realizing the increasing power of conservative, oil, aircraft, and cotton interests in Texas, LBJ voted for the antilabor Taft-Hartley bill, opposed civil-rights legislation, and strongly supported the Cold War and the domestic anticommunist agenda. In 1948 he again campaigned for the Senate and this time squeaked through the Democratic primary by eighty-seven votes (after an additional two hundred Johnson votes were reported from a notoriously corrupt precinct three days after the election).

"The Treatment." LBJ early learned the value of working his political opponents and fellow democrats — skills that served him well in the White House.

"Landslide Lyndon" was on his way to the U.S. Senate, where his political career would flower.

Johnson looked out for Texas oil interests to ensure his reelection but steered a nondoctrinaire middle course in the Senate. Moreover, by adroitly tiptoeing between his party's conservative and liberal factions, he managed to gain favor with both diehard southern reactionaries such as Richard Russell of Georgia and northern reformers such as Hubert Humphrey of Minnesota. He made it his business to know all his Democratic colleagues' likes and dislikes and learned how to ingratiate himself with them. Unlike John F. Kennedy, who in eight years in the Senate never became one of "the boys," Lyndon Johnson emerged as the dominant insider. In 1952 his colleagues elected him Democratic whip. The following year he was chosen as minority leader, and when the Democrats regained control of the Senate in 1955, LBJ became majority leader.

No one before or since has dominated the U.S. Senate as Johnson did. Recognizing Eisenhower's immense popularity, he collaborated with the Republican administration, particularly on matters of foreign affairs and national defense. Johnson aspired to the presidency and, realizing that no southerner could win that office without endorsing civil rights, in 1957 and 1960 he painstakingly pushed compromises between reluctant southerners and northern liberals that permitted the first civil-rights legislation since Reconstruction. He also encouraged the creation of the National Aeronautics and Space Administration (NASA) after the *Sputnik* launching. Finally, he propelled such moderately liberal measures as an increase in the minimum wage, a public-housing bill, and the addition of disability payments to the Social Security system.

Johnson persuaded not through public debate but through behind-the-scenes manipulation. ''The Johnson Treatment,'' according to columnists Rowland Evans and Robert Novak, ''could last ten minutes or four hours'' and could occur ''whenever Johnson might find a fellow Senator within his reach. Its tone could be supplication, accusation, cajolery, exuberance, scorn, tears, complaint, the hint of threat. . . . Interjections from the target were rare. Johnson anticipated them before they could be spoken. . . . The Treatment was an almost hypnotic experience and rendered the target stunned and helpless.'' By 1960 such tactics and legislative successes had made Lyndon Johnson the most influential Democrat in Washington. Now he craved the presidency.

However, the style that had served him so well in the Senate did not garner him public appeal, and his temperament, regional background, and personal ways ill suited him as a presidential candidate. Easily defeated by the charismatic Kennedy and his lavishly financed, well-oiled political machine, Johnson accepted JFK's offer of the vice-presidential nomination and helped to secure the Democrats' triumph, particularly as they carried Texas.

Kennedy and Johnson never developed a close working relationship. LBJ was disconsolate in office and hated taking orders from the young president and erstwhile insignificant senator. Frustrated by the lack of opportunity to exercise power, ill at ease and insecure among the brilliant and glamorous denizens of ''Camelot,'' Johnson later recalled detesting ''every minute'' as vice president. All this changed on that fateful November 22, 1963. . . .

Lyndon Johnson once compared Americans at the time of Kennedy's assassination to ''a bunch of cattle caught in the swamp, unable to move in either direction, simply circling 'round and 'round. . . . I knew what had to be done. There is but one way to get the cattle out of the swamps. And that is for the man on the horse to take the lead, to assume command, to provide direction. In the period of confusion after the assassination, I was that man.'' Almost immediately after Kennedy's death, Johnson contacted important labor, civil-rights, religious, educational, and political leaders and urged them to ''put aside their selfish aims in the larger cause of the nation's interest.'' The morning following the assassination, the new president even sent a telegram to folk singer Joan Baez assuring her that the grand gala at which she had agreed to perform for Kennedy would go on ''just as the late beloved President Kennedy would have wanted it to be.''

In his State of the Union address in January 1964, Johnson stressed three major legislative priorities: civil rights, a tax cut, and what he termed ''an unconditional war on poverty.'' The climate of national remorse, combined with Johnson's resourcefulness, won him a series of spectacular legislative victories in 1964. By summer, his three priorities would become laws.

The tax cut, based on Keynesian principles and first proposed by Kennedy in January 1963, aimed to use deficit spending to stimulate economic growth and to smooth the cycle of boom and bust. Enacted in February 1964, the measure slashed corporate and individual taxes by more than $11.5 billion. The bill soon achieved the results that Walter Heller and other economists had predicted. In 1965 the GNP grew by 8 percent; in 1966, by 9 percent. By 1968 average real annual family income stood at $8,000, exactly doubled from a decade earlier. Unemployment had fallen to less than 4 percent, and, because of heightened productivity, federal tax revenues rose and kept federal deficits low. Americans luxuriated in the biggest boom of the postwar period.

Yet true national prosperity, Johnson believed, necessitated aiding those at the

Poverty Amid Abundance. The dilapidated tenement on the right that was occupied by African-Americans contrasts markedly with the modern high-rise apartment on an adjacent Chicago street.

bottom of the economic ladder. The vast funds pouring into the federal treasury made it seem possible to eliminate poverty and to fund an array of social programs without undue sacrifice from the rest of the population. With high confidence, Johnson and his advisers, mostly Kennedy technocrats, began planning the all-out war against want.

Johnson himself had witnessed hardship. As a young teacher in the late 1920s, he noted that his students, mostly Mexican-Americans, "often came to class without breakfast, hungry. They knew even in their youth the pain of injustice. . . . Somehow you never forget what poverty and hatred can do when you see its scars on the hopeful face of a young child."

In the midsixties, as now, poverty wrought immense suffering in America. When Johnson began his crusade, destitution plagued a whopping one in four Americans. Postwar affluence had reduced the percentage of the populace living in want but had not created an equitable distribution of income. At the time of Kennedy's murder, the richest 20 percent of Americans owned 77 percent of the nation's wealth, whereas the poorest 20 percent possessed a mere 0.05 percent. Industrial automation; lack of adequate education; poor health; and discrimination based on race, gender, class, and age all worsened the problem. Certain areas of America, such as the languishing mill towns of the Northeast, the Rust Belt cities of the Midwest, and rural Appalachia, were particularly depressed. Johnson assumed that the nation had amassed enough abundance to aid these unfortunates and pledged an all-out "War on Poverty."

In March 1964, the president introduced the economic opportunity bill. Passed in August, the act created the Office of Economic Opportunity, which, headed by Kennedy's brother-in-law Sargent Shriver, coordinated the antipoverty activities of various federal agencies. The law established the Job Corps to teach marketable skills to youths between ages sixteen and twenty-five. It also created VISTA (Volunteers in the Service of America), a domestic version of the Peace Corps that sent young recruits to work in poverty-stricken areas, and the Community Action Program, which encouraged the "maximum feasible participation" of the poor in making decisions that affected them. The bill offered loans to businesses hiring the chronically unemployed and other educational and job-training benefits. Congress later added the Head Start program to aid preschool children and the Upward Bound program that offered promising but impoverished high schoolers a chance at college. With high optimism and an initial budget of $800 million, social workers and economists set out to vanquish poverty.

Conceived by task forces staffed largely by academic social scientists, this omnibus antipoverty program exemplified midsixties liberals' faith in social engineering. Economic growth, they assumed, would generate sufficient tax revenue to pay for a broad spectrum of social welfare measures, abolish destitution, and open up economic opportunity. Liberal intellectuals and politicians believed that government programs would lead the way to a more decent and equitable America without resorting to redistributing wealth from rich to poor.

The final key victory for Johnson in 1964 came with the passage of the Civil Rights Act, to which he had brought a convert's zeal. As we have seen, LBJ rolled over legislative roadblocks and built enough crucial Republican support to pressure Congress into enacting a law considerably stronger than Kennedy's original plan.

Election '64

By the time Congress adjourned in October 1964, President Johnson had achieved most of his legislative goals. In addition to his three major priorities—civil rights, the War on Poverty, and the tax cut—he had pushed through a mass-transit bill, an expanded food-stamp program, increased federal aid to higher education, a $1 billion housing program, and a wilderness-preservation act.

Most of Johnson's 1964 legislation derived from plans drawn up during the Kennedy years. Although LBJ initially had presented himself as the executor of Kennedy's policies, increasingly he wished to distinguish his administration from his predecessor's New Frontier. In a May 1964 commencement address at the University of Michigan, Johnson, determined to put his own stamp on the presidency, offered his Great Society vision: "We have the opportunity to move not only toward the rich society and the powerful society, but upward to the Great Society." He spoke of an America of "abundance and liberty for all" with "an end to poverty and racial injustice." In this idyllic world, people would be "more concerned with the quality of their goals than the quantity of their goods."

To make his vision real, Johnson foresaw a major expansion of federal functions. Not only would government accept responsibility for the poor, it would grapple with the very quality of life. He envisioned an America where "the city of man serves not only the needs of the body and the demands of commerce but the desire for beauty and hunger for community." Indeed, by the 1960s, the idea of using the state to improve the lives of its citizens had been ripening for nearly a century. As individuals grappled with economic forces over which they had little control in an increasingly complex urban-industrial society, reformers from the late nineteenth century on had advocated an activist government to intervene on behalf of the less fortunate. The Progressive movement of the early twentieth century strengthened government's welfare and regulatory functions, but it was Franklin Roosevelt's New Deal that brought the government directly into American lives as never before. From Social Security and unemployment insurance through various public works and welfare programs, the New Deal eased human suffering and convinced millions of the goodness of government.

Not all Americans agreed. In the nineteenth century, liberals had espoused laissez faire, the belief in a limited role for government. Over the twentieth century, however, as liberals increasingly endorsed the welfare state, conservatives, who had once venerated state power, adopted the laissez-faire philosophy. In the flush of enthusiasm for government programs that Roosevelt's New Deal created, it was easy to overlook the deep fear of big government that many Americans harbored. Nevertheless, these apprehensions persisted in the postwar years and surfaced in the later sixties in opposition to LBJ's Great Society.

Oblivious to such conservative qualms, Lyndon Johnson plunged ahead with his reformist plans. Having come to political maturity as a staunch New Dealer, he, far more than Kennedy, believed in the benevolence of big government. He remembered the New Deal positively and now wished to surpass the reform record of his mentor, Franklin Roosevelt. No longer forced to cater solely to his Texas constituents, he could abandon the cautious politics of his past and forge on with his grandiose dream.

The first test of the popularity of Johnson's policies and proposals came during the November 1964 election. Fearing that his political rival, attorney general Robert Kennedy, would seek the vice-presidential nomination, LBJ announced the exclusion of any member of his cabinet from consideration for the second spot on the ticket. He then dominated the Democratic convention, which met in late August at Atlantic City. With two forty-foot portraits of himself towering above the convention rostrum and delegates dutifully singing the convention theme song, "Hello, Lyndon," to the tune of the Broadway show song "Hello, Dolly," LBJ easily won the nomination on the first ballot. He then chose Minnesota Senator Hubert Humphrey as his running mate.

One note of discord disturbed the Atlantic City celebration, however: the determined delegates from the Mississippi Freedom Democratic party (see Chapter 4) challenged the right of the all-white official delegation to represent the state. The president's supporters forced through a compromise, antagonizing civil-rights activists and white southern politicians alike. Jubilant Democrats paid little heed to these dissensions, but disgruntled black militants and conservative southerners foreshadowed the strife that lay ahead as LBJ set out to build his Great Society.

As another indication that not all Americans shared the president's vision, a white backlash against civil rights emerged. Johnson's racial liberalism naturally alienated southern segregationists, but the strong showing of Alabama's avowedly racist governor George Wallace in northern Democratic primaries in the spring of 1964 revealed substantial white reaction there as well. In early April, Wallace surprised political analysts by winning 34 percent of the votes cast in Wisconsin's Democratic primary. Soon he garnered nearly 30 percent of the vote in Indiana and almost 43 percent in Maryland. Wallace ran particularly well in white, working-class, "ethnic" neighborhoods but also earned substantial backing among middle-class suburbanites, especially in Wisconsin and Indiana, where state laws permitted Republicans to vote in the Democratic primary.

This backlash against racial equality proved only one facet of a burgeoning conservatism in midsixties America. Since the late forties, a number of conservative intellectuals had challenged America's postwar consensus on foreign, domestic, and even moral issues. Instead of containment, conservatives sought victory over communism; in place of the welfare state, they advocated laissez faire; in lieu of what they viewed as the moral relativism and mass culture of the postwar years, they embraced the absolute moral standards of Christianity and the genteel traditions of Western civilizations. This self-styled new conservatism dated back to 1944 with the publication of Friedrich von Hayek's *The Road to Serfdom*. A Viennese refugee from Nazism, Hayek had warned Americans of the threat to freedom that he found inherent in social planning. Political liberty, he argued, depended on economic freedom. In his view, the growth of the welfare state in the United States, if not stopped, would lead inexorably to totalitarianism of either the Nazi or Soviet variety.

In the postwar years, conservatives, influenced by Hayek, came to see the fight against the welfare state as vitally linked to the struggle against international communism. In the late forties and fifties, a number of influential publications combined the call for militant anticommunism with economic libertarianism and cultural traditionalism. Among the most important conservative books were Richard Weaver's *Ideas Have Consequences* (1949), ex-communist Whittaker Chambers's *Witness* (1952), Russell Kirk's *The Conservative Mind* (1953), Clinton Rossiter's *Conservatism in America* (1956), and William Buckley's *Up from Liberalism* (1959). In 1955 Buckley launched the *National Review,* which soon became the most influential journal of conservative opinion. On a more popular level, the *Reader's Digest* brought conservative views to millions of American households.

In addition to an intellectual Right, the late fifties and early sixties saw the emergence of an extremist ''Radical Right'' that viewed the world in conspiratorial terms. By 1964 literally hundreds of organizations had cropped up that identified with the Radical Right. Among the best known were Robert Welch's John Birch Society, Reverend Billy Joe Hargis's Christian Crusade, and Dr. Frederich Charles Schwartz's Christian Anti-Communist Crusade. These groups believed that communists aimed to destroy America and that an eastern liberal establishment supported this conspiracy. They opposed the United Nations, foreign aid, civil rights, the income tax, Social Security, and especially Earl Warren and his liberal Supreme Court. With access to TV and radio, best-selling books such as Hargis's *Communist America: Must It Be?* and even a cadre of about thirty thousand armed and trained anticommunist minutemen, the Radical Right had become a powerful force.

Conservatism also flourished on college campuses. As early as 1952, libertarian Frank Chodorov had founded the Intercollegiate Society of Individualists (ISI) with the stated purpose of fomenting ''the organization of campus cells for the study and discussion of Individualist ideas and theories.'' By the late fifties, ISI was sending out thousands of pieces of literature and had established conservative clubs at more than a hundred colleges and universities. Youthful conservatism received a further boost with the founding of Young Americans for Freedom in 1960. Launched under the guidance of William Buckley, Jr., with generous funding from conservative corporate and banking interests, YAF pledged to save the free-market economy and to triumph over communism. YAF became one of the fastest growing campus organizations in the early sixties and worked to nurture conservatism within the Republican party.

By the early sixties, many older Republicans also had grown disenchanted with moderate Republicans such as Eisenhower, who had accepted the basic reforms of the

Campaign '64. Democratic campaign posters such as these associating Republican presidential candidate Barry Goldwater with the extreme right and nuclear war helped to carry Lyndon Johnson to a landslide election victory.

New Deal. Believing that Nixon's defeat in 1960 had stemmed from the GOP's catering to New York governor Nelson Rockefeller and other liberal eastern Republicans, conservatives began a grass-roots campaign to gain control of the party and to nominate a conservative. In the July 1964 Republican convention, they jubilantly named Senator Barry Goldwater of Arizona as their party's presidential candidate.

Whereas Johnson looked forward to extending vastly the role of government through social and economic reforms, Goldwater challenged the very concept of liberalism. Except for a strong military, Goldwater believed that federal functions should be strictly limited. In his book, *The Conscience of a Conservative* (1960), he had advocated abolishment of the graduated income tax, the sale of the Tennessee Valley Authority, and the gradual abandonment of federal social and welfare programs, including Social Security.

Although not a member of the organized Radical Right, Goldwater shared many of their views, and at the Republican convention his supporters decisively defeated a liberal resolution denouncing "extremist groups" like the Birch Society. In his acceptance speech, Goldwater thrilled the Radical Right with his avowal that "extremism in the defense of liberty is no vice, . . . moderation in the pursuit of justice is no virtue."

Millions of Americans shared Goldwater's views, yet he faced manifold obstacles in the election. Because he stood decidedly to the right of the mainstream, Democrats portrayed him as dangerous and easily exploited popular fears about a Republican victory. His candidacy allowed Johnson to champion the social reforms of his Great Society while still appearing moderate next to Goldwater. Moreover, Goldwater's opposition to civil-rights laws alienated black voters and supporters of the freedom movement. The aged feared that he would dismantle Social Security, and labor took alarm at his advocacy of right-to-work laws. Even his views on foreign policy came back to haunt him. Goldwater had voted against the nuclear-test-ban treaty and had talked of giving commanders of the North Atlantic Treaty Organization (NATO) control over nuclear weapons. He also favored escalation of the war in Vietnam, now heating up, and criticized the Democrats for failing to pursue total victory there. Democrats hurried to depict him as a "trigger-happy" warmonger. While Republican billboards proclaimed, "In Your Heart You Know He's Right," Democrats countered with bumper stickers reading, "In Your Guts You Know He's Nuts" and "In Your Heart You Know He Might." One powerful Democratic TV ad pictured a child picking off daisy petals; the scene then dissolved into an ominous mushroom cloud. Republican protests forced the removal of the ad, but the Democrats had made their point: Goldwater was the dangerous extremist; Johnson, the restrained moderate.

The president also painted himself as the peace candidate, although LBJ and his closest advisers had already formulated plans for expanding America's role in Vietnam, as we shall see in Chapter 6. "We seek no wider war," he assured the people. "We are not going to send American boys nine or ten thousand miles from home to do what Asian boys ought to be doing for themselves."

The overall strategy worked. Johnson polled over 61 percent of the popular vote and carried forty-four states, losing only five states in the Deep South and Goldwater's home state of Arizona. In the new Congress, Democrats fared equally well, surging to a majority of 68–32 in the Senate and an overwhelming 295–140 edge in the House. Not since 1936 had a president enjoyed such congressional advantages. Elected in his own right by a huge popular vote and presiding over a liberal Congress, LBJ seemed ready to realize his Great Society vision.

At the time, most commentators saw the Republican debacle as the final discrediting of conservatism. Yet the support that Goldwater gathered among white southerners, as well as northern blue-collar workers and white-collar suburbanites, revealed a growing trend toward grass-roots conservatism. Although branded a reactionary who would dismantle the welfare system and bring on World War III, Goldwater still won some 27 million votes. Developments in the later sixties would spur the growth of this constituency. Indeed, Hollywood actor Ronald Reagan became one immediate beneficiary of the Goldwater campaign. Reagan's well-publicized TV speech for Goldwater late in the campaign transformed the actor into a political figure and launched him in politics, gaining him the governorship of California two years later.

Liberalism Triumphant

In his January 1965 State of the Union address, Lyndon Johnson scarcely touched on foreign affairs and made no mention whatever of John F. Kennedy. "We're only at

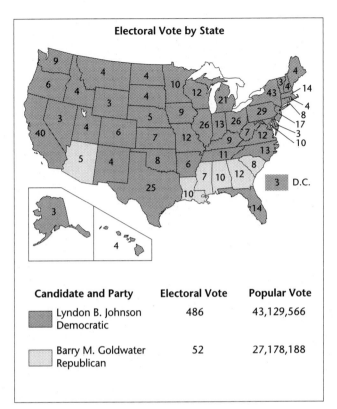

Electoral Vote by State

Presidential Election of 1964.

Candidate and Party	Electoral Vote	Popular Vote
Lyndon B. Johnson Democratic	486	43,129,566
Barry M. Goldwater Republican	52	27,178,188

the beginning of the road to the Great Sociey," he announced. "Ahead now is a summit where freedom from the wants of the body can help fulfill the needs of the spirit."

Eager to capitalize on his lopsided victory, Johnson established task forces staffed by equally eager liberal social scientists convinced that prosperity could transform American society without undue class conflict. "Hurry, boys, hurry," Johnson exhorted his aides. "Get that legislation up to the hill and out. Eighteen months from now ol' Landslide Lyndon will be Lame-Duck Lyndon." The president's boundless vision included providing federal funds to support the arts, scientific research, and the poor; additional and better schools; racial equality; clean air and water; free health care for the aged and impoverished; and improved highways stripped of unsightly billboards. All this and more seemed within reach.

Impressed by the Johnson mandate and swelled with newly elected liberals, the Eighty-ninth Congress rallied to the presidential program. Nearly every Johnson request became law. Only half in jest, *New Yorker* political correspondent Richard Rovere wrote, "If the President decides that it would be nice to have a coast-to-coast tunnel, he need only call in some engineers and lawyers to put the scheme in order, advise Congress of his wishes, and begin letting contracts." During the congressional session of 1965–1966, some forty major laws were enacted, the greatest torrent of domestic reform since the midthirties.

Several more important measures included Medicare, a program of health insurance for the aged, and Medicaid, medical assistance for the poor. An elementary- and secondary-education act provided $1.3 billion in federal aid for low-income pupils in both public and private schools. The Higher Education Act granted scholarships and loans for university students. As part of the War on Poverty, Congress voted over $1 billion for the regional development of an eleven-state Appalachian Mountain area and granted the Office of Economic Opportunity expanded functions and higher finances. A housing and urban development act made funds available for new housing, contributed rent supplements for the poor, and created the new cabinet-level Department of Housing and Urban Affairs. A model-cities bill authorized $1 billion for slum clearance and the construction of model communities. Congress also raised and broadened both the minimum wage and Social Security.

As part of Johnson's emphasis on improving the quality of life, legislation encouraged the beautification of highways and established restrictions on air and water pollution. The National Foundation of the Arts and Humanities Act instituted federal support for artistic and cultural activities. Truth-in-lending and packaging bills aided consumers, as did the Highway Safety Act, which set automobile and highway safety standards. This latter bill derived in large measure from the influence of Ralph Nader's widely read critique of the auto industry, *Unsafe at Any Speed* (1965). Congress also repealed the discriminatory national-origins system for determining immigration quotas.

The Voting Rights Act passed, too, less a result of long-range Great Society planning than the response to the pressures of the civil-rights movement. Nevertheless, the Johnson administration took full credit when the new law helped to reconstruct the South. To emphasize further his commitment to African-American political equality, LBJ appointed Robert Weaver, the first black cabinet officer, to head the new Department of Housing and Urban Affairs, and named former NAACP lawyer Thurgood Marshall as the first black Supreme Court justice.

In addition to the plethora of liberal legislation in the midsixties, the Supreme Court also played a major role in strengthening American liberalism. Beginning in 1954 with the crucial *Brown* decision, the Court, headed by Chief Justice Earl Warren, continued its liberal, activist role. In decisions handed down in 1956–1957, the Court had upheld the rights of alleged communists, and so incurred the wrath of the Radical Right. By the time Kennedy took office, the John Birch Society had dotted the land with billboards demanding IMPEACH EARL WARREN.

In the sixties, the addition of two Kennedy and two Johnson appointees—Byron White, Arthur Goldberg, Abe Fortas, and Marshall—fortified the liberal bent of the Court. That tribunal upheld the sit-ins of the early 1960s and validated the Civil Rights Act of 1964 and the Voting Rights Act of 1965. In *Engel* v. *Vitale* (1962), the justices prohibited prayer in the classroom. In *Baker* v. *Carr* (1962) and a series of later cases, the Court struck down legislative malapportionment and declared population the only basis for representation. A 1966 decision outlawed the poll tax in all elections.

The Court further enraged conservatives with a series of decisions broadening the rights of accused criminals. In *Gideon* v. *Wainwright* (1963), it decreed that poor defendants charged with a felony must have an attorney; *Escobedo* v. *Illinois* (1964) declared that police must permit alleged offenders to consult with lawyers during interrogation; and in *Miranda* v. *Arizona* (1966), the Court required police to warn all arrested suspects that any statement that they make can be used against them and that they have the right to remain silent and to obtain free legal counsel. Like Johnson's

Great Society legislation, these judicial decisions aimed at benefiting the underprivileged and powerless. But by shaping national policy without legislative mandate, the Supreme Court provoked a conservative backlash that still affects American politics.

Despite indications of a rising antiliberal reaction, by the end of the legislative session of 1966, elated liberals looked forward to the speedy end of poverty, racism, and other forms of discrimination. With an activist Court and Congress, led by a president committed to social justice, America's long reformist tradition seemed to have reached fruition. Applauding the accomplishments of the Eighty-ninth Congress, House Speaker John McCormack called it "the Congress of accomplished hopes" and "realized dreams." Lyndon Johnson bragged to senators in 1966, "They say Jack Kennedy had style, but I'm the one who got the bills passed."

The president had reason to be proud. His Great Society programs, although flawed, alleviated some of the nation's worst social and economic ills. The Johnson legislation gave nonwhites legal equality and greater access to political power. The War on Poverty and other social and welfare programs redressed some problems of privation. Between 1964 and 1969, the number of people officially classified as poor dropped from more than 42 million to about 25 million. Government programs also eased some of the worst conditions attendant to poverty, among them inadequate medical care, malnutrition, and overcrowded and substandard housing. The Head Start program provided thousands of low-income children with early educational opportunities and increased the potential of these children for later educational and employment success. Job training taught thousands of unemployed teens and adults employable skills. African-Americans particularly advanced their economic status. In 1965 black-family income had averaged only 54 percent of white-family income, but by 1969 it had climbed to 60 percent. Although these improvements derived partly from the larger economic boom, Great Society programs strengthened them. Equally important, Johnson's legislation sharpened Americans' awareness of poverty and racism.

The Dream Fizzles

Before the election of 1964, Johnson's friend and speechwriter Horace Busby had warned the president of a potential white backlash to his civil-rights and antipoverty programs. "America's real majority," he claimed, "is suffering a minority complex of neglect. They have become the real foes of Negro rights, foreign aid, etc., because . . . they feel forgotten." Going on to win his landslide election and ignoring Busby's warning, LBJ hoped that his programs' success would unite behind him a solid consensus of contented Americans.

Yet regardless of the flood of liberal legislation, by 1966 all was not as the president had hoped. The consensus that he so desired began to give way to disorder and doubt. Part of the problem stemmed from the reaction that Busby had prophesied. Numerous Americans resented programs aimed to benefit the poor in general and nonwhites in particular. A fall 1966 Gallup poll found 52 percent of white respondents critical of the administration for pushing too hard on civil rights, whereas only 10 percent answered that Johnson was not acting fast enough.

That year's November elections reflected this backlash. Except in the Deep South, most candidates were too subtle to denounce nonwhites openly, but many Republicans campaigned against "crime in the streets" and "open-housing" legislation. The Democrats lost forty-seven seats in the House, a shift that protected their substantial majority, yet ended the brief period of liberal dominance in Congress. In California, conservative Republican Ronald Reagan defeated liberal Democratic incumbent governor Pat Brown by nearly a million votes. In Illinois, longtime liberal stalwart Paul Douglas lost his bid for a fourth term in the Senate.

White reaction was not the only factor undermining Johnson's efforts. The domestic effects of the Vietnam War lay behind much of the disquiet brewing throughout the nation. In 1966 Johnson spent over twenty times more money to wage the war in Vietnam than he spent for his War on Poverty. Vietnam hurt the poor by curbing funds for antipoverty programs and unleashed an inflationary spiral. When Johnson began escalating the war in 1965, he felt confident that the nation could afford both warfare and welfare. Yet by 1966, with the United States spending nearly $20 billion on the conflict in Southeast Asia, federal budget deficits rose—and so did inflation. About 2.5 percent in 1966, inflation climbed to 3 percent annually by 1967 and over 5 percent by 1968. Although low compared with later times, these numbers marked the end of several years of relative price stability. From the midsixties on, wage earners' purchasing power, which for most workers had risen since World War II, began to level off and in some cases even to decline. This start of what would become the Great Inflation fueled the widespread discontent of the time, undermined Johnson's popularity, and weakened support for his domestic reforms.

Even without war and white backlash, it is doubtful that Johnson could have made his Great Society vision real. Throughout the Kennedy-Johnson years, a large gap yawned between the promise of poverty and civil-rights programs and their actual achievements. The two presidents had pledged to create an egalitarian society, but they hoped to reach this radical goal through modest and essentially conservative means. Believers in the corporate/capitalist economic system, they had faith that moderate government action would suffice. Instead of seeking a redistribution of wealth or income, they sought to finance domestic reform through economic growth: the pie would get bigger, they expected, so that although the slices for the rich would remain disproportionately large, at least the poor would get more of a taste. In practice, funds for poverty and civil-rights programs proved rather meager. Even at the height of Johnson's War on Poverty, all poverty programs together cost the country far less than 1 percent of the GNP.

Underfunding of antipoverty measures was only part of the problem. Many of the programs themselves were misconceived and then mismanaged. In their haste to rush legislation to Congress, Johnson's aides had little time for thoughtful, careful planning as they drafted bills. As a result, dozens of antipoverty and welfare measures passed based on a wide range of largely untested and sometimes inconsistent theories. In the words of journalist David Broder, Johnson had thrown together his reforms with "no pause to consider how each of the new Federal programs meshed with all the others, or whether the function was one the national government could most appropriately undertake."

Many legislated programs ostensibly aimed to help the poor but ultimately benefited the well-to-do. The massive government effort to uplift impoverished people of Appalachia provides an apt example. Nearly a hundred federal programs sought to ease the area's chronic poverty. The government spent billions constructing public works such as expressways, airfields, and dams. Yet these short-run projects scarcely changed the region's fundamental economic distress. Beyond the smooth new interstate highways that sped middle-class drivers to scenic vacation spots, the same old tarpaper shacks remained visible. What new jobs the programs created tended to be temporary and seldom went to the truly destitute. "All we're doing for the poor," lamented a federal antipoverty worker in Kentucky, "is making the poverty more bearable."

Moreover, because the government theorized that poverty stemmed from cultural deprivation, it emphasized education and other self-help measures. As Sargent Shriver, director of the Office of Economic Opportunity, noted, the War on Poverty was "not a handout program." Instead it sought to change "indifference to interest, ignorance to awareness, resignation to ambition." For some poor, of course, acquiring middle-class aspirations sufficed to lift them above the poverty line. But for millions more, whether they were ambitious had little bearing on their lack of economic success. For them, the antipoverty program seemed paternalistic and irrelevant.

African-Americans in particular fumed at the Johnson administration's analysis of the causes of black poverty. In a speech delivered at Howard University in June 1965, LBJ contended that black destitution came from a "devastating heritage of long years of slavery" and "the breakdown of the Negro family structure." Johnson drew his ideas from a report by Daniel Patrick Moynihan, a social scientist, assistant secretary of labor, and one of the chief theoreticians of the War on Poverty. Moynihan argued that black culture derived from a "social pathology" fed by the unstable black family. Antipoverty programs, he judged, would provide little help to blacks until "a stable Negro family structure" existed. Although Moynihan's report used a wealth of statistical data to prove the precariousness of the black family, it implied that white middle-class ways set the standards and that until blacks adopted them they could not expect to better their lot. When this confidential document leaked to the press, which oversimplified and sensationalized it, black leaders exploded. "One can't talk about pathologies of Negroes," retorted Whitney Young of the Urban League, "without talking about the pathologies of white society. If Negroes are sick socially, then whites are sick morally." "It's the damned system that needs changing"—not African-American society—charged CORE's Floyd McKissick. The acrimonious debate further weakened the War on Poverty.

The Job Corps was another administration antipoverty program that met with disappointing results. Created by Congress as part of the Economic Opportunity Act, the Job Corps sought to recruit unemployed young people, house them in training centers removed from slum environments, and teach them marketable skills. When Sargent Shriver launched the corps with much fanfare in 1965, some ten thousand volunteers signed up; in 1966, the corps recruited an additional forty-five thousand. The government housed trainees in special instructional centers where, at an average annual cost exceeding $8,000 per person, they learned such skills as welding, auto-body repair, janitoring, and carpentry. Yet homesick and chafing under the unaccustomed discipline, more than two-thirds of the trainees dropped out before completing the program. Half a year after participating in the course, even among those who had graduated, only one-third held jobs related to their training, and 28 percent were unemployed. Furthermore, because the Job Corps trained young people to fill only existing positions, it is doubtful that the program had any long-lasting impact on the unemployment rate. This experiment made a mere dent in the more than one million youths, ages sixteen through twenty-one, who lacked jobs in the midsixties.

The most radical and controversial of Johnson's antipoverty measures became the Community Action Program (CAP). Also part of the Economic Opportunity Act, CAP called for the establishment of community-action agencies "developed, conducted, and administered with the maximum feasible participation of residents of the areas and members of the groups served." In other words, CAP aimed to bring the poor into the community power structure by setting up new local agencies or reforming existing ones. By 1966 the government funded more than a thousand such organizations.

Many CAP agencies made important contributions, including the establishment of birth-control programs, community health centers, and free legal services for the poor. Head Start and Upward Bound, two particularly valuable CAP initiatives, respectively aimed to improve the cognitive skills and health of impoverished preschool children and provide low-income teenagers with the competence and incentive to attend college. CAP's emphasis on the participation of the poor in decisionmaking, although not effective everywhere, gave many indigent people some control over matters directly affecting them. Indeed, CAPs became an important training ground for a generation of black, urban politicians.

A majority of Community Action Programs were well run and improved the lives of thousands. Yet from the outset, controversy dogged the programs. In community after community, disputes erupted between mayors and CAP reformers that pitted white-dominated city governments against an emerging black political leadership. In cities where the poor gained control over CAP agencies, they often challenged the status quo by organizing rent strikes, picketing city hall, or attempting to control welfare agencies and local school boards. In a few communities, black militants commandeered the programs. In Harlem, a CAP-subsidized theater project produced a LeRoi Jones play in which Jack Benny's docile and comic servant Rochester turned and killed his white oppressors. In San Francisco, CAP-employed black radical Charles Sizemore and a band of some thirty toughs marched into city hall and threatened mayor John Shelley until he promised $45,000 for CAP's summer project.

Not surprisingly, city and other establishment leaders fought back. To Chicago's mayor Richard Daley, allowing the poor to run the antipoverty agencies seemed "like telling the fellow who cleans up [at the newspaper] to be the city editor." Daley did everything in his power to limit the participation of the poor in local decisionmaking and to impede institutional change. In Chicago and several other cities, antipoverty money found its way into the pockets of local politicians and their cronies. Elsewhere, internal bickering, poor planning, and outright fraud squandered funds. In 1968 African-American sociologist Kenneth Clark sadly concluded about the Harlem project that "none of it worked, and the $20 million that went into it has disappeared without a trace." A federal official described the results of the Harlem community-action agency as "a lot of garbage."

Johnson and his advisers had launched the war against poverty with high confidence and trust in expanding federal revenues, and treated the challenge as a technical problem, much like putting a man on the moon. But poverty proved far more intractable than the White House experts imagined, and by 1967 the entire effort stood in disarray. Johnson saw himself as America's savior, and with his ego tied to his Great Society programs, he resisted admitting that his ideas had flaws. The president instead kept defending his vision, and his supporters produced impressive statistics on the programs' achievements.

Although the War on Poverty scored some success, the slums of urban America and the shacks of rural America remained, and several members of Johnson's administration began reappraising the programs. Presidential adviser Moynihan concluded that the government had oversold and underperformed its antipoverty efforts. "The program," he noted, "was carried out in such a way as to produce a minimum of the social change its sponsors desired, and to bring about a maximum increase in the opposition to such change."

The Johnson administration had raised the hopes of millions of destitute Americans. Resentment mounted when the various programs' actual impact proved marginal to the lives of most poor people. Nowhere did the anger and frustration erupt more fiercely than in the black urban ghettoes.

The Black Revolution

Lyndon Johnson did more to aid African-Americans than any other president except Lincoln, and like Lincoln he wished to be remembered as a great emancipator. But here, too, events would shatter his hopes. LBJ had ascended to the presidency at the height of the civil-rights movement and had thrown his support behind the crusade for racial justice. The 1964 Civil Rights Act, the 1965 Voting Rights Act, and many antipoverty programs aimed to win equality for African-Americans. Yet racism, like poverty, was stubborn. During Johnson's presidency, the civil-rights movement increasingly gave way to black militancy and urban violence that in the end would intensify the white backlash and hamstring LBJ's efforts.

In the summer of 1964, while the president celebrated the passage of the Civil Rights Act, angry African-Americans rioted in Harlem and several other northern cities. On August 11, 1965, just five days after Johnson signed the Voting Rights Act, violence erupted in the Watts area of Los Angeles. Touched off when white police attempted to arrest a young black man for drunken driving and then scuffled with his mother, the Watts riot raged for six days and nights as blacks rampaged through the ghetto, looting and burning. To restore order, more than sixteen thousand national guardsmen and police occupied the district. In the end, the uprising became one of the most destructive outbreaks of urban violence in American history, costing thirty-four deaths, nearly nine hundred injuries, and $35 million in property damage.

Watts turned out to be only the prelude to a succession of "long hot summers" as black bitterness escalated. While a stunned nation viewed the Watts riot on TV, Chicago's blacks exploded on August 12 after a fire-truck accident killed an African-American woman. Police and national guardsmen had barely begun to quell the burning, looting, and shooting in Watts and Chicago when the August 14 arrest of a group of blacks gathered outside a nightclub in Springfield, Massachusetts, triggered a new outburst.

Coinciding with Lyndon Johnson's drastic escalation of the Vietnam War and burgeoning antiwar protest at home, between 1965 and 1968 almost three hundred race riots, involving an estimated half-million blacks, shook cities across the nation. The summers of 1966 and 1967 especially witnessed scores of such uprisings. Scarcely a day passed without the evening news showing film clips of furious African-Americans rampaging through city streets, smashing windows, looting stores, overturning cars,

Exploding Cities. August 16, 1965, a national guardsman stands ready for further trouble in the strife-torn Watts district of Los Angeles. It took some ten thousand police and national guard soldiers to quell the six days of violence in this predominantly black community.

and hurling bricks at police. Millions of alarmed whites hardened their hearts to the plight of blacks.

The worst riot broke out in Detroit during the strife-torn summer of 1967. Ignited by police arrests of blacks attending an after-hours bar, a week of rioting left the city devastated. Forty-three died and more than a thousand suffered injuries; nearly four thousand fires destroyed thirteen hundred buildings. After Detroit, President Johnson appointed the National Advisory Commission on Civil Disorders, headed by Illinois governor Otto Kerner, to investigate the urban crises. The Kerner commission report, issued in 1968, detected a pattern to the riots. In no instance did investigators find evidence suggesting that ghetto explosions were planned. Rather, they had erupted spontaneously, usually in response to perceived incidents of police brutality. Despite the racial overtones of the riots, they were all confined to black neighborhoods. Seldom had rioters directly attacked whites. Instead, they vented their rage and despair against ghetto symbols of white exploitation—tenements and white-owned stores. Most of the dead and wounded in fact were African-Americans, shot by police and national guardsmen.

The Kerner report blamed the riots on an "explosive mixture" of poverty, unemployment, slum housing, segregated education, and antagonistic police-community relations. The underlying cause, claimed the commission, was "white racism," and the situation was worsening: "Our nation is moving toward two societies, one black, one white—separate and unequal." To end what the commission described as "the destruction and the violence, not only in the streets of the ghetto, but in the lives of people," the report recommended the creation of two million new jobs in the ghetto, an assault on *de facto* school segregation, construction of six million new units of public housing, and the enactment of a "national system of income supplementation."

But when the Kerner report came out, the majority of white Americans opposed massive new federal programs to aid African-Americans. The backlash that Busby warned about in 1964 had escalated sharply with the rise of urban violence, and reaction coursed through the country. People demanded stronger law enforcement with additional staffing and riot-control weapons, not new government programs to improve ghetto life. Working-class whites, many of them members of eastern or southern European groups struggling financially themselves and living near black slums, particularly resented measures aimed to help nonwhites.

Even northern white liberals proved more reluctant to fight racism in the North than they had been in the South. Many of the same whites who had approved the civil-rights struggle in Alabama and Mississippi exhibited racial prejudice when their own neighborhoods and schools faced integration. Supporting voting rights for peaceful protesters in Selma was one thing; busing black students from downtown Detroit to schools in all-white Grosse Pointe or Dearborn seemed quite another matter. Northern whites had difficulty accepting the conclusions of the Kerner commission: that the United States was a racist society and that, by implication, the riots were justified. In a national opinion poll shortly after the release of the commission's report, fewer than one-third of whites questioned agreed with the experts' findings.

The militancy brewing among African-Americans within the civil-rights movement further alienated white liberals. Even before the Watts fires illuminated black rage, veterans of the civil-rights struggle had begun to rethink strategy. Soon the emergence of the Black Power movement would parallel the fury that urban violence unleashed. From the midfifties to the midsixties, the civil-rights movement had adhered to a liberal philosophy of interracial cooperation. Blacks and whites had worked together, with nonviolent resistance as their tactic and integration as their goal. In retrospect, the 1963 March on Washington stands out as its apogee, as thousands of blacks and whites, hands joined, sang "We Shall Overcome." Martin Luther King, Jr., had offered America a sublime vision. "The Negro dream," he had declared at the march, "is rooted in the American dream." Through Christian love and nonviolent protest, he promised the transformation of the nation and urged Americans to transcend their racist past and to craft an integrated utopia in which race no longer mattered. For Reverend King and most of his SCLC followers, nonviolence formed the core of their Christian way of life.

But for numerous younger civil-rights activists in SNCC and CORE, nonviolence had never been more than a tactic. During the Mississippi Freedom Summer of 1964, protesters had begun to question just what nonviolence had achieved. They had witnessed too many beatings, too many bombings, too many murders. They knew that to turn the other cheek all too often invited more white brutality. By the time Watts went up in flames in August 1965, SNCC and CORE field workers in the Deep South routinely carried guns. White liberals, frightened by intensifying black militancy and trusting that civil-rights laws and federal programs would prevail, began to withdraw their support. At the same time, black activists increasingly rejected the strategy of nonviolence, cooperation with whites, and the goal of integration. The hitherto dominant philosophy of Martin Luther King, Jr., faded, eclipsed by the ideas of black nationalist Malcolm X.

Black nationalism had deep roots among northern urban blacks, dating back to the movement that Marcus Garvey led in the 1920s. In the 1950s and early 1960s, it had gained new adherents through the Nation of Islam, commonly known as the Black Muslims. Led by Elijah Muhammad, the Black Muslims proclaimed whites devils and blacks Allah's chosen people. Preaching black separatism, self-discipline, and self-defense, this faith rehabilitated many young, black drug addicts, alcoholics, and criminals. Few whites had heard of the Muslims until 1959, when Mike Wallace and Louis Lomax aired an inflammatory documentary on CBS-TV, "The Hate That Hate Produced." Soon Muslim membership more than doubled, although the white press continued to depict the organization as fanatical and violent.

By the early sixties, media attention focused particularly on Malcolm X. Born Malcolm Little in Lansing, Michigan, the future black nationalist had endured prejudice from birth. Whites had murdered his father, a minister in the Garvey movement. Although an outstanding student, Malcolm's teachers discouraged his aspirations to become a lawyer. As a young man, he drifted into a life of petty crime, drug addiction, and menial labor. In prison, he accepted the Muslim faith and cast off his "slave-master" name to become Malcolm X. A persuasive speaker and charismatic leader, Malcolm X more than anyone else brought black nationalism to public attention. His angry eloquence attracted a substantial following, particularly among younger urban blacks. Unlike King, he opposed integration and advocated self-defense rather than nonviolence, declaring, "I don't see any American dream; I see an American nightmare." He ridiculed the March on Washington, demanding, "Who ever heard of angry revolutionists all harmonizing 'We Shall Overcome . . .' while tripping and swaying along arm-in-arm with the very people they were supposed to be angrily revolting against?" Above all, Malcolm taught racial pride.

Late in 1963, Elijah Muhammad, jealous over Malcolm X's prominence, tried to silence his minister. Rebuffed, Malcolm broke from the Nation of Islam. The following year, he traveled widely in Africa, where he concluded that the economically oppressed of all races the world over should work together against the oppressor. He moved toward socialism and came to see the African-American revolt as a global class rebellion of "the exploited against the exploiter." Early in 1965 he created the Organization of Afro-American Unity. Then on February 21, 1965, three Black Muslims, outraged at his defection from their organization, gunned him down as he approached the lectern in Harlem's Audubon Ballroom. Malcolm X's assassination left his organization without effective leadership; yet his greatest influence was still to come, most notably through his remarkable *Autobiography,* posthumously published and widely read. In death, Malcolm X articulated the anger among younger blacks in the ghettoes and the movement. He became the martyred prince whose message trumpeted pride in blackness, pride in African-Americans' roots, pride in blacks' abilities to control their destinies.

The rebelliousness of some blacks stemmed partly from a shift in focus from the South to the North during the midsixties. The passage of the 1964 Civil Rights Act and the 1965 Voting Rights Act appeared to complete the southern civil-rights agenda. Now the movement turned its spotlight on the urban North, where racism, although less blatant, remained insidious. Southern blacks had a rich religious tradition and had warmed to King's call for nonviolent resistance. Long accustomed to contact between

Black Rebelliousness. A persuasive speaker and charismatic leader, Malcolm X brought black nationalism to public attention. Unlike King, he opposed integration and advocated self-defense rather than nonviolence, and after his assassination, he became a symbol for black pride.

the races, integration for them seemed a natural goal. Northern urban blacks, on the other hand, less rooted in Protestantism and segregated in ghettoes, harbored more hostility toward whites and had less interest in integration than did southern blacks. Indeed, the core issues of concern differed markedly between the two regions. In the South, gaining equal access to public facilities and the voting booth mattered hugely to blacks. In the North, African-Americans already enjoyed these freedoms. For them, the much-heralded civil-rights and voting-rights legislation only swelled expectations and raised frustration. Northern blacks wanted better housing, schools, and economic opportunities—immediately.

With the movement's shift to the North, black radicalism intensified. In a series of staff meetings and national conventions held during 1965 and early 1966, a majority within both SNCC and CORE rejected nonviolence, integration, and interracialism and replaced pacifists John Lewis and James Farmer as national directors. The new leaders, Stokely Carmichael and Floyd McKissick, epitomized the groups' militant course. McKissick called nonviolence "a dying philosophy" that had "outlived its usefulness." Carmichael declared, "I'm not going to let somebody hit up the side of my head for the rest of my life and die. No! You got to fight back." In addition to Malcolm X's *Autobiography*, SNCC radicals read Frantz Fanon's *Wretched of the Earth*. Fanon, a black French psychiatrist and supporter of the Algerian fight for independence, extolled Third World revolutionary movements and decreed violence as both a tactic for achieving liberation and a way for the oppressed to affirm their courage. Reading Fanon, many black militants came to see African-America as an internal colony within the United States and to equate their struggle with that of all oppressed colonial peoples.

In June 1966, a confrontation arose between King, Carmichael and McKissick, and their opposing philosophies. That month, James Meredith, who had integrated the University of Mississippi in 1962, set out on a solitary march from Memphis to Jackson in an effort to encourage blacks to register to vote. Ten miles into his march, a white man, waiting in ambush, shot and seriously wounded him. Civil-rights leaders hurriedly gathered in Memphis and decided to carry on what they now called the Meredith March Against Fear. Each evening on the many days of the march, crowds gathered to hear King, Carmichael, McKissick, and other speakers. But whereas King still preached nonviolence, Carmichael shouted, "The Negro is going to take what he deserves from the white man!" In Greenwood, Mississippi, Carmichael exhorted a large rally, "The only way we gonna stop them white men from whippin' us is to take over. We been saying freedom for six years and ain't got nothin'. What we gonna start saying now is Black Power!" SNCC worker Willie Ricks leaped to the podium and yelled, "What do we want?" The crowd shouted back, "Black Power! Black Power!" A forceful new slogan was born and made headlines across the country the next day.

King insisted that "we must never seek power exclusively for the Negro, but the sharing of power with white people"; nevertheless, Carmichael and McKissick carried the day. When the fifteen thousand marchers reached Jackson on June 26, they roared, "Black Power! Black Power! Black Power!" Addressing the closing rally, McKissick avowed: "1966 shall be remembered as the year we left our imposed status as Negroes and became *Black Men* . . . 1966 is the year of the concept of Black Power."

The goal of Black Power quickly replaced integration among most younger activists. Carmichael defined Black Power as "a call for black people in this country to unite, to recognize their heritage, to build a sense of community. It is a call for black people to define their own goals, to lead their own organizations and to support those organizations. It is a call to reject the racist institutions and values of this society." The West Indian–born, Howard-educated Carmichael offered not only a plea for self-determination but also a critique of integration. "The goal of black people," he wrote, "must *not* be to assimilate into middle-class America, for that class—as a whole—is without a viable conscience as regards humanity." Instead, he argued, blacks should build their own institutions—their own businesses, their own political party, their own culture and history.

Like Malcolm X, Carmichael did not rule out the use of force. Frequently beaten by southern whites while working for SNCC in the early sixties, Carmichael had concluded that it was "the right of black men everywhere to defend themselves when threatened or attacked. . . . Responsibility for the use of violence by black men, whether in self-defense or initiated by them, lies with the white community." H. Rap Brown, Carmichael's successor as chairman of SNCC, was even blunter: "Violence is necessary and it's as American as cherry pie." He urged black audiences "to get some guns. . . . I mean, don't be trying to love that honky to death. Shoot him to death."

Reflecting the new combative mood in October 1966, Huey Newton and Bobby Seale founded the Black Panther party in Oakland, California. Sporting black berets, black leather jackets, and black pants and bandoliers, the gun-toting Panthers marched about the Oakland ghetto attempting, in Newton's words, to defend "our black community from racist police oppression and brutality." The group attained national notoriety from a series of bloody shoot-outs with police.[2]

Black Power catalyzed important political, cultural, and psychological changes. Unlike earlier phases in the civil-rights movement that appealed mostly to blacks with

---

[2]For more on the Black Panther party, see Chapter 10.

middle-class status or aspirations, Black Power reached into the ghettoes and mobilized scores of new enthusiasts. It encouraged community organization and a new spirit of self-reliance. Black Power politicized African-Americans, particularly on the local level. Above all, the new creed made African-Americans proud to be black. A true revolution in perception, this change was necessary for blacks to achieve real equality. Centuries of racist oppression had conditioned most blacks to accept white standards as right. Now black became beautiful. As James Brown's hit song expressed it, "Say It Loud—I'm Black and I'm Proud."

Signs of this new pride popped up everywhere. Ghetto sales of skin bleaches and hair straighteners plummeted. "Afro" hairstyles and dashikis exhibited blacks' new-found fascination with their African heritage. Blacks took Islamic names. Basketball star Lew Alcindor converted from Christianity to Islam and changed his name to Kareem Abdul-Jabbar. Young, outspoken, heavyweight boxing champion Cassius Clay joined the Black Muslims and became Muhammad Ali. "Soul" food, "soul" music, black theater and dance, black dialect, indeed, all aspects of black culture gained legitimacy as blacks reclaimed and celebrated their uniqueness. Black pride in turn stimulated renewed interest in the African-American past. Scholars revamped the writing and teaching of history and acknowledged the long-neglected black experience. Under pressure from Black Power activists, universities established black studies programs. By the late sixties, racial consciousness had grown; the crippling self-hatred of earlier decades had given way to self-esteem. The Black Power movement also inspired other American minorities to develop self-pride and to demand their rights.

Yet although Black Power launched a revolution of consciousness and elevated some black, urban politicians to prominence, it produced few tangible changes in economic institutions and in fact dealt a devastating blow to the civil-rights cause. The antiwhite connotations of Black Power drove numerous sympathetic whites out of the movement and scared off financial backers. By 1967 both SNCC and CORE were moribund. Even mainstream, moderate organizations like SCLC, the NAACP, and the Urban League, although they still pushed for affirmative action and integration, had lost members and funding. Urban rioting, coinciding with the violent rhetoric of Black Power advocates and the emergence of paramilitary groups such as the Black Panthers, served to fuel the white backlash. In August 1966, angry mobs shouting "White Power" assaulted and stoned Martin Luther King, Jr., and other SCLC pacifists demonstrating in Chicago for open housing.

• • •

Caught between spiraling black fury and white backlash, the Johnson administration floundered. LBJ's efforts to build his Great Society based on social justice and racial harmony, all overwhelmingly supported by his cherished consensus, had failed. White sympathy for the black movement ebbed, and in 1966, for the first time in a decade, Congress rejected a civil-rights bill. By 1967 civil rights were clearly in retreat. In his State of the Union message, President Johnson devoted only forty-five words to racial issues. Later that year, Congress ousted Harlem representative Adam Clayton Powell, Jr., for fraudulent payroll practices frequently tolerated among white congressmen. Also in 1967, Congress defeated a plan to control rats in the ghettoes, a bill that one southern representative jeeringly dismissed as a "civil-rats bill."

From the late fifties through the midsixties, the civil-rights movement had stood as the supreme driving force for social change in America. The decline of the movement now stalled crusades for both racial equality and other social and economic reforms. Johnson's popularity plummeted, and his liberal legislation came under attack.

But black militancy, white backlash, and resurgent conservatism made up only part of the picture of the nation's growing discord and disillusionment. By June 1966, while the fiery Stokely Carmichael thrilled his listeners with shouts of "Black Power," the Johnson government was pouring more than $2 billion a month into the escalating war in Vietnam. A year later, a despondent Martin Luther King, Jr., told Americans, "The bombs in Vietnam explode at home. They destroy the hopes and possibilities of a decent America." King prophesied correctly. More than anything else, the Vietnam War sabotaged the promise of the Great Society and ultimately ruined the presidency of Lyndon Baines Johnson.

Selected Bibliography

Lyndon Johnson's memoir, *The Vantage Point* (1971), although reserved and self-serving, has value. More candid is Lady Bird's engaging *A White House Diary* (1970). Critical counterbalances include Paul K. Conkin, *Big Daddy from the Pedernales* (1986), and Frank Cormier, *LBJ: The Way He Was* (1977). More interesting reading is Doris Kearns, *Lyndon Johnson and the American Dream* (1976); Kearns's psychological analysis is based on extensive interviews with the president. Another insider's account is Eric F. Goldman, *The Tragedy of Lyndon Johnson* (1969). Goldman served briefly as Johnson's historian-in-residence and sheds light particularly on the president's uneasy relationship with the intellectual community. Somewhat more favorable insiders' memoirs are George E. Reedy, *Lyndon Johnson* (1982); Jack Valenti, *A Very Human President* (1976); and Harry McPherson, *A Political Education* (1972). LBJ's prepresidential life and career are examined in great detail in Robert A. Caro, *The Years of Lyndon Johnson: The Path to Power* (1982), and his hostile *Means of Ascent* (1990). Also valuable on this topic is Ronnie Dugger, *The Politician* (1982). Johnson's powers of political persuasion are examined by journalists Rowland Evans and Robert Novak in *Lyndon Johnson and the Exercise of Power* (1966). LBJ's changing political ideology is analyzed in Joe B. Frantz, "Opening a Curtain: The Metamorphosis of Lyndon B. Johnson," *Journal of Southern History* 65 (February 1979), 3–26. Serious students of Johnson's presidency should consult *Public Papers of the Presidents: Lyndon B. Johnson* (5 vols., 1964–1970).

Vaughn Davis Bornet, *The Presidency of Lyndon B. Johnson* (1983), although poorly written and insufficiently analytical, is reliable on specific details of legislation and agencies. Briefer but more informed is Jim R. Heath, *Decade of Disillusionment: The Kennedy-Johnson Years* (1975). Robert Divine, ed., *Exploring the Johnson Years* (1981), is a collection of interpretive essays based on material in the Johnson Library.

The 1964 election is masterfully reported in Theodore H. White's *The Making of the President, 1964* (1965). The rise of postwar conservatism is examined in George H. Nash, *The Conservative Intellectual Movement Since 1945* (1976); Paul Gottfried and Thomas Fleming, *The Conservative Movement* (1988); and William Blumenthal, *The Rise of Counterestablishment: From Conservative Ideology to Political Power* (1986). For an understanding of Barry Goldwater's political philosophy, see his *The Conscience of a Conservative* (1960). William A. Rusher, *The Rise of the Right* (1984), sympathetically studies the emergence of the Radical Right; more critical is Michael W. Miles, *The Odyssey of the American Right* (1980).

Controversy still swirls around the Great Society social programs. On the basis of limited evidence, John E. Schwarz, *America's Hidden Success* (1983), judges sixties domestic reforms a great success. Charles Murray, *Losing Ground* (1984), on the other hand, is sharply critical. Allen J. Matusow's detailed examination of liberalism in the 1960s, *The Unraveling of America* (1984), also concludes that liberal reforms failed. Unlike Murray, however, who questions the very premises of liberalism, Matusow faults liberal leaders for not going far enough with their reforms. More favorable assessments of Johnson's antipoverty programs are Michael Katz, *The Undeserving Poor: From the War on Poverty to the War on Welfare* (1989), and Sara A. Levitan and Robert Taggart, *The Promise of Greatness* (1976). Charles R. Morris, *A Time of Passion: America 1960–1980* (1984), offers a sympathetic evaluation by a former welfare administrator. Marvin E. Gettleman and David Mermelstein, eds., *The Great Society Reader: The Failure of American Liberalism* (1967), is a contemporary collection of critical essays and documents.

The seminal book that originally focused national attention on poverty is Michael Harrington's *The Other America* (1962). James T. Patterson, *America's Struggle Against Poverty* (1981), and Michael B. Katz, *In the Shadow of the Poorhouse* (1986), place sixties antipoverty programs in a larger historical perspective. Katz has also edited a collection of essays useful for understanding the emergence of new forms of urban poverty in the postwar years and policy responses to urban poverty: Michael B. Katz, ed., *The "Underclass" Debate* (1993). Additional worthwhile studies of poverty issues are Stephen M. Rose, *The Betrayal of the Poor: Transformation of Community Action* (1972); Oscar Lewis, *La Vida: A Puerto Rican Family and the Culture of Poverty* (1966); Harry Caudill, *Night Comes to the Cumberlands* (1963); and Ben Seligman, *Permanent Poverty* (1968). An important study of Kennedy-Johnson economic policies and the emergence of the "new economics" is Herbert Stein, *The Fiscal Revolution in America* (1969).

The role of the Earl Warren–led Supreme Court in the sixties is examined in Bernard Schwartz, *Super Chief: Earl Warren and the Supreme Court* (1983); Archibald Cox, *The Warren Court* (1968); Philip B. Kurland, *Politics, the Constitution, and the Warren Court* (1970); and Alexander Bickel, *The Supreme Court and the Idea of Progress* (1970).

The Kerner commission's *Report of the National Advisory Committee on Civil Disorders* (1968) is filled with useful data on the midsixties urban riots. A good overall analysis of the ghetto riots is Robert Fogelson, *Violence as Protest* (1971); see also Joe F. Feagin and Harlan Hahn,

Ghetto Revolts: The Politics of Violence in American Cities (1973). The Watts riot is detailed in Robert Conot's *Rivers of Blood, Years of Darkness* (1968); on the 1967 Detroit riot, see Sidney Fine, *Violence in the Model City: The Cavanagh Administration, Race Relations, and the Detroit Riot of 1967* (1988), and John Hersey's *The Algiers Motel Incident* (1971). Tom Hayden's *Rebellion in Newark* (1970) is an insiders' look at the 1967 Newark riot.

Two insightful articles on the demise of the nonviolent civil-rights movement and the emergence of Black Power are Allen J. Matusow, "From Civil Rights to Black Power: The Case of SNCC, 1960–1966," in Barton J. Bernstein and Matusow, eds., *Twentieth Century America: Recent Interpretations* (1969), and Vincent Harding, "Black Radicalism: The Road from Montgomery," in Alfred Young, ed., *Dissent: Explorations in the History of American Radicalism* (1968). James Baldwin's *The Fire Next Time* (1963) foretold rising black militancy. Malcolm X's influence is examined in Archie Epps, *Malcolm X and the American Negro Revolution* (1969), and Peter Goldman, *The Death and Life of Malcolm X* (1979 ed.). *The Autobiography of Malcolm X,* as told to Alex Haley (1965), is essential reading for comprehending Malcolm X's life and philosophy.

Books helpful for understanding Black Power are Nathan Wright, Jr., *Black Power and Urban Unrest* (1967); Stokely Carmichael and Charles V. Hamilton, *Black Power: The Politics of Liberation in America* (1967); Lewis Killian, *The Impossible Revolution: Black Power and the American Dream* (1968); and Thomas L. Blair, *Retreat to the Ghetto* (1977). William VanDeburg, *A New Day in Babylon* (1992), emphasizes the cultural aspects of Black Power.

Revealing personal accounts of the radicalization of African-American activists include Cleveland Sellers, *The River of No Return: The Autobiography of a Black Militant and the Life and Death of SNCC* (1973); Julius Lester, *Look Out Whitey! Black Power's Gon' Get Your Mama* (1968); Eldridge Cleaver, *Soul on Ice* (1968); H. Rap Brown, *Die Nigger Die* (1969); Stokely Carmichael, *Stokely Speaks* (1971); and James Forman, *The Making of Black Revolutionaries* (1985).

CHAPTER

6

VIETNAM AND AMERICAN SOCIETY, 1945 – 1967

On April 8, 1963, the *New York Times* published a letter by noted British philosopher Bertrand Russell denouncing the United States for "suppressing the truth about the conduct of [the Vietnam War]," which, he claimed, involved the use of "napalm jelly gasoline" and "chemical warfare." The *Times* contemptuously dismissed the British philosopher as a man living in "never-never land" and unthinkingly subscribing "to the most transparent Communist propaganda." Indeed, at that time, only a few radical American pacifists shared Russell's concerns. Although the civil-rights struggle had galvanized numerous Americans, the nearly two-decades-old conflict in Vietnam had escaped the nation's attention. Most Americans had no idea where Vietnam was, let alone that the United States had sent some sixteen thousand military advisers there. Besides, frequent encouraging reports from high-ranking American officials soothed any qualms.

The blissful ignorance could not last. After 1963, the United States plunged deeper and deeper into what would become the longest, most controversial, and only losing war in its history. By late 1967, nearly half a million American troops were fighting some nine thousand miles from U.S. shores, for unclear purposes. From the time of Lyndon Johnson's escalation of the war in 1965 until the last Americans withdrew from South Vietnam in 1975, the Vietnam War took center stage in

American history and divided the country more than any other issue. Over 58,000 Americans perished in the conflict; Indochinese deaths surpassed 1.5 million. Combat deaths, however, were only part of the picture. The war turned thousands of verdant acres of Vietnam into a wasteland and devastated much of the rest of Southeast Asia. It wrenched the American people apart, undermined liberal domestic programs, and touched off more than a decade of inflation. Traditional notions of America's innocence, invincibility, benevolence, and moral superiority died. The war also spawned a crisis of leadership. All too often during the extended conflict, political and military leaders acted without consulting elected representatives. Congress and the public were deceived and manipulated, and dissent was stifled in the name of patriotism. These bitter events engendered a deep and chronic distrust of government leadership and dealt a crushing blow to national self-confidence.

The war was not an aberration. Growing directly out of America's Cold War ideology and post–World War II global strategy, it capped a series of decisions made during more than two decades, each of which seemed logical at the time. Vietnam bedeviled the Truman, Eisenhower, and Kennedy administrations and ultimately destroyed the presidencies of Johnson and Nixon. This chapter tells the story of deepening U.S. involvement in Vietnam and its consequences for American society through 1967.

The Kennedy Inheritance

When John F. Kennedy took office in January 1961, he inherited a dilemma that had long roots in U.S. history. American policymakers had first become concerned with Vietnam during World War II. With France's fall in 1940, Japan gained major influence in this former French colony, but a nationalist guerrilla movement challenged their position. Led by Ho Chi Minh, a gentle, scholarly revolutionary and dedicated communist, Vietnamese guerrillas, with the assistance of the American Office of Strategic Services (OSS), gained control of six northern provinces of Vietnam. On September 2, 1945, following Japan's defeat, Ho Chi Minh proclaimed the independence of a "free Vietnam." An avid student of U.S. history, Ho announced the birth of the Vietnamese republic with the familiar words of the Declaration of Independence: "We hold these truths to be self-evident: That all men are created equal." During independence celebrations that day in Hanoi, American army officers stood proudly on the reviewing stand and U.S. planes flew overhead. As a Vietnamese band played the "Star-Spangled Banner," Vietnamese officials spoke affectionately of their "particularly intimate relations" with the United States.

But American and Vietnamese amity was not to be. Between September 1945 and February 1946, Ho sent eight letters to President Harry Truman, appealing to the Americans as "guardians and champions of world justice" to support Vietnamese independence. Ho's letters went unanswered as the Truman administration instead approved the restoration of French rule, for several reasons. First, U.S. policymakers deemed French support and cooperation essential in the emerging Cold War struggle over Europe. In addition, Vietnam produced large quantities of rice, rubber, tin, tungsten, and other resources considered crucial to the industrialized nations of the West. Moreover, all of Southeast Asia appeared strategically vital to the defense of Japan and the Philippines against Soviet expansionism. Finally, and most important, Ho Chi Minh was a communist. Although OSS officers' reports stressed Ho's fervent nationalism, the Truman administration concluded that the United States could not ''afford to assume that Ho is anything but Moscow-directed.'' Looking at events through a Cold War lens, American policymakers chose to ignore the domestic origins of the nationalist rebellion and knew nothing of the historical tenacity of the Vietnamese in resisting foreign domination.

Assisted by the United States and Great Britain, the French returned to Vietnam in September 1945 and by the spring of 1946 had regained control of Saigon and the surrounding southern provinces. In November 1946 the French bombed the northern port of Haiphong, killing some six thousand civilians and provoking Ho's forces, the Vietminh, to fight back. Focused on the fate of Europe and wary of intervening on the side of France in a colonial war, the United States stayed in the background.

But with the triumph of communism in China in 1949 and the outbreak of the Korean War the following year, American policymakers came to see all of Southeast Asia as strategically vital to the containment of communism. In 1950 the Truman White House made two fateful decisions. First, it recognized the French-sponsored Vietnam government of Bao Dai, a westernized playboy who had collaborated with both the Japanese and the French. In the eyes of the Vietminh and most Vietnamese people, the United States by this act allied itself with the hated colonialist French. Second, the Truman administration began supplying French forces with military aid, a policy that Eisenhower augmented. All told, between 1950 and 1954 the United States spent more than $2.6 billion in an effort to bolster the French and ''save'' Vietnam.

Despite these expenditures, the French steadily lost ground to the Vietminh and in the spring of 1954 agreed to peace talks in Geneva. On May 7, 1954, envoys from France, the United States, the Soviet Union, Britain, the People's Republic of China, Laos, and Cambodia convened with representatives of the warring Vietnam regimes of Ho Chi Minh and Bao Dai to discuss Indochina's fate. That same day, the Vietminh captured a major French fortress at Dien Bien Phu in northwest Vietnam. France, having lost the will to fight, granted full independence to Laos and Cambodia. Vietnam, too, received independence but was to be temporarily divided. The Soviets, hoping to ease international tensions after Stalin's death in 1953, pressured the Vietminh into accepting the momentary division of Vietnam at the seventeenth parallel, with Ho's government confined to the north. The agreement specifically stated that this division was ''provisional and . . . not in any way to be interpreted as constituting a political or territorial boundary''; further, the arrangement provided for internationally supervised elections to be held in 1956 to reunify Vietnam. Before 1956 neither zone was to accept foreign troops, military personnel, or arms.

Even with the concession of a temporary division between a diplomatically concocted North and South Vietnam, the Eisenhower administration feared that the Geneva agreements would ultimately give rise to a communist Vietnam. As Ike saw it, having ''lost'' China to ''Communist dictatorship,'' the United States ''simply can't afford greater losses.'' Nor was Vietnam the only territory at risk, warned Eisenhower. Should that nation fall to the communists, the rest of Southeast Asia would ''go over very quickly,'' like a ''row of dominoes'' when ''you knock over the first one.'' The United States, which had never signed the Geneva accords, moved to establish an independent, anticommunist government in South Vietnam and to harass Ho Chi Minh's North Vietnam. Frustrated by the stalemated Cold War in Europe but elated at the easy successes of CIA-directed coups in Iran and Guatemala, the Eisenhower government saw Vietnam as another developing country that it could manipulate through covert operations. Soon CIA operatives entered Vietnam with instructions to use "all available means" to subvert Ho's government in Hanoi and to make South Vietnam "the cornerstone of the Free World in Southeast Asia." CIA teams moved to launch clandestine sabotage missions against North Vietnam.

In South Vietnam, the United States set out to establish an independent, anticommunist government. In place of the French puppet Bao Dai, the Eisenhower administration helped to put Ngo Dinh Diem in power. An aristocratic scholar, Diem was a staunch anticommunist, and because he had spent the years of the French-Indochina war in exile, mostly in the United States, he was untainted by close association with the French. However, as a Roman Catholic in a predominantly Buddhist country, he had slim prospects of earning the Vietnamese people's approval.

Nevertheless, with American aid, Diem managed to bring a semblance of order to this chaotic, artificially created country. In 1956 he blocked the national elections to reunify Vietnam, as required by the Geneva agreements. In this action, too, he had the complete support of the Eisenhower administration, whose diplomatic advisers knew full well that the charismatic Ho would have won an overwhelming victory. From 1955 to 1961, the United States poured close to $2 billion in aid into South Vietnam, most of it military. In an effort to build a stable anticommunist nation, American advisers organized and trained the South Vietnamese army. Under special contract from Washington, police experts from Michigan State University instructed a secret police force. American agriculturalists and engineers offered technical assistance. For a time, the U.S. gamble appeared to be working. The massive infusion of American aid enabled South Vietnam to survive and develop what promised to be a viable nation-state and a bulwark against communism. The American media referred to Diem as the "tough little miracle man."

Appearances deceived, however. American aid, though it propped up the Diem government, fostered South Vietnam's dependency on the United States rather than economic self-sufficiency. The political reality of South Vietnam proved even less stable than its economic base. An elitist with little understanding of the needs and problems of the Vietnamese people, Diem spurned U.S. requests for land reform. Instead he abolished village elections and appointed only his loyal supporters to public office. His government threw thousands of dissenters into jail and shut down critical newspapers. Diem's brother, Ngo Dinh Nhu, headed the Vietnam Bureau of Investigation, which ruthlessly rooted out suspected subversives. More than twenty thousand Vietnamese—communists and noncommunists alike—were herded into government "re-education centers." Increasingly alienated from the people, Diem grew more and more suspicious and dictatorial.

Not surprisingly, resistance to Diem's repressive regime began to percolate. Thousands of Vietminh had remained in South Vietnam at the time of partition in 1954. By 1957 these guerrilla fighters had mobilized opposition to the government and embarked on a program of terror, assassinating hundreds of Diem's hated village officials. Initiated as an indigenous response to Diem's oppressiveness, this rebellion grew without significant support from Ho Chi Minh's government in North Vietnam. In 1959, however, the Hanoi regime began secretly supplying arms and men to support the ongoing struggle in South Vietnam. By then, local insurgents already controlled much of the countryside.

In December 1960, with backing from the North, southern revolutionaries founded the National Liberation Front (NLF), whose guerrilla fighting force came to be labeled the Vietcong (VC).[1] Although spearheaded by the communists and having close affiliation with Hanoi, the NLF attracted a broad coalition of South Vietnamese disaffected with Diem. Its platform promised sweeping land reform, return to village rule, and true democratic government. Throughout the country, thousands of recruits joined the makeshift VC army, and revolutionary activity in the South intensified.

The rising insurgency in 1960 alarmed Washington and jeopardized the Eisenhower experiment in anticommunist nation building. From Saigon, American ambassador Elbridge Durbrow cabled Washington that the Diem regime was in "serious danger" and that "prompt and even drastic action" was required to save it. Durbrow called for additional military aid coupled with extensive reforms of the South Vietnamese government. In October, with Eisenhower's approval, he urged Diem to broaden his government, relax censorship, restore village elections, and initiate land reform. Diem agreed with these proposals, but in the next months his administration introduced no reforms and clamped down even harder on dissent.

The United States found itself in a bind. Diem seemed the only alternative to a communist Vietnam, yet the more American support he received, the more corrupt, isolated, and unpopular his government became. Partly because of more pressing problems elsewhere in the world and because of the upcoming presidential election in November 1960, the Eisenhower government avoided reconsidering America's huge investment in Diem's South Vietnam. When John F. Kennedy took office in January 1961, he inherited the problem.

Since Kennedy's days as a senator in the fifties, he had shared Eisenhower's conviction that Vietnam represented "the cornerstone of the Free World in Southeast Asia" and that if the "red tide of Communism" were allowed to advance, it might swallow much of Asia. Calling Vietnam's "political liberty" an "inspiration to those seeking to obtain or maintain their liberty in all parts of Asia," Senator Kennedy had concluded, "It is our offspring, we cannot abandon it, we cannot ignore its needs."

In his first State of the Union address on January 30, 1961, Kennedy implied that the Cold War had come to a crucial crossroads. Throughout the developing regions of the world, new nations struggled to break from their colonial past and to establish modern institutions. The administration assumed that the Soviet Union would try to take advantage of the chaos. Nikita Khrushchev's January 1961 endorsement of wars of national liberation struck the New Frontiersmen as a virtual declaration of war against the West in these nations. Only the United States had the capacity to defend freedom. Should America fail, Kennedy avowed, "the whole world, in my opinion, would inevitably begin to move toward the Communist bloc."

Several Cold War perceptions shaped Kennedy's policies toward Vietnam. Like Eisenhower, JFK unquestioningly accepted the premise, largely erroneous, that South

---

[1] The term *Vietcong* was a pejorative one Diem coined to mean Vietnamese communist. Because not all those opposing the Saigon regime and the U.S. presence were communist, the term is misleading.

Vietnam was the victim of communist aggression instigated by the North Vietnamese, whom—the administration believed—Moscow and Beijing controlled. Despite dawning recognition of a Sino-Soviet rift, communism, wherever it appeared, remained a monolithic conspiracy to Kennedy and most of his advisers. Kennedy also shared Ike's belief in the domino theory.

Further, like most of the generation that had come to political maturity during the Second World War, Kennedy firmly believed that only a show of force could halt aggression. In Kennedy's mind, compromise with Ho Chi Minh in Vietnam would be like the appeasement of Hitler at Munich. Instead, not only would the Kennedy administration contain communism, it also pledged to "move forward to meet Communism, rather than waiting for it to come to us and then reacting to it."

Finally, as a young congressman in 1949, Kennedy had joined in the attacks on the Truman administration for having "lost" China to the communists. He knew the political damage that the loss of additional Asian territory to the enemy ideology could cost. The humiliations of the Bay of Pigs and the Berlin Wall during his first year in office further convinced him that losing Vietnam would fatally injure America's credibility. As JFK confessed to John Kenneth Galbraith, "There are just so many concessions that one can make to the communists in one year and survive politically."

Although Vietnam served a key purpose for Kennedy, neither he nor his foreign-policy advisers knew anything of the Vietnamese people, their history, or their culture. Additionally, accurate information about the fighting was difficult to obtain, with on-the-scene reports from American officials consistently confusing and often contradictory. Vice President Lyndon Johnson, on a fact-finding visit to Saigon in the spring of 1961, pronounced Diem "the Churchill of Asia." Yet that same spring, a State Department intelligence report informed Kennedy that Diem's "reliance on virtual one-man rule" and "toleration of corruption" had opened an "extremely critical period." On another occasion, Kennedy received simultaneous briefings from a general and a State Department official, with the general assuring that the war was going well and that the Diem government remained stable, and the other adviser reporting South Vietnam near collapse. "You two did visit the same country, didn't you?" quipped Kennedy. To JFK and his policymakers, Vietnam was less a real country than a pawn in the international Cold War. As Kennedy's secretary of defense Robert McNamara put it, America had "to prove in the Vietnamese test case that the free world can cope with Communist 'wars of liberation' as we have coped successfully with Communist aggression at other levels."

Besides viewing the conflict in Southeast Asia as a trial of the United States' ability to defeat wars of liberation, the Kennedy White House also saw the war as an opportunity to test the effectiveness of the new administration's counterinsurgency theories and tactics. Having criticized the Eisenhower administration's lack of a flexible military response, the New Frontiersmen decided to use Vietnam to confirm their military analysis. Indeed, the idea of developing a select antiguerrilla force capable of fighting unconventional wars fascinated JFK, and soon after taking office he bolstered the army's Special Forces. The young president even helped to select the forces' equipment and designated the elite corps' unique green beret.

Trained at Fort Bragg on texts reflecting the views of such experts on guerrilla warfare as Mao Zedong and Che Guevara, the Green Berets became Camelot's knights-errant. In addition to military training, they studied espionage, survival skills, medicine, and exotic languages. They could swing through trees, live on snake meat, and rally peasants against Marxism-Leninism. The administration eagerly anticipated verifying the proficiency of these Special Forces. The deployment of antiguerrilla specialists, according to Kennedy's chief military adviser, General Maxwell Taylor, would convince the Soviets that wars of national liberation were not ''cheap, safe, and disavowable [but] costly, dangerous, and doomed to failure.''

In May 1961, Kennedy ordered five hundred Green Berets to Vietnam and reinstituted clandestine operations against the North. In the fall of 1961, after reading a report on the worsening conditions in South Vietnam from White House advisers Walt W. Rostow and General Maxwell Taylor, Kennedy sent additional troops and supplies. Although he rejected Rostow's and Taylor's recommendation to ship eight thousand troops, more than three thousand Americans, referred to as ''advisers,'' served in Vietnam by December 1961.

Kennedy's actions represented a compromise between the extremes of negotiation on the one hand and massive troop build-up on the other. Yet his commitment of arms and advisers, however cautious, marked a turning point. At the time of the Rostow/ Taylor report, Undersecretary of State Chester Bowles and veteran diplomat W. Averell Harriman called for negotiations, warning against further support for what Harriman termed a ''repressive, dictatorial and unpopular regime.'' Bowles stated bluntly that additional aid to Diem would head the United States ''full blast up a dead end street.'' Convinced, however, that American credibility demanded a show of force, Kennedy flatly rejected a negotiated settlement. The president's circumscribed commitment, once made, could not easily be controlled. Continuing setbacks in South Vietnam led him to send in still more Americans. By late 1962, U.S. forces there numbered more than 9,000, and by October 1963, this figure had mushroomed to more than 16,700. That year, 489 Americans died in Vietnam.

Although still listed as advisers, American forces increasingly played a major fighting role. U.S. helicopter and fighter-bomber crews flew combat support missions, American ground troops fought skirmishes, and the Green Berets and CIA operatives continued their campaigns of covert warfare against North Vietnam. The U.S. government kept these activities secret from the public. Kennedy also tried to curb unfavorable newspaper reports of America's military activity in South Vietnam. He even personally, albeit unsuccessfully, pressured *New York Times* publisher Arthur Hays Sulzberger to terminate the Vietnam assignment of David Halberstam, an American journalist critical of U.S. policy. Thus the Kennedy White House, like the later Johnson and Nixon administrations, distorted the truth about America's role in Vietnam. Moreover, U.S. generals and other officials regularly filed overly optimistic battle reports. McNamara talked of ''tremendous progress,'' while Kennedy in his January 1962 State of the Union address claimed that ''the spearhead of aggression has been blunted in Vietnam.''

During JFK's presidency, American and South Vietnamese forces developed methods of warfare that fanned the flames of popular hostility toward the Saigon government and later outraged the antiwar movement after Lyndon Johnson's escalation of the conflict. These tactics included the use of napalm, a petroleum jelly that burned at 1,000 degrees and clung to whatever it splattered on, including human flesh; the dropping of chemical defoliants to denude the countryside and deprive the Vietcong of natural cover; and a "strategic hamlet" program that forcibly removed people from their sacred ancestral villages and relocated them to protected enclaves to prevent infiltration by the Vietcong.

As the war escalated, hatred of the Diem regime intensified. The Kennedy government pressured Diem to make political and economic reforms but met with no more success than the Eisenhower administration had. Instead of reaching out for popular support, Diem's government grew only more tyrannical and isolated. Diem, his brother Nhu, and Nhu's wife—nicknamed the "Dragon Lady" after a popular cartoon character—formed a narrow, despotic family oligarchy. Public gatherings of all sorts, even weddings and funerals, were prohibited unless approved in advance by the government. The regime also imposed strict censorship on the media. In the name of freedom and democracy, Kennedy, again like Ike before him, had become hostage to a dictatorial regime. Preoccupied with the Cuban missile crisis and other issues throughout 1962, JFK failed to heed Chester Bowles's call for an "agonizing reappraisal" of America's Vietnam policy. The president continued, in dissident reporter David Halberstam's words, to "sink or swim with Ngo Dinh Diem."

In the spring of 1963, South Vietnam erupted when Buddhists throughout the region demonstrated against the Diem regime. On May 8, government troops fired into a crowd of Buddhists gathered in the ancient city of Hué to protest Diem's orders forbidding the display of flags on the anniversary of Buddha's birth. The shootings touched off nationwide demonstrations as Buddhists demanded an end to the government's religious persecution. Buddhist leaders staged hunger strikes, and on June 11 a monk named Thich Quang Duc, seated in the lotus position—the pose of the Buddha—poured gasoline on his robes, set fire to himself, and died in front of passing crowds on a busy Saigon street. The following day, newspapers around the world featured pictures of the self-immolation. That summer several other monks burned themselves in protest, riveting U.S. and international attention on the crisis. Madame Nhu mocked the self-immolations as "barbecues," while Diem denied any religious persecution and blamed the disorders on the Vietcong. But the antigovernment demonstrations gained momentum. On August 21, Nhu's secret police raided and ransacked hundreds of Buddhist pagodas and they arrested more than fourteen hundred Buddhist protesters.

By this time the Kennedy government concluded, belatedly, that Diem must go. Through the newly appointed ambassador to Vietnam, Henry Cabot Lodge, and the CIA, the United States encouraged disaffected South Vietnamese generals to stage a coup. On November 1, 1963, the generals struck, capturing Diem and Nhu and brutally murdering them in the back of an armored personnel carrier. At the time of the coup, Madame Nhu and her daughter were in the United States to defend the Diem government. They would never return to Vietnam. In Saigon, news of the coup brought jubilant crowds into the streets.

It is impossible to know what path Kennedy's policies might have taken after Diem's death. Just three weeks later, the young American president himself fell victim to an assassin's bullets. Kennedy partisans contend that had the president lived, he would have found a way out of the Vietnam quagmire, but most evidence suggests otherwise. Because Kennedy expanded the American presence in Vietnam, directed Americans to engage in actual combat, and shared complicity in Diem's death, he had transformed what had been a "limited-risk gamble" under Eisenhower into a major

Crisis in South Vietnam. Buddhist monk Quang Duc immolates himself to protest the anti-Buddhist policies of South Vietnamese president Ngo Dinh Diem. Protests such as this one shocked the world and awakened American policymakers to the growing crisis in South Vietnam.

American commitment. At the time of Kennedy's murder, the United States stood firmly committed to what a prescient *New Republic* reporter described in October 1963 as "the war [that] cannot be won."

The Alamo Revisited: Johnson and Vietnam

Lyndon Johnson inherited from Kennedy problems far worse than Eisenhower had bequeathed JFK, but he also received an opportunity to extricate the United States from the quagmire in Southeast Asia. With new governments in Saigon and Washington, a reassessment of the crisis appeared possible. The Vietcong, North Vietnam, France, United Nations general secretary U Thant, and others encouraged negotiations. Because of the rift between the Soviet Union and the People's Republic of China, both Moscow and Beijing favored a settlement as well. A chance thus arose to establish a coalition government in South Vietnam. Nevertheless, Johnson refused to cooperate. "We do not believe in conferences called to ratify terror," he sniffed. And he vowed to Ambassador Lodge two days after Kennedy's assassination, "I am not going to lose Vietnam. I am not going to be the president who saw Southeast Asia go the way China went." He instructed Lodge to "go back and tell those generals in Saigon that Lyndon Johnson intends to stand by our word." Several days later, LBJ approved a memorandum stating that the purpose of the American presence in Vietnam was "to assist the people and

Government of that country to win their contest against the externally directed and supported Communist conspiracy.''

Johnson had inherited both the war and its logic from earlier administrations. By the time he came to the White House, three presidents had sanctioned U.S. involvement in Vietnam, and the doctrine of containment and the domino theory had become the creed of virtually all American policymakers. Indeed, it is doubtful that any mainstream politician of the midsixties would have had the wisdom and courage to extricate the United States from Vietnam. Still alarmed by the ''loss'' of China and the stalemate in Korea, the Johnson administration insisted that no more Asian territory yield to the communists. As Johnson later recalled, ''I knew that all these problems, taken together, were chicken shit compared to what might happen if we lost Viet Nam.'' Democrats in particular feared being seen as ''soft'' on communism, lest another right-wing red scare undermine domestic reform and drive them from office.

Yet unlike Kennedy, for whom foreign affairs held a fascination, Johnson concerned himself mostly with domestic reforms. Like Truman, he came to the presidency having little direct experience with or knowledge of foreign-policy matters. Nevertheless, he possessed firm convictions and saw the world in simple ''us versus them'' terms. A supporter of the Cold War consensus, Johnson held rigidly to notions of American superiority, the global threat of communism, and the need for the United States to police the world. Reaching political maturity in the crisis atmosphere of World War II and the Cold War, LBJ accepted American foreign policies. Patriotism, in his mind, required bipartisan support of these policies.

For Johnson, Vietnam represented more than Cold War orthodoxy: it called up issues of personal honor and credibility. Like all other Texas schoolchildren, he had learned early the story of heroic resistance at the Alamo. Vietnam, he once told the National Security Council, ''is just like the Alamo.'' LBJ also assumed that his political enemies would seize advantage of any sign of weakness in his handling of Vietnam. He confided to an aide and later biographer Doris Kearns a recurrent nightmare in which Robert Kennedy accused him of having ''betrayed John Kennedy's commitment to Viet Nam'' and called him ''a coward. An unmanly man. A man without spine.'' For personal and political reasons, then, Johnson could see no alternative to ''sticking it out'' in Vietnam. Surrounded by Kennedy-appointed advisers such as Robert McNamara and Dean Rusk, who had helped to chart the course of deepening American involvement, Johnson understandably heeded their advice.

From the outset, LBJ's administration faced volatile conditions in Vietnam. After Diem's death, instability and disorder reigned. During 1964 alone, seven different governments came to power in South Vietnam. Nevertheless, the United States stepped up aid to Saigon. ''As far as I am concerned,'' Johnson cabled Lodge in April 1964, ''you must have whatever you need to help the Vietnamese do the job, and I assure you that I will act at once to eliminate obstacles or restraints wherever they may appear.''

Early in 1964, to show American resolve, Johnson sent five thousand additional troops to Vietnam. In February, the president approved Operation 34-A, a covert maneuver against North Vietnam involving intelligence gathering and sabotage. But the war still fared badly for the South. By spring, the Vietcong controlled more than half of South Vietnam, and new troops and supplies from the North more than countered U.S. increases. American policymakers came to believe that only by carrying the war directly to the North could the South triumph. Administration strategists responded by planning retaliatory air strikes against North Vietnamese targets, although National Security Adviser McGeorge Bundy suggested obtaining a congressional resolution supporting any future escalation of the war. In May, Johnson's tacticians drafted such a resolution and waited for an opportunity to implement it.

In August 1964 an incident in the Gulf of Tonkin off the coast of North Vietnam gave the administration the occasion to effect the planned expansion of the war with congressional backing. On the night of August 2, the U.S. destroyer *Maddox*, participating in South Vietnamese commando raids against North Vietnam, came under attack from northern patrol boats. The *Maddox* returned the fire, sinking one of the North Vietnamese boats and driving off the others. The *Maddox* suffered no damage except for a half-inch bullet hole found later in an outside bulkhead. Angered at the allegedly "unprovoked" attack, President Johnson ordered a second destroyer to join the *Maddox* and to continue patrolling North Vietnamese waters. On the night of August 4, during a severe thunderstorm, sonar technicians reported what they believed were enemy torpedoes. The *Maddox* and its companion ship began firing. Yet no one on the American ships actually saw any hostile vessels, and soon after the supposed attack, the captain of the *Maddox* radioed that "many reported contacts and torpedoes fired appear doubtful." Blaming "freak weather effects" and an "overeager sonar-man," the captain called for a "complete evaluation before any further action."

Despite his awareness of the dubious nature of the second attack, LBJ never acknowledged that the U.S. ships took part in covert raids against North Vietnam, and he charged the Hanoi regime with "open aggression on the high seas." In retaliation, he ordered air attacks against North Vietnamese naval bases and an oil-storage depot. Unnerved by the crisis, the misinformed U.S. Congress overwhelmingly passed the Gulf of Tonkin resolution, based on the document drawn up months earlier. This sweeping resolution authorized the president to "take all necessary measures to repel any armed attack against the forces of the United States and to prevent further aggression." Reflecting the foreign-policy consensus, the measure passed in the House by a vote of 416–0; in the Senate, the vote was 88–2. Only Democrats Wayne Morse of Oregon and Ernest Gruening of Alaska opposed it. The Gulf of Tonkin resolution was the closest the United States ever came to declaring war on North Vietnam, and it formed the basis of President Johnson's (and later President Richard Nixon's) prosecution of the war in the face of growing opposition in and out of Congress. A delighted LBJ compared the decree to "grandma's nightshirt—it covered everything." Most Americans, too, applauded the resolution.

In September, a month after the Tonkin resolution passed, Johnson's strategists completed plans for sustained bombing of North Vietnam, to begin sometime early in 1965. The administration kept the scheme secret, however, because LBJ was running as the peace candidate against Barry Goldwater, whom they were pillorying as being "trigger happy." In his campaign, Johnson played down the American role in Vietnam. "I have not thought we were ready," he promised in a September speech, "for American boys to do the fighting for Asian boys. . . . We are not going north and drop bombs at this stage of the game."

The election of 1964 offered voters a seemingly clear choice on Vietnam. Johnson assured the public that he wanted "no wider war"; he would neither deploy American troops to fight in South Vietnam nor extend the war by bombing North Vietnam. Goldwater, on the other hand, told voters, "We must have the will to win that war," and gave the impression that, if elected, he would use any means, including nuclear weapons, to achieve victory. In a bitter irony, the overwhelming majority vote for LBJ proclaimed a mandate for peace.

"Waist Deep in the Big Muddy"

In his inaugural address on January 20, 1965, Johnson made scarce mention of Vietnam, except to state that "to ignore aggression would only increase the danger of a larger war." The United States, he claimed, was "free, growing, restless, and full of hope" and with his programs and leadership would soon blossom into the Great Society. A week later the president received a memo from McGeorge Bundy warning of worsening conditions in Vietnam and imminent "disastrous defeat." Buddhist and student strikes disrupted South Vietnam throughout January, and Saigon newspapers called for "negotiated settlement." In Hué some five thousand students sacked the United States Information Service library. Bundy's memo urged an escalation of the war through systematic air attacks on North Vietnam.

On February 6, 1965, when the Vietcong attacked an American base at Pleiku in the central highlands of South Vietnam, Johnson immediately ordered retaliatory air raids against North Vietnam, a nation that he privately referred to as a "raggedy-ass little fourth-rate country." Justifying the raids to the American people, LBJ reverted to a frontier metaphor: "We have kept our gun over the mantel and our shells in the cupboard for a long time now. And what was the result? They are killing our men while they sleep at night."

A week after the retaliatory strikes, the president took the advice of New Frontiersmen Bundy, McNamara, Rusk, and other top officials and approved Operation Rolling Thunder, the long-planned systematic bombing of North Vietnam. By July 1965 American planes were flying more than nine hundred sorties a week over North Vietnam; by December, more than fifteen hundred. In addition to bombing North Vietnam, the United States used heavy bombing to support ground operations in South Vietnam and to destroy suspected enemy infiltration routes in neighboring Laos. During 1966 U.S. bombing raids quadrupled, and by the end of the year more bombs had fallen on Southeast Asia than had exploded throughout the Pacific theater during all of World War II. By late 1968 U.S. pilots had detonated more than 3.2 million tons of explosives, far more than the combined totals used on all fronts of World War II and in the Korean War.

In February 1965 the State Department issued the White Paper, which claimed that the North Vietnamese "inspired, directed, supplied, and controlled" the Vietcong. "A Communist government," the document further asserted, "has set out deliberately to conquer a sovereign people in a neighboring state." As "incontrovertible evidence" of North Vietnamese aggression, the White Paper claimed that during the preceding eighteen months, U.S. and South Vietnamese troops had captured from the Vietcong 179 weapons manufactured in communist countries.

Like the official information supplied at the time of the Gulf of Tonkin crisis, this State Department publication manipulated the truth, downplaying the fact that nearly 98 percent of seized Vietcong arms had come from noncommunist manufacturers. Most, in fact, were American-made weapons that the Vietcong had captured from South Viet-

Operation Rolling Thunder. The sustained heavy bombing of North Vietnam by the United States forced the North Vietnamese to devise means of protecting civilian populations and industries. Here, kindergarten children evacuated from Hanoi attend an outdoor classroom near an air-raid shelter. The children wear wicker helmets for protection against splinters and shrapnel.

namese forces. Indeed, the whole thesis that the war in the South was ''inspired, directed, supplied, and controlled'' by North Vietnam was largely false, and the Johnson administration knew this. Confidential U.S. intelligence before the systematic American air attacks against the North had regularly reported that ''the primary sources of Communist strength in South Vietnam are indigenous.'' North Vietnam had sent advisers and aid to the insurgents in the South as early as 1959, with cadres in place there by 1964. But not until April 1965, well after the bombing had begun, did the CIA report the regular presence of a North Vietnamese regiment fighting in South Vietnam.

The White Paper provided the public rationale for the bombings. Their real purpose was to ''break the will of North Vietnam,'' claimed General Maxwell Taylor, JFK's former military adviser, whom LBJ appointed to replace Lodge as ambassador to South Vietnam. The even larger purpose, according to McGeorge Bundy, was to demonstrate American willingness to use sustained bombing to counter wars of national liberation. This strategy, he contended, ''will set a higher price for the future upon all adventures of guerrilla warfare.''

The Johnson administration launched Operation Rolling Thunder with high optimism. LBJ himself spent many evenings in the White House basement going over aerial photographs and personally picking out targets. Yet from the outset, the new strategy failed. Instead of bringing North Vietnam to the conference table on terms favorable to the United States, the bombings strengthened Hanoi's resolve and brought the North fully into the war. Although the raids aimed to destroy the military industries of North Vietnam, Vietnamese workers rebuilt these small-scale facilities or moved them underground. Nor did extensive U.S. bombing of the Ho Chi Minh Trail close this infiltration route, which the North Vietnamese used to transport men and supplies to the South. A labyrinth of jungle trails modernized into a logistics network capable of handling large trucks, the Ho Chi Minh Trail, although repeatedly devastated by B-52s, was kept open by thousands of North Vietnamese laborers, many of them women and children. When American bombers destroyed concrete and steel bridges, workers hurriedly replaced the structures with bamboo pontoon bridges that could be sunk during the day to avoid detection. Driving at night with headlights off, in trucks camouflaged with palm fronds or banana leaves, the North Vietnamese stepped up their infiltration into South Vietnam after the air strikes began. The American attacks also impelled the Soviet Union and the People's Republic of China to bolster their aid to North Vietnam.

In January 1965, a month before committing the United States to the air war, President Johnson admitted to General Taylor that bombing in itself would not suffice to win the war. Victory, he predicted, would require "appropriate military strength on the ground." LBJ's launching of Operation Rolling Thunder led inexorably to his escalation of American military operations in the South. Soon after the bombing started, veteran political analyst Walter Lippmann argued in a television interview that regular air attacks on North Vietnam would cause the Hanoi regime to move its army into South Vietnam, a shift that would lead to demands for American ground troops. "What then?" the interviewer asked. "At first," Lippmann answered, "if the war hawks prevail and we become involved in a big war, they will rejoice, but in the end the people will weep."

Lippmann would prove a prophet. In early March 1965, as the air strikes escalated, some fifteen hundred marines in full battle gear splashed ashore near Da Nang. Welcoming bands played, U.S. officials held a large sign reading "Welcome to the Gallant Marines," and South Vietnamese girls passed out flowers to the warriors. The scene was a happy beginning of what would become a nightmare for both nations.

On April 1, Johnson acquiesced to the request of General William Westmoreland, the new head of U.S. forces in Vietnam, that American troops be allowed to take offensive action in so-called search-and-destroy missions. In these sorties, helicopters would carry American units into an area to locate the enemy, engage him, and bring in artillery or aircraft fire to destroy him. A few days later, LBJ approved an additional twenty thousand troops. This fateful commitment of U.S. forces ended all pretext that the Americans in South Vietnam served only in an advisory capacity. The United States had lost the chance to withdraw easily and had committed itself to escalation. When Johnson had delivered his optimistic inaugural address in January 1965, about 20,000 U.S. forces served in South Vietnam; by the end of the year, they numbered 185,000.

That same April, Johnson also dispatched marines into the economically depressed Dominican Republic, which had been unstable since the 1961 assassination of long-time dictator Rafael Trujillo. In 1962 a popular reform government headed by Juan Bosch, a social democrat and intellectual, had been freely elected, but a right-wing coup had ousted him the following year. In late April 1965, hostilities broke out between forces supporting the return of Bosch and those backing the conservative army generals. Fearing that a Bosch government might pursue reforms detrimental to American business interests, President Johnson, in violation of Dominican sovereignty, sent in the U.S. Marines on April 28. Soon some 22,000 American troops occupied the Caribbean country. The Bosch reformist faction was routed, and the United States helped to place in power a military dictatorship under General Antonio Imbert. Juan Bosch sadly noted, "This was a democratic revolution smashed by the leading democracy in the world."

As with the escalation in Vietnam, LBJ defended his actions before Congress and the public through deceptive statements. Initially Johnson announced that he had dispatched troops to protect American nationals. At one press conference, he claimed that the insurgents had beheaded hundreds of innocent people and that the U.S. ambassador had phoned him from beneath an embassy desk as bullets whizzed through the windows. Johnson was lying; there were no beheadings, no shots fired at the American embassy. The president offered a second justification. On May 2 he charged that "what began as a popular democratic revolution" had fallen "into the hands of a band of Communist conspirators." On-the-scene reports and later scholarly evaluations denied communist control of the Bosch movement, but Johnson, like Kennedy, was obsessed with Castroism in Latin America and had long since concluded that only the decisive use of military prowess would avert communist expansion. "The real danger," LBJ told a newsman, "is that the other side is going to underestimate us. . . . The danger is that they'll think we are fat and fifty—just the country club crowd."

Johnson's military adventure in the Dominican Republic paid off as far as the administration was concerned. Within a year a degree of order was restored and an elected anticommunist government installed. Yet among knowledgeable Americans, the feeling grew that LBJ and other government officials were not being honest. In addition to undermining LBJ's credibility, the incident disclosed disturbing aspects of Johnson's handling of foreign affairs. Shortly after the episode, Adlai Stevenson confided to a friend, "When I consider what the administration did in the Dominican Republic, I begin to wonder if we know what we are doing in Vietnam."

Lyndon's War

By the summer of 1965, the war in Southeast Asia had become America's war. The South Vietnamese army (ARVN) continued to battle the North; in the end it would suffer far more casualties than Americans. Nevertheless, because countless U.S. advisers had failed to train, equip, and motivate ARVN troops enough to ensure their victory, the Johnson administration now resorted to sheer military might. According to General William Depuy, the United States would simply employ "more bombs, more shells, more napalm . . . 'til the other side cracks and gives up."

The thousands of American combat troops who landed in South Vietnam that summer radiated optimism and eagerness. Few were prepared for Vietnam's tropical climate, dense jungles, murky rivers, flooded rice paddies, and exotic customs and language. Unique in American military history, the conflict lacked overt clashes or battle fronts in the usual sense. Even when U.S. forces seized territory in an occasional open confrontation, they soon lost it. Indeed, the Vietcong and North Vietnamese regulars avoided direct combat. They excelled instead at ambush and at setting traps, often devastating American patrols while remaining invisible. The enemy also could disappear mysteriously among the population. Friend and foe looked alike to the American GIs. A young boy might have a grenade; an old woman might be a walking boobytrap.

U.S. soldiers, with their substantial numbers and superior weaponry, had expected decisive victories on the battlefield—a military solution. "My generation," one soldier recalled, "came of age totally post–World War II. We were the savior democracy . . . and I was bred to believe that . . . you served your country." But as the war dragged on, frustration mounted. Philip Caputo, a marine lieutenant, aptly summed up the disillusionment of the American infantry: "When we marched into the rice paddies on that damp March afternoon, we carried, along with our packs and rifles, the implicit convictions that the Vietcong would be quickly beaten. We kept the packs and rifles; the convictions, we lost."

Most American draftees and enlistees came from working-class families who were ineligible for deferments because they did not attend college. A 1968 study of deferment policies and income levels showed that a high-school dropout from a low-income family had a 70 percent chance of serving in Vietnam, compared with a 64 percent chance for a high-school graduate and a 42 percent chance for a college graduate. Nonwhites were disproportionately represented, particularly in the early years of the war. In 1965 blacks, although comprising only 12 percent of the U.S. population, accounted for 23.5 percent of all American combat deaths. The African-American community protested the shocking percentage, and in 1966 the Pentagon pressured the military to reduce the black casualty rate. By the end of the war, the percentage had dropped to 12.5, only slightly higher than the black proportion of the national population. Despite the lower figures, however, draft policies reflected racial and class bias throughout the conflict. One Vietnam-era study of the draft concluded, "Factory neighborhoods, slums [and] Negro ghettos were the draft boards' happy hunting grounds."

For most of these eighteen- and nineteen-year-old soldiers, boot camp and Vietnam were their first experiences away from home. They went to war armed with patriotism, but for many of them, Vietnam turned into a nightmare. "Going crazy," wrote journalist Michael Herr, "was built into the tour." One soldier told a reporter, "The off times are just as insane as the on-duty times. We'd get in fights and blow things up. . . . We didn't make much distinction about who the enemy was. . . . All you were supposed to do over there was be crazy."

Once initiated, escalation took on a life of its own. As U.S. casualties mounted, those who favored broadening the war used the logic of redemption; the underlying motivation for the war shifted from saving Vietnam to repairing America's national pride. Johnson saw the war as a test of U.S. will and credibility: "Ike . . . made a promise. I have to keep it." The real threat in Vietnam, according to Johnson, was not just the NLF or North Vietnam. China had successfully exploded an atomic bomb in 1964, and LBJ asserted that "over this war, and all Asia, is another reality, the deepening shadow of Communist China."

Time and again the Johnson administration acquiesced to General Westmoreland's request for additional U.S. troops, and with every American escalation, military and government officials' optimism grew. As early as 1952, Truman's secretary of state, Dean Acheson, had insisted that the American-aided French war effort "appears to be developing favorably." Ten years later Robert McNamara stated flatly, "We're win-

Deep in the Big Muddy. A GI applies a make-shift bandage to the head of a wounded buddy while keeping an eye out for the enemy during fighting "outside the wire" of U.S. Special Forces camp at Ben Het.

ning this war." With Johnson's escalation, the promises became more strident and frequent, while the number of American troops steadily climbed. By the end of 1966, the total stood at 385,000; a year later, more than 485,000. What had started as a limited short-term war now seemed to have no end.

Unable to win decisive battles or to pacify the countryside, McNamara and General Westmoreland tried to prove U.S. success through the "body count"—a daily total of supposed enemy killed in combat. Death became a numbers game; the body count made the foe impersonal and the concept of victory in battle nonsensical. Under pressure to produce higher and higher counts, unit commanders offered prizes for the most kills. Charts posted in regimental headquarters listed enemy dead, as one might list baseball batting averages. The body count became an end in itself. American units routinely counted civilian casualties as Vietcong dead. "If it's dead and Vietnamese, it's VC, was a rule of thumb in the bush," recalled marine lieutenant Caputo. Padding of figures became customary; in 1965, when 1,365 American soldiers died, the body count certified 35,000 dead Vietcong. By late 1967, U.S. officials listed more than 220,000 VC dead and promised imminent U.S. victory.

Even had the death count been accurate, it is doubtful that the U.S. strategy of attrition would have succeeded. Each year during the escalation, an estimated two hundred thousand North Vietnamese reached draft age, enabling Hanoi to replace its losses and to match the U.S. build-up easily. Moreover, the North Vietnamese seemed prepared to fight indefinitely. The American public, on the other hand, would soon protest the casualties and costs.

Ironically, as American officials busily counted bodies, they also spoke of "winning the hearts and minds" of the Vietnamese people. America's role in Vietnam, in the words of McNamara's assistant John McNaughton, was that of a "good doctor." In reality, the war wrought more and more wanton destruction on the people of Vietnam, both North and South. Although the administration claimed that the multiplying air strikes over North Vietnam were carried out with surgical precision against military targets only, in fact American bombers caused thousands of civilian casualties.

Even in South Vietnam, American policymakers designated huge areas as "free-fire" zones. U.S. troops forcibly moved civilian populations to supposedly safe areas, then burned the abandoned villages and destroyed crops. Much of the devastation in both North and South came from huge B-52 bombers' flying at thirty thousand to fifty thousand feet, trying to hit unseen targets such as jungle hideouts, "suspect" villages, trucks, and even bicycles. As with the body count, officials kept statistics on the number of bombing sorties, as if the figures documented American success.

The U.S. Air Force sprayed millions of gallons of chemical defoliants on the forests and crops of South Vietnam, a tactic begun during the Kennedy years and continued under presidents Johnson and Nixon. All told, American pilots dumped nearly nineteen million gallons of toxic herbicides between 1962 and 1971. Called Operation Ranch Hand, the program defoliated nearly 20 percent of the South Vietnamese countryside, a land area about the size of Massachusetts. Defoliation aimed to eliminate jungles and forests where the enemy might hide and to destroy rice crops to starve the VC. Like bombing, however, the tactic harmed the civilian population but failed to halt the VC and North Vietnamese. Most of the spraying used a dioxin known as Agent Orange, later found to damage human health and the environment.

Despite bombs, defoliants, and the devastation of the countryside, the mounting body counts of presumed VC and North Vietnamese dead, and the ringing reassurances of American leaders, the United States and its South Vietnamese ally could not crush the enemy. Gaining peasant loyalty was crucial to American success, yet U.S. and South Vietnamese policies and operations consistently alienated the local population. Allied forces demolished hundreds of villages, turned thousands of acres of rich cropland into wasteland, and killed thousands of civilians. They forced millions more to leave their homes and the ancestral grave sites so important to Vietnamese culture and relocated them in barbed-wire-encircled "strategic hamlets" that the Vietcong and North Vietnamese compared to concentration camps. As war veteran John Kerry later recalled, "In Vietnam, the 'greatest soldiers in the world,' better armed and better equipped than the opposition, unleashed the power of the greatest technology in the world against thatch huts and mud paths. In the process we created a nation of refugees, bomb craters, amputees, orphans, widows, and prostitutes." Not surprisingly, the Vietcong and even the North Vietnamese regulars garnered support in the countryside and thus moved freely among the people.

In short, an array of peasants with limited heavy artillery, operating largely without

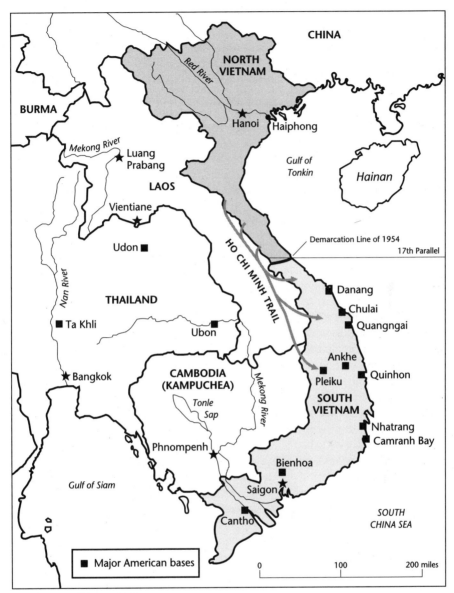

The Vietnam War to 1968.

an air force or a navy, stymied the most powerful country in history, a nation that possessed the most advanced technological weaponry ever employed. The United States found itself trapped in a strategically insignificant country less than half the size of California, more than nine thousand miles away. The bizarre predicament bled away American power and prestige. LBJ's escalation diverted funds and energy from his War on Poverty and Great Society programs, unleashed spiraling inflation, and wrought the most severe divisiveness in American society since the Civil War. In April 1965, less than a month after the first marine battalions debarked at Da Nang, Senator Wayne Morse swore that Vietnam would send Johnson "out of office the most discredited President in the history of the nation." At the time, both the war and the president enjoyed firm popular backing, and Morse's prediction struck many as farfetched and unpatriotic. In the end, however, the senator's prophecy would prove correct.

Vietnam at Home

World War II had inspired national unity, but Vietnam only reinforced manifold divisions in American society: minorities against the dominant culture, young people against the establishment, liberals against conservatives, class against class. The war protesters who shouted "Hell No, We Won't Go!" and the war supporters whose bumper stickers retorted, "America, Love It or Leave It!" might have hailed from separate nations, so different were their viewpoints. From 1965 until America's final withdrawal from South Vietnam in 1975, the nation split sharply into supporters and critics of the war, the hawks and the doves.

In Congress and the country at large, hawks initially predominated, endorsing LBJ's policies with fervor. Most of them accepted at face value the administration's argument that the U.S. presence in Vietnam mainly aimed to defend a democratic ally from the external communist aggression of North Vietnam. Hawks further assumed that Moscow and Beijing supplied and encouraged the Hanoi regime. Adhering to the domino theory and scorning a Munich-style appeasement, they saw the Vietnam War as an essential model for containing communist expansion everywhere. Indeed, some hawks viewed the president's policies as too limited and restricted; these critics called for yet additional troops and bombs, which they were sure would lead to quick victory. Some even advocated the use of nuclear weapons.

From today's perspective, it is tempting to judge hawks as misinformed, devious, or downright evil. However, in view of the dominant Cold War ideas, values, and policies characteristic of the time, involvement in Vietnam made sense. In fact, numerous well-meaning and well-informed people strongly supported the war. Vietnam, viewed from the global perspective of postwar American foreign policy, struck many as a logical and justifiable effort to contain world communism. LBJ's escalation thus appears not the tragic policy of an isolated president but a natural development of two decades of incremental decisions made in accordance with the prevailing Cold War consensus. When the Johnson administration began to expand the U.S. role in the war, the great majority of the public and politicians alike approved.

Doves, however, perceived the issue in profoundly different ways. Although initially a small minority, their numbers and influence grew steadily. In the long run, the dove critique of the war would challenge not only specific policies in Vietnam but the entire Cold War consensus on which those policies rested. Liberal and radical doves did not see the war as a simple struggle between democracy and communism. They realized that Diem and his successors were dictatorial and corrupt. Moreover, they knew that much of the opposition to the South Vietnamese government was motivated not by communism but by Buddhist and Confucian hatred of Catholic dominance and by a desire to end the economic and social oppression of the Saigon regime. Doves viewed the struggle as a civil war, with large-scale support for the NLF coming from North Vietnam only after the United States began bombing the North. These critics also recognized that, historically, Vietnam was a single nation: the divisions of North and South were creations of the 1954 Geneva conference, which had called for elections to reunite the country in 1956. In addition, doves disagreed with the administration's assumptions that North Vietnam was the pawn of the Chinese or the Soviets, and that if South Vietnam fell, all Southeast Asia would follow. War protesters grew incensed by mounting American casualties, rising draft quotas, and the spiraling cost of the war, which slashed funds available for domestic social and welfare programs.

Above all, critics condemned the war's brutality and immorality evidenced by the daily body counts, the published photos and reports of torture and mutilation, the burning and bombing of villages, the herding of civilians into refugee camps, and the use of napalm and toxic defoliants. Doves came to believe that, in the name of anticommunism, the United States was destroying an ancient civilization and its people. Reflecting the doves' moral critique of the war, *New York Times* correspondent Neil Sheehan wrote of witnessing "the bombed-out peasant hamlets, the orphans begging and stealing in the streets, and the women and children with napalm burns lying on the hospital cots." Like most other doves, Sheehan questioned "whether the United States or any other nation has the right to inflict this suffering and degradation on another people for its own ends."

Although direct American involvement in Vietnam began with the defeat of the French in 1954, not until the early 1960s did a significant number of Americans become concerned about the U.S. presence there. Protests against the build-up of American advisers in Vietnam first cropped up during Kennedy's presidency and Johnson's first year in office. Pacifist groups such as the War Resisters League, Fellowship of Reconciliation, Committee for Non-Violent Action, the American Friends Service Committee, the Catholic Worker, and Women Strike for Peace, all active in the "Ban the Bomb" movement in the fifties and early sixties, led the way in trying to educate the public on the realities of U.S. involvement in Southeast Asia. On December 19, 1964, peace groups and the Socialist party sponsored an outdoor antiwar rally in New York City's Washington Square. About fifteen hundred people turned out to hear speeches by veteran pacifists A. J. Muste, A. Philip Randolph, and Norman Thomas. Peace groups held similar small demonstrations that day in Boston, Philadelphia, Chicago, San Francisco, and Seattle. The purpose of these gatherings, in Muste's words, was "to keep the issue of Vietnam before the public, and before the Administration."

The demonstrations drew little notice at first, but the public's focus shifted within a few months, as Johnson's escalation during the winter and spring of 1965 brought Vietnam to the nation's attention. By spring, antiwar activism had spread well beyond the tiny, traditional peace movement. War protesters came to include a broad cross-section of Americans, but it was on college campuses that the indictment against Johnson's war crystallized. Within the universities, the civil-rights movement already had stirred thousands of students to activism. These youths thrilled to President Johnson's call for a Great Society, and many of them had supported him as the "peace" candidate in the 1964 election. Now in 1965, when LBJ adopted the very policies for which he had condemned Goldwater, his supporters felt betrayed.

The initial manifestation of growing antiwar sentiment within universities took the form of "teach-ins," the first of which occurred at the University of Michigan on

March 24, 1965. More than three thousand students and some fifty faculty attended the all-night session designed to educate on Vietnam. The teach-in movement soon blossomed. From the University of Maine in Orono, where about three hundred gathered for an evening teach-in, to Berkeley, where some twelve thousand University of California students and faculty attended a two-day event, war critics held hundreds of these sessions. Although organizers tried to present all sides of the conflict, few administration supporters participated. As a result, most teach-ins became as much antiwar rallies as educational seminars. At the University of Wisconsin, some five thousand students heard Professor William Appleman Williams denounce American policy as an attempt "to thwart and abort an indigenous social and political revolution." At Rutgers University, another radical historian, Eugene Genovese, sparked a furor when he told cheering students, "I do not fear or regret the impending Vietcong victory in Vietnam, I welcome it." Addressing a crowd at the University of Oregon, Senator Wayne Morse accurately prophesied, "Twelve months from tonight there will be hundreds of thousands of American boys fighting in Southeast Asia—and tens of thousands of them will be coming home in coffins."

The spring 1965 teach-ins played an important role in collectivizing intellectual opposition to the war and legitimizing dissent, persuading large numbers of students and faculty to reconsider America's role in Vietnam. This shift also led people to reevaluate America's basic Cold War assumptions. For many, Vietnam became a symbol of deeper ills afflicting American society.

Initially the Johnson administration tried to ignore the teach-ins. However, Secretary of State Dean Rusk soon spoke out, blaming the teach-ins on "the gullibility of educated men" with their "stubborn disregard of plain facts." A Senate subcommittee headed by Connecticut senator Thomas Dodd went so far as to label the teach-ins a communist plot. In May the administration sent so-called truth teams from the State Department to universities to present the government's case. Everywhere the government representatives encountered tough questions and hecklers, and after three weeks the administration called in the teams. On May 15, 1965, a national teach-in gave the antiwar movement crucial television coverage. McGeorge Bundy was to have defended the administration but backed out because of the Dominican crisis. His replacement, Robert Scalapino, a prowar Berkeley professor, proved no match for an antiwar panel composed of foreign-policy and Asian specialists.

The spring of 1965 also witnessed the first mass antiwar demonstration. Late in 1964, Students for a Democratic Society (SDS), a small, radical campus and community-action organization, called for a protest gathering in Washington the following spring. Held on Easter Sunday, April 17, 1965, the event astounded its organizers when nearly thirty thousand students and adults showed up. The day of the march dawned warm and sunny, and folk singers Joan Baez and Judy Collins entertained the crowd with freedom songs. There followed speeches by Yale historian Staughton Lynd, Alaska senator Ernest Gruening, radical journalist I. F. Stone, and two young representatives of the New Left—Paul Potter of SDS and Bob Moses of SNCC.

After the successful Easter protest, antiwar activists staged a series of additional national demonstrations. That summer, various antiwar groups formed the National Committee to End the War in Vietnam; on October 15–16, this committee sponsored the First International Days of Protest. Demonstrations involving more than a hundred

Hawks. While demonstrations protesting the Vietnam War are in progress around the world on October 21, 1967, this group of high school and college students holds a patriotic vigil in New York's Battery Park, expressing their support for the war.

thousand people sprang up throughout the country. High-school and college students joined with middle-aged parents and senior citizens in a coalition bound by their opposition to the war. That weekend witnessed similar protests in London, Stockholm, Copenhagen, Brussels, and Tokyo. Clearly opposition to the Vietnam conflict had spread beyond the ranks of committed pacifists and student radicals.

Liberal intellectuals played an increasingly important role in the antiwar coalition. When LBJ began bombing North Vietnam in February 1965, the *New Republic,* a major liberal journal, and Americans for Democratic Action, the most influential liberal political organization, called for a negotiated settlement. Hoping to woo intellectuals, Johnson, at the suggestion of administration historian Eric Goldman, sponsored a White House Festival of the Arts for June 1965. Invitees included cultural icons such as distinguished American poet Robert Lowell. In a much-publicized letter to the president, however, Lowell declined the invitation and warned that America was "becoming an explosive and suddenly chauvinistic nation" that "may even be drifting . . . to the last nuclear ruin." Other intellectuals and artists followed Lowell's example. Infuriated at these "sons-of-bitches" who had been so obeisant at Camelot, LBJ nearly canceled the festival.

Many influential black leaders also came to oppose the war, specifically the incredible sacrifices that African-Americans were making in Vietnam and the war's undermining of domestic reforms. The war and racial injustice, claimed Martin Luther King, Jr., were "inextricably bound together." Some blacks saw the wanton destruction of Asians as racially motivated. "Vietnamese are being murdered," stated an official

SNCC resolution, "because the United States is pursuing an aggressive policy in violation of international law." CORE gave its support to "the men in this country who are unwilling to respond to a military draft." In mid-1965, blacks in McComb, Mississippi, distributed a pamphlet stating that "no Mississippi Negroes should be fighting in Viet Nam for the White man's freedom, until all the Negro People are free in Mississippi."

In Congress, criticism of the war, nearly absent at the time of the Tonkin Gulf resolution, grew with Johnson's escalation. In 1965 Senators George McGovern and Frank Church, both Democrats, denounced the bombing of North Vietnam and called for negotiations. Senators Eugene McCarthy, Gaylord Nelson, and Stephen Young soon joined them. In addition, both Senate majority leader Mike Mansfield and chairman of the Senate Foreign Relations Committee J. William Fulbright privately expressed their misgivings to the president.

Partly to minimize growing skepticism among these and other Democrats, LBJ halted the bombing of North Vietnam on Christmas Eve 1965 and called for negotiations, only to resume the attacks on January 29, 1966. Dismissing Johnson's bombing halt as a propaganda ploy, additional liberals disparaged the president's policies. Fulbright now openly joined the doves, and in February 1966 his Foreign Relations Committee held televised hearings on the war. In this forum, Secretary of State Dean Rusk and U.S. ambassador to Vietnam Maxwell Taylor presented the administration's case. George Kennan, the originator of the containment doctrine, in the 1940s, told the committee that preoccupation with Vietnam weakened the United States in more strategic areas of the world. America, he concluded, could win in Vietnam only "at the cost of a degree of damage to civilian life and of civilian suffering, generally, for which I would not like to see this country responsible."

Although the dignified Fulbright hearings failed to resolve the dilemma, they further legitimized dissent. Indeed, Fulbright's reconsideration of the administration's Vietnam policies led him to rethink American postwar foreign policy in general. In a series of lectures at Johns Hopkins University during the spring of 1966 that were later published in book form, he attacked America's "arrogance of power" and warned against blindly opposing all revolutionary movements in the name of anticommunism. American leaders, he concluded, were not "qualified to play God." A seething LBJ began snidely referring to his former friend as Senator "Halfbright."

But even more annoying to Johnson than Fulbright's defection was the emergence early in 1966 of Robert Kennedy, now a senator from New York, as a leading Senate dove. Johnson detested Kennedy and feared him politically. Although Bobby Kennedy had somewhat of a reputation as a ruthless political operator, he had inherited his brother's political aura. For those who cherished the Camelot legend, Robert Kennedy offered the hope of restoration. Moody, temperamental, and private, Kennedy nevertheless began to emerge as a liberal champion. His brother's murder, the era's racial struggles, and Vietnam had combined to move Kennedy to the left. Becoming a genuine supporter of nonwhites and the poor, he followed his emotions and took political risks. Kennedy not only called for including the NLF in the South Vietnamese government, he also supported blood donations to the Vietcong, traveled to South Africa to stand with opponents of apartheid, and flew to California to aid labor leader Cesar Chávez in his efforts to unionize grape pickers.

Enraged by Kennedy, Fulbright, and the increasing number of dissenters within his own party, Johnson lashed out at his critics. In a May 1966 speech, he defended the war as a patriotic duty. ''There will be some 'Nervous Nellies,' '' he charged, ''and some who will become frustrated and bothered and break ranks under the strain, and some will turn on their leaders, and on their country, and on our own fighting men. . . . But I have not the slightest doubt that the courage and the dedication and the good sense of the wise American people will ultimately prevail.''

Despite Johnson's outbursts, opposition to the war expanded and even surfaced within the administration. Undersecretary of State George Ball, a longtime advocate of a negotiated settlement, resigned in frustration. LBJ's press secretary, Bill Moyers, whom Johnson regarded almost as a son, quit over the war. National Security Adviser McGeorge Bundy, one of the war's architects, came to have reservations and quietly left the administration to take a job with the Ford Foundation.

The highest-ranking policymaker to reconsider his original support of the war was Secretary of Defense Robert McNamara. After years of believing the optimistic reports routinely issued by U.S. military officials, McNamara began to harbor doubts. Somehow the policies that he had helped to set in motion had failed to achieve their objectives. Even his own son had joined the antiwar movement. In June 1967, McNamara ordered a special assistant in the Defense Department, Daniel Ellsberg, to lead a secret investigation of the history of U.S. involvement in Vietnam. The Ellsberg team's careful study uncovered classified documents and chronicled a long history of official deception of the public. Alarmed by his findings, Ellsberg defied security rules and in 1971 released his classified report to the *New York Times,* where it was published as *The Pentagon Papers* and would be used to spur the antiwar effort during the Nixon years. Meanwhile, McNamara's misgivings deepened and led him to support a negotiated settlement. In mid-November 1967, soon after McNamara had told LBJ that the administration's strategy in Vietnam was ''dangerous, costly, and unsatisfactory,'' Johnson announced that the secretary of defense would be resigning to head the World Bank. The president replaced McNamara with his friend and supporter Clark Clifford, but the defection of original Kennedy appointees such as McNamara and Bundy weakened Johnson's claim that his policies represented the continuation of JFK's strategies.

In the country at large, dissent broadened and intensified during 1966–1967. Clergy held peace vigils; students at Union Theological Seminary circulated a petition requesting that draftees be allowed to choose some form of alternative service; professors took out newspaper ads against the war; Women Strike for Peace lobbied Congress for ''a peaceful solution''; college students at Bryn Mawr, Haverford, and Swarthmore fasted for peace; members of SANE began a national campaign for the election of antiwar congressional candidates.

Personal acts of opposition proliferated as well. Singer Eartha Kitt denounced the war at a White House luncheon given by Lady Bird Johnson. When called for induction in April 1967, heavyweight champion Muhammad Ali, a powerful symbol of black pride and accomplishment, set an example for other African-Americans by refusing to be drafted to fight in a ''white man's war.'' Authorities stripped him of his title and sent him to prison at the height of his boxing career. Also that month, folk singer Pete Seeger, appearing on national TV for the first time since being blacklisted as a red in the early fifties, attacked the war in a song called ''Waist Deep in the Big Muddy''

("And the old fool says 'Push on' "). In a more sarcastic vein, that spring the Fugs, an underground rock group, released a song called "Kill for Peace":

Kill, kill, kill for peace.

If you don't kill them then the Chinese will.

If you don't want America to play second fiddle.

Kill, kill, kill for peace.

Kill, kill, kill for peace.

If you let them live they might subvert the Prussians.

If you let them live they might love the Russians.

Kill, kill, kill for peace.

The mass antiwar demonstrations rolled on. On March 25–26, 1966, the Second International Days of Protest again saw rallies throughout the United States and around the world. On August 6, Lyndon Johnson's daughter Lucy's wedding day and the anniversary of Hiroshima, protesters carrying two coffins draped with Japanese and North Vietnamese flags greeted the reception guests. The largest antiwar demonstrations to date took place on April 15, 1967. Sponsored by a coalition of antiwar groups called the Spring Mobilization to End the War in Vietnam, protests in New York and San Francisco drew combined crowds of more than half a million, twice as many as had attended the famed 1963 civil-rights march. That October, more than a hundred thousand participated in a demonstration in Washington that included a group of self-described "witches, warlocks, holymen, seers, prophets, mystics, saints, sorcerers, shamans, troubadours, minstrels, bards, roadmen and madmen" who attempted to levitate the Pentagon and exorcise its evil spirits, flinging "mighty words of white light against the demon-controlled structure."

Antiwar activists came from all walks of life: young and old, black and white, and every shade in the liberal-radical political spectrum. Demonstrators were suburban mothers pushing baby carriages, priests and nuns, tweedy professors, aristocratic octogenarians, blue-suited businessmen, blue-collar union members, Vietnam veterans, blacks wearing dashikis and sporting Afro hairstyles, bearded young men, and long-haired young women carrying daisies and chanting "Flower Power." More than 150 organizations threw their support behind the major antiwar marches. These groups ran a broad gamut that included religiously motivated traditional peace groups such as the American Friends Service Committee and the Catholic Worker, old-line pacifist organizations such as the War Resisters League and the Committee for Nonviolent Action, respected middle-class organizations such as SANE and Women Strike for Peace, militant civil-rights groups such as SNCC and CORE, New Left student-oriented societies such as SDS and the Student Peace Union, and Marxist youth groups such as the communist W. E. B. Du Bois Club and the Maoist Progressive Labor party. In addition, thousands of people participated in demonstrations motivated by individual concern rather than group affiliation.

Unfortunately for the effectiveness and credibility of the antiwar movement, the media focused on its militant and outrageous youthful participants from the New Left and counterculture. The uninformed public thus gained the mistaken impression that

Reprinted through the Courtesy of Bil Canfield and the *Newark Star-Ledger*.

the war's opponents consisted largely of unpatriotic kooks, hippies, flower children, communists, and cowards out to avoid the draft. Although the media presented a distorted picture of the movement, militancy did grow among antiwar activists during 1966–1967. Frustrated by Johnson's apparent indifference to peaceful demonstrations and by the continued escalation of the war, "From protest to resistance!" increasingly became the rallying cry. Youthful demonstrators chanted, "Hey, Hey, LBJ, How Many Kids Did You Kill Today?" Some protesters waved North Vietnamese flags and chanted "Ho, Ho, Ho Chi Minh, the Vietcong Is Gonna Win." On college campuses, students harassed recruiters from organizations such as the CIA and Dow Chemical, which manufactured napalm. Reserve Officers Training Corps (ROTC) programs came under fire, and on a few campuses, activists attacked and even burned ROTC buildings. High-level government officials making public appearances routinely faced masses of hecklers. When Robert McNamara visited Harvard University in November 1966, an angry student mob surrounded his limousine and forced a confrontation.

The draft in particular stirred student militancy. Although the majority of draft-age men complied with the Selective Service throughout the war years, a significant minority did not. Some went to jail; thousands more fled, especially to Canada. Others, because of deferment policies, stayed out of the military by remaining in college or graduate school. More militant protesters expressed their outrage by turning in or publicly burning their draft cards, despite Congress's passing a law making the act a felony. In the tradition of Thoreau and Gandhi, young men claimed to defy the law in the name of higher moral principles. "To destroy one's draft card, to place one's conscience before the dictates of one's government," declared one card burner, "is in the highest tradition of human conduct."

Beginning in California in 1967, students formed the Resistance to give direction to the antidraft movement. "The War in Viet Nam is criminal," the group announced. "We must act together, at great individual risk, to stop it. . . . To cooperate with conscription is to perpetuate its existence, without which the government could not wage war. We have chosen to openly defy the draft and confront the government and its war directly." Women participated by counseling draft resisters, organizing and participating in draft protests, and playing an important part in the antidraft movement in various other ways. In addition to encouraging massive defiance of the draft, the Resistance attempted to close down an induction center in Oakland, California, in October 1967, catalyzing a week of violent confrontation with police.

Militant students were not the only Americans who turned to civil disobedience as the war's devastation and costs mounted. That same October, Father Philip Berrigan, a Roman Catholic priest and World War II veteran, and three other men broke into a Baltimore draft office and drenched the files in their own blood. The following May, Berrigan, out on bail, was joined by his brother, Daniel, a Jesuit priest, and seven other Catholic priests and lay people. Together, they destroyed the draft records in Catonsville, Maryland. "An unthinkable Asian war," imputed Daniel Berrigan soon after his arrest, "once a mere canker on the national body . . . has festered and flowered . . . until only Jeremiah and Kafka can encompass its irrational horror."

Academics, too, grew radical. On October 12, 1967, "A Call to Resist Illegitimate Authority," signed by 121 university professors and other intellectuals, was published in the *New York Review of Books.* The document pledged the signers to raise money "to organize draft resistance unions, to supply legal defense and bail, to support families and otherwise aid resistance to the war in whatever ways may seem appropriate." Protesters circulated and signed similar petitions at large universities and small colleges throughout the country.

Morally outraged by the war, millions of Americans also took alarm at its economic costs. When Lyndon Johnson began the escalation in 1965, he mistakenly deemed the economy sufficiently sound to fund both Great Society programs and the expanding military effort. But by January 1966, Johnson himself admitted that "because of Vietnam, we cannot do all that we should, or all that we would like to do." Martin Luther King, Jr., more blunt, described the antipoverty program as "broken and eviscerated, as if it were some idle political plaything of a society gone mad on war." By 1967 annual spending on the war surpassed $30 billion, nearly two-and-a-half times the scant $12 billion spent on domestic social programs.

Not only did the war hurt the poor by curbing funds for poverty programs, it also unleashed an inflationary spiral that plagued all Americans. Early in 1966, the Council of Economic Advisers warned President Johnson that increased military appropriations had created deficits that in turn had overstimulated the economy and spurred inflation. Now, less than two years after LBJ had pushed through a tax cut to stimulate the economy, the council recommended tax increases. Johnson delayed, preferring not to raise taxes during an election year. Meanwhile, war costs, the deficit, and inflation continued to mushroom, and a decade of relative price stability ended. What would become twenty years of sustained inflation only aggravated the widespread discontent of the time. Not until August 1967 did Johnson call for a tax increase, but nearly a year would pass before Congress agreed to a 10 percent surcharge on personal and corporate incomes. By then economic problems had advanced too far to be checked by taxation.

In 1964 Lyndon Johnson had received one of the greatest popular mandates in election history. Even as late as January 1966, polls showed that 63 percent of the people approved his handling of the presidency. But by October 1966, his rating had fallen to 44 percent; he would never again enjoy majority support. Always insecure, LBJ worried obsessively that "liberals" and "intellectuals" plotted his demise, and that fairweather friends had abandoned him. Embittered, his cherished Great Society programs at a standstill, and his popularity steadily waning, Johnson grew more and more secretive and peevish. As ghetto riots, inflation, and bitter divisions over the war closed in on him, the president's political savvy deserted him. By 1967 he was a virtual captive in the White House, limiting his public appearances to places, such as military bases, unlikely to include protesters.

"The major threat we have is from the doves," LBJ told his advisers in September 1967. Setting out to destroy the peace movement, he had the CIA and the FBI establish surveillance programs and compile thousands of files on antiwar activists. The CIA and FBI infiltrated the peace movement so as to disrupt and discredit it. At the same time, the White House launched an all-out public-relations campaign to build popular support for the war. The government helped to establish the Committee for Peace with Freedom in Vietnam, an ostensibly private organization that aimed to win the backing of America's "silent center." LBJ ordered the embassy and military command in Saigon to "search urgently for occasions to present sound evidence of progress in Viet Nam." Reports of rising enemy body counts were dutifully documented. "I am very, very encouraged," General Westmoreland told Congress in November 1967. "We are making real progress. . . . The enemy's hopes are bankrupt."

Nevertheless, the president's popularity continued to plummet, barely touching 28 percent that fall. For the first time, polls indicated that a majority of Americans judged U.S. intervention in Vietnam a mistake. Both in and out of government, opposition to the war intensified daily. "Vietnam," maintained Johnson aide Jack Valenti soon after resigning his post, "was a fungus slowly spreading its suffocating crust. . . . No matter what we turned our hands and minds to, there was Vietnam, its contagion infecting everything that it touched, and it seemed to touch everything." Confessing to having once been an "all-out hawk," Republican senator Thruston Morton of Kentucky claimed that the United States had painted itself into a corner in Vietnam. Robert Kennedy, too, sensed America's anguish. On national television, he announced, "The people are terribly disturbed across this country. There is general dissatisfaction . . . with our society. . . . I am dissatisfied with our country."

All the antiwar clamor baffled Johnson. His escalation of the conflict had grown naturally out of the Cold War ideology of the bipartisan consensus that had dominated the foreign-policy decisionmaking of every administration since World War II. The containment theory expounded in the Truman Doctrine of 1947, supported by Eisenhower in the 1950s and reconfirmed by Kennedy in the early 1960s, had pledged the United States to oppose the advance of communism anywhere in the world. Over these years, Vietnam had served as a test case of America's ability to defeat a communist-backed guerrilla movement in a Third World nation. Johnson never questioned that responsibility. "Why are we in Vietnam?" he asked rhetorically in 1965. "We are there because we have a promise to keep. . . . To leave Vietnam to its fate would shake the confidence of all these people in the value of American commitment.'' Armed with his convictions, Johnson pushed on. By late 1967, he had expanded troop strength in Vietnam to half a million.

● ● ●

Johnson's Vietnam policy, based on assumptions that had gone uncontested since the late forties, now met with widespread criticism. Many liberals, alarmed by the crisis, had broken with the administration and rejected the simplistic anticommunism that had served as orthodoxy for so long. Millions of other Americans had come to see the war as a threat to their moral standards, economic well-being, and social stability. Moreover, nightly television coverage of the conflict revealed the error of official optimism. LBJ's frequent efforts to deceive Congress and the American people further eroded support for his war policies. As antiwar sentiment mounted, the public's confidence in government withered. This shift in turn encouraged criticism of both the war and Great Society domestic programs.

The Tet Offensive early in 1968—a massive North Vietnamese and Vietcong assault on American and ARVN forces throughout South Vietnam (see Chapter 8)—would deal the final blow to Johnson. Soon after Tet, LBJ chose not to run again for the presidency, his political career and liberal vision casualties of war. He would exit the White House in disgrace, with the fighting still raging in Southeast Asia and the United States split asunder.

Selected Bibliography

An excellent introduction to American involvement in Vietnam and its ultimate failure is George C. Herring, *America's Longest War* (1986 ed.). Stanley Karnow, *Vietnam* (1983), features a detailed history of the war by the chief correspondent for the PBS television series on Vietnam. *The Vietnam War: An Almanac* (1985), edited by John S. Bowman, is a useful chronology of the war and other events in Vietnam from World War II to 1984. George McT. Kahin's *Intervention* (1986) is excellent on the early years of U.S. involvement in Vietnam, the nature of Diem's rule, and the insurgency against it. Two first-rate critical accounts of the U.S. role in Vietnam in the context of American culture are Gabriel Kolko's *Anatomy of a War: Vietnam, the United States, and the Modern Historical Experience* (1985), and Loren Baritz's *Backfire* (1985). A controversial defense of U.S. policies based on classified military records is Guenter Lewy, *America in Vietnam* (1978). Although few other scholars would agree, Lewy argues that the war should have been fought and could have been won; he also defends the United States against

charges of war crimes. Jeffrey P. Kimball, ed., *To Reason Why: The Debate About the Causes of U.S. Involvement in the Vietnam War* (1990), and David Levy, *The Debate Over Vietnam* (1991), offer several interpretations of why American policymakers acted as they did. Three outstanding studies that give equal weight to the Vietnamese and the American sides are Frances FitzGerald, *Fire in the Lake* (1972); James Pinckney Harrison, *The Endless War* (1982); and Marilyn Young, *The Vietnam Wars, 1945–1990* (1991). Paul M. Kattenburg's *The Vietnam Trauma in American Foreign Policy, 1945–75* (1992) places U.S. policy toward Indochina in the broader context of American policy worldwide.

The controversial *Pentagon Papers* (1971) document the history of American involvement in Vietnam from the Truman years through the Johnson presidency. Other revealing collections of documents are Garth Porter, ed., *Vietnam: A History in Documents* (1979); Steven Cohen, ed., *Vietnam: Anthology and Guide to a Television History* (1983); Marvin E. Gettleman et al., eds.,

Vietnam and America: A Documented History (1985); and Robert McMahon, ed., *Major Problems in the History of the Vietnam War* (1995).

Insiders' defenses of American policies in Vietnam include Lyndon Johnson, *The Vantage Point* (1971); William C. Westmoreland, *A Soldier Reports* (1976); Townsend Hoopes, *The Limits of Intervention* (1969); Maxwell Taylor, *Swords and Ploughshares* (1972); Walt W. Rostow, *The Diffusion of Power* (1972); and Dean Rusk, *As I Saw It* (1990). A lively indictment of these policymakers can be found in David Halberstam's prize-winning *The Best and the Brightest* (1972) and his earlier *The Making of a Quagmire* (1965). James William Gibson in *The Perfect War* (1986) argues that American civilian and military commanders lost sight of realities and became victims of their own technocratic assumptions. In *The Arrogance of Power* (1966), former chair of the Senate Foreign Relations Committee J. William Fulbright critically reassesses American foreign policy and Vietnam.

Philip Caputo, *A Rumor of War* (1977), is a marine lieutenant's personal account of the corrupting and disillusioning impact of Vietnam. Ron Kovic, *Born on the Fourth of July* (1976), is a moving autobiographical account of one soldier's journey from patriotic marine to antiwar veteran paralyzed from the chest down. Mark Baker's *Nam* (1982) conveys how the war felt to American soldiers. Christian Appy, *Working Class War: American Combat Soldiers and Vietnam* (1993), a fine analysis of the experiences of combat soldiers, argues that fully 80 percent of soldiers serving in Vietnam came from working-class or poor families. Wallace Terry, *Bloods* (1984), examines the experiences of black veterans. *Dispatches* (1968) by Michael Herr is a brilliant journalistic description of the war that inspired the 1979 movie *Apocalypse Now*. In his novel *Dog Soldiers* (1975), Robert Stone investigates the parallels between the war and the home front. Neil Sheehan's *A Bright Shining Lie: John Paul Vann and America in Vietnam* (1988) focuses on the war through the experiences of a career army man who entered the conflict in 1962. Firsthand accounts of American participants in the war have been anthologized in J. V. B. and J. Dann, eds., *In the Field of Fire* (1987), and H. Maurer, *Strange Ground: Americans in Vietnam, 1945–1975: An Oral History* (1989). D. D. Duncan, *War Without Heroes* (1972), and Mark Jury, *The Vietnam Photo Book*

(1971), document the war in pictures. An important corrective to the above works by American participants is the memoir of a Vietnamese peasant woman, Le Ly Hayslip (with Jay Wurts), *When Heaven and Earth Changed Places* (1989), made into the 1993 movie *Heaven and Earth.*

The two best analyses of the impact of the Vietnam War on American society are Thomas Powers, *The War at Home* (1973), and Alexander Kendrick, *The Wound Within* (1974). The war's damage to the American economy is the subject of Robert Warren Stevens, *Vain Hopes, Grim Realities* (1976). The antiwar movement is covered in Nancy Zaroulis and Gerald Sullivan, *Who Spoke Up? American Protest Against the War in Vietnam, 1963–1975* (1984); Melvin Small, *Johnson, Nixon, and the Doves* (1988); and Charles DeBenedetti and Charles Chatfield, *An American Ordeal: The Antiwar Movement of the Vietnam Era* (1990). Also helpful on that topic are participants Alice Lynd's *We Won't Go* (1968); David Harris's *Dreams Die Hard* (1982); and Michael Ferber's and Staughton Lynd's *The Resistance* (1971). A fine collection of documents from the antiwar and draft resistance movements is Louis G. Heath, ed., *Mutiny Does Not Happen Lightly* (1976). The draft is the focus of Lawrence Baskin and William Strauss, *The Draft, the War, and the Vietnam Generation* (1978).

Anthony Austin's *The President's War* (1971) and John Galloway's *The Gulf of Tonkin Resolution* (1970) document the Johnson administration's misleading of Congress and the American public at the time of the Gulf of Tonkin incident. Kathleen J. Turner, *Lyndon Johnson's Dual War* (1985), and Clarence R. Wyatt, *Paper Soldiers* (1993), examine the Johnson presidency in relation to the press and the Vietnam War. Michael J. Arlen, *Living-Room War* (1969), and especially Daniel Hallin, *The "Uncensored War": The Media and Vietnam* (1986), are essential reading for an understanding of press and TV coverage of the war. For Americans' perceptions of the war, see John E. Mueller, *War, Presidents, and Public Opinion* (1973). Larry Berman's two books, *Planning a Tragedy: The Americanization of the War in Vietnam* (1982) and *Lyndon Johnson's War* (1989), explore LBJ's escalation of the war and its consequences. Also enlightening on that topic is Herbert Y. Schandler, *Lyndon Johnson and Vietnam: The Unmaking of a President* (1977).

CHAPTER

7

THE MOVEMENT

As 1967 opened, *Time* magazine broke with its forty-year tradition of selecting its "Man of the Year" by instead saluting an entire generation: Americans "Twenty-Five and Under." The children of the postwar baby boom had come of age. *Time* touted them as "well educated, affluent, rebellious, responsible, pragmatic, idealistic, brave, 'alienated' and hopeful." Despite this admiring tone, unrest simmered within America's youth.

Two weeks after the *Time* article, young people in the San Francisco Bay region celebrated themselves in a ritual that baffled most adults. Billed as "A Gathering of the Tribes for the First Human Be-In," the event featured a crowd of some twenty thousand who thronged to Golden Gate Park. Proclaiming the Be-In "a union of love and activism" that would unite "political activists and the hip community," organizers exuberantly heralded the event as a "spiritual revolution" that would "shower the country with waves of ecstasy and purification."

The day of the Be-In dawned unseasonably warm and sunny. Poets Allen Ginsberg and Gary Snyder arrived hours early to perform a "purificatory circumambulation," a Hindu ritual aimed at driving off evil spirits. Soon the park swarmed with young people dressed in what San Francisco *Chronicle*'s music critic Ralph Gleason described as "a wild polyglot mixture of Mod, Palladin, Ringling Brothers, Cochise, and Hell's Angel's Formal." People wandered about, many high on marijuana and LSD, some sporting painted faces. Others wore bells, beads, and buttons reading "Freak Freely" or "Make Love,

Not War.'' One group set up tables and distributed thousands of free turkey sandwiches; others handed out drugs, feathers, flowers, incense, and poems.

On the makeshift stage, local bands—the Grateful Dead, Quicksilver Messenger Service, Jefferson Airplane, Big Brother and the Holding Company, and Country Joe and the Fish—pounded out rock. Between sets, Ginsberg led the audience in chanting a Buddhist mantra. Snyder blew on a conch shell, and drug advocate Timothy Leary entreated people to ''turn on to the scene, tune in to what is happening, and drop out—of high school, college, grad school, junior executive—and follow me, the hard way.'' The head of the Berkeley Vietnam Day Committee, Jerry Rubin, condemned the war in Southeast Asia. Toward evening, Ginsberg, facing the setting sun, led the chant of ''Om Shri Maitreya'' to the Coming Buddha of Love and then led the merrymakers in picking up the afternoon's trash.

The media pondered the Be-In's meaning. In a cover story on the event, *Newsweek* writers described it as ''a love feast, a psychedelic picnic, a hippie happening'' and struggled to identify its deeper significance. Clearly the growing war in Vietnam and racial injustice at home troubled the nation. But most adults believed the United States stood at the pinnacle of its power, on the verge of the Augustan Age that poet Robert Frost had predicted at the Kennedy inaugural. The GNP and the stock market had climbed steadily. Liberal legislation aimed at creating the Great Society had poured from Congress. What, then, explained why hundreds of thousands of young people—in most cases the children of the well-off middle class—challenged mainstream America's most cherished values?

Indeed, as the decade progressed, many youths tossed aside sacred, traditional verities and adopted shocking new values. The family itself, the bulwark of bourgeois life, came under fire. Defying their parents, some children, made highly visible by the media, dressed as they wanted, grew their hair long, smoked marijuana, and abandoned college or career to become radical political activists or to live as hippies. For many more, the importance of chastity before marriage evaporated. Couples lived together openly, a few even communally or in homosexual relationships. Blacks, women, and various other groups demanded liberation. People demonstrated in the streets, threw away their bras, called police ''pigs,'' and even attempted to levitate the Pentagon. Patriotism, too, came under assault: young men publicly burned their draft cards; soldiers deserted the armed forces; teens flaunted American flags on the seats of their jeans.

During the mid- to late sixties, this upheaval crested. Although only a minority of young Americans participated, nevertheless, by the time of the Be-In, a sizable group of political radicals known as the New Left had emerged, along with a related and equally formidable number of cultural radicals called the counterculture. This rebellion comprised a mix of populist, democratic ideas; concern about the equality of blacks, women, gays, Hispanics, and Native Americans; opposition to the Cold War and Vietnam; communitarian and drug experimentation; transformation of sexual mores; and an almost religious quest for ''authenticity'' and ''personal fulfillment.'' Whether expressed through marijuana use, massive antiwar demonstrations, rock music, or civil-rights activism, the shift was of one piece. By the late sixties, advocates of both the new politics and culture spoke fervently of ''the Movement,'' even ''the Revolution.'' Rooted in the dissent of the fifties, the Movement gathered momentum in the sixties as young people's unique response to specific events, personal experiences, and broad cultural forces crystallized.

The New Left and counterculture reflected long-term trends in American society. With the relaxation of Cold War tension after the 1963 nuclear test-ban treaty, for example, along with the Sino-Soviet split and Johnson's 1965 escalation of the Vietnam War, many liberal intellectuals began to question America's anticommunist orthodoxy. The New Left's antiwar stand and sharp criticism of Cold War dogma paralleled this larger reassessment of postwar foreign policy. Similarly, the counterculture's liberated lifestyle and emphasis on personal fulfillment hastened trends already transforming mainstream society. Postwar American capitalism had generated unprecedented affluence that supplanted the traditional doctrines of thrift and delayed gratification. The children of the prosperous postwar generation led the way in the assault on old verities. Secure in their pampered sphere, suspended between childhood and adult responsibility, they explored a taboo-defying world of drugs, sex, and rock and roll. Few dreamed that one day the dominant culture would absorb the more hedonistic and narcissistic aspects of the counterculture—and no one could foresee the conservative backlash that would arise in response.

The wave of idealism and activism that swept American society in the 1960s was not unprecedented. Similar torrents of youthful enthusiasm, utopianism, and radicalism had brimmed in the 1840s and again in the 1910s, before America's entry into World War I. In the sixties, just as in previous such periods, the Movement's activists were only a minority of the population, yet their numbers continued to grow, and they would wield a far greater impact than in earlier times. Although their vision of a complete regeneration of America would not find fulfillment, Movement members nevertheless transformed society and politics. They helped to liberalize racial and sexual attitudes, hastened the demise of the liberal consensus, and inadvertently fostered a conservative revival. Thus the New Left and the counterculture, though transitory and directly involving only a fraction of the population, shook the very foundations of American life.

"The Times They Are A-Changin'"

On February 1, 1960, four neatly dressed black students had made history by insisting on being served at a segregated lunch counter in Greensboro, North Carolina. But racial equality was only one issue engaging the previously passive student generation during the spring of 1960. In May, San Francisco and Berkeley students demonstrated against the House Un-American Activities Committee (HUAC), the chief symbol of the postwar witch-hunts. At the time, HUAC was holding hearings in San Francisco on alleged communist activities in the Bay Area. On Friday May 13, hundreds of students gathered to protest at San Francisco's City Hall. Barred from entering the hearing room, anti-HUAC demonstrators ''sat in'' peaceably in the hallway and on the marble stairs leading up to the building. As protesters sang the thirties' union song ''We Shall Not Be Moved,'' police in riot gear hosed and clubbed them, claiming later that the demonstrators were communist inspired. Demonstrator Betty Denitch watched in horror as her cohorts were ''dragged by their hair, dragged by their arms and legs down the stairs so that their heads were bouncing off the stairs.'' The next day, five thousand angry

Bloody Friday. Demonstrators peacefully protesting hearings of the House Un-American Activities Committee held in San Francisco's City Hall on Friday, May 13, 1960, are sprayed with water hoses. Witnessing the event, *Nation* reporter Jessica Mitford affirmed that these student protesters had "gone far to shake the label of apathy and conformity that had stuck through the fifties."

students gathered at city hall. "That was the start of the sixties for me," recalled Denitch.

A new mood spread across the country. In June 1960, Tom Hayden, a student at the University of Michigan, hitchhiked to California, inspired by Jack Kerouac's *On the Road.* Arriving in Berkeley only weeks after the anti-HUAC demonstrations, Hayden met some of the student radicals there. "What Berkeley did," he later remembered, "was define my politics, and turn me on to the idea of student power. . . . You could feel a sense of power and excitement at the prospect of young people being able to change things drastically."

Several other challenges to the status quo emerged in the early sixties, although their significance would not come to light until later. Michael Harrington, for example, investigated the persistence of poverty amid the nation's plenty. Ralph Nader, a young lawyer, discovered that many American-made automobiles were "unsafe at any speed." Marine biologist Rachel Carson amassed evidence of the deadly effects of pesticides on the environment. Writer Betty Friedan pondered the debilitating costs of "the feminine mystique" for women. And in the same month as the HUAC demonstrations, the U.S. Food and Drug Administration announced its approval of an oral contraceptive for women. News of "the Pill" was relegated to page 75 of the *New York Times,* but the drug would soon revolutionize sexual relations and ease the age-old fear of pregnancy.

As protest singer Bob Dylan would soon sing, the times were "a-changin'." For many people, particularly the young, 1960 opened a new era of hope, rich with promise. The election of John F. Kennedy that November amplified this sense, as the vital, glamorous new president spoke of a New Frontier. Embodying the energy, idealism, and confidence needed to ''get America moving again,'' JFK truly appeared able to make American realities live up to American dreams. Kennedy still mouthed the Cold War platitudes of the past, yet he detected the awakening aspirations of younger Americans. While campaigning at the University of Michigan in mid-October, he had proposed the Peace Corps, in which citizens could volunteer to aid developing nations directly. Seven hundred Michigan students promptly signed up for this as-yet nonexistent agency. Throughout the remainder of the campaign, youthful enthusiasm for the Peace Corps bubbled at every Kennedy stop. To the young especially, Kennedy's election symbolized the end of fifties complacency.

Not just in America, but throughout the world, the young grew aware of their political clout. In 1960 alone, major student demonstrations shook the governments of Korea, Japan, Turkey, and Venezuela. In Great Britain, marches organized by the Campaign for Nuclear Disarmament drew college-age crowds. In the United States, civil rights spearheaded the transformation of the Eisenhower era's ''silent generation'' into the activist idealists of the Kennedy years. As the sit-in movement spread through the South, the courage of the young blacks inspired the nation and stirred white students to action. To a generation emerging from the more languid fifties, the chance to leave a mark on history proved exhilarating.

From 1960 through 1964, the civil-rights movement served as the major outlet for the growing mood of commitment. Young whites from affluent backgrounds, working on such projects as the 1964 Mississippi Freedom Summer, learned about racist violence and subjugation first hand. Witnessing daily violations of America's democratic creed, activists bristled with outrage. Participation in the civil-rights movement also taught them the tactics of protest. Equally important, racist resistance and liberal politicians' failure to step into the fray disgusted many civil-rights workers and precipitated their own disaffection from the American consensus.

Nevertheless, the dominant attitude among activists during the early sixties was liberal, idealistic, and optimistic—not revolutionary. The folk-music revival of the time reflected this quality. The proliferation of coffeehouses and nightclubs, spawned by the Beat movement in the late fifties, catalyzed interest in this genre. In 1958 the Kingston Trio's recording of ''Tom Dooley'' sold more than two million copies. Although the trio's rendition was more show biz than folk, the song's success fueled the folk fad. Through the midsixties, folk music's popularity soared, particularly among college students. Older singers such as Pete Seeger, Josh White, Burl Ives, and Dave Van Ronk gained new audiences, and younger singer-composers Bob Dylan, Joan Baez, Judy Collins, Buffy Saint-Marie, Odetta, Phil Ochs, and Tom Paxton achieved stardom. The ABC-TV program ''Hootenanny'' furthered folk music's appeal, though because the network blacklisted Seeger for his Old Left affiliations, stars such as Baez, Ochs, and Paxton refused to appear as guests.

Folk music's strong emphasis on lyrics lent itself to message and protest songs. Indeed, folk songs became a staple of every demonstration. ''We Shall Overcome'' emerged as the anthem of the civil-rights movement, and ballads such as Pete Seeger's ''Where Have All the Flowers Gone,'' Bob Dylan's ''A Hard Rain's A-Gonna Fall,'' and Malvina Reynolds's ''What Have They Done to the Rain'' captured the pacifism of the early sixties antinuclear movement.

Folk's popularity coincided with the early years of the New Left and the growth of the counterculture and had close ties to both. The genre evoked community, purity, sincerity, and moral purpose and revealed an almost naive faith that the mere exposure of evil through song would bring justice. The liner notes to Peter, Paul, and Mary's first album, released in 1962, read: "The news that something this *Good* can be as popular as this is can fill you with a new kind of optimism. Maybe everything's going to be all right. Maybe mediocrity has had it. Maybe hysteria is on the way out. One thing is for sure in any case: Honesty is back. Tell your neighbor."

On occasion, impatience with the adult generation's shortcomings and hypocrisies broke through, as in Bob Dylan's biting 1963 generational anthem "The Times They Are A-Changin' ":

Come mothers and fathers
Throughout the land
And don't criticize
What you can't understand
Your sons and your daughters
Are beyond your command.
There's a battle
Outside and it's ragin'
It'll soon shake your windows
And rattle your walls . . .
For the times they are a-changin'!

Dylan's ominous note would grow louder as the decade progressed.

The New Left Ascendant

When the sixties began, what came to be called the New Left was more a mood than a systematic, nationally organized ideology. The traditional Marxist Old Left in America, plagued by factional strife, McCarthyism, and the revelations of Soviet communist atrocities committed under Stalin, had virtually disappeared by the midfifties. In 1956 the Labor Youth League, the Communist party youth group, disbanded. By 1960 only the Socialist party's Young People's Socialist League (YPSL) and the Socialist Workers party's Young Socialist Alliance (YSA) continued to offer college students Old Left Marxist analyses. YPSL, the larger and more moderate, had a membership of only about three hundred at the start of the sixties and in 1964 broke up.

New Marxist-oriented youth groups such as the communist W. E. B. Du Bois clubs and the Maoist Progressive Labor party would emerge during the decade, but most young activists of the early sixties had little use for what they saw as the enfeebled dogmas of Marx, Lenin, and Trotsky. Few of them knew more about the Stalinist, Trotskyite, and Social Democratic debates from the thirties than what they learned in the classroom. In place of Marx and Lenin, emerging student radicals found mentors in prophets of a humanitarian, non-Marxian Left such as C. Wright Mills and Paul Goodman. Rather than some abstract belief in "the proletariat" as the instrument of revolutionary change, issues—racism, poverty, and nuclear testing—galvanized these activists. Instead of attacking capitalism as exploitative, they reviled it for its creation of a materialistic culture that alienated the individual and created false values. They rejected Marx's class analysis yet had no desire to restore economic competition and possessive individualism. Offering a new vision, they sought the social commitment and the creation of a "beloved community" such as they believed SNCC activists had established.

Radical students always remained in the minority, even at Berkeley, Michigan, Wisconsin, Columbia, and other campuses renowned as hotbeds of militant protest. Nevertheless, in the words of *Village Voice* writer Jack Newfield, they were "a prophetic minority" whom their generation came to view as its spokespeople. Children of the postwar baby boom would make up a large segment of the Movement from the midsixties through the midseventies, but the first wave of activists were born in the late thirties or early forties and came of age during the fifties.

A disproportionate number of these early 1960s radicals were the children of Old Left or progressive, well-educated, professional parents. Many came from Jewish, agnostic, or liberal Protestant families. Numerous activists were outstanding students and attended the nation's most prestigious universities. With their affluent upbringing and strong ethical values, they tended to major in the liberal arts and focused on issues of morality and altruism.

Yet an array of other individuals had grown disenchanted with Cold War liberalism, and shared many of the Left's values. Although such supporters seldom participated in protests, they felt themselves part of the Movement, and their support widened the Movement's impact. Sympathizers cropped up in the ranks of younger journalists, lawyers, college professors, graduate students, publishing-house employees, and even members of government agencies.

The new radicalism that emerged in the early sixties was ideologically ill defined and had no single organizational base. In 1957 left-of-center students at the University of California in Berkeley had founded a student political faction called SLATE, which campaigned to abolish compulsory participation in ROTC and to establish a cooperative bookstore. SLATE had helped to organize the HUAC protests in May 1960. Other left-leaning campus political parties—Tocsin at Harvard, Polit at Chicago, ACTION at Columbia, and VOICE at the University of Michigan—had arisen by 1960. At many universities, single-issue groups also flourished, focusing on causes such as civil rights and nuclear testing. For many later New Left members, Fair Play for Cuba Committees, which decried American policy toward the Castro revolution, provided their first political experience. At the University of Wisconsin, radical students inspired by historian William Appleman Williams published *Studies on the Left,* and University of Chicago students turned out *New University Thought.* Similar journals cropped up at Columbia, Harvard, and other colleges.

The largest campus-based radical organization in the early sixties was the Student Peace Union (SPU). Founded in 1959 at the University of Chicago, the SPU by the end of 1961 had more than fifteen hundred dues-paying members in dozens of chapters on campuses throughout the Midwest and the Northeast. Clearly these figures represented a minuscule fraction of the millions enrolled in universities. Yet membership numbers told only part of the story. For every card-holding member of any New Left organization, hundreds more felt the tremors of change and empathized with the activists. As an example, in February 1962, when SPU and another small peace group, Student SANE, sponsored a two-day demonstration against continued nuclear testing, more than six thousand students made their way to the nation's capital to participate. SPU membership peaked at about four thousand in 1963.

Nevertheless, the signing of the Nuclear Test Ban Treaty in August that year defused the movement, and both SPU and Student SANE dwindled. With campus peace groups languishing, Students for a Democratic Society emerged in the midsixties as the embodiment of the white New Left student movement. SDS had begun as the student affiliate of the League for Industrial Democracy, an Old Left organization founded before World War I. Originally called the Student League for Industrial Democracy (with the unfortunate acronym SLID), the tiny group adopted its new name in January 1960 to declare its independence from the sectarian Old Left. SDS leaders hoped that the reorganized group would direct the student movement and, in the words of one member, formulate "radical alternatives to the inadequate society of today."

At the time, such expectations appeared grandiose. In June 1960, SDS could boast of only eight campus chapters with a combined membership of 250—hardly a mass movement. The most active SDS chapter was at the University of Michigan in Ann Arbor, from which emerged the two most important early leaders of SDS, Al Haber and Tom Hayden.

Born in 1936, Robert Alan Haber was the son of an eminent liberal economist and labor arbitrator. The elder Haber had taught at the University of Michigan, and Al enrolled there in 1954. A well-read intellectual who wore a beard (rare at that time) and dark, horn-rimmed glasses, the intense, brooding Haber by 1960 had entered his graduate studies with a reputation as Ann Arbor's resident radical. As head of Michigan's SDS chapter, he organized the conference on Human Rights in the North in the spring of 1960, which attracted more than 150 students from southern and northern schools. Speakers included black leader James Farmer, socialist Michael Harrington, and several Greensboro sit-in heroes. Participants discussed racism on campus and in northern communities and explored ideas for supporting the southern sit-ins. Elected national SDS president soon after, Haber helped to recruit Tom Hayden to the organization that fall.

Hayden would become a very influential New Left leader. Despite his atypical working-class, Irish-Catholic background, his development otherwise paralleled that of the emerging New Left. Ironically, he grew up in Royal Oak, Michigan, an all-white suburb of Detroit, where he served as an altar boy in the Shrine of the Little Flower Church, still presided over by the infamous 1930s antisemitic radio priest Father Charles Coughlin. In high school, Hayden's chief interests lay in sports and the student newspaper. He identified with J. D. Salinger's Holden Caulfield and James Dean in *Rebel Without a Cause* and was an avid reader of *Mad* magazine. Hayden even founded his own underground paper, the *Daily Smirker*. Entering the University of Michigan in 1957, Hayden gained notoriety as a brilliant student of philosophy and an outstanding reporter for the student newspaper, the *Michigan Daily*. Initially more bohemian than political, he became radicalized by the sit-in movement and his experiences in California during the summer of 1960. That fall he joined Haber in SDS.

Both men saw the southern civil-rights crusade as a major vehicle for encouraging students to work for social change. In the fall of 1961, Tom Hayden, who had recently married SNCC activist Sandra "Casey" Cason, traveled South to be with Casey and

The Radicalization of Tom Hayden. October 1961, punched by an assailant while demonstrating for civil rights in McComb, Mississippi, SDS leader Hayden came to the conclusion that "this is not just a movement but a revolution."

to serve as SDS's liaison to SNCC. There he experienced the dangers that civil-rights workers regularly encountered. In McComb, Mississippi, white racist toughs savaged him as he participated in a peaceful demonstration; in Albany, Georgia, officials jailed him for freedom riding. These experiences furthered Hayden's radicalization. He wrote of a "crazy new sentiment that this is not just a movement but a revolution" and came to agree with what SNCC workers already believed: that "beyond lunch counter desegregation there are more serious evils which must be ripped out by any means: exploitation, socially destructive capital, evil political and legal structure, and myopic liberalism which is anti-revolutionary." Hayden's published reports from the South, including a letter smuggled out of the Albany jail, made him a hero to the emerging student movement and boosted SDS's reputation.

Haber and Hayden wanted SDS to address broader questions of human and economic rights rather than to serve as merely a white information and support group for the civil-rights movement. In late December 1961, SDS's National Executive Committee decided to draw up "a political manifesto of the Left" to express the group's ideas and vision. The members tapped Hayden to compose a draft and called for a week-long national convention the following June to debate and refine the document.

Hayden had little faith in America's two-party system, and he realized that "the socialistic parties are in a shambles. The working class . . . is just not the missionary force we can count on." He admired the militancy and determination of the civil-rights movement but did not wish to limit SDS to a single issue. "I have the impression," he wrote, "that we have been our own leadership to a far greater degree than most 'student radicals' of the past.'' Yet he did in fact have some important mentors. In preparation for writing the SDS manifesto, he read a multitude of philosophical and political thinkers, including Marx, John Stuart Mill, John Dewey, Albert Camus, and especially C. Wright Mills, whom Hayden would choose as his master's-thesis subject. As he recalled:

> Mills's analysis validated us not only personally, but as a generation and as activist-organizers, the political identity we were beginning to adopt. We tried as organizers to penetrate what Mills called the private ''milieu'' of those we were trying to reach, whether southern blacks or the students next door to us. Such people often felt helpless, or blamed themselves for their fate, too isolated to identify and blame larger institutions. . . . We attempted to show that the power elites were to blame for seemingly individual troubles, and communicated that they had to take back power and responsibility over their lives.[1]

Hayden's planned twenty-page document ballooned to nearly seventy pages. In early June, fifty-nine delegates convened at an AFL-CIO camp on the shores of Lake Huron just north of the Michigan city of Port Huron. For five days and nights, the group debated and revised, and out of this intense communal experience emerged the *Port Huron Statement,* the manifesto of the emerging student Left. In an impassioned appeal for social change, the *Port Huron Statement* urged both personal and political metamorphosis:

> We are people of this generation, bred in at least modest comfort, housed now in universities, looking uncomfortably to the world we inherit. . . . Many of us began maturing in complacency. As we grew, however, our comfort was penetrated by events too troubling to dismiss. First, the permeating and victimizing fact of human degradation, symbolized by the Southern struggle against racial bigotry, compelled most of us from silence to activism. Second, the enclosing fact of the Cold War, symbolized by the presence of the Bomb, brought awareness that we ourselves, and our friends, and millions of abstract ''others'' we knew more directly because of our common peril, might die at any time.

In terms of concrete proposals, the document advocated little more than political realignment to oust conservatives from the Democratic party, the enactment of such liberal measures as health insurance, expanded public housing and antipoverty programs, and a thaw in the Cold War. But on a deeper level, the *Port Huron Statement* was radical and utopian. The treatise presented a moral critique of American society and a moving vision of a regenerated society. It attacked liberals who failed to end racism and the Cold War, and it denounced anticommunism as mindless paranoia, although it faulted the Old Left for having been ''perverted by Stalinism.'' It glorified individual empowerment, personal authenticity, and community.

---

[1] Hayden read of Mills's premature death of a heart attack as he wrote the SDS manifesto. He felt that Mills had been ''broken by the attempt to wake up America.'' For more on Mills, see Chapter 2.

At the core of the manifesto lay a call for a new kind of democracy. Hayden deplored the notion that a person was ''a thing to be manipulated'':

> We would replace power rooted in possession, privilege, or circumstance by power and uniqueness rooted in love, reflectiveness, reason and creativity. . . . We seek the establishment of a democracy of individual participation, governed by two central aims: that the individual share in those social decisions determining the quality and direction of his life; that society be organized to encourage independence in men and provide the media for their common participation.

''Participatory democracy'' implied that people, liberated from hierarchic bureaucracies, would control their own lives.

How this transformation of corporate America into decentralized democratic communities would take place remained vague, but Hayden's document suggested that students would serve as the key agents of change. In this point he again drew from Mills, who had pinned his hopes on ''the young intelligentsia.'' Hayden recalled: ''We believed students could be the catalysts for change in the world. They were volunteering for the Peace Corps, they were the moving force in the civil rights movement, they were shaking up governments around the world. It seemed that students could awaken other classes of people to participate in the democratic process.''

The *Port Huron Statement* depicted universities as having ''a permanent position of social influence . . . functionally tied to society in new ways.'' SDS harbored ambivalence toward these institutions, however. On one hand, universities supplied the engineers and technicians to serve the needs of the Cold War and the corporations. On the other hand, if students and faculty could ''wrest control of the educational process from the administrative bureaucracy,'' then the universities would become ''new levers for change.'' With a strong base in the university, students could reach out to other dissenting groups—blacks, the poor, pacifists, liberals—and create a broad movement that would revitalize American democracy.

Soon after the Port Huron meeting, SDS distributed mimeographed copies of the manifesto to members, civil-rights workers, student leaders, and delegates attending the National Student Association (NSA) meeting in Columbus, Ohio, that summer.[2] The document's moral urgency and sweeping vision captured the attention of its readers. Within four years, more than sixty thousand copies had circulated, and eager recruits founded a string of new SDS chapters.

Through 1963, SDS had served as little more than a national forum for ideas, yet members hungered for direct action. Despite the *Port Huron Statement*'s emphasis on universities as the locus of social change, the national leadership decided to abandon the campus and embark on building an ''interracial movement of the poor'' in northern slums. In the summer of 1964, while other northern students joined the freedom fight in Mississippi, SDS, with a $5,000 grant from the United Auto Workers, launched its Economic Research and Action Project (ERAP). Young volunteers established projects

---

[2]The NSA had been founded in 1947 as a forum for student leaders and by the early sixties had become the nation's most influential student organization. Although few knew it at the time, the NSA was funded and manipulated by the CIA.

in Newark, Cleveland, Chicago, Philadelphia, Baltimore, and other northern cities. They moved into the ghettoes, lived on meager wages, and set out to organize the poor.

SDS had chosen ERAP over campus activity for several reasons. First, it looked to ERAP to provide a test for participatory democracy. The young volunteers hoped to create community unions through which the poor could control their housing, services, and jobs. SDS activists also strove to practice participatory democracy themselves. They downplayed leadership and engaged in endless hours of discussion trying to arrive at consensus. Indeed, ERAP members in Cleveland once spent twenty-four hours debating whether they should take a day off to go to the beach. Like the SNCC workers whom they so admired, ERAP participants lived communally and shared the hardships of the people whom they hoped to help. The slum work also allowed them to jettison their guilt over their privileged backgrounds. Indeed, Todd Gitlin, who worked in the Chicago project, later admitted that ERAP "was built on guilt." Finally, although SDS had begun as a campus-based movement, by 1963 most of its old guard had graduated, and though some enrolled in graduate school, mostly at the University of Michigan, they realized that the movement would have to reach beyond the universities to score a true success.

In a few cities, ERAP volunteers, after much hard work, won minor victories on issues such as garbage collection and traffic lights. But organizing the poor and overcoming the intransigence of local bureaucracies proved far more difficult than these idealists had expected. By late summer of 1965, most projects had collapsed. In the end, the ERAP experience had its greatest impact on the participants themselves by providing opportunities for personal growth; SDS women especially thrived as ghetto organizers. Participation in ERAP also further radicalized SDS members and alienated them from establishment liberals. Last, ERAP anticipated the Community Action Program that would spring up in 1965 in connection with President Johnson's War on Poverty. Yet the short-lived ERAP projects did little either to help the poor or to win new recruits. SDS still had only a few dozen chapters and no more than fifteen hundred members. There was no national student movement.

Jamming the Gears: Revolt on the Campus

In 1965 SDS shifted its focus back to campus and became the major New Left organization, spurred by campus unrest, the struggle for racial equality, and above all the Vietnam War. At its height in 1968, SDS boasted more than one hundred thousand members, with strong influence over thousands, perhaps even millions, more. Nor was SDS alone; more than a thousand Movement organizations competed for youthful allegiance.

A major population shift in the sixties provided a key reason for this phenomenal growth of the New Left. Indeed, some have suggested that the difference in values and culture between the fifties and the sixties can best be explained demographically. Although it overstates the case, such an interpretation has merit. In the fifties, owing to a high birthrate after the First World War followed by a decline of births during the Depression, the median age of the population climbed to more than thirty-five years. By the sixties, however, the huge postwar baby-boom generation lowered America's mean age. By 1968 over half the population was under twenty-five, and as the nation grew younger, youthful attitudes and values gained influence.

Born in the prosperous postwar period, hailing largely from the suburbs or cities, and raised on television and under the somewhat permissive guidance of Dr. Benjamin Spock, this unique population segment exercised vast power by its sheer numbers. These youngsters reached late adolescence just as momentous questions of civil rights and war rent the nation. Not surprisingly, many of them attacked the compromises and inadequacies of adult authority. Although not all baby boomers chafed against the values of their Depression- and war-torn parents, generational conflict had become a phenomenon by the sixties, especially on college campuses.

The baby boom combined with prosperity and Cold War and corporate needs to transform the American university system. College enrollments soared in the postwar years. By 1965 some 6.5 million youths attended institutions of higher learning, compared to only 2.2 million in 1950. As universities expanded, they grew more bureaucratic and impersonal, yet they retained strict codes of student behavior. Moreover, as they took on more and more importance, their focus shifted; liberal-arts colleges providing general humanistic education to an elite gave way to complex institutions responsible for conducting research and training large numbers of skilled workers for industry and government. Accordingly, federal expenditures for higher education during the sixties, much of it spent on military-related research and special Cold War projects, rose from $6.7 billion to $24.7 billion.

These changes in the structure and purpose of the university, coinciding with burgeoning student activism and idealism, created a volatile brew. From the late fifties on, students had periodically protested required military training, compulsory chapel, dress codes, and dormitory regulations. The first massive student upheaval struck during 1964–1965 at the University of California Berkeley.

In 1964 Berkeley, with its enormous enrollment of some 27,500 students and world-renowned faculty, stood as one of the country's most impressive universities. Headed by liberal economist Clark Kerr, Berkeley appeared a model institution. Kerr had presided over its expansion and rise to international prominence and lauded the school as a "multiversity" and "knowledge factory" serving the needs of business and government. Yet discontent had long simmered. In 1962 David Horowitz, a Berkeley graduate student, had compared the university's educational system to an assembly line. "A man is not a product," he wrote, "nor is he an IBM record card." In a 1963 lecture, "The Uses of the University," even Kerr admitted that the multiversity's role as "a prime instrument of national purpose" exacted a price. With soaring student enrollments, classes had grown large and impersonal. Faculty, hired for their research accomplishments rather than their teaching abilities, relegated more and more undergraduate instruction to overloaded teaching assistants. Kerr confessed that in a large university like Berkeley, the student "has problems of establishing his identity and a sense of security." Thus, it is not surprising that the university itself became the focus of a major student protest—the Berkeley Free Speech Movement (FSM).

Like other students throughout the country, many at Berkeley had watched fascinated as the drama of the civil-rights movement unfolded. Beginning in December 1963, Jack Weinberg, a Berkeley graduate student and head of the Berkeley chapter of CORE, organized some 150 students to picket downtown stores and demand more minority hiring. In February 1964, CORE protesters devised the "shop-in." Directed against Lucky's groceries, a regional chain that hired almost no nonwhites, demonstrators entered a store and loaded their carts with groceries. At the checkout counters, they abandoned the filled carts, announcing that they refused to buy groceries where blacks could not work. That March, as many as fifteen hundred protesters targeted the Sheraton-Palace Hotel in San Francisco. After several days of picketing by demonstrators and the arrest of nearly eight hundred of them, the hotel signed a minority hiring agreement. The protests radicalized many participants. In the spring of 1964, when recruiters for SNCC's Mississippi Freedom Summer project arrived on campus, about sixty local activists signed up.

This new militancy alarmed local business leaders and conservative politicians, who charged that the university had become the staging ground for radical agitators. Soon after the Palace Hotel protest, a pressured Kerr announced that students faced "grave consequences" for their actions. In particular, he established new restrictions on their political activity. Although politics had been banned on the campus since the 1930s in reaction to fear of communist student movements, for years students had used a strip of sidewalk at the juncture of Bancroft Way and Telegraph Avenue, just outside the main campus gate, to display political literature, collect donations, give speeches, and enlist volunteers. The university had long tolerated this small strip of free speech. Now, however, the administration extended the ban on political activity to include the Bancroft strip.

Infuriated students returning in the fall of 1964 immediately formed a coalition of campus political organizations, running the gamut from communists to youth for Goldwater, to defy the ban and carry on their politicking at the proscribed location. At first the administration attempted to mollify them by promising a moderate interpretation of the ban. Then on October 1, police arrested Jack Weinberg as he staffed the CORE table on the strip. When officers ushered Weinberg into an awaiting squad car, a sea of students surrounded the auto and sat down. Soon thousands of students gathered about the immobilized vehicle.

As the officers and the administration pondered their predicament, Mario Savio, a Berkeley philosophy major who had just returned from working on SNCC's Mississippi Freedom Summer, stepped from the crowd. Politely removing his shoes, he climbed onto the roof of the police car. Shy to the point of stuttering in private conversation, Savio in public proved an electrifying speaker who soon emerged as the major leader of the student movement. "Last summer," he told those assembled, "I went to Mississippi to join the struggle there for civil rights. This fall I am engaged in another phase of the same struggle, this time in Berkeley. The two battlefields may seem quite different to some observers, but this is not the case. The same rights are at stake in both places—the right to participate as citizens in a democratic society."

Negotiations between students and university officials began, but the police car, with Weinberg still inside, would remain in the students' captivity for thirty-two hours. Through the first afternoon and long into the night, numerous speakers climbed atop the vehicle's increasingly sagging roof. It was dark when Bettina Aptheker ascended this rooftop rostrum. The daughter of prominent communist parents, Aptheker was a longtime civil-rights activist and had been arrested while picketing the Palace Hotel. Quoting the great nineteenth-century abolitionist Frederick Douglass, she urged students to stand firm and advised them that "power concedes nothing without a demand." She, too, emerged a leader of the newborn movement.

The following evening, Savio, who had been negotiating with Kerr and other administrators, announced an agreement. Student protesters freed the police car and

Student Power. Berkeley Free Speech Movement leader Mario Savio addressing a crowd before the student takeover of Sproul Hall. Events at Berkeley would reverberate in colleges and universities throughout the country.

agreed to pay for the repair of its dented roof; in return, Kerr promised not to take disciplinary action against Jack Weinberg or others, to support the university's deeding of the Bancroft strip to the city so that it would fall outside campus jurisdiction, and to establish a tripartite committee composed of administrators, faculty members, and students to work out permanent rules for political activity on campus.

Nurturing their momentum, students organized the FSM to ensure that the administration adhered to the pact. Members represented the full range of the political spectrum, but from the outset, New Left activists wielded the most influence. With an executive committee comprising representatives of various concerned student organizations and a smaller steering committee elected by the executive committee, the FSM put into practice the participatory democracy advocated in the *Port Huron Statement*.

Subsequent actions by the university administration nudged the Free Speech Movement further left. During October and November, the October 2 agreement unraveled when, underestimating the FSM's commitment, Kerr attempted to manipulate the tripartite committee. Increasingly, FSM students, as well as many faculty, charged Kerr with acting in bad faith. "We were constantly betrayed," recalled Barbara Garson, the editor of the FSM newsletter. "Three months of this helped most people overcome their naiveté, and after a while we began to hold noon rallies on the Sproul Hall [the administration building] steps every time the administration double-crossed us and constant meetings in classrooms across the campus." The more the administration equivocated on the free-speech issue, the more support the FSM garnered.

On December 2, soon after the administration had announced new disciplinary action planned against Mario Savio and other Free Speech leaders, the FSM held a massive noon rally in Sproul Plaza. In words reminiscent of Henry David Thoreau, Savio told the crowd: "There is a time when the operation of the machine becomes so odious, makes you so sick at heart, that you can't take part. . . . You've got to put your bodies upon the gears and upon the wheels, upon the levers, upon all the apparatus and you've got to make it stop. And you've got to indicate to the people who run it, to the people that own it, that unless you're free, the machines will be prevented from working at all.'' More than a thousand students marched into Sproul Hall and sat in on the administrative "gears" of the university. Sustained by peanut-butter sandwiches, they spent the night singing, discussing, and watching Charlie Chaplin movies in a relaxed, festive atmosphere.

Then the police came. By morning, the combined units of the Berkeley and Oakland forces had cleared the building and arrested nearly eight hundred demonstrators. Sit-in participant Barbara Zahn recorded her reaction to the police arrest in her diary:

> Nine A.M. and they have started arresting my floor. I watch them move closer and closer, dragging people away. . . . I'm tired, dirty, scared, but most of all proud . . . and we sit and sing. . . . They asked me my name, and then if I would walk or must I be dragged. I had just watched Ruth, my best friend, being dragged away, and I replied, "I must be dragged." They grabbed me and almost threw me down the corridor.

The use of outside police further undermined Kerr's moral authority. Enraged faculty members arranged bail money for the jailed protesters. Even moderate students supported the FSM's call for a strike that virtually shut the university down. Dismissing his American history class, professor Leon Litwack snapped, "It hardly behooves us to study, if not to celebrate, the rebels of the past while we seek to silence the rebels of the present."

On December 8, the Academic Senate voted overwhelmingly in favor of FSM demands. Students gathered outside the meeting hall and formed an aisle through which the faculty marched. "Many of us were crying, and so were many of them," noted Aptheker. "There were many among them and among us who finally came to believe that the repression of the 1950s was truly at an end." The administration soon capitulated, and by early January 1965, political advocacy was once more permitted on campus. Jerry Rubin, an FSM activist, hailed the victory; ex-radical and Berkeley faculty member Lewis Feuer, on the other hand, charged the FSM with initiating a "juvenocracy" that undermined the entire purpose of the university. Both supporters and detractors, however, acknowledged the FSM's potential power.

Although the conflict had centered on free speech, other concerns surfaced during these months. Students protested the impersonal, bureaucratic nature of the university and voiced their feelings of alienation. Dissidents demanded more voice in their education, with fewer requirements or restrictions. Most important, the FSM radicalized students who realized that Kerr and the majority of their on-campus opponents were not ideological conservatives but liberals. "Liberalism," claimed Jack Weinberg, "is a trap. . . . Cowardice has always been the characteristic of the American liberals. They are willing to take a principled stand, as long as there is no risk involved." Like the militant supporters of the Mississippi Freedom Democratic party who trudged home from the Democratic convention in the summer of 1964 utterly disillusioned, so too did the FSM represent a radical critique of mainstream liberalism.

During the winter of 1965, the Free Speech Movement degenerated into the Filthy Speech Movement when some students claimed their right to exclaim certain four-letter words publicly. Nevertheless, the FSM had altered life on the campus and beyond. The Berkeley struggle had intrigued the media and stirred students nationwide. Between the outbreak of the Free Speech Movement in the fall of 1964 and the pivotal upheaval at Columbia University during the traumatic spring of 1968, several hundred major campus demonstrations broke out as universities became physical and ideological battlegrounds. On most campuses, faculty felt forced to choose sides. Many professors supported the student demands and even joined in active protest; others saw the demonstrations as a threat to the very function of the university, including the free exchange of reasoned ideas. By the late sixties, numerous departments had become so polarized that a vote on something as innocuous as whether to purchase a new coffee machine would split along ideological lines.

Despite the friction, the protests yielded substantive reforms. Students gained more freedom and some voice in academic governance. Many universities encouraged innovative teaching methods and flexible grading systems, added courses in such new areas as black history and women's studies, and reduced the number of required courses. Where reform lagged, radical students and faculty established "free universities" and "alternative classrooms" to discuss subjects not traditionally taught, such as the ideas of Paul Goodman and Herbert Marcuse or the disciplines of hatha-yoga and Tai Chi. True, the value of altering the traditional curriculum, decreasing mandated classes, and catering to students' concern for "relevance" remains highly controversial. Yet these changes unquestionably made universities more democratic and more responsive to student needs than before.

Students Against the War

The years of university disruption paralleled the escalation of the Vietnam War. Indeed, the two battlegrounds were not unrelated. In December 1964, the same month as the Berkeley Free Speech Movement's sit-in and strike, SDS decided to hold a springtime antiwar demonstration in Washington. By the time the event took place on April 17, 1965, Lyndon Johnson's air war against North Vietnam and his commitment of marines to South Vietnam had evoked widespread antiwar sentiment, especially in the universities where the teach-in movement had spread (see Chapter 6). Instead of the few thousand demonstrators whom SDS had expected, nearly thirty thousand people participated. It was the first national protest against the war and the largest antiwar gathering that the country had ever seen. SDS suddenly made national news, and new members flocked to the organization.

The conflict in Vietnam created a highly favorable climate for the growth of the New Left. From 1965 on, the war provided the central issue and organizing principle around which various discontents coalesced. Opposition to U.S. involvement in Vietnam gave moral purpose to student dissidents and intensified their belief in universities' complicity in the war. After all, the schools encouraged military-related research, maintained ROTC programs, and allowed on-campus recruiters from companies that profited from war.

More than moral outrage at America's conduct of the war animated these young people. The Vietnam conflict affected their personal lives directly. The threat of being drafted, or of having boyfriends or brothers drafted, loomed large. When the United

States began to escalate the war in the spring of 1965, monthly draft quotas stood at about seven thousand. By December, the Selective Service System had called up some forty thousand young men. In 1966, with more than a quarter of a million American soldiers in Vietnam, the government instituted the Selective Service College Qualification Test, making students ranking in the lower levels of their class eligible for the draft.

On college campuses throughout the country, protests against the war and the draft erupted among students and faculty. Objection took the form of teach-ins, mass antiwar demonstrations, draft-card burnings, sit-ins, and picketing of local draft boards. In response, Congress passed a law making violations of Selective Service laws punishable by a fine of up to $10,000 and five years in prison. Besides arresting draft-card burners and draft resisters, the government imprisoned hundreds of other antidraft demonstrators for such offenses as interfering with the operation of a draft board and, in one case, for wearing a jacket adorned with the words "Fuck the Draft."

Only a small minority of young people publicly defied the draft, but thousands more draft-age men found ways to avoid conscription. Perhaps as many as a quarter of a million did not register as required by law on their eighteenth birthday. Others, helped by an expanding number of draft-counseling centers and antiwar lawyers, brought legal challenges against the Selective Service System. In one example, nine University of Michigan students were reclassified I-A, the highest category of draft eligibility, after having been arrested for participating in a December 1965 sit-in. They succeeded in having their reclassification overturned in court.

As draft quotas rose, draft evasion became an obsession among college students, even though this activity could put a serious blot on a young man's record and compromise his ability to obtain a job later. One effective way of beating the draft was to fail the preinduction physical. Some students obtained falsified medical reports from antiwar doctors. Others faked mental or physical illness. Some jabbed pins into their arms to give the impression that they were heroin addicts. One student ate three large pizzas every night until his weight exceeded the military limit for his height. Another common tactic was to make a sexual pass at one of the soldiers on duty at the examination center. In a few extreme cases, potential draftees chopped off toes to flunk the physical. "Use any means," advised the student newspaper at the University of Florida. "Get stoned. . . . Say you're a schizoid, a queer. Refuse to sign a disclaimer that you are not a member of any subversive organization. File as a conscientious objector. It takes more time. You can't be classified and drafted during an appeal." Many nonprotesting students avoided service in Vietnam by remaining in college and graduate school and receiving deferments or by joining the National Guard. A more radical solution was to flee the country. At least one hundred thousand—about half of them draft evaders, half military deserters—went into exile in Canada, Sweden, and elsewhere.

By 1966 the draft had become a major driving force behind the younger generation's opposition to the war. Discontent with university administrations' compliance with Selective Service spawned sit-ins and other forms of protest from Brooklyn College to San Francisco State. At the University of Chicago, students occupied the administration building for five days. A number of college administrations relented to the pressure and refused to rank students for the Selective Service. Many sympathetic professors leniently graded draft-age males.

As the Vietnam War intensified and the civil-rights movement turned to Black

Power and ghetto rioting, student militancy burgeoned. Early in 1967, SDS leader Greg Calvert called on students to move "from protest to resistance," paralleling a shift taking place throughout the country. In addition to Berkeley, Wisconsin, Michigan, Columbia, and Harvard, schools such as the University of Maine, the University of Nebraska, Kentucky State, North Carolina A&T, and numerous other colleges saw student-led militant confrontations against war research and ROTC. Demonstrators particularly targeted campus recruiting by the military, the CIA, and Dow Chemical, whose flesh-burning napalm symbolized the butchery of Vietnam. At Cornell, a "We Won't Go" group organized collective draft-card burning. In California, David Harris and others founded "the Resistance" to oppose the draft even if it meant, as it did in Harris's case, going to jail.

Despite the growing militancy of the antiwar movement, most students protested nonviolently. In 1967, for instance, more than twenty thousand students joined "Vietnam Summer." Modeled on Mississippi Freedom Summer, student volunteers trudged door to door in an effort to bring their antiwar message to mainstream Americans. The media, however, paid less attention to peaceful protesters than they did to the more militant minority. As a result, the public received a largely negative image of the antiwar movement. Television news focused on events such as "Stop the Draft Week" in October 1967, when Berkeley students, in an effort to close the Oakland induction center, grappled with police in open street warfare. For many Americans, TV film clips of student demonstrators blurred with ghetto rioters and Black Power advocates in a fuzzy but frightening image of violence.

Yet negative publicity did not prevent the antiwar movement from flourishing throughout the country in the latter half of the sixties, drawing support from citizens of every stripe.[3] But it was on the nation's campuses that opposition to the Vietnam conflict proved most vocal. Even at universities where antiwar activists were in the minority, majorities opposed the war and generally sympathized with the protesters. Channeling this sentiment into an effective organization proved extremely difficult. SDS, the organizers of the first major national demonstration against the war in April 1965, had attracted waves of new members in the wake of this event. Of all campus-based New Left organizations, it appeared to have the most potential to consolidate antiwar, racial, and university issues into a general New Left movement. By the end of 1967, SDS had an estimated membership of 100,000 in more than 300 chapters located in every state except Alaska. During the mid- to late sixties, nearly 20 million postwar baby boomers turned eighteen. Millions of these adolescents attended universities, and, having come of age in the era of civil-rights, antiwar, and student-power demonstrations, thousands of them questioned the Cold War consensus. Many found a home in SDS.

Nevertheless, even as the New Left began to assume the dimensions of a mass movement led by SDS, problems of goals, tactics, and leadership plagued the budding crusade. Part of the predicament lay in the very nature of SDS. As developed in the early sixties by Haber, Hayden, and others, SDS was a small group of radical intellectuals who for ideological and personal reasons opposed hierarchical leadership. Participatory democracy, the philosophy espoused in the *Port Huron Statement,* worked well

---

[3]The antiwar movement is examined in more detail in Chapter 6.

within the close and often communal networks of early SDS. But after 1965, as opposition to the war attracted new recruits in unprecedented numbers, SDS found itself lacking the power to give coherent direction to the Movement.

To make matters worse, SDS's original old guard became increasingly estranged from the eager young recruits. Although a few years scarcely qualifies as a generation, something like a generation gap nonetheless developed in SDS. In addition to being younger, the new SDS members tended to be less intellectual, had fewer personal or family connections with the Old Left, and felt a greater affinity for the liberated lifestyle of the emerging counterculture. Earlier recruits had come mainly from prestigious eastern and midwestern universities, whereas later members typically sprang from less eminent public and private colleges scattered across the country. To them the old guard seemed an elitist old-boy network tied to ''all that thirties horseshit.''

Many idealistic values held by SDS's early leaders had grown naturally from their parents' radical or liberal views, but a large number of the newer recruits came from conservative, middle-American families. To these adolescents, the discoveries of the injustice of racism and the immorality of war came as a revelation. Their disillusionment with America and their estrangement from their families became complete. Even more than the original SDS members, they distrusted all authority, including that of the old guard itself.

Jeffrey Shero typified the newcomers. The son of an air force colonel stationed in Texas, Shero had led the fight to desegregate toilets at the University of Texas, rallying his followers with the memorable slogan, ''Let my people go.'' As he described it, joining SDS in Texas ''meant breaking with your family, it meant being cut off—it was like in early Rome joining a Christian sect—and the break was so much more total. . . . Your mother didn't say, 'Oh, isn't that nice, you're involved. We supported the republicans in the Spanish Civil War and now you're in SDS and I'm glad to see you're socially concerned.' In most of those places, it meant '*You Goddamn Communist.*' ''

New recruits infused SDS with energy and enthusiasm for direct action, but they also burdened it with their almost anarchistic disdain for leadership and organization. Elected vice president of SDS in June 1965, Jeff Shero introduced ''an experiment in office democracy'' to SDS's national office. To root out ''elitism,'' all work within the office was to be shared equally. After the spring march and the explosion of publicity that SDS drew, letters poured into the national office asking for information, literature, and membership applications. Disaffected adolescents throughout the country wrote in: ''Please send me anything you have about the war.'' ''I heard from a friend what kind of things you're doing, and I'd like to join.'' With no one delegating responsibilities and with few members of the understaffed office enjoying running mimeograph machines and stuffing envelopes, little mail got answered.

SDS flourished despite these problems, but it grew on local campuses with scant regard to the national organization. No longer a self-selected community of friends, SDS became an assortment of loosely bonded, independent campus chapters. At national conventions, growing factionalism made the rule-by-consensus ideal of participatory democracy all but impossible.

The war clearly stood as the most pressing concern of alienated youth, but even here SDS failed to maintain leadership. Many of the old guard, though utterly opposed to the war, still hoped to make projects like the ERAP the focus of SDS. They also worried about becoming a single-issue organization. ''We really screwed up,'' recalled early SDS leader Paul Booth. ''We had the opportunity . . . to make SDS *the* organizational vehicle of the antiwar movement. It was ours. We had achieved it. Instead, we chose to go off in all kinds of different directions.'' Most new recruits vehemently opposed the war and saw it as a natural outgrowth of ''the system.'' Many of them, however, had become so alienated from what they contemptuously referred to as ''Amerika'' that they condemned even the antiwar movement as working within the hated system. Instead, they harbored romantic visions of revolution, and idealized African-American ghetto fighters and Third World revolutionaries such as Ho Chi Minh and Che Guevara.

Thus, leadership of the antiwar movement slipped from SDS's grasp. With little direction from the national office, local chapters were left to pick their own issues. Members continued to participate in antiwar and antidraft activities, but leadership passed to groups such as the Resistance, SANE, Women Strike for Peace, and various ad hoc national committees. By the end of 1967, Students for a Democratic Society had become a large, loosely connected collection of campus chapters that looked healthy on the surface but would soon splinter. The New Left would survive, but it never developed a single effective organization.

''Sex, Drugs, and Rock 'n' Roll'': The Rise of the Counterculture

The radicalization of youth coincided with the build-up of the war in Vietnam and with the wave of urban riots. Yet four pivotal cultural phenomena—an increase in drug use, the resurgence of rock music, the revolution in sexual mores, and the rise of an underground media—also spurred the growth of the counterculture.

A portentous event in the revolution in drug use occurred one summer day in August 1960, when Harvard psychologist Timothy Leary, vacationing in Cuernavaca, Mexico, ingested some hallucinogenic psilocybin mushrooms. ''The revelation had come,'' he declared. ''The veil had been pulled back. The classic vision. The full blown conversion experience. . . . God had spoken.'' Back at Harvard that fall, Leary devoted himself to experiments with hallucinogens. One of the first people whom he contacted was English author Aldous Huxley. In 1954 Huxley had published *The Doors of Perception,* an account of a profound mystical awakening that he had experienced under the influence of mescaline, a powerful hallucinogen synthesized from the peyote cactus. Huxley felt that he had viewed ''what Adam had seen on the morning of creation'' and touted mind-expanding drugs as a way ''to be shaken out of the ruts of ordinary perception, to be shown for a few timeless hours the outer and the inner world . . . as they are apprehended, directly and unconditionally, by Mind at Large.'' Leary hoped to bring Huxley's mystical message to the world.

That December, Beat poets Allen Ginsberg and Peter Orlovsky participated in the Harvard professor's drug sessions. High on psilocybin, dancing naked in Leary's kitchen, Ginsberg declared himself the messiah and proposed a phone hookup with novelists William Burroughs, Jack Kerouac, and Norman Mailer, and with Kennedy and Khrushchev, to ''settle all this about the Bomb once and for all.'' Like Leary, Ginsberg would become a prophet of the psychedelic revolution.

Soon Leary's journey led him to the much more powerful synthetic hallucinogen

LSD (lysergic acid diethylamide), discovered by a Swiss chemist in 1943 and many times more potent than all other known hallucinogens; a mere 300 millionths of a gram of this colorless, odorless substance—little more than a speck—could produce a profound or frightening psychedelic experience. Psychologists and psychiatrists had begun using LSD in the late fifties as a possible cure for schizophrenia.[4] But as the sixties began, few outside of psychiatric circles knew of the drug, though it was legal. Enraptured by his initial experiments with LSD, Leary hailed the drug as a breakthrough comparable to the discovery of fire.

Drug taking was nothing new in 1960. In the nineteenth century, opium, morphine, heroin, and cocaine were common ingredients in patent medicines. But during the twentieth century, two factors inhibited American drug use: legislation that made most mind-altering drugs illegal and an association of drugs with outcast minorities such as African-Americans and Chinese or with disreputable people like prostitutes and underworld figures. For law-abiding, middle-class Americans, alcohol had remained the drug of choice, although some used medically prescribed tranquilizers and amphetamines.

In the sixties, drugs appealed to young rebels for the very reasons that their respectable parents feared them. They gave adolescents a sense of flouting adult taboos while participating in a secret outlaw community. The state of mind that drugs induced also attracted members of the sixties' counterculture. Marijuana, peyote, mescaline, and LSD, devotees claimed, created a new state of being—deeper and yet more passive. By the midsixties, drugs had become an integral part of the revolt against dominant social values. Rejecting the striving competitiveness and individualism of the larger society, sixties drug prophets spoke in visionary terms of a higher consciousness focused on sharing, cooperation, and the mystical union of the self with nature. Psychedelic drugs, claimed Leary, stimulated "contemplation, meditation, sensual openness, artistic and religious preoccupation."

Marijuana, the most available and least harmful of illegal drugs, had become nearly as commonplace among college students as alcohol by the later sixties. Generally friends introduced first-time users to the drug. Inhaled in the right setting, "pot" or "dope" induced a mild state of euphoria and a sense of heightened perception. Smoking it was almost always a shared experience, with hand-rolled "joints" passed around among a group. Marijuana smoking spread rapidly through the youth culture, filtering from college campuses into the high schools and the armed forces as well. In 1967 more United States troops in Vietnam were arrested for using marijuana than for any other crime.

To the young, marijuana seemed far less harmful than alcohol; to ban one and encourage the other struck them as one more example of adult hypocrisy. Once initiated into the world of dope smoking, young people became potential recruits for the counterculture, not so much because of the drug's effects as because of its cultural associations and illegality. Michael Rossman, a leader of the Berkeley Free Speech Movement, explained: "When you smoked dope, you inhaled an entire complex of attitudes and culture. . . . You couldn't smoke dope without being an outlaw and being against the state, because the state was out to get your ass."

---

[4]The CIA also conducted numerous secret LSD experiments in the fifties in what the agency termed "research in the manipulation of human behavior."

LSD's High Priest. Timothy Leary entreated Americans to "tune in, turn on, drop out."

Drug use widened the generation gap. Middle-class adults were horrified that their sons and daughters were indulging in illegal substances. Even those aware of the differences among drugs developed something of a domino theory: the belief that however mild a drug might be, its user would invariably seek stronger, more addictive substances. The first puff of marijuana, they thought, would almost certainly lead to heroin addiction. Their argument had some merit. Although sixties youth rarely used heroin, many did proceed from pot to more potent hallucinogens, particularly LSD, the second most-popular drug among counterculture people.

Timothy Leary and novelist Ken Kesey emerged as the most widely known advocates of LSD. Leary's early Harvard scientific experiments soon became drug-induced religious experiences. Fired from Harvard in 1963, Leary established a religious commune based on drugs in an old mansion in Millbrook, New York. In 1966 he founded the League for Spiritual Discovery (LSD) and began proselytizing for the drug in conjunction with his quasi-religious sect. Traveling about the country with a multimedia show, Leary sported long, white robes and flowing, snowy hair. His simple sermon exhorted ''Tune In, Turn On, Drop Out'': listen to your inner spiritual self, take LSD to reach that true self, and withdraw from the mainstream.

If Leary became LSD's high priest, Ken Kesey waxed as its Pied Piper. While attending graduate school at Stanford University in 1959, Kesey first took LSD as part of a medical experiment, an experience that forever changed his perception. In 1963 he used profits from his successful first novel, *One Flew Over the Cuckoo's Nest,* to found a drug commune at La Honda, California. There the Merry Pranksters, as Kesey and his followers called themselves, crafted a world of drugs, music, and sex. They wore lurid costumes and motored around in a 1939 International Harvester bus painted in Day-Glo colors and outfitted with speakers, tapes, and microphones. The bus driver was Neal Cassady, the hero of Kerouac's adventures described in *On the Road.*

To spread their vision of the cosmic consciousness further, Kesey and the Pranksters began a series of multimedia shows called "acid tests" in 1965. The largest of these, the Trips Festival held in San Francisco's Long Shoremen's Hall during January 1966, drew a crowd of more than twenty thousand people. Sporting everything from Civil War uniforms to Indian headdresses, audiences gyrated to the heavily amplified music of the Grateful Dead and other local rock groups, while strobe lights, taped sounds, and slide shows piled on further stimulation. The event organizers distributed LSD freely.

By the time the Trips Festival ended, LSD had become a national concern. *Life, Newsweek,* and the *Saturday Evening Post* ran lurid cover stories on the drug. *Life's* headline read: "LSD: The Exploding Threat of the Mind Drug That Got Out of Control." Congress rapidly outlawed the chemical, but by this time, the youthful counterculture had their own chemists clandestinely churning out quantities of the now illicit drug.

The most legendary of these underground chemical wizards was Augustus Owsley Stanley III, known simply as Owsley. The grandson of a United States senator from Virginia and a college dropout, Owsley set up a lab near Berkeley in 1964 and began mass-producing high-quality LSD. During the Free Speech Movement, he even soaked the pages of a Bible with acid and smuggled it into the Berkeley jail for the spiritual enlightenment of imprisoned FSM students. Over the next few years, Owsley turned out an estimated ten million "tabs" of LSD. Like Leary and Kesey, he saw himself as an "architect of social change" with a mission "to change the world." He supplied the LSD for Kesey's acid tests. He also paid for the expensive sound equipment used by the Grateful Dead. Naively but sincerely, Owsley, Leary, Kesey, and thousands of youthful participants believed that a drug like LSD held the key to a new and elevated consciousness.

For adults appalled at the thought of their children's taking drugs, the shifting nature of popular music in these years only worsened their fears. During the early sixties, optimistic protest and moral witness had flourished. Folk music provided the perfect expression of these ideals, at a time when many youths expected sincerity and commitment to change the world. Remnants of 1950s rock and roll coexisted with the folk scene. Some of it, like the southern California "surfing" sound as exemplified by the Beach Boys, earned an enthusiastic following, as did the Twist dance craze and other dance fads, such as the Mashed Potato, the Stroll, and the Loco-Motion. Teens also enjoyed the relatively innocuous pop music of Dick Clark's "American Bandstand," and black entrepreneur Barry Gordy of Detroit's Motown Records produced memorable rhythm and blues hits such as Smokey Robinson and the Miracles' "Shop Around" (1960) and Martha and the Vandellas' "Heat Wave" (1963). Overall, however, popular music seemed to stagnate during the early sixties.

Then came 1964 and the arrival of the Beatles. Educated by classic African-American rhythm and blues and fifties rock and deriving their name from the Beats, the Beatles developed their musical style through years of playing clubs in their native Liverpool, England, and in Hamburg, Germany. They hit the American rock scene in January 1964 with the release of their first U.S. single, "I Want to Hold Your Hand."

Within five days, the song had sold an incredible 1.5 million copies and had jumped to the top of the national charts.

At 1:35 P.M., February 7, 1964, Pan Am flight 101 touched down at Kennedy Airport, and the Beatles began their first American tour. More than ten thousand screaming teens greeted the plane. Two nights later, an estimated 73 million Americans, an astounding 60 percent of the viewing public, watched the Beatles' first of three appearances on the ''Ed Sullivan Show.'' Everywhere the band traveled, hordes of shrieking fans mobbed them. Beatlemania swept America like nothing before or since in the history of popular culture. By April 1964, Beatles songs held the five top places on the record charts. Later that year their first movie, *A Hard Day's Night,* packed in enthusiastic young audiences and also won critical acclaim.

The Beatles brought lightness, exuberance, and melodic happiness to rock, comforts that young Americans needed after the Kennedy assassination. From working-class backgrounds, the group had grown up in an atmosphere characterized by irreverence toward established authority. When asked at their first American press conference: ''What do you think of Beethoven?'' drummer Ringo Starr replied: ''I love him, especially his poems.'' In answer to a reporter's query of John Lennon as to whether his family was in show business, Lennon smiled slyly: ''Well, me dad used to say me mother was a great performer.'' The cynicism and disillusionment toward mainstream society that white, middle-class American youths were learning painfully from the lessons of Dallas, Mississippi, Watts, and Vietnam came naturally to the Beatles. Yet they expressed their alienation cheerfully and offered their audiences images of love, pleasure, and freedom.

Their contagious vitality and wit—combined with Lennon's and Paul McCartney's brilliant song writing, an intense stage presence, and a polished musical style—delivered the Beatles' message to millions. They even initiated eccentric fashions and the trend of long hair for men. In fact, the Beatles' influence on the generation of Americans that came of age in the midsixties is incalculable. They embodied the playful, hedonistic, utopian sensibilities so central to the youth revolt.

The Beatles' phenomenal success led to a veritable invasion of the United States by other British rock groups—the Dave Clark Five, the Yardbirds, Herman's Hermits, the Animals, the Who, the Moody Blues, and the Rolling Stones, second only to the Beatles. In the midsixties the Beatles and the Stones stood as the yin and yang of the American rock scene—the Beatles projecting whimsical, youthful charm, the Stones exuding aggressive, hostile rebelliousness. Both groups drew their initial inspirations from classic American rock, but the eclectic Beatles constantly experimented with new forms, while the Stones retained a strong allegiance to the black rhythm-and-blues tradition. The Beatles sang of teen love; the Stones explored anguish, alienation, and sexuality in songs such as ''Satisfaction,'' ''19th Nervous Breakdown,'' and ''Get Off My Cloud.'' Yet the Stones' scorn and contempt and the Beatles' irreverence and playfulness reflected two aspects of the same rebellion. By 1965 the success of these two British groups had inspired a major resurgence of American rock.

Bob Dylan emerged as the central American contributor to this rock revival. On the night of July 25, 1965, Dylan performed at the Newport Folk Festival, the mecca of folk-music purists. Having jettisoned the jeans, workshirt, and acoustic guitar that he had made famous as a folk singer, Dylan strode out on stage clad in a black leather

Bob Dylan, America's Foremost Folk-Rock Poet. Seen here at the Newport Folk Festival, July 1965, Dylan shocked the audience as he belted out his rock classic "Maggie's Farm" accompanied by electric guitar and backed by the Paul Butterfield Blues Band.

jacket, black slacks, and high-heeled, pointy-toed black boots. Plugging in his new electric guitar with the Paul Butterfield Blues Band behind him, Dylan launched into "Maggie's Farm," a rock song that bid a disrespectful farewell to the middle-class world. Although the uncomprehending Newport audience of folk purists booed Dylan off the stage, his transformation symbolized the end of the folk era. Rock once again took first place as the undisputed music of youth.

Dylan shifted not only from folk to rock but also from liberal protest to cultural radicalism. Much of Dylan's music from this period struck an intense, creative, private, almost surrealistic note, yet it had a radical bite. His bitter song of alienation, "Like a Rolling Stone" ("How does it feel / To be on your own / With no direction home / Like a complete unknown / Like a rolling stone"), leaped to the top of the charts in the summer of 1965. "Desolation Row" depicted America as a crazed society run by madmen. "Highway 61 Revisited" conjured up images of the American road—not the wild, romantic road of Kerouac and Cassady but a road of shattered hopes, headed toward destruction. As America's rock poet, Dylan made the personal universal. His music expressed the longings, fears, joys, and battle cries of a generation at war.

Through numerous performers, rock evolved from pure entertainment to an intrinsic component of the new culture of drugs and radical politics. Nowhere was this more true than in San Francisco. By the midsixties, the San Francisco region had become the recognized center of cultural and political rebellion. The young rebels had various names—"flower children," "love generation," "freaks"—but the term *hippie,* a diminutive of the black jazz term *hip,* stuck. The Bay Area teemed with these young men and women flaunting long hair, beads, bangles, and unusual costumes—middle-class youth who had dropped into a subculture of drugs, sex, and rock. The Haight-Ashbury district of San Francisco became a veritable hippie city—a colorful street scene of communal "pads," "head" shops, free stores, and chanting Hare Krishnas.

Rock served as a focal point of hippie culture. Away from the mainstream of the commercial pop-music business, San Francisco developed a unique rock style. The Jefferson Airplane, the Grateful Dead, and Big Brother and the Holding Company, featuring the powerful blues renditions of Janis Joplin, performed regularly at San Francisco's Fillmore Auditorium and Avalon Ballroom. These musicians sang of a loving, communal society, as in the Jefferson Airplane's enticement: ''C'mon people now / Smile on your brother / Everybody get together / Try and love one another right now.'' Such music appealed especially to drug-taking audiences. The Airplane's 1967 hit ''White Rabbit,'' for instance, used the Alice in Wonderland story to advocate drugs:

One pill makes you larger

And one pill makes you small

And the ones that mother gives you

Don't do anything at all.

Go ask Alice

When she's ten feet tall.

. . . Remember what the dormouse said

Feed your head.

The San Francisco sound, featuring a simple melodic line and beat, was electronically distorted, played at an eardrum-shattering volume, and enhanced by light shows calculated to simulate a psychedelic drug experience. Kesey's legendary acid tests took place in this sensation-filled setting. The dazzling interplay of sights and sounds climaxed in a total sensory experience for listeners.

San Francisco rock, sometimes called acid rock, had originated within the local hippie community, but its fame and influence soon spread. Promoter Bill Graham opened Fillmore East to bring the West Coast experience to hip New Yorkers. San Francisco bands started recording and touring, joining the ranks of rock's superstars. They influenced the Beatles, who in 1967 released perhaps the greatest rock album of the sixties, *Sergeant Pepper's Lonely Hearts Club Band.* With songs like ''Lucy in the Sky with Diamonds,'' *Sergeant Pepper* celebrated the drug experience, inspiring Timothy Leary to proclaim the Beatles ''evolutionary agents sent by God, endowed with mysterious power to create a new human species.''

By the time of the Golden Gate Park Be-In in 1967, the idea of rock as a liberating revolutionary force had won popularity among those wishing to believe it. San Francisco rock critic Ralph Gleason claimed that ''at no time in American history has youth possessed the strength it possesses now. Trained by music and linked by music, it has the power for good to change the world.''

One of rock's major themes centered on sexual liberation. The real power of a group like the Rolling Stones derived less from their radical stance than from their blatant sexuality, particularly as manifested by lead singer Mick Jagger. With his tight costumes, snarling, sultry leers, and uninhibited gestures and lyrics, Jagger exuded sex. Jim Morrison of the Doors, whom police arrested on two occasions for exposing himself on stage, described Doors concerts as erotic odysseys. "My music," summed up Janis Joplin, "isn't supposed to make you riot. It's supposed to make you fuck."

Naturally, youthful sexuality predated the sixties by several millennia, but postwar affluence had turned Americans' attention to leisure and pleasure, and thus to new attitudes about sex. The incredible success of Hugh Hefner's *Playboy* highlighted the growing candor about sexuality. Started on a shoestring in the fall of 1953, *Playboy*'s first issue, featuring a famous nude calendar photo of Marilyn Monroe, sold some fifty-three thousand copies. By 1956 circulation surpassed six hundred thousand, making *Playboy* second only to *TV Guide* as the most spectacular magazine success story of the fifties.

But though Hefner's preaching of the pleasures of sex weaned many Americans away from their puritanical past, fear of pregnancy, moral and religious principles, parental disapproval, and lack of opportunity kept millions of unmarried adolescents chaste before the sixties. All this changed when reliable contraceptives freed individuals to explore their sexuality without risk of unwanted conception. By the midsixties, the Pill, first marketed in 1960, had achieved wide use. Other women came to rely on intrauterine devices that prevented conception and could be left in place for extended periods of time. As fear of pregnancy diminished, sexual activity increased. At the same time, new scientific studies emphasized that women had much greater sexual capacities and needs than anyone hitherto had believed or acknowledged. The findings of Dr. William Masters and Virginia Johnson, widely publicized after their book *Human Sexual Response* appeared in 1966, even suggested that women are capable of multiple orgasms.

Affluence and the explosion of campus populations also fueled the sexual revolution. Owing to the Berkeley Free Speech Movement and subsequent protests, many universities relaxed their rules about curfews and dormitory visits, allowing students more opportunity for sex than previous generations had enjoyed. More collegians than ever before lived off campus, many with their lovers. This generation, which had never known the hardships of depression and seldom thought in terms of saving for hard times, developed a hedonistic and permissive ethic. "Get it while you can," as a Janis Joplin song proclaimed, became the rallying cry of sixties' youth. Sexual gratification, like drug taking and music, took its place in this new outlook.

Besides the quest for personal pleasure, ideology also drove the sexual revolution. Many counterculture youth viewed sexual freedom as part of the larger movement to liberate America. Although the individual philosophies of older intellectual gurus like Paul Goodman, Norman O. Brown, Herbert Marcuse, and Wilhelm Reich varied considerably, these radical Freudians all associated sexual repression with capitalistic exploitation and political authoritarianism. Unrepressed sexuality therefore represented both a personal act of liberation and a form of radical politics. Counterculture youth embraced this philosophy and came to associate casual sex with freedom and with feeling good about one's body. They identified monogamy and jealousy, on the other hand, with hierarchical authoritarianism. Youthful rebels perceived public nudity and the use of four-letter words not as mindless vulgarities but as direct challenges to puritanical, fascistic, "uptight Amerika." Sex, they believed, was as natural as any other bodily function, and, if practiced outside the confining, bourgeois bonds of matrimony, it made a revolutionary statement as well. "The arousal of prurient interest," claimed counterculture spokesperson Paul Krassner, "is, in and of itself, a socially redeeming act.'' Promiscuous sex, in short, promised both personal pleasure and cultural liberation.

As the schism widened between the counterculture and the establishment, many members of the new culture came to distrust the mainstream media. An underground press sprang up in the midsixties that knit together the various strands of cultural and political dissent. In 1962 the appearance of the short-lived *Fuck You: A Magazine of the Arts* previewed the sixties underground. *Fuck You* supported ''pacifism, unilateral disarmament . . . non-violent resistance . . . multilateral indiscriminate aperture conjugation, anarchy, world federalism . . . the LSD communarium . . . and group-gropes.''

In 1964 the *Los Angeles Free Press* became the first sustained sixties underground paper. Soon, with the growth of the New Left and counterculture, other underground papers proliferated. In California, the *Free Press* was joined by the Berkeley *Barb,* which emerged in the wake of the Free Speech Movement, and the San Francisco *Oracle,* a Haight-Ashbury paper filled with multicolored, swirling psychedelic art designed, according to the editor, ''to aid people on their trips.'' In New York City's East Village, the East Coast hippie capital, the *East Village Other (EVO)* began publication in the fall of 1965. Like many subsequent underground papers, *EVO* blended cultural and political radicalism. Alongside antiwar articles and pictures of LBJ as Hitler ran drug analyses and reports on avant-garde art happenings. Each week the paper featured a ''Slum Goddess'' and zany, sexy comics.

Soon underground papers proliferated in cities and college towns throughout the country. The new publications included the *Great Speckled Bird* (Atlanta), the *Fifth Estate* (Detroit), *The Paper* (East Lansing, Michigan), *Kaleidoscope* (Milwaukee), *Seed* (Chicago), *Phoenix* (Boston), *Chinook* (Denver), and *The Rag* (Austin, Texas), to name just a few. Underground papers even showed up in high schools and on army bases. Various radical organizations published their own papers: *New Left Notes* (SDS), *Challenge* (Progressive Labor), *Insurgent* (W. E. B. Du Bois Club), *Resist* (the Resistance), and *Black Panther.* In 1966 radical journalists founded the Underground Press Syndicate (UPS) to give papers a collective identity and to allow them to reprint each other's articles freely. The following year, counterculture journalists Ray Mungo and Marshall Bloom launched Liberation News Service to dispatch features on the Movement worldwide to the undergrounds. By the late sixties, more than four hundred underground papers had sprung up, with an estimated readership of nearly thirty million.

For guidance, the underground press looked in part to such earlier left-leaning publications as the *Village Voice,* the literate, artistic Greenwich Village paper that Norman Mailer had helped to found in 1955; *Liberation,* the radical-pacifist magazine begun in 1956 by A. J. Muste, Dave Dellinger, and Bayard Rustin; *I. F. Stone's Weekly,* Stone's radical, investigative political paper launched in 1953; and Paul Krassner's satirical, atheistic *Realist* started in 1958. They borrowed from these journalistic precursors and then developed a more radical and more alienated style, focusing on political issues such as the Vietnam War and racial justice and on a variety of cultural issues. They attacked middle-class mores and supported liberation through drugs, music, and sex. ''Our fight,'' proclaimed a 1966 issue of San Francisco's *Digger Papers,* ''is with those who would kill us through dumb work, insane war, dull money morality.'' Unlike the Old Left socialist and communist press, which subordinated every subject to the class struggle and took a rather puritanical view of such matters as drugs, sex, and avant-garde art, the New Left press had little faith in the working class but high optimism about the truly liberated individual. Spontaneity, sexuality, community, rock, experimental art, and all things "natural" were celebrated. Underground reporters, seldom professionals, often participated actively in the demonstrations, festivals, and events that they covered. Making no pretext of being objective, they used the press to propagandize.

This extensive medium lent validity to dissent and gave participants a sense of belonging to a true cultural movement. The papers exhibited a crude vitality and stimulated feelings of community. As they furthered political and cultural change, they boosted the counterculture's confidence in its ability to reshape society. The undergrounds' treatment of issues and ideas differed wildly from the establishment press. As *Seed* editor Abe Peck put it: "Mainstream newspapers ran crime news and arts reviews and *Dick Tracy*. Underground papers ran demonstration news and rock reviews and *The Fabulous Furry Freak Brothers,* a comic about three amiable 'heads' Tracy would have busted for their rampant pot-smoking. The dailies carried ads for pots and pans and suits; the undergrounders sold rolling papers, LPs, and jeans as they criticized the money economy." A number of issues that later became national concerns—women's rights, gay liberation, environmentalism, holistic medicine—first gained exposure in the New Left press.

Radical magazines also proliferated in the mid- to late sixties. The two most important, the *New York Review of Books* and *Ramparts,* intellectual journals with a national adult readership, offered critiques of American society and official government policies that further legitimized protest and undermined the liberal establishment. In 1966 *Ramparts* revealed the involvement of Michigan State University in training South Vietnam's secret police. The following year, the magazine unmasked CIA funding of the National Student Association. These and other disclosures radicalized many students and campus papers.

Other nationally circulated publications appealed directly to the interests of the new youth culture. In 1967 twenty-one-year-old hippie Jann Wenner founded *Rolling Stone* to celebrate the rock and counterculture scene. By the end of the decade, *Rolling Stone* had built a circulation of over a quarter of a million. In 1968 Stewart Brand, who with Ken Kesey two years before had organized the infamous Trips Festival, brought out the *Whole Earth Catalog.* Published in oversize-book format, *Whole Earth* promoted an alternative culture with practical information on living off the land. With rural communes springing up throughout the country, the *Catalog* served a useful purpose. By the early seventies, this survival primer in its various editions had sold some two million copies.

Comics (or "comix," as counterculture papers called them) also flourished in the underground media, proving ideal for reaching large, youthful audiences and preaching rebellion and liberation. Jules Feiffer, the *Village Voice* cartoonist from the midfifties on, and *Mad* magazine had pioneered the use of comics for radical political and cultural purposes. But underground comix artists of the sixties, with almost unlimited artistic freedom, pushed well beyond Feiffer or *Mad* in defying social conventions. Drawing characters from hippie life, cartoonists depicted all varieties of sexual, drug, and other taboo-breaking experiences. The *East Village Other* ran the continuing saga of Spain Rodriguez's *Trashman,* a revolutionary who fought the police. The *Free Press* carried Ron Cobb's single-panel cartoons; one showed a frazzled middle-class American wandering about with a television set searching for an electrical outlet in a postnuclear

Underground Comix. Underground comix artists preached rebellion and liberation. Their widely read depictions of hippie life helped to legitimize the counterculture. (Jim Mitchell. ''Teen-Age Horizons of Shangrila,'' No. 1. Copyright 1970 Denis Kitchen. By permission of Denis Kitchen.)

wasteland. In 1967 Robert Crumb published the first full-length underground comix book, *Zap #1*. Through his characters Fritz the Cat, Flakey Foont, and Mr. Natural, Crumb presented caricatures of various counterculture types. Soon *Zap* and other underground comic books such as Bill Griffith's and Jay Kinney's *Young Lust* series were selling hundreds of thousands of copies and became staples of hippie life.

The counterculture explored other media as well. Listener-sponsored, commercial-free radio stations, begun in the postwar period, continued to play an important role, particularly WBAI in New York and KPFA and KPFK in San Francisco and Los Angeles, respectively. Many student-run campus stations programmed rock albums, eager to promote their drug-inspired sounds and socially conscious lyrics. A number of commercial FM stations also adopted this format to win youthful audiences. Underground theater, too, flourished with plays such as Barbara Garson's *MacBird,* an angry satire of Lyndon Johnson based on Shakespeare's *Macbeth.* New Left acting troops thrived. The two most famous were the Living Theater, whose performances involved radical dialogues, sex, and direct encounters with the audience; and the San Francisco Mime troupe, which performed regularly at major antiwar rallies.

Film became an important underground medium as well. Lacking access to major studios and most commercial theaters, young film makers produced low-budget movies in 16 mm and 8 mm and showed them in lofts, art galleries, and college film societies.

As with the underground press, counterculture movie makers explored radical demonstrations, drugs, sex, and rock. Pop artist Andy Warhol, in a New York loft that he dubbed The Factory, turned out numerous underground movies, one of which, *The Chelsea Girls,* grossed more than a million and a half dollars. Sensing a new source of profit with the explosion of the counterculture, major studios by the late sixties produced a number of films directed at this audience. Some of the more successful included *The Graduate, Blow-Up, Easy Rider, Alice's Restaurant,* and an X-rated movie cartoon version of Robert Crumb's *Fritz the Cat.*

In short, from the mid- to late sixties, the underground media proliferated, offering a wide range of alternative visions and values. On any given day, people in most cities and college towns could read a radical paper or magazine, attend an underground film, witness an experimental play, tune in to rock radio, or laugh at the taboo-defying antics of comic characters. The media lent the counterculture unity and purpose and infused it with youthful optimism.

New Left and Counterculture: Two Faces of a Movement

From the mid- to late sixties, America stood polarized as a separate nation teemed within the larger society. The New Left and counterculture concerned themselves with Vietnam, civil rights, and the role of the universities; strove to create alternative institutions; and challenged some of the most cherished values of the dominant culture. Insurgent youth had instigated a rebellion against what they saw as the alienating and destructive values of science and technology. Rather than expecting individuals to adjust to the rational, mechanized needs of technological society, they stressed the priority of human needs and feelings. Advocating cooperation, love, sexuality, participatory democracy, immediate gratification, and community, they charged mainstream society with competitiveness, violence, and repression, and they spurned its hierarchical authoritarianism, striving, and individualism.

Although the values and life-styles of many Americans overlapped old culture and new, this cultural division was nevertheless very real. America had developed a sizable and vocal alternative society easily distinguishable from the mainstream by such superficial signals as dress and hair length and by more serious aspects like politics and values. In the late fifties, Beat novelist Jack Kerouac had predicted a "rucksack revolution" in which alienated youth would take to the road. A decade later, young, backpack-toting rebels hitchhiked about the country, finding welcome refuge with like-minded youths in experimental rural communes or in less formal communal houses in college towns and major cities. They flashed peace signs, passed joints, and considered themselves part of a new and better community. Nor was this an American phenomenon only. By the late sixties, the entire industrialized world contained an international youth culture built on radical politics, drugs, rock, and alternative institutions.

Many scholars assessing this turbulent time have made a sharp distinction between the political radicals and the cultural rebels. This is a serious misinterpretation. Certainly some New Left protesters oriented themselves solely along political lines, and some counterculture proponents focused only on personal life. A publication like *New Left Notes,* for example, the organ of SDS, devoted most of its pages to political analyses, whereas Haight-Ashbury's *Oracle* dealt almost exclusively with drugs, sex, and rock. But publications like *Rag,* a paper out of the University of Texas at Austin that synthesized politics and culture, proved more typical. *Rag* even sponsored an event called "Gentle Thursday," a day of peace and sharing when the old jet parked in front of the ROTC building was draped with a sign saying "Fly Gently, Sweet Plane." As one of the paper's editors declared, "We probably have the most political hippies and the most hip politicos around."

To a large extent, political radicals and cultural rebels were the same people. Most New Left–counterculture advocates drew little distinction between a political act, like picketing the Pentagon, and a cultural act, such as smoking marijuana. Both deeds, they believed, furthered the Movement or the Revolution, commonplace terms in the underground media by the mid- to late sixties. Political and cultural radicals alike felt alienated and believed that the whole system would benefit from transformation. They fought the same battle, though sometimes on different fronts and with different weapons.

The hippie counterculture owed a great debt to the Beat movement of the late fifties. Yet in many ways the early New Left also prefigured the counterculture. Both SNCC and SDS in their first years adopted alternative lifestyles that included freer sexual relationships, communal living, marijuana smoking, and love of folk and rock music. For these young radicals, personal liberation ranked almost as high in importance as their larger political goals. Like the nineteenth-century transcendentalists Thoreau and Emerson, they sought a change of consciousness and a new way to relate to each other. The "freedom houses" of the idealistic black SNCC workers in Mississippi were the sixties' first intentional communes, which in turn influenced the SDS ghetto communes of the ERAP. Finally, a close reading of SDS's famed *Port Huron Statement* reveals that it is as much a counterculture document as a New Left political manifesto. Participatory democracy summoned people to transform the hierarchical political structure into a decentralized, humane world of egalitarian communities. Throughout the document runs a lamentation against the depersonalization and alienation of citizens in a world dominated by technology and bureaucracy.

Part of the entwining of the New Left and counterculture entailed a new definition of politics. Most young radicals made no distinction between the personal and the political, believing that one's whole life held political meaning, a view that later became central to the women's movement. As Berkeley Free Speech activist Michael Rossman expressed it, "Reconstructing the society, reconstructing the self . . . can happen simultaneously, interpenetrating as they must." Linked to the notion that "politics is how you lead your life" was a strong desire to create the future in the present. Whether by means of sit-ins and freedom rides or drug trips and rock shows, the New Left and counterculture, in Rossman's words, acted "as if we could make our own future." This ethic of immediacy led to the formation of numerous counterinstitutions and social forms: SNCC freedom schools, SDS's community unions, underground papers, free universities, free stores, thousands of communes, and "happenings."

Sometimes tension marred the relationship between radical activists and hippie dropouts. The Marxist-Maoist group Progressive Labor, for example, denounced sex, drugs, and rock as mere bourgeois indulgences that detracted from the class struggle. PL members practiced a rigid Puritanism. But most radicals shunned such asceticism and saw no barrier between their activism and the joys of hippie life. And even the least political of hippies placed themselves outside the law because of their illicit drug consumption. Drug use and other symbols of defiance such as long hair and strange clothes admitted them into the political war against the authorities.

• • •

The synthesis of the political and cultural movements comes to light in many ways. The slogan "Make Love, Not War," frequently displayed at antiwar demonstrations, made both a political and a cultural statement. Most underground papers treated New Left activities and the new lifestyle equally. The Berkeley *Barb,* with no sense of incongruity, might print an editorial analysis of American imperialism on the same page as a first-person account of an acid trip. Rock music not only provided a central expression of the counterculture but delivered a biting antiwar message. The career of Bob Dylan revealed how easily political activism could veer into cultural rebellion. And when Berkeley radical Jerry Rubin ran for mayor of that city in 1967, he called for an end to the war, support of Black Power, and the legalization of marijuana. Later Rubin helped to found the Yippies, to turn radical protest into hippie street theater. Even Tom Hayden, the esteemed New Left political leader, had begun the sixties as a follower of the Beats and ended the decade living in a counterculture Berkeley commune. Surely the New Left and counterculture displayed immense naiveté, but a great many radicals believed that any act of defiance, from burning a draft card to dancing naked in a public park, furthered the revolutionary cause. John Sinclair, a rock promoter and founder of the politically oriented New Left White Panther party, was not atypical when he advocated playing rock music, smoking dope, and engaging in public copulation to foment the Revolution.

By 1967 the sheer numbers of radicalized youth, the mass antiwar demonstrations, the flood of drugs, the sexual revolution, the loud reverberations of rock, and the general assault against authority gave many young people—and some of their adult supporters—the sense that political and cultural rebellions were fusing into one powerful Movement that would soon remake the world.

Selected Bibliography

The 1967 San Francisco Be-In and the hippie world of Haight-Ashbury are chronicled in Charles Perry, *The Haight-Ashbury* (1984). General studies of the 1960s offering useful material on the New Left and counterculture include Barbara L. Tischler, ed., *Sights on the Sixties* (1992); Edward P. Morgan, *The 60s Experience* (1991); David Chalmers, *And the Crooked Places Made Straight: The Struggle for Social Change in the 1960s* (1991); Stewart Burns, *Social Movements of the 1960s* (1990); Allen J. Matusow, *The Unraveling of America* (1984); Milton Viorst, *Fire in the Streets* (1979); Morris Dickstein, *Gates of Eden* (1977); Godfrey Hodgson, *America in Our Time* (1976); and William L. O'Neill, *Coming Apart* (1971). Former president of Students for a Democratic Society Todd Gitlin combines

scholarly analysis with personal biography in his study of the Movement years, *The Sixties: Years of Hope, Days of Rage* (1987). In *The Whole World Is Watching* (1980), Gitlin explores the influence of the media on the history of SDS. Sohnya Sayres et al., eds., *The 60s Without Apology* (1984), is a sympathetic collection of retrospective articles on the sixties upheavals. For opposing views, see Joseph Conlin, *The Troubles* (1982), and the even more caustic diatribe by former activists turned conservatives Peter Collier and David Horowitz, *Destructive Generation: Second Thoughts About the Sixties* (1989).

Kirkpatrick Sale, *SDS* (1973), is a thorough, sympathetic history of the rise and fall of the major New Left organization. An excellent biographical study focusing on early SDS is James

Miller's *"Democracy Is in the Streets"* (1987). George Vicker's *The Formation of the New Left* (1975) also concentrates on the early years of the Movement, as does Jack Newfield's perceptive midsixties assessment, *A Prophetic Minority* (1966). Central SDS figure Tom Hayden tells his own story in *Reunion: A Memoir* (1988). Maurice Isserman's *If I Had a Hammer* (1987) examines the links between the Old Left and New. Wini Breines compassionately explores the issues of *Community and Organization in the New Left* (1982). Less sympathetic studies of the New Left are Edward J. Bacciocco, Jr., *The New Left in America* (1974), and Irwin Unger, *The Movement* (1974). The best books on the psychological, social, and historical factors contributing to the radical commitments of American youth are Kenneth Keniston, *Young Radicals* (1968), and former SDS member and now sociology professor Richard Flacks, *Youth and Social Change* (1971). These studies should be contrasted with the uncomplimentary psychological and religious interpretation of Stanley Rothman and S. Robert Lichter in *Roots of Radicalism: Jews, Christians, and the New Left* (1982), and Cyril Levitt's unflattering *Children of Privilege: Student Revolt in the Sixties* (1984).

Collections of New Left and counterculture essays, speeches, manifestos, and other primary documents are Judith Clavir Albert and Stewart Edward Albert, eds., *The Sixties Papers* (1984); Mitchell Goodman, ed., *The Movement Toward a New America* (1970); Gerald Howard, ed., *The Sixties* (1982); Massimo Teodori, ed., *The New Left* (1969); and Paul Jacobs and Saul Landau, eds., *The New Radicals* (1966). In addition to Hayden's and Gitlin's books, other worthwhile personal accounts by Movement participants include David Harris, *Dreams Die Hard* (1983); Joan Baez, *And a Voice to Sing With* (1987); Don McNeill, *Moving Through Here* (1970); Abbie Hoffman, *Revolution for the Hell of It* (1968); Jerry Rubin, *Do It!* (1970); and Paul Cowan, *The Making of an Un-American* (1970). Novels by counterculture participants—Richard Brautigan's *Trout Fishing in America* (1967) and Richard Fariña's *Been Down So Long It Looks Like Up To Me* (1965)—capture the whimsy, alienation, and freedom expressed by youthful rebels.

Lawrence Lader, *Power on the Left: American Radical Movements Since 1946* (1979); Milton Cantor, *The Divided Left: American Radicalism, 1900–1975* (1978); James Weinstein, *Ambiguous Legacy: The Left in American Politics, 1900–1975* (1975); and John P. Diggins, *The American Left in the Twentieth Century* (1973), place the Movement in the larger context of the Left in the twentieth century.

The Berkeley Free Speech Movement elicited a number of contemporary analyses. See particularly Harold Draper, *Berkeley: The New Student Revolt* (1965); Seymour M. Lipset and Sheldon S. Wolin, eds., *The Berkeley Student Revolt* (1965); and Michael V. Miller and Susan Gilmore, eds., *Revolution at Berkeley* (1965). Slightly later evaluations include Max Heirich, *The Spiral of Conflict: Berkeley, 1964* (1968); Sheldon S. Wolin and John H. Schaar, *The Berkeley Rebellion and Beyond* (1970); and Michael Rossman, *The Wedding Within the War* (1971). W. J. Rorabaugh's *Berkeley at War: The 1960s* (1989) places the Free Speech Movement in the larger context of Berkeley in the sixties. Lewis Feuer, a Berkeley sociologist at the time of the Free Speech Movement, in a massive history of student movements, *The Conflict of Generations* (1969), offers a negative Freudian analysis of student rebels. More balanced general accounts of university protests are Seymour Martin Lipset, *Rebellion in the University* (1971), and Samuel Lubell and Irving Kristol, eds., *Confrontation: Student Rebellion in Universities* (1971).

The two best studies of the impact of the Vietnam War on the student generation and American society generally are Thomas Powers, *The War at Home* (1973), and Alexander Kendrick, *The Wound Within* (1974). For the antiwar and antidraft movements, see Nancy Zaroulis and Gerald Sullivan, *Who Spoke Up? American Protest Against the War in Vietnam, 1963–1975* (1984); Melvin Small, *Johnson, Nixon, and the Doves* (1988); Charles DeBenedetti and Charles Chatfield, *An American Ordeal: The Antiwar Movement of the Vietnam Era* (1990); Lawrence Baskin and William Strauss, *The Draft, the War, and the Vietnam Generation* (1978); Alice Lynd, *We Won't Go* (1968); and Michael Ferber and Staughton Lynd, *The Resistance* (1971). Louis G. Heath, ed., *Mutiny Does Not Happen Lightly* (1976), is a collection of documents from the antiwar and draft resistance movements. Kenneth J. Heineman, *Campus Wars* (1993), examines the peace movement at several northern state universities.

Influential, positive, contemporary analyses of the counterculture still worth reading are Theodore Roszak, *The Making of a Counter Culture* (1969); Philip Slater, *The Pursuit of Loneliness* (1970); and Charles Reich, *The Greening of America* (1970). A sociological analysis of the youth culture is Milton Yinger, *Countercultures* (1982).

Jay Stevens's *Storming Heaven* (1987) offers the most thorough investigation of LSD and its popularity in the sixties. Other helpful studies of the sixties drug scene are William Novak, *High Culture* (1980), and David Musto, *The American Disease* (1973). See also James T. Carey, *The College Drug Scene* (1968), a sociological study that focuses on Berkeley. Timothy Leary tells his story in *High Priest* (1968) and *The Politics of Ecstasy* (1973). Ken Kesey and his Merry Pranksters are the subject of Tom Wolfe's entertaining *Electric Kool-Aid Acid Test* (1968). Documents on the drug culture have been collected in D. Salamon, ed., *The Marijuana Papers* (1970), and Harrison Pope, Jr., *Voices from the Drug Culture* (1971).

Jerome Rodnitzky examines the early sixties folk-music revival in *Minstrels of the Dawn* (1976). R. Serge Denisoff's *Great Day Coming: Folk Music and the American Left* (1971) views the folk revival in the larger context of the long history of protest songs. Books attempting to place rock music into a broader culture of the sixties are Herbert London, *Closing the Circle: A Cultural History of the Rock Revolution* (1985); John Orman, *The Politics of Rock Music* (1985); Bruce Pollock, *When the Music Mattered: Rock in the 1960s* (1983); David Pichaske, *A Generation in Motion: Popular Music and Culture in the Sixties* (1979); and R. Serge Denisoff and Richard A. Petersen, eds., *The Sounds of Social Change* (1972). Valuable insights into the rock scene can also be gleaned from Greil Marcus, *Mystery Train* (1975); Jim Miller, ed., *The Rolling Stone's Illustrated History of Rock and Roll* (1980 ed.); and Jonathan Eisen, ed., *The Age of Rock* (1970). Richard Goldstein, *Goldstein's Greatest Hits* (1970), and Robert Christgau, *Any Old Way You Choose It* (1973), are collections of review essays by two informed sixties rock critics. Useful studies of individual artists are Philip Norman, *Shout! The Beatles in Their Generation* (1981); Hunter Davies, *The Beatles* (1978); Stanley Booth, *Dance with the Devil: The Rolling Stones and Their Times* (1984); Anthony Scaduto, *Dylan* (1973); and Ralph Gleason, *The Jefferson Airplane* (1972).

Herbert Hendin's *The Age of Sensation* (1975) treats the sexual revolution, and pollster Daniel Yankelovich documents changes in sexual attitudes in *The New Morality* (1974). Richard King's *The Party of Eros* (1978) analyzes the radical Freudian advocates of sexual freedom Paul Goodman, Herbert Marcuse, and Norman O. Brown. Abe Peck, *Uncovering the Sixties* (1986), and Lawrence Leamer, *The Paper Revolutionaries* (1972), record the history of the underground media. A representative sampling of underground writings can be found in Thomas King Forcade, ed., *Underground Press Anthology* (1972). Underground comix receive their due in Mark James Estren, *A History of Underground Comics* (1974).

CHAPTER

8

1 9 6 8

As with many other areas of South Vietnam, American commanders had ordered Quang Ngai province "sanitized": kill the Vietcong, destroy homes and crops, and remove the civilian population to "strategic hamlets." An area of lush, green rice paddies and small villages on the northeast coast, Quang Ngai province had endured repeated bombing, defoliation, and napalm attacks. U.S. firepower already had destroyed 70 percent of the province's dwellings, rendering nearly 140,000 civilians homeless, when in December 1967, the U.S. Army sent in Charlie Company, First Battalion, Twentieth Infantry, to complete the sanitizing operation. On February 25, 1968, land mines fatally injured six members of Charlie Company and wounded twelve others. A VC booby trap killed a sergeant and severely wounded one of his men on March 14.

Two days later, Charlie Company's commander, Captain Ernest Medina, ordered a platoon led by Second Lieutenant William L. Calley, Jr., to attack the small Quang Ngai province hamlet of My Lai. According to later testimony, Medina gave orders to destroy the village and to kill "anybody that was running from us, hiding from us, or who appeared to us to be the enemy." Making no effort to distinguish between civilians and combatants, Calley's platoon launched a vicious onslaught. One soldier slashed an old man with his bayonet and threw another man down a well. The soldiers shot women and children kneeling in prayer around a temple. Calley and others threw grenades into houses and fired as the desperate inhabitants darted from the dwellings. As a baby tried to open her slain mother's blouse to nurse, a soldier stabbed the infant. The men raped a thirteen-year-old girl and then murdered her. Laughing infantryman tossed mutilated bodies about and herded fleeing villagers into a large drainage ditch, where Calley directed their slaughter. Helicopters gunned down others who had managed to escape the ground troops.

A front-page story in the next day's *New York Times* credited Charlie Company with killing 128 "Vietcong," and the head of U.S. military operations in South Vietnam, General William Westmoreland, sent a congratulatory message. In truth, American soldiers killed nearly five hundred people at My Lai, most of them women, children, and old men. It would be more than two years before investigative reporter Seymour Hersh, in a May 1970 article in *Harper's* magazine, revealed the full horrors of that day.

As a direct result of Hersh's report, in 1971 a military court sentenced Lieutenant Calley to life in prison for his part in the murders. Nevertheless, millions of Americans who supported the war saw Calley not as a villain but as a hero. President Richard Nixon ordered Calley released from a military stockade and returned to his officers' quarters. Nixon also assured the public that as commander-in-chief he would make the final disposition in Calley's case.

The My Lai atrocities symbolized the violence and chaos of 1968, a year in which a series of crises rocked the United States and the rest of the world. The first shock hit on January 23, when North Korean patrol boats in the Sea of Japan seized the American naval spy vessel the USS *Pueblo*. The eighty-three-man crew would be held prisoners for almost a year. One week later, North Vietnamese and Vietcong forces launched the largest and best coordinated offensive of the war to date, corroding Americans' confidence in their policymakers' judgment. As the year ground on, Lyndon Johnson withdrew from the presidential race; Martin Luther King, Jr., and Robert Kennedy fell to assassins' bullets; widespread rioting shook the nation's cities; student demonstrations broke out at universities throughout the world; and violence tainted the Democratic presidential nominating convention in Chicago. The traumas at home and abroad ripped American society apart and exposed social, cultural, and generational fissures far wider than anyone had imagined.

All of these forces converged in the most divisive presidential campaign since the election of Lincoln in 1860 sparked the Civil War. By the end of this climactic year, those on the Left who had hoped to secure their goals through the political system would fall to defeat. The country would swing decidedly to the Right and elect Republican Richard M. Nixon. Although after 1968 Americans repudiated the Left, they could no longer agree on national purpose and values. The long-dominant postwar consensus crumbled, and faith in a pure and indomitable America evaporated. Disillusionment with public institutions and leaders spread, and the nation's fragmentation accelerated.

Tet

In an address to the nation on January 17, 1968, Lyndon Johnson cockily pledged U.S. victory in Vietnam. In his year-end assessment of the war ten days later, General William Westmoreland concluded that "the enemy . . . has experienced only failure." The general expressed "optimism for increased successes in 1968," thanks in part to "a greatly improved intelligence system." Three days later, North Vietnamese and Vietcong forces launched the Tet Offensive, their most massive military effort of the war to date.

Tet, the Vietnamese lunar new year, is normally a festive time when families gather in the villages of their ancestors. In previous years, an undeclared cease-fire had prevailed during the holiday. But on the evening of January 30, 1968, North Vietnamese and Vietcong soldiers disguised as South Vietnamese troops or as civilians returning from holiday visits infiltrated cities throughout South Vietnam. Many of them carried weapons hidden in baskets and vegetable carts. Late that night, a nineteen-man VC squadron blasted a hole in the wall surrounding the U.S. embassy in Saigon and rushed into the courtyard of the compound. Unable to break through the embassy's heavily reinforced walls and door, the attackers pounded the building with rockets and exchanged gunfire with a small detachment of military police. The siege lasted for more than six hours before U.S. paratroopers, landed by helicopter on the embassy roof, overpowered the intruders. All but two of the nineteen Vietcong died in the fighting; five Americans perished.

Because of the twelve-hour time difference between Saigon and the eastern United States, it was midafternoon before news of this assault on a key symbol of the American presence in Vietnam reached Washington and New York. Walter Cronkite, America's most trusted TV anchor, was preparing for the ''CBS Evening News'' when he read the Associated Press bulletin. ''What the hell is going on?'' he demanded. ''I thought we were winning the war.''

The dramatic night at the embassy in fact made up only a small part of the Tet Offensive, an extensive series of coordinated, nationwide attacks on South Vietnam's cities and military bases. Overnight, jungle guerrillas had become urban street fighters. On January 30 and 31, North Vietnamese and Vietcong soldiers hit virtually every key South Vietnamese city, including sixty-four district capitals, thirty-six provincial capitals, fifty hamlets, and most major military bases. Saigon itself, hitherto unscathed by a full-scale VC offensive, staggered when more than four thousand guerrilla fighters descended on major public buildings and military installations. Although repelled from the American embassy, the presidential palace, and the airport, the Vietcong seized temporary control of Saigon's radio station and large areas of the city itself.

The offensive caught the United States and South Vietnam utterly off guard. Communist rockets destroyed grounded planes on American air bases and blew up an ammunition dump at the ground-forces base at Long Binh. About seventy-five hundred North Vietnamese and Vietcong troops captured the ancient city of Hué. Farther north they overran all five provincial capitals. Fierce fighting raged from the Mekong Delta in the South to the demilitarized zone in the North.

Within days, though, despite early Vietcong gains, American and South Vietnamese forces turned the tide. Relying on fierce artillery fire and air bombardments, they retook city after city. The Vietcong held out longest in Hué, but after three weeks of heavy bombing and intense house-to-house fighting, U.S. and ARVN troops prevailed. The once-beautiful city that had graced the banks of the Perfume River was reduced, in the words of one observer, to a ''shattered, stinking hulk, its streets choked with rubble and rotting bodies.''

In purely military terms, Tet ended in an American victory. U.S. and South Vietnamese troops had routed the enemy, and the estimated number of VC and North Vietnamese dead totaled thirty-three thousand compared with the loss of thirty-four hundred allied forces. But these figures omitted the larger story. Despite the United States' claim that it sought to protect the South Vietnamese people's freedom, Americans had resorted to their modern weaponry under the pressure of Tet. Artillery shells and bombings had taken an immense toll on civilian lives, not just in Hué but throughout South Vietnam. American pilots had even bombed areas of downtown Saigon. Nowhere was the futility of the U.S. effort to "save" Vietnam more clearly illustrated than in Ben Tre, the capital of Kien Hoa province in the Mekong Delta. As AP reporter Peter Arnett viewed the rubble of what had once been a thriving city of 35,000, an American major told him: "It became necessary to destroy the town to save it." Before Tet ended, more than 12,500 civilians had died, and more than a million Vietnamese had become refugees.

In other ways, too, media images from Tet belied America's stated aim to defend a democracy in Vietnam. On the fourth day of the fighting, AP photographer Eddie Adams, walking through Saigon with NBC correspondent Howard Tuckner and his cameraperson, spotted General Nguyen Ngoc Loan, the chief of South Vietnamese national police, leading a suspected VC prisoner. As the horrified Americans watched, General Loan brought his pistol up to the bound man's head and fired. The shocking public execution, captured both in Adam's Pulitzer Prize–winning photograph and on TV, further damaged America's rationale for the war.[1]

General Westmoreland and Lyndon Johnson proclaimed Tet a great victory. In the president's words, it was "the most disastrous Communist defeat of the War in Vietnam." "The enemy is on the ropes," affirmed Westmoreland. "Tet was his last gasp." But Americans had heard optimistic reports before and knew better. Nightly TV coverage of the bloody fighting revealed that no area of Vietnam was secure. How could the United States be winning this war, people wondered, when enemy snipers had killed marines within the very compound of the American embassy? Even U.S. soldiers in the field distrusted their leaders' reassuring accounts. In reaction to Westmoreland's assurance that he saw "light at the end of the tunnel," one battle-hardened marine noted for his skill at ousting Vietcong from their underground hideouts demanded: "What does that asshole know about tunnels?"

At home, the Tet Offensive altered attitudes toward the war. Public opinion polls that March revealed more doves than hawks for the first time since the United States had gone to war. The consensus on foreign policy that had dominated since the end of World War II began to collapse. In the words of the *New York Times*, the majority of Americans concurred "that the price of rescuing Vietnam from Communism had outrun the benefit and should not be paid."

The media, particularly television, played a major role in shifting public outlook on the war. By the 1960s, virtually every U.S. family owned a TV set, and viewers formed their opinions about Vietnam through this medium. In 1963 the major networks revamped the evening news, expanding their fifteen-minute presentations to a half-hour. Two years later came color TV. These innovations, combined with newly available satellites that allowed instant transfer of film tapes from Vietnam and around the world to studios in New York, transformed the far-off conflict into what *New Yorker*

---

[1] The Vietcong and North Vietnamese were as brutal as the South Vietnamese, and maybe even more so, but they committed most of their atrocities well out of sight of foreign photographers.

correspondent Michael Arlen called "the Living-Room War." When the United States began escalation in the midsixties, most TV and news journalists in the field accepted the optimistic official reports and presented supportive coverage. Because the war had few real fronts and much of the fighting took place in remote jungles, the TV audience thus saw only infrequent battle pictures.

Tet changed all this. Suddenly some sixty million viewers were bombarded nightly with such images as bodies strewn in the embassy compound, the public execution of a suspected VC, and U.S. bombing and shelling of Saigon and Hué. The graphic coverage made a mockery of the rosy appraisals by the administration and the military. TV newsmen themselves came to question the wisdom of the war, with CBS anchor Walter Cronkite delivering the most significant reevaluation.

A dentist's son born in 1916 in St. Joseph, Missouri, Cronkite dropped out of the University of Texas in his junior year and worked as a radio sportscaster and, later, as a reporter for the *Houston Post*. In 1942 he shipped off to become a World War II battlefield correspondent for the United Press. He joined CBS in 1950 and rose to fame with TV's soaring postwar popularity. In 1962 he accepted the newly named post of anchorman for the "CBS Evening News." With his commanding voice and soothing manner, the fatherly, gray-haired Cronkite soon earned a reputation as "the most trusted man in America."

Before Tet, Cronkite had supported American actions in Southeast Asia. After a trip to Vietnam in 1965, he praised the Johnson administration for having "made the courageous decision that communism's advance must be stopped in Asia and that guerrilla warfare as a means to a political end must be finally discouraged." Like most other citizens, Cronkite greeted the outbreak of Tet with astonishment and disbelief. On the tenth day of the offensive, he announced his plans to visit Vietnam for a personal look. Soon after his return, on the night of February 27, he broadcast a well-publicized special, "Who, What, When, Where, Why: Report from Vietnam by Walter Cronkite." Like Edward R. Murrow's televised exposé of Joseph McCarthy some fourteen years earlier, Cronkite's courageous report held devastating consequences.

With vivid film footage, he described the widespread destruction, the countless casualties, and the plight of refugees. The program opened with a shot of the CBS anchor standing in a bombed-out urban area. His rich, deep voice explained, "These ruins are in Saigon, capital and largest city of South Vietnam. . . . Like everything else in this burned and blasted and weary land, they mean success or setback, victory or defeat, depending upon whom you talk to." An interview with an American captain working on the rural pacification project revealed the breakdown of that effort.

At the program's end, filmed at his studio desk in New York, Cronkite delivered his conclusions:

> We have been too often disappointed by the optimism of the American leaders, both in Vietnam and Washington, to have faith any longer in the silver linings they find in the darkest clouds. . . . It seems now more certain than ever that the bloody experience of Vietnam is to end in a stalemate. . . . For every means we have to escalate, the enemy can match us . . . and with each escalation, the world comes closer to the brink of cosmic disaster. . . . To say that we are mired in stalemate seems the only reasonable, yet unsatisfactory, conclusion. . . . It is in-

creasingly clear to this reporter that the only rational way out will be to negotiate, not as victors, but as an honorable people.

As a furious Lyndon Johnson watched CBS's prime-time assault on administration policy, he resignedly observed, ''Well, if I've lost Cronkite, I've lost Middle America.''

Nor was Cronkite the only defector from the mainstream media. After Tet, many other respected TV and newspaper journalists spoke out against the war. Four days before Cronkite's Vietnam special, the *Wall Street Journal,* the cautious voice of American capitalism, lambasted LBJ's war: ''We think the American people should be getting ready to accept . . . the prospect that the whole Vietnam effort may be doomed.'' In a special edition on the war early in March, *Newsweek* editorialized: ''Unless it is prepared to indulge in the ultimate, horrifying escalation—the use of nuclear weapons—it now appears that the U.S. must accept the fact that it will never be able to achieve decisive military superiority in Vietnam.'' Throughout the mainstream media, calls reverberated for reassessment and negotiation.

Tet catalyzed serious doubts about the war within the administration as well. In the Defense Department, Paul Warnke, an assistant secretary in charge of international security affairs, argued that the Tet Offensive revealed American military strategy to be ''foolish to the point of insanity.'' Undersecretary of Defense Paul Nitze concurred and warned against the ''unsoundness of continuing to reinforce weakness.'' Even General Earle Wheeler, chairman of the Joint Chiefs of Staff, who continued to support the war, described the enemy as ''operating with relative freedom in the countryside'' and admitted that the Tet Offensive almost succeeded.

On March 10, when the *New York Times* leaked the story that the administration was considering a request from General Westmoreland to send an additional 206,000 troops to Vietnam, it set off a barrage of protests nationwide. That evening on an NBC-TV special focused on Vietnam, Frank McGee bluntly stated that ''the war, as the administration has defined it, is being lost. . . . Laying aside all other arguments, the time is at hand when we must decide whether it is futile to destroy Vietnam in the effort to save it.'' In Congress the prospect of another major troop increase provoked heated debate and a call for a full review of American policy in Vietnam. In the country at large, public opinion polls showed that support of Johnson's handling of the war had plummeted to an all-time low of 26 percent. This discontent would soon manifest itself in the race for the presidency.

Eugene McCarthy and the Children's Crusade

Well before Tet, in the summer of 1967, some liberal, antiwar Democrats seriously considered challenging LBJ's renomination. Allard Lowenstein, vice-chairman of Americans for Democratic Action, led the drive to ignite a ''dump Johnson'' movement, but he had trouble finding a replacement candidate. Although antiwar Democrats disliked and distrusted Johnson, opposing an incumbent president of one's own party could lead to political suicide. Lowenstein's first choice, Robert Kennedy, refused to run. Dove senators George McGovern and Frank Church also declined.

In late October, however, Eugene McCarthy, senior senator from Minnesota, agreed to enter the race. Announcing his candidacy on November 30, 1967, McCarthy declared: "There is growing evidence of a deepening moral crisis in America—discontent, frustration and a disposition to take extra legal . . . actions to manifest protest. I am hopeful that this challenge . . . may alleviate . . . this sense of political helplessness and restore to many people a belief in the processes of American . . . government." Pledging to halt the bombing, declare a cease-fire, and negotiate a settlement in Vietnam, Eugene McCarthy set out on a seemingly quixotic crusade to topple Johnson.

Furious at McCarthy's audacity, LBJ and others within the administration nevertheless failed to take him seriously. A practicing poet with an enduring interest in theology, McCarthy despised the daily routine of politics and often came across as arrogant and aloof. He could deliver brilliant speeches but more frequently bored his audiences. According to columnist I. F. Stone, McCarthy seemed "to lack heart and gut" and gave one "the uneasy feeling that he really doesn't give a damn."

Yet McCarthy was not without assets. He possessed charm, wit, and a keen intellect; he was tall and handsome, exuded a professional air, and looked presidential. These attributes, plus his antiwar platform, attracted some support from the educated middle class, particularly among college students opposed to the war. But with few funds and only a makeshift organization of amateur volunteers, McCarthy's chances of blocking Lyndon Johnson's renomination appeared minimal, and no serious political analyst gave him a chance. In January 1968, a White House poll of New Hampshire voters, who held the earliest presidential primary, showed McCarthy receiving a meager 6 percent of the vote, against LBJ's 76 percent.

Then came Tet. Suddenly thousands of college students, some from as far away as California, deserted the classrooms and descended on New Hampshire to work for McCarthy. Bright and eager, they threw themselves into the fray as if on a crusade. Most of these volunteers had long opposed the war. For many of them, McCarthy's campaign represented one last push to stop Vietnam from within the traditional political system. To sway conservative New Hampshire voters, young men cut their hair and shaved their beards, becoming "clean for Gene." Men and women packed away their blue jeans and donned suits and ties, skirts and blouses. A powerful camaraderie united these young workers. For some campaigners, McCarthy became almost a surrogate father. As one volunteer recalled, "There was the whole 'children's crusade' aspect, with Gene as the father whom we would have liked to have. Instead of having this warmonger redneck [LBJ], we had an educated, gentle man. Instead of an eagle, we had a dove."

Functioning on little sleep and virtually no pay, the students canvassed the state from door to door, ran mimeograph machines, arranged meetings, sent out mailings, and answered phones. *Newsweek* reporter Mary McGrory described the scene at McCarthy headquarters in Concord, New Hampshire as "one thousand percent activity. I hadn't seen so many people in a political headquarters since I could remember. It was just so immense you figured it had to make a difference."

McGrory's first story on the "children's crusade," entitled "Going Straight in New Hampshire: The 'Hairies' Learn How to Help McCarthy," appeared in *Newsweek* on March 5, 1968, just a week before the primary. "What is phenomenal," she claimed, "is the reception [the students] have been accorded by reputedly hawkish natives who are traditionally unfriendly to strangers." Until this time, the major media had largely ignored the McCarthy campaign. Now TV news celebrities such as Mike Wallace, Chet Huntley, and David Brinkley flocked to New Hampshire. Movie stars, too, came to

The Children's Crusade. Four college students, some of the more than 5,000 unpaid volunteers who descended on New Hampshire, do their part to aid Senator Eugene McCarthy in his presidential bid.

work for McCarthy. "I didn't come here to help Gene McCarthy," Paul Newman told a cheering crowd, "*I* need McCarthy's help. The country needs it." Money now poured into the campaign. One McCarthy supporter even placed a $10,000 bet that his candidate would get over 30 percent of the vote and pledged his winnings to the campaign. The incredulous bookie gave him twelve-to-one odds.

Two days before the New Hampshire primary, the *New York Times* released the story of Westmoreland's request for additional troops and hinted at the heated debate that it had stirred within the administration. Tet, the student volunteers, media attention, and now the furor over more Americans going to Vietnam caused McCarthy's stock to soar. Writing on the eve of the primary, McGrory saluted McCarthy as

> a political star of the first magnitude. Violet-eyed damsels from Smith are pinning McCarthy buttons on tattooed mill-workers, and Ph.D.s from Cornell, shaven and shorn for world peace, are deferentially bowing to middle-aged Manchester [New Hampshire] housewives and importuning them to consider a change of commander-in-chief. . . . A kind of reconciliation process between the generations has begun. . . . McCarthy is leading the children back into the political process and thus willy-nilly into communication with their elders.

McGrory noted a rumor that Robert Kennedy was reconsidering his earlier decision to stay out of the presidential race. She asked some young volunteers how they felt about this and found them contemptuous of the New York senator: "He wasn't there when we needed him," voiced a Cornell senior. "He's a moral slob." McGrory concluded that "whatever else happens on Tuesday, Senator McCarthy has taken the place of Robert Kennedy as the symbol of hope and change among America's bright children. The question is being openly asked whether Lyndon Johnson can put the Democratic Party back into the LBJ bottle. The top is off here."

A week before the primary, New Hampshire's Democratic governor, John King, predicted that McCarthy would garner no more than 28 percent of the vote. Instead, outperforming virtually everyone's expectations, the antiwar candidate received a whopping 42.4 percent and, in a separate simultaneous election for Democratic National Convention delegates, McCarthy supporters won twenty out of twenty-four positions.

President Johnson came out ahead with 49.5 percent of the vote, and it was later learned that many of those voting for McCarthy supported the war; nevertheless, the media and much of the nation interpreted New Hampshire as a crushing repudiation of LBJ and his efforts in Vietnam. If nothing else, this first primary revealed the president's unpopularity and political vulnerability.

An exultant McCarthy told reporters: "People have remarked that this campaign has brought young people back into the system. But it's the other way around: The young people have brought the country back into the system." Looking ahead, he reflected, "If we come to Chicago [site of the upcoming Democratic National Convention] with this strength, there will be no violence and no demonstrations but a great victory celebration." In the postprimary euphoria, it seemed that Americans could peacefully turn the country around. Through the electoral process, observers believed, McCarthy's supporters would reunite disaffected young with the mainstream, end Johnson's disastrous policies, and restore peace in Vietnam. No one knew that these dreams of a restorative "new politics" would die in this strange year.

RFK and LBJ

On March 16, four days after McCarthy's strong showing in New Hampshire, New York senator Robert F. Kennedy entered the race. McCarthy and his followers fumed. Alone and at great political risk, McCarthy had succeeded in putting the war on the national agenda and in proving the president's unpopularity. Now Bobby Kennedy rushed in to seize the spoils. "We woke up after the New Hampshire primary like it was Christmas Day," a distressed McCarthy worker charged. "And when we went down to the tree, we found Bobby Kennedy had stolen our Christmas presents." In the media, Kennedy's actions provoked accusations of blatant opportunism. Murray Kempton, liberal columnist for the *New York Post,* called Kennedy a coward who had come

> down from the hills to shoot the wounded. He has, in the naked display of his rage at Eugene McCarthy for having survived on the lonely road he dared not walk himself, done with a single great gesture something very few public men have ever been able to do: In one day, he managed to confirm the worst things his enemies have ever said about him.

Although many liberals condemned Robert Kennedy's actions and worried that his candidacy would divide the peace vote, Jacqueline Kennedy had another reason to rue her brother-in-law's decision to run. To historian Arthur Schlesinger, Jr., a Kennedy family friend and later biographer of RFK, she fearfully predicted that "the same thing that happened to Jack" would happen to Bobby. "There is so much hatred in this country, and more people hate Bobby than hated Jack." When she expressed her worry directly to Bobby, he dismissed it as "fatalistic."

Kennedy found it hard to dispel the widespread charges of opportunism. He explained that he had considered challenging Johnson for several months but had refrained out of fear of splitting the Democratic party. He now presumed that McCarthy's success had legitimized his entry into the race and that the public should perceive his campaign as based on issues rather than on personal ambition or as an anti-Johnson vendetta. "We've got to get out of that war," he told reporters. "It's destroying the country." Just two days before announcing his candidacy, Kennedy had privately presented LBJ's new secretary of defense, Clark Clifford, with an offer: if Johnson appointed an outside commission to review American policy in Vietnam and made "a public statement that his policy had been in error," Kennedy would agree to stay out of the race. Clifford and President Johnson flatly rejected the imperious proposition.

Even today it is hard to judge Kennedy's motives for throwing his hat into the ring. Perhaps he could see no alternative. As *Time* magazine analyzed it on March 22, "Events were passing him by. Kennedys are supposed to stand for courage; the antiwar parade marshaled by a lonely Gene McCarthy was trampling that profile." At the time, Robert Kennedy was forty-two, the same age his brother Jack had been when he initiated his run for the presidency. Possessed of the Kennedy competitiveness and charisma, RFK probably longed to revive Camelot. He loathed Lyndon Johnson and deemed him incapable of running the country. And even if by some miracle McCarthy should win the presidency, Kennedy judged him unfit for the office.

McCarthy's youthful supporters disliked Kennedy for trying to steal the prize from their hero, and many older, liberal intellectuals harbored a distrust of RFK that dated back to the early fifties when he had served on Senator Joe McCarthy's staff. For years his critics had perceived him as brash, arrogant, cocky, and ruthless in his pursuit of his brother's or his own goals. This caricature contained some truth, yet Robert Kennedy had also changed since his brother's assassination. JFK's murder had plunged him into a profound despair. He became introspective and reflective, spending hours alone reading Greek tragedies, existential philosophy, and religion. His sympathies for the sufferings of the underclasses of the world markedly deepened, and he questioned what right the United States had to kill tens of thousands in Vietnam and to make millions of people refugees. The Tet Offensive, he claimed, had "finally shattered the mask of official illusion with which we have concealed our true circumstances, even from ourselves."

In addition to his growing criticism of Johnson's actions in Vietnam, he also attacked the administration's Latin American policy as a betrayal of his brother's Alliance for Progress. In RFK's view, instead of furthering land reform and political democracy, the Johnson administration supported military dictatorships. "The responsibility of our time," he argued before a student audience in Peru, "is nothing less than a revolution— peaceful if we are wise enough; humane if we care enough; successful if we are fortunate enough. But a revolution will come whether we will it or not." Even the threat of Cuba's Fidel Castro, who had so obsessed his brother's administration, had diminished in Bobby Kennedy's eyes.

During a trip to South Africa, Kennedy denounced apartheid and urged a commitment to social justice. He implored his audience not to believe that "there is nothing one man or woman can do against the enormous array of the world's ills—against misery and ignorance, injustice and violence. . . . Few will have the greatness to bend history itself; but each of us can work to change a small portion of events, and in the totality of all those acts will be written the history of this generation."

At home, too, Kennedy increasingly became, in Schlesinger's words, the "tribune of the underclass." Although cautious to an extreme in confronting civil-rights issues as his brother's attorney general, as a senator he threw his full support behind the cause of racial equality. He visited urban ghettoes, met with black leaders, and sponsored legislation aimed at ending economic and racial injustice. He championed the cause of other nonwhites as well. "Today in America," he claimed, "we are two worlds." Many Americans belonged to the comfortable middle class, but there was another world of "the Negro, the Puerto Rican, and the Mexican American . . . a dark and hopeless place." Kennedy had traveled to California to hold hearings on conditions among migrant farm workers. There he endorsed the efforts of Cesar Chávez, the charismatic leader of the largely Chicano United Farm Workers Union that had launched a strike against grape-vineyard owners. Kennedy, declared Chávez, saw "things through the eyes of the poor. . . . It was like he was ours." In addition, Kennedy investigated poverty, malnutrition, and educational deprivation on Indian reservations and won strong support among Native Americans. "Spiritually," affirmed Indian activist and author Vine Deloria, "he was an Indian!"

Kennedy's sympathy for the poor had made him increasingly critical of the Johnson administration, for the war in Vietnam drained dollars from badly needed social programs at home. In February 1968, the Kerner commission, established following the summer riots of 1967, had issued its report, recommending the creation of two million new jobs in the inner cities, an assault on *de facto* school segregation, construction of six million new units of public housing, and the institution of a "national system of income supplementation." Johnson, embroiled in the crisis of Tet, ignored these recommendations. "The President is just not going to do anything more," charged Kennedy. "That's it. He's through with the domestic problems, with the cities." Several factors finally persuaded RFK to run, among them LBJ's rejection of further help for the poor, Tet and the continuing crisis of Vietnam, McCarthy's showing in New Hampshire— and personal ambition. He plunged into the campaign, confirming Lyndon Johnson's worst nightmares.

LBJ had won election by a vast majority in 1964, but by March 1968 his popularity had plunged to record depths. Jeered by antiwar critics whenever he appeared in public, he had become a virtual prisoner in the White House. The physical strain showed on his face, prompting his wife, Lady Bird, to note in her diary of March 10 that his eyes had become "red and swollen and painful." She compared his tribulations with the biblical Job's. Soon after RFK entered the race, Johnson confessed to his confidante Doris Kearns,

> I felt that I was being chased on all sides by a giant stampede. I was being forced over the edge by rioting blacks, demonstrating students, marching welfare mothers, squawking professors, and hysterical reporters. And then the final straw. The thing I feared from the first day of my presidency was actually coming true. Robert Kennedy had openly announced his intention to reclaim the throne in the memory of his brother. And the American people, swayed by the magic of the name, were dancing in the streets.

The fate of his besieged presidency and the war, two interrelated issues, absorbed Johnson. Immediately following Tet, the president remained hawkish. He ordered an additional 10,500 men to Vietnam and insisted in a speech to the nation in late February, "There will be blood, sweat, and tears shed . . . but persevere in Vietnam we will and we must." Nevertheless, conditions in South Vietnam continued to deteriorate. After

Vietnam Brings Down a President. With the war going poorly and his popularity plummeting, Lyndon Johnson sits dejected. On March 31, 1968, he announced he would not seek reelection.

Tet, morale among U.S. soldiers plummeted, desertions rose, as did drug use, and in some units, discipline broke down altogether, with enlisted men refusing to obey officers' orders. Some soldiers even killed their officers. Anti-Vietnamese feeling also intensified among the American troops. A joke circulating in GI barracks and bars proposed a solution to the Vietnam problem: "What you do is, you load all the Friendlies onto ships and take them out to the South China Sea. Then you bomb the country flat. Then you sink the ships." On March 16, the My Lai massacre occurred.

The clamor to reassess American policy in Vietnam grew louder in March. McCarthy's and Kennedy's campaigns focused attention on the war; so, too, did the media. Throughout the country, debate raged. George Kennan, the father of America's Cold War containment policy and a respected foreign-policy expert, called the war "a massive miscalculation and error of policy, an error for which it is hard to find any parallel in our history."

Still, Johnson held his ground. In response to a memo from UN ambassador Arthur Goldberg urging a halt to the bombing and negotiation, LBJ admonished his advisers, "Let's get one thing clear. I am not going to stop the bombing. I have heard every argument on the subject and I am not interested in further discussion. I have made up my mind." On March 18, two days after Kennedy announced his candidacy, Johnson called on Americans to join "in a *total national effort* to win the war, to win the peace, and to complete the job. . . . Make no mistake about it . . . we are going to win."

But by this time, even the president's closest advisers no longer counted on victory. Tet and particularly General Westmoreland's request for additional troops stirred dissent within the administration. At the center of the debate stood newly appointed secretary of defense Clark Clifford. An adviser to Democratic presidents since Truman and a close friend of Johnson, Clifford had earned a reputation as a hard-liner on the war. But on assuming leadership of defense on March 1, he decided to reassess Vietnam policy before agreeing to any substantial troop increase. After a week of talks with high-level military and civilian officials, Clifford concluded that ''we had no real plan to win the war. All we were gong to do was just keep pouring men in there and hopefully attrition would finally wear down the enemy to the point where they would come forward and say, 'Let's negotiate.' '' LBJ's trusted hawk metamorphosed into a dove.

Alarmed at Clifford's defection and the growing antiwar sentiment within his administration, Lyndon Johnson made a last effort in late March to win support for his policies. He removed the controversial Westmoreland from command, promised a major speech on the war for March 31, and summoned a high-level group of military, political, and business leaders to appraise administration policy in Vietnam. The so-called Wise Men included, among others, Dean Acheson, who had served as Truman's secretary of state when American involvement in Vietnam began; General Maxwell Taylor, the former ambassador to Vietnam; McGeorge Bundy, JFK's national security adviser; Supreme Court justice Abe Fortas; and noted Democratic diplomat Averell Harriman. Architects and longtime supporters of the war, these men had evaluated Vietnam in November 1967 and given their approval of the president's policy. LBJ hoped once again to secure the support of these prestigious minds.

To Johnson's alarm, when the Wise Men met on March 25–26, virtually to a man they joined the growing dissent. Present policy, they concluded, was bankrupt and lacked the support of the American people. In the words of Dean Acheson, the United States could ''no longer do the job we set out to do in the time we have left and we must begin to take steps to disengage.'' Although not advocating immediate withdrawal, the group called for de-escalation and negotiation. Their decision pointed to the end of an era: no longer would America's most influential opinionmakers give their unconditional support for the containment of communism throughout the world. Johnson reportedly charged, ''The establishment bastards have bailed out.''

Keeping his options open, LBJ had speechwriter Harry McPherson draw up two versions of his scheduled national address—a patriotic harangue proposing the call-up of fifty thousand reserves and a second draft initiating a partial bombing halt and espousing new peace initiatives. On the evening of March 31, Lyndon Johnson spoke to the American people. His face sagging, his eyes pained, he launched into his speech: ''Tonight, I want to talk to you of peace in Vietnam and Southeast Asia.'' He announced a halt to the bombing of North Vietnam except for the area just north of the demilitarized zone and asked Ho Chi Minh ''to respond positively, and favorably, to this new step toward peace.'' Even this limited bombing of North Vietnam would end, he pledged, ''if our restraint is matched by restraint in Hanoi.'' He urged strengthening of the South Vietnamese army and turning more of the fighting over to them, a shift that the next president would call Vietnamization.

Concluding his speech, Johnson explained that in thirty-two years of service to his country he had always put the unity of the people ahead of partisan politics:

> There is divisiveness among us all tonight. And holding the trust that is mine, as President of all the people, I cannot disregard the peril to the progress of the American people and the hope and the prospect of peace for all peoples. . . . Believing this as I do, I have concluded that I should not permit the Presidency to become involved in the partisan divisions that are developing in this political year. . . . Accordingly, I shall not seek, and I will not accept, the nomination of my party for another term as your president.

A stunned America collectively gasped. The man who less than four year earlier had received the largest electoral mandate in the history of American two-party politics had abdicated; the consensus that he had so craved had shattered beyond repair. Lyndon Johnson's tragedy was America's tragedy. Seeking to contain communism abroad and to reform society at home, he had made huge strides in fulfilling that liberal vision. His Great Society programs had sought to heal the sick, feed the poor, and eradicate racial and sexual discrimination. But by the time of LBJ's withdrawal, Vietnam had blighted his vision.

At first many members of the antiwar movement believed that Kennedy or McCarthy could win the election and return the nation to peace and unity. On the night of Johnson's announcement, spontaneous candlelight marches sprouted up on college campuses across the country. In front of the White House, activists gathered to sing, "We *have* overcome." The next morning the stock market surged ahead twenty points in the largest volume since Black Tuesday in 1929. But the cataclysmic year of 1968 would dash these hopes. Johnson's fall did not prove cathartic, and his capitulation failed to ease the country's bitter divisiveness. Eugene McCarthy would rightly come to call 1968 "the hard year." On April 4, just four days after the president's surprise announcement, an assassination in Memphis revealed anew the tensions rending American society.

The Death of a King

Early in 1968, Martin Luther King, Jr., had begun planning what he envisioned as a major new campaign: an interracial coalition of the oppressed in a forceful but peaceful Poor People's March on Washington. "We can't live with another summer like the last," he vowed. After helping to launch the civil-rights movement in the 1955–1956 Montgomery bus boycott, King, more than anyone else, had held together the civil-rights coalition responsible for the enactment of the 1964 Civil Rights Act and 1965 Voting Rights Act. Through courage, energy, intelligence, and oratory, he had united more blacks and whites in the moral cause of racial equality than any other American since Lincoln.

Yet at the height of his success in the midsixties, King's constituency was deserting him. Denigrated by younger, more militant blacks as a pawn of the white establishment, King grew equally estranged from the Johnson administration after his outspoken criticism of the Vietnam War. Through these years, the FBI continued to hound him. The agency's head, J. Edgar Hoover, developed an obsessive hatred for King, whom he referred to as "the burrhead." Years later, the FBI's former chief of domestic intelligence, William Sullivan, admitted to Congress that "no holds were barred" in the bureau's crusade to destroy King, and he attributed Hoover's vendetta to "racial bias." Indeed, in the midsixties, the only African-Americans the FBI employed were Hoover's five personal servants.

Harassed by the FBI, his civil-rights leadership challenged by Black Power militants, and the war in Vietnam dividing him from the administration, King grew despondent. He watched horrified as bombs in Vietnam and fires in America's ghettoes destroyed his dream of a nonviolent world. But like Robert Kennedy, whose sympathies for the poor blossomed during the period of despair following his brother's death, King focused more sharply on the economic roots of racial injustice. Hitherto centered on ending legal discrimination against blacks, King came to realize that abolishing Jim Crow laws in no way eliminated the economic inequality of the races. In 1967 he argued, "We must recognize that we can't solve our problems now until there is a radical re-distribution of economic and political power." He came to see racism, poverty, militarism, and materialism as interrelated flaws "rooted deeply in the whole structure of our society." The only solution, as he saw it, lay in a "radical reconstruction of society itself."

To dramatize the plight of the impoverished of all colors, King organized the Poor People's Campaign, scheduled to establish an encampment in the nation's capital during the spring of 1968. In late March, he took time away from planning this demonstration to lend his support for striking sanitation workers in Memphis. There, on the evening of April 3, King delivered a powerful and prophetic sermon to a mass rally at the Masonic Temple:

> We've got some difficult days ahead. But it really doesn't matter with me now, because I've been to the mountaintop . . . and I've looked over, and I've seen the promised land. I may not get there with you. But I want you to know tonight, that we, as a people, will get to the promised land. And so I'm happy tonight.

The next evening, as King stood talking with friends on his motel balcony, a white sniper killed him.[2] Predictably but ironically, King's murder touched off the worst wave of urban rage in American history. "Dr. Martin Luther King was the last prince of nonviolence," cried Floyd McKissick, the militant head of CORE. "Nonviolence is a dead philosophy, and it was not the Black people that killed it." At a press conference, former SNCC leader Stokely Carmichael vowed, "When white America killed Dr. King last night, she declared war on us. We have to retaliate for the deaths of our leaders. . . . The only way to survive is to get some guns. . . . We are going to stand up on our feet and die like men. If that's our only act of manhood, then goddammit, we're going to die."

Upheavals wracked 168 cities. In Chicago, looters and arsonists laid to waste large areas of the downtown business area. Mayor Richard Daley gave police orders to "shoot to kill" all arsonists. "A fascist's response," charged Jesse Jackson, a young SCLC activist. "The mayor may have a killing program for the dreamers, but he has no program that can kill the dreams." Rioting in Baltimore led Maryland governor Spiro Agnew to lash out at "local Black Power advocates and known criminals." Hardest hit was the nation's capital, where twelve died and more than seven hundred fires raged. Soldiers toting machine guns set up defenses around the Capitol and the White House. It took nearly fifteen thousand federal troops and national guardsmen to quell the week-long frenzy involving an estimated twenty thousand rioters.

"Martin's memory is being desecrated," deplored NAACP leader Roy Wilkins. Smoking cities stood as shameful testimonies to the collapse of King's peaceful vision and the failure of Lyndon Johnson's Great Society expectations. Liberalism in general

---

[2] King's assassin, James Earl Ray, was a habitual criminal who had recently escaped from a Missouri prison. Although the full truth may never be known, in all likelihood Ray was a hired hit man.

and civil rights in particular had come unglued. The efforts of Ralph Abernathy, Dr. King's right-hand man, to carry on with the Poor People's March on Washington proved a fiasco. The nation paid scant attention to the muddy shantytown called Resurrection City that demonstrators established near the Lincoln Memorial. Eventually the government arrested SCLC leaders and drove the encamped demonstrators off. Few protested.

New York and Paris

In the polarized and volatile world that took shape after King's assassination, the prospect that a new politics of peace and racial justice might triumph and rebuild consensus in America faded. Robert Kennedy, on whose shoulders rested the hopes of millions for a better America, heard the news of King's death while traveling by plane to address a rally in the black ghetto of Indianapolis. He appealed to his African-American audience for restraint: "What we need in the United States is not division; what we need in the United States is not hatred; what we need in the United States is not violence or lawlessness, but love and wisdom and compassion toward one another and a feeling of justice toward those who still suffer within our country, whether they be white or they be black." The next day in Cleveland, as urban America blew up, Kennedy warned that "violence breeds violence, repression brings retaliation, and only a cleansing of our whole society can remove this sickness from our soul."

Yet the strife that Robert Kennedy condemned seemed almost endemic to American society by the apocalyptic year 1968. The war, the assassinations, and the riots had torn surface civilities asunder to reveal an underlying culture of violence. It saturated the TV screen, not only in news films about Vietnam and the ghetto riots but in popular police and detective shows too. From the midsixties on, a culture of confrontation and violence emerged. LBJ had his *war* in Vietnam and his *war* on poverty. Antiwar activists chanted, "Hey, hey LBJ, how many kids did you kill today!" Black militants shouted, "Burn, Baby, Burn!" and "Off the Pig!" SNCC leader H. Rap Brown called violence "as American as cherry pie." Black Panthers paraded through city streets brandishing rifles and bandoliers. Songs such as Barry McGuire's "Eve of Destruction" (1965), the Doors' "The End" (1967), and the Rolling Stones' "Street Fighting Man" (1968) snarled defiance and death. The nonfiction best-seller of 1966, Truman Capote's *In Cold Blood,* recounted the brutal and senseless murder of a happy American family. In the wildly popular 1967 movie *Bonnie and Clyde,* director Arthur Penn choreographed brutal killing as an art form; the film's last scene shows a fusillade of bullets ripping into the two protagonists in slow motion. That August even the intellectually respectable *New York Review of Books* printed a diagram of a Molotov cocktail on its cover; inside, an article by radical journalist Andrew Kopkind asserted that "morality, like politics, starts at the barrel of a gun." By 1968 talk of revolution had become commonplace in the Movement, and for many black and white militants, a clenched fist had replaced the "V" for peace as a greeting. Psychologist Kenneth Keniston claimed that "the issue of violence is to this generation what the issue of sex was to the Victorian world." Even Martin Luther King, Jr., had confided privately to Ralph Abernathy just weeks before his murder: "Maybe we just have to admit that the day of violence is here. . . . The nation won't listen to our voice; maybe it'll heed the voice of violence. Maybe we just have to give up and let violence take its course."

In 1968 angry young protesters worldwide, many of them affluent university students, chose the course of confrontation in what a San Francisco underground paper called "The Year of the Barricades." New Left students attacked the established order from New York to Tokyo, San Francisco to Paris. In October 1967, while American protesters assaulted the Pentagon and the Oakland induction center, student demonstrators in Prague launched a democratic Czechoslovak revolution. On January 19, 1968, Japanese students broke into the foreign ministry in a mass rally against the visit of the USS *Enterprise*. On January 30, police in Warsaw arrested students protesting the closing of a classic nineteenth-century anti-Russian play. The consequent wave of unrest culminated in mid-March when all of Poland's universities went on strike. That March, Italian demonstrators forcibly closed a dozen universities as more than half a million students demanded educational reforms. On March 17, some 25,000 young protesters, including a Rhodes scholar named Bill Clinton, marched on the American embassy in London's Grosvenor Square, many of them chanting "Ho-Ho-Ho Chi Minh! We will fight, we will win!" Five days later, French students, led by Daniel Cohn-Bendit, occupied the administration building at Nanterre University. Their initial complaints centered on dormitory overcrowding and the segregation of the sexes, but students would soon challenge the very structure of French society.

Similar student rebellions over local, national, and international issues broke out in West Germany, the Netherlands, Belgium, Yugoslavia, Uruguay, and Mexico. Radical students came to see themselves as part of an international movement and drew inspiration from one another. When on April 11, 1968, a would-be assassin badly wounded Germany's most influential student radical, Rudi Dutschke, rioting and demonstrations erupted in New York, Berkeley, Toronto, London, Paris, Rome, Milan, Belgrade, Prague, and other cities. Although the issues of the Vietnam War and civil rights carried less weight outside the United States, the war, imperialism, and racism nevertheless had become international concerns. Students everywhere felt alienated and fought intransigent bureaucracies, inhumane technologies, and antidemocratic institutions.

In the United States, between January and June 1968, more than two hundred major student demonstrations broke out, including fifty-nine cases in which protesters occupied campus buildings. The unrest here centered on Black Power, student rights, and above all the war. The most publicized and explosive university upheaval took place at Columbia and encompassed all three issues.

On April 9, the day of Martin Luther King, Jr.'s funeral in Atlanta, Columbia University held a memorial service for the slain civil-rights leader in the college's St. Paul's Chapel. In the midst of the service, student members of the local SDS stormed the pulpit and wrested the microphone from the startled chaplain. Columbia was racist, they charged, and had no right to honor King. The accusation stemmed from the university's beginning construction of a gymnasium in Morningside Park, a sloping hillside that separated Columbia from Harlem below. The administration had authorized the work despite the protest of black community groups. African-American activists dubbed the project "Gym Crow" and demanded that construction halt, but the university ignored them. SDS and Columbia's Students' Afro-American Society (SAS) seized upon the gym conflict as a way to radicalize the student body.

Other issues plagued the university as well. A private, Ivy League school, Columbia was run by a traditional and autocratic administration. Not even the faculty, let alone students, had much to say about university governance. Presided over by sixty-seven-year-old Grayson Kirk, who castigated students as "potentially dangerous" nihilists "whose sole objectives are destruction," Columbia in the April of the chapel fracas disciplined a Barnard student (Columbia's women's college) for living with her Columbia boyfriend. This infringement on what most students considered a basic freedom led sixty additional Barnard women to come forward and taunt the administration by admitting that they too had live-in lovers.

University complicity in the war also angered students. In March, SDS activists created a sensation on campus by throwing a lemon meringue pie in the face of a visiting colonel from Selective Service. Columbia's affiliation with the Institute for Defense Analyses (IDA) particularly rankled radical students. The IDA conducted weapons research and counterinsurgency studies for the Pentagon, and Grayson Kirk served on the IDA's governing board. On March 27, six Columbia students demonstrated against IDA in the administration building, violating a recent decree banning such activities. Asked to report to their deans for disciplinary action, the IDA six refused. On April 22, one of the protesters, Mark Rudd, threw down the gauntlet in the form of an open letter to Kirk:

> Grayson, I doubt if you will understand any of this . . . you call for order and respect for authority; we call for justice, freedom, and socialism. There is only one thing left to say. It may sound nihilistic to you, since it is the opening shot in a war of liberation. I'll use the words of LeRoi Jones, whom I'm sure you don't like a whole lot: "Up against the wall, motherfucker, this is a stick-up."

Rudd, described by a Columbia professor as "a tall, hulking, slack-faced young man with a prognathic jaw and blue-gray eyes so translucent that his gaze seems hypnotic," would soon emerge as an international symbol of the radical student movement. The son of a retired army officer, Rudd was a third-generation Jewish-American who grew up in a comfortable middle-class neighborhood in suburban Maplewood, New Jersey. A Boy Scout and serious student in high school, Rudd entered Columbia in the midsixties and, like many of his generation, became quickly radicalized. He joined SDS and soon earned recognition as the leader of the so-called action faction. Rudd believed that only disruptive deeds would radicalize the student body. In March 1968, soon after his return from a visit to Castro's Cuba, Rudd won election as president of Columbia's SDS chapter.

Enraged by the university's harassment of the IDA six and by the continued construction of the gym, SDS and SAS called a noon rally on April 23 at the Sundial in the campus center, followed by a march of several hundred students to the gym construction site, where they tore down part of a fence and tussled with police. Returning to campus, students began a sit-in at Hamilton Hall. They took a dean hostage and issued a list of demands, including that Columbia sever all ties with IDA, end construction of the gym, and grant amnesty for themselves.

Late that night, the African-American students occupying Hamilton, influenced by the Black Power movement, asked the whites to leave. "If you want to do something that's relevant," SAS leader Bill Sales told the whites, "grab as many other buildings as you can. But you guys got to leave. This is ours." Rudd and about 130 white students marched from Hamilton and at 5:30 A.M. broke into Low Library, the university's administrative center. They smoked Kirk's cigars, sipped his sherry, and rifled his files, uncovering information about secret grants for military research that they later released to the underground press.

That morning students occupied three more buildings. The administration hesitated to take action, fearful that ousting the students by force might divide the campus further and even ignite a Harlem riot. Although organized student opposition to the protesters formed, the majority of Columbia students supported the demonstrators, and many joined the occupation. Columbia attracted national and international attention. Well-known radicals Stokely Carmichael, H. Rap Brown, and Abbie Hoffman visited the scene. Tom Hayden merged with the students occupying Mathematics Hall and was joined there by an anarchistic group of Lower East Side artists and street fighters known as the Motherfuckers. The Grateful Dead put on a free concert for the rebels.

Over the next week, the occupied buildings became student communes managed by the principles of participatory democracy. Debate ran almost around the clock. ''The political discussions,'' one student recalled, ''were like nothing I'd ever heard before. It was like blowing away these cobwebs from the dark corners of the attic of the past, and having the world make perfect sense to me.'' Tom Hayden remembered the ''intense relationships, the joy of singing, an atmosphere of caring for each other's feelings during the debates.'' There was even a wedding in the midst of this war. More than five hundred students celebrated as a chaplain, helped in through a window to perform the ceremony, proclaimed the young couple ''children of the new age.''

A week of negotiations, with many faculty members acting as intermediaries, came to naught. In the early hours of April 30, more than a thousand police stormed the occupied buildings. Largely from working-class backgrounds, the cops resented the privileged Ivy League students and took the opportunity to strike and kick them and drag them from the buildings. The police also indiscriminantly clubbed professors who attempted to assist injured students.

The nationally televised brutality further radicalized students and turned much of the faculty against the administration. A strike of university classes virtually closed Columbia, and a ''liberation school'' of impromptu classes took the place of regular instruction. ''It was exhilarating,'' claimed a graduate student. ''There was suddenly a tremendous explosion of opportunities for learning. . . . Faculty people were being drawn into debate with graduate and undergraduate students. That's where the barriers and hierarchies just fell apart.'' In the end the protesters triumphed. They forced the abandonment of the gym project and Columbia's withdrawal from IDA. In August, Grayson Kirk resigned, and his successor dropped all charges against the arrested students.

The Columbia uprising intensified the nation's already strong sense of polarization, alarming millions of Americans. Campaigning for the Republican presidential nomination, Richard Nixon called Columbia ''the first major skirmish in a revolutionary struggle to seize the universities of this country and transform them into sanctuaries for radicals and vehicles for revolutionary politics and social goals.'' The backlash against student militancy that had simmered since the midsixties gathered steam.

The much-publicized contention at Columbia was only one of many outbreaks that spring. On April 26, while protesters occupied Columbia's buildings, more than a million American students, and many more worldwide, went on strike as part of the Day

Columbia University Student Uprising, April 30, 1968. In the aftermath of a predawn raid in which police arrested hundreds of protesters, student dissidents and sympathizers attempt to form a human barricade around the university. They launched a strike that virtually closed Columbia for the remainder of the spring semester.

of Resistance to the Vietnam War. Columbia seemed to spawn a string of campus revolts that mad spring. Over one hundred riots erupted in U.S. colleges, from Stanford to Michigan State to Harvard.

Nor were disruptions at American universities the only cause for alarm. Events in Europe, particularly in Paris, soon overshadowed the American student movement. During May, as Columbia closed, French students catalyzed the largest general strike in that nation's history and nearly brought down the government of General Charles de Gaulle. Their audacity electrified the American New Left. "Holy shit!" a Columbia protester blustered. "Look what we set off!"

The strike began in Paris on May 3 with a bloody clash between demonstrators and police. On May 10, students erected a series of street barricades in Paris's Latin Quarter and fiercely battled police. Soon the working class joined the university dissidents. Unlike in the United States, where workers resentful of privileged protesters often supported reactionary movements, in France the sight of the defiant students standing up to the authorities aroused strong labor support. French workers, oppressed by their nation's bureaucratization and hierarchy, working forty-eight hours a week, and subjected to the lowest wage rates in industrialized Western Europe, were ripe for revolt. In mid-May, a wave of strikes hit the country. Teachers, artists, architects, atomic-energy employees, civil servants, and even some physicians joined the movement. By May 22 more than nine million workers had walked off the job. "The aim is now the overthrow of the government," announced student leader Cohn-Bendit.

But the revolutionaries' elation soon deflated. France's Communist party refused to support the more militant workers and students, and the movement weakened. In late May, the tottering de Gaulle regime regained control. The strikes continued even when the government agreed on May 27 to large wage increases and fringe benefits for the unions, but worker enthusiasm for revolution cooled. On May 30, de Gaulle addressed the nation with a call for law and order. He falsely blamed the communists for the crisis and accused them of planning a totalitarian dictatorship. The revolutionary mood dissipated, and as elsewhere during the chaos of 1968, a conservative reaction set in. Parliamentary elections in late June gave the Gaullist party a clear majority. By this time, New Left dreams born of the Paris spring had shattered and, as in the United States, counterrevolution held sway.

Los Angeles and Chicago

For some, the events of 1968 suggested that the United States had lost the ability to govern itself. In March, *New York Times* columnist James Reston wrote, "The main crisis is not Vietnam itself, or in the cities, but in the feeling that the political system for dealing with these things has broken down."

With Johnson no longer a contender, the Democratic race stood wide open. The candidacies of Eugene McCarthy and Robert Kennedy had offered an alternative to the war and thus had defused some of the explosive mood among antiwar activists. Yet the two men's bitter rivalry threatened to fragment the peace vote. The independent candidacy of Black Panther leader Eldridge Cleaver running against the war on the radical Peace and Freedom party ticket complicated the campaign.[3] In the meantime, Vice President Hubert Humphrey joined the race. Announcing his candidacy on April 27, less than a month after King's murder and as students occupied buildings at Columbia, Humphrey fatuously bubbled: "Here we are, the way politics ought to be in America, the politics of happiness, the politics of purpose and the politics of joy."

Once a hero to liberal Democrats, Humphrey's role as Johnson's toady and his unequivocal public support of the war had badly tarnished his image. His candidacy generated little popular enthusiasm; indeed, he struck many people as insensitive and out of touch with the harsh realities of 1968. Even LBJ, who ostensibly supported him, described the vice president as "just too old-fashioned, he looks like, he talks like he belongs to the past."

Despite these judgments, party regulars regarded Humphrey as a safe, loyal Democrat. He particularly appealed to prowar Democrats, party bosses, and most labor leaders. "I will not run away from the record of this administration," Humphrey proclaimed. "I will do everything in my power . . . to carry the record of the Johnson-Humphrey administration to the people in the months ahead." Avoiding the primaries, he relied on the power of party bosses to deliver sufficient convention votes in nonprimary states to win him the nomination. Opinion polls showed him well behind both

---

[3]The day after King's death, Cleaver was wounded in a shootout with the Oakland police. Appeals kept Cleaver out of jail until the November election, after which he fled into exile.

To Restore Camelot. Robert Kennedy's 1968 presidential campaign, shown here in South Dakota, generated ardent support among his followers.

Kennedy and McCarthy, yet as the two peace candidates battled in the primaries, Humphrey quietly and efficiently began lining up delegates.

The media and most of the public, however, focused on the Kennedy-McCarthy struggle. Although these two Irish-American Catholics shared a loathing for Johnson and the war, their campaigns differed dramatically in content and in style. On announcing his candidacy, RFK had declared, "I run to seek new policies, policies to end the bloodshed in Vietnam and in our cities, policies to close the gap that now exists between black and white, between rich and poor, between young and old in this country and around the rest of the world." Like his brother in 1960, Bobby Kennedy plunged vigorously into the primary battles. Unlike JFK, however, he championed social reform, not global containment. His jacket off, sleeves rolled up, tie loose, RFK moved audiences with his infectious enthusiasm. Kennedy thrilled listeners with emotional pleas for social justice and national unity and charmed them with his self-deprecating wit. When speaking in agricultural Nebraska, a small piece of paper blew out of his hand: "That's my entire farm program," he quipped. Everywhere he spoke, frenzied crowds pressed close. Americans, weary of the decade's traumas, craved a heroic savior. Even newsmen who first judged RFK an opportunist were touched by his campaign. "Quite frankly," *New York Times* correspondent Tom Wicker noted, "Bobby Kennedy was an easy man to fall in love with."

Whereas Kennedy exuded evangelical zeal, McCarthy emanated arrogant disdain.

His campaign focused less on winning than on making a personal statement, as he dwelled on himself and his moment in history. Instead of broad new social programs, McCarthy promised to limit the power of the presidency. Yet to many of his student volunteers, the aloof and philosophical McCarthy possessed an aura of authenticity, and they identified with him. To them, he was a daring hero who, without sacrificing his principles, had ousted a president and awakened a nation. Yet McCarthy clearly felt uneasy in the company of the underprivileged, and as a consequence his campaign held little appeal for blacks or other nonwhite minorities. He did, however, earn a strong following among educated middle-class people who opposed the war—a strong constituency made up of what his wife described as "thoughtful America and troubled America."

The first head-to-head contest between the two antiwar Democrats came on May 7 in Indiana, a state with a diverse population of inner-city blacks, white ethnic factory workers, rural farmers, and comfortable suburbanites. RFK hired the famous Wabash Cannonball and rode the train on a series of whistle-stops throughout the state. "We have to convince the Negroes and poor whites that they have common interests," he told a reporter. "If we can reconcile those two hostile groups, and then add the kids, you can really turn this country around." On primary day, Kennedy outpolled McCarthy by nearly two to one. A week later he scored a similar triumph in rural Nebraska. The Kennedy bandwagon rolled on, apparently unstoppable. McCarthy, gloated RFK's press secretary, Pierre Salinger, was "no longer a credible candidate."

In Oregon, however, the mostly white middle-class voters remained cool to Kennedy's fervent attacks on racism and poverty, whereas McCarthy's wry humor and intelligent critique of the war won him widespread support. He defeated Kennedy 45 percent to 39 percent, marking the first time that any Kennedy had lost an election. This turnabout made the June 4 California primary crucial for both candidates. McCarthy had momentum, and with thousands of enthusiastic volunteers working out of some 150 local campaign headquarters, he threatened to replicate his Oregon upset. But Kennedy had the support of powerful speaker of the state assembly Jesse Unruh, who moved to unite party regulars behind his candidacy. African-American leaders Charles Evers of Mississippi and SNCC's John Lewis campaigned in the black communities for Kennedy. Cesar Chávez lobbied among Hispanics in the barrios. Kennedy himself campaigned vigorously throughout the state and shone in a televised debate with McCarthy held the Saturday before the election. On June 4, Kennedy polled 46 percent of the vote to McCarthy's 42, with Humphrey's stand-in receiving a humiliating 12 percent.

That night, a jubilant Bobby Kennedy addressed the crowd gathered in the ballroom of his Los Angeles hotel. He congratulated McCarthy for having broken "the political logjam" and asked him and his followers to join him. "What I think is quite clear," he told the applauding audience, "is that what has been going on within the United States over a period of the last three years . . . the divisions, whether it's between blacks and whites, between the poor and the more affluent, or between age groups or on the war in Vietnam—is that we can start to work together." Kennedy ended with the exhortation, "On to Chicago and let's win there!"

Moments later, gunfire crackled, and Kennedy sank fatally wounded to the floor, shot by fanatic Arab nationalist Sirhan Sirhan.

The previous February, Kennedy had prophetically written: "We seem to fulfill the vision of Yeats: 'Things fall apart, the center cannot hold;/mere anarchy is loosed upon the world.' '' For the fourth time in less than five years, a young, charismatic American leader had fallen to an assassin's bullets. Robert Kennedy's death, only two months after King's, traumatized the country anew.

Had Robert Kennedy lived, he might well have won both the nomination and the presidency. By force of personality and family aura, he had pulled together a coalition of poor, nonwhites, workers, and youth in a campaign to end the war abroad and poverty and racism at home. Intelligent and energetic, courageous and compassionate, he might have made a great president. Even socialist Michael Harrington, looking back on the sixties, saw Kennedy as ''the man who actually could have changed the course of American history.'' The tearful presence of archenemies Chicago political boss Richard Daley and New Left leader Tom Hayden before Kennedy's coffin in St. Patrick's Cathedral testified to RFK's wide-ranging appeal. According to Hayden, that coffin contained ''all that remained of last night's hopes of the poor. Nothing left of that hope now, gone in a coffin while crews hammered away and police awaited the crowd. I started to cry hard.''

The assassination took the heart out of McCarthy's campaign. Although the senator pledged to continue to fight for the nomination, he lacked zest. Even his victory in the New York primary on June 18 failed to encourage him. He still drew large crowds, and polls showed him running ahead of Humphrey, but he had minimal support among party regulars. This last obstacle, combined with his lackadaisical performance, doomed the effort to end the war through electoral politics. Well before the Democratic convention met in Chicago late in August, Hubert Humphrey, without having run in a single primary, had amassed a sufficient number of nonprimary delegates to ensure his nomination.

With King and Kennedy dead, the movement for peaceable change within the political system splintered. Among nonwhite minorities, despair reigned. ''I won't vote,'' an African-American told a pollster. ''Every good man we get they kill.'' Within the New Left, frustration led many to give up altogether on mainstream politics. Some radicals dropped out and joined the counterculture world of drugs and communal living. Others developed fantasies of becoming guerrilla fighters and overthrowing the hated ''Amerika.''

As Humphrey's momentum gathered, a despondent McCarthy, sensing impending trouble, urged his youthful volunteers not to come to Chicago. Hundreds of them nevertheless insisted on attending. Having driven Lyndon Johnson from office, they were appalled that LBJ's chosen successor was about to win the nomination, and they nurtured hope for some sort of last-minute miracle.

Whereas McCarthy volunteers came to Chicago in an effort to make the political process work, other young activists gathered to demonstrate against the war and what they saw as the undemocratic two-party system. These antiwar militants converged on the city, organized by the National Mobilization Committee to End the War in Vietnam (Mobe) and led by New Leftists Tom Hayden and Rennie Davis and veteran pacifist Dave Dellinger. A group of self-styled Yippies joined them. The brainchild of Abbie Hoffman and Jerry Rubin, the Yippies promised a ''Festival of Life'' in Chicago, to contrast with what they called the Democrats' ''Festival of Death.'' Hoffman, Rubin, and their supporters joked about putting LSD into Chicago's water system and sending ten thousand nude Yippies wading in Lake Michigan. They nominated a pig, ''Pigasus,'' for president, who ran on the ''garbage'' ticket and attracted intense media attention.

Chicago's mayor Richard Daley, an old-fashioned political boss, loathed the young radicals. Proud of his city and its selection as the site for the convention, he cracked down on the dissidents, refusing to issue parade permits or to allow the demonstrators to sleep in city parks. As the convention date neared, he ordered Chicago's twelve thousand police officers to work twelve-hour shifts. In reserve, he held six thousand army troops, five thousand national guardsmen, and thousands of state and county police. Hundreds of FBI and Secret Service agents were also on hand, many working undercover.

The Chicago underground paper *Seed* warned: ''Don't come to Chicago if you expect a five-day Festival of Life, music and love.'' For those determined to attend, the *Seed* offered this bit of advice: ''If you're going to Chicago, be sure to wear armor in your hair.'' The Festival of Life, announced a Chicago Yippie, could well become a ''Festival of Blood.'' Instead of the tens of thousands of demonstrators that Mobe and Yippie leaders had expected, only about five thousand arrived from out of town; about an equal number from the Chicago area joined them.

On August 20, Soviet tanks rumbled through the streets of Prague, crushing the nascent Czechoslovak democracy that the Czech student movement had inspired. Five days later, when the Democratic convention opened, Daley's minions unleashed their own violence on the streets of Chicago. Ranging through the city, law-enforcement officials savaged demonstrators and anyone else who stood in their way. Norman Mailer, in Chicago to report on the convention, described the scene: ''The police attacked with tear gas, with Mace, and with clubs, they attacked like a scythe through grass, lines of twenty and thirty policemen striking out in an arc, their clubs beating, demonstrators fleeing.''

The police descended on protesters, reporters, cameramen, and bystanders with equal abandon. Shouting ''Kill!'' ''Commie!'' and ''Pussy!'' rampaging cops, many having removed their badges, battered the children of the middle class. Hayden, Davis, Rubin, and Hoffman were beaten. A priest suffered a fractured skull. *Playboy* mogul Hugh Hefner was clubbed. French writer Jean Genet, in Chicago to cover the convention for *Esquire,* was badly tear-gassed; he subsequently marched with the Yippies and called the cops ''mad dogs.'' Police invaded McCarthy headquarters on the fifteenth floor of the Hilton Hotel and clubbed the campaign volunteers working there. Even on the convention floor, Daley's guards punched CBS reporter Dan Rather when he questioned their tactics, and they dragged fellow reporter Mike Wallace from the hall. When Connecticut senator Abraham Ribicoff in a televised speech from the podium turned toward Daley to denounce the ''Gestapo tactics,'' cameras showed the mayor, snarling like an enraged bulldog, shaking his fist and mouthing, ''Fuck you, you Jew son of a bitch!'' ''In Chicago,'' wrote respected columnist Stewart Alsop, ''for the first time in my life it began to seem to me possible that some form of American fascism may really happen here.'' ''Welcome to Czechago,'' a protester's placard proclaimed.

The violence climaxed on the evening of Humphrey's nomination. Watching, veteran political writer Theodore White jotted in his notebook, ''The Democrats are finished.'' With national attention focused more on the bloody streets than on the conven-

Showdown in Chicago. The sign over the archway leading to the International Amphitheatre welcomes delegates to the 1968 Democratic National Convention, as a swarm of helmeted Chicago police stand guard. Throughout the convention, police vented their rage against antiwar demonstrators, news reporters, and anyone else who got in their way.

tion proceedings, a grim-faced but tenaciously garrulous Humphrey accepted the nomination. His campaign promise of "a politics of joy" seemed a mockery. The Democrats battered and split, tainted by Johnson's unpopularity and the war, Humphrey had lost touch with the passions and issues surging through the politics of 1968.

The systematic repression in the streets of Chicago radicalized millions of young Americans. In a survey of college students, over half called the United States "sick"; two-thirds believed that Vietnam was a mistake; a majority said they preferred Che Guevara to Lyndon Johnson or Richard Nixon. For the more militant New Leftists, Chicago was a watershed. Before Daley's carnage, the Movement had sought to stop America's war in Vietnam; now the New Left took a stance against America itself. "The battle for Chicago," wrote bloodied *East Village Other* editor Allen Katzman, "will be remembered in heavy years to come as the beginning of a Revolution." Yippie Jerry Rubin hailed Chicago as a victory:

> We wanted exactly what happened. We wanted the tear gas to get so heavy that the reality was tear gas. We wanted to create a situation in which the Chicago police and the Daley administration and the federal government and the United States would self-destruct. We wanted to show that America wasn't a democracy, that the convention wasn't politics. The message of the week was of an America ruled by force.

Chicago transformed American perceptions, but not in the way that militants had hoped. Initially the media mostly condemned the actions of Daley's cops. Walter Cronkite referred to the police as "thugs"; *Newsweek* denounced "Mayor Daley's beefy cops, who went on a sustained rampage unprecedented outside the most unreconstructed boondocks of Dixie." The National Commission on Violence officially labeled the episode a "police riot."

But despite the media coverage, only 19 percent of polled respondents thought that the police used "too much force"; 70 percent supported their actions. Chicago had scared Middle America. Television had brought the New Left to life for them. Yet rather than seeing heroic youth, bloodied in their efforts to make a moral stand against the war, they saw a mob of unkempt, long-haired kids waving North Vietnamese flags and hurling curses at the cops. Like Mayor Daley and his police, the majority of Americans hated the defiant protesters. Indeed, the backlash against radical dissent accelerated after Chicago. More and more ordinary Americans demanded "law and order," even if it meant clubbing some of the nation's privileged youth. The real victors in Chicago were not Rubin and Hoffman and Hayden, but Richard Daley, his police, and the nation's conservative politicians.

R N

What Mailer termed "the siege of Chicago" boosted the hopes of Republican presidential candidate Richard Nixon. Four years earlier, after the Goldwater debacle, the GOP looked moribund. In 1968, however, with the Democrats self-destructing, Republican chances revived, along with Richard Nixon's career. Following his close loss in the 1960 presidential election, Nixon had tried to rebuild his political reputation by running for the governorship of California in 1962. Again he suffered defeat, and after a petulant farewell to the press, his political career seemed over. Joining a lucrative New York law firm, Nixon nevertheless continued to work hard at advancing his position in the party. In 1964 he campaigned for Goldwater. In 1966 he stumped the country on behalf of Republican congressional candidates, received much of the credit for the party's resurgence that year, and emerged as a serious contender for the 1968 nomination. Michigan governor and former American Motors president George Romney stood as the major obstacle in Nixon's path. However, Romney's confusing pronouncements on Vietnam and his confession to an interviewer that he had been "brainwashed" by the diplomats and military officers who had briefed him on the war discredited his candidacy. Now the odds-on favorite for his party's nomination, Nixon did well in the primaries. At the Republican convention in Miami, he easily outmaneuvered the last-minute efforts of conservative Ronald Reagan and liberal Nelson Rockefeller to win a first-ballot nomination.

The GOP convention appeared as bland as the Democratic one had been violent. Mailer, who covered both, likened the Miami meeting to a group of Rotarians gathered in a cemetery. But the convention's placidity gave Nixon the chance to project a vision of stability, order, and traditional values. The Republican candidate's campaign workers and the press spoke of a "new" Nixon, presumably wiser and more mature.

The chaos of this election year, from Tet through Chicago, buttressed the Republi-

can campaign. Nixon had merely to blame the unpopular Johnson-Humphrey administration for the nation's various ills. Although earlier he had taken a more hawkish
position on Vietnam than Johnson had, he realized the swelling antiwar sentiment and
now claimed to have a "secret plan" to end the war. Capitalizing on fears generated
by the domestic strife, Nixon pledged "the restoration of law and order." He also
sensed the growing conservative backlash against Great Society domestic programs,
particularly supposed preferential treatment for nonwhites. Promising to reduce spending for such measures, he charged that "it is gross irresponsibility to promise billions
of new Federal dollars for the cities, or even for the poor." Instead of special programs
for nonwhites, Nixon touted "black capitalism" and promised to relax federal pressures
in race relations and to eliminate mandated busing of children as a means of integrating
schools. To woo southern and "law and order" votes, he chose as his running mate
Maryland governor Spiro Agnew, noted for his advice to shoot urban rioters and his
attacks against black civil-rights leaders and student dissidents. Nixon and Agnew
claimed to speak for "the Forgotten Americans . . . those who do not break the law,
people who pay their taxes and go to work, who send their children to school, who go
to their churches." These people, they asserted, "cry out . . . that is enough, let's get
some new leadership."

Nixon gained support in northern white urban areas too because of the Democratic
party's identification with civil rights. Although racism clearly played a role in this
political shift among northern workers, blatant bias offers only a partial explanation.
Rightly or wrongly, millions of lower-income whites had concluded that liberal Democrats wanted to uplift nonwhites but do nothing on their behalf. Furthermore, urban
"ethnics" frequently bore the brunt of racial change. Blacks seeking better housing
and schools, for example, tended to migrate to nearby poorer white neighborhoods,
spurring resentment among longtime residents. As a white construction worker living
in the Canarsie section of Brooklyn told an interviewer, "The rich liberals, they look
down on my little piece of the American dream, my little backyard with the barbecue
here. The liberals and the press look down on hard hats like me, but we've invested
everything we have in this house and neighborhood." Blue-collar voters, once a mainstay of the Democratic coalition, increasingly turned to the right.

Former Alabama governor George Wallace, heading a strong third-party movement, further complicated the election. Like Nixon, Wallace and his American Independent party hoped to capitalize on the white backlash. Articulating the resentments and
frustrations of many less-educated whites, Wallace declared after the Chicago Democratic convention that the police "probably showed too much restraint." On other
occasions he pledged that "if any demonstrator ever lays down in front of my car, it'll
be the last car he'll ever lay down in front of."

Strongly supported in the white South because of his overt racism and his populist
politics, Wallace also showed growing strength among white, northern blue-collar
workers. His political organization succeeded in placing his American Independence
party on the ballot in all fifty states. From only a 9 percent voter rating in polls taken
in May 1968, by mid-September Wallace had climbed to 21 percent, his success building on bitterness bred of rapid racial and cultural change. Like country singer Merle
Haggard, whose songs "Okie from Muskogee" and "Welfare Cadillac" attacked intellectuals, hippies, pacifists, and welfare recipients, Wallace, too, played on people's
fears. He denounced "pointy-headed professors" who "don't even know how to park

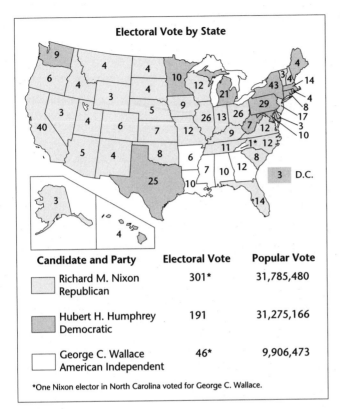

Electoral Vote by State

Candidate and Party	Electoral Vote	Popular Vote
Richard M. Nixon Republican	301*	31,785,480
Hubert H. Humphrey Democratic	191	31,275,166
George C. Wallace American Independent	46*	9,906,473

*One Nixon elector in North Carolina voted for George C. Wallace.

Presidential Election of 1968.

a bicycle straight'' and promised that come election day, people were ''going to find out there are a lot of rednecks in this country.''

Thus the campaign commenced with two candidates capitalizing on a white conservative backlash and fear of disorder, while the third spoke absurdly of a politics of joy. None of the three was truly popular. Polls showed Nixon well in the lead, but his carefully planned and heavily financed campaign, though it effectively exploited the national malaise, aroused little real excitement. Wallace's campaign, run like an old-fashioned revival with ministers and country singers, created a dedicated following, but most Americans found him shrill and negative. Hubert Humphrey had neither the large numbers enjoyed by Nixon nor the impassioned, smaller following of Wallace. Despite some of Humphrey's personal misgivings about the war, his belligerent defense of Johnson's policies had alienated most antiwar Democrats. Plagued by a divided party, meager crowds, and little money, Humphrey's campaign floundered. Antiwar hecklers harassed him at every campaign stop. In the first month after the Democratic convention, he lost ground to both Nixon and Wallace. Polls showed him trailing Nixon by 15 percent and ahead of Wallace by only 7 percent.

On September 30, a desperate Humphrey tried a new tactic. Speaking on national television from a lectern stripped of the vice-presidential seal, he announced that he would ''stop the bombing of North Vietnam as an acceptable risk for peace.'' This statement put some distance between Humphrey and the president and quieted antiwar critics. His campaign took on sudden life. Labor leaders, fearful of a Nixon victory, contributed money and effort to win workers back from Wallace. Northern union members and ethnics rejoined the Democratic fold, as did antiwar liberals. Even Eugene McCarthy belatedly came out in favor of Humphrey. When Lyndon Johnson announced a complete bombing halt over North Vietnam on October 31, antiwar support for the vice president gathered further strength.

As Humphrey picked up momentum, Wallace lost ground. The pull of party loyalties and voter fears of wasting a ballot hurt him. So too did the Alabaman's selection of General Curtis LeMay as his running mate. LeMay, reportedly the model for the deranged general in the 1964 film *Dr. Strangelove,* blithely advised bombing North Vietnam "back to the Stone Age." Humphrey began referring to Wallace and LeMay as the "bombsy twins." Nixon's vice-presidential candidate, Spiro Agnew, also drove voters back to the Democrats with his tasteless ethnic slurs and crude attacks on liberals, intellectuals, and protesters.

By election day, polls showed Humphrey and Nixon nearly even. Nevertheless, the vice president's last-minute efforts to rebuild the traditional Democratic coalition fell short. Nixon won, though by the smallest plurality since the election of 1912, earning 43.4 percent to Humphrey's 42.7 percent. Wallace came in a distant third with less than 14 percent of the vote and victories in only five states of the Deep South. Nixon ran well in the upper South, Midwest, and West, though he failed to carry a single major city.

Those who had hoped that Americans would use the political process in 1968 to achieve world peace and social justice reeled at the election results. *Village Voice* writer Jack Newfield, who had strongly supported Robert Kennedy, lamented, "The stone was at the bottom of the hill and we were alone." In his memoir, *Reunion,* Tom Hayden summed up the feelings of the idealists who had committed themselves to creating a better world:

> Rarely, if ever, in American history has a generation begun with higher ideals and experienced greater trauma than those who lived fully the short time from 1960 to 1968. Our world was going to be transformed for the good, we let ourselves believe not once but twice, only to learn that violence can slay not only individuals, but dreams. After 1968, living on as a ruptured and dislocated generation became our fate, having lost our best possibilities at an early age, wanting to hope but fearing the pain that seemed its consequence.

• • •

And so as a chaotic year closed late in a decade of protest, change, and violence, power passed to conservative Republican Richard Nixon, a man who had built his career on anticommunist witch-hunts and Cold War confrontations. The Vietnam War would drag on for four more years, and another twenty thousand American soldiers would die. The 1964 Democratic plurality of sixteen million votes had evaporated. War, inflation, racial strife, campus unrest, and distrust of presidential leadership had destroyed Lyndon Johnson's dreams of becoming the greatest president since Franklin Roosevelt. Not since Herbert Hoover exited the White House during the Great Depression had a president's departure gone as unlamented as Johnson's.

Nixon Triumphant. Richard Nixon, fingers spelling out V for victory, cheers on his supporters in the 1968 campaign.

At the time, most political analysts concluded that the swing to the right and Nixon's election sprang from the aberrant circumstances of 1968. Nixon, after all, could hardly be said to have a popular mandate, and many voters distrusted both major parties. Only 61 percent of those registered to vote bothered to cast ballots; Nixon thus won with the support of only about 27 percent of the eligible electorate. The Democrats still controlled Congress, retaining majorities in both the House and Senate.

Observers have since realized that Nixon's election reflected a long-term trend toward conservatism. Together, Nixon and Wallace polled just under 57 percent of the popular vote, marking an undeniable shift to the right. New Deal–type liberalism was in retreat. Millions of Americans had lost faith in legislated civil rights, expensive welfare programs, the ''new'' economics, and big government. Frightened by violence amplified by TV, numerous people rejected reform movements that had dominated the sixties political agenda. Radical protest and counterculture lifestyles also provoked what Nixon termed the ''silent majority,'' and the counterrevolutionary backlash gathered speed. Much of the South had already defected from the Democrats to vote for Goldwater in 1964 and Wallace and Nixon in 1968. Northern ethnic working-class voters, the traditional mainstay of the Democrats in industrialized urban areas, also deserted the party in droves.

In retrospect, the Johnson years stand as a turning point in the role of government in America. LBJ launched his administration auspiciously with a massive liberal consensus to create the Great Society at home and to police the world abroad. Four years later, his vision lay in ruins. Liberalism, though far from dead, had gone on the defensive. Moreover, with the U.S. death toll in Vietnam surpassing thirty thousand, and with still more than half a million American troops there, a constrained view of the nation's world role gained favor. The sense of omnipotence abroad faded in the jungles of Vietnam, while the ideal of the Great Society at home shattered in the streets of Watts, Detroit, Washington, and Chicago. By the end of 1968, America faced the first major realignment in party politics since the Great Depression.

Selected Bibliography

The 1960s remain on people's minds, and in 1988, the twentieth anniversary of America's most traumatic postwar year, a spate of books dealing with this pivotal year poured from publishing houses. The best of these are David Caute, *The Year of the Barricades: A Journey Through 1968* (1988), and Ronald Fraser et al., *1968: A Student Generation in Revolt* (1988). Both books treat events worldwide, as does Robert V. Daniels's absorbing *Year of the Heroic Guerrilla: World Revolution and Counterrevolution in 1968* (1989), which went to press too late to meet the 1988 rush. Historians Irwin and Debi Unger focus on the American scene in *Turning Point: 1968* (1988), as does Charles Kaiser in *1968 in America* (1988). More general books with analyses of 1968 are Edward P. Morgan, *The 60s Experience* (1991); David Chalmers, *And the Crooked Places Made Straight: The Struggle for Social Change in the 1960s* (1991); Stewart Burns, *Social Movements of the 1960s* (1990); Allen J. Matusow, *The Unraveling of America* (1984); Milton Viorst, *Fire in the Streets* (1979); Godfrey Hodgson, *America in Our Time* (1976); William H. Chafe, *The Unfinished Journey* (1995 ed.); and William L. O'Neill, *Coming Apart* (1971).

Journalist Seymour Hersh, who first called attention to My Lai, wrote an excellent book on this subject: *My Lai 4: A Report on the Massacre and Its Aftermath* (1970). Reporter Don Oberdorfer in *Tet* (1971) documents the events and repercussions of that major offensive. A broader study of the dire consequences of the Vietnam War for the Johnson presidency is Herbert Y. Schandler, *Lyndon Johnson and Vietnam: The Unmaking of a President* (1977).

Three fine, nearly contemporaneous books examine the 1968 election. Theodore H. White, *The Making of the President 1968* (1969), is the most balanced and detailed. *An American Melodrama* (1969), by British journalists Lewis Chester, Godfrey Hodgson, and Bruce Page, is less balanced than White's study but often more insightful. The most lucidly written yet opinionated account is Norman Mailer's *Miami and the*

Siege of Chicago (1969). Eugene McCarthy, *The Year of the People* (1969), is a personal account of McCarthy's candidacy. McCarthy is also the subject of Jeremy Larner's *The Man Nobody Knows* (1974). Robert F. Kennedy's tragic campaign is well presented in the relevant chapters of Arthur M. Schlesinger, Jr.'s *Robert Kennedy and His Times* (1978), and in Jack Newfield's *Robert Kennedy: A Memoir* (1976). More focused on RFK's last days is Jules Witcover's *Eighty-Five Days: The Last Campaign of Robert F. Kennedy* (1970).

The assassination of Martin Luther King, Jr., and its aftermath are studied in the last chapters of the major King biographies: David Garrow, *Bearing the Cross* (1986); Stephen B. Oates, *Let the Trumpet Sound* (1982); and David L. Lewis, *King* (1970).

The official report on the Columbia University uprising was compiled by a group headed by legal professor Archibald Cox: Cox Commission, *Crisis at Columbia: Report of the Fact-Finding Commission Appointed to Investigate the Disturbances at Columbia University in April and May 1968* (1968). For students' versions of what happened, see Jerry L. Avorn et al., *Up Against the Ivy Wall: A History of the Columbia Crisis* (1968), and James Kunan, *The Strawberry Statement* (1968). See also Roger Kahn, *The Battle for Morningside Heights* (1970), and Stephen Spender, *The Year of the Young Rebels* (1969). English poet Spender also covers student demonstrations in Paris and elsewhere abroad, as do the books by Caute, Fraser, and Daniels cited above. General campus dissent was the subject of an official investigation: William Scranton et al., *The Report of the President's Commission on Campus Unrest* (1970).

The best study to date of the 1968 Chicago Democratic convention is David Farber, *Chicago '68* (1988). Mailer's book, cited above, also gives a dramatic account of the violence in Chicago. The official report on the Chicago riots is Daniel Walker et al., *Rights in Conflict* (1968). The role of Alabama governor George Wallace in the 1968 campaign is discussed in Marshall

Frady's *Wallace* (1970). Nixon's version of the election is recorded in his *RN: The Memoirs of Richard Nixon* (1978). Kevin Phillips in *The Emerging Republican Majority* (1969) interprets Nixon's election as the beginning of a new, dominant conservative coalition. The tactics of the Nixon campaign are well documented in Joe McGinnis, *The Selling of the President* (1969). A good starting point for understanding Nixon the man is Garry Wills's irreverent and penetrating *Nixon Agonistes* (1970). Also helpful is Bruce Mazlish's psychohistorical portrait, *In Search of Nixon* (1972).

Sociological studies of the white ethnic voters and Middle Americans and why they were attracted to Nixon and Wallace include Michael Novak, *The Rise of the Unmeltable Ethnics* (1973); Richard Scammon and Benjamin Wattenberg, *The Real Majority* (1974); Andrew Levison, *The Working Class Majority* (1974); and Jan Erickson and Robert Coles, *Middle Americans* (1973).

CHAPTER

9

THE NIXON
COUNTERREVOLUTION

Only six months after entering the White House, President Richard Nixon and the nation celebrated the first successful manned space mission to the moon. Seven years after President John F. Kennedy had launched a massive effort to meet the Soviet challenge in space, *Apollo 11* landed its lunar module on a rock-strewn plain on the moon's Sea of Tranquility. On July 21, 1969, astronaut Neil Armstrong set foot on the moon's surface and heralded to a worldwide television audience back on earth: ''That's one small step for man, one giant leap for mankind.'' After taking rock and soil samples, Armstrong and Buzz Aldrin planted an American flag and a plaque reading: ''Here men from planet earth first set foot on the moon, July 1969 A.D. We came in peace for all mankind.'' The astronauts returned to earth as national heroes, and Americans swelled with pride in the shared achievement. Some people celebrated the fact that the United States had come from behind to win the space race. Others thrilled at the human and technological triumph.

But the sense of national unity proved ephemeral. The Vietnam War and domestic turmoil continued to divide the nation during the Nixon years. Having promised to ''bring Americans together again,'' Nixon in office appealed to what he termed the nation's ''silent majority'' with calls for law and order, patriotism, and traditional middle-class values. Using opposition to civil rights, assaults on the Supreme Court's liberalism, and repression of radical protesters, he sought to forge a new conservative Republican majority.

Nixon's strength lay in his foreign-policy successes. Indeed, his trips to China and the Soviet Union inaugurated a relaxation of tensions—détente—with those two communist powers. Reelected in 1972 by a landslide, his presidency nevertheless disintegrated under the most appalling of scandals. A break-in at the Democratic National Committee headquarters in Washington's Watergate building during the 1972 campaign, and a subsequent White House cover-up, proved part of an elaborate and illegal pattern of spying, sabotage, and lies that threatened the foundation of American government. Ultimately, the Nixon administration would see twenty-five of the president's top aides jailed for criminal activity. Facing impeachment, Nixon resigned in disgrace on August 9, 1974.

Watergate, coming on the heels of defeat in Vietnam and the upheavals of the sixties, left the nation in shambles. Inflation spiraled into double figures, unemployment climbed, and contempt for the political system ran rampant. Many Americans, despairing of the larger political world, turned inward and sought personal fulfillment. Others, still motivated by the expectations of the sixties, applied themselves to community organizing, feminism, ecology, and antinuclear protest. The Democrats would rebound after Watergate and elect Jimmy Carter to the presidency in 1976, but their gains proved short-lived. Persistent economic decline at home and crises abroad undermined the Carter administration. In 1980 Americans completed the conservative revolution begun by Nixon and put actor-politician Ronald Reagan into the White House.

Conservatism Resurgent

By the time Nixon took office in January 1969, the contentment and confidence that had bathed the early sixties had given way to anguish and bitterness. The long, frustrating Vietnam War, the relative decline of America's international prestige, violence and crime at home, rising prices, unemployment, poverty, protests, water and air pollution—these burdens and more induced a profound pessimism. In his inaugural address, Nixon acknowledged the despondency of a nation "rich in goods, but ragged in spirit; reaching with magnificent precision for the moon, but falling into raucous discord on earth. . . . We are torn by division, wanting unity. We see around us empty lives, wanting fulfillment." An astute politician, Nixon promised "an answer of the spirit" to lift America out of its "crisis of the spirit."

Others were less hopeful. In 1970, political scientist Andrew Hacker claimed that "what was once a nation has become simply an agglomeration of self-concerned individuals." America, Hacker continued, no longer had "the will to carry out a worldwide mission of redemption and reform." His conclusion was sobering:

> America's history as a nation has reached its end. The American people will of course survive; and the majority will continue to exist quite comfortably, at least in the confines of their private lives. But the ties that make them a society will grow more tenuous with each passing year. There will be undercurrents of tension and turmoil, and the only remaining option will be to learn to live with these disorders.

Despite the pervasive social discord, few other Americans were as despairing as Professor Hacker. Many liberals and radicals, still excited by the sixties sense of possibilities, looked forward to a "New Politics," an alliance of liberal and radical intellectuals with nonwhite minorities, feminists, environmentalists, the young, and the poor. Sixties activist Jack Newfield declared in the *Village Voice* that the New Politics would comprise a coalition of "campus, ghetto and suburb." Robert Kennedy, liberals believed, would have forged such an alliance in 1968 had he lived. Optimistic leftists such as Newfield viewed Nixon's election as the result of the unusual circumstances surrounding the 1968 campaign, not as part of a larger swing to the right. Liberalism, they assumed, still stood as America's dominant ideology and would quickly revive.

These dreams proved ill founded, for the dark clouds that hung over the nation's future remolded traditional political affiliations. The years of upheaval rent the liberal consensus and catalyzed a conservative revival. Indeed, to many people, New Frontier–Great Society programs aimed at ending racism and poverty seemed only to compound these targeted problems, and Americans had begun to grumble about higher taxes and burgeoning government bureaucracy. In January 1969, Kevin Phillips, a young lawyer who had worked on the Nixon campaign, published *The Emerging Republican Majority*, a book that interpreted Nixon's narrow election as the beginning of a new conservative majority. Whereas the Democrats had held the reins of power from the Depression through the late sixties, except for the Eisenhower presidency, Phillips argued that two major trends would likely ensure the Republican party's ascendancy in the future. First, Phillips stressed the appeal of conservatism to the growing population of the Sun Belt, an area stretching from Florida across Texas and the Southwest to California. In the generation following World War II, these states had nearly doubled in population. Houston jumped from fewer than 400,000 inhabitants to nearly 1.4 million; Phoenix, from 65,000 to 755,000. During these years, the Sun Belt attracted new high-tech industries in aerospace, electronics, computers, chemicals, and plastics. Traditionally suspicious of "big government" and what was perceived as the elitist dominance of the Northeast, the Sun Belt population became a seedbed for political conservatism.

The second trend Phillips cited was the new prosperity among white "ethnic" workers, many of whom had recently fled the cities for the suburbs and in the process had adopted conservative values. "The great political upheaval of the nineteen-sixties," he wrote, "is not that of Senator Eugene McCarthy's relatively small group of upper-middle-class and intellectual supporters, but a populist revolt of the American masses who have been elevated by prosperity to middle-class status and conservatism. Their revolt is against the caste, policies and taxation of the mandarins of Establishment liberalism."

Even among certain influential liberals, a discernible rightward shift emerged by the late sixties. In September 1967, prominent liberal sociologist Daniel Patrick Moynihan shocked fellow members of the liberal-intellectual organization Americans for Democratic Action when he called on ADA to make a political alliance with conservatives. Liberals, warned Moynihan, must "divest themselves of the notion that the nation—especially the cities of the nation—can be run from agencies in Washington." He concluded that liberals had to admit that problems existed that "we do not fully understand and certainly do not know how to solve."

In 1969 Democrat Moynihan became an adviser to Republican Nixon. By then, Moynihan's heretical critique of liberal orthodoxy had gathered steam. Indeed, a number of former liberals became neoconservatives and rejected the liberal doctrine that all social problems lend themselves to rational solutions by politicians and planners.

The Conflict of Cultures. So vociferous were the generational and ideological tussles of the late sixties that they even appeared on advertising billboards.

Big government came under attack as disillusioned liberals discovered the anguish of the middle class and the need for decentralization. Reflecting on the sixties from the perspective of 1970, journalist Peter Schrag wrote, "It is ten years later, and the great dream has come to an end. We thought we had solutions to everything—poverty, racism, injustice, ignorance; it was supposed to be only a matter of time, of money, of proper programs, of massive assaults. . . . It is now clear that the confidence is gone, that many of the things we *knew* no longer seem sure or even probable." Neoconservative criticisms of liberal programs lent credence to more traditional conservative assaults on social reform.

The resurgent conservatism of the late sixties and early seventies comprised very disparate elements: ex-liberals disillusioned with Great Society programs; libertarian individualists distraught over infringements on free enterprise; hard-line Cold Warriors yearning for victory in Vietnam; fundamentalist Protestants and traditional Catholics distressed by changing moral standards; states-rightist southerners disturbed by court-ordered school desegregation; "ethnics" disgruntled over inflation, taxes, and New Left protest. Apostles of nearly anarchistic individualism were thrown together with religious and social authoritarians. This diversity of the Right made it nearly impossible for conservatives to agree on a coherent philosophy of government. Whereas most favored the idea of a free-market economy, they were united more by prejudices and preferences than by well-thought-out programs.

Sensing the intense emotion simmering among these various groups, the Nixon administration hoped to weld together a new majority of the Right primarily by appealing to conservative biases and fears. In his victory statement the day after the election, a beaming Nixon pledged that the great objective of his administration would be "to bring the American people together." He urged Americans to stop shouting at each other and "speak quietly enough so that our words can be heard as well as our voices."

Yet Nixon's real strategy was less to end dissension than to capitalize on it. By lashing out against student militants, Black Power advocates, welfare cheaters, and drug users, the Nixon administration in effect exploited polarizations to create a solid majority of what the president called "the Forgotten Americans." "Our fundamental values," claimed Nixon in a June 1969 speech, are "under bitter and even violent attack. . . . We live in a deeply troubled and profoundly unsettled time. Drugs, crime, campus revolts, racial discord, draft resistance—on every hand we find old standards violated, old values discarded."

Rather than addressing the causes of dissent, however, the administration focused its attack on the dissenters themselves, with Vice President Spiro Agnew serving as its chief voice. When he labeled antiwar organizers "hard-core dissidents and professional anarchists," referred to liberal intellectuals as an "effete corps of impudent snobs," or condemned the press as "nattering nabobs of negativism," he was reading from prepared texts written by the president's speechwriters and approved by the White House. The vice president's bombast revealed the true nature of the Nixon regime. Rather than conciliation and unification, Agnew called "for a positive polarization." Now was the time, he added, "to rip away the rhetoric and divide on authentic lines. . . . When the President said 'bring us together' he meant the functioning, contributing portions of the American citizenry."

Repressing the Left, Wooing the Right

Political repression and surveillance took place under all the postwar presidents. During the late forties and fifties, the FBI and other federal agencies concentrated on ferreting out supposed communists. In the early sixties, the government targeted the civil-rights movement and, from the midsixties on, the antiwar movement. In May 1968, in response to the Columbia uprising, FBI director J.Edgar Hoover launched a program aimed at disrupting the entire New Left. In a secret directive, Hoover stated:

> *The purpose of this program is to expose, disrupt, and otherwise neutralize the activities of the various new left organizations, their leadership and their adherents.* It is imperative that activities of those groups be followed on a continuous basis so we may take advantage of all opportunities for counter intelligence and also *inspire action where circumstances warrant. . . . We must frustrate every effort of these groups and individuals to consolidate their forces or to recruit new or youthful adherents. In every instance, consideration should be given to disrupting organized activity of these groups and no opportunity should be missed to capitalize on organizational or personal conflicts of their leadership.* [italics in original]

Richard Nixon inherited these repressive programs and pushed them to further extremes. Indeed, the antiradicalism of the Nixon years proved as pervasive and insidious as the more notorious McCarthy era. Elected after a law-and-order campaign amid the social chaos of 1968 and supported by Americans recoiling from student demonstrators, antiwar protesters, black militants, urban rioters, and promiscuous hippies, Nixon had no qualms about using the federal powers, both legal and illegal, to suppress the Left. Having written off the votes of rebellious students, blacks, and liberal intellectuals, the president moved to solidify a political coalition of traditional conservatives, southern whites, and ethnic blue-collar workers.

During 1969 and 1970, Nixon's first two years in office, the antiwar movement flourished, attracting more and more middle-class Americans and college students. On October 15, 1969, numerous members of Congress, as well as other respected national leaders, joined millions of Americans across the country in Vietnam Moratorium Day, the largest antiwar observance in the nation's history to that time. Movements demanding the rights of women, Native Americans, Chicanos, and homosexuals also gained prominence. Awareness of environmental problems grew, and concern about racial injustice continued.[1] Hundreds of campus demonstrations disrupted and threatened universities. At Cornell, black students outraged by racist cross burnings, the dearth of black professors, the lack of a black-studies program, and limited admissions of African-American students, took over the student union. Later they marched out before the TV cameras holding rifles and capturing national attention. The thriving of counterculture communes and collectives throughout the country also highlighted opposition to mainstream America.

Many Americans, including Richard Nixon, had difficulty distinguishing among these developments. From the outset of his presidency, Nixon and his close advisers tended to identify dissent with disloyalty. Hoping to prove that America's communist enemies in China, North Vietnam, or Cuba planned and financed the home-front opposition, Nixon called on the FBI, the CIA, and the Defense Intelligence Agency to investigate. In June 1969, these agencies reported that though some New Left leaders and black militants had traveled to communist countries, they could find no "ironclad" proof of any foreign funding. Nixon insisted that the agencies keep looking.

Even before Nixon came to power, the government had indicted Tom Hayden, Dave Dellinger, Rennie Davis, Abbie Hoffman, Jerry Rubin, Bobby Seale, and two other dissidents for "conspiracy" in the Chicago convention riots of 1968. The trial of the Chicago Eight took place in the fall and early winter of 1969–1970.[2] Vice President Spiro Agnew referred to the defendants as "kooks" and "social misfits," and the presiding judge even had Bobby Seale, the only black defendant, chained and gagged in the courtroom after he objected to not being allowed to serve as his own defense council. Although the trial ended with a guilty verdict, the blatant bias of the judge and prosecutor led a higher court to reverse the decision.

The Nixon administration nonetheless continued to manipulate the judicial system to harass New Left activists. Nixon's closest adviser, Attorney General John Mitchell, used the Internal Security Division of the Justice Department to conduct more than a hundred grand juries, which called thousands of witnesses and returned four hundred

---

[1] The movements for Native American, Chicano, and gay rights are treated in Chapter 10; feminism and the environmental movement are covered in Chapter 11.

[2] Black Panther Bobby Seale was eventually tried separately; and the remaining defendants came to be called the Chicago Seven.

indictments against members of the antiwar, women's, Chicano, Black Power, and American Indian movements. Senator Sam Ervin of North Carolina, a noted constitutional lawyer, accused the Nixon White House of using its "law-and-order slogan" to rationalize a "fundamental negation of America's constitutional traditions."

Had Ervin or other congressional critics known the full extent of Nixon's tactics, their condemnation of the administration would have been much harsher. In May 1969, the president personally ordered the illegal wiretapping of five news reporters and thirteen members of his own National Security Council. Although the CIA was legally prohibited from internal security investigations, Nixon authorized that agency to spy on Black Power groups, the antiwar movement, the underground press, and various other New Left organizations. By the time of Nixon's resignation in 1974, the CIA would hold secret files on about a thousand groups and more than three hundred thousand individuals. The FBI compiled dossiers on more than a million Americans. Both agencies also carried out immense operations to subvert left-wing organizations by inserting undercover agents into their ranks, spreading false information, encouraging factionalism, and provoking violent confrontations that justified police reprisals. Nixon encouraged army intelligence, the National Security Agency, and the Internal Revenue Service (IRS) to spy on and harass dissidents. The IRS used its legally confidential records to compile files on supposed subversives and conducted tax audits to pester left-leaning taxpayers. In 1976 the Senate Select Committee to Study Government Operations concluded that the FBI during the Nixon years "went beyond excessive information-gathering and dissemination to the use of secret tactics designed to 'disrupt' and 'neutralize' domestic intelligence targets."

In June 1970, Nixon pushed further to gain control over the mushrooming domestic spying operations. He ordered a meeting of the directors of the CIA, the National Security Agency, the Defense Intelligence Agency, and the FBI with White House aide Tom Huston to create the secret Interagency Group on Domestic Intelligence and Internal Security. According to Huston, the former director of the conservative Young Americans for Freedom, the president had decided that "everything is valid, everything is possible" in dealing with domestic dissent. Nixon promised authorization for opening mail, tapping telephones, even breaking into suspects' homes and offices. "The discussions were open and frank," Huston informed Nixon's chief of staff, H. R. Haldeman. "All were delighted that an opportunity was finally at hand to address themselves jointly to the serious internal security threat that exists." Although none of the agency directors expressed any misgivings about the illegal powers offered, the scheme broke down because J. Edgar Hoover did not want the other agencies intruding on what he deemed FBI turf.

Undaunted, the president next organized a secret investigative unit dubbed the "Plumbers" in 1971. Directed by his special assistant John Ehrlichman and staffed by men such as ex-CIA agent E. Howard Hunt and former FBI operative G. Gordon Liddy, the Plumbers carried out such illegal activities as falsifying Kennedy administration diplomatic records, tapping reporters' telephones, hiring thugs to attack antiwar demonstrators, and practicing political espionage. In an effort to obtain material damaging to former Defense Department employee Daniel Ellsberg, on trial for having released the classified *Pentagon Papers,* the Plumbers burglarized the office of Ellsberg's psychiatrist. This same group later got caught breaking into Democratic National Headquarters in the Watergate complex in Washington, D.C.

In addition to overt repression of dissent, the government found another way to weaken the Left: intimidating the media. Nixon employed Vice President Agnew to lead the fight. In a speech written by presidential speechwriter Patrick Buchanan and delivered in Des Moines, Iowa, on November 13, 1969, Agnew lashed out at what he termed the "small and unelected" group of "elitist snobs" of the media who have the power to "distort our national search for internal peace and stability." The president, claimed Agnew, should not have to "contend with a gaggle of commentators raising doubts." The Nixon-appointed chair of the Federal Communications Commission (FCC) praised the vice president's message as worthy of "careful consideration."

The pressure yielded immediate results. Two days after Agnew's harangue, an immense antiwar demonstration took place across the country. Organized by longtime antiwar activists calling themselves the New Mobilization Committee, more than a hundred thousand demonstrators turned out in San Francisco; nearly half a million gathered in the nation's capital. In a moving ceremony, over forty thousand people marched in single file from Arlington National Cemetery past the Lincoln Memorial and the White House to the steps of the Capitol. There, each marcher read the name of one American soldier killed in Vietnam and deposited that name in a small wooden coffin. None of the three major television networks presented any live coverage of the demonstration, and newspapers and news magazines gave only scant notice to the protest.

While Agnew continued challenging the media, Nixon urged the FCC to threaten investigations into news-gathering practices. Because the FCC has the power to revoke a network's broadcasting license, TV executives took heed. In addition to withholding coverage of antiwar demonstrations, TV also overlooked other radical protests. The executive producer of NBC's "Nightly News" specifically proscribed airing film of black radicals. Throughout the sixties, media attention, especially via television, had stimulated the growth of dissent as well as stirred hostility toward the dissenters. From 1969 on, however, the media toned down its attention to antiwar protesters and other militants. According to a recent study, only 10 percent of all "severe protests" received national coverage in 1970–1971, as compared with 40 percent in 1968–1969.

As early as 1961, public opinion polls had revealed that a majority of Americans received their information about the world primarily from TV. After the major networks doubled the length of their nightly news programs in 1963, people more than ever perceived the pivotal events of the midsixties—from JFK's assassination to the 1968 Democratic convention in Chicago—through the filter of television. The power of this medium to create news is immense. TV defined the issues for the public and to a large extent influenced trends in the print media and radio as well. It was TV that made people aware of the ghetto riots, Black Power salutes, student demonstrations, feminist rallies, and mass antiwar protests. As the networks reduced or eliminated their coverage of these events, TV viewers concluded that dissent was disappearing, an impression that eventually became something of a self-fulfilling prophecy.

In part, Nixon's success in muzzling the media stemmed from the fact that both television and print news had begun modifying their coverage of demonstrations and the war even before Agnew's harangues and FCC pressures. Mayor Daley's assaults on journalists and camera crews had already persuaded key media leaders to temper the emphasis on violence in the news. The editors of the nation's leading newspapers, including the *New York Times,* the *Washington Post,* and the *Chicago Daily News,* joined the executive heads of the three TV networks and the editors of *Time* and *Newsweek* in sending a telegram to Mayor Daley condemning the way in which reporters "were repeatedly singled out by policemen and deliberately beaten." "The obvious purpose," the telegram argued, "was to discourage or prevent reporting of an important confrontation between police and demonstrators which the American public as a whole has a right to know about."

Media moguls soon learned, however, that the great majority of Americans supported the police and denounced the demonstrators. "We got thousands of calls," recalled CBS Washington bureau chief Bill Small, "from people saying they didn't believe their eyes, accusing us of hiring cops to beat up kids." The media reconnoitered. Three weeks after the convention, the *Washington Post* exonerated police actions on the grounds that the officers had a natural antipathy to bearded men. Two weeks before this capitulation, influential syndicated columnist Joseph Kraft anticipated Agnew's argument when he chided the media for being too elitist and not sufficiently cognizant of the values of "Middle America." "The most important organs of press and television," he claimed, "are, beyond much doubt, dominated by the outlook of the upper-income whites. . . . In the circumstances, it seems to me that those of us in the media need to make a special effort to understand Middle America. Equally it seems wise to exercise a certain caution, a prudent restraint, in pressing a claim for a plenary indulgence to be in all places at all times the agent of the sovereign public."

At President Nixon's inaugural in January 1969, demonstrators held an elaborate "counterinauguration" to protest the war. The chastened media largely ignored them. In fact, NBC news strictly prohibited any TV coverage. As NBC president Reuven Frank admitted, "An atmosphere [of] . . . self-censorship" had developed. The media had caved in to the pressures of the Nixon government with only minor resistance. By 1972 professor of journalism Ben H. Bagdikian, writing in the *Columbia Journalism Review,* noted that "a sample study of leading papers and network specials during the presidential campaign makes it clear that the Nixon Administration's three year war against the media has succeeded."

The consequences of the government's muffling of the media came to light particularly in coverage of the Vietnam War. From the escalation in 1965 through the Tet Offensive in 1968, Vietnam had been America's "living-room war." Indeed, TV coverage probably had done as much to foster the growing moral outrage against the war as had the antiwar movement, and by the time Nixon took office, the majority of Americans opposed U.S. involvement in Vietnam. In the midst of the massive antiwar demonstrations in the fall of 1969, President Nixon, aware of public sentiment, told a national TV audience that "we are Vietnamizing the search for peace." Nixon pledged to bolster the South Vietnamese army and to turn the bulk of the fighting over to them. Yet the war would rage on for four more years; by 1973 the administration had dropped four million tons of bombs on Indochina, including those used in secret missions against Cambodia and Laos. All told, the bombing during the Nixon years amounted to twice the tonnage dropped during Johnson's presidency and one and one-half times the total exploded over Europe and Asia in World War II and the Korean War combined. But Nixon's escalation only occasionally made the nightly news. By withdrawing American troops, speaking of Vietnamization, and claiming to work toward "peace with honor," Nixon convinced a majority of Americans of his intention to end the war.

Fearing an FCC investigation and wary of alienating advertisers and Nixon's "silent majority,'' the TV networks supported the president. In 1969 Av Westin, executive producer of ABC's "Evening News," sent a directive to all correspondents: "I have asked our Vietnam staff to alter the focus of the coverage from combat pieces to interpretive ones, pegged to the eventual pullout of the American forces." Westin ordered the Saigon bureau to "shift our focus . . . to themes and stories under the general heading: We Are On Our Way Out of Vietnam." Other networks followed suit, and Americans began seeing footage of returning GIs, reunions, and peace negotiations rather than bombings, battles, and torture. As with the peace movement, changes in television coverage gave the public a distorted impression—in this case, that the end of the war was imminent.

Besides employing repressive tactics against protesters and the media, the administration aimed to weaken the civil-rights drive so as to win conservative support. Having polled only 13 percent of the black vote in 1968, Nixon chose to ignore African-American as well as liberal voters in favor of Middle America: southern whites, Sun Belt suburbanites, and white blue-collar workers. Few of these voters looked favorably on various programs designed to benefit nonwhites. Nixon particularly wished to win the support of the white South. The civil-rights revolution of the fifties and sixties, combined with prosperity and population shifts, had loosened the Democratic party's hold on the region. Nixon and his advisers designed a ''southern strategy'' to gain the support of conservative and racist voters. Part of this strategy involved curtailing civil-rights programs.

Although President Nixon spoke of "black capitalism" as the answer to racial inequalities, the administration allocated few funds to develop black businesses. At the same time, the White House cut other federal programs aimed at aiding nonwhites. Nixon even opposed extending the 1965 Voting Rights Act and lobbied Congress to defeat the fair-housing enforcement program. Further, the president and his advisers argued against court-ordered school busing, and when the Supreme Court in 1971 upheld busing as both constitutional and necessary to achieve racial balance in the schools (*Swann* v. *Charlotte-Mecklenburg Board of Education*), Nixon condemned the ruling on national TV and asked Congress to pass a moratorium on the policy. When the Labor Department called for proportional minority hiring on federal construction jobs, Nixon characterized quotas as ''a dangerous detour away from the traditional value of measuring a person on the basis of ability.'' As a result, minority representation was declared a ''goal'' rather than a ''requirement.'' The president hamstrung the civil-rights offices within the Justice and Health, Education and Welfare departments and fired government officials seeking to implement integration. Queried about making Martin Luther King, Jr.'s birthday a national holiday, Nixon wrote, underlining both words: ''*No never!*'' ''For the first time since Woodrow Wilson,'' the NAACP's president charged, ''we have a national administration that can rightly be characterized as anti-Negro.''

Nixon bolstered his southern strategy through his nominations to the Supreme Court. Ever since the 1954 *Brown* desegregation decision, the Court, headed by Chief Justice Earl Warren, had come under attack by the American Right. In addition to criticizing the Court for opening the door to the civil-rights revolution, conservatives faulted it for abolishing school prayer, reapportioning state legislatures, and protecting the rights of those charged with committing illegal acts. Conservatives blamed the Court for both increases in crime and social permissiveness. Soon after Nixon took office in 1969, Earl Warren retired; the president replaced him with Warren Burger, a conservative federal judge from Minnesota.

Even before Burger had won confirmation, judicial activist Abe Fortas resigned from the Court. Nixon quickly nominated Clement Haynsworth, a South Carolina judge with a record of segregationist and antilabor decisions. Pressured by civil-rights and labor lobbyists, the Senate rejected Haynsworth after lengthy debate. Seventeen Republicans had joined the Democrats in overturning the president's choice. Infuriated, Nixon named an even more conservative southerner, G. Harrold Carswell of Florida. Close investigation found Carswell utterly unqualified for the Supreme Court. An avowed segregationist, he had helped to transfer a Tallahassee golf course from municipal to private ownership to prevent its being integrated. Carswell, claimed the dean of the Yale Law School, had "more slender credentials than any nominee for the Supreme Court put forth in this century." Nine out of fifteen University of Florida law professors opposed his nomination. Staunch Nixon supporters cast about for ways to defend him. "Even if Carswell were mediocre," suggested Republican senator Roman Hruska, "there are a lot of mediocre judges and people and lawyers. They are entitled to a little representation, aren't they?" The Senate once more blocked confirmation.

Nixon shrewdly used this second rebuff to advance his southern strategy. In a public statement, he praised the "admirable dignity" displayed by judges Carswell and Haynsworth in the face of "vicious assaults on their intelligence . . . and their character." The real reason for their rejection, he claimed, was "the fact that they had the misfortune of being born in the South. . . . I understand the bitter feeling of millions of Americans who live in the South about the act of regional discrimination that took place in the Senate yesterday."

Having pleased the white South, Nixon finally filled the Court vacancy with Harry Blackmun, a more reputable and moderate federal judge from Minnesota. Before the end of his first term, the president appointed two additional conservative justices, Lewis Powell, Jr., and William Rehnquist. Although the relatively moderate Burger Court annoyed Nixon by deciding in favor of abortion (*Roe* v. *Wade,* 1973), it generally followed a more cautious course than the Warren-led Court had. Supreme Court decisions of the midseventies, for instance, allowed states to reintroduce the death penalty, gave communities a local option on obscenity and pornography censorship, and disallowed busing between separate school districts as a means of achieving racial balance.

In the 1968 campaign, Nixon had charged the Supreme Court with giving a "green light" to "criminal elements." Once in the White House, he introduced a new crime bill for the nation's capital. The proposed legislation empowered judges to send criminal suspects to jail for sixty days before trial and allowed police to break into private residences without a warrant. The administration knew that both measures violated the Bill of Rights, but it had two purposes in mind. First, it hoped that the bill would suggest a tough law-and-order demeanor to Americans anxious about crime. Second, it wanted to embarrass Democrats, who were expected to vote against the unconstitutional measure. Instead, Democrats, fearful of appearing to coddle criminals, joined Republicans in supporting the law. Nixon had made his symbolic gesture and would again attack the courts when they later declared the law unconstitutional.

The administration's success in slowing the pace of the civil-rights campaign, reshaping the Supreme Court, and passing a symbolically tough anticrime law strongly appealed to conservative Americans. But whether the Right indeed constituted a silent majority remained to be seen. The first test of the administration's popularity came with the 1970 off-year elections. White House insiders were optimistic. "This country," exclaimed John Mitchell, "is going so far right you are not going to recognize it." A memorandum prepared by White House assistants H. R. Haldeman and Jeb Magruder laid out the theme of the Republican campaign: "The Democrats should be portrayed as being on the fringes: radical-liberals who bus children, excuse disorders, tolerate crime, apologize for our wealth, and undercut the President's foreign policy." Following this script, Agnew asked in a September speech, "Will America be led by a President elected by a majority of the American people, or will we be intimidated and blackmailed into following the path dictated by a disruptive, radical, and militant minority—the pampered prodigies of the radical liberals in the United States Senate?" Agnew crisscrossed the nation. Greeted by audiences holding signs declaring "Spiro Is My Hero," the vice president assailed students as "parasites of passions," Democrats as "sniveling hand-wringers," and newscasters as "curled-lip boys in eastern ivory towers."

Nixon struck similar themes as he decried the "creeping permissiveness" of the courts, the legislatures, and the universities: "All over this country today, we see a rising tide of terrorism, of crime, and on the campuses . . . we have seen those who . . . engage in violence. . . . It's time to draw the line and say we're not going to stand for that! . . . It's time for the great silent majority of Americans to stand up and be counted."

Democrats countered Republican slanders by themselves denouncing crime, drugs, and the new morality while blaming the Nixon government for inflation and recession. In the end, however, the election proved little. Republicans managed to limit the usual off-year losses in the House to nine seats and actually gained two Senate seats. The Democrats retained control of Congress and won eleven additional governorships.

Despite the ambiguity of the 1970 results, the president interpreted the election as a conservative mandate. He continued to cut federal expenditures for liberal social programs, impounded funds already authorized by Congress, and fired liberal Republicans George Romney and Robert Finch from his administration. Then he and his advisers set out to win a decisive victory in the 1972 presidential election. As his initial strategy, he gave top priority to foreign affairs, an area where he could exert presidential initiative and play the role of international statesman, above congressional and domestic squabbles. But before Nixon could implement his plan, he had to address disturbing economic trends at home.

Hard Times

"The period of 1945 to 1970," claimed social critic Michael Harrington, was "the time of the Keynesian euphoria" when "it seemed that the business cycle had been conquered." With moderate inflation and relatively full employment in these years, the American economy had stood as the envy of the postwar world. In the prosperous sixties, U.S. economic output had grown by 47 percent, generating a 35 percent jump in disposable income after adjustments for inflation. In the midsixties, eighty-seven companies worldwide did an annual business of a billion dollars or more; sixty of these were American. Such prosperity convinced policymakers such as Kennedy and Johnson that America had the bounty to uplift the poor and police the world.

Climbing the political ladder during these plentiful times, Richard Nixon, like most other Americans, assumed that the abundance would continue. Nixon also felt much more comfortable attending to foreign affairs than to the domestic economy. The chairman of his Council of Economic Advisers described the president's attitude toward economic issues as "somewhat like that of a little boy doing required lessons." Yet at about the time he took office, the economy began to falter. The problem in part stemmed from the Johnson administration's policies, particularly LBJ's attempt to finance both the War on Poverty and the Vietnam War, a strategy that had prompted a rise in both the national debt and inflation. When Nixon assumed the presidency, he faced what at that time was considered a huge budget deficit of over $25 billion and an alarming annual inflation rate of 5 percent.

Following traditional Republican policies, Nixon raised interest rates and reduced the money supply, hoping to cool the economy and dampen inflation. Instead, soaring interest rates virtually halted residential construction and brought a sharp drop in industrial production. Unemployment, which had been idling at a postwar low of 3.3 percent, jumped to 6 percent. Americans found themselves in the midst of the worst recession since the last years of the Eisenhower administration. Yet contrary to conventional economic wisdom, inflation continued to spiral upward. By 1970 Democratic chairman Larry O'Brien gloated that "Nixonomics" meant that "all the things that should go up—the stock market, corporate profits, real spending income, productivity—go down, and all the things that should go down—unemployment, prices, interest rates—go up."

Fearing the political consequences of a deepening recession, Nixon abandoned his conservative economic principles early in 1971 and announced to a bewildered nation, "I am now a Keynesian." Adopting a favorite tactic of liberal Democrats, he proposed an unbalanced federal budget in the hopes that deficit spending would revive the economy and calm unemployment before the 1972 presidential election. But the antirecession spending only caused prices to spiral and barely made a dent in unemployment.

In August 1971, Nixon again changed course. After the Commerce Department announced that for the first time since 1890 the United States was running a trade deficit, the president declared virtual economic war on other industrial nations. He devalued the dollar by allowing it to "float" in international money markets, hoping to improve American exports' competitiveness on the world market. To encourage consumption of domestic goods, he levied a 10 percent surcharge on imports. As part of what he termed his "New Economic Policy," Nixon then shocked conservative Republicans again by declaring a ninety-day freeze on wages, prices, and rents, to be followed by federally imposed controls setting a maximum of 5.5 percent annual increases for wages and 2.5 percent for prices and rents.

These policies scored some success in the short run. The stock market rallied, sending the Dow Jones industrial index to new heights. The foreign trade deficit, inflation, and unemployment all registered slight declines. The administration continued to pump money into the economy, ignoring the costs of budget deficits. As Secretary of Defense Melvin Laird recalled, "Every effort was made to create an economic boom for the 1972 election. The Defense Department . . . bought a two-year supply of toilet paper. We ordered enough trucks . . . for the next several years." By the November election, Nixon's policies had worked sufficiently to defuse economic tensions.

Once safely into his second term, Nixon dropped mandatory wage, price, and rent ceilings and called for "voluntary" restraints. As always when price controls lapse, inflation promptly skyrocketed, hitting nearly 10 percent in 1973 and racing past 12 percent in 1974; it would remain in double figures throughout the rest of the decade. Farm prices alone rose an incredible 23 percent in just one month in 1973. By this time, Nixon, increasingly embroiled in the Watergate debacle, abandoned his efforts to solve the nation's mounting economic problems. In August 1974, when he resigned, the economy was in far worse shape than when he first took office five and a half years earlier. Inflation had become endemic, and unemployment and trade deficits continued apace.

Although Nixon's inconsistent policies unquestionably aggravated matters, America's economic downturn in the 1970s also reflected a confluence of long-term factors. Indeed, the United States' economic dominance in the two decades after World War II had derived from historic circumstances. Of the world's major industrial nations, only the United States had emerged from the war with its economy booming and its industrial capacity unscathed. In the 1950s, about 40 percent of all manufactured goods were American made. Gradually, however, other nations began catching up. With American aid, war-devastated Japan, Germany, and Western Europe had rebuilt their economies virtually from scratch, and by the sixties, these nations had regained a major share of the world market. In many cases, products produced in older American factories failed to compete well with manufactures from the more modern factories in Europe and Asia. Foreign producers began to insinuate themselves into the American domestic market. In 1960, imported automobiles had accounted for only 4 percent of the U.S. market; by 1970 this figure had expanded to 17 percent. During the same decade, the foreign share of America's consumer electronics business ballooned from 4 to 31 percent.

As foreign competition stiffened, the United States' share of the world market shrank. Whereas in 1955 American manufactures had made up 32 percent of the world market, by 1970 this number had fallen to 18 percent. As Americans spent more and more money overseas both to buy foreign goods and to support the war in Vietnam and other worldwide military activity, the enormous trade surplus that the United States had enjoyed shriveled and disappeared. By 1971, when Nixon devalued the dollar and tried to discourage imports with a surcharge, the United States had racked up a $10 billion balance-of-payments deficit.

A final factor undermined America's postwar economic reign: the nation's increasing dependence on the resources and raw materials of other countries, particularly oil. Cheap oil had fueled the United States' postwar prosperity, as gasoline consumption swelled from 1 billion barrels in 1950 to 2.25 billion barrels by 1971. Largely self-sufficient through the early sixties, American oil production failed to keep pace with demand. Yet rather than looking for ways to cut back on oil use, Americans turned to oil from the Middle East. By 1973 one-third of the nation's oil supply, although still purchased at low prices, came from overseas.

All this changed in October 1973. Angered by American support of Israel in the Arab-Israeli Yom Kippur War, the oil-producing Arab states embargoed shipments of crude oil to the United States and its allies. By the time the embargo ended in March 1974, the Organization of Petroleum Exporting Countries (OPEC) had quadrupled the price of oil. For the rest of the decade, OPEC prices kept mounting. Oil that had cost less than two dollars a barrel in 1970 cost more than twenty dollars by the end of the

Energy Crisis. To conserve gas, a driver pushes his car in a long line at a Water-town, Massachusetts, filling station during the 1974 fuel crisis.

seventies; during these same years, the price that the United States paid for imported oil leaped from only $4 billion to $90 billion.

America's unchallenged global economic dominance had ended. Dependent on oil imports, the United States no longer commanded its own economic fate. The high cost of oil reverberated through the entire economy, driving up inflation and unemployment and slowing overall economic growth. Sales of large gas-guzzling American automobiles plummeted, and recession hit the auto industry. Other heavy industries suffered in turn, particularly steel. By 1975 unemployment topped 9 percent, and millions of young people entered the job market for the first time with few employment prospects.

Détente

Although Nixon came to the White House during a period of intensifying economic problems and roiling domestic unrest, foreign affairs absorbed him most. The nation "could run itself domestically without a President," he claimed. "All you want is a competent Cabinet to run the country at home. You need a President for foreign policy." Like John F. Kennedy, Nixon saw the presidency primarily as a platform for foreign-policy leadership and hoped to achieve historic greatness through his handling of international affairs. Long associated with bellicose anticommunism, Nixon as president nevertheless proved more of a realist than an ideologue. Recognizing that the Vietnam War had eroded America's position as the world's supreme power, he admitted in 1970 that "the postwar period in international relations has ended." The current challenge, he believed, would center on adjusting to the emerging limits of power without sacrificing the security of the United States or its allies. He also realized that the deepening Sino-Soviet split would allow the United States to rethink its relations with the communist nations and to reduce international tensions.

Nixon sought to concentrate foreign-policy decisionmaking authority in the White House rather than in the State Department. He distrusted Secretary of State William Rogers and Secretary of Defense Melvin Laird, his own cabinet appointees. Instead, he chose Henry Kissinger to carry out his objectives. A Jewish refugee from Nazi Germany, Kissinger had become a renowned Harvard professor of international politics. He had served as an occasional consultant to both the Kennedy and Johnson administrations during the sixties and had advised New York's Republican governor Nelson Rockefeller on foreign-policy matters. In the 1968 campaign, Kissinger secretly offered his services to both the Humphrey and Nixon camps and even passed confidential information to the Nixon people on Johnson's plans for peace overtures to the North Vietnamese. Soon after the election, Nixon named Kissinger his national security adviser. With the president's blessing, Kissinger reorganized the National Security Council so as to exclude the State and Defense departments from any significant role in shaping policy.

Witty and gregarious, Kissinger stood in marked contrast to the dour, reticent Nixon. Yet both men mistrusted the existing foreign-policy bureaucracy and shared a fondness for intrigue. Determined to make history, the duo ruthlessly removed obstructions to their ambitions. According to Kissinger's close aide Lawrence Eagleburger, "Kissinger and Nixon both had degrees of paranoia. It led them to worry about each other, but it also led them to make common cause on perceived mutual enemies. They developed a conspiratorial approach to foreign policy management." In his memoirs, Kissinger claimed that Nixon had a "powerful tendency to see himself surrounded by a conspiracy reaching even among his Cabinet colleagues." He further admitted that, to secure the president's favor, he fell "in with the paranoid cult of the tough guy." For his part, President Nixon once expressed concern to White House adviser John Ehrlichman that Kissinger needed psychiatric care.

Kissinger's foreign-policy strategy, he later explained, was to attempt "to relate events to each other, to create incentives or pressures in one part of the world to influence events in another." Like Nixon, he realized that the dualistic worldview that had dominated the thinking of postwar policymakers was no longer tenable. Instead of the Free-World/communist-bloc division and the supremacy of the two superpowers, Kissinger saw five major power centers: the United States, the Soviet Union, China, Japan, and the NATO nations of Western Europe. Rather than seeking to contain communism, Kissinger and Nixon now looked to reestablish the classical idea of a balance of power.

The most positive result of this new thinking came with U.S. rapprochement with the two communist powers. After much preparation, including a Chinese tour by the U.S. Ping-Pong team and a secret visit by Kissinger, President Nixon traveled to China in February 1972. The highly publicized visit eased more than two decades of Sino-American hostility. The United States agreed that American troops would eventually be removed from Taiwan and that the Chinese should settle the island's future. As Nixon and Kissinger saw it, improved relations with China would limit Soviet influence in Asia and open vast new markets for American manufactures. The Chinese wanted to boost trade and looked to American friendship to counterbalance the Soviet Union, whose troops were massed on their border. The United States and China agreed to a cultural exchange, pledged themselves to "peaceful mutuality," and in the spring of

1973 established informal diplomatic missions. Official diplomatic recognition came in 1979.

Closer relations with Beijing strengthened Washington's diplomatic bargaining position with Moscow, and in May 1972 Nixon followed his triumphant tour of China with an equally productive visit to the Soviet Union. The deepening Sino-Soviet split had made the Soviets eager for better relations with the United States, and the possibility of a Sino-American alliance lent this Soviet goal even more urgency. Moreover, with the United States and the Soviet Union spending upward of $130 billion annually for armaments, slowing the arms race appealed to both countries. Since 1969 the Soviets and Americans had held a series of Strategic Arms Limitations Talks (SALT). During Nixon's visit, he and Soviet leader Leonid Brezhnev signed two arms-control treaties, the initial results of the SALT negotiations. The first agreement limited each nation to two hundred antiballistic missiles (ABMs). The second froze each side's intercontinental ballistic missiles at the existing ratio for a five-year period. Neither agreement reduced existing armaments or prevented development of new weapons systems. Both superpowers already possessed sufficient nuclear warheads to destroy the world many times over, and the arms race ground on. But the SALT agreements symbolized a first step toward limiting nuclear weapons and signified the United States' and the U.S.S.R.'s desire to settle their differences peacefully.

Other agreements from the Nixon-Brezhnev summit pledged the two nations to cooperation in medical research, space exploration, and environmental protection. In addition, the heads of state assented to improved trade relations, which soon yielded massive American grain sales to the Soviets at bargain prices. In 1971, a year before the summit, the perennial problem of Berlin and the two Germanies had found resolution when the superpowers recognized the legitimate existence of two distinct German states and established improved communications between West Germany and Berlin. This thaw in the Cold War came to be referred to as détente, something that Kissinger hoped would "give the Soviets a stake in international equilibrium." The Cold War was by no means over, but at least America's peaceful coexistence with the communist nations now seemed protected.

Nixon's War

By building détente with the Soviet Union and China, Nixon and Kissinger also sought to persuade these nations to pressure North Vietnam into accepting peace terms that would allow the United States to extricate itself honorably from the quagmire in Indochina. Vietnam had become what a White House aide referred to as "the bone in the nation's throat." President Nixon judged Vietnam only a short-term problem; Kissinger dismissed it as a historical footnote. But after nearly twenty-five years of determined fighting, the Hanoi regime was not about to be commanded by the Nixon administration or the communist superpowers. The Vietnam War did not respond to Henry Kissinger's global manipulations and in fact would remain the thorniest problem of the Nixon White House throughout the president's first term.

Johnson's abdication and the election of Nixon, with his "secret plan" to end the Vietnam War, struck most political observers as a mandate for peace. Even before

Johnson left office, his administration had begun negotiations with the North Vietnamese in Paris, peace talks that continued under Nixon. "I'm not going to end up like LBJ," boasted Nixon, "holed up in the White House afraid to show my face on the street. I'm going to stop that war. Fast." Yet like his predecessors, Nixon searched for a way to preserve the United States' image abroad. "I will not be the first President of the United States to lose a war," he told Republican congressional leaders. "Precipitate withdrawal," he instructed the American people, would be a "popular and easy course," but such a surrender, he claimed, would "cause a collapse of confidence in American leadership." The goal of the United States, added Kissinger, should be "to withdraw as an expression of policy and not as a collapse." This aversion to losing face burdened the nation with four more years of fighting in Southeast Asia.

In July 1969 the new president announced the Nixon Doctrine: the United States would now serve as supportive partner in the Third World, not as military protector. "Asian hands," he proclaimed, "must shape the Asian future." The new plan recognized that the United States could no longer afford to police the world and that henceforth America would rely on regional allies to maintain an anticommunist global order. To implement the doctrine, the administration began a gradual withdrawal of American troops from Vietnam while supplying the South Vietnamese army with massive quantities of weapons.

Despite "Vietnamization," the American military role in Vietnam continued, and the war in fact widened. In March 1969 the president secretly ordered the bombing of the neutral nation of Cambodia, concealing his actions from Congress and the American public through a complex system of false bombing reports. Ongoing air strikes against North Vietnam and Laos were also stepped up. This "jugular diplomacy," as Kissinger called it, had a twofold purpose: to destroy North Vietnamese bases and supply routes in Cambodia and Laos and to force concessions from North Vietnam by giving the impression that the new president was a "mad bomber":

> I want the North Vietnamese to believe I've reached the point where I might do *anything* to stop the war [Nixon told an aide]. We'll just slip the word to them "for God's sake, you know Nixon is obsessed about communism. We can't restrain him when he's angry—and he has his hand on the nuclear button"—and Ho Chi Minh himself will be in Paris in two days begging for peace.

Although Nixon bombed Cambodia for fourteen months, the tactic failed to achieve the administration's objectives. North Vietnam continued to deliver men and supplies to the South and refused concessions at the negotiating table. The bombings destroyed countless Cambodian villages, killing hundreds of civilians and precipitating a brutal civil war in Cambodia between pro-American and communist forces. The North Vietnamese aided the Cambodian communists, the ruthless Khmer Rouge, and persisted in using the tiny nation as a staging area for attacks on South Vietnam. On April 30, 1970, Nixon announced a full-scale incursion into Cambodia by U.S. and South Vietnamese forces.

The invasion yielded some caches of enemy weapons but failed to coerce North Vietnam into concessions. Indeed, the move ended any pretext of Cambodian neutrality, forced that nation even closer to North Vietnam, and furthered the cause of the Khmer Rouge. Nations throughout the world condemned the American aggression. At home, the invasion touched off the most widespread antiwar protests in American history, as people nationwide vehemently denounced the new phase of the war (see Chapter 10). Congress attacked Nixon's broadening of the war by repealing the 1964 Gulf of Tonkin resolution and considering various proposals to cut off further funding of the war.

Antiwar sentiment also flared in 1970 when Americans learned the shocking details of the 1968 My Lai massacre. The army's official inquiry found the U.S. troops guilty of "individual and group acts of murder, rape, sodomy, maiming and assault on noncombatants and the mistreatment and killing of detainees." At the trial, one officer testified, "Every unit of brigade size had its My Lai hidden someplace." These revelations stunned a nation accustomed to seeing itself as the upholder of justice and decency. Opinion polls taken soon after the public learned of My Lai reported that 65 percent of respondents considered it "morally wrong" for Americans to be fighting in Vietnam.

Opposition to "Nixon's war" mounted in June 1971 when the *New York Times* began to publish the *Pentagon Papers,* a classified, official study of U.S. decisions in the Vietnam conflict. Commissioned by Robert McNamara in 1967 when he began to harbor doubts about American policy, the *Pentagon Papers* documented the war's long history of concealments, mistaken assumptions, and deceptions. Although the study focused on American involvement in Vietnam before Nixon's administration, the president correctly surmised that publication of these documents would further erode support for his conduct of the war. Citing national security, the Justice Department obtained an injunction ordering the *Times* to cease publishing the papers. The *Times* immediately appealed, and on June 30, 1971, the Supreme Court ruled against the government and praised the *Times* "for serving the purpose that the Founding Fathers saw so clearly."

Nixon and Kissinger turned their wrath against Daniel Ellsberg, the former Defense Department employee who had leaked the *Pentagon Papers* to the *Times.* Kissinger denounced Ellsberg as an "unbalanced" drug abuser. Suspecting that Ellsberg was part of an antiwar conspiracy, Nixon recalled being "furious and frustrated. . . . I wanted someone to light a fire under the FBI. . . . If a conspiracy existed, I wanted . . . the full resources of the government brought to bear in order to find out." In addition to instituting court proceedings against Ellsberg for theft of classified documents, the White House ordered the Plumbers to break into the office of Ellsberg's psychiatrist in the hopes of finding incriminating evidence.[3]

Ignoring the intensifying antiwar sentiment, Nixon and Kissinger escalated the conflict yet further. In February 1971, the president authorized a South Vietnamese invasion of Laos with American air support; the ARVN troops were soon routed. By the spring of 1972, the war faring badly, Nixon risked disrupting his summit with the Soviets by ordering the mining of North Vietnamese ports and the bombing of densely populated areas of that country on the eve of the Moscow meeting. U.S. targets included North Vietnamese rail lines running into China. Ultimately Soviet and Chinese leaders showed less concern for North Vietnam than for their own national interests, and détente survived. But despite the mines and massive bombings, the American and South Vietnamese military position steadily deteriorated.

Fearing the effects of Vietnam on the 1972 presidential election, the Nixon admin-

---

[3] At Ellsberg's trial in May 1973, the judge dismissed all charges when the Plumbers' break-in was revealed.

istration made major concessions to the North Vietnamese at the long-stalemated Paris peace talks. The United States agreed to allow the North Vietnamese army to remain in South Vietnam after the withdrawal of American forces and promised to aid in the reconstruction of North Vietnam. In return, the Hanoi regime accepted the American proposal that a cease-fire would precede a final political settlement. On October 26, a week before the election, a beaming Kissinger announced that "peace is at hand." Although his announcement proved premature—the South Vietnamese government objected—it served to undermine the peace candidacy of Democratic presidential nominee George McGovern.

In December 1972, with peace talks once more bogged down but Nixon safely reelected, the president ordered renewed bombings of North Vietnam. These "Christmas bombings" became the most intensive in military history. The United States also rushed more than a billion dollars' worth of weapons to South Vietnam and pressured that government to accept the peace agreement. Finally, on January 23, 1973, a peace treaty was signed in Paris. The accord contained little that could not have been negotiated many years earlier.

The Nixon-Kissinger agreement was a thinly disguised surrender that they called "peace with honor." By the end of 1975, not only South Vietnam but also Cambodia and Laos had fallen to communist-led nationalist forces. Although they toppled like the dominoes that American policymakers had long imagined, their collapse largely stemmed from nationalist revolutions stirred by American intervention, not some grand communist design.

America had capitulated in what had been the longest, most unpopular war in its history, and Nixon's "peace with honor" had exacted a staggering price. In the four years since he had come to office promising to end the war, an additional 20,553 Americans had died in Vietnam, bringing the total to more than 58,000. The burden of the war, of course, fell hardest on the people of Southeast Asia. By 1973 Indochinese deaths exceeded 1.5 million. The tonnage of bombs dropped on North and South Vietnam, Cambodia, and Laos during the Nixon years far surpassed that of the Johnson presidency, left millions homeless, and wrought untold devastation and ecological damage. At home, the war had divided the American people and polluted the political atmosphere as no other issue had since slavery and the Civil War. With its price of more than $150 billion, the conflict had brought inflation, retrenchment from social reform, and attacks on civil liberties.

The psychic wounds for a generation of young men were particularly severe. All told, some 2.8 million Americans served in Vietnam. Their tours of duty left many of them traumatized. In addition to the horror of the war itself, soldiers endured indifference, even hostility, on coming home. Never in U.S. history had society so scorned its returning military men. To some veterans, it seemed that they had become the scapegoats for the nation's humiliation. There were few public parades and no generous GI Bill such as World War II veterans had enjoyed. One prisoner of war called "the pain and the loneliness . . . shallow compared to finding yourself stripped of all entitlement to reputation, love, or honor at home." Readjusting to everyday life brought a new round of problems. Testifying before the Senate Foreign Relations Committee, John Kerry, a member of Vietnam Veterans Against the War and former lieutenant and future U.S. senator, told the nation, "We wish that a merciful God could wipe away

Honoring the Dead. The Vietnam War Memorial in Washington, D.C., was completed in November 1982, seven years after the conclusion of the war.

our own memories of service as easily as this Administration has wiped away their memories of us.''

Despite a government study's finding that nearly 60 percent of Vietnam veterans suffered medical or psychological disorders—alcohol and drug abuse, disease, nervous conditions, recurring nightmares—Congress and the Veterans Administration dragged their feet in providing help. Not until 1979 did Congress appropriate funds for an outreach program. The following year, the American Psychiatric Association labeled the condition afflicting many veterans as "posttraumatic stress disorder." Moreover, only after a long court battle did the government acknowledge responsibility for illnesses caused by Agent Orange, the deadly defoliant used to level the jungles of Vietnam. Not until 1982 would the nation formally recognize those who died in Vietnam with the dedication of the Vietnam Veterans Memorial in Washington, D.C. The memorial, two polished granite walls set in a low embankment and bearing the names of all Americans who died in Vietnam, gave symbolic acknowledgment to the dead and attempted to heal the wounds of the living.

Veterans were not the only ones whose lives had been disrupted by the war. Women in the antiwar movement, widows of war dead, and families of returning GIs all paid a high price. To this day, the families and friends of the nearly 2,400 Americans officially listed as missing in action seek word of the fate of their loved ones. Those who resisted the draft and refused to fight also suffered. Some went to jail; thousands more escaped underground or fled the country. Even after the war had ended, the debate over giving amnesty to some 570,000 "draft offenders" continued to divide the nation.

The Vietnam War also took its toll on Richard Nixon and his administration. By the time of the cease-fire agreement in January 1973, presidential adviser Charles Colson described the White House inner circle as a "small band of tired, dispirited sometimes mean and petty men, bickering among themselves, wary and jealous of one another." Indeed, the severe steps that Nixon had taken to protect his Vietnam policies against real and imagined foes led to the Watergate crisis that would ultimately compel his resignation. As much as any other issue, then, the Vietnam War destroyed the Nixon presidency.

Dirty Tricks: Scheming Toward Watergate

In his perceptive 1970 biography of Richard Nixon, historian Garry Wills described the president as "the least 'authentic' man alive." Conservative Republican Barry Goldwater recalled Nixon as "the most dishonest individual I have ever met in my life. . . . Nixon lied to his wife, his family, his friends . . . his own political party, the American people, and the world." His rise from a lower-middle-class background through the political ranks reads like a Horatio Alger story, yet Nixon remained acutely insecure and perceived his life as a series of crises. His craving for power, recognition, and approval seemed insatiable. Paranoia plagued him. Ill at ease with others, as president he avoided contact with most of his staff and cabinet members and instead chose to contemplate affairs in isolation.

Nixon believed that his adversaries were plotting his political demise. To protect his position, he kept an "enemies' list" and hunted for opportunities to thwart his opponents. Presidential adviser Charles Colson later described the Nixon White House as haunted by "a siege mentality. . . . It was now 'us' against 'them.' Gradually, as we drew the circle closer around us, the ranks of the 'them' began to swell." Nixon's paranoia drove Watergate, a small crime that evolved into the most momentous constitutional crisis since the Civil War. Ultimately, this scandal threatened the very legitimacy of the American political system.

In addition to Nixon's character, two long-term developments contributed to Watergate. First, during the twentieth century, the authority and stature of the presidency had expanded. Various crises, from World War I to Vietnam, furthered the aggrandizement of the presidency. The postwar prominence of international affairs had also elevated the executive branch far above Congress. The president conducted American diplomacy, planned the nation's defense, and served as commander-in-chief in time of war. Television, in making the president visible to the public, further heightened the chief executive's stature. By the 1960s, these circumstances had created what historian Arthur Schlesinger, Jr., termed "the imperial president."

Second, owing to the postwar obsession with national security, Americans had grown accustomed to espionage, surveillance, and secrecy in the conduct of national affairs. Cold War anticommunist fears had made the public tolerant of violations of individual civil liberties committed in the name of security. Operating with little congressional control, the FBI and the CIA had vastly strengthened their surveillance roles in the years preceding the Nixon presidency, using wiretaps, bugging devices, infiltrations, and other illegal means to investigate suspected subversives and political opponents, usually in the name of national security.

That Nixon, with his penchant for secrecy and intrigue, augmented this spying is not surprising. The president limited policy discussions to within his own tightly controlled White House bureaucracy, and there his power reigned unchecked. Indeed, from the outset of his administration, Nixon determined to suppress challenges to his authority by whatever means, legal or illegal. His first major presidential act was to authorize the secret bombing of Cambodia. When news of the attack leaked and was published in the *New York Times,* Nixon and Kissinger had the FBI place wiretaps on several State Department officials and on a member of Kissinger's own staff.

The road to Watergate began in 1971 when Nixon established the Plumbers, the secret group that burglarized the office of Daniel Ellsberg's psychiatrist and tapped Ellsberg's telephone. The Watergate scandal itself began as an incident in Nixon's reelection campaign. On the night of June 17, 1972, police arrested five men equipped with electronic bugging devices and cameras after they had broken into the Democratic National Committee offices in Washington's Watergate building. One of the burglars, James McCord, was the security chief of the Committee to Re-Elect the President. This committee, soon popularly referred to as CREEP, was headed by John Mitchell, who had resigned as attorney general to direct Nixon's campaign. Mitchell promptly denied any involvement on CREEP's part.

Ironically, the break-in occurred at a time when Nixon's reelection appeared assured. The president, however, sought a vast popular mandate, to mitigate his nagging insecurity and ensure his place in history as both a great and a well-liked leader. He left nothing to chance. Well before the Democrats chose a candidate, the Committee to Re-Elect the President had accumulated vast sums of money from corporations and other organizations and individuals seeking government favors. A new campaign finance law went into effect in April 1972 calling for full disclosure of large campaign contributions, and Nixon's campaign officials set out to gather as much cash as possible before the deadline. They threatened corporations and wealthy individuals with government harassment if they did not make large contributions. Shipbuilder and later New York Yankees owner George Steinbrenner was informed that the IRS, the Justice Department, and the Commerce Department would investigate his business dealings if he failed to donate handsomely to the Republican cause. ''It was a shakedown. A plain old-fashioned Goddamn shakedown,'' griped Steinbrenner to a friend. The administration rewarded major contributors with special favors. As one example, the president expressed his appreciation for a hefty contribution from the three major dairy corporations by raising government support of milk prices.

The Nixon campaign raised more than $20 million before the April 7 deadline, much of it in cash. CREEP kept much of the money secret and had it ''laundered'' through Mexican banks. Nixon's close aides then used these funds for covert operations against potential Democratic contenders. As early as 1970, the White House had secretly channeled some $400,000 into the Alabama gubernatorial primary in an unsuccessful effort to unseat Governor George Wallace.

As the 1972 election approached, CREEP conducted clandestine intelligence investigations of leading Democratic candidates, including careful scrutiny of the sexual and drinking habits of high-ranking Democrats. In addition, CREEP established a special ''dirty tricks'' unit to harass Democrats through such means as issuing false literature ''signed'' by Democratic candidates or publishing smear letters from supposedly concerned citizens. In one especially effective ploy, CREEP placed spurious letters in a New Hampshire newspaper charging the then front-running Democrat, Edmund Muskie, with making derogatory remarks about New Englanders of French-Canadian ancestry. The letters also claimed that Muskie's wife drank heavily and used crude language. Muskie's tearful denial of the false charges shattered his image as a mature statesman and destroyed his candidacy.

The Watergate break-in was only part of CREEP's larger program of "dirty tricks," spying, and sabotage. In January 1972, Plumber saboteur G. Gordon Liddy had proposed a plan to destroy the Democrats with kidnappings, hijackings, and wiretaps. John Mitchell rejected the scheme as too complicated but in March approved a plan for wiretapping the Democratic National Committee. A first break-in succeeded; however, the wiretap malfunctioned, prompting the second break-in on June 17, in which the burglars got caught. The cover-up began at once. Mitchell lied about CREEP's connection; Nixon's press secretary, Ronald Ziegler, dismissed Watergate as a "third-rate burglary attempt." A week after the break-in, Nixon himself secretly ordered CIA director Richard Helms to inform the FBI that Watergate involved national security and to demand that the bureau drop its investigation. White House aides and campaign officials also approved the payment of more than $200,000 "hush money" to the Watergate Plumbers. The White House claimed to be conducting a thorough probe into the Watergate affair. At the August news conference, Nixon assured the nation that a full investigation had been made and that "I can state categorically that no one in the White House staff, no one in this administration, presently employed, was involved in this very bizarre incident." For a time the cover-up succeeded, and Nixon scored his long-coveted triumph in the November election.

Election '72

Nixon's Democratic opponent in the 1972 election, Senator George McGovern of South Dakota, won nomination partly because of circumstances that hobbled other leading Democrats. Senator Edward Kennedy, the younger brother of John and Robert, undoubtedly would have been the party favorite if not for an auto accident on July 18, 1969, on Chappaquiddick Island off Martha's Vineyard. There, under mysterious circumstances, Kennedy's car had plunged off a bridge into the water. A young woman riding with Kennedy drowned while he fled the scene. The senator never adequately explained either the accident or his subsequent behavior. Muskie's campaign, meanwhile, failed to recover from his public display of emotion in New Hampshire. Hubert Humphrey's candidacy generated little enthusiasm, for he was still too closely associated with the defeat of 1968 and the Vietnam War. Finally, George Wallace, who had run well in the spring primaries as a Democrat on an antibusing platform, was crippled by a would-be assassin's bullets that May and forced to drop out.

McGovern also benefited from new convention rules adopted by the Democrats after the disastrous 1968 Chicago convention. Each state delegation now had to give proportional representation to minority voter groups such as the young, women, blacks, and Hispanic Americans. Delegate Shirley MacLaine described California's pro-McGovern delegation as looking "like a couple of high schools, a grape boycott, a Black Panther rally, and four or five politicians who walked in the wrong door." Indeed, many longtime Democratic political leaders failed to get in by any door. Even Chicago mayor Richard Daley was denied a seat on the Illinois delegation for violating the new reforms. Daley and his entire delegation were unseated and replaced by a delegation led by Jesse Jackson, a black preacher and former associate of Martin Luther King, Jr. With the convention dominated by reformers, McGovern easily won on the first ballot. But the slighting of traditional party leaders—city bosses, union heads, and southerners—would greatly weaken the Democrats' chances in November. Bosses such as Daley sat on their hands during the campaign, and even the AFL-CIO declined to endorse McGovern.

McGovern's candidacy represented the "New Politics" that had emerged from the New Left critique of American society in the sixties. A "politics of conscience," his campaign stressed immediate peace in Vietnam, a reduced American world role, amnesty for draft resisters and army deserters, racial integration through school busing, welfare and tax reforms, women's rights, environmental and consumer protection, and enlarged civil liberties. Conservatives cringed when exuberant McGovern delegates openly debated abortion, gay rights, and the legalization of marijuana.

In marked contrast to Nixon, George McGovern was a decent man. Politically, however, his idealism and naiveté cut him off from mainstream America. He campaigned for bold new social and welfare programs at a time when much of the public shied from big government and high taxes. McGovern's efforts to create a new coalition of youth, women, nonwhites, the poor, and radicalized intellectuals may have been doomed from the start, for the majority of American voters were neither poor, nor black, nor radical, nor intellectual. Many traditional Democrats, especially white southerners, Catholics, and working-class "ethnics," felt deserted by the party; they either sat out the election or voted for Nixon. McGovern backers had counted heavily on the votes of young people, yet although 1972 was the first national election in which eighteen-year-olds could participate, an unexpectedly small percentage of the young bothered to go to the polls.

Had McGovern proved as electrifying a campaigner as John and Robert Kennedy had been, he might have stood a chance, but his speeches lacked flair, and he often seemed indecisive. McGovern particularly hurt himself when newspapers revealed that his choice for vice-presidential candidate, Senator Thomas Eagleton of Missouri, had been hospitalized on several occasions for depression. At first McGovern gave Eagleton his "1,000 percent" endorsement. Later he bowed to pressures and dumped Eagleton in favor of Sargent Shriver, a Kennedy brother-in-law and former director of the Peace Corps and the Office of Economic Opportunity. McGovern's reputation suffered irreparable damage from this about-face.

The Nixon people delighted in McGovern's candidacy, depicting the Democratic nominee as a dangerous radical and linking him with campus unrest, street rioting, draft-card burning, and disrespect for traditional values. Even before McGovern's nomination, CREEP, believing that McGovern would be the easiest Democrat for Nixon to defeat, had ordered its tricksters to "lay off" the South Dakota senator.

In his nomination acceptance speech, Nixon implored the nation to "reject the policies of those who whine and whimper about our frustrations and call on us to turn inward. . . . Let us not turn away from our greatness." Playing the role of statesman above mere politics, Nixon let McGovern's apparent extremism become the main issue of the campaign. McGovern cited Watergate and called the Nixon administration "the most corrupt in history." However, the cover-up was working, and few Americans believed the Democrat's charges. McGovern might have gained advantages as the peace candidate, but even here Republican strategy foiled him: just before the election, Kissinger announced that peace in Vietnam was at hand.

Although he never won America's heart, Nixon's strategy scored a spectacular success. Polling 60.8 percent of the vote, the president's popular landslide ranked second only to that of Lyndon Johnson in 1964. In the electoral college, his margin of victory surpassed LBJ's as McGovern managed to carry only Massachusetts and the District of Columbia. Voting patterns appeared to bear out Kevin Phillips's earlier predictions of an "emergent Republican majority." Whereas the Democrats did well among the young, blacks, Jews, and low-income voters, the GOP reversed Democratic dominance among white "ethnics" and gained the support of a majority of Catholic voters. Republicans also made significant gains in the South and West and predominated in the populous Sun Belt. Yet while voters unmistakably repudiated McGovern, Democrats nevertheless retained control of Congress. Political alignments were shifting, but because only 55 percent of registered voters actually cast ballots, these patterns would not yet emerge in sharp focus.

The contrast between his 1968 and 1972 victories nevertheless elated Nixon. He now believed that he had won a mandate to rule as he saw fit. When the Vietnam cease-fire was signed at the beginning of his second term, he appeared in complete command. His approval rating in January 1973 stood at 70 percent in national polls, and on New Year's Day, *Time* named the president and Kissinger its "Men of the Year." Only weeks later, the trial of the Watergate burglars would begin, and Watergate would turn into what Nixon's counsel John Dean labeled a "cancer on the presidency."

Nixon Laid Low

If not for the diligent efforts of two young *Washington Post* reporters, Bob Woodward and Carl Bernstein, and federal judge John J. Sirica, Nixon might well have disguised his involvement in Watergate and the other illegal activities of his administration. Beginning in late September 1972, Woodward and Bernstein published allegations about the cover-up. Although these revelations had little impact initially, continuing articles by the reporters detailed how John Mitchell, White House chief of staff H. R. Haldeman, domestic affairs adviser John Ehrlichman, and various other high-ranking officials had participated in the break-in or deception. Judge Sirica presided at the trial of the Watergate burglars. Convinced that the full story was not being told, he threatened the burglars with long jail terms unless they talked. James McCord yielded to the pressure and gave the judge a letter implicating "higher-ups" at CREEP and the White House. The Senate then appointed a special committee, chaired by North Carolina Democrat Sam Ervin, to look into Watergate.

By this time, the cover-up supplanted every other concern confronting the administration. "I don't give a shit what happens," Nixon told Mitchell in late March. "I want you all to stonewall it, let them plead the fifth amendment, cover-up or anything else, if it'll save it." By April, however, the lies began to unravel. Mounting evidence implicated top White House advisers. Nixon fired White House counsel John Dean and allowed Haldeman, Ehrlichman, and Attorney General Richard Kleindienst to resign. All previous White House statements on Watergate, Nixon's press secretary blandly announced, were "inoperable." In an effort to preserve his credibility, Nixon agreed to the appointment of Archibald Cox of Harvard Law School as Watergate special prosecutor.

On May 17, 1973, Sam Ervin convened the Senate committee investigating Watergate. The televised hearings proved as spectacular and influential as the Army-McCarthy hearings of 1954 and made Watergate the national obsession. The cover-up crumbled, not just concerning Watergate but the entire hidden history of the Nixon years. Witness after witness revealed the administration's illegal efforts to destroy its political opponents. Charges included wiretapping, sabotage, espionage, blackmail, forgery, burglary, bribery, perjury, obstruction of justice, illegal offers of executive clemency, even subversion of the Constitution. The public learned of Nixon's "enemies' list"; they heard how the IRS had been used to harass opponents; they became aware of CREEP's multimillion-dollar political-sabotage fund. Although previous campaigns had resorted to "dirty tricks," the tactics of the Nixon White House showed unprecedented illegality and misuse of presidential authority. Ultimately Watergate was revealed to be no third-rate burglary at all but part of a systematic plot to undermine a presidential election.

In early July, lawyers for the Ervin committee held a preliminary hearing to interrogate Alexander Butterfield, the former head of day-to-day White House operations. In response to an innocent question from the chief Republican counsel, Butterfield revealed that for two years Nixon had secretly taped his own White House conversations. The irony was perfect: the president who spied on so many others had provided the basis for his own undoing by bugging himself. Nixon began a new cover-up and withheld the tapes for, he claimed, reasons of national security and executive privilege.

In October 1973, the president's position deteriorated further. On October 10, Spiro Agnew resigned the vice presidency after pleading *nolo contendere* (no contest) to charges stemming from years of taking bribes and evading income taxes. The man who had smeared the Democrats and the courts for supposedly coddling the criminal element was himself revealed as a common criminal. Two days after Agnew's disgrace, a court of appeals decision ordered certain White House tapes turned over to Judge Sirica; Nixon again refused to comply. On October 20, the president shocked the nation by firing special Watergate prosecutor Cox, as well as his attorney general and deputy attorney general, who had refused to carry out the order to fire Cox. The "Saturday Night Massacre" provoked what one Nixon adviser called a "firestorm" of protest. More than half a million telegrams poured into the White House. Newspapers and magazines called on Nixon to resign. The House began impeachment proceedings. Under the mounting pressure, Nixon agreed to release nine tapes and to appoint a new special prosecutor, Leon Jaworski.

But the president's troubles only multiplied. Sirica soon learned that two of the requested tapes had not been released and that another crucial tape had an eighteen-and-a-half-minute gap, the result of several erasures. The public also found out that Nixon, like Agnew, had avoided paying some income taxes and had become a millionaire through dubious means while in office. Moreover, he had spent millions in taxpayers' money on refurbishing his California and Florida houses.

Through revelation after revelation, Nixon clung to his office. Each new disclosure of misconduct, in the words of one congressman, was like waiting for the other shoe to drop—on a centipede. "I am not a crook," the president protested. In April 1974, in a last-ditch effort to delay the inevitable, Nixon released a printed version of the

Mandate the Magician. As Watergate relentlessly unraveled, President Nixon on several occasions appealed to the American people on national television, insisting on his non-involvement in the scandal. Draper Hill's January 1974 cartoon mocks these presidential efforts. (Courtesy of Draper Hill, Memphis, Tennessee. Copyright *The Commercial Appeal*, Memphis.)

tapes. Even this heavily edited transcript exposed the president's petty, vulgar, vindictive nature. The conservative and usually pro-Nixon *Chicago Tribune* was stunned: "We have seen the private man and we are appalled. He is humorless to the point of being inhuman. He is devious. He is vacillating. He is profane. . . . His loyalty is minimal."

The end loomed. On July 24, 1974, the Supreme Court, four of whose members were Nixon appointees, voted unanimously that the president must turn over all the tapes. Three days later, the House Judiciary Committee in televised hearings adopted the first article of impeachment. Finally waking up to the hopelessness of his position, on August 8, 1974, Richard Nixon announced his resignation as president of the United States effective at noon the next day.

Some twenty-five top administration officials eventually would go to prison, including Nixon's closest advisers Ehrlichman, Haldeman, and Mitchell. The president, however, refused to admit his own guilt. His resignation speech admitted only to "errors in judgment" and claimed that he was stepping down because he "no longer [had] a strong political base in Congress." The president who had promised "law and order" turned out to be the most lawless and shameless of national leaders.

• • •

Watergate, following on the heels of the deceptions and defeat of Vietnam, left Americans disillusioned. As one elderly Washington, D.C., cab driver expressed on the day of Nixon's resignation, "You don't get to the top in politics without doing a lot of crooked stuff." Poet Adrienne Rich eloquently summed up the prevailing cynicism

Exit RN. Having resigned the presidency, Richard Nixon bids an emotional farewell to members of his staff and cabinet in the East Room of the White House, August 9, 1974.

toward politics and politicians: "We assume that politicians are without honor. We read their statements trying to crack the code. The scandals of their politics: not that men in high places lie, only that they do so with such indifference, so endlessly, still expecting to be believed."

After Watergate, the Democrats emerged as the short-term winners. In the 1974 elections they would pick up forty-nine House seats and five in the Senate, and in 1976 Georgia Democrat Jimmy Carter, untainted by any connection with Washington politics, would win the presidency. In the long run, however, the Democrats came out the losers because of their association with big government. By furthering popular distrust of government, Watergate actually aided the swing to the right that had sprung from the governmental programs and social upheavals of the sixties. By 1980, with the election of Ronald Reagan to the presidency, the conservative reaction seemed to crest. Blaming big government for society's problems, conservatives promised to beef up the military while diminishing social spending, deregulating business, and cutting taxes, all in the name of restoring traditional family values, prosperity, and world prestige.

Yet for liberal supporters, the story was not yet over. Despite Nixon's triumphs in 1968 and 1972 and the successes of Reagan and George Bush in the eighties, the nation elected Democrat Bill Clinton president in 1992. To some, Clinton's victory presaged a revival of liberalism. Furthermore, as Chapters 10 and 11 and the Epilogue discuss, the influence of the social movements of the sixties extended well beyond 1970. Indeed, radical activism and conservative politics coexisted throughout the seventies and eighties as feminism, environmentalism, gay rights, antinuclear protest, and a host of other causes came to the forefront. The Movement's visibility and intensity may have lessened, but the lid that conservatives attempted to close on it has refused to stay shut.

Selected Bibliography

Andrew Hacker's pessimistic prophecies about America's future are contained in his *The End of the American Era* (1970). For a far more sanguine appraisal of the United States at the beginning of the seventies, see Ben J. Wattenberg, *The Real America* (1974). Kim McQuaid, *The Anxious Years* (1989), presents an overview of American society from 1968 through Nixon's resignation in 1974. The Republican southern strategy of the Nixon years was first spelled out in Kevin P. Phillips, *The Emerging Republican Majority* (1969). Kirkpatrick Sale, *Power Shift* (1975), documents the growing political significance of the Sun Belt.

A spate of sociological studies appeared in the early seventies trying to explain the political and cultural reactions of white "ethnics" and other "middle Americans" to the upheavals of the sixties. The best of these include Michael Novak, *The Rise of the Unmeltable Ethnics* (1971); Jan Erickson and Robert Coles, *Middle Americans* (1973); Richard Lemons, *The Troubled Americans* (1970); Andrew Levison, *The Working Class Majority* (1974); Peter Binzen, *Whitetown, U.S.A.* (1970); Michael Wenk et al., eds., *Pieces of a Dream: The Ethnic Workers' Crisis with America* (1972); Sar Levitan, ed., *Blue Collar Workers: A Symposium of Middle America* (1971); and Patricia Cayo Sexton and Brandon Sexton, *Blue Collars and Hard Hats* (1971).

Long-range political trends responsible for the demise of liberalism and the rise of conservatism are the subject of Steve Fraser and Gary Gerstle, eds., *The Rise and Fall of the New Deal Order, 1930–1980* (1989); Alonzo L. Hamby, *Liberalism and Its Challengers: From F.D.R. to Bush* (1992 ed.); E. J. Dionne, *Why Americans Hate Politics* (1991); Martin P. Wattenberg, *The Decline of American Political Parties, 1952–1980* (1984); and Everett Ladd, Jr., *Transformation of the American Party System: Political Coalitions from the New Deal to the 1970s* (1978).

The rise of conservatism during the Nixon years is best discussed in James Reichley, *Conservatives in an Age of Change* (1981). See also George Nash, *The Conservative Intellectual Movement in America* (1979); Paul Gottfried and Thomas Fleming, *The Conservative Movement* (1988); Allan Crawford, *Thunder on the Right* (1980); William A. Rusher, *The Rise of the Right* (1984); Kevin P. Phillips, *Post-Conservative America* (1982); William B. Hixson, Jr., *Search*

for the American Right Wing: An Analysis of the Social Science Record, 1955–1987 (1992); Michael Miles, *The Odyssey of the American Right* (1980); and Robert W. Whitaker, *The New Right Papers* (1982). Peter Steinfels, *The Neoconservatives* (1979), critically analyzes the renewed interest in conservatism among certain liberals. Important books by such neoconservative liberals include Nixon's most influential domestic adviser Daniel P. Moynihan's critique of the Great Society, *Maximum Feasible Misunderstanding* (1969), and his memoir of White House service under Nixon, *Coping* (1973); Norman Podhoretz, *Breaking Ranks* (1979); Daniel Bell, *The Cultural Contradictions of Capitalism* (1978); and Irving Kristol, *Two Cheers for Capitalism* (1978).

Books documenting the repressive tactics of the Nixon administration include Athan Theoharis, *Spying on Americans: Political Surveillance from Hoover to the Huston Plan* (1974); Jonathan Schell, *The Time of Illusion* (1975); and Tom Shachtman, *Decade of Shocks* (1983). Robert J. Goldstein's *Political Repression in Modern America: From 1870 to the Present* (1978) places the repression of the Nixon years in a larger perspective. Judy Clavir's and John Spitzer's edited transcripts of the conspiracy trial of those accused of crossing state lines to foment riot at the 1968 Chicago Democratic convention were published as *The Conspiracy Trial* (1970). Tom Hayden's *Trial* (1970) is his account of the proceedings.

Todd Gitlin's *The Whole World Is Watching* (1980) presents an excellent analysis of the pressures on TV and other media to change their coverage of the Vietnam War and protests and the effect of diminished coverage on the New Left. Also insightful on this topic are Eric Barnouw, *The Image Empire* (1970) and *Tube of Plenty* (1975); Michael J. Arlen, *Living-Room War* (1969); Daniel Hallin, *The "Uncensored War": The Media and Vietnam* (1986); and Godfrey Hodgson, *America in Our Time* (1976).

An excellent introduction to Nixon and his presidency is Herbert Parmet, *Richard Nixon and His America* (1990). A good starting point for understanding Nixon's complex personality is Gary Wills, *Nixon Agonistes* (1970). Bruce Mazlish, *In Search of Nixon* (1972), and Fawn Brodie, *Richard Nixon* (1980), present psychohistorical interpretations. The most thorough biography to date is Stephen Ambrose, *Nixon*

(3 vols., 1987–1991). Also useful is Roger Morris, *Richard Milhous Nixon* (1989). Self-serving but revealing are Nixon's own accounts: *Six Crises* (rev. ed. 1978) and *RN: The Memoirs of Richard Nixon* (1978). William Safire, *Before the Fall* (1975), and Raymond Price, *With Nixon* (1977), are insightful memoirs by White House aides. Leonard Silk, *Nixonomics* (1972), and Herbert Stein, *Presidential Economics* (1984), cover Nixon's economic policies.

On Nixon-Kissinger foreign policies and the search for détente, see Tad Szulc, *The Illusion of Peace* (1978); Stanley Hoffman, *Primacy of World Order* (1978); Lloyd Gardner, *A Covenant with Power* (1984); Robert Litwack, *Détente and the Nixon Doctrine* (1984); and Henry Brandon, *The Retreat of American Power* (1973). Henry Kissinger tells his story in *The White House Years* (1979) and *Years of Upheaval* (1982). These boastful memoirs should be read in conjunction with the critical analyses by Roger Morris, *Uncertain Greatness* (1977), and particularly Seymour M. Hersh, *The Price of Power* (1983).

On Nixon and Vietnam, in addition to the literature cited for Chapter 6, see Ronald Spector, *After Tet* (1993); David W. Levy, *The Debate over Vietnam* (1991); A. E. Goodman, *The Lost Peace* (1978); Earl C. Ravenal, *Never Again* (1978); Gareth Porter, *Vietnam* (1979); and Timothy Lomperis, *The War Nobody Lost—and Won* (1984). William Shawcross, *Side-Show* (1979), is a devastating indictment of the Nixon administration's actions in Cambodia. Nixon's own post-presidential evaluation of Vietnam is found in his *The Real War* (1980). The problems of returning Vietnam veterans are considered in Lawrence Baskir and William A. Strauss, *Chance and Circumstance* (1978), and Paul Starr, *The Discarded Army* (1973).

The election of 1972 is the subject of Hunter S. Thompson's scathing, sacrilegious *Fear and Loathing: On the Campaign Trail '72* (1973). For a more traditional analysis, see Theodore H. White, *The Making of the President 1972* (1973).

Watergate and the crimes of the Nixon presidency are revealed in three fascinating compilations of primary sources assembled by the staff of the *New York Times: The Watergate Hearings* (1973), *The White House Transcripts* (1974), and *The End of a Presidency* (1974). The Watergate ignominy gave rise to a large number of personal and journalistic accounts. The best of these remain the books of the *Washington Post* reporters who penetrated the cover-up: Bob Woodward's and Carl Bernstein's *All the President's Men* (1974) and *The Final Days* (1976). Revealing memoirs of Nixon aides include John Dean, *Blind Ambition* (1976); H. R. Haldeman, *The Ends of Power* (1978); John Ehrlichman, *Witness to Power* (1982); and Maurice Stans, *The Terrors of Justice: The Untold Story of Watergate* (1984). Special prosecutor Leon Jaworski tells his story in *The Right and the Power: The Prosecution of Watergate* (1976). Judge John Sirica's *To Set the Record Straight* (1979) tells of the role of the judiciary in unraveling Watergate. Informative secondary accounts of Watergate include Theodore H. White, *Breach of Faith: The Fall of Richard Nixon* (1975); Jimmy Breslin, *How the Good Guys Finally Won* (1975); J. Anthony Lukas, *Nightmare: The Underside of the Nixon Years* (1976); Jonathan Schell, *The Time of Illusion* (1976); Jim Houghan, *Secret Agenda: Watergate, Deep Throat and the CIA* (1984); and Stanley I. Kutler, *The Wars of Watergate* (1990).

CHAPTER

10

TWILIGHT OF THE MOVEMENT

On September 26, 1970, the *New Yorker* published lengthy excerpts from the newly released *The Greening of America*, a book that promptly hit the best-seller list. Written by Yale law professor Charles Reich, *The Greening of America* announced the imminent victory of the "revolution of the new generation." Young people's "protest and rebellion, their culture, clothes, music, drugs, ways of thought, and liberated lifestyle," Reich argued, "are not a passing fad . . . , nor are they in any sense irrational. The whole emerging pattern, from ideals to campus demonstrations to beads and bell bottoms to the Woodstock Festival, makes sense as part of a consistent philosophy. It is both necessary and inevitable, and in time will include not only youth, but all people in America."

According to Reich, the United States' "whole perception of reality" was shifting. In his version of cultural history, Americans had passed through two stages of consciousness. The first stage, "Consciousness I," expressed the mind-set of frontier, preindustrial America and "focused on self . . . cut off from the larger community of man, and from nature." In the post–World War II years, the new "Consciousness II" had gained dominance as "a response to the realities of organization and technology." In this stage, the "corporate state" united business and government in a "mindless" system in which "technology, organization and administration" ran "for their own sake" with no concern for "human ends." People who played the game were rewarded with money and status but lacked meaningful control over their lives. Consciousness II yielded war, domestic dissension, poverty, powerlessness, and a dominant, dehumanizing technology.

Rebelling against both Consciousness I and especially Consciousness II, the emerging youth movement of the mid- to late sixties had created a new stage of development, "Consciousness III." "What happens is simply this," Reich explained. "In a brief span of months, a student, seemingly conventional, changes his haircut, his clothes, his habits, his interests, his political attitudes . . . his whole way of life." This lifestyle alteration, Reich claimed, represented the outward manifestation of a profound change of consciousness. As the young entered adult life and as older Americans began to emulate them—to listen to rock, smoke marijuana, join communes, and open themselves to "dread, awe, wonder, mystery, . . . magic"—then a true "greening" of corporate America would come.

One reviewer found that Reich's study had touched a national nerve. The media bestowed much attention on the book. The *New York Times* alone printed three articles by Reich explaining his thesis and four scholarly assessments. Published after five years of intensifying war in Vietnam and civil unrest at home, *Greening* offered a benign vision of a new millennium. Adults could now see their long-haired, dope-smoking children not as dangerous, deviant dropouts but as harbingers of hope. Even critical reviewers treated Reich's book seriously.

The idea that the Movement would radically change American values and institutions predated Reich by several years, first taking hold among youthful participants themselves around the time of the January 1967 Human Be-In. The following year, the musical *Hair* presented this thesis in a popular format that reached adult audiences. Opening on Broadway amid the chaos and violence of the spring of 1968, *Hair,* billed as "the Tribal Love-Rock Musical," announced "the dawning of the Age of Aquarius," a time when "peace will guide the planets and love will steer the stars." The musical predicted a blissful era of "harmony and understanding," celebrated the culture and values of liberated youth, and satirized war, pollution, the American flag, and middle-class goals. In one scene the entire cast—men and women, blacks and whites—stripped naked and danced joyously while singing of "beads, flowers, freedom, happiness." *Hair* shocked audiences, yet scored a hit. Performed more than eighteen hundred times on Broadway, touring companies also delivered the new-age extravaganza across the nation. Four of the show's songs became Top-10 singles. Even Clive Barnes, theater critic for the staid *New York Times,* called *Hair* "brilliant" and described it as "the first Broadway musical in some time to have the authentic voice of today."

Soon the larger message of Hair—that rebellious youth would usher in a glorious new era—found supporters beyond the ranks of the disaffected young themselves. By the end of the sixties, Reich and a number of other adult intellectuals looked to the Movement as the vanguard of a better America. Historian Theodore Roszak, in a sympathetic and influential 1969 book, *The Making of a Counter Culture,* compared alienated young to the earliest Christians. He praised "the strange youngsters who don cowbells and primitive talismans and who take to the public parks or wilderness to improvise outlandish communal ceremonies . . . seeking to ground democracy safely beyond the culture of expertise." Discerning a religious bent in the Movement, he prophesied "a new heaven and a new earth so vast, so marvelous that the inordinate claims of technical expertise must of necessity withdraw to a subordinate and marginal status in the lives of men." Roszak argued, as Reich would later, that young Americans had emerged as a new social class opposed to the technological values of advanced industrial society. It was not the New Left's politics of confrontation that impressed these authors. The hope for America, as they saw it, lay in the counterculture's efforts (in Roszak's words) to "discover new types of community, new family patterns, new sexual mores, new kinds of livelihood, new esthetic forms, new personal identities on the far side of power politics, the bourgeois home, and the consumer society."

In a similar vein, classics scholar Philip Slater in his *The Pursuit of Loneliness* (1970) described U.S. society as "at the breaking point." "We live in the most affluent society ever known," he wrote, yet "the sense of deprivation and discomfort that pervades it is also unparalleled." Americans, dominated by a traditional scarcity-oriented culture that stressed property over human rights, technological requirements over human needs, competition over cooperation, violence over sexuality, means over ends, social forms over personal expression, and striving over gratification, had become a grim and grasping people. Yet amid the individualistic and lonely populations, a youthful counterculture had emerged. Communal, nonviolent, pleasure-oriented, these deviants offered a way for Americans to recapture bodily and sensory experience. Through emulating the counterculture, Slater prophesied, "we may again be able to take up our original utopian task" of creating a cooperative, peaceable society.

Prepared by *Hair*, Roszak, Slater, Reich, and other prophets of the coming Eden, and by the abundance that made counterculture values appealing, many Americans embraced the hopeful message of a peaceful revolution. However, as the seventies began to unfold, it became apparent that the Revolution would not materialize. The Nixon years discouraged large-scale dissent. People came to have second thoughts about America's "greening." In March 1971, radical journalist Andrew Kopkind confessed that "revolution is a longer and harder road than any of us wanted to think, and . . . hippies aren't going to man the FBI." Soon communes dispersed as more and more young people shed their counterculture clothes and joined the work force. By the time Nixon resigned from office in August 1974, only remnants of the New Left and counterculture remained, and Reich, Roszak, Slater, and others of their ilk had fallen into disrepute.

Recent historians who write of these authors' grandiose expectations routinely ridicule their naiveté. Certainly it took a credulous mind to expect, as Reich did, that youths wearing curious clothing, sporting long hair and beards, smoking marijuana, and enjoying unwedded sex heralded a higher level of consciousness. In predicting that the self-liberation of counterculture youth would provide the lever for freeing American society, Reich, Roszak, and Slater were proved wrong. The Revolution failed to take shape. Although the moral and cultural revolt of the sons and daughters of the most privileged Americans gained some support among an educated elite, the Movement largely failed to win working-class backing. In addition, it managed to outrage the mass of citizens who increasingly demanded a return to traditional family values and "law and order." Within a few years, the New Left and counterculture, along with their great expectations, would fade, and its dreams of a new-age utopia remain unfulfilled. In the long run, however, this tumultuous minority, the radical fringe of a wider and deeper change, would profoundly alter American society. Although the Age of Aquarius never dawned, those who prophesied its coming were not as foolish as some have claimed.

Woodstock, August 1969. Nearly half a million young people reveled in three days and nights of "sex, drugs, and rock 'n' roll" that quickly became a metaphor for a generation.

Woodstock or Altamont?

The violence in Chicago in August 1968, claimed the editors of *Rolling Stone,* were "only the labor pains. The inheritors came to life outside the village of White Lake." In mid-August 1969, White Lake, near the town of Bethel in upstate New York, hosted the "Woodstock Music and Art Fair, An Aquarian Exposition"—three days and nights of "sex, drugs, and rock 'n' roll" that became the metaphor for a generation.

Organized by twenty-four-year-old entrepreneur John Roberts as a money-making extravaganza, the ticket-selling system broke down when nearly half a million young people converged on the farm that Roberts had leased for the occasion. Woodstock became a free concert and for the duration of the event the third largest city in the state of New York. Braving rain, mud, heat, and shortages of food, shelter, and sanitation facilities, audiences thrilled to the music of Jefferson Airplane, Sly and the Family Stone, the Grateful Dead, the Who, Janis Joplin, Jimi Hendrix, Joe Cocker, John Sebastian, Santana, and Crosby, Stills, Nash, and Young.

Despite numerous cases of drug and alcohol overdoses, the docility of the crowd amazed the media and the police. No one reported so much as a fistfight. According to a state police lieutenant, "There hasn't been anybody yelling pig at the cops and when they ask directions they are polite and none of them has really given us any trouble yet." Indeed, for a few days, Woodstock became a community. "All those people," one participant recalled, "stoned in the mud. Maybe they'd have one biscuit, but they'd take that biscuit, break it up and give it to the person to the left of them and the person to the right. . . . The music became a sound track for that incredible rush of sharing." At the festival's conclusion, Yippie Abbie Hoffman announced "the birth of the Woodstock Nation and the death of the American dinosaur."

The mainstream media hesitated over what to make of Woodstock. Initially the *New York Times* struck a hostile note. "The dreams of marijuana and rock music," a commentator wrote, "had little more sanity than the impulses that drive lemmings to march to the sea. They ended in a nightmare of mud and stagnation." The next day, however, the *Times* editors took a more sanguine view, informing readers that "the rock festival begins to take on the quality of a social phenomenon. . . . And in spite of the prevalence of drugs it was essentially a phenomenon of innocence" where young people came "to enjoy their own society, free to exult in a lifestyle that is its own declaration of independence."

The media soon made Woodstock the symbol of the young generation. The event heralded the flowering of a cultural revolution, promising a spiritual America bursting with love and sharing, drugs and music. "The festival," reported *Time*, "turned out to be history's largest happening. As the moment when the special culture of U.S. youth of the '60s openly displayed its strength, appeal and power, it may well rank as one of the significant political and sociological events of the age."

Woodstock suggested paradise found. But less than four months later, at the Altamont Raceway near San Francisco, another massive free rock concert came to symbolize paradise lost. On December 6, the Rolling Stones offered their fans a free concert to celebrate a successful U.S. tour.[1] Hoping to recreate the beloved community of Woodstock, some 300,000 young people crammed the concert site. LSD spiked with amphetamines circulated through the crowd, causing numerous "bad trips." The stockcar raceway site was cheerless, the vibrations ominous. One Berkeley activist, high on acid, had an insight that "everyone was dead."

In return for $500 worth of beer, the Stones hired the notorious Hell's Angels motorcycle gang to guard the stage. High on bad dope, beer, and Red Mountain vin rosé, and armed with weighted pool cues sawed off to the length of billy clubs, the Angels terrorized the crowd, beating anyone whom they deemed offensive. They knocked out the teeth of a fat man dancing naked in front of the stage. Screams and violence spread through the audience. Then fights broke out. Someone threw a full beer bottle, striking a woman on the head and nearly killing her. When the Jefferson Airplane's Marty Balin tried to stop an Angel from clubbing a fan who had climbed on stage, he was knocked unconscious. Later, as Mick Jagger and the Stones performed "Sympathy for the Devil," Angels kicked and stabbed a young black man to death, an event captured on the Stones' documentary film of the concert, *Gimme Shelter*. Before the concert ended, the Angels assaulted many more; a car ran into the crowd, killing two people; and a man high on drugs fell into an irrigation ditch and drowned.

Only a few months earlier, the media praised the "Woodstock Nation"; now the headlines read, "Altamont Death Festival." Underground papers expressed the most outrage, some going so far as to call the disaster the death of the Movement. In an article written for Liberation News Service, New Left leader Todd Gitlin lamented

---

[1] Although admission to the concert was free, the Stones planned to use the occasion to make a profitable film cheaply.

"The End of the Age of Aquarius." The *Los Angeles Free Press* printed a full-page cartoon showing Jagger wearing a Hitler-like mustache and linking arms with a Hell's Angel as long-haired hippies gave them a Nazi salute. *Rolling Stone* devoted eighteen pages to the event, decrying the violence, greed, carelessness, and callousness. Altamont, according to *Rolling Stone* editor Jann Wenner, "ended certain notions about how groovy everything was, and how everything was going to take care of itself."

At the time of the ill-fated concert, the most popular movie among counterculture youth was *Easy Rider,* featuring two hippies, played by Dennis Hopper and Peter Fonda, who traverse America on a drug-enhanced motorcycle odyssey. They celebrate the free and independent life, but everywhere they go they meet the harsh realities of conformity, materialism, authority, and violence. "This used to be a helluva country," snarls their friend (Jack Nicholson). In the end the saintly hippie (Fonda) admits the youthful rebels' failure: "We blew it."

Altamont forced many Movement members to similar conclusions. Other omens too signaled trouble within the love generation. The fate of the Haight-Ashbury section of San Francisco provided one early example. From the midsixties on, this former working-class neighborhood of reasonably priced Victorian houses located just to the south of Golden Gate Park had become the center of the burgeoning Bay Area hip scene. The Human Be-In of January 1967 had brought Haight-Ashbury to national attention, and the Haight's hippie lifestyle soon became a media sensation. TV and news reporters titillated their audiences with accounts of thousands of "flower children" who shared drugs and living quarters, rang bells, danced ecstatically in the streets, and handed incense to police. The Haight gave birth to the sixties first full-blown counterculture, a world of psychedelic "head" shops, leather and bead emporia, "mod" clothing boutiques, organic and macrobiotic restaurants, and chanting Hare Krishnas. A carnival atmosphere hung over Haight Street, the Fifth Avenue of this hippie mecca. At any time of day or night, a bizarre cast of characters paraded about dressed in every imaginable costume. Long-haired, mustached young men with names like "Geronimo" or "Mud" pranced with braless, barefooted young women called "Sunshine" or "Evening Star." Strangers smiled at one another. A group called the Diggers—named after the seventeenth-century English radicals who opposed private property—distributed free food and clothing. Residents had access to a free medical clinic and a free legal-aid organization. They called the local mailman "Admiral Love."

This hippie wonderland fascinated Americans, particularly the young, who had dubbed the summer of 1967, a time of intensifying ghetto riots and war in Vietnam, the "Summer of Love." Haight-Ashbury ("Hashbury," some called it) became the destination of choice among youths. In the *East Village Other,* Walter Bowart declared the seven-hilled San Francisco to be "the Rome of a future world founded on love . . . the love-guerrilla training school for drop-outs from mainstream America." That spring, a little-known singer, Scott MacKenzie, scored a hit with his song "Are You Going to San Francisco?" which encouraged new arrivals to wear flowers in their hair. Soon thousands, then tens of thousands, of young people began flocking to the Haight. They hitchhiked, often getting rides in crowded vans adorned with psychedelic, Day-Glo art. Like Dust Bowl victims in the thirties, they migrated to the promised land of California—but with rather different goals in mind.

The Summer of Love proved the undoing of the Haight. As newcomers poured into the area, its already fragile economy and ecology began to collapse. Hippie living quarters overflowed, forcing young people into the street, where inadequate sanitation facilities and scarce food worsened matters. Plentiful but often tainted drugs subjected hapless users to "bad trips." Underage runaways wanted by law-enforcement officials hid among the crowds, prompting police to make routine sweeps of the area. The number of undercover narcotics agents working the district also increased. In the wake of the young innocents came drug addicts and pushers and a legion of thieves and psychopaths. Crime became endemic and rape a constant danger. Racial tension flared as black gangs from the nearby Filmore district, resentful of the largely white middle-class hippies pretending to be poor, rampaged through the Haight. "Love is the password in the Haight-Ashbury," observed hip reporter Hunter Thompson, "but paranoia is the style."

Under the glaring eye of the media and gawking tourists on sightseeing buses, the dream of a nonviolent city of youth turned into a nightmare. A prominent black drug dealer known as Superspade was found dead; he had been stabbed and shot, then thrust into a sleeping bag and hung from a cliff top. A sixteen-year-old girl reportedly was drugged with amphetamines and raffled off in the streets for sex. By late August, one participant in the Haight's Summer of Love recalled: "Everybody knew that the scene had gotten so big that they'd destroyed it. Too many people. Too many runaways. Drugs were getting pretty bad. Heroin was showing up. The street carnivals were crazy."

When fall came, the human tide of love children receded, leaving behind a community that never recovered. The Diggers stopped serving free food; the free clinic closed; most of the shops shut down; the more responsible citizens had fled; and the tour buses stopped coming. Drug dealers and criminals stayed behind. "Haight got fucked over by people like me," recalled one former hippie resident. "Haight-Ashbury was a nice stable Italian neighborhood before we took it over. It's a no-man's land now. You should see it. All the windows are boarded up. Nobody goes there now."

Charles Manson had lived in the Haight during its deterioration. On December 8, 1969, two days after Altamont, California police arrested Manson and other members of his obscure hippie commune for a series of murders, including the grisly killings of actress Sharon Tate and four friends. In August, the same month as Woodstock, the victims' grotesquely positioned bodies were found in Tate's Bel-Air mansion in the hills of Los Angeles; Tate had been eight months pregnant.

A neglected child, Manson had passed from juvenile delinquency to more serious crime and spent seven years in jail during the sixties for forgery. On his release in 1967, he hung around the Haight, participating in a satanic drug cult known as the Process. Long-haired and bearded, with an intense, almost demonic stare, Manson had gathered a devoted following of nine young women and five young men. In 1968 they left Haight-Ashbury to form a communal family in the mountains north of the San Fernando Valley. Like many others in the counterculture, Manson believed in free love, drugs, rock, and mysticism, but he was also psychotic. The Beatles song "Helter Skelter" convinced him that a war between the races was imminent, and he and his followers began arming themselves in anticipation. They also committed capricious, monstrous, ritualistic murders.

Although the Manson murders were the work of a deranged few, people in this highly polarized period saw larger historical significance in isolated events. For those alarmed by hippies, Charles Manson became the symbol of counterculture evil—the monster lurking beneath the facade of flowers and love. As *Rolling Stone* noted, the mass media almost gloated that "after a five-year search, [the establishment] finally found a longhaired devil you could love to hate."

The mainstream media's use of Manson to condemn the whole hippie lifestyle led some counterculture people to defend him. *Tuesday's Child,* a small Los Angeles underground newspaper, proclaimed Manson its "Man of the Year" and pictured him as a hippie on a cross. Jerry Rubin, after visiting Manson in jail, wrote: "I fell in love with Charlie Manson the first time I saw his cherub face and sparkling eyes on national TV." Such pronouncements only further discredited the "love generation."

And so as the sixties ended, millions of Americans concluded that an era had closed. The "Woodstock Nation" delusion had died on the drag strip of Altamont and in Sharon Tate's home. Yet this symbolic account of the decade's finish, though attractive to the media and much of the public, is simplistic. In retrospect, the Movement's complexity and diversity become clear, and neither Woodstock nor Altamont serves as an adequate symbol for this phenomenon. Nor did it all come unraveled in 1970. The demise of SDS and the Black Power movement at this time, however, revealed clear signs of disintegration within the Movement.

SDS and Black Power Collapse

From 1965 to 1968, SDS virtually led the New Left, playing a major role in campus protest and the national antiwar movement. By 1968 the organization boasted more than a hundred thousand members and millions more sympathizers. That year SDS served as a catalyst for campus demonstrations at Columbia and hundreds of other universities across the country. Student interest in SDS stood at an all-time high. Yet despite the appearance of strength, the organization had begun to self-destruct. The warm camaraderie that had characterized early SDS had long since given way to factionalism. From 1965 on, the free and easy New Left of Port Huron days came more to resemble the rigid and dogmatic Old Left of the thirties. Variants of Marxism and revolutionary radicalism displaced the philosophies of nonviolence and participatory democracy, just as internecine squabbling superseded consensus. SDS was about to implode.

Much of the bitter divisiveness within the organization came with the efforts of a group known as the Progressive Labor party (PL) to seize control. Founded in 1962 by youths expelled from the Communist party for ultraleftism, PL inherited the worst traits of the Old Left and few of its virtues. PL professed to follow the teachings of Chinese communist leader Mao Zedong and drew inspiration from his *Little Red Book* of quotations. Yet the group saw the industrial American working class, not Third World peasants, as the key to the overthrow of the capitalist system. In 1966 PL members gave up on organizing their own youth group and began infiltrating SDS. Like Old Left Marxists from the thirties, PL people eschewed the liberated lifestyle of the counterculture. Their puritanical asceticism and doctrinaire ideology alienated most SDS members. However, as Marxism's influence grew, the disciplined PL faction gained a degree of power within SDS.

Progressive Labor forced SDS members to become more conscious of ideology and thus further fragmented the organization. "Sitting in an SDS gathering," complained a longtime member, had become "a hellish agony." "Intellectualization and parliamentary manipulation" had replaced "a sharing of experiences and consensus decision-making." In opposition to PL's working-class analysis, some SDSers, influenced by Herbert Marcuse, looked to students, intellectuals, and younger professionals as a "new working class" to lead the revolution. Some members focused on aiding the Black Power struggle; still others began devoting their attention to the emerging women's movement. Finally, frustrated by years of mustering massive demonstrations and protests with no tangible results, some SDS people became attracted to the idea of shedding their white, middle-class guilt and waging guerrilla warfare as espoused by such international figures as Che Guevara and Ho Chi Minh.

At its June 1969 national convention, held in the cavernous Chicago Coliseum just seven years after the *Port Huron Statement,* SDS fell apart. Various contingents contested for control, among them anarchistic and Marxist groups, all claiming to hold the true ideology. The organization splintered into hostile factions, the best known of which was called the Weatherman. Although individual campus chapters of SDS would continue to flourish and squabbling sects would persist in tussling over the skeleton of the national organization, the withdrawal of the Weatherman in effect signaled the end of the largest organization of the sixties New Left.

The Weatherman, named after a line from Bob Dylan's "Subterranean Homesick Blues" ("You don't need a weatherman to know which way the wind blows"), continued to function as a small revolutionary fighting force of white youth. In their analysis, the United States was an imperialist "worldwide monster" beyond hope of redemption. Third World guerrillas and an "internal black colony" within the United States, as they saw it, had already set in motion the struggle against the American empire. The Weatherman's job was to form alliances with groups like the Black Panthers and a militant, Chicago-based Chicano group, the Young Lords. They also hoped that by demonstrating their bravery as outlaw guerrillas within urban America they would enlist younger working-class whites in the revolution. Their goal was to create a "mass revolutionary movement" that would "bring the war home to Amerika."

On the night of October 8, 1969, the Weatherman launched what they called the "Days of Rage" in Mayor Daley's Chicago. Armed with helmets, baseball bats, and arrogance, they set out to "tear pig city apart." They smashed some windows on Chicago's Loop, but Daley's cops soon overwhelmed them, arresting more than three hundred. The remaining Weatherman members went underground. They claimed credit for blowing up some buildings and for freeing Timothy Leary from a minimum-security prison in California, where he had been jailed for possession of marijuana. On March 6, 1970, an explosion in a Greenwich Village townhouse used as a Weatherman bomb factory killed three revolutionaries. Although the group perpetrated a few acts of guerrilla violence after this fiasco, the New York explosion marked the end of the Port Huron dream.

Like white protest, black militancy also subsided during this period. Neither SNCC nor CORE survived the sixties. Both organizations lost liberal, white financial support when they adopted the Black Power slogan and came out against the Vietnam War in the midsixties. Plagued by declining memberships, loss of revenues, internal dissension, and external repression, the two groups quietly expired. By the late sixties, the Black Panthers had become the most visible militant African-American organization, but they too suffered from internal quarreling. One faction, led by Eldridge Cleaver, broke with

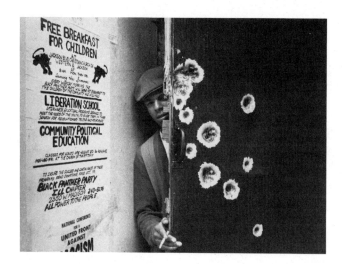

Annihilating the Black Panthers. Chicago, 1969: An unidentified Black Panther peeks around a bullet-pocked door, which police blasted with gunfire during a predawn raid.

Huey Newton and the main Panther group. In November 1968, Cleaver fled into exile to avoid a jail sentence and the wrath of his Panther opponents. More than any other radical group of the sixties, the Black Panthers fell victim to violent government repression. Although the Panthers sustained a number of community programs aimed to help black ghetto youth, their paramilitary style and ''self-defense groups'' alarmed most white Americans.

When Richard Nixon took office in January 1969, he stepped up FBI surveillance and encouraged government agents to infiltrate Panther ranks. Informers and agents provocateur working undercover penetrated the organization, providing detailed intelligence and instigating confrontations in order to legitimize police violence. In 1969 alone, the FBI and local police killed twenty-eight Panthers; hundreds of others were imprisoned. On the morning of December 4, 1969, two days before the violence at Altamont, police working in cooperation with the FBI broke into a Chicago apartment and murdered Illinois Panther chairman Fred Hampton and his associate Mark Clark. Hampton died in his bed. Although the police claimed that the Panthers had started the shootout, subsequent investigations revealed that at most the Panthers had fired two shots while the police had riddled the apartment with hundreds of bullets. By 1970, deaths, imprisonments, and exile had virtually annihilated the Panther organization.

Backlash: The War Against the Left

The destruction of the Panthers provided the most blatant example of government repression, but every dissident group endured official harassment. Nor was the Nixon administration alone in its desire to squelch dissent. Federal repression was replicated on the state level. By the late sixties, most state police forces had so-called Red Squads—secret units that investigated supposed subversives. Like their federal counterparts, the Red Squads compiled dossiers, infiltrated New Left organizations, planted bugging devices, disseminated misinformation, and in other ways tried to disrupt the

Movement. State and local police forces in turn cooperated with federal agents in crackdowns against dissidents.

Violent repression also manifested itself on the state level. One of the worst instances occurred in Berkeley in the spring of 1969. After the Free Speech Movement, Berkeley had maintained its position in the vanguard of the New Left and counterculture. The community had a major underground newspaper, the *Barb;* a nonprofit, left-wing radio station, KPFA; a Free Clinic; a Free Church; a free university and free schools; collectives of architects, doctors, film makers, lawyers, and mechanics; various communes; and numerous active political groups. Most students identified with the Movement; fraternity and sorority memberships dwindled.

The center of Berkeley's hip life lay along Telegraph Avenue just south of the main campus. Here a bustling world thrived—a cornucopia of sidewalk cafés, art cinemas, a repertory theater, book stores, "head" shops, boutiques, craft shops, and bulletin boards plastered with broadsides. Hippies, radicals, students, professors, runaways, and dropouts thronged the avenue.

Alarmed by the growth of this radical community, the university in 1967 exercised its right of eminent domain to buy a three-acre residential area just off Telegraph. A year later the university ousted the area's student and hippie residents and demolished its houses. Seeing no immediate use for the land, the Berkeley administration allowed it to become a makeshift parking lot and an eyesore of old foundations, trash, weeds, and mud.

On April 13, 1969, local activists met to discuss the site. Mike Delacour, proprietor of the Red Square dress shop, proposed that the community build a park. Five days later, an anonymous story appeared in the *Barb* under the name "Robin Hood's Park Commissioner," calling for a public gathering on Sunday, April 20, to begin transforming the muddy ruins. "The University," Berkeley's Robin proclaimed, "has no right to create ugliness as a way of life." The *Barb* had a circulation of nearly 100,000, and the article reached a wide audience. That Sunday, hundreds of people showed up wielding hoes, picks, and shovels. One person brought a tractor, which volunteers used to remove old foundations and grade the land. With money donated by local merchants, the park builders purchased and carted in a truckload of sod and plants.

The scheme generated lively enthusiasm. For some the ecological benefit—creating a site with grass and flowers amid the urban blight—mattered most. Others saw the park as a place for community gatherings and concerts. Over the next weeks, several thousand people joined in the project, among them hippies, housewives, professors, students, and older neighborhood residents. Despite the lack of an overall plan and occasional disputes, work progressed smoothly. People laid sod and planted trees, shrubs, flowers, and vegetables. They built a wading pool and a sandbox and installed swings and slides. Volunteers cooked huge communal meals. One radical activist eulogized the park "as substance and sign of a possible participatory order, as the living proof that necessary institutions need not be overplanned, absentee-owned, hierarchical—as such the Park came to stand in many minds as one tantalizing trace of a good society." On Sunday, May 11, the Reverend Richard York of the Free Church officially consecrated the "People's Park."

University officials brooded about how to stop the project. At first Berkeley chancellor Roger Heyns stalled, hoping that some sort of compromise would avert a showdown. However, under strong pressure from conservative governor Ronald Reagan and the university regents, Heyns on May 15 authorized the closing of the park. Before dawn, police cordoned off an eight-block area while work crews bulldozed the grounds and erected an eight-foot fence around the area.

At 10:00 A.M. Chancellor Heyns rejected a last-ditch appeal from faculty members of the College of Environmental Design to declare the site an experimental field station. By noon, several thousand irate people gathered for a rally in front of Sproul Hall. Speakers denounced the university's actions, and soon with shouts of "Take the park!" the crowd surged down Telegraph Avenue, where they were met with a barrage of police tear-gas canisters. Next a special unit of Alameda County sheriff's deputies showed up and stunned even the most battle-hardened protest veterans when they raised shotguns and fired into the crowd. As people fled, the deputies kept shooting, wounding 110 people, including reporters and bystanders. No one fired at the police. An artist named Alan Blanchard was permanently blinded. A load of buckshot ripped open spectator James Rector's stomach as he watched the riots from a nearby rooftop. He died in hospital.

Governor Reagan declared martial law and dispatched three thousand rifle-toting national guardsmen to keep order. During the next week, police arrested more than a thousand people. On May 20 guardsmen blocked access routes to and from the campus while a helicopter sprayed a peaceful crowd of demonstrators with tear gas. As the gas blanketed the campus, people scattered, screamed, and vomited. The chemical even afflicted patients in the university hospital.

Ten days later on Memorial Day, an estimated thirty to fifty thousand people staged a peaceful march to the park, where the National Guard defended the fence. Quakers distributed thousands of daisies, which marchers passed out to guardsmen and even placed in their rifle barrels. Many participants carried green flags made from old Girl Scout uniforms. "The green flag," predicted one of the demonstrators, symbolized "new indelible connections in the mind which will re-color popular protest in every country in the world, from this time on." There was no violence that day. When the march ended, the fence remained standing. To this date, the university has made no use of the vacant land.

In Berkeley even conservatives expressed outrage at the police savagery and the occupation of the community. Nationally, however, the establishment media and much of the public applauded the actions of Governor Reagan and the forces of law and order. The battle of Berkeley and the fall of People's Park laid bare the growing antiradical, antihippie reaction.

After the bloodshed at Berkeley, students nationwide stepped up their radicalism and their opposition to Vietnam. By the fall of 1969, a Gallup poll reported that 69 percent of them called themselves doves; the figure had doubled since the spring of 1967. Demonstrations, mostly against the war, cropped up on hundreds of campuses; more than seven hundred of them drew police reprisals and arrests. On April 8, 1970, Ronald Reagan gave the young people an ultimatum: "If it takes a bloodbath, let's get it over with. No more appeasement."

On April 30, Richard Nixon announced what he termed the American incursion into Cambodia. In his televised speech, the president warned: "We live in an age of anarchy both abroad and at home. We see mindless attacks on . . . great universities and small nations. . . . If, when the chips are down, the world's most powerful nation, the United States of America, acts like a pitiful, helpless giant, the forces of totalitarianism and anarchy will threaten free nations and free institutions around the world."

Kent State Killings. Holding her head in anguish, a coed reacts with horror upon seeing the body of a student who was shot and killed by national guardsmen during an antiwar rally at Kent State University, May 4, 1970.

Depicting the war as a test of the nation's "will and character," he concluded: "We will not be humbled. We will not be defeated."

Somehow the war in Vietnam and its extension into Cambodia had become linked in Nixon's mind with campus unrest as a challenge to American credibility. Even Nixon's chief foreign-policy adviser, Henry Kissinger, later deemed the president's speech delusionary. The following day Nixon ranted about "these bums . . . blowing up the campuses" and told his staff: "Don't worry about divisiveness. Having drawn the sword . . . stick it in hard."

Nixon had guessed rightly that his invasion of Cambodia would exacerbate tensions at home. Millions of Americans nationwide protested the president's action, as did the *New York Times, Wall Street Journal, Washington Post,* and numerous other respected papers. On college campuses, the invasion of Cambodia touched off a wave of antiwar demonstrations. At Kent State, a university in northern Ohio, a series of student protests, including the burning of the ROTC building, led Governor James Rhodes to call out the National Guard and declare martial law. In words reminiscent of Nixon, Agnew, and Reagan, Rhodes denounced the demonstrators as "worse than the brown shirts and the Communist elements." Calling them "the worst type of people we harbor in America," he pledged "to eradicate the problem." In the early afternoon of May 4, as demonstrators held a peaceful rally, national guardsmen opened fire, killing four students and wounding nine. Two of the dead had been walking to class at the time. Nixon told Americans that the Kent State massacre "should remind us all . . . that when dissent turns to violence it invites tragedy." Vice President Agnew dismissed the deaths as "predictable and avoidable" given the "traitors and thieves and perverts . . . in our midst." Ten days later, at historically black Jackson State in Mississippi, police fired into a student gathering, killing two. The war had come home.

That May, student-led demonstrations and strikes broke out at nearly 60 percent of the nation's twenty-five hundred colleges, from elite public and private schools to church-affiliated colleges, and at numerous high schools. Even students at Nixon's alma mater, Whittier College, went on strike. Protesters bombed or burned ROTC buildings at Idaho, Utah, and some thirty other schools. Police wounded a dozen demonstrators at the State University of New York at Buffalo and bayoneted ten at the University of New Mexico. On May 9, more than a hundred thousand marchers converged on Washington; police arrested about ten thousand of them. Similar mass demonstrations took place in London, Paris, and Berlin. A Harris poll that May revealed that more than three-fourths of a national sample of students believed that the system needed "basic changes." Many universities closed down completely that spring. Others adopted the "Princeton Plan," giving students a two-week leave in the fall to work in the 1970 congressional campaigns.

Antiwar activists and liberals condemned the Kent State and Jackson State shootings and other manifestations of repressive violence. In New York City, Mayor John Lindsay denounced the Nixon administration for driving the country to "the edge of spiritual—and perhaps even a physical—breakdown." Yet a majority of Americans continued to support Nixon's view that student demonstrators deserved brutal treatment. On May 8, encouraged by the White House, some two hundred hard-hatted construction workers shouting, "Kill the Commie bastards!" brutally attacked an antiwar rally near Wall Street as police looked on. Nixon sent a secret message of solidarity to the workers and a few days later met with "loyal" union leaders and publicly accepted a hard hat inscribed "Commander-in-Chief." In *Joe,* a popular Hollywood movie that summer, the protagonist, a resentful, blue-collar worker, conspires with an upper-middle-class executive to take revenge on Movement members. In a murderous rage, they kill young hippies, even accidentally the wealthy man's daughter.

An Ohio jury acquitted the National Guard of all charges stemming from the Kent State slayings. A decade that had opened on a note of exhilaration and optimistic idealism ended in bloodshed and hate.

Co-opting the Counterculture

Violence and repression were not the only ways in which old and new cultures interacted. Offsetting the tension, television made the conflict of cultures humorous. Early in 1971, Norman Lear's weekly comedy series "All in the Family" debuted and scored an instant hit. Archie Bunker, the family patriarch, typified the stereotypical working-class bigot with values rooted in the past. He disliked liberals, blacks, modern women, gays, hippies, protesters—the entire new culture. His daughter Gloria and her husband, Michael (whom Archie referred to as "Meathead"), personified the liberated new society. Archie's wife, Edith, stood caught between her husband and children: loyal to Archie, she nevertheless favored more liberal trends. Amazingly, the show appealed to Americans of all stripes. Liberals and counterculture types saw it for what Lear intended—a satire on social prejudice—while millions of other Americans readily identified with Archie. One railroad worker told a *Life* reporter: "You think it, but ole Archie he *says* it, by damn." "All in the Family" exposed the issue of social prejudice, but because the characters seldom changed their basic positions from week to week, the problem never reached resolution.

In the early seventies, however, America's Archie/Meathead war deescalated as mainstream society gradually co-opted the new ways. In part, the direct influence of the dissenters prompted this adaptation. More important, postwar prosperity encouraged a leisurely, self-indulgent lifestyle. The traditional Protestant ethic of hard work and thrift no longer served the needs of corporate America, and advertisers, as much as the liberated young, encouraged excess. Although this trend would undermine the uniqueness of the counterculture, it also prodded the larger society in a pleasure-oriented, pluralistic, and tolerant direction. In midcentury American advertising had been a bulwark of conformity, but by the late sixties and early seventies, many major firms, staffed by young, creative people, embraced the youth culture. The "Pepsi Generation" emerged with beards, beads, and peace symbols; Dodge touted a "Revolution"; cigarette ads featured counterculture couples on motorcycles. Advertisers nationwide suddenly strove to identify their products with youth.

In the late sixties, obvious visual signs had revealed the conflict of cultures. One could judge a person's politics and values fairly accurately by such superficial evidence as hair length and dress. By the early seventies, however, physical trademarks of the counterculture began to spread into the surrounding society. Hair provides one example. Long hair for both young men and women, as well as beards, had served as a badge of radical politics and the counterculture lifestyle. But because American society puts a premium on youthfulness and advertisers increasingly featured the young, adults came to emulate them. Middle-aged business executives let their hair grow over their ears and sported sideburns and mustaches. Even Lyndon Johnson in retirement grew his graying mane nearly to his shoulders. Increasingly, hair length became more a matter of style than politics.

Clothing followed a similar pattern. Hippie garb, like hairstyles, had consciously evolved as a societal criticism. Blue jeans, army-surplus wear, tie-dyed T-shirts, beads and bangles, long or short dresses and skirts—almost any costume sufficed. Cheap, colorful, and functional counterculture clothes made a statement. But they also lent themselves to easy copying by the fashion industry. In the seventies, styles that had originated as odd outfits thrown together by youthful rebels scrounging through attics and surplus stores now showed up in expensive boutiques. Inexpensive, all-purpose hippie blue jeans transformed into suburbanites' costly designer jeans. Visual distinctions between old and new cultures still existed, but fashion changes blurred the sharp edges and dulled the confrontation between the two.

Mainstream society even assimilated elements at the heart of the counterculture: drugs, rock, liberated sex, and the underground media. Drug use, once the most shocking aspect of counterculture life to traditional Americans, changed in two ways. First, the promised nirvana through chemistry preached by sixties drug prophets never materialized. Timothy Leary and Ken Kesey both spent time in jail and in exile. "Acid" turned out to have negative long-term effects, occasionally even permanent brain damage. Too many bad trips and muddled minds had dimmed the naive notion that a drug like LSD would usher in the millennium, and by the early seventies, acid use had declined markedly.

Second, at the same time that LSD lost favor, marijuana smoking spread from the counterculture to more affluent, educated segments of adult society as well as to younger members of the working class. These groups, too, had begun to emphasize pleasure over self-restraint. Millions of Americans, including President Nixon, persisted in labeling any use of illegal drugs as immoral, yet the widespread acceptance of marijuana, combined with the decline of LSD, moderated drugs' frightening image and bridged the culture gap. In more recent times, drugs such as cocaine, "crack" cocaine, and heroin have become serious problems. But despite conservative claims to the contrary, current drug use did not spring directly from the sixties counterculture. Drugs today are neither the exclusive preserve of alienated youth nor are they widely touted as holding the key to a higher perception.

Mainstream America found rock music one of the easiest aspects of the new culture to absorb and commercialize. From the invasion of the Beatles in 1964 through the Woodstock Festival of 1969, young people had perceived rock as much more than music. Hostile adult reactions convinced rebels that rock was a major weapon in their antiestablishment arsenal. The underground media, and rock musicians who invariably presented themselves as agents for change, only encouraged this belief. Indeed, many important rock groups of the sixties grew directly from the hippie subculture and dedicated their efforts to its precepts. Their music promised political and cultural liberation and proffered community, love, and revolution.

But like drugs, rock failed to transform society. Some stars—Janis Joplin, Jimi Hendrix, and Jim Morrison—died of drugs and alcohol. More typically, however, rock idols capitulated to commercialism. Although most of them viewed themselves as radical leaders of cultural change, they succumbed to the lure of wealth and fame. Rock became more and more a business. As one example, in a typical six-week U.S. tour, the Rolling Stones earned millions. Even Woodstock, the ultimate expression of rock as community, had a major commercial purpose. Although the concert itself became free out of necessity, the promoters made a handsome profit through producing a documentary film and records based on the festival. As rock grew more business-oriented, its popularity soared, but it lost its power to make a political statement. By the early seventies, one could hear most forms of rock at suburban parties and on commercial radio. By then, few people on either the Right or Left regarded the music as a revolutionary force. Rock finally came to be recognized for what it always had been—a form of popular entertainment.

The liberalized sexual mores preached and practiced by the counterculture also spread through the population, again especially among the more affluent and educated. Traditionalists still complained of declining moral standards, but most Americans paid little heed. During the sixties, sex increasingly saturated American culture. As early as 1960, federal courts judged D. H. Lawrence's *Lady Chatterley's Lover* not obscene, and soon publishers dared to print other long-banned books. By the end of the decade, pornography had virtually disappeared as a legal concept.

The new sexual freedom became big business. In 1968 the movie industry adopted a code to separate family movies (rated G) from sexually revealing films (rated R) and sexually explicit films (rated X). Adult audiences could watch anything from a sophisticated comedy about wife swapping, *Bob and Carol and Ted and Alice* (R), to *Deep Throat* (X), a graphic depiction of oral sex. Sexual liberation in live theater also increased. The nude dancing in *Hair* was soon surpassed by plays such as *Oh! Calcutta* and *Che* that broke some of the last theatrical taboos by simulating sexual acts on stage.

Nightclubs began featuring topless waitresses and dancers; even topless shoeshine parlors emerged. Magazines such as *Playboy* and *Penthouse* grew more blatantly sexual—and more popular. These publications in turn now competed with more hardcore, often explicitly antiwoman magazines such as *Screw, Suck, Gay,* and *Hustler.*

By the early 1970s, the new promiscuity was by no means limited to the rebellious young. Casual premarital, extramarital, and gay sex became more commonplace and more publicly accepted than ever. Moralists' efforts to restore puritanical standards persisted after 1970 and would play an important role in the conservative political revival, but the battle over sexual standards would no longer divide exclusively along generational lines.

The final mainstay of the sixties counterculture, the underground media, also lost its distinctive role as the voice of dissenting youth during the seventies. From the outset, a lack of capital had hampered virtually all undergrounds. Newspapers, film companies, radio stations, and theater troupes all scrounged to survive, and even at the height of the Movement in the late sixties, many of them failed for lack of funds. The Movement's fragmentation also weakened the underground media. As blacks split off from whites, women from men, gays from straights, and as these groups in turn splintered, they created new, narrow media to support their particular causes. These divisions only intensified economic pressures. Some underground publications and radio stations managed to survive by paying low wages and accepting advertising only from counterculture businesses. Still, the mortality rate was high, and going ''commercial'' proved all too tempting.

Rolling Stone provides an apt example. Founded in 1967 by Jann Wenner with $7,500 of borrowed money, *Stone* by 1970 boasted a circulation of over 250,000 and lucrative advertising contracts with national record companies. As the magazine gained popularity, it toned down its radical image. ''Rock-and-roll is now the energy core of change in American life,'' Wenner explained to a *Time* reporter in 1969. ''Capitalism is what gives us the incredible indulgence of this music.'' For *Rolling Stone,* youth culture had become a marketable commodity to be packaged for pecuniary gain. Similarly, Stewart Brand's *Whole Earth Catalog,* the bible of those seeking an alternative to materialistic America, was snapped up by Random House. It became a best-seller and even won the prestigious National Book Award in 1972.

Some underground papers survived into the seventies by accepting sex ads. The *Los Angeles Free Press,* the *Berkeley Barb,* and the *East Village Other* all suffered this fate, running classified ads such as this one from the *Barb:* ''Get laid! $5 tells you where . . .'' Although these papers initially justified the ads as part of the counterculture's libertarian attitude toward sex, they increasingly served the commercial sex industry and catered to an adult audience titillated by hippie sexuality.

Alternative viewpoints had a voice in the years after 1970 but never again on the broad scale of the late sixties. Drugs, music, sexual openness, and the underground media all endured into the new decade but not as part of a unique oppositional culture. The assimilative powers of the dominant culture had triumphed, though that culture also changed in the process. Indeed, by 1979 historian Christopher Lasch would describe middle-class life as the ''culture of narcissism.'' In values, morals, and outlook, the younger generation and mainstream America came to resemble one another more than ever.

Communes. Spurning modern technology and the traditional nuclear family, thousands of young Americans attempted to create ideal communal societies. Here, members of the New Buffalo commune make adobe bricks.

The Movement Ebbs

Aside from repression and co-optation, sheer exhaustion also undermined the youth rebellion in the early seventies. Dissenters had tried to use nonviolence to stop the war in Vietnam, racial injustice, and other perceived evils. For many, hopes of working through the political system died with Robert Kennedy and the election of Richard Nixon in 1968. In desperation, the Movement's radical fringe had turned to violence. Their tactics failed and served only to undermine the moral authority of the protesters. Students in the early seventies still deplored the war in Vietnam, and major antiwar mobilizations continued. But with little media coverage and no effective national organization to focus the Movement and maintain continuity, campus protest quietly subsided.

The counterculture lingered longer. Communes and counterinstitutions proliferated in the early seventies as hippies removed themselves from urban America to rural outposts: Cape Breton Island in Nova Scotia; Washington County in Maine; the mountains around Frazer, Colorado; Taos County in New Mexico; and Santa Cruz, Sonoma, and Modoc counties in California. An austere socialistic life based on organic farming and crafts provided an escape from the nine-to-five job, just as communal living created a sexual alternative to the nuclear family. Getting back to the land had strong romantic appeal but proved difficult to sustain over time, and communes collapsed like children's blocks. Those surviving the longest typically had strong religious commitments and charismatic leaders. Although the thousands of communes provided a lifestyle alternative and encouraged environmental awareness, their overall impact on the larger society remained limited.

The New Left's inability to develop a widely accepted alternative ideology beyond liberalism on the Right and Marxism on the Left also spurred its collapse. With its patriotic air and radical ring, along with its appealing ambiguity, participatory democracy as advocated in the *Port Huron Statement* came closest to providing an ideological basis for a uniquely American New Left. Yet it contained seeds of future trouble. To some, the idea implied getting citizens involved in a system of representative democracy. In a more radical view, expressed by early SDS tactician Richard Flacks, it "meant an exciting transformation of the meaning of socialism . . . [and] extending principles of democracy from the political sphere into other institutions, like industry, like the university." In practice, participatory democracy came to entail rule by consensus. As long as SDS and other New Left organizations remained small groups of like-minded friends, face-to-face decisionmaking worked well. But the method's inherent distrust of leadership and structure made creating an effective national political organization virtually impossible. Moreover, with the rapid expansion of membership in New Left organizations following the midsixties escalation of the Vietnam War, consensus invariably gave way to conflict.

By the late sixties, many New Leftists had reverted to traditional Marxist analysis in place of participatory democracy. According to the Progressive Labor party, the working class would provide the lever for revolutionary change. Yet the Movement failed to win significant support from workers. As it turned out, American unions in the postwar era believed in harmony between business and labor. Of course, many younger workers did drop out and join the Movement, and a worker-published underground newspaper, the *Stranded Oiler,* even appeared at Standard Oil. But workers' most serious concerns—wages, inflation, line speed-ups, work boredom, job insecurity, and occupational dangers—seldom turned them into revolutionaries. On the contrary, many blue-collar employees vilified the politics and lifestyles of the middle-class rebels. Like the New York construction workers, innumerable workers believed the government's claim that America had gone to Vietnam to stop communist aggression. Even laborers who harbored doubts about the war often viewed antiwar protesters as unpatriotic.

The winding down of the Vietnam conflict also weakened the Movement. Lyndon Johnson's 1965–1968 escalation of the war had turned the nascent New Left into a mass crusade. But because the Movement lacked an agreed-upon ideology, opposition to the war became the most important issue uniting the New Left. With Nixon's troop reductions and talk of Vietnamization, as well as diminished TV coverage, the urgency of the issue subsided. Fewer troops in action let the administration reduce draft quotas. The government also introduced a lottery system for selecting draftees. Instead of allowing college students automatic deferments, the Selective Service now conducted recruitment by lot. The reduced number of inductees and fairer selection process moderated the draft's power to radicalize. In 1973 American involvement in the war and the draft ended, removing the New Left's major unifying cause.

Nixon also inadvertently defused the New Left by pursuing détente with China and the Soviet Union. From the time of the *Port Huron Statement* through the sixties, the New Left had attacked America's oversimplified Cold War stereotypes. Unlike most other Americans, the radicals did not view communism as evil per se, nor did they judge communism a monolithic force controlled and directed by Moscow and bent on world domination. By the midsixties, many establishment liberals had come to similar conclusions. But ironically, it was Nixon, the longtime, hard-line Cold Warrior, who acted on these New Left perceptions. With his rapprochement with China and improved relations with the Soviet Union (see Chapter 9), Cold War tensions eased. The conflict endured, but détente, combined with the gradual withdrawal of U.S. forces from Vietnam, deprived dissenters of a reason to attack the government's foreign policy.

The Sino-American accord particularly stunned many within the New Left. During the sixties, as young radicals grew increasingly disenchanted with the United States, they had idealized Mao's China and believed it would lead a world revolution of op-pressed peoples. American New Leftists had thrilled at the student-led Chinese Cultural Revolution of the late sixties, which they erroneously saw as analogous to their own rebellion. Via communications satellite in late February 1972, an astonished world watched pictures of Chinese Chairman Mao Zedong and Premier Zhou En-lai drinking a toast to Richard Nixon. To appalled American radicals, it now appeared as if the Chinese hope had been an illusion all along. To some, this ''sellout'' dashed their revolutionary dreams.

Economic developments hammered the last nail into the coffin of the New Left and counterculture. In part the Movement represented a revolt against the materialism of mainstream society. Yet the sheer existence and even the values of the youth culture depended on affluence. The counterculture's concentration on pleasure and self-ful-fillment could occur only in a society of abundance. Indeed, the alternative lifestyles attracted large numbers of prosperous adults, and corporate advertisers encouraged these hedonistic values. Most participants in the youth culture had grown up in comfort-able middle-class homes. They had difficulty comprehending their parents' obsession with economic security and material possessions. Going off to live in voluntary poverty in New York City's East Village or the hills of Vermont gave them a way to flout parental values, but they could always fall back on wealth. Not a few college students dropped out and joined the new culture for a time, only to return to school, graduate, and take a well-paying mainstream job. A prosperous and expanding economy made this choice possible.

But by the time Nixon took office, the economy had begun to slip, and war-related inflation had struck. Interest rates and unemployment rose; the stock market fell. By the end of 1970, the Gross National Product declined for the first time since 1938. The United States had plunged into a recession, and yet, to the astonishment of economists and politicians alike, inflation remained high. OPEC's 1973 price hikes delivered the final blow. The economic downturn made the hippie ethic, with its presupposition of limitless abundance, less tenable. Furthermore, unemployment hit hardest among young adults looking for their first full-time jobs. Increasingly, college graduates hoping for professional positions in teaching, science, or engineering found scarce opportunities. Understandably, many of them turned their focus to grades and careers.

The Movement had rested on hope and utopian visions. During the early seventies, this vision shrank. Possibilities that once looked limitless came to have boundaries. People drew inward, and for many of them, personal introspection replaced social com-mitment. By the time Richard Nixon resigned from the presidency in August of 1974, only remnants of the great youth rebellion remained.

Legacies

''Are the vulgar narcissism of the seventies and a few new wrinkles in men's fashion all that the Movement accomplished?'' asked historian Joseph Conlin. ''Pretty much so,'' he concluded. ''In terms of real social change, its consequences were nil.'' The brevity and uniqueness of the youth upheaval led many observers to dismiss it as an aberrant era of little lasting significance. To conservative William Buckley, the sixties were ''the crazy years''—superficial and violent, even silly. Even some radicals came to regard the Movement as an interlude. Today's nostalgists see the sixties as drugs, rock, sex, and outlandish costumes—a quaint "lifestyle" suitable for theme parties. These views deny the long-range significance of the period.

Active participants in the New Left and counterculture never ranked in the majority, even among college students. Yet this "prophetic minority" raised issues that often mirrored mass attitudes or spoke to mass frustrations. The Movement faded and the old culture reasserted itself, but the sixties upheaval has survived as more than a memory. Even today it continues to influence American society and culture. In rebelling against elitism, militarism, racism, sexism, technocracy, bureaucracy, paternalism, and the dehumanization of life, the counterculture pointed the way to new priorities, forcing Americans to recognize social injustice and highlighting the emptiness of material progress as a goal. Although the dominant culture's values did not disappear, the Movement created alternative values that would persist. In this sense, the sixties added new, permanent choices to people's stock of options. In the years since the decade of upheaval, many Americans have continued to question competition, the work ethic, racism, the feminine mystique, and whether unlimited growth is "progress." Numerous people have also retained liberated social and sexual mores. Although the sexual revolution has subsided somewhat, largely because of AIDS, Americans have not returned to the repressive, puritanical standards of the fifties. Casual and unconventional lifestyles have remained alternatives, and the push for self-fulfillment is still alive.

Like the pre–Civil War abolitionist crusade that forced the nation to confront the issue of slavery, the civil-rights focus of the Movement sharpened Americans' awareness of racial issues and inaugurated the irreversible entry of African-Americans and other nonwhites into the mainstream. Beginning in 1955 in Montgomery, with blacks asking only for decent treatment on buses, a decade of activism led to demands for full equality. At great personal sacrifice and against formidable odds, blacks and whites changed the nation's consciousness and destroyed the century-old system of segregation and disfranchisement of African-Americans. There have been backlashes. Racism still mars America's democratic ideals, and nonwhite urban ghettoes persist. Nevertheless, the sixties reinstigated the long-delayed drive for racial equality.

The antiwar movement, too, had major impact. Although it antagonized and alienated many people, it also brought to the forefront for millions of Americans the immoral and senseless nature of U.S. involvement in Vietnam. Undoubtedly, the movement shortened the war and encouraged the United States to reflect before shipping troops abroad at every perceived provocation. The antiwar movement also served to weaken the Cold War consensus that had dominated American thinking since the late 1940s. The New Left's assaults on Cold War attitudes contributed to a reassessment of America's world role, stabilization of relations with the Soviet Union and China, and the ultimate end of the Cold War itself.

The Movement left a legacy of skepticism about those in authority. In institution after institution, those in power have been pressured to answer to their associates and to the public. In politics, business, labor unions, universities, and churches, decisionmaking is more democratic today than before the sixties revolution. In addition, by forcing people to choose sides, that decade made many individuals aware of their values and beliefs. Even the tactic of direct action would continue as a way of expressing grievances.

The sixties upheavals particularly influenced America's university system. After the Free Speech Movement and subsequent university protests, students gained more freedom and some voice in academic governance. No longer do universities play the role of *in loco parentis* for their students. Regulations concerning such issues as dormitory visiting hours and dress codes have been dropped and the number of required courses reduced. At many colleges, compulsory military training programs have been eliminated. Universities also have grown wary of accepting government contracts for weapons research.

In the long run, the most significant campus changes involved college curricula. Traditionally focused on the great, white, male thinkers of Western civilization, most universities have revamped their general education classes. Under pressure, universities have broadened curricula to include a range of minority voices and have increased the number of courses in non-Western studies. Most larger universities have added majors in African-American and women's studies. Within the humanities and social sciences, professors in both their teaching and scholarly research show a new concern for race, gender, class, and ethnicity. Historians have shifted their concentration from political and cultural elites to the social and often private experiences of ordinary citizens. In English departments, younger scholars have added hitherto neglected writings of women and minorities to the literary canon. Feminist and Marxist theories have become common analytical tools. Naturally, traditionalists have denounced this refocusing, arguing that it undermines high culture and its values. Such critics claim that today's universities offer students little more than a superficial smorgasbord of courses lacking depth and focus. But whatever merit exists in such criticisms, clearly there will be no reverting to the elitist white male perspective that reigned unchallenged before the sixties.

In society generally, the sixties forced Americans to recognize the United States for what it truly is: a pluralistic, heterogeneous society. The decade shattered the long-dominant melting-pot image of America as a consensual, homogeneous, middle-class society with white, Anglo-Saxon, Protestant values as the only norm. First African-Americans and then various ethnic groups and other minorities developed a strong sense of their own cultural identities. Many have continued to emphasize their group solidarity and to demand their rights.

Hispanic Americans have taken a new pride in their heritage and have struggled to gain a place for themselves. In the sixties, Cesar Chávez attracted nationwide attention to the plight of Mexican-American migrant workers in California by organizing the United Farm Workers (UFW) union. An admirer of Martin Luther King, Jr., and the black civil-rights movement, Chávez drew strength from his Roman Catholic faith. Through a series of strikes, marches, fasts, and well-publicized boycotts of grapes and lettuce, Chávez created a massive labor and civil-rights movement that ultimately forced California's powerful agricultural conglomerates to recognize the UFW.

Chávez's success gave dignity and hope not only to farmworkers but to all Mexican Americans. In the late sixties, young Mexican-American activists insisted on being called *Chicanos* as a term of respect. They pressured schools to adopt bilingual and bicultural education in predominantly Mexican-American schools, and they succeeded in getting Chicano-studies programs established in a number of universities. In New Mexico, Reies Lopez Tijerina led the Alianza, a nationalist movement demanding the return of lands historically belonging to Mexicans. In Texas, Colorado, and California, Mexican Americans established an independent political party, La Raza Unida. More militant young Chicanos in California organized the Brown Berets, modeled on the Black Panthers, and embarked on a search for "Chicano Power." In Chicago, the Young Lords formed a similar militant organization.

In the seventies, immigration and a high birthrate made Hispanics the fastest-growing minority in America. Between 1970 and 1980, the number of Spanish-speaking people officially living in the United States increased from nine million to more than twenty million. In addition, several million illegal aliens made Hispanics the nation's second-largest minority group behind blacks. However, the potential political power of Hispanics was weakened by the language barrier, the lack of citizenship for illegal immigrants, and the diversity of Spanish-speaking people. But in areas of the country with heavy concentrations of Hispanics, they have gained some access to power. In California and the Southwest, Mexican Americans eventually won a federal mandate for bilingual education. On the East Coast, millions of Puerto Ricans in New York and Cubans and other Latin American refugees in Florida have won rights and some cultural autonomy. Yet cut off from the dominant society by language and culture, Hispanics have faced hard obstacles in their drive for equality. Poverty, ghetto housing, and menial jobs continue to plague this group. But like African-Americans before them, Spanish-speaking Americans have taken new interest in their heritages. "We have been trying to become American for too long," proclaimed a New York Puerto Rican woman, "and we are forgetting our roots, culture, and values of our nationality."

Native Americans, too, began to recall and respect their past. Popular books such as Vine DeLoria, Jr.'s *Custer Died for Your Sins* (1970) and Dee Brown's *Bury My Heart at Wounded Knee* (1970) retold American history from an Indian perspective. During the fifties, the Eisenhower administration had sought to end Indian tribal affiliations and to assimilate Native Americans into the urban mainstream, a policy that wrought suffering and drastic disruption in Indian life. In 1961 representatives of sixty-seven tribes met in Chicago and drew up a Declaration of Purposes demanding a change of policy and the "right to choose our own way of life" and to preserve "our precious heritage." In 1965 Indians pressured President Johnson to establish the National Council on Indian Opportunity to direct antipoverty funds into Native American communities.

By the late sixties, more militant, younger Indians asserted "Red Power" and insisted on being designated "Native Americans." In 1968 militant Indians clashed with officials of the state of Washington over native fishing rights promised in an old treaty. The following year Indians dramatized the Red Power movement by seizing Alcatraz Island in San Francisco Bay and occupying the site of an abandoned federal penitentiary for nearly two years. Our battle, claimed Indian leader Richard Oakes, is "not just on Alcatraz, but every place else, the Indian is in his last stand for cultural survival." After Alcatraz, Native American activists became even more militant. Radical younger Indians led by Russell Means and Dennis Banks organized the American Indian Movement (AIM). In 1972 AIM dramatized their grievances by occupying the Bureau of Indian Affairs in Washington, D.C., charging the white-dominated bureaucracy with having "stultified our ambitions, corrupted our society, and caused creeping paralysis to set in—economically and socially." The following year AIM militants captured Wounded Knee, South Dakota, where U.S. troops had crushed the last major pan-Indian resistance movement in the 1890s. Although none of these actions did more than symbolize Native American disquiet, during the seventies and eighties a series of

The Second Battle of Wounded Knee. Demanding basic reforms in federal Indian policy and tribal governance, in 1973, members of the American Indian Movement staged a 71-day protest at Wounded Knee, South Dakota, the site of the 1890 massacre of 200 Sioux by U.S. soldiers.

court rulings supported some Indian land claims. Nevertheless, poverty, unemployment, limited education, and poor health still plague Native Americans.

Various white ethnic groups also came to stress their distinctiveness after the sixties. Irish-Americans, Italian-Americans, Polish-Americans, German-Americans, and various others took new interest in their national backgrounds. In the seventies, millions of Americans self-consciously searched for their roots and celebrated their distinctive birthrights, inspired by African-American author Alex Haley's *Roots* (1976) and the 1977 television miniseries based on the book. *Roots* attempted to trace Haley's ancestry from Africa through slavery to the present. An estimated 130 million viewers watched the eight-part series, making it the most popular television show up to that time. "Roots" sensitized TV audiences to the trials of slavery and racism and encouraged Americans to search for their own pasts. The melting-pot ideal gave way to a celebration of pluralism.

Along with the new claims made by ethnic and racial minorities, the Movement encouraged social minorities to demand equal rights. Homosexuals and lesbians, long discriminated against or forced to hide their sexual preferences, asserted themselves. In 1965 homosexuals, employing the black civil-rights sit-in tactic, staged a "sip-in" at a New York bar and sought to test a 1965 rule imposed by the New York State Liquor Authority that prohibited more than three homosexuals in a bar at one time. This protest, combined with the American Civil Liberties Union's threat of a lawsuit, forced the Liquor Authority to rescind its discriminatory policy. Harassment of gays and lesbians, however, remained routine.

On the night of June 27, 1969, the gay-rights movement took a militant turn when police raided the Stonewall Inn, a popular homosexual bar in New York's Greenwich Village. Police crackdowns had been commonplace for years, but that night at the Stonewall, gays fought back. A riot ensued, which according to a *Village Voice* reporter "was a kind of liberation, as the gay brigade emerged from the bars, back rooms and bedrooms of the Village and became street people.'' Within days, activists organized a variety of homosexual- and lesbian-rights groups. The most important of these, the Gay Liberation Front (GLF), called for ''complete sexual liberation for all people'' and sought to affiliate with the radical New Left. ''Gay is Good,'' they declared in their publication *Gay Flames.*

Soon gays and lesbians marched in antiwar demonstrations under banners reading ''Homosexuals Against the War.'' In June 1970, the GLF organized the first Gay Pride Week with the motto ''Out of the Closets and into the Streets.'' The movement continued to grow in the seventies as homosexuals and lesbians gained self-confidence. In response to these pressures, some communities and states changed their practices and laws. Although hostility toward homosexuals persists and a backlash against gay rights has manifested itself, tolerance toward gays has grown. Today most people regard homosexual and lesbian relationships as matters of personal choice, and not as a symptom of sin or mental illness.

• • •

The sixties' upheavals, then, have pushed America in a more pluralistic and less prejudicial direction. Writing nearly two decades after his role in the Berkeley Free Speech Movement, Mario Savio claimed that ''the rising of Black People, which brought on the '60s, marked the historic end of the viability of social oppression in America. Thereafter one oppressed group after another—American Indians, Latinos, Women, Homosexuals, etc., collectively threw off the yoke.'' People have relaxed about such matters as communist China, premarital sex, as well as homosexuality—taboo topics before the sixties.

These major legacies confirm the Movement's significance. The sixties will likely endure as a model for American thought and behavior, just as the 1930s typified an earlier generation. For all its transience and excess, the youth rebellion led to a fundamental reappraisal of American values and institutions. Moreover, although the Movement was short-lived, it raised issues that are still timely. As the next chapter discusses, the women's movement and environmental concerns are two such ongoing developments.

Selected Bibliography

Although a thorough history of the decline and legacies of the New Left and counterculture has yet to be written, most general histories of the sixties and larger studies of the postwar years attempt such analyses. See particularly Edward P. Morgan, *The 60s Experience* (1991); David Chalmers, *And the Crooked Places Made Straight: The Struggle for Social Change in the 1960s* (1991); William H. Chafe, *The Unfinished Journey* (1995 ed.); Stewart Burns, *Social Movements of the 1960s* (1990); Douglas T. Miller, *Visions of America: Second World War to the Present* (1988); Todd Gitlin, *The Sixties: Years of Hope, Days of Rage* (1987); Morris Dickstein, *Gates of Eden* (1977); Godfrey Hodgson,

America in Our Time (1976); and William L. O'Neill, *Coming Apart* (1971).

The influential, positive, contemporary analyses of the counterculture discussed in the text are Charles Reich, *The Greening of America* (1970); Theodore Roszak, *The Making of a Counter Culture* (1969); and Philip Slater, *The Pursuit of Loneliness* (1970).

The story of the Woodstock Festival is told in Robert Stephen Spitz, *Barefoot in Babylon* (1979). For Altamont, see Jonathan Eisen, ed., *Altamont: Death of Innocence in the Woodstock Nation* (1970). Both the Woodstock and Altamont concerts are scrutinized in Robert Santelli, *Aquarius Rising: The Rock Festival Years*

(1980); John Orman, *The Politics of Rock Music* (1985); and Herbert London, *Closing the Circle: A Cultural History of the Rock Revolution* (1985).

The fate of Haight-Ashbury is chronicled in Charles Perry, *The Haight-Ashbury* (1984). The Manson murders are the subject of Movement activists Ed Sanders's *The Family* (1972), and policeman Vincent Bugliosi's *Helter Skelter* (1975).

Kirkpatrick Sale documents the decline of Students for a Democratic Society in *SDS* (1973). Harold Jacobs, ed., *Weatherman* (1970), is a collection of documents from this radical offshoot of SDS. Life in the Weatherman underground is personally recounted in Susan Stern's *With the Weatherman* (1975). The demise of the Black Panthers and other Black Power groups is treated in Harvard Sitkoff, *The Struggle for Black Equality, 1954–1992* (1993); James Button, *Black Violence: Political Impact of the 1960s Riots* (1978); and Cleveland Sellers, *The River of No Return: The Autobiography of a Black Militant and the Life and Death of the SNCC* (1973).

The story of People's Park and its repercussions is best told in W. J. Rorabaugh, *Berkeley at War: The 1960s* (1989). The Kent State killings are the subject of Joseph Kelner and James Munves, *The Kent State Coverup* (1980); Joe Eszterhas and Michael D. Roberts, *Thirteen Seconds* (1970); I. F. Stone, *The Killings at Kent State* (1971); James A. Michener, *Kent State* (1971); and Richard E. Pelerson and John A. Bilorusky, *May 1970: The Campus Aftermath of Cambodia and Kent State* (1971). Antiwar protest during the Nixon years is covered in Alexander Kendrick, *The Wound Within* (1974); Kenneth J. Heineman, *Campus Wars* (1993); and Nancy Zaroulis and Gerald Sullivan, *Who Spoke Up?* (1984).

No adequate study of mainstream America's assimilation of counterculture styles and values exists, though Douglas T. Miller, *Visions of America* (1988); Godfrey Hodgson, *America in Our Time* (1976); and Peter Clecak, *America's Quest for the Ideal Self* (1983), touch on this subject. The commercialization of the underground media is well presented in David Armstrong, *A Trumpet to Arms* (1981). Estelle Freedman and John D'Emilio, *Intimate Matters* (1988), and Daniel Yankelovich, *The New Morality* (1974), investigate changing sexual mores.

Evaluations of the economic downturn of the Nixon years include Richard J. Barnet, *The Lean Years* (1980); Robert L. Heilbroner and Lester C. Thurow, *Five Economic Challenges* (1983); and David Calleo, *The Imperious Economy* (1982).

Studies of the growing assertiveness of Hispanic-Americans include Carlos Muñoz, Jr., *Youth, Identity, Power: Chicano Movement* (1989); Mario García, *Mexican-Americans: Leadership, Ideology, and Identity* (1989); Rudolfo Acuna, *Occupied America: The Chicano's Struggle Toward Liberation* (1972); Matt Meier and Feliciano Rivera, *The Chicanos* (1972); and Jacques Levy, *Cesar Chávez* (1975). The Native American cultural and political resurgence is appraised in Peter Matthiessen, *In the Spirit of Crazy Horse* (1991 ed.); Stan Steiner, *The New Indians* (1968); Alvin Josephy, Jr., *Red Power* (1972); Donald Berthrong, *The American Indian* (1973); Vine DeLoria, Jr., *Behind the Trail of Broken Treaties* (1974), and with Clifford M. Lytle, *The Nations Within: The Past and Future of American Indian Sovereignty* (1984). The best studies of the new ethnic pluralism are Michael Novak, *The Rise of the Unmeltable Ethnics* (1973), and Richard Krickus, *Pursuing the American Dream: White Ethnics and the New Populism* (1976). The gay rights movement is addressed in Barry D. Adam, *The Rise of a Gay and Lesbian Movement* (1995 ed.); John D'Emilio, *Sexual Politics, Sexual Communities* (1984); Dennis Altman, *The Homosexualization of America* (1982); and Jonathan Katz, *Gay American History* (1976).

FEMINISM AND ENVIRONMENTALISM
ENDURING BEQUESTS OF THE SIXTIES

"Of all the accomplishments of the American woman,'' claimed the editors of *Life* in a special 1956 Christmas issue devoted to women, ''the one she brings off with the most spectacular success is having babies.'' At the time, very few Americans, women or men, questioned *Life*'s jubilant pronouncement. Feminism, which had flourished in the early years of the twentieth century, was in the doldrums. Indeed, the popular culture bombarded women with countless variants of the message that only in childrearing and homemaking could they find true fulfillment. Even in wild fantasies, no one guessed that, within a decade and a half, women would picket the Miss America pageant, fight for the right to abortion on demand, and extol lesbianism as the ''road to freedom from oppression by men.''

Environmentalism fared no better than feminism in the postwar period. Accustomed to the scientific and technological miracles of the war years, Americans looked forward to a future of abundance: plusher and more powerful automobiles, jet planes, and helicopters; modern houses in suburban settings filled with labor-saving appliances; television, record players, and portable radios; wonder drugs; DDT; and ample nuclear energy.

When Pacific Gas and Electric announced plans in 1958 to build a nuclear power plant at Bodega Head, California, on a site less than a thousand feet from the San Andreas fault, few people expressed concern at the dangers in combining an earthquake zone with an atomic installation. To most Americans, nuclear reactors promised inexhaustible, cheap energy to fuel the expanding economy. "With the device of the reactor," the *Walt Disney Story of Our Friend the Atom* (1956) assured young readers, "we hold the Atomic Genie under safe control. He comes forth at the beckoning of modern science—a smiling, magic servant to all mankind." This promise was not reserved for children alone. As a supporter of nuclear power plants stated in 1957, "Atomic energy can be applied to peaceful purposes without serious hazard to the public or its employees." Only years later would determined environmentalists succeed in stopping construction of the proposed Bodega Head plant.

Both the women's-rights and environmental movements emerged from the ferment of the 1960s, propelled by the struggles for civil rights and peace and by the new values and lifestyle of the counterculture. Yet while the civil-rights and antiwar movements and the counterculture all appeared in disarray by the end of that stormy decade, feminism and environmentalism gathered strength and wielded their greatest influence in the early 1970s. By the midseventies, these movements would spawn a new round of massive opposition, just as the earlier movements had. Nevertheless, they continue to influence American society today and hence endure as major legacies of the sixties.

The Status of Women: The Kennedy Commission

Insiders knew John F. Kennedy as a womanizer and as a man entrenched in the gender traditions of his day. Raised in a competitive, patriarchal family, JFK accepted socially dictated sex roles without question. With his beautiful, fashionable wife, Jacqueline, by his side and two small children, a girl and a boy, he appeared the embodiment of the American domestic ideal. In his efforts to staff his administration with "the best and the brightest," he drew from elite educational and corporate institutions that employed few women, leading columnist Doris Fleeson to remark, "It appears that for women the New Frontiers are the old frontiers."

Kennedy's first 240 appointees included only 9 women, of whom Assistant Secretary of Labor and Director of the Women's Bureau Esther Peterson was the highest ranking. A strong Kennedy supporter and longtime labor lobbyist, Peterson persuaded the president to initiate a commission to investigate women's standing in American society. Established by executive order in December 1961, the President's Commission on the Status of Women was authorized to examine "the story of women's progress in a free democratic society" and to recommend remedies to combat the "prejudices and outmoded customs [that] act as barriers to the full realization of women's basic rights." Inadvertently, Kennedy had laid one brick in the foundation of the women's movement.

Although women had held the right to vote since ratification of the Nineteenth Amendment in 1920, they remained outside the political power structure. In 1960 fewer than 5 percent of all state lawmakers were women, and when JFK came to office in 1961, only seventeen women served in the House and two in the Senate. Moreover, in every state, widespread legal discrimination against women persisted. Several states, for example, prohibited women from serving on juries, and numerous state laws interfered with a married woman's rights to own property, enter into business, sign contracts, or even control her own wages. But women faced more than legal limitations. Many prestigious universities excluded women altogether; professional schools of law, medicine, and business routinely admitted only a tiny quota of women. Even many college bands excluded female members. Women could not serve as pages in Congress, or as members of the National Press Club in Washington, D.C., nor could they buy a drink at New York's famed McSorley's or sit at a bar in Connecticut.

After the Depression and World War II, renewed public articulation of what Betty Friedan labeled the "feminine mystique" had emerged—the pervasive cultural message that "the highest value and only commitment for women is the fulfillment of their own femininity." Americans overwhelmingly assumed that nature decreed women to be wives and mothers and that they should stay contained in the domestic sphere.

Yet despite the dominance of the feminine mystique, more and more women had entered the work force after the late forties. By 1960 nearly 40 percent of all women held jobs, and women constituted one-third of the total labor force. Furthermore, contrary to popular stereotypes, more than half of these female employees were married, and more than one-third had children. Nevertheless, opinionmakers and the media ignored women's increasing presence in the labor market and continued to designate homemaking and childrearing as the primary female responsibilities. Further, because society expected women neither to be breadwinners nor to seek careers, employees felt little pressure to pay women high wages. As a result, most women who worked held low-paying, low-status jobs. In 1960 full-time women workers received only 60 percent of the pay that full-time male employees earned.

Discontent among women had surfaced since the midfifties, but because they lacked a clear feminist perspective, most women concluded that their dissatisfaction came from their own maladjustment. Only a small number of older feminists, led by Alice Paul of the National Women's party (NWP), had lobbied Congress from 1923 on to pass the equal rights amendment (ERA) outlawing discrimination on the basis of sex. Although the NWP had the equal rights amendment introduced in Congress every year and had persuaded both parties since 1944 to include the ERA in their platforms, few women knew anything of the amendment or the NWP. In fact, a 1962 Gallup poll revealed that two-thirds of female respondents did not believe that discrimination against American women existed.

Such were circumstances when the President's Commission on the Status of Women began its hearings. Chaired by Eleanor Roosevelt until her death in 1962, when she was succeeded by Peterson, the commission documented the forms of prejudicial treatment that women faced in government, education, and employment. Because the commission did not advocate equal rights between the sexes, it was not feminist. Indeed, Kennedy had created it in part to head off demands for the ERA. Although JFK had endorsed the amendment during his campaign, he agreed with Roosevelt and Peterson that the ERA would be detrimental to women because it would void protective labor laws. The commission's report in 1963 recognized the expanding position of married women in the economy but reaffirmed woman's primary role as wife and mother and emphasized "society's stake in strong family life." The report denied the necessity for the ERA, arguing that the Fifth and Fourteenth amendments provided women with sufficient protection.

Despite the report's cautious tone, the president's commission nevertheless constituted a crucial step in the emergence of the modern women's movement. As the first official government body to investigate the position of women in the United States, it legitimized women's aspirations for equality. In addition, its report documented the low status of women in the labor market, the problems confronting women in education, and the persistence of discriminatory state and federal laws. The commission endorsed legal changes to ameliorate these problems. In response, Congress in 1963 passed the Equal Pay Act, requiring employers to pay men and women equally for performing the same work. Because most women worked in predominantly female occupations such as clerical and service positions, however, this law barely made a dent in the wage differential between the sexes. Nevertheless, it helped some women, and, more important, it focused public attention on sex discrimination.

The Kennedy commission encouraged the rebirth of feminism in two other ways: it spurred the development of a women's network concerned with feminist issues, and it inspired creation of similar bodies at the state level. Although the original commission consisted of only fifteen women and eleven men, various subcommittees cropped up that ultimately involved more than a hundred politically active women. The very existence of the federal commission generated interest in women's issues, and even before it disbanded in 1963, a number of states followed in the federal wake and launched their own studies on the status of women. By 1967 all fifty states had such commissions. Composed primarily of women, the state agencies compiled massive evidence of the legal and economic barriers to women's full equality and convinced many previously uninterested Americans of the need for reform. Beginning in 1964, members of the state commissions held annual conferences at which hundreds of women from across the country shared their distress over sex discrimination.

Unveiling the Mystique

At about the time that the Kennedy Commission on the Status of Women issued its report in October 1963, Betty Friedan's *The Feminine Mystique* hit the best-seller list. The timing of this book was exquisite. Not only had the president's project stirred national concern about women's rights, but the civil-rights movement, cresting in 1963, had awakened all Americans to the issue of equality.

The Feminine Mystique sharply attacked the overwhelming emphasis on female domesticity that had permeated American culture in the postwar generation. Friedan ridiculed the common notion that biology determined women's position in society. Referring to the suburban home as a ''comfortable concentration camp,'' Friedan asserted that it was foolish for women to feel ''like freaks for not having that orgiastic bliss while waxing the floor.'' Her book indicted educators, social scientists, Freudian psychologists, corporate advertisers, and the mass media for pushing the message that women could find fulfillment only in domesticity. ''The core of the problem for women today,'' she argued, ''is not sexual but a problem of identity—a stunting or evasion of growth that is perpetuated by the feminine mystique.''

Although the book failed to examine the particular problems of nonwhite and working-class women, it struck a chord for millions of educated, middle-class housewives. Friedan urged women to break loose from their domestic confines, return to school, seek a career, and gain a sense of independence. The book showed that women's problems were social, not personal. Nationwide, suddenly discontented

Launching the Women's Movement. Betty Friedan's *The Feminine Mystique* (1963) captured a mass audience. Three years later, Friedan and others founded the National Organization for Women (NOW).

women found their voices. *The Feminine Mystique* awakened many future feminists and won its controversial author instant celebrity status.

Friedan's groundbreaking tract opened the door for other feminist publications. In the spring of 1964, the prestigious *Daedalus* magazine published a special issue devoted to women in America. It included Erik Erikson's reflections on woman's "Inner and Outer Space," Esther Peterson's study of working women, and, most influential, sociologist Alice Rossi's "Equality Between the Sexes: An Immodest Proposal," which emphasized the "need to reassert the claim to sex equality and to search for the means by which it can be achieved."

Shortly after the special issue of *Daedalus* appeared, feminists received unexpected assistance from Congress when women were included in protections under the 1964 Civil Rights Act. Title VII of this act prohibited discrimination in employment on the basis of "race, color, religion, national origins or sex." The inclusion of "sex" had resulted from an unlikely coalition of conservative southern congressmen opposed to civil rights and feminists who favored equality for both blacks and women. As the bill stood before the House Judiciary Committee, National Women's party members induced the committee chair, Howard W. Smith, to introduce an amendment adding "sex" to Title VII. A chivalrous southern gentleman and longtime supporter of ERA, Smith, a Democratic representative from Virginia, believed that white women deserved legal protections. But his primary motive in introducing the sex amendment was to get the bill defeated.

When House debate on the amended version of Title VII began, Smith and other male "supporters" treated the inclusion of sex as a joke; the media also derided it. Smith provoked raucous laughter when he began his defense of the amendment by reading a letter from an Omaha spinster calling for an additional amendment that would protect the "'right' of every female to have a husband of her own."

Women representatives found nothing funny in the debate. Led by Martha Griffiths, a Michigan Democrat, they pushed the amendment's passage. "I presume that if there had been any necessity to have pointed out that women were a second-class sex,'' argued Griffiths, ''the laughter would have proved it.'' With the tacit support of the Johnson administration, the amended bill passed the House. In the Senate, Republican Margaret Chase Smith of Maine spearheaded passage of the bill with the sex provision intact. On July 2, 1964, Lyndon Johnson signed the landmark Civil Rights Act into law. Both black civil rights and women's equality of opportunity were now endorsed by the federal government.

To implement the new law and to handle complaints of discrimination under Title VII, the government established the Equal Employment Opportunity Commission (EEOC). From the outset, the EEOC took issues of race discrimination seriously, but it treated sex discrimination with indifference. EEOC's first executive director, Herman Edelsberg, referred to the inclusion of sex under Title VII as a ''fluke . . . conceived out of wedlock.'' The commission's refusal to outlaw employment ads listing positions by sex infuriated feminists, as did Edelsberg's glib remark that ''men were entitled to female secretaries.'' In a June 20, 1966, speech on the House floor, Representative Griffiths charged EEOC with ''casting disrespect and ridicule on the law.'' African-American lawyer Pauli Murray, a member of the original Kennedy commission, argued the need for a women's organization to force the government to attend to women's rights just as civil-rights organizations helped blacks.

When the Third National Conference of the State Commissions on Women met in Washington, D.C., late that June under the auspices of the Labor Department, impatience boiled over among the delegates. On June 30, the last day of the conference, feminists drafted a resolution demanding that the EEOC treat sex discrimination as seriously as race discrimination; the federal officials running the conference retaliated by informing them that delegates were not allowed to pass resolutions. Infuriated, a number of women gathered at the conference's closing luncheon and planned a women's-rights organization. Betty Friedan, present at the luncheon, described what happened:

> We all chipped in $5.00, began to discuss names. I dreamed up N.O.W. on the spur of the moment, which everybody seemed to like, and Kay [Clarenbach, head of the Wisconsin commission on the status of women] agreed to be temporary Chairman since she had the facilities to get the clerical work done during the first months. We all agreed, that noon, on our main purpose—''to take action to bring women into full participation in the mainstream of American society now, assuming all the privileges and responsibilities thereof in truly equal partnership with men.''

Thus the National Organization for Women (NOW) was born. Over the summer, the original twenty-eight members sought recruits, and when they held an organizing conference the following October 29–30, NOW boasted some three hundred women and men as charter members. They elected Friedan as president and Clarenbach as chairman of the board. Other NOW participants included former members of the EEOC who had resigned in frustration, representatives of state commissions on women, and persons from the professions, labor, government, and the communications industry.

With the creation of NOW, feminism had a national focus. ''We, men and women,'' began NOW's statement of purpose, who hereby constitute ourselves as the National Organization for Women, believe that the time has come for a new movement toward true equality for all women in America, and toward a fully equal partnership of the sexes, as part of the world-wide revolution of human rights now taking place within and beyond our national borders. . . . We organize to initiate or support action, nationally or in any part of this nation, by individuals or organizations, to break through the silken curtain of prejudice and discrimination against women in government, industry, the professions, the churches, the political parties, the judiciary, the labor unions, in education, science, medicine, law, religion and every other field of importance in American society. . . . We do not accept the traditional assumption that a woman has to choose between marriage and motherhood, on the one hand, and serious participation in industry or the professions on the other.

NOW grew slowly, but by the early seventies it had fifty chapters and a combined membership of more than five thousand. Like Friedan, most of them were middle-class professionals and reformers. They hoped to win for women equal protection before the law and equal rights to participate fully in the nation's economic, political, and social life. Despite its lack of a mass membership, NOW soon developed into a highly effective political lobby.

Establishing a number of task forces, NOW tackled such issues as gender-specific employment ads, discrimination in employment and education, women's image in the media, and marriage and divorce laws. In October 1967, only a year after its founding, NOW won a major victory when it persuaded President Johnson to issue an executive order barring sexual discrimination in federal contracts. The order also required the federal government as well as private employers with federal contracts to establish affirmative-action programs. Firms with government contracts and the government itself now had to prove that they hired, trained, and promoted women as well as minority men.

Other successes soon followed. NOW won a lawsuit against the EEOC's upholding of sex-segregated employment ads. The organization compelled airlines to rescind their policy of retiring female flight attendants who married or turned thirty-two. In December 1967, NOW engaged in direct-action protest when members picketed EEOC offices in New York, Washington, D.C., Pittsburgh, Chicago, and San Francisco.

NOW also took an active role in electoral politics. At its November 1967 national conference, it adopted the Bill of Rights for Women, pledging to ''cross party lines to work for and support those candidates who will commit themselves to our Bill of Rights and defeat those who are its enemies.'' The Bill of Rights called for:

    I. Equal Rights Constitutional Amendment

    II. Enforcement of Laws Banning Sex Discrimination in Employment

    III. Maternity Leave Rights in Employment and in Social Security Benefits

    IV. Tax Deduction for Home and Child Care Expenses for Working Parents

    V. Child Care Centers

    VI. Equal and Unsegregated Education

    VII. Equal Job Training Opportunities and Allowance for Women in Poverty

    VIII. The Right of Women to Control Their Reproductive Lives

Although the convention adopted the Bill of Rights, the first and last proposals provoked bitter dissension. Some union women opposed the ERA because it would eliminate protective labor legislation for women. NOW's call for repeal of restrictive abortion laws and support of a woman's right to control her own body sparked even greater controversy. Some women who denounced abortion withdrew from NOW and formed a new organization, the Women's Equity Action League (WEAL). In the words of its first president, Nancy Dowding, WEAL sought to avoid issues "that polarize people—like The Pill or abortion or husbands washing dishes." More cautious than NOW, WEAL nonetheless took on such projects as eliminating sex-role stereotyping in elementary and secondary schools, analyzing the effects of credit and banking practices on women, advocating divorce reform, and leading a major campaign against sex discrimination in colleges and universities.

WEAL members and union women found NOW's approach too radical and controversial, yet some younger women perceived NOW as overly prudent and hierarchical. In October 1968, led by twenty-nine-year-old Ti-Grace Atkinson, president of NOW's New York chapter, a number of these women abandoned NOW and reconstituted themselves as the Feminists. In an effort to avoid entrenched leadership, the Feminists chose officers by lot and rotated these positions frequently. To facilitate equal participation in discussions, they adopted a system whereby each member would be given an equal number of chips at the outset of a meeting. Each time anyone spoke, she handed in one of her chips. Once the chips were gone, that person could no longer speak. Unlike NOW, the Feminists also rejected the participation of men and went so far as to attack marriage as an "inherently inequitable" institution. The organization praised the rejection of marriage as "a primary mark of the radical feminist."

By the time the Feminists had split from NOW, similar clusters of younger radical women were forming local groups in various parts of the country. Many of these women had come to feminism through their experiences in civil-rights and New Left protest movements. Ultimately they would push the women's movement beyond Friedan's goal of bringing women into the male mainstream and launch a comprehensive attack on all aspects of sexism. By contrast, groups such as NOW and WEAL lacked the grass-roots support and social activism necessary to convince politicians and public of the urgency of their cause. As a Justice Department official in the Civil Rights Division stated, "We respond to social turmoil. The fact that women have not gone into the streets is indicative that they do not take employment discrimination too seriously." Radical feminists would create the mass-based insurgency essential to place women's rights on the political agenda.

The Power of Sisterhood

In November 1964, the staff of SNCC, weary from the travails of Mississippi Freedom Summer and the rejection of the Mississippi Freedom Democrats at Atlantic City, held a retreat in the Gulf Coast town of Waveland, Mississippi. Frustrated by years of nonviolently confronting Mississippi's brutal white racism, they met to discuss the organization's future goals and tactics. Some forty position papers were submitted by staff members before the meeting, one of them on the status of women in SNCC.

Written by long-time activists Mary King and Casey Hayden and submitted anonymously to avoid ridicule, the paper charged that "assumptions of male superiority are as widespread and deep-rooted and every . . . [bit] as crippling to the woman as the assumptions of white supremacy are to the Negro." Why was it, King and Hayden asked, that "women who are competent, qualified, and experienced are automatically assigned to the 'female' kinds of jobs such as: typing, desk work, telephone work, filing, library work, cooking, and the assistant kind of administrative work but rarely the 'executive' kind?" Fearing that discussion of their paper would provoke laughter, they still hoped that "sometime in the future . . . all of us [would] gradually come to understand that this is no more a man's world than it is a white world." Both of their predictions proved true.

The laughter came first. One night a number of SNCC staffers relaxed on a pier jutting out into the gulf, enjoying each other's company as they passed around a jug of wine. The gregarious Stokely Carmichael regaled the group with a monologue worthy of a professional stand-up comedian. After telling some jokes, the standing Carmichael, smiling at King, Hayden, and the rest of the crowd stretched out on the pier, asked: "What is the position of women in SNCC?" Answering himself, he announced, "The position of women in SNCC is prone!" Carmichael and his audience roared with laughter.

Despite the flippant dismissal, women in the southern civil-rights struggle and in the student New Left had awakened to sexual discrimination within the Movement. Six months before King's and Hayden's paper, black women in SNCC's Atlanta office staged a half-serious sit-in to protest being delegated traditional female jobs. A few months later, when the Socialist Workers party in Seattle refused to consider "the woman question," female members defected and formed their own Freedom Socialist Club. These were isolated instances, but they revealed a rising feminist consciousness among Movement women.

Mary King and Casey Hayden persisted. In November 1965, a year after their first paper, they circulated "A Kind of Memo" to women in SNCC, SDS, the Student Peace Union, and several other New Left organizations. Complaining of "a common-law caste system" that forced women "to work around or outside hierarchical structures of power," they called for opening dialogue among women. "Perhaps we can start to talk with each other more openly than in the past," they urged, "and create a community of support for each other so we can deal with ourselves and others with integrity."

The King-Hayden memo won a positive response, particularly among women in SDS. At a national SDS conference that December, female members organized the New Left's first workshop on women to discuss their grievances and build solidarity. The experiences of women in SDS's Economic Research and Action Projects in northern ghettoes had roused them to recognize their own strengths. As Marya Levensen testified, "[We] became much stronger. . . . We learned how to fight." Such women became the vanguard of the women's liberation movement.

Organizations like SNCC and SDS were not more sexist than mainstream society, nor did women completely lack power in them. Founded on democratic and egalitarian principles, both SNCC and SDS had tried to create communities in which all members shared in decisionmaking. Furthermore, both groups developed an androgenous lifestyle that would later be associated with the counterculture. In place of the usual sex roles, these radicals stressed what tradition deemed the "feminine" values of nurturance and love. Civil-rights activist Martha Norman recalled SNCC as "the singularly most liberating environment'' of her life. Writing of her experiences in the University of Texas's chapter of SDS, Judy Pardun claimed, ''We treated each other with affection and respect. . . . We had a real alternative to the present American society. . . . Without verbalizing it, somehow we all felt it was necessary to treat people as individuals, not things; that in order to achieve our goals one had to, as much as possible, live them as we were fighting for them.'' Even Casey Hayden spoke of the ''empowerment'' that she experienced in the movement. When queried about women's roles in Mississippi, she asserted, ''Nobody cleaned the freedom house.''

Yet however well intentioned young idealists in the peace and freedom movements were, they could not entirely escape the gender stereotyping of the larger society. In theory participatory democracy made all people equal, but in practice men, culturally conditioned to be assertive, tended to dominate discussions. The freedom struggle had instilled in women the leadership skills and personal strength to challenge male supremacy.

Nevertheless, just as a feminist consciousness surfaced in the midsixties, the Movement grew even more male dominated and sexist. As the civil-rights struggle turned to Black Power and ghetto rage, the ideals of nonviolence, sharing, and community dissipated. SNCC became increasingly militant and refused to allow further white involvement, even ousting women such as King and Hayden. At the same time, SDS and other New Left groups multiplied rapidly in opposition to the Vietnam War and the draft. Small communal chapters gave way to raucous, unwieldy units in which shrill voices competed for attention. In an atmosphere of ghetto riots, escalation in Vietnam, and government repression, white male radicals increasingly adopted the revolutionary rhetoric and machismo posturing of the black militants. Women's issues ranked as low priority as the war and particularly draft resistance absorbed the New Left. Although women played crucial roles in organizing antidraft activities, the fact that they could not be drafted excluded them from the heroic status of male draft resisters, and they were expected to participate in the resistance through their men. A popular Movement slogan tellingly proclaimed, ''Girls Say Yes to Guys Who Say No!''

Women's tenacity in raising feminist issues earned them only ridicule. In June 1967, when a Women's Liberation Workshop held at the SDS national convention demanded that men confront their male chauvinism ''in their personal, social and political relationships'' and called for the full participation of women in SDS, many male members responded wth catcalls and derision. A report on the workshop published in SDS's organ, *New Left Notes,* appeared alongside a demeaning cartoon of a girl in a polkadot minidress with underpants exposed, holding a placard declaring: ''We Want Our Rights and We Want Them Now.''

That September activists held the National Conference for New Politics in Chicago, an abortive effort to pull together a viable political Left out of some two-hundred-odd civil-rights, antiwar, and other radical organizations. At the conference, women's exasperation with the Movement came to a boil. When several members of the radical women's caucus attempted to grab the microphone to present a resolution, the chairman patted one of them on the head saying, ''Cool down, little girl, we have more important things to talk about than women's problems.'' The ''little girl,'' Shulamith Firestone, did not cool down. A few days later, Firestone, Jo Freeman, and others organized the first autonomous women's group in Chicago. Modeling themselves on Black Power, they argued in a mimeographed paper, addressed ''To the Women of the Left,''

"Women must not make the same mistake the blacks did at first of allowing others . . . to define our issues, methods and goals. Only we can and must define the terms of our struggle."

Later that fall, Firestone and Pam Allen founded New York Radical Women. Soon similar groups sprang up in Boston, Washington, D.C., New Orleans, San Francisco, and other cities. A dam had broken. Within a year, hundreds of liberation groups attracted thousands of women. Loosely connected through a network of personal friendships and feminist publications, these women discovered an exhilarating sense of sisterhood. At first some Movement veterans felt hesitant. As civil-rights activist and founder of a Washington, D.C., women's group Charlotte Bunch remembered, "We spent months convincing ourselves that it was politically okay to meet separately as women and to focus on women's concerns. We felt somewhat more secure because we saw a parallel to the arguments of blacks who had been establishing their right and need to have their own space." But as women's liberation grew, such doubts evaporated in the heat of feminist elation. "It was something that we had all been waiting for, for a long time," claimed seasoned New Left activist Mime Feingold. "It was a really liberating experience for all of us. . . . This was finally permission to look at our own lives and talk about how unhappy we were."

Yet the movement needed an effective tactic for turning discontent into a feminist perspective. It hit on "consciousness raising," derived in part from SNCC's testimonials on racism and the long "rap" sessions that typified SDS's ERAP collectives and the Resistance. Radical feminists went further and made consciousness raising a major recruitment method, a means for molding politics and ideology, a stratagem for uniting women in an egalitarian community, and a prelude to feminist activity. Emphasized at the First National Women's Liberation Conference held in Chicago in 1968, consciousness raising entailed small groups of women meeting regularly for discussion. Charlotte Bunch described the impact of such sessions: "Women begin to discover ourselves as an oppressed people and struggle against the effects of male supremacy on us. . . . When we describe and share our individual problems . . . we can understand the universality of our oppression and analyze its social roots." When New York antiwar activist Rosalyn Baxandall joined a women's group, "it was instantaneous love," she recalled, "and I never missed a meeting for two years. . . . I'd never talked to people at that level and it just seemed incredible." Through consciousness raising, women realized that other women shared their problems, and they demanded a collective solution. Launched by radical women, thousands of consciousness-raising groups had sprung up by the early seventies attracting women from young, militant New Leftists to middle-aged suburban housewives.

Having cut their teeth on the civil-rights and antiwar movements, radical feminists acquired an ideology and the political skills, strategies, and tactics of organized dissent. Adopting the Movement ploy of direct-action protest, women's liberationists announced themselves to the world on prime-time TV in September 1968. Some two hundred women picketed the Miss America pageant in Atlantic City. They targeted it, claimed protest organizer Robin Morgan, because it was

> patently degrading to women (in propagating the Mindless Sex Object Image); it
> has always been a lily-white, racist contest (there has never been a black finalist);
> the winner tours Vietnam, entertaining the troops as a Murder Mascot; the whole

Feminists Mock the Miss America Pageant, 1968. This early women's rights protest targeted society's portrayal of women as "Mindless Sex Objects."

gimmick of the million-dollar Pageant Corporation is one commercial shill-game to sell the sponsors' products. Where else could one find such a perfect combination of American values—racism, militarism, capitalism—all packaged in one "ideal" symbol, a woman.

To dramatize their protest, women auctioned off a dummy Miss America, crowned a live sheep as the winner, and tossed such demeaning items as dishcloths, steno pads, women's magazines, girdles, bras, high heels, "and other instruments of torture" into a "Freedom Trash Can."[1]

Diverse militant demonstrations ensued. The following month, a Marxist feminist group, WITCH (Women's International Terrorist Conspiracy from Hell), lampooned the capitalist system by holding a Halloween witches' dance on Wall Street. The stock market slumped five points after the hexing. That fall, women at the University of Chicago seized a university building to protest the firing of a radical feminist professor. In 1969 Redstockings, a New York women's group, disrupted a state legislative committee hearing on abortion law reform. When the committee, consisting of fourteen men and a nun, refused to listen to their testimony, Redstockings held a public meeting, where women testified to the humiliation, danger, and suffering that they had endured through illegal abortions.

Other women's groups intruded on bridal fairs, "liberated" male-only bars and social clubs, and demonstrated at various professional associations deemed prejudicial

---

[1]Reporting this protest, the *New York Post* erroneously referred to the demonstrators as "bra burners," linking their militancy with antiwar protesters who burned draft cards. Although no bras in fact were burned, the media myth of bra-burning "women's libbers" stuck.

to the hiring and advancement of women. In Boston, the women of Bread and Roses stormed a radio station after an on-air announcement that "chicks" were wanted as typists. In New York, liberationists staged a "mill-in" at the *Ladies' Home Journal* and exacted a concession to have a future supplement devoted to women's rights. At Grove Press, militant women occupied executive offices and insisted that the millions earned from pornographic books degrading to women be used to establish child-care centers.

By 1970, as other New Left and Black Power organizations faded, women's liberation gained formidable momentum. On August 26, in commemoration of the fiftieth anniversary of woman suffrage, tens of thousands of women nationwide joined in the Women's Strike for Equality, demanding equal employment, the sharing of domestic duties, and legal abortions. By then, radical feminists had created a host of alternative women's institutions—community women's centers, health clinics, child-care co-ops, bookstores, shelters for battered women, rape crisis centers, abortion-counseling services, craft stores, and music collectives. Professional women in the American Historical Association, the American Political Science Association, the Anthropological Association, the Modern Language Association, and various other academic organizations launched women's caucuses to advance feminist scholarship and to urge the hiring and advancement of women in these professions. Thousands of women found the new feminism infectious. "Once I let feminism in," noted former SDS activist Rayna Rapp, "I reorganized everything I understood about the world. That was my conversion experience—it was natural and it was quick." In the fall of 1970, even the outgoing Miss USA succumbed. In her televised farewell address, instead of performing the expected grateful gushings, she shocked her audience by denouncing the commerical way in which she had been exploited.

The emergence of radical feminism prompted mixed media reactions. When women's liberation first came to public attention in 1968, the media paid scant attention, and when reporters covered events such as the demonstrations at the Miss America pageant, their tone tended toward condescension and ridicule. "The media-created woman," according to one outraged feminist, appeared as "a total weirdo—a bra-burner, man-hater, lesbian, sickie!" But as the movement mushroomed, media coverage increased in quantity and quality. Frequently pressured by feminists within their organizations, TV, news magazines, and newspapers began to reevaluate and legitimize women's rights. The change in media coverage also stemmed in part from the policy of most radical feminist groups to speak only with women reporters, a great many of whom were sympathetic to the movement. By the spring of 1970, virtually ever major magazine had run cover stories on the women's movement, and feminists had become a regular part of TV's nightly news. Following the extensively covered August 26 strike, a poll determined that four out of five adults had "read or heard about women's liberation." The publicity accelerated the growth of the movement.

Despite the more favorable mainstream press coverage, radical women, like their male New Left counterparts, distrusted the establishment media and instituted feminist underground papers. In March 1968, Jo Freeman and the Chicago women's liberation group inaugurated the first of these, *Voice of the Women's Liberation Movement*. By the end of 1970, more than one hundred feminist papers and journals flourished, running the gamut from amateur, mimeographed local sheets to professional-quality, national journals. Such publications provided a crucial nationwide communications link. Articles covered historical feminist movements; discussions of theoretical issues; personal testaments on such problems as employment discrimination, abortion, and rape; practical information on how to fix a leaky faucet or change a flat tire; and movement news from around the world.

Radical feminists also swayed the older underground press, most dramatically when a coalition of women's liberationists seized control of the New York undergrounder *Rat* in January 1970 and reconstituted it as a collectively run women's newspaper. "Women are Something Else," wrote Robin Morgan in celebration of the takeover of *Rat.* "This time, we're going to kick out all the jams, and the boys will just have to hustle to keep up, or else drop out and openly join the power structure of which they are already the illegitimate sons. . . . Women are the real Left. We are rising powerful." Women needed less drastic measures than the *Rat* coup to persuade other radical papers to take women's liberation seriously. Underground papers began featuring feminist articles; many such papers ceased portraying women as sex objects and no longer accepted pornographic advertising.

In addition to feminist papers, women's liberationists established publishing collectives that printed feminist literature, political essays, and nonsexist children's books. In 1970 Kate Millett's *Sexual Politics,* an attack on the sexist literary tradition of D. H. Lawrence, Henry Miller, and Norman Mailer, became a national best-seller, and *Time* magazine featured a cover story on the author. Other important feminist tracts soon followed, including Shulamith Firestone's *The Dialectic of Sex* (1970), Robin Morgan's *Sisterhood Is Powerful* (1970), and Germaine Greer's *The Female Eunuch* (1971). A handbook on women's health, *Our Bodies, Our Selves* (1971), issued by a women's health collective, sold more than a million copies. In 1972 Gloria Steinem founded *Ms.,* the first feminist magazine to gain a large national audience. That same year, academic feminists launched three scholarly women's studies journals. In 1973, Erica Jong's *Fear of Flying* and the first American edition of Sylvia Plath's *The Bell Jar* became best-selling novels. By then feminist rock groups, theater troupes, speakers' bureaus, and films had proliferated.

From WITCH to WEAL: Feminism Assessed

By 1970 feminism had swelled into a vital social movement, espousing a multitude of issues from equal pay to the ERA, and pushing women's rights to the forefront of the national agenda. Women's groups ran the gamut from WITCH, with its condemnation of marriage as "legal whoredom" and denunciation of men as creators of "the Imperialist Phallic Society," to WEAL, composed largely of affluent professionals concerned with issues such as discrimination against female academics and the effects of credit and banking practices on women. In general, younger participants who came to feminism from civil-rights and New Left organizations adopted a radical political perspective, whereas older feminists in NOW and other liberal groups took a moderate, pragmatic approach to reform.

A gulf divided radical from liberal feminists, but major differences also separated the numerous radical women's groups. As one example, radical feminists took several positions regarding marriage and the family. Some argued that the traditional nuclear family needed to be replaced by communal arrangements. Others viewed any heterosexual relationship as inherently oppressive. Such women regarded men as the enemy and patriarchy as the system that must be destroyed. Some radical feminists carried this argument to its logical conclusion and advocated lesbianism as a liberating, political act. Marxist feminists, on the other hand, insisted that the capitalist economic system perpetrated women's oppression. For them, liberation would come only through a movement of all oppressed peoples, male and female, to create a classless, socialist society. Liberal feminists considered all of these positions extreme; they accepted marriage, the family, and capitalism as long as women's legal rights stood equal to those of men.

Although divergent visions, goals, and methods at times made it hard for women to unite in support of national objectives, on balance the diversity appears to have strengthened the movement. The proliferation of local organizations in the late sixties and early seventies lent the movement vitality and allowed women to raise a wide variety of issues and to experiment with feminist lifestyles. The grass-roots nature of modern feminism gave women an array of groups from which to choose. Furthermore, despite ideological and organizational differences, the sundry radical and liberal groups reinforced one another. By the early seventies, these two strands had grown closer together, forming an eclectic, creative, and powerful force. Influenced by younger radicals, NOW endorsed gay rights in 1973 and two years later elected Karen DeCrow president on the slogan, "Out of the Mainstream, Into the Revolution."

The new feminism, though by no means unopposed, chalked up dramatic successes because the issues that it raised had close links to changing social developments. More and more women were joining the work force, a trend that accelerated during the economic downturn in the seventies. To preserve living standards threatened by inflation, many middle-class wives took jobs, and by the midseventies, the two-income family had become the norm. Even women with young children increasingly sought employment; by the end of the seventies, more than half of mothers with children under age six engaged in gainful employment outside the home. Consequently, feminist demands for equal pay, an end to job discrimination, the establishment of child-care centers, paid maternity leaves, the sharing of child-raising and household responsibilities with husbands appealed to the needs of a growing number of working women.

The declining birthrate also had connections to the revival of feminism. The postwar baby boom had peaked around 1957. A decade later, the birthrate had plummeted to Depression levels, and it continued to fall. By the midseventies, the country had reached what demographers call zero population growth, when the birthrate and death rate coincide. Improved methods of birth control, the rising number of working women, growing awareness of worldwide overpopulation, and the economic insecurities of the seventies all influenced the declining birthrate. But so too did the women's movement with its emphasis on the right of choice—in career, marriage, and family life. Women exercised this choice by delaying marriage and childbearing, and many had fewer children than in previous generations.

By the early seventies, the women's movement enjoyed a strong national lobby in NOW, numerous local feminist organizations, and the tacit support of millions of Americans not directly affiliated with organized feminist groups. A 1971 report revealed that even among the Future Homemakers of America, the ideas of women's liberation exerted a "definite influence." Millions of Americans, men and women, found themselves, often for the first time, debating such feminist issues as household

Androgenous America. Unisex fashions of the early 1970s reflected the blurring of traditional sex roles that the women's movement encouraged.

responsibilities, child care, abortion, and the ERA. Perhaps the feminist critique reached a large audience by the seventies in part because the nation overall displayed less dominant, less stereotypically masculine attitudes. The turmoil of the sixties, the prolonged tragedy of Vietnam, and the economic problems of the seventies made many Americans—men and women—feel vulnerable and hence attuned to issues of power.

As one indication of changing sexual perceptions, distinctions blurred between men and women in the world of fashion. This melding began among New Left and counterculture youth in the mid- to late sixties and rapidly spread through society. The look for the 1970s, prophesied the *National Observer,* "will be natural, the sex indeterminate." "Unisex," the word coined to describe this new fashion, featured slacks, pantsuits, and short hair for women; colorful clothing, longer hair, jewelry—even colognes—for men. Unisex fashion, like all other fashions, would change with time, but the deeper mitigation of sex differences that the women's movement inspired would prove long lasting. Although sex roles obviously have not vanished, since the sixties America has become more androgynous than before. Men have felt freer to develop what were once perceived as "feminine" traits, and women have adopted more "masculine" characteristics. No longer is it taboo for a man to cry or to nurture a child, or for a woman to compete in sports or to seek sexual gratification. Large numbers of men and women have embraced the idea of sharing the tasks of homemaking, childrearing, and earning a living.

Two of the foremost goals of the women's movement—passage of an equal rights amendment and the legalization of abortion—had won widespread support by the early seventies. The ERA, a simple statement that "equality of rights shall not be denied or abridged by the United States or any state on account of sex," had been repeatedly blocked in Congress since first being introduced in 1923. In 1972, however, with the women's movement swelling, ERA easily sailed through Congress, and by 1975, it had been ratified by thirty-four states. With only thirty-eight states needed for final adoption of ERA, victory seemed assured.

The women's movement was even more successful in its fight for control over reproduction. Under growing pressure from feminists, several states liberalized their abortion laws in the late sixties and early seventies. Finally, in 1973 the Supreme Court found a constitutional basis for abortion. In *Roe* v. *Wade,* the Court deemed abortion a private matter between doctor and patient, safeguarded by the implied constitutional protection of privacy. This decision in effect legalized the procedure. In other decisions, too, the Court came to interpret women's rights as among those civil rights protected by the equal-protection clause of the Fourteenth Amendment.

Additional achievements brought about by the new feminism included state and national victories in sex-discrimination cases, affirmative-action programs, revisions of state rape laws, easing of divorce requirements, and removal of discriminatory aspects of other laws. Recognizing the political clout of the women's movement, the EEOC finally began investigating women's complaints of discrimination in the workplace. Title 9 of the 1972 Education Act barred sex discrimination by colleges and universities receiving federal aid. Indeed, this law went so far as to ensure female college athletes the same financial support as male athletes. The number of females competing in school and college athletics rose from 7 percent in 1972 to 33 percent by 1980. Women's sports and feminism also received a boost when tennis star Billie Jean King soundly defeated former champion Bobby Riggs in a nationally televised 1973 match billed as "The Battle of the Sexes." Soon after, the prestigious U.S. Open tennis tournament offered women the same prize money as men.

With the mushrooming movement, women garnered political clout. In 1971 feminists founded the National Women's Political Caucus and successfully pressed both parties to add women's-rights planks to their platforms. At the 1972 Democratic and Republican conventions, women comprised 40 and 30 percent of the delegates, respectively, up from 13 and 17 percent four years earlier. Between 1972 and 1974, the number of women candidates for state legislative offices soared 300 percent.

Above all, the women's movement affected the way Americans thought about gender relations. In a 1970 opinion poll, women respondents split evenly over whether they supported the movement for equality. By 1974 those answering the same question endorsed the goal by two to one. The women's movement exorted its greatest impact among the young, especially in the universities. A survey of college freshmen in 1970 found that half of the men and one-third of the women endorsed the statement, "The activities of married women are best confined to home and family." Five years later, only one-third of the men and one-fifth of the women took the same position. By 1977 fewer than 16 percent of American households followed the traditional family pattern of husband as sole breadwinner supporting a full-time homemaker wife and at least one child.

Yet although feminism emerged from the sixties as the most powerful ongoing social movement and won a series of triumphs in the early seventies, significant obstacles remained. Part of the problem lay within the movement itself. In addition to conflicts among radical cliques and between radicals and liberals, feminist groups, whatever their politics, almost exclusively comprised white, educated, middle-class women. A 1972 Harris poll showed black females more supportive than white females of "efforts to strengthen and change women's status," but African-American women did not flock to the feminist movement. For most nonwhite women, discrimination on the basis of gender seemed less significant than racial oppression. Also, nonwhite women believed the elevation of their entire race or ethnic group more important than the separate struggle for women's rights. Among poor minority women—whether African-American, Hispanic, or Asian—respect for family and customary sex roles were widely accepted cultural traditions that white-dominated feminist organizations appeared to challenge.

Overt racial bias among white feminists was extremely rare, yet a kind of covert racism surfaced. Women's liberation groups spoke of careers, seldom jobs, and they paid scant attention to issues such as the plight of welfare mothers or domestic servants. Celebrating the ideal of "sisterhood," it was easy for educated, affluent, white feminists to assume that all women shared their concerns. However, a number of prominent blacks such as novelist Alice Walker and Congresswoman Shirley Chisholm did support women's rights, and in 1973 black women founded the National Black Feminist Organization. In more recent years, nonwhites have played an important role in the movement.

A far more serious challenge to the women's movement came with the emergence of an emphatic antifeminist crusade. Numerous Americans, men and women alike, recoiled from modern feminism. Concerns about the challenge to traditional "masculine" and "feminine" roles ran deep. To many people, the issues raised by the women's movement seemed to threaten the family and their religious beliefs, as well as their personal and social identities. Housewives long devoted to traditional roles considered feminism a direct attack on their own experiences. Many women feared losing the protections and benefits of marriage and clearly enjoyed the special treatment that came with being "feminine." Marabel Morgan, founder of the "Total Woman" movement, extolled the joys of female subordination: "A Total Woman caters to her man's special quirks, whether it be in salads, sex, or sports." "Don't Liberate Me, Love Me," sang country star Tammy Wynette. Millions of women seemed to agree.

The flush of feminist success in the early seventies obscured the powerful, gathering counterattack. Stunned by the plethora of liberation movements in the sixties and early seventies, conservative Americans increasingly saw feminism as the essence of all that threatened long-established American verities. President Nixon catered to this backlash: in 1972 he vetoed a bill that would have established a national network of day-care centers. Its "communal approach to child-rearing," he asserted, was "family weakening."

Antifeminists coalesced in their opposition to abortion and the ERA. Conservative Illinois lawyer Phyllis Schlafly led the fight against ERA. Turning debate from economic and political rights to the protection of marriage and family, she falsely claimed that the amendment would legalize homosexual marriage, prohibit separate public toilets, abolish alimony, and require women as well as men to be drafted into the military. "Women's lib," Schlafly charged, "is a total assault on the role of the American woman as wife and mother and the family as the basic unit of society." Conservatives such as Schlafly defined women by their reproductive, sexual, and childrearing roles within the family and saw the ERA as a threat to the "natural" division of spheres. To many conservatives, women's unique place within the family was divinely ordained. As the reverend Jerry Falwell, founder of the evangelical Moral Majority, asserted, ERA spurns the mandate that "the husband is the head of the wife, even as Christ is the head of the church." A final conservative argument impugned the ERA as an unwarranted expansion of federal power into areas best reserved either to the states or to the family. Senator Sam Ervin of Watergate fame charged that "the Equal Rights Amendment will convert the States from sovereign authorities in the constitutional field now assigned to them into rather meaningless zeroes on the nation's map."

Such campaigning mustered strong support for the STOP-ERA forces. Despite the fact that polls consistently showed an overwhelming majority favoring the amendment, anti-ERA activists, in an often vicious single-issue crusade, successfully persuaded several key state legislatures to vote no. The measure died in 1982, when at the end of an extended deadline, it remained three states short of the necessary three-quarters required for ratification. We "have repudiated this fraudulent proposal prompted by a little bunch of militant radicals," gloated Schlafly. Feminists determined to fight on.

Abortion sparked even greater controversy. Catholics and fundamentalist Protestants asserted the rights of the unborn fetus, the family, and society over those of the mother. Feminists judged abortion a woman's basic right to protect her own body; antifeminists vilified it as murder. As with the ERA, conservatives perceived abortion as an attack on the family because it placed women's individual rights ahead of that institution. Supporting "the right to life of all innocent persons from conception to natural death," this movement lobbied, demonstrated, and pressed for laws against abortion, including a constitutional amendment. Although unsuccessful in overthrowing the 1973 Supreme Court decision that legalized abortion, the right-to-life movement pressured Congress to cut off most Medicaid funds for abortions and unleashed an emotional campaign that has driven political debate from the early seventies to the present.

Jolted by the antifeminist backlash and continued internal dissension, the women's movement lost momentum in the midseventies. But unlike most other social movements of the sixties, organized feminism has remained a force in American life. In November 1977, for instance, more than twenty thousand women gathered in Houston for a federally sponsored National Women's Conference. "We are here to move history forward," declared the document drawn up by the conference delegates. Responding to a federal government request to "identify the barriers that prevent women from participating fully and equally in all aspects of national life," the convention drew up a comprehensive agenda of reform. With near unanimity, delegates supported such measures as passage of the ERA, the establishment of national day-care centers, the creation of shelters for battered women, and greater rights for minorities, including homosexuals. The movement continued to swell in the late seventies. Between 1977 and 1982, NOW's numbers exploded from 65,000 to 230,000. Although the organization's membership has declined somewhat more recently, NOW continues to champion ERA; abortion rights; a federally funded, national child-care system; maternity and family leave; affirmative action; the elimination of pay inequality; and strong laws against rapists and abusive men.

The women's movement persists as one of the major legacies of the sixties. Feminist action over the past quarter century has moved America closer than ever to gender equality. Barriers that once denied women access to educational and occupational opportunities have fallen. Increasingly, women have entered such traditionally "masculine" fields as architecture, business, engineering, law, and medicine. Moreover, women's studies have become an integral component of university curricula, and feminist scholarship has revamped and revitalized the liberal arts and social sciences. Feminism has made society aware of sexism and has changed media images of women, language habits, school textbooks, and child-rearing practices. Abortion continues as a legal alternative to unwanted pregnancy, and women have gained choices in terms of lifestyle and sexual behavior. Now women govern states, serve in the cabinet and on the Supreme Court, anchor TV news programs and host talk shows, and drive trucks.

Still, women continue to encounter obstacles in their quest for equality. Female employment remains largely sex segregated, with women concentrated in low-paying secretarial, service, nursing, and noncollege teaching jobs. At the end of the seventies, just as in 1960, women workers still took home only sixty cents to every male worker's dollar. Low wages, combined with a dramatic increase in single-woman households, has led to the feminization of poverty; in recent years more than three-quarters of welfare recipients have been women. Even affluent career women married to successful men often face a "second shift": the double burden of cleaning, cooking, and caring for children in addition to holding full-time jobs, for many husbands fail to assume their share of household responsibilities. The feminist agenda thus remains far from fulfilled.

To Save the Planet

Like women's liberation, the environmental movement began in the sixties, reached its broadest base in the early seventies, and by the midseventies faced serious opposition. Indeed, the two movements shared common values and rejected the tradition of human domination of nature. Radical feminist Robin Morgan wrote in 1970, "The only thing I know for certain is that *this* time we women must seize control over our own lives and try, in the process, to salvage the planet from the ecological disaster and nuclear threat created by male-oriented power nations. It is not a small job, and it does seem as if women's work is never done." Rather than emulating the aggressive "male mystique," feminists advocated the transformation of society according to a "female" ethic of caring and cooperation. As once-militant-radical Jane Alpert, who emerged from the New Left underground in the early seventies as a cultural feminist, wrote in 1973, "Could it not be that just at the moment that masculinity has brought us to the brink of nuclear destruction or ecological suicide, women are beginning to rise in response to the Mother's call to save Her planet and create instead the next stage of evolution?"

Traditionally, Americans thought of the world's resources as unlimited, put there by providence for their ever-expanding needs. By the end of the sixties, the United States, with less than 6 percent of the world's population, consumed 40 percent of the world's resources annually and produced 50 percent of the world's yearly pollution. Americans had always believed that they could shape their own destinies and, in a larger sense, control history itself. The nation's physical frontier may have ended in the 1890s, but the frontier mentality persisted well into the 1960s. It was a mentality of growth, conquest, and exploitation—the nation's masculine mystique.

Most Americans viewed their history as the progressive conquest of the continent by a hardy race of pioneers. Forests had been felled, swamps drained, rivers confined, minerals extracted, savages tamed, vermin and weeds exterminated, all in the quest to make America the most enterprising, successful nation on earth. In the expansive nineteenth century, a few lonely voices questioned this exploitive ethic. Henry David Thoreau in the 1850s called for the creation of "national preserves" of wilderness. "What is the use of a house," he asked, "if you haven't got a tolerable planet to put it on?" In the post–Civil War years, George Perkins Marsh, appalled at how humans had ravaged nature, warned that "the earth is fast becoming an unfit home for its noblest inhabitant." By the progressive years of the early twentieth century, people had begun to heed the call for conservation. With the frontier gone, groups such as the Sierra Club, founded in 1892, and the Audubon Society, launched in 1905, called for the preservation and protection of undeveloped habitats. A major conservation movement swelled. Yet as historian Samuel Hays has pointed out, this movement became "an effort on the part of leaders in science, technology, and government to bring about more efficient development of physical resources." The government set aside vast tracts of public land that mostly benefited large mining, ranching, and timber businesses. Exploitation of the environment continued.

After World War II, matters worsened. Ecologist Barry Commoner charged,

> Most of our environmental problems are the inevitable result of sweeping changes in the technology of production after World War II: the use of new, large, high-powered, smog-generating automobiles; the shift from fuel-efficient trains to gas-guzzling trucks and cars; the replacement of biodegradable and less toxic natural products with nondegradable and hazardous petro-chemical products; and the substitution of chemical fertilizers for manure and crop rotation. By 1970 it was clear that these changes in technology of production were the *root cause* of modern environmental pollution.

As early as 1948, Fairfield Osborn's *Our Plundered Planet* had expressed alarm over accelerating environmental damage. A year later, Aldo Leopold's *A Sand County Almanac* called for the development of a "land ethic" that would recognize the interdependence of human life with "soils, waters, plants, and animals." The Princeton conference report, *Man's Role in Changing the Face of the Earth* (1956), offered similar counsel. But with the Cold War deepening, policymakers ignored such admonishments and in the late fifties and early sixties stressed economic growth as the highest priority.

In 1962, as the Kennedy White House urged Americans on to New Frontiers, biologist Rachel Carson's *Silent Spring* revealed the deadly effects that pesticides such as DDT had on the environment. Her work helped to launch the modern environmental movement. Within two years, forty states passed laws restricting pesticide use, and in 1969 the Department of Agriculture prohibited further domestic applications of DDT.

By then many Americans had grown painfully aware that environmental damage involved much more than pesticides. The nation's growth and technological prowess had proved a mixed blessing. National debate over the perils of nuclear fallout that preceded the test ban treaty of 1963 increased public awareness of the dangers of atomic

Environmental Disaster. In March 1967, the grounded oil tanker *Torrey Canyon* split in half and spewed forth a filthy tide of congealing oil. Such accidents spurred the environmental movement.

radiation. That same year, the surgeon general's report linked cigarette smoking to lung cancer and other illnesses. Three days of smog alerts in the Los Angeles area in October 1965 made some Americans mindful of another great danger—air pollution—caused by extensive reliance on private automobiles. The following year, pictures of dead fish and expert testimony informed Americans that Lake Erie was dying from nitrogenous wastes that encouraged algae growth, which in turn absorbed oxygen. Other waterways such as Cleveland's Cuyahoga River had become so polluted with industrial wastes as to constitute a fire hazard. On October 5, 1966, the Enrico Fermi breeder-type nuclear power plant just outside Detroit narrowly averted disaster when the reactor overheated and a portion of the core melted down. In March 1967, a giant oil tanker, *Torrey Canyon,* struck a reef off the coast of England, spilling over 100,000 gallons of oil into the sea. Within weeks, oil scum coated beaches as far away as Cape Cod and New Jersey. In January 1969, an offshore oil-drilling rig six miles off the coast of Santa Barbara erupted, disgorging some 235,000 gallons of oil that left dead birds and black slime over an eighty-mile stretch of heavily populated California coast. "The present course of environmental degradation," chided Commoner at the end of the sixties, "is so serious that, if continued, it will destroy the capability of the environment to support a reasonably civilized human society."

Mindful of the disasters and public pressures, the Johnson administration initiated a series of environmental reforms. Cleaning up the water and air, preserving wilderness and scenic areas, and saving endangered species dovetailed well with LBJ's emphasis on improving the quality of life in his Great Society. New legislation vastly extended the role of government in protecting the environment. The Wilderness Act of 1964 established a system of congressionally designated wilderness areas. In 1965 Congress set up the Land and Water Conservation Fund, in which federal revenues were allocated for both state and federal use in acquiring wildlands. The Clean Water Act of 1965 and Clean Air Act of 1967 established standards to measure water and air pollution and regulatory agencies to combat polluters. Endangered-species laws in 1964 and 1968 created the Office of Endangered Species to identify species at risk for extinction and to preserve safe habitats. Answering to the demands of canoers, hikers, and other nature lovers, in 1968 Congress passed the National Wild and Scenic Rivers Act and the National Trails Act. That same year, the North Cascades and the Redwood national parks came into being, the latter over the objections of the lumber industry and California governor Ronald Reagan.

The sixties also witnessed a remarkable growth of organizations concerned with preserving wildlands and improving environmental quality. Membership mushroomed in older national societies—the Sierra Club, the Audubon Society, the National Wildlife Federation, the Wilderness Society, and the Isaac Walton League—and important new groups emerged—Friends of the Earth, the Environmental Defense Fund, and the Natural Resources Defense Council, and the more radical groups, Greenpeace and Earth First. In addition, more than twenty-five hundred community- and campus-based environmental organizations sprang up. Generally focusing on regional problems, these small groups often collapsed as rapidly as they had risen, yet many people advanced from participating in local organizations to joining national groups.

By the time Richard Nixon took office in 1969, the environmental movement had developed into a major crusade. On July 20 that year, American astronaut Neil Armstrong became the first human to walk on the surface of the moon. This technological triumph capped John F. Kennedy's New Frontier–Cold War philosophy: an American hero had conquered the frontier of space. But for millions of Americans, the pictures of the living Earth taken from the dead blackness of space served as a dramatic reminder of the planet's beauty and fragility. Stewart Brand soon used a photograph of earth taken from the moon—a blue orb in a sea of blackness—on the cover of the *Whole Earth Catalog,* the bible of counterculture youth trying to live in harmony with nature.

As in the civil-rights, antiwar, and women's movements, young people played an important role in environmental activism. From the fifties Beats through the sixties counterculture, many youthful rebels had judged American materialism appalling. Rejecting the values of acquisitiveness and utility, the counterculture embraced a philosophy of simplicity and respect for nature as Thoreau had. In the late sixties and early seventies, a back-to-the-land communal movement flourished. "The return to the land is happening," affirmed an *Oracle* writer in 1967. "Land is being made available at a time when many of us in the Haight-Ashbury and elsewhere are voicing our need to return to the soil, to straighten our heads in a natural environment, to straighten our bodies with healthier foods and Pan's work, toe to toe with the physical world, just doing what must be done." Repelled by the horrors of a technological war in Vietnam and influenced by Eastern religions and Native American philosophies, thousands of counterculture youth came to see nature as a vital force to live with in peace, not as a resource to be conquered. For these people, reverence for nature was spiritual. Many such counterculture youth joined the back-to-the-land movement; they resided in rural communes, farmed with organic materials, and lived simply, usually as vegetarians, with few possessions.

By 1970 environmental concerns had spread well beyond counterculture youth to become one of the more powerful political forces of the postwar era. "There is a new kind of revolutionary movement under way in this country," claimed Washington senator Henry Jackson. "This movement is concerned with the integrity of man's life support system—the human environment." On April 22, 1970, environmentalists sponsored the first Earth Day, a national "teach-in," modeled on the antiwar movement, to publicize environmental problems, pressure politicians to pass legislation, and encourage the clean-up of the landscape. Congress adjourned that day, and an estimated ten million schoolchildren and adults participated. By then millions of Americans had come to question the wisdom of unlimited economic growth and technological development. The term *ecology,* meaning the interdependency of all things in nature, came into vogue.

Environmentalists took action on many fronts. They blocked the building of a jetport in the Everglades, kept wetlands in New Jersey wild and free from development, and halted dam construction on the Snake River in Idaho and the New River Gorge in West Virginia. Local environmental groups lobbied and launched recycling and educational programs. Realizing the swelling political clout of environmentalists, President Nixon declared the "Environmental Decade" and signed even more sweeping environmental legislation than had LBJ. Congress amended and made more stringent existing laws to improve air and water quality and to save endangered species. In 1969 Congress passed the National Environmental Policy Act, mandating that every federally funded or federally sponsored project file environmental-impact studies. The following year, Nixon established the Environmental Protection Agency to enforce various environmental laws. Also in 1970, Congress created the Occupational Safety and Health Administration to protect workers' health, and, over Nixon's objections, voted to cease funding supersonic air transport on environmental grounds.

Under pressure from environmentalists, other changes unfolded: the government decreed the use of less polluting lead-free gasoline and required various antipollution devices in new cars; some states passed laws dictating returnable, recyclable containers; others banned the use of nonbiodegradable detergents. Although helpful, these various regulations served as only a piecemeal attack on the problem. As Barry Commoner cautioned, "The solution of the environmental crisis is not to be found in new kinds of automobile mufflers or in legal constraints on waste emissions but in the radical reorganization of national economies and international commerce along lines that make ecological sense."

Ecologists such as Commoner hoped for a sea change in public consciousness. As Rockefeller University scientist René Dubos defined it, ecological responsibility demanded "a new social ethic," a "religion . . . based on harmony with nature as well as man." Environmentalists became particularly critical of economic growth and stressed the need to "live lightly on the earth." Americans, one ecologist warned, "must either undergo a major change in the direction of living more rewarding lives with fewer material demands, or the nation is headed toward endless and escalating crises." Yet although millions of Americans drew inspiration from the environmental movement, the extent of their commitment varied considerably. For many people, being environmentally active meant little more than picking up litter or recycling; for others the movement created new values that sharply challenged long-dominant doctrines of growth and development.

The publication of the Club of Rome's *The Limits to Growth* in 1972 stirred widespread debate. Authored by a group of MIT computer experts under the auspices of a prestigious international group of scientists and business executives, this report projected that global economic and population growth would rapidly deplete the earth's resources. Without sharp checks on growth, they prophesied a grim future of mass starvation, diminishing resources, lethal pollution, and war between rich and poor nations. Initially, the Club of Rome distributed some twelve thousand copies of the tract to influential state, industrial, and labor leaders. Soon the book sold more than two million copies in twenty-seven languages. Even some esteemed economists who had hitherto championed growth became converts of the antigrowth message. Robert Heilbroner, for instance, changed from optimistic Keynesian to pessimistic ecologist. His 1974 book, *Inquiry into the Human Prospect,* predicted that ''the industrial growth process, so central to the economic and social life of capitalism and Western socialism alike, will be forced to slow down.''

Sensing the radical challenge of environmentalism and resenting the increase in government regulations, corporate America increasingly opposed the movement. Although few industrialists spoke out directly in defense of pollution, strong antienvironmental arguments nevertheless evolved. Critics complained that environmental regulations slowed growth, weakened industries, caused unemployment, prevented needed development, and blocked the economic advancement of lower-income groups. Business leaders argued that the costs of meeting stringent environmental standards would make U.S. industries less competitive internationally and thereby worsen the already serious balance-of-payments deficit. By 1972 the Nixon administration, which had supported the early ecological crusade, became openly hostile. ''We are not going to allow the environmental issue to be used,'' Nixon asserted, ''basically to destroy the system.'' Under the president's prodding, the Environmental Protection Agency grew lax in enforcing existing regulations.

In the fall and winter of 1973–1974, the conflict between ecology and production intensified with OPEC's price hikes. The resulting ''energy crisis'' catalyzed serious fuel shortages, inflation, and recession in the United States. Long accustomed to abundant energy at low prices, Americans woke up to the fact that natural resources had limits. ''Although it's positively un-American to think so,'' one observer noted, ''the environmental movement and energy shortage have forced us all to accept a sense of our limits, to lower our expectations, to seek prosperity through conservation rather than growth.'' Congress cut highway speeds to fifty-five miles per hour and asked people to lower their thermostats. Conservationists encouraged research on alternative, renewable, nonpolluting energy sources such as wind and solar power.

Yet if the energy crisis stimulated heightened ecological awareness for some Americans, overall it weakened the environmental movement. Many people saw the ''crisis'' as a ruse by the oil companies to raise prices. Others blamed environmental regulations for America's economic woes. The Nixon administration responded to the energy crisis by authorizing construction of the Alaska oil pipeline despite serious environmental objections. The trucking industry received permission to use larger trucks, and auto manufacturers were allowed more time to meet emission standards.

By 1974 the worst recession of the postwar years gripped the United States. The beleaguered government paid less heed to environmental concerns and allowed public utilities to resume burning coal to produce electricity. To supply the utilities and meet other domestic energy needs, the administration encouraged coal production, including the use of the environmentally devastating technique of strip mining. The government also authorized and advocated the building of nuclear-power plants, assuring the public that nuclear energy would prove safe, clean, and cheap and would free the United States from dependence on foreign oil.

But as with the women's movement, the midseventies setbacks for environmentalists in no way ended the debate. Indeed, the hazards of nuclear power aroused the most massive outpouring of protest to take place in the later seventies. Reliance on nuclear power alarmed environmentalists for several reasons. First, real possibility existed of a major accident, a ''meltdown'' that would release radioactive poison into the environment. Second, even without a serious accident, it was known that nuclear plants emitted small amounts of radiation, and, as most scientists agreed, there was no such thing as a ''safe'' amount of radiation poisoning. Finally, the problem of storing the tons of radioactive waste generated annually by each reactor remained unsolved. With a toxic life of an estimated half-million years, finding feasible, permanent, and safe storage sites seemed impossible.

On Washington's birthday in 1974, former antiwar acitivist Sam Lovejoy chopped down a utility weather tower on the site of a planned nuclear power plant near Montague, Massachusetts. ''Communities have the same rights as individuals,'' Lovejoy declared on his arrest. ''We must seize back control of our community.'' In a much publicized trial, a local jury acquitted Lovejoy, who quickly became a movement hero. Antinuclear organizations sprang up throughout the country. Supported by major national environmental groups and such well-known celebrities and activists as Tom Hayden, Jane Fonda, Robert Redford, Benjamin Spock, and Ralph Nader, the antinuclear movement's greatest strength resided in local organizations. These groups worked through the courts, lobbied Congress, circulated petitions, held local and state referenda on nuclear plants, gave testimony before hearing boards, and propagandized for solar and wind power.

When all else failed, the movement resorted to the sixties tactic of direct action. Beginning in April 1976, a coalition of some thirty-five New England groups formed the Clamshell Alliance and staged sit-ins and other forms of nonviolent civil disobedience at a nuclear-plant construction site near the small coastal town of Seabrook, New Hampshire. A Seabrook sit-in during the spring of 1977 led to more than fourteen hundred arrests. Like the SNCC workers of the early sixties, many of those arrested at Seabrook refused bail and chose to remain in jail to dramatize their protest. Clamshell Alliance protests and court actions halted construction at Seabrook, albeit temporarily, and inspired similar regional antinuclear coalitions and demonstrations elsewhere.

In May 1979, more than a hundred thousand activists representing over ninety organizations converged on Washington, D.C., for the largest antinuclear protest to date. ''The history of the nuclear power industry,'' Ralph Nader told the throng of demonstrators, ''is replete with cover-ups, deceptions, outright lies, error, negligence, arrogance, greed, innumerable unresolved safety questions, and a cost-plus accounting that taxes our citizens as consumers and taxpayers.''

By the time of this demonstration, public concern over the dangers of nuclear power had reached a peak. The year had opened with the release of the popular Hollywood film *The China Syndrome*. Starring Jane Fonda, Jack Lemmon, and Michael Douglas, the movie dramatizes the fictional story of a near disaster in a nuclear power plant. At one point in the film, a physicist makes the dire prediction that a core meltdown would ''render an area the size of Pennsylvania permanently uninhabitable.'' Late that March, in an actual plant at Three Mile Island, Pennsylvania, a stuck valve overheated the reactor core and threatened to blanket the countryside with radiation. For two weeks, engineers worked feverishly to prevent a meltdown. More than a hundred thousand residents were forced to flee their homes. Although calamity was nar-

Antinuclear Demonstration, May 1979. In the aftermath of the near-disaster at Three Mile Island, more than one hundred thousand demonstrators converged on Washington, D.C., to protest both nuclear power plants and weapons. Tom Hayden and Jane Fonda (at left of stage) address the throng.

rowly averted, a member of the presidential commission that investigated the accident confessed, "We were damn lucky."

Three Mile Island intensified public awareness of the dangers of nuclear power, but by the late seventies, another factor aided the antinuclear cause. Quite apart from safety, nuclear energy had failed to be cost-efficient. Initial construction entailed staggering expenditures, and once in operation, no nuclear plant ever performed consistently up to expectations. By 1980 power companies dropped some twenty planned projects, and the industry grew wary of further investment in nuclear facilities.

Although the antinuclear movement and economic considerations largely halted new construction of nuclear power plants, the victory amounted to only a partial triumph for environmentalists. Increasingly, the electric power industry turned to cheaper coal-fired plants that produce the pollutant sulfur dioxide. Furthermore, during the 1980s, the Reagan administration launched an all-out attack against nearly two decades of environmental programs, slashing environmental budgets and turning most environmental agencies over to their confirmed opponents.

• • •

As with women's equality, the ultimate environmental goal of a healthy planet remains elusive. Each year brings new global tragedies, sad reminders of the earth's fragility. Nevertheless, like the women's movement, the environmental crusade of the sixties and seventies has wielded a profound impact on American society. Today the United States has basic laws aimed at eliminating air and water pollution and ridding the environment of toxic chemicals and other wastes. Federal and state agencies enforce these laws; strong environmental lobbies and national and local organizations have proliferated. Environmental issues have won a permanent place on the political agenda. Both feminism and environmentalism sharply challenge long-established institutions and values, and both should endure as legacies of the sixties.

Selected Bibliography

General surveys of women's history in twentieth-century America include Wiliam H. Chafe, *The Paradox of Change: American Women in the 20th Century* (1991 ed.); Robert Daniel, *American Women in the Twentieth Century* (1987); Lois W. Banner, *Women in Modern America* (1995 ed.); and Sheila M. Rothman, *Woman's Proper Place* (1978). Two valuable collections of essays and documents on women's experience in America are Linda Kerber and Jane De Hart, eds., *Women's America: Refocusing the Past* (1991 ed.), and Mary Beth Norton, ed., *Major Problems in American Women's History* (1989).

Betty Friedan's catalytic polemic, *The Feminine Mystique* (1963), remains a worthwhile source for the history of women in the postwar years. However, the book should be supplemented by Elaine Tyler May's *Homeward Bound* (1988), a fascinating study of the connections between the Cold War and America's domestic ideology. The fate of feminism in the fifties is the subject of Leila Rupp and Verta Taylor, *Survival in the Doldrums: The American Women's Rights Movement, 1945 to the 1960s* (1987); Eugenia Kaledin, *Mothers and More: American Women in the 1950s* (1984); and Cynthia Harrison, *On Account of Sex: The Politics of Women's Issues, 1945–1968* (1988).

A growing body of scholarship exists on the emergence of feminism in the sixties. Especially helpful are Jo Freeman's inside account, *The Politics of Women's Liberation* (1975); Maren Lockwood Carden, *The New Feminist Movement* (1974); Judith Hole and Ellen Levine, *Rebirth of Feminism* (1971); Barbara Deckard, *The Women's Movement* (1983); Myra Marx Ferree and Beth B. Hess, *Controversy and Coalition: The New Feminist Movement* (1994 ed.); Flora Davis,

Moving the Mountain: The Women's Movement in America Since 1960 (1991); Blanche Linden-Ward and Carol Hurd Green, *Changing the Future: American Women in the 1960s* (1992); Gayle Graham Yates, *What Women Want: The Ideas of the Movement* (1975); and William Chafe, *Women and Equality* (1977). Sara Evans, *Personal Politics* (1979), documents radical feminism's emergence from the civil-rights movement and the New Left. Mary King's autobiography, *Freedom Song* (1987), movingly narrates one feminist's experiences in SNCC. The various strands of radical feminism in the late sixties and early seventies are painstakingly delineated in Alice Echols, *Daring to Be Bad* (1989). A good overview of feminism and its opposition in the 1970s is Winifred D. Wandersee, *On the Move: American Women in the 1970s* (1988). Steven M. Buechler, *Women's Movements in the United States* (1990), is a comparative study of the first and second waves of the women's movement.

Radical feminist Robin Morgan's anthology of articles and manifestos, *Sisterhood Is Powerful* (1970), contains an outstanding collection of primary documents written during the first flush of feminist activism. Other important documentary collections include Leslie Tanner, ed., *Voices from Women's Liberation* (1970), and Anne Koedt, Ellen Levine, and Anita Rapone, eds., *Radical Feminism* (1973). Kate Millett, *Sexual Politics* (1970); Shulamith Firestone, *The Dialectic of Sex* (1970); and Germaine Greer, *The Female Eunuch* (1971), are important feminist tracts. Best-selling feminist novels, Erica Jong's *Fear of Flying* (1973), and Sylvia Plath's *The Bell Jar* (1973), are also informative sources. Betty Friedan's ambivalent relationship to the movement that she helped to launch is conveyed in her two autobiographical works, *It Changed My Life* (1976) and *The Second Stage* (1981). Another valuable autobiography is Gloria Steinem, *Revolution from Within* (1992).

To understand the complex relationship of black women to feminism, see Barbara Smith, ed., *Home Girls: A Black Feminist Anthology* (1983); Michele Wallace, *Black Macho and the Myth of the Superwoman* (1979); Gloria Joseph and Jill Lewis, *Common Differences: Conflicts in Black and White Feminist Perspectives* (1981); Bell Hooks, *Ain't I a Woman? Black Women and Feminism* (1981); and Paula Giddings, *When and Where I Enter: The Impact of Black Women on Race and Sex in America* (1984). Also valuable is Elaine Brown's autobiography, *A Taste of Power: A Black Woman's Story* (1992).

Kristin Luker has probed both sides of the issue in *Abortion and the Politics of Motherhood* (1984). Also rewarding on this subject are Dallas A. Blanchard, *The Anti-Abortion Movement and the Rise of the Religious Right* (1994); Marion Faux, *Roe v. Wade* (1988); and Rosalind Pollack Petchesky, *Abortion and Women's Choice* (1984). On the issue of rape, see Susan Brownmiller, *Against Our Will: Men, Women, and Rape* (1975).

The best studies of the ERA struggle are Gilbert Steiner, *Constitutional Inequality: The Political Fortunes of the Equal Rights Amendment* (1985); Mary Frances Berry, *Why ERA Failed* (1986); Jane J. Mansbridge, *Why We Lost the ERA* (1986); Joan Hoff Wilson, ed., *Rights of Passage: The Past and Future of ERA* (1986); and Donald G. Mathews and Jane Sherron De Hart, *Sex, Gender, and the Politics of ERA* (1990). The anti-ERA campaign is covered in Carol Felsenthal, *The Sweetheart of the Silent Majority: The Biography of Phyllis Schlafly* (1981), and in Schlafly's own account, *The Power of the Positive Woman* (1977). More general studies of antifeminism include Rebecca E. Klatch, *Women of the New Right* (1987); Susan Faludi, *Backlash* (1991); and Pamela Johnston Conover and Virginia Gray, *Feminism and the New Right: Conflict over the American Family* (1983).

Books on the changing political fortunes of women include Susan Tolchin and Martin Tolchin, *Clout: Womanpower and Politics* (1974); Ellen Boneparth, ed., *Women, Power and Policy* (1982); Ethel Klein, *Gender Politics: From Consciousness to Mass Politics* (1984); Karen Leigh Beckwith, *American Women and Political Participation* (1986); and particularly Susan M.

Hartmann, *From Margin to Mainstream: American Women and Politics Since 1960* (1989).

Environmental issues first attracted national attention with the publication of Rachel Carson's *Silent Spring* (1962). Later influential books include Georg Borgstrom, *The Hungry Planet* (1967); Paul R. Ehrlich, *The Population Bomb* (1968); Barry Commoner, *The Closing Circle* (1971); Donella Meadows et al., *The Limits to Growth: A Report for the Club of Rome's Project on the Predicament of Mankind* (1972); Theodore Roszak, *Where the Wasteland Ends* (1973); Robert Heilbroner, *An Inquiry into the Human Prospect* (1974); E. F. Schumacher, *Small Is Beautiful: Economics As If People Mattered* (1974); and Victor Ferkiss, *The Future of Technological Civilization* (1974). Nineteenth-century progenitors of the environmental movement, Henry David Thoreau and George Perkins Marsh, are best studied through their writings, especially Thoreau's *Walden* (1854) and his essay "Walking" (1862), and Marsh's *The Earth as Modified by Human Action* (1874). See also Douglas T. Miller, *Henry David Thoreau: A Man for All Seasons* (1991).

The best recent historical accounts of environmental issues are Samuel P. Hays, *Beauty, Health, and Permanence: Environmental Politics in the United States, 1955–1985* (1987), and Roderick Nash, *The Rights of Nature* (1989). Other insightful studies include Donald Worster, *Turning to the Land: Environmental History and the Ecological Imagination* (1993); Martin V. Melosi, *Coping with Abundance: Energy and Environment in Industrial America* (1985); Richard H. K. Vietor, *Energy Policy in America Since 1945* (1984); Lester Milbrath, *Environmentalists: Vanguard for a New Society* (1984); Craig R. Humphrey and Frederick R. Buttel, *Environment, Energy, and Society* (1982); Rice Odell, *Environmental Awakening: The New Revolution to Protect the Earth* (1980); and Sam H. Schurr, ed., *Energy, Economic Growth, and the Environment* (1972). Carolyn Merchant, ed., *Major Problems in American Environmental History* (1993), is an outstanding collection of documents and essays.

Roderick Nash, *Wilderness and the American Mind* (1982 ed.), traces Americans' changing perceptions of wilderness. Beneficial studies of the struggles to preserve the wilderness are Craig Allin, *The Politics of Wilderness Preservation* (1982), and Michael Frome, *Battle for the Wilderness* (1974). For the history of the creation of national parks, see Alfred Runte, *National Parks* (1979 ed.). Susan R. Schrepfer's *The Fight to*

Save the Redwoods: A History of Environmental Reform, 1917–1978 (1983) documents the controversy surrounding the establishment of Redwoods National Park. Friends of the Earth leader David Brower, a leading figure in the fight to preserve America's wilderness areas, is the subject of John McPhee's delightful biography, *Encounters with the Archdruid* (1972).

The conflict over pesticide use sparked by Carson's *Silent Spring* is traced in Thomas Dunlap, *DDT: Scientists, Citizens, and Public Policy* (1981); John Perkins, *Insects, Experts, and the Insecticide Crisis* (1982); Robert Van Den Bosch, *The Pesticide Conspiracy* (1978); and Frank Graham, Jr., *Since Silent Spring* (1970). Charles O. Jones, *Clean Air* (1975), examines the problems and politics of air pollution.

For an understanding of the energy crisis and its impact, read Barry Commoner, *The Politics of Energy* (1979), and Richard J. Barnet, *The Lean Years* (1980). Insight into the protest against nuclear power can be gleaned from Gerard H. Clarfield and William M. Wiecek, *Nuclear America: Military and Civilian Nuclear Power in the United States, 1940–1980* (1984); Langdon Winner, *The Whale and the Reactor: A Search for Limits in an Age of High Technology* (1986); Anna Gyorgy et al., *No Nukes* (1979); Michael Mandelbaum, *The Nuclear Question* (1979); and Steve Ebbin and Raphael Kasper, *Citizen Groups and the Nuclear Power Controversy* (1974). The Three Mile Island crisis is assessed in Mark Stephens, *Three Mile Island* (1980), and Daniel F. Ford, *Three Mile Island* (1982).

The Reagan administration's assault on environmental reform is appraised in Jonathan Lash, *A Season of Spoils: The Story of the Reagan Administration's Attack on the Environment* (1984), and Joan Claybrook, *Retreat from Safety: Reagan's Attack on America's Health* (1984).

E P I L O G U E

It had been ten years with little in the way of simple summations to explain it once it was over. The best and the worst in us had fought it out with the best and the worst in ourselves. No one had won and no one had lost. Nothing had changed but everything was different.

David Harris, *Dreams Die Hard* (1982)

The Movement: Perceptions and Realities

For some observers today, the sixties appear to have been little more than a boisterous party that came to a bad end. Judged superficially, this view seems plausible. If four college students sitting in at the lunch counter in Greensboro, North Carolina, symbolized the decade's heartening beginning, four college students lying dead in Kent, Ohio, marked its fatal end. What began with utopian visions of the beloved community based on pure democracy expired in authoritarian ideologies and violence. Events propelled the idealistic Movement toward its rendezvous with rage: the assassinations of two Kennedys, Malcolm X, and King; the racist savagery in the South; government repression; the ghetto flare-ups; and above all the infernal war in Vietnam.

Flaws within the Movement, too, hastened its demise. The sixties social movements exhibited the idealism, enthusiasm, and energy of youth but also its adolescent impatience, shortsightedness, and self-righteousness. In the short run, the Movement proved more adept at protesting wrongs than at planning long-range strategies or building coalitions based on compromise. Too often the New Left adopted an ethic of immediacy and lived in the present. For many, direct action became an end in itself. When such tactics failed to abolish racism or end the war, frustration mounted. Participatory democracy's rejection of hierarchy and its ineffectiveness in large-scale organizations also left the Movement without strong direction. Covert leaders nevertheless emerged or were elevated to that status by the media, yet such leadership was neither accountable nor institutionalized. In addition, participatory democracy allowed well-organized factions to wrest power within New Left groups.

And so, driven by the frenzy of the times and youthful

337

intolerance, many in the Movement lost touch with American realities. Their adoption of alien Marxist ideologies or romantic notions of Third World guerrilla fighting speeded the Movement's collapse. Former SDS president Todd Gitlin recalled the anxiety and despair of the Movement's demise: "My world had exploded, ten years of the movement; I had lost the ground I walked on." In 1970 the Beatles, perhaps the greatest cultural icons of the sixties, broke up. Former Beatle John Lennon declared that "the dream is over." Bob Dylan, another eminent cultural idol, announced that the gates of Eden had been replaced by the "day of the locust." Like many other Movement veterans surviving into the seventies, Lennon and Dylan looked to private domestic life as the only alternative to hopelessness. "I just believe in me / Yoko and me," sang Lennon. Dylan intoned: "Build me a cabin in Utah / Marry me a wife and catch rainbow trout / Have a bunch of kids who call me pa / That must be what it's all about." The "Me" Decade had opened.

In this version of the Movement's history, the years of protest served only to delegitimize liberalism and fuel the rise of conservatism. Through constant condemnation of the New Left, the black movement, feminism, gay rights, and the counterculture, the New Right and neoconservatives asserted their hegemony, beginning with the election of Richard Nixon in 1968 and culminating in the Reagan and Bush triumphs of the 1980s.

This view of the sixties Movement is widely held, particularly among conservatives. Yet there is another analysis of the decade's freedom movements and their contributions and legacies. Judging effectiveness, of course, is difficult, especially when assessing the impact of grass-roots social movements at such close range. Because the government enacted and executed the most publicized reforms involving civil rights, women's rights, and environmental protection, it is easy to overlook the role that social protest played in molding public opinion, the media, and ultimately the politicians. Yet throughout American history, social movements have provided the major motivation for such significant reforms as abolishing slavery, enfranchising blacks and women, regulating corporations, and granting rights to working people.

In the sixties and early seventies, the various peace and freedom movements played key roles in toppling white supremacy; liberating women; protecting the environment; improving the lot of Hispanic-Americans, Native Americans, gays, and other minorities; ending the war in Vietnam; and challenging Cold War orthodoxies. Not only did these movements apply the necessary pressures to win legislative victories, they also altered the moral and cultural landscape and gave rise to new values and policies. Indeed, one of the most positive legacies of the sixties was the emergence of an altered national consciousness regarding race, gender, class, ethnicity, sexual preference, and lifestyle.

Certainly the Movement had its self-righteousness, inflammatory rhetoric, and violence. Not all activists were noble idealists, nor were all their opponents bigoted reactionaries. Although excesses of moral smugness, drugs, and violence abounded, so too did ideals of community and equality. For a time, idealism and the hope for change challenged the very foundations of American society. Although instrumental in the ouster of two presidents, the system nevertheless remained intact, and the sixties revolution fell short of its overarching objective. Yet in the long run it scored some triumphs. Today, many basic rights enjoyed by nonwhites, women, gays, and various minorities owe their emergence to the sixties. Concern for the environment, tolerance of different values and lifestyles, and greater cultural pluralism all flourish despite efforts of recent conservative administrations to reverse these trends. Clearly the Movement has left its mark on the nation. It also profoundly influenced the lives of its participants.

Activism in the "Me" Decade

By the midseventies, the traumas of the sixties, defeat in Vietnam, the Watergate scandal, and stubborn economic woes appeared to have sapped the public's passion for social commitment. The political pendulum swung to the right, and for many Americans, possibilities seemed to contract. People who had always believed in the gospel of progress now began to see the future as a threat, with time and resources running out.

One reflection of this national exhaustion in the seventies was the emergence of an intense nostalgia, especially for the 1950s. As the sixties and early seventies receded in violence, repression, anguish, and disillusionment, the fifties loomed as a blank screen on which people could project fantasies of a better America. Television shows such as "Happy Days" and "Laverne and Shirley" and movies like *American Graffiti* and *Grease* recreated an idyllic world of youth and innocence. Excessive, sentimental nostalgia generally occurs during times of perceived crises, and the seventies was no exception. The rise of enthusiasm for the fifties coincided with widespread disillusionment and burgeoning conservatism. For many people, the 1950s came to symbolize a golden age of happiness and simplicity—the antithesis of social turmoil.

In addition to becoming retrospective, millions of Americans also grew introspective. The seventies witnessed a widespread retreat from the public world to purely personal preoccupations. "The 1970s," wrote social chronicler Tom Wolfe in an influential 1976 article, "will come to be known as the Me Decade." "The new alchemical dream," he claimed, "is: changing one's personality—remaking, remodelling, elevating, and polishing one's very *self* . . . and observing, studying, and doting on it (Me!)." One indication of this personal preoccupation was Robert Ringer's best-seller *Looking Out for No. 1* (1974), a book that spawned a small library of self-respect volumes.

A host of self-awareness disciplines also competed for the privilege of putting people in touch with their true selves. Transcendental meditation, a yogic discipline, drew nearly half a million adherents to its more than two hundred teaching centers; EST (Erhard Seminars Training) self-discovery programs grossed $10 million a year by 1975. On a beautiful cliffside overlooking the Pacific at Big Sur, California, Esalen Institute, which Wolfe described as "the Harvard of the Me Decade," helped people to learn about themselves through encounter sessions, massage, and group touching. Such therapies, or what came to be called the "human potential movement," taught that one could determine one's fate. Interest in things outside the self diminished.

While many Americans insulated themselves from the larger world through therapeutic self-absorption, others made moral sense of their lives through religion. A 1977 survey reported that seventy million Americans identified themselves as "born-again" Christians. This statistic constituted more than one of every three adults and, in addition to President Jimmy Carter, included such figures as former Watergate criminals Charles Colson and Jeb Magruder, ex–Black Panther militant Eldridge Cleaver, football hero Roger Staubach, and singers Pat Boone, Johnny Cash, and Bob Dylan. Spurred by a number of TV and radio revival programs and stations, evangelical, fundamentalist Christianity, once dismissed by sophisticated Americans as part of a dying, superstitious past, grew spectacularly from the late sixties through the early eighties.

Most of the search for spiritual solace took place within the framework of organized Christian churches, but the quest also spawned various new sects and cults, generally headed by charismatic leaders. Buffeted by international and domestic crises, alarmed at social and moral chaos, some Americans surrendered their personal wills to spiritual masters. The Reverend Sun Myung Moon, Korean founder of the Unification Church, converted thousands of young Americans to his religion, a blend of Christian faith and anticommunism that worshipped the Reverend Moon as the new messiah. Others became disciples of the Maharaj Ji, the young "perfect master" from India who established the Divine Light Mission. Zen Buddhism and other Eastern religions and practices also enlisted enthusiastic followers.

Whereas millions of Americans sought spiritual or psychic well-being in the seventies, millions more devoted themselves to perfecting their physical bodies. "I hear America puffing," exclaimed *Newsweek* in a May 1977 cover story on the national exercise craze. Concern for physical fitness dominated American culture in the seventies and long after. Millions of hitherto sedentary citizens took to running, hiking, biking, swimming, and cross-country skiing. Health, tennis, and racquetball clubs flourished. "We are discovering," claimed George Leonard, author of *The Ultimate Athlete* (1975), "that every human being has a God-given right to move efficiently, gracefully and joyfully." To the prophets of the new athleticism, competition seemed less significant than the physical and spiritual benefits of exercise. "Sports," asserted Leonard, "may open the door to infinite realms of perception and being."

Concern for physical fitness also brought about a new awareness of the importance of diet. Although the vast increase in the consumption of fast foods belied this trend, millions of Americans nevertheless took a closer look at what they ate. Realizing that careless eating habits contributed to heart disease and cancer, health-conscious consumers chose to limit the amounts of fat, sugar, and salt in their diets. "Natural" foods, without preservatives or excessive processing, became popular. Americans also changed their drinking habits. Per-capita consumption of hard liquor and regular beer dropped, and sales of low-calorie "light" beer and wine coolers soared.

To what purpose were Americans leading more healthful and "spiritual" lives? Commenting on the proliferation of therapeutic, religious, and fitness fads, social critics such as Tom Wolfe and Christopher Lasch expressed alarm at what Lasch labeled "the culture of narcissism." "To live for the moment," complained Lasch, "is the prevailing passion—to live for yourself, not for your predecessors or posterity. We are fast losing the sense of historic continuity, the sense of belonging to a succession of generations originating in the past and stretching into the future." America, such critics contended, had turned into a fragmented nation of fractious individualists. To Irving Louis Horowitz, writing in 1977, the United States had "become a Hobbesian rather than a Marxian nation, a place where the war against all is conducted with a ferocity that makes nineteenth-century class warfare seem tame in comparison."

Critics who saw the seventies as a decade of solipsistic selfishness contrasted this era with the activist political concerns of the Vietnam years. "After the political turmoil of the sixties," claimed Lasch, "Americans have retreated to purely personal preoccupations. Having no hope of improving their lives in any of the ways that matter, people have convinced themselves that what matters is psychic self-improvement: getting in touch with their feelings, eating health food, . . . immersing themselves in the wisdom of the East, jogging, learning how to 'relate,' overcoming the 'fear of pleasure.'" All of this, Lasch concluded, signified "a retreat from politics and a repudiation of the recent past."

Such criticisms of the new consciousness were not without merit. Certainly much that took place in the seventies was banal, selfish, hedonistic, apolitical, and often downright silly. Yet such an interpretation of seventies America contains serious flaws. For one thing, the dichotomy that Lasch and others made between a politicized sixties and a personalized seventies fails to hold up under close scrutiny. What historian Peter Clecak described as "the quest for the ideal self" was not unique to the seventies but grew quite naturally from the sixties counterculture. Indeed, the counterculture stressed personal liberation as a basic aim. Aided by drugs, music, meditation, organic foods, and communal living, thousands of radical youths of the sixties had sought psychic and spiritual awareness and physical well-being. In this respect, the main difference between the decades was that, by the seventies, people pursued personal fulfillment with more intensity and on a far wider scale than they had in the sixties. During the seventies, the human potential movement came to affect virtually every sector of American society.

Nor was the consciousness revolution of the seventies as solipsistic and selfish as critics claimed. Lasch insisted that "narcissism holds the key to the consciousness movement and to the moral climate of contemporary society." Yet as Theodore Roszak, a proponent of the new consciousness, noted in 1977, critics tended to generalize on the basis of the movement's "worst excesses of silly self-indulgence and commercial opportunism." In his 1978 book *Person Planet,* Roszak claimed that Americans searched not merely for personal salvation but "for a new reality principle to replace the waning authority of science and industrial necessity." To Clecak, Americans were making a "quest for personal fulfillment," but one conducted "within a small community (or several communities) of significant others." The search for meaningful community as an end to separation and alienation underlay seventies culture.

A final fault of the Wolfe/Lasch schema of the seventies is that political activism in fact did not end with the Vietnam War. Although the political pursuit of change became less vociferous and less well publicized in the post-Vietnam, post-Watergate years, it nevertheless remained alive. Throughout the seventies, the environmental, feminist, gay-rights, antinuclear, and peace movements flourished. Thousands of communes, women's centers, free schools, alternative publishers, food cooperatives, and various other counterinstitutions proliferated. However, disillusionment with national politics and the inadequacies of past federal programs increasingly led seventies activists to concentrate on the community or state as arenas for change. As Milton Kotler, director of a coalition of community groups, claimed, "There's a new recognition that the country's not going to be saved by experts and bureaucrats. It's going to be saved by some moral vision and some moral hope coming from the grass-roots and the neighborhoods."

By the end of the seventies, an estimated twenty million Americans had participated in various community-action programs. In hundreds of cities, groups toiled to restore urban neighborhoods, rebuilding existing buildings rather than following the traditional bulldozing patterns of urban renewal. In addition, grass-roots groups improved public spaces, experimented with alternative energy, created crisis-intervention centers, established abortion and birth-control clinics, and promoted consumer advocacy. "The media is selling us on this notion of apathy and paralysis in the country," criticized former antiwar activist Sam Lovejoy. "The movement did not die. It did the most intelligent thing it could do; it went to find a home. It went into the community. It's working, unnoticed, in the neighborhood."

Sixties activists continued to play important roles in the social movements of the seventies and more recently. Scholars who debunk the sixties and find few lasting legacies of the Movement frequently cite the postsixties experiences of a few well-known activists who "sold out" to the establishment. Most frequently presented as evidence of the ephemeral nature of sixties activism is the career of Yippie leader Jerry Rubin. After becoming a New Left media celebrity through such antics as wearing revolutionary battle dress into an HUAC hearing, trying to levitate the Pentagon, throwing money onto the floor of the New York Stock Exchange, and nominating a pig for president, Rubin immersed himself in the human potential movement. In the end, he settled down and became a Wall Street stockbroker.

Others who gave up the radical quest for social justice included Black Panther Eldridge Cleaver who, in addition to becoming a born-again Christian, attempted to reap the benefits of capitalism by marketing men's pants with polyester codpieces. Panther Bobby Seale, after an unsuccessful run for mayor of Oakland, authored a cookbook, *Barbecuing with Bobby*.[1] Rennie Davis, an early SDS leader and one of the Chicago Eight, became a follower of the guru Maharaj Ji. Radical *Ramparts* writers Peter Collier and David Horowitz reemerged as Reagan supporters and wrote a scathing attack on the sixties as the "Destructive Generation."

Historian Joseph Conlin, whose book *The Troubles* (1982) presents an unrelenting diatribe against the Movement, offers the story of Charles C. "Chip" Marshall III as representative. An organizer for SDS and one of the "Seattle Eight" jailed for conspiring to destroy federal property, Marshall by 1980 had become the director of a major private housing development company. In a *Time* story that Conlin quotes, Marshall claimed that "liberal economics just doesn't work. . . . Self-reliance, productivity and independence are important. . . . Business interests me." Conlin concludes, "Now there is how a chap named Chip ought to talk! Just like fellows with names like Jerry Rubin."

There were, of course, hundreds of Marshalls and Rubins—socially conscious youths who later became conservative capitalists and avid consumers. However, these examples do not paint an accurate portrait of what became of the core of the generation of sixties activists. The Movement left an indelible imprint on most members. Like the nineteenth-century transcendentalist Henry David Thoreau, Movement participants had acted as moral witnesses against what they perceived as an unjust society. Their individual rebellions led innumerable activists to a higher level of consciousness, a democratic vision that would remain with them. Not surprisingly, a great many of them have continued to work for social justice. As one would expect, most youthful rebels eventually settled down and chose careers, yet they did so less to make money than to serve society and to find self-fulfillment—to do good rather than to do well. Studies

---

[1] Seale, however, has remained a staunch supporter of racial justice.

of Mississippi Freedom Summer volunteers, for instance, indicate that whereas only 7 percent entered the business world, about half went into helping professions, with teaching, social service, law, and medicine the most popular. They often worked with the poor in inner cities. They taught African-American and women's history, ran legal aid and medical clinics, and established housing and job-training programs. Many found employment as social workers, counselors, and planners in the various government agencies established by the Economic Opportunity Act. Sociologist Joseph R. DeMartini, summarizing the findings of research on the postsixties careers of participants in the civil-rights, antiwar, and Free Speech movements, concluded that "former activists' current political beliefs are consonant with those held by activists during the 1960s." Thus, unlike the Old Left of the thirties, which witnessed dramatic deconversions when that group hit middle age in the postwar years, members of the New Left remained remarkably true to their early ideals.

Moreover, many New Leftists returned to school, earned Ph.D.s, and became university professors, bringing a radical perspective to their fields. Three early SDS leaders, Bob Ross, Todd Gitlin, and Richard Flacks, became professors at major universities. Ross's work has focused on creating a model for a humanistic international capitalism. Gitlin and Flacks have written well-received books about the Movement. Bernice Johnson Reagon, who joined the sixties crusade for racial justice in Albany, Georgia, became director of the Black American Culture program at the Smithsonian Institute. SNCC activist Joyce Ladner today is a well-known sociologist at Howard University specializing in race relations. Indeed, at colleges and universities across the country, former Movement people, both leaders and rank and file, can be found in disproportionate numbers in the liberal arts and social sciences.

Other sixties activists settled into careers as authors, investigative reporters, documentary film makers, high school teachers, clergy, labor organizers, urban planners, health and child-care workers, and various social-service professions. Some have chosen physical labor, such as carpentry or farming. SDS founder Al Haber, for example, works as a cabinetmaker. He lives in Berkeley and remains involved in radical organizing and protest.

A number of black leaders entered politics. SCLC staffers Jesse Jackson and Andrew Young came to play important national roles. Jackson today is recognized as one of the leading voices for African-Americans within the Democratic party. Young has twice served as mayor of Atlanta, has been a congressman, and was Jimmy Carter's ambassador to the United Nations. SNCC's first chairman, Marion Barry, went on to be elected mayor of Washington, D.C. SNCC leaders John Lewis and Julian Bond have had illustrious careers. Bond served for many years as a Georgia state senator and more recently as a visiting professor at Harvard; Lewis today is a respected member of the U.S. House of Representatives.

Although fewer white New Leftists entered politics, Tom Hayden did. Elected to the California state legislature, he has led the Campaign for Economic Democracy— later renamed Campaign California—a network of grass-roots citizen-action groups that have taken up such measures as rent control, energy conservation, clean air, and opposition to environmentally destructive development. Still evoking the ideals of participatory democracy, Hayden recently stated, "The process of trying to find a consensus rather than going ahead with a slim majority still strikes me as key." Although scarcely a Movement leader, Bill Clinton, an antiwar activist, draft evader, and casual marijuana smoker in the sixties, is the first member of the Movement generation to have won election to the presidency, and his administration includes a number of former Movement members.

In addition to picking helping professions, numerous sixties activists have continued to volunteer their services in environmental, feminist, antinuclear, consumer, and community service movements. Even most of those no longer active in progressive organizations have absorbed sixties values and lead lives in which they remain conscious of environmental and equal-rights issues. They recycle, share in household tasks, and strive to raise socially and environmentally aware children.

Although it would be presumptuous to pick the postsixties career of any single individual as representative of the Movement generation, certainly one could do better than Chip Marshall or Jerry Rubin. Heather Tobis Booth makes an excellent choice. In 1964, Tobis, a student at the University of Chicago, joined other northern volunteers and traveled to Mississippi for Freedom Summer. Back in Chicago, she joined SDS and took an active role in the antiwar, women's-rights, and various local movements. She married Paul Booth, a former SDS national secretary and in more recent years a union organizer. In 1973 she founded the Midwest Academy in Chicago, which became the training center for Citizen Action, a national federation of grass-roots citizen organizations.

Over the years, Booth's Midwest Academy has trained thousands of community activists in organizing; raising funds; establishing networks; and holding public hearings, demonstrations, and petition drives. Former SDS leader Steve Max has served as the academy's curriculum director for years, stimulating what he calls "resurgent populism." Academy-trained activists have aided the causes of environmentalists, feminists, the poor, trade unionists, small businessmen, tenants, and peace groups. Citizen Action has furthered the sixties goals of social change and personal empowerment, but this time with the necessary clout to win lasting victories.

Numerous Movement veterans have preserved and nurtured the values of the sixties. With maturity, their objectives have become less grandiose and their tactics more pragmatic than before, yet the goals of social justice and real democracy remain strong. Aquarian dreams have been tempered but not abandoned.

Selected Bibliography

Tom Wolfe's flippant criticisms of self-absorption appear in his influential article "The 'Me' Decade and the Third Great Awakening," *New York*, August 23, 1976. Christopher Lasch's *The Culture of Narcissism* (1979) is a more sustained attack on the narcissistic self-involvement that he found so predominant in the seventies. Peter Clecak's *America's Quest for the Ideal Self* (1983), on the other hand, is more positive about the seventies search for personal fulfillment. It also detects strong continuities between the sixties and seventies. Other studies of merit on changing cultural values and new personal preoccupations include Theodore Roszak's very positive *Person Planet* (1978); Daniel Yankelovich's survey-based *New Rules: Searching for Self-Fulfillment in a World Turned Upside Down* (1982); Jim Hougan's *Decadence: Radical Nostalgia, Narcissism, and the Decline in the Seventies* (1975); and Edwin Schur's *The Awareness Trap: Self-Absorption Instead of Social Change* (1976). Peter N. Carroll, *It Seemed Like Nothing Happened* (1982), is a good general survey of American life in the 1970s.

For the religious revivals and movements of the seventies, see Martin E. Marty, *A Nation of Believers* (1976); Steven M. Tipton, *Getting Saved from the Sixties: Moral Meaning in Con-*

version and Cultural Change (1982); Richard Quebedeaux, *The New Charismatics* (1976); and David Edwin Harrell, Jr., *All Things Are Possible: The Healing and Charismatic Revival in Modern America* (1975).

The growth of community activism in the seventies is detailed in Harry C. Boyte, *The Backyard Revolution* (1980). Urban reform is the subject of Robert Cassidy, *Livable Cities* (1980). For the women's, environmental, and antinuclear movements in the seventies, see the Selected Bibliography for Chapter 11.

Joseph Conlin's *The Troubles* (1982), on the basis of slight, impressionistic evidence, portrays sixties activists as typically having joined the money-making mainstream, a view also stressed in Peter Collier and David Horowitz, *Destructive Generation* (1989). However, studies based on interviews, questionnaires, and other systematic surveys all conclude that sixties activists did not experience a generational selling out but instead to a remarkable extent have remained true to their political visions. See Doug McAdam, *Freedom Summer* (1988); Jack Whalen and Richard Flacks, *Beyond the Barricades: The Sixties Generation Grows Up* (1989); Sara M. Evans and Harry C. Boyte, *Free Spaces: The Sources of Democratic Change in America* (1986); Joseph R. DeMartini, "Social Movement Participation: Political Socialization, Generational Consciousness, and Lasting Effects," *Youth and Society* 15 (December 1983); James M. Fendrich, "Keeping the Faith or Pursuing the Good Life: A Study of the Consequences of Participation in the Civil Rights Movement," *American Sociological Review* 42 (February 1977); Stephen I. Abramowitz and Alberta J. Nassi, "Keeping the Faith: Psychosocial Correlates of Activism Persistence into Middle Adulthood," *Journal of Youth and Adolescence* 10 (1981); William Greider, "The Rolling Stone Survey," *Rolling Stone,* April 7, 1988; Margaret M. Braungart and Richard G. Braungart, "The Effects of the 1960s Political Generation on Former Left- and Right-Wing Youth Activist Leaders," *Social Problems* 38 (August 1991); David DeLeon, ed., *Leaders from the 1960s: A Biographical Sourcebook of American Activism* (1994); Rex Weiner and Deanne Stillman, *Woodstock Census: The Nationwide Survey of the Sixties Generation* (1979); and Annie Gottlieb, *Do You Believe in Magic? The Second Coming of the Sixties Generation* (1987).

The Language
of the Sixties

acid: LSD

acidhead: a frequent LSD user

acid rock: music associated with the San Francisco drug culture; also known as *psychedelic music*

Amerika: radical spelling of *America,* intended to emphasize the nation's fascist tendencies

bad: good

bad trip: an unpleasant experience, especially with drugs

bag: an interest, as in, "Music is her bag"

ball: to have sexual intercourse

blasted: intoxicated by drugs or alcohol

blow: to smoke drugs; to fail, as in, "We blew it"; to perform cunnilingus or fellatio

blow one's mind: to have an intense drug experience

bread: money

brother: a male member of the Movement

bummer: an unpleasant episode, especially a bad drug experience

burned: cheated, usually by being sold phony drugs

busted: arrested

cat: a hip male

chick: a female, usually young

clean: not in possession of illegal drugs

cool: a superlative used to describe any positive experience or circumstance

cool it: to stop doing something

cop out: to violate one's values

crash: to experience a letdown after using drugs; to fall asleep

crash pad: a place to sleep

deal: to sell drugs

dig: to like; to understand

dope: any drug

downer: a barbiturate; a negative experience

drop out: to withdraw from the establishment

far out: a superlative meaning "amazing" or "incredible"

flower children: media's term for members of the counterculture

freak: a drug user; a member of the counterculture

grass: marijuana

groovy: very good

hassle: an argument or a problem

head: a heavy drug user

head shop: a store selling drug paraphernalia

heavy: serious, important

high: a happy state of mind induced by drugs or other stimuli

hip: in the know, aware

hippie: a member of the counterculture

holding: possessing illegal drugs

Jesus freak: one who finds Christ the "ultimate trip"

joint: marijuana cigarette

junk: heroin

karma: fate

lay it on: to give someone something; to tell a contrived story

liberate: to steal

lid: an ounce of marijuana

make it: to have intercourse

man: a common greeting or interjection

mindblower: an overwhelming experience usually induced by drugs

mindfuck: an upsetting experience

munchies: marijuana-induced hunger

off: to kill

old lady: girlfriend

old man: boyfriend
out front: honest, open
pad: apartment
pig: police
Pill, the: oral contraceptive
plastic: artificial, cheap
pot: marijuana
pothead: a frequent marijuana user
psychedelic: art or music related to LSD
rap: to talk
right on: correct, accurate, perceptive
rip off: to steal
roach: the butt of a marijuana cigarette
roach clip: a holder used for smoking marijuana butts
scene: a total setting and mood
shit: heroin
sister: female member of the cause
snow: cocaine
spaced out: high on drugs
speed: amphetamines
split: to leave
stash: a personal supply of drugs
stoned: high on drugs
straight: term describing a member of the establishment; one who does not use drugs; one who is not homosexual

street people: nonstudents who hang out in university towns
trip: a drug experience, especially with LSD; to become totally immersed in something
turn off: something disgusting or uninteresting
turn on: something stimulating
underground: antiestablishment, often used in reference to the media; in hiding
unreal: a superlative meaning unbelievable or amazing
up: high on drugs
up front: open and honest
uppers: amphetamines
uptight: tense, angry, suspicious, or puritanical
vibes, vibrations: a shared mood, as in, ''The concert had good vibes''
wasted: excessively high on drugs
weed: marijuana
wiped out: very tired
wired: high on amphetamines
YIPPIE: Youth International party
zap: to perform a quick action, as in, ''He zapped to the store''
zonked: very tired owing to drugs

Acknowledgments

p. 1, Lyrics from "Woodstock" by Joni Mitchell, © 1969 Siquomb Publishing Corp. All Rights Reserved. Used By Permission.

p. 1, "Ohio" performed by Neil Young, © 1970 Cotillion Music, Inc. & Broken Fiddle. All rights administered by Warner-Tamberlane Publishing Corp. All Rights Reserved. Used By Permission.

p. 19, Lyrics from "Eisenhower Blues" by J. B. Lenoir. © 1970 Arc Music Corporation. Used by permission. All rights reserved.

p. 37, Lyrics from "Shake, Rattle and Roll" Charles Calhoun. © 1954 Unichappell Music Inc. (Renewed). All Rights Reserved. Used By Permission.

p. 43, Lines from "Howl" from *Collected Poems 1947–1980* by Allen Ginsberg. Copyright © 1955 by Allen Ginsberg. Reprinted by permission of HarperCollins Publishers, Inc.

p. 48, Lines from "The Applicant" from *Ariel* by Sylvia Plath. Copyright © 1963 by Ted Hughes. Copyright Renewed. Reprinted by permission of HarperCollins Publishers, Inc.

p. 172, "Kill for Peace" words and music by Tuli Kupferberg, a Fugsong, 1966. Used with permission.

p. 205, Lyrics from "Let's Get Together" © 1963, Renewed 1991, Irving Music Inc. (BMI). All Rights Reserved International © Secured. Used by Permission.

p. 205, Lyrics from "White Rabbit" by Jefferson Airplane. © 1966, Renewed 1994, Irving Music Inc. (BMI). All Rights Reserved International © Secured. Used by Permission.

Photo Credits

CHAPTER 1
p. 11, UPI/Bettmann; p. 16, The Bettmann Archive; p. 20, The Bettmann Archive; p. 22, Archive Photos/Lambert; p. 27, AP/Wide World Photos

CHAPTER 2
p. 38, UPI/Bettmann Newsphotos; p. 41, Archive Photos; p. 44, The Bettmann Archive; p. 47 (left), The Bettmann Archive; p. 47 (right), FPG International; p. 50, Pictorial Parade; p. 59, Dan Weiner—Courtesy of Sandra Weiner

CHAPTER 3
p. 67, AP/Wide World Photos; p. 70, The Bettmann Archive; p. 79, Photo No. ST-C267-5-63 in the John F. Kennedy Library; p. 85, © Bob Henriques/Magnum Photos; p. 90, UPI/Bettmann Newsphotos

CHAPTER 4
p. 96, UPI/Bettmann; p. 103, UPI/Bettmann; p. 107, © Eve Arnold/Magnum Photos; p. 109, UPI/Bettmann; p. 110, Max Scheler/Black Star

CHAPTER 5
p. 123, Archive Photos/Burchman; p. 125, AP/Wide World Photos; p. 129, Max Scheler/Black Star; p. 138, UPI/Bettmann; p. 141, Archive Photos

CHAPTER 6
p. 155, AP/Wide World Photos; p. 159, UPI/Bettmann; p. 163, UPI/Bettmann; p. 169, UPI/Bettmann

CHAPTER 7
p. 182, UPI/Bettmann; p. 187, UPI/Bettmann; p. 193, AP/Wide World Photos; p. 201, Richard Scott Smolan/FPG International; p. 204, © Alice Ochs/Michael Ochs Archives/Venice, CA

CHAPTER 8
p. 222, AP/Wide World Photos; p. 226, Jack Kightlinger/LBJ Library Collection; p. 234, UPI/Bettmann; p. 236, UPI/Bettmann; p. 240, UPI/Bettmann; p. 245, Archive Photos

CHAPTER 9
p. 252, Peter L. Gould/FPG International; p. 263, Spencer Grant/FPG International; p. 269, Magnum Photos; p. 277, UPI/Bettmann Newsphotos

CHAPTER 10
p. 284, © J. Laure/The Image Works; p. 290, UPI/Bettmann; p. 293, UPI/Bettmann; p. 298, © Lisa Law/The Image Works; p. 304, Michael Abramson/Black Star

CHAPTER 11
p. 311, AP/Wide World Photos; p. 318, UPI/Bettmann; p. 322, Archive Photos; p. 328, UPI/Bettmann; p. 333, UPI/Bettmann

With special thanks to Debbie Goodsite at The Bettmann Archive for her assistance with the research.

INDEX

Poor People's Campaign of, 229
  on Vietnam War, 169, 174, 228
  on violence, 230–231
King, Mary, 99, 100, 314–315
Kingston Trio, 183
Kinney, Jay, 209
Kinsey, Alfred, 47–48
Kirk, Grayson, 232, 233
Kirk, Russell, 128
Kissinger, Henry, 264, 265, 266, 267, 271, 274,
  293
Kitt, Eartha, 171
Kleberg, Richard, 122
Kleindienst, Richard, 274
Knowland, William, 123
Kopkind, Andrew, 230, 283
Korean War, 10, 27–28, 30, 149
Kotler, Milton, 341
Kraft, Joseph, 257
Kramer, Hilton, 2
Krassner, Paul, 53, 206–207
Ku Klux Klan, 57, 108, 112

Labor unions, 17–18, 273
Labor Youth League, 184
Ladner, Joyce, 343
Lady Chatterley's Lover (Lawrence), 296
Laird, Melvin, 261, 264
Land and Water Conservation Fund, 328
Landau, Saul, 51
Lane, Mark, 90
Laos, 267, 268
Lasch, Christopher, 297, 340–341
"Laverne and Shirley," 339
Lawrence, D. H., 296, 320
Lawson, James M., 95, 99, 100
League for Industrial Democracy, 186
League for Spiritual Discovery (LSD), 201
Lear, Norman, 294
Leary, Timothy, 180, 199–201, 202, 205, 289,
  295
Lee, Herbert, 106
LeMay, Curtis, 243
Lemmon, Jack, 332
Lennon, John, 203, 338
Lenoir, J. B., 19
Leonard, George, 340
Leopold, Aldo, 327
Lerner, Max, 48, 56
Levensen, Marya, 315
Levitt, William, 21
Lewis, John, 94–96, 97, 102, 103, 104, 105,
  109, 114, 141, 237, 343
Liberalism, 4–5, 6
  during Cold War, 49–53
  during Johnson administration, 127–128, 130–
  133

  during Kennedy administration, 78–83
  during Nixon administration, 251
  See also New Left
Liberation magazine, 52–53
Lichter, S. Robert, 3
Liddy, G. Gordon, 255, 272
"Like a Rolling Stone" (Dylan), 204
Limits to Growth, The (Club of Rome), 330–
  331
Lippmann, Walter, 9, 26, 160
Listen Yankee (Mills), 50
Literature
  Beats, 34, 35, 42–45, 51
  civil-rights movement and, 54
  feminist, 320
  of liberal writers, 51–53
  See also specific works
Little, Malcolm (Malcolm X), 140, 141
Little Red Book (Mao Zedong), 288
Little Richard, 37
Little Rock civil-rights confrontation, 67–68
Lodge, Henry Cabot, Jr., 73, 154, 155, 156
Lomax, Louis, 140
Lonely Crowd, The (Riesman), 24
Looking Out for No. 1 (Ringer), 339
Lopez Tijerina, Reies, 302
Los Angeles Free Press (underground newspa-
  per), 207, 208–209
Lovejoy, Sam, 332, 342
Lowell, Robert, 62, 169
Lowenstein, Allard, 220
Loyalty program, 11–14, 29
LSD, 200, 201, 202, 295
Luce, Clare Booth, 69
Luce, Henry, 9
Lymon, Frankie, 40
Lynd, Staughton, 168

MacArthur, Douglas, 10
MacBird (Garson), 209
MacDarrah, Fred, 52
MacKenzie, Scott, 286
MacLaine, Shirley, 272
Maddox (destroyer), 157
Mad magazine, 41, 62, 186, 208
Magruder, Jeb, 260, 339
Mailer, Norman, 51, 52, 62, 65–66, 75, 83, 199,
  207, 239, 241, 320
Making of a Counter Culture, The (Roszak), 3,
  282–283
Malcolm X, 140, 141
Manhattan Project, 13
Mansfield, Mike, 170
Manson, Charles, 5, 287–288
Man's Role in Changing the Face of the Earth,
  327
Mao Zedong, 10, 288, 300